*The Safer Society Handbook of
Assessment and Treatment of Adolescents
Who Have Sexually Offended*

The Safer Society Handbook of Assessment and Treatment of Adolescents Who Have Sexually Offended

Edited by Sue Righthand, PhD
and William D. Murphy, PhD

A GIFR PROFESSIONAL BOOK

GLOBAL INSTITUTE
OF FORENSIC RESEARCH

PRESS

Brandon, Vermont

Project Management: Collette Leonard
Design and Composition: Edgeworks Creative
Copy Editing: Laura Jorstad
Proofreading: Susannah Noel
Indexing: Elizabeth Hoff

Library of Congress Cataloging-in-Publication Data
Names: Righthand, Sue, editor. | Murphy, William D., Ph. D., editor. | Safer
  Society Foundation. | Safer Society Press, issuing body.
Title: The Safer Society handbook of assessment and treatment of adolescents
  who have sexually offended / edited by Sue Righthand, William D. Murphy.
Other titles: Handbook of assessment and treatment of adolescents who have
  sexually offended | Assessment and treatment of adolescents who have
  sexually offended
Description: First edition. | Brandon, Vermont : Safer Society Press, [2017]
  | Includes bibliographical references and index.
Identifiers: LCCN 2016050259 | ISBN 9781940234069
Subjects: | MESH: Sex Offenses--psychology | Psychology, Adolescent
Classification: LCC RC560.S47 | NLM WM 605 | DDC 616.85/83--dc23
LC record available at https://lccn.loc.gov/2016050259

P.O. Box 340
Brandon, Vermont 05733
(802) 247-3132
www.safersociety.org

GLOBAL INSTITUTE
OF FORENSIC RESEARCH
www.gifrinc.com

Safer Society Press is a program of the Safer Society Foundation, a 501(c)3 nonprofit dedicated to the
prevention and treatment of sexual abuse. For more information, visit our website.

The Safer Society Handbook of Assessment and Treatment of Adolescents Who Have Sexually Offended
Order #WP 176

Contents

Part III Intervention

Part IV Special Issues

Part I
Characteristics of Adolescents Who Sexually Offend

CHAPTER 1

Adolescent Development and Clinical and Legal Implications

CHAPTER 2

Adolescent Sexual Development and Normative Behavior

CHAPTER 3

Juveniles Who Sexually Abuse: The Search for Distinctive Features

CHAPTER 4

A Developmental Life Course View of Juvenile Sexual Offending

Adolescent Development and Clinical and Legal Implications

Kathryn L. Modecki

Funding: Portions of the work described here were supported by a grant from the Australian Institute of Criminology through the Criminology Research Grants Program to Kathryn Modecki, Bonnie Barber, and Wayne Osgood. The views expressed are the responsibility of the author and are not necessarily those of the AIC.

Who we "are" in adolescence does not foretell our adulthood. Because adolescence is a time of immense physiological, cognitive, and social change, teenagers confront daily challenges in navigating their shifting internal and external landscapes. These developmental shifts, and the resources needed to successfully pilot them, strain adolescents' capacity for adaptive and prosocial decision making in the context of risky or antisocial opportunities they confront (Centifanti, Modecki, MacLellan, & Gowling, 2014; Chein, Albert, O'Brien, Uckert, & Steinberg, 2011). As a result of these and other age-based demands, the risks for engaging in behaviors such as violence, sexual risk taking, substance use, school dropout, and other antisocial activities is higher during adolescence than any other developmental period (Bongers, Koot, Van Der Ende, & Verhulst, 2004).

That said, maturation during adolescence around self-identity, cognitive abilities, and moral reasoning skills also provides a solid foundation for intervention during this time. In fact, neurological and psychosocial changes are tightly paired during adolescence, and this can set the stage for malleability in some key factors that contribute to antisocial behavior, such as affective decision making, emotional valence, and susceptibility to peer influence (Modecki, 2008; 2009; Monahan, Steinberg, Cauffman, & Mulvey, 2009). For this reason, prevention of adolescents' antisocial behaviors and settings, and programs that diminish their occurrence, are of sizable interest to researchers, policy makers, and practitioners.

In this chapter, I briefly lay out theory and empirical research across major areas of psychology to help explicate the unique role of "adolescence" in the occurrence of risky and antisocial behaviors. I then tie our developmental understanding of adolescents' decision making and behavior to the legal arena, where considerations of teenagers' normative development should arguably impact their legal treatment. Finally, I briefly discuss policy and practice implications for adolescent antisocial behavior, broadly speaking, with a final note on areas for future research.

CURRENT THEORY

Are adolescents mature decision makers? Research that seeks to answer this question provides a lens through which we view and treat our adolescents (Jacobs-Quadrel, Fischhoff, & Davis, 1993; Steinberg & Lerner, 2004). Here, a tension exists between two poles: one viewing adolescents as "older children" with fewer rights and responsibilities and in need of legal safeguarding and protections, versus another viewing them as "younger adults" with rights to make their own choices and to fully bear the consequences of those decisions (see Steinberg, Cauffman, Woolard, Graham, & Banich, 2009, for a full discussion). This tension is especially visible in the criminal arena, in part because adolescence is linked to a major uptick in antisocial activity, and in part because the impact on adolescents regarding how these activities are legislated is sizable. Where society views adolescents as competent, rational decision makers, they are judged to be mature and responsible enough to be held fully culpable for their criminal behaviors (Grisso, 1997). This can translate to sanctioning that is decidedly punitive, including adult-like sentencing and deterrence strategies designed to prevent others from committing crimes by exemplifying possible negative outcomes. On the other side, where society views adolescents as immature decision makers who are unduly impacted by the challenging nature of their developmental stage, they are deemed less competent to make criminal decisions and thus not fully culpable for their actions (Woolard, Reppucci, & Redding, 1996). Such assessments of developmental immaturity usually translate to more rehabilitative sentencing aims and treatment approaches (Grisso, 1996). In all, adolescents' perceived maturity, and the degree to which the unique time period of adolescence is seen to contribute to their proclivity for antisocial behavior, has vast implications for how we seek to punish youth for their offenses (whether sexual in nature or not) and for how we seek to prevent them from engaging in these types of behaviors in the first place.

Over the last two decades, research has coalesced in support of the idea that adolescents are not simply younger versions of adults (e.g., Cauffman & Steinberg, 2000;

Chassin et al., 2010; Collwell et al., 2005; Dmitrieva, Monahan, Cauffman, & Steinberg, 2012; Grisso et al., 2003; Modecki, 2009; 2008; Monahan et al., 2009; 2013; Steinberg & Cauffman, 1996). Rather, adolescents tend to lack maturity and judgment in settings characterized by heavy social and affective rewards, and, in particular, those offering antisocial opportunities. In fact, recent advances in the psychological sciences point to a confluence of influences that converge during adolescence to generate a "perfect storm" of risk for initiation and escalation of risky, delinquent, violent behaviors (e.g., Crone & Dahl, 2012; Luciana, 2013; Romer, 2010). As will be discussed, major theories, including dual-systems theory, coping with inputs, and maturity of judgment, point to a constellation of forces that can impact risky and antisocial decision making during this time, and may do so in a manner and to a degree that is fairly unique to this developmental period. Because individuals are far more likely to engage in antisocial behavior during adolescence than any other period of their life (Kann et al., 2014), and because the costs of adolescent crime for society are considerable (Piquero, Jennings, & Farrington, 2013), understanding underlying factors that serve to trigger or exacerbate offending during this time period is of substantial practical importance.

Neurobiological Theories

Neurobiological research has advanced our understanding of adolescent antisocial behavior in important ways, and continues to fine-tune explanations for why teenagers are especially likely to make decisions that are contrary to their long-term interests. One of the major theoretical arms that has generated rapid-fire developments within the field of developmental psychology is dual-systems models (e.g., Durston & Casey, 2006; Somerville, 2013). In general, dual-systems theories assert a developmental incongruity between adolescents' highly active and fully mature reward system, which drives youth toward the "plunders" of antisocial behavior, and adolescents' slow-to-engage and still-developing cognitive control system, which curbs youthful impulses and deters them from risky choices. In these models, the socio-emotional affective system, driven by the "hot" limbic system, takes precedence over the "cold" cognitive control system undergirded by the prefrontal cortex (Steinberg et al., 2008). As a result, during adolescence, antisocial and risky decisions are largely driven by possible rewards, including "the rush" of breaking rules, excitement, and improved social status with friends (Shulman & Cauffman, 2013; Modecki, 2009).

More recently, the field has expanded on dual-systems frameworks to derive increasingly nuanced neurobiological models. These models implicate "hot" and "cold" systems, but also highlight continued maturation in underlying circuitry and their connections, rather than viewing one key part of the adolescent brain as especially undeveloped as had been thought in the past. In these models, adolescent decision making is challenged by a less networked or fine-tuned, though relatively well-developed cognitive control system (Crone & Dahl, 2012). Developmental immaturity, in these models, translates to poor executive function in which prefrontal systems are not yet strongly connected. They are also less deeply circuited, meaning that various distinct areas associated with impulse control cannot yet fully cooperate across different regions of the brain. As a result, prefrontal systems experience difficulties that dynamically inhibit risk-taking behaviors (Hwang, Velanova, & Luna, 2010).

In a somewhat similar interpretation, "coping" frameworks assert that the prefrontal system is overridden with social and emotional inputs during adolescence, including fluctuating emotions, new and unfamiliar social contexts, and hassles and stressors associated with navigating adolescent life (Luciana, 2013; Luciana & Collins, 2012). Here, the intense social and emotional demands of adolescence coupled with a not yet fully networked prefrontal system render adolescents less able to direct information and cope with risky opportunities (Modecki, Zimmer-Gembeck, & Guerra, in press; Modecki & Uink, in press). Again, progressive maturation in the intricate connections within and across adolescents' brain circuitry is implicated in reduced abilities to process decisions and, ultimately, to make "good" decisions in risky and antisocial contexts (Casey, 2015).

A key takeaway from each of these models is that unlike that of adults, adolescents' cognitive control system does not operate on automatic at "full throttle"; it is neither quickly nor automatically deployed when adolescents seek to respond and make decisions within "hot" emotion-laden contexts. Instead, its still-maturing connections render it very flexible, so that is it not deployed routinely, across all of the contexts that youth encounter. Indeed, the malleability of this system is reflected in the very fact that its deployment is so highly context-dependent (Crone & Dahl, 2012). In particular, the motivational salience—the emotional and social rewards—of a given context will influence the executive systems' capacity to come online. That is, strong emotions, possible rewards, and social demands make it less likely that the "brakes" of the cognitive control system will be quickly or fully deployed.

Although this chapter covers adolescent risk behavior and antisocial decision making, broadly, it is worth noting that risky sexual decision making also happens under strong emotional, physiological, and motivational arousal. Though little research exists in relation to neural and cognitive factors that influence adolescents' decision making regarding sexual activity (Ewing et al., 2016), there is some early research pointing to similarities in normative sexual risk taking and other aspects of risky and antisocial decision making described below. Studies on developmentally typical sexual risk taking (measured in terms of riskiness of contraceptive method used at time of last sexual intercourse) report associations with diminished recruitment of brain regions associated with control of impulses and emotions. Sexually riskier teens show less recruitment of frontal regions implicated in impulse control and cognitive control of emotion regulation (Goldenberg, Telzer, Lieberman, Fuligni, & Galván, 2013). In terms of sexual offending, more specifically, many of the risk factors for adolescent sexual offending do overlap with general criminogenic offending, such as antisocial tendencies, conduct problems, and general delinquency risk factors (Lussier & Chouinard Thivierge, this volume; Seto & Lalumière, 2010; Wijk & Boonmann, this volume). In fact, adolescents who sexually offend are three to four times more likely to reoffend non-sexually than they are sexually (Caldwell, 2010), so clearly there are co-occurring risks. Thus, programs for adolescents who sexually abuse should be grounded in current understanding of adolescents' development and antisocial behavior, and the sexual nature of adolescents' crimes should arguably take less precedence than is normally the case (Fanniff, Schubert, Mulvey, Iselin, & Piquero, 2016). That said, meta-analytic work does describe some specificity to adolescent sexual offending, including atypical sexual interests, sexual abuse history, and social isolation, and these appear to have fairly strong correlations with male adolescent sexual offending (Seto & Lalumière, 2010). Although developmental research is required to disentangle whether atypical interests and social isolation, for instance, precede or are outgrowths of sexual offenses, it is unlikely that broad-spectrum antisocial development explanations alone can fully explain sexual offending during adolescence (Seto & Lalumière, 2010). Rather, developmental explanations are required that are predicated on more precise understanding of the unique developmental paths that lead certain adolescents to sexually offend, and not others. Because no studies described here have examined adolescent development in relation to sexual offending, the research described and implications discussed can only provide one perspective through which such explicit understanding of sexual offending might be conceptualized.

Sources of Bias

Because the major neuropsychological theories described above are all in agreement that certain factors have an especially strong pull on adolescents' executive systems, and in turn their antisocial behavior, researchers are now seeking to delineate sources of such bias in teenagers' choices. That is, across these theories, affective and motivations demands appear to override adolescents' executive system (Luciana & Collins, 2012). Thus, even if the prefrontal systems are fully developed and resourced, demands on that system are excessively high (Luciana & Collins, 2012). Here anticipated rewards, emotions, and approach toward novelty (incentive motivation; Luciana

& Collins, 2012) all appear to overwhelm adolescents' capacity for overseeing their decision-making process. As a result, they play an outsized role in adolescents' risky decisions, and to the extent that we can conceptualize and model their impacts, it is possible to translate such knowledge for policy and prevention.

First, adolescents' disproportionate involvement in antisocial behavior has been attributed to their heightened sensitivity to rewards. Adolescents are more behaviorally disposed toward attaining social and affective rewards than any other age group (Barkley-Levenson & Galván, 2014; Galván et al., 2007). In fact, the still-maturing teenage brain appears to be "hardwired" to seek out rewards at its resting, baseline state. For example, in lab tasks, adolescents respond more quickly to stimuli that have been associated with rewards in the past than do adults, and they are more sensitive to the changing value of rewards than are adults (e.g., Barkley-Levenson & Galván, 2014; Cohen et al., 2010). That said, it is also becoming increasingly clear that rewards don't just impel risky decision making. Rather, when rewards are linked with accurate performance in laboratory tasks, adolescents actually improve their decision making (Teslovich et al., 2014). It is possible that when paired with certain stimuli, then, rewards may also work to enhance adolescents' inhibitory control (Geier, Terwilliger, Teslovich, Velanova, & Luna, 2009). Thus taking advantage of adolescents' preference for rewards, and pairing rewards with legally desired outcomes, may be a useful avenue for future intervention.

A second major source of bias in adolescents' decision making is their strong experiencing of emotion. Immaturity in their prefrontal systems hampers youth's ability to effectively down-regulate strong emotions—whether positive or negative. Their continued need to "level" these emotional ups and downs creates an underlying tax on executive control resources. As a result, adolescents are especially likely to rely on "feeling" instead of "thinking" in contexts that place heavy demands on their system, such as those that are exciting, with friends or peers, or otherwise offer potential social or affective rewards (e.g., Shulman & Cauffman, 2014). In these instances, adolescents are particularly likely to consult their emotional experience to guide their behavioral choices (Modecki, 2009). Just as positive emotions play a role in overriding adolescents' executive system, so too do negative emotions, and the experience of threat and negative affect is also amplified during adolescence (Crone & Dahl, 2012). For example, adolescents experience momentary surges in emotion in response to daily hassles (Uink, Modecki, & Barber, 2016) and youth who are high in externalizing symptomology are especially challenged in "bouncing back" from negative experiences across their day (Uink, Modecki, & Barber, under review). Thus, emotional experiences associated with stressful events may also contribute to adolescents' further engagement in antisocial behaviors.

In fact, stressors and challenges, and the strong negative emotion associated with stressful experiences, may amplify perceptions that antisocial behavior is a good idea (Galván & McGlennen, 2012). That is, negative emotional arousal experienced in the moment may alter decision making and signal to youth that antisocial behavior will be rewarding (Cooper et al., 2000). Accordingly, the experience of negative emotional arousal also makes it difficult for adolescents to exert cognitive control and tamp down on rewarding and antisocial tendencies (Galván & McGlennen, 2012; Modecki et al., in press). For instance, preliminary research shows that adolescents make riskier decisions on days they experience high levels of stress than on low-stress days (Galván & McGlennen, 2012). All told, adolescents' antisocial choices are arguably more strongly influenced by both positive and negative emotions than are those of children or adults. This means that emotions—and adolescents' ability to regulate them—should be a core component of rehabilitative programs working with adolescents.

Third, adolescents appear to be hardwired to approach novel stimuli, and embedded within the neuropsychological findings described above is evidence of increased activation within the "valuing" systems of the teen brain. Thus, adolescents appear to be heavily sensitive to understanding sources of reward and threat, especially in relation to their social contexts (Crone & Dahl, 2012). Given adolescents' developmental mandate to try out new behaviors and settings in anticipation of moving into adulthood, responsiveness to environmental cues that could offer either prizes or penalties makes a certain amount of evolutionary sense (Casey, 2015). Their susceptibility to strong appetitive-approach demands, which tends to translate to seeking out novel and exciting contexts, may be one evolutionary mechanism to compel adolescents to learn about their awaiting adult world. Increasingly, research is highlighting how contexts can play a key role in contingencies associated with risk and rewards, which arguably can translate to teens' risky and antisocial decision making in the real world.

The Role of Contexts

As a result of increasing appreciation for the role of contexts in shaping adolescents' decision contingencies, research is converging at a rapid pace to detail the role of social situations in shifting adolescents' risk choices. In a keystone study, for example, Gardener and Steinberg (2005) highlighted a unique impact of peers on adolescents' risk taking. This work experimentally manipulated the presence versus absence of same-aged peers, and compared the role of peer influence on risky (simulated) driving for children, adolescents, and young adults. Relative to other age groups, adolescents' risky decision making was intensified by having same-aged peers nearby. Steinberg's lab has duplicated this effect of exacerbated peer influence on adolescent risk taking across a number of paradigms, including situations in which an anonymous peer watches a risk task silently, through a window (Weigard, Chein, Albert, Smith, & Steinberg, 2014). These researchers suggest that the peer-presence effect can be attributed to peers' activation of reward regions of the adolescent brain, again pointing to a possibly substantial role of adolescents' socio-emotional valuing systems in their risk behaviors (Chein et al., 2011).

While research clearly highlights that the presence of peers can activate adolescent risk taking, social contexts don't just push teenagers toward risk; they can also pull them toward more conservative decisions. Illustratively, when adolescents are surrounded by friends who are less risky than they are, they make decisions on lab-based tasks that are more risk-averse (Centifanti et al., 2014). Likewise, experimental research demonstrates that when adolescents are grouped with a slightly older adult, their level of risk taking diminishes, and they make similar choices as if they were alone (Silva, Chein, & Steinberg, 2016). Not only do slightly older adults appear to help mitigate risky choices, but parents, in particular, seem to have an influential effect on adolescents' decisions. Specifically, mothers appear to diminish the rewarding nature of risk taking; in lab-based tasks, when adolescents make decisions in the presence of their mother, these tend to be less risky (Telzer, Ichien, & Qu, 2015). Interpretations regarding the brain regions activated during these tasks suggest that arguably, a mother's presence may simply render risk taking less fun.

Maturity and Psychosocial Theory

One of the reasons that brain-based research over the last two decades has been so important to our notions of adolescents' decision making in risky and antisocial contexts is that previous to this, interested scholars had focused mainly on cognitive aspects of decision making. This work pointed to few differences between adolescents and adults (e.g., Inhelder & Piaget, 1958). That is, many cognitive capacities undergo rapid developmental change prior to adolescence, during middle childhood. Thus, in the developmental buildup to adolescence, children are increasingly able to manipulate information. Their flexibility, goal-setting, and information-processing skills undergo critical progression. These improved cognitive abilities are also mirrored in other ways as social beliefs begin to gel and internal standards for achievement grow progressively more influential (see Guerra, Modecki, & Cunningham, 2014, for a brief reveiew). Thus, in lab-based tasks of "cold" decision making, few differences between adolescents and adults tend to emerge (Jacobs & Klaczynski, 2002).

As a result of their strong performance on "cold" cognitive tasks, up until relatively recently (and in some circles, ongoing today) the prevalent assumption was that adolescents were comparatively mature in their decision-making abilities. That is, their ability to make reasonable decisions in relation to their antisocial and criminal conduct was generally similar to that of adults. Here, the assumption was generally that, by adolescence, youth presented with risky and antisocial opportunities were capable of mature judgment (Steinberg & Cauffman, 1996; Cauffman & Steinberg, 2000). By extension, justice systems, especially in the United States, held (and in some instances continue to hold) adolescents as equally responsible for their crimes, implicitly if not explicitly (Cepparulo, 2006; Gardner, 1989; Shapiro, 2012; Steinberg & Cauffman, 1999). Although rates of juvenile detention have been declining since 1999, the US remains the forerunner in youth incarceration rates among industrialized nations (Annie E. Casey Foundation, 2013). Later, I touch on notions of adolescent criminal responsibility in two contexts, the US and Australia, to illustrate this idea. However, as described below, the idea that adolescents are equivalent to adults in their ability to navigate and manage antisocial contexts fails to align with what we know about their psychosocial functioning.

Building on new indications that adolescence is, contrary to previous understanding, a period of rapid brain development (e.g., Spear, 2000), a body of psychosocial research has coalesced to explicate how adolescents' immaturity might be reflected in their criminal decisions (e.g., Cauffman & Steinberg, 2000; Fried & Reppucci, 2001; Modecki, 2008; 2009; Monahan et al., 2009; 2013). This literature, sometimes described as "immaturity of judgment" research, emphasizes influences on decision making as it occurs outside "cold" laboratory contexts in the real world. For example, as adolescents navigate day-to-day life, they face difficulties in tempering their emotional responses; they carry a shortened future-time perspective in which their focus is on short-term gains instead of long-term outcomes; and their decisions tend to be shaped by concerns about fitting in with peers and desires to impress them and so they are not always self-reliant or autonomous in making choices (Cauffman & Steinberg, 2000; Scott, Reppucci, & Woolard, 1995).

Of course, plenty of adults fail to temper their emotions. Many of us overlook the long-term consequences of our behaviors; we want to fit in with others and can forgo our responsibilities. The crux of the immature-judgment argument, though, is that adolescents have a developmental proclivity toward these characteristics, because of their maturational stage. That is, by the nature of their developmental stage, on average adolescents tend to be characterized by deficits in decision-making competencies needed to navigate antisocial contexts. In these settings, adolescents' choices can be unduly influenced by factors such as impressing their friends and the need for excitement. Here, although some adults continue to demonstrate inadequacies in making decisions around risky or antisocial opportunities, this can be attributed to their own actions, and is not linked to their developmental stage

(Modecki, 2009). Adult decisions are believed to reflect their own choices and preferences, whereas adolescent choices are made within the framework of their developmental (in) competencies (Steinberg & Scott, 2003).

As described earlier, immature judgment may perhaps be undergirded by brain-based changes that take place during adolescence. Indeed, during adolescence, youth continue to experience significant growth in cognitive abilities such as abstract reasoning, particularly in their meta-level cognitive systems, which allow them to reflect on their own mental processes and strategies (Flavell, 1979; Kuhn, 2006). These upgrades in higher-order cognitive functioning allow youth to direct their own learning and mental life, choosing how and where to apportion their mental effort (Durston & Casey, 2006). Advances in abstract thinking allow them to step outside both themselves and others and take a "third-person" or societal perspective. What this means is that adolescents are making gains in their ability to think through the perspective of others and consider the long-term and broader impacts of their decisions (Modecki, 2008; 2009). But these abilities are not necessarily automatic and are only building, as youth slowly evolve into the emotional, social, and behavioral roles of adulthood. This is a time of transition; youth are preparing to "leave the nest" and meet the demands of adult roles. This developmental mandate means that teens are putting themselves in novel situations, trying out new roles, identities, and peer groups, and generally "practicing" independence. Yet in doing so, many adolescents are limited by their reduced capabilities in withstanding psychosocial stimuli and making prosocial decisions (Scott et al., 1995).

Research on immaturity of judgment has aimed to encapsulate these psychosocial factors that unduly impact adolescents' antisocial decisions and may, in turn, suggest mitigated responsibility for criminal conduct. These psychosocial dimensions include factors such as autonomy, independence, emotional temperance, future-time perspective, perspective of others, and peer influence. In normative (non-justice-system-involved populations sampled from high school and university settings), cross-sectional comparisons show that immature judgment peaks around age 15 and then dissipates during the university years (Cauffman & Steinberg, 2000). Indeed, adolescents are less mature than university students, young adults across their 20s, and adults, and factors such as emotional temperance continue to mature through young adulthood (Modecki, 2008). Likewise, moral reasoning in relation to why youth chose not to engage in illegal behavior also continues to increase through young adulthood (Modecki, 2009), making it clear that decision-making competencies are still developing during adolescence. This developmental staging is important, because research demonstrates that immature judgment predicts antisocial decision making (Cauffman & Steinberg, 2000) as well as actual engagement in delinquent behavior (Modecki, 2008). For example, among adolescent boys, adolescents who engage in a great deal of delinquent behavior have less mature judgment relative to those who engage in very little (Modecki, 2008).

Indeed, one large-scale study (n = 1,354), Pathways to Desistance (see Mulvey, 2011), has tracked maturity of judgment among juvenile offenders across adolescence and young adulthood and has garnered valuable insight into its developmental progression and links to crime. This research indicates that psychosocial maturity continues to develop across adolescence, through to the mid-20s (Monahan, Steinberg, Cauffman, & Mulvey, 2009; 2013). Importantly, too, findings show that different developmental patterns of psychosocial maturation can be mapped for youth who desist versus those who persist in their antisocial behavior. In particular, youth who continue to engage in antisocial activities tend to show a pattern of suppressed maturation in relation to their emotional temperance through late adolescence (Monahan et al., 2009). Overall, too, juvenile offenders who are still engaging in antisocial behavior even later, during young adulthood, show overall deficits in development of psychosocial maturity, relative to youth who are no longer persisting in their antisocial activities (Monahan et al., 2013).

Tracking the development of psychosocial maturity is especially informative in relation to juvenile offenders because findings have implications for how we treat juvenile crime. That said, it is also important to consider how incarceration, rehabilitation, and related risk factors for antisocial behavior might serve to impact change in maturity of judgment. Other findings from the Pathways to Desistance study (Mulvey, 2011) indicate that time spent incarcerated in secure settings does indeed impact the rate at which youth mature, and at least in the short term. Here, time in secure settings seems to slow the developmental of psychosocial maturity, relative to time in residential treatment facilities (Dmitrieva et al., 2012). Somewhat surprisingly, the total amount of time a youth spends within a residential treatment facility also has a negative impact on development of psychosocial maturity. This dampened effect of residential treatment on growth in psychosocial maturity may possibly be related to the fact that many residential treatment facilities offer drug and alcohol treatment services, and there are links between substance use and diminished maturity of judgment. Among male juvenile offenders, use of alcohol and marijuana prospectively predicts lower psychosocial maturity in the short term, and elevated or increasing adolescent substance use over the long term is associated with significant parallel declines in maturity (Chassin et al., 2010).

These studies and others make clear that adolescents have diminished maturity of judgment relative to adults, and correspondingly such psychosocial immaturity is related to engaging in and persisting with antisocial behaviors. Importantly, the arc of brain-based changes described earlier and of psychosocial maturation described here shows that this development spans through late adolescence and into early adulthood. However, it is important to recall that during young adulthood (past age 18), some developmental improvements have occurred and, too, that other factors that help offset psychosocial immaturity are already in place. As one example, young adults are more established in their character and identity, and this should help to counterbalance some of the appeal, excitement, and potential for impressing peers of antisocial choices. This idea is supported by research findings. In cross-sectional comparisons, the impact of psychosocial factors (anger, sensation seeking, peer pressure, short-term benefits) on criminal behavior is noticeably stronger for adolescents than for adults (Modecki, 2009). Although young adults are also somewhat psychosocially immature, the impact of immaturity of judgment on their criminal conduct is, statistically speaking, no different than it is for adults. Thus, adolescence is a unique stage in terms of mitigating psychosocial influences on decisions and behavior. As a result, understanding developmental contributors to adolescent antisocial decision making is integral to improved treatment and prevention of juvenile crime (Modecki, 2016; Shulman & Cauffman, 2013).

Relevant Policy Issues

Criminal Responsibility

How do these biological and psychosocial changes experienced by adolescents translate to legal treatment of their antisocial behavior? In general, there are "threads" woven within many juvenile justice policies that speak to the fact that adolescents are not yet adults and should be treated differently in relation to their crimes. Many juvenile justice systems, however, have not yet adopted policies or treatments that acknowledge our fuller understanding of adolescent development, much of which has been spawned by physiological and psychosocial evidence generated in the last two decades (Annie E. Casey Foundation, 2013). The United States is particularly punitive in relation to juvenile crime (Annie E. Casey Foundation, 2013), but even in relatively less punitive environments such as Australia, notable gaps exist between policy and developmental understanding. Below, I briefly sketch juvenile justice policies concerning adolescent crime in two Western industrialized nations, the US and Australia, and highlight several gaps between empirical evidence and legal considerations of adolescent development in relation to sentencing. It is worth noting that a number of gaps exist between empirical understanding and policies in regard to how justice systems question, detain, and treat juvenile offenders (e.g., Grisso et al., 2003; Salekin, Yff,

Neumann, Leistico, & Zalot, 2002). Here, however, I cover only briefly some major disparities in relation to sentencing.

In the United States, to be held fully criminally responsible under law, someone must willingly engage in a criminal activity and, while doing so, possess a guilty or "criminal" mind-set (Weithorn, 1984). Traditionally, it was assumed that children (aged 14 and below) were not capable of possessing a guilty mind-set, although evidence to the contrary might be evaluated in specific cases (Weithorn, 1984). This assumption is known as the infancy defense, akin to the adult defense of insanity, and has been reasoned to compel reduced punishment (Bonnie, Coughlin, Jeffries, & Low, 1997). However, infancy is not allowable as a defense in juvenile court (Bonnie et al.), because the system exists to accommodate the notion that juveniles are indeed less mature than adults, and thus inherently less culpable for their crimes (Scott & Grisso, 1997). Still, given that many jurisdictions focus on punishment of juvenile offenders rather than their rehabilitation, this founding assumption of the juvenile court may be overlooked.

With the formalization of the modern US juvenile justice system in 1967, *In re Gault,* the Supreme Court maintained that youth required procedural and substantive protections distinguishing between juveniles' and adults' developmental maturity (Buss, 2003). Importantly, the court differentiated juveniles as being more amenable to treatment and less criminally responsible than adults. The Supreme Court decision *Roper v. Simmons* (2005) maintained this notion more than 10 years ago by outlawing the juvenile death penalty as cruel and unusual punishment. More recently, the court made some further (though only partial) strides in *Graham v. Florida* (2011), indicating that life in prison without the possibility of parole for crime committed as a juvenile was also deemed cruel and unusual punishment—however, only in the cases of non-homicide offenses. One year later, in *Miller v. Alabama* (2012), the court held that a statute mandating a sentence of life in prison without the possibility of parole for homicide further constituted cruel and unusual punishment, and instead mitigating factors need to be considered. Thus, there is a thread underlying current US juvenile justice policies acknowledging that juvenile offenders cannot be presumed to be future hardened criminals caught early.

That said, depending on the jurisdiction and the type of crime in question, this thread can be hard to identify. Mechanisms have long been in place that allow for similar handling of juvenile and adult crimes, through juvenile waiver to adult court (Salekin, 2002; see Grossi, Brereton, & Prentky, this volume, for a discussion). Since 1991, almost every US state has widened the extent to which juveniles are processed by adult criminal courts as opposed to juvenile or family courts (Griffin, Addie, Adams, & Firestine, 2011). However, rates of judicial waiver have declined subsequently, due in part to decreases in juvenile crime (Redding, 2008), rates of violent crime in particular (Puzzanchera & Addie, 2014). Importantly, when adolescents are transferred to adult court, the infancy claim described above is no longer extraneous. Although it is often assumed that criminal courts consider adolescent immaturity as a mitigating factor (Slobogin, Fondacaro, & Woolard, 1999), research suggests that this is not always the case (Scott & Grisso, 1997). In fact, juveniles transferred to criminal court are often punished more severely than young adults for similar crimes (Kurlychek & Johnson, 2004). Some research suggests that judges may view transferred adolescents as more culpable for their crimes than adult defendants (Kurlychek & Johnson. 2004); other studies argue that this may not necessarily be the case (see Kurlychek & Johnson, 2010, for a discussion). It is worth noting, too, that although automatic transfer is more typical for serious offenses such as murder and assault (Brannen et al., 2006), youth are also waived to adult court through official proceedings for a range of offenses, including drug, property, public order, and person offenses. Although previously property offenses were more common, person offenses now make up roughly half of the waived cases in the United States (Puzzanchera & Addie, 2014).

Despite the fact that these transfer policies assert adolescents' culpability for their crimes, there is little developmental evidence to support this idea (Woolard et al., 1996). Instead, given that adolescents' antisocial decisions are characterized as lacking maturity, this notion is largely undermined, as indicated by the psychological evidence described earlier (Scott et al., 1995; Woolard, Fondacaro, & Slobogin, 2001). Recall that this research describes adolescents' immaturity when making antisocial decisions, and supports their reduced criminal responsibility (Woolard et al., 1996). Importantly, this does not imply lack of responsibility or accountability, only that legislation and policy aimed toward rehabilitation instead of punishment is warranted. Also, if "adult crime" begets "adult time," it is crucial to point out that there is no evidence at all to suggest that more punitive treatment of adolescent offenders leads to any improvements in their antisocial decision making (Monahan et al., 2013) or their recidivism (Redding, 2008).

As a second example of legal treatment of juvenile crime, Australia's approach to juvenile offending is comparatively liberal relative to the United States'. Generally, adolescents are processed in child-specific courts until they reach the age of 18 (17 in Queensland), unless the offense is highly serious, such as murder, in which case their trial could possibly take place in adult court (Crofts, 2008). In Australia, this question is not up for debate and there are few questions about the appropriateness of this age; nor are there calls for a younger age at which an offender could be tried as an adult. However, the age at which a child can be held culpable for criminal behavior and thus convicted of an offense and liable to punishment is more often subjected to criticism. Illustratively, there have been repeated calls for more severe treatment of juvenile offenders in Australia, based on the assumption that young people are akin to adults in their "moral understanding" of crime. As a result, highlighting the mitigating role of adolescent development in relation to juvenile crime is still important, even within this relatively more liberal juvenile justice context.

Currently in Australia, children are presumed incapable of criminal responsibility until they have reached 10 years old, and from the ages of 10 to 13 they are conditionally presumed incapable of criminal responsibility (Crofts, 1998; 2008). This conditional age limit allows children to be held criminally responsible if there is proof that they were developed enough to understand that their crime was "seriously wrong, as distinct from an act of mere naughtiness or childish mischief" (*BP v. R,* 2006: 27) alongside proof of the criminal act and any necessary mens rea, such that the child must understand that the act it was wrong according to the ordinary standards of reasonable people (*R v. M,* 1977: 589).

Between ages 14 and 18, youth are presumed to be responsible for their crimes, and there is no consideration of their level of development when holding them accountable for a criminal offense. As explicated above, this does not mean that the special treatment of children within the criminal justice system ends at age 14. Usually, until reaching adulthood (age 18 or 17 in Queensland) adolescents are tried in specific juvenile courts with modified sanctions.

Because Australian law interprets adolescent criminal responsibility in terms of "understanding that [the criminal act] was wrong according to the ordinary standards of reasonable people," two important factors are at play. First, a misunderstanding exists when policies such as this conceptualize "ordinary standards" as simply knowing the difference between right and wrong. This is because developmental differences exist in relation to moral reasoning. Children and adolescents consider the moral implications of antisocial decisions in different ways than do older individuals (e.g., Hains & Ryan, 1983). Indeed, as noted earlier, moral reasoning progresses developmentally (Tapp, 1976); youth increasingly consider the moral consequences of antisocial behavior with age (Modecki, 2009). Second, moral standards of behavior alone do not adequately define adolescent maturity in relation to their criminal responsibility. For instance, many adolescents view risky, aggressive, and delinquent behavior as personal decisions, rather than moral decisions, and delinquent youth often show significant delays in their development of moral reasoning (Guerra, Nucci, & Huesmann, 1994). Thus, even within a national context in which adolescents are on surer ground in terms of justice policies and legal treatment that differentiates adult crime from that of juveniles, room for improvement still exists. Further consideration of adolescents' underlying development and the ways in which this impacts their criminal responsibility and treatment is certainly warranted, in Australia and the United States as well as in other industrialized and non-industrialized nations.

IMPLICATIONS FOR PRACTITIONERS AND ADMINISTRATORS

A constellation of forces shapes risky and antisocial decision making during adolescence, in a manner that is unique to the developmental period. Teenagers are influenced by strong and fluctuating emotions, poor self-control, a desire to impress peers, and other psychosocial pressures. Susceptibility to these psychosocial influences peaks in the middle-teen years and begins to diminish during late adolescence. During young adulthood, although these pressures have some impact albeit smaller, their influence on crime appears to be mitigated by a more coherent identity, improved moral reasoning, enhanced self-esteem, and other factors that take ascendance during this time (e.g., work, marriage, and having children; for example, see Lussier & Chouinard Thivierge, this volume).

Although adolescents are still building their sense of self and "who they are," and are clearly at a decision-making disadvantage given their developmental stage, the research discussed here should not be interpreted to mean that their capacities are so reduced as to render them "frontal lesion patients" (Lucina, 2013). Rather, when considering adolescent development in relation to policy, prevention, and intervention, one must overlay any snapshot of present functioning and limitation with an understanding that there also exists a dynamic of underlying change. The picture during adolescence is not yet fully formed, and some risk (and protective) factors will remain stable, while others will change.

Based on the underlying age-related influences described here, which are known to impact adolescents' risk for initiation and escalation of antisocial behavior, programs are arguably going to be more effective when couched within a developmental perspective toward initiating behavioral improvements. There is no consensus about how best to do so, or to prevent or diminish delinquency more generally, but I offer several observations. First, cognitive-behavioral treatments represent one of our most effective tools for decreasing youth delinquency (Izzo & Ross, 1990; Koehler, Lösel, Akoensi, & Humphreys, 2013; Landenberger & Lipsey, 2005). Given that these types of programs tend to be implemented to target youth's "cold" risk perceptions, they could be updated to better recognize the activating influence of emotion (including anger control) and perceived rewards on adolescents' antisocial choices (Guerra, Williams, Tolan, & Modecki, 2008; Landenberger & Lipsey, 2005). Second, as mentioned earlier, one of the ways scholars currently conceptualize the adolescent brain in relation to externalizing psychopathology is in terms of working in overdrive to "cope with stressors" (Luciana, 2013). This is a useful framework for interventionists, because it highlights the myriad ways that "life" can trigger adolescents' acting out (Modecki & Uink, in press; Modecki et al., in press). Helping adolescents to better cope with and process emotions (Zimmer-Gembeck & Skinner, 2011), teaching them to make thoughtful decisions in the face of exciting rewards (Modecki, 2009; 2016), and helping them to navigate and resist antisocial peer influence (Steinberg & Monahan, 2007) are some examples of how adolescents can be taught to diminish sources of stress on their executive capacities. Adolescents also need to be taught how to avoid creating or contributing to circumstances that will add to their challenges and stress (e.g., Evans & Kim, 2012; Galván & McGlennen, 2012). To the extent that programs can cultivate and support adolescents' ability to connect with prosocial peers and adults (e.g., Burrus, 2012; Williamson, Modecki, & Guerra, 2014), these positive relationships can help buffer against future challenges and roadblocks that might further ensnare youth within a problematic life pathway (e.g., DuBois, Holloway, Valentine, & Cooper, 2002; Modecki, Barber, & Eccles, 2014).

Of course, the basic tenet of prevention is to avert antisocial behaviors in the first place. Ideally programs and policies will harness youth, family, and community resources to improve youth functioning during childhood, before initiation and escalation of antisocial behavior. One of the most effective ways to intervene with children is to improve skills in a parent or carer, who can then scaffold protective factors in youth (Sandler, Schoenfelder, Wolchik, & MacKinnon, 2011). Even during adolescence, programs that target youth in conjunction with their caregivers or other important adult role models can still be useful, as they create a safe space for adolescents to scaffold and practice any skills that are being programmatically nurtured (Modecki et al., in press).

Recommendations for Future Research

Although scholars have made exciting advances in explicating adolescents' increased penchant for antisocial behavior, further research is needed to translate research knowledge to the prevention and treatment of antisocial behavior. Research points to the benefits of attending to the risk-need-responsivity principles (Andrews & Bonta, 2010; Lowenkamp, Latessa, & Holsinger, 2006), systemic intervention, and strong adherence to program fidelity in implementation, and these standards are clearly filtering through to programs and settings (e.g., Landenberger & Lipsey, 2005; Lipsey, 2009). That said, such programs could arguably improve their effectiveness by expanding their focus to the role of coping with inputs, executive function, and the impact of psychosocial functioning on externalizing psychopathology (e.g., Eisenberg, Spinrad, & Eggum, 2010; Riggs, Greenberg, Kusché, & Pentz, 2006). One example of the manner in which these types of mechanisms might be targeted is via "add-on" modules to existing cognitive-behavioral programs that are already known to be relatively effective. Here, comparisons of program effectiveness and, ideally, testing mechanisms of effective program change might better highlight the ways in which developmental features contribute to adolescents' initiation and persistence in crime.

In all, translating psychological understanding of adolescent and young adult development to youth rehabilitation represents a strategic investment. As research continues to elucidate the pathways by which youth are led to initiate and escalate their delinquency, policies and programs can only serve to benefit. Just as important is continued research that highlights youth resilience (e.g., Gardner, Dishion, & Connell, 2008), and the pathways by which youth facing considerable risks are somehow able to avoid these pitfalls.

REFERENCES

Andrews, D. A., & Bonta, J. (2010). Rehabilitating criminal justice policy and practice. *Psychology, Public Policy, and Law, 16*(1), 39–55.

Barkley-Levenson, E., & Galván, A. (2014). Neural representation of expected value in the adolescent brain. *Proceedings of the National Academy of Sciences, 111*, 1646–1651.

Bongers, I. L., Koot, H. M., Van Der Ende, J., & Verhulst, F. C. (2004). Developmental trajectories of externalizing behaviors in childhood and adolescence. *Child Development, 75*, 1523–1537. doi: 10.1111/j.1467-8624.2004.00755.x

Bonnie, R.J., Coughlin, A.M., Jeffries, J.C., & Low, P.W. (Eds.). (1997). *Criminal Law.* Westbury, NY: The Foundation Press.

BP v R [2006] NSWCCA 172.

Brannen, D. N., Salekin, R. T., Zapf, P. A., Salekin, K. L., Kubak, F. A., & DeCoster, J. (2006). Transfer to adult court: A national study of how juvenile court judges weigh pertinent Kent criteria. *Psychology, Public Policy, and Law, 12*, 332–355.

Burrus, B., & Community Preventive Services Task Force. (2012). Person-to-person interventions targeted to parents and other caregivers to improve adolescent health: a community guide systematic review. *American Journal of Preventive Medicine, 42*(3), 316–326. doi: 10.1016/j.amepre.2011.12.001

Buss, E. (2003). The missed opportunity in Gault. *The University of Chicago Law Review, 70*, 39–54.

Caldwell, M. F. (2010). Study characteristics and recidivism base rates in juvenile sex offender recidivism. *International Journal of Offender Therapy and Comparative Criminology, 54*, 197–212.

Casey, B. J. (2015). Beyond simple models of self-control to circuit-based accounts of adolescent behavior. *Annual Review of Psychology, 66,* 295–319.

Cauffman, E., & Steinberg, L. (2000). (Im)maturity of judgement in adolescence: why adolescents may be less culpable than adults. *Behavioral Sciences & the Law, 18*(6), 741–760. doi: 10.1002/bsl.416

Centifanti, L. C. M., Modecki, K. L., MacLellan, S., & Gowling, H. (2016). Driving under the influence of risky peers: An experimental study of adolescent risk taking. *Journal of Research on Adolescence, 26*(1), 207–222.

Cepparulo, E. (2006). Roper v. Simmons: Unveiling juvenile purgatory: Is life really better than death. *Temple Political & Civil Rights Law Review, 16,* 225–256.

Chassin, L., Dmitrieva, J., Modecki, K., Steinberg, L., Cauffman, E., Piquero, A. R., & Losoya, S. H. (2010). Does adolescent alcohol and marijuana use predict suppressed growth in psychosocial maturity among male juvenile offenders? *Psychology of Addictive Behaviors, 24,* 48–60.

Chein, J., Albert, D., O'Brien, L., Uckert, K., & Steinberg, L. (2011). Peers increase adolescent risk taking by enhancing activity in the brain's reward circuitry. *Developmental Science, 14*(2), F1–F10.

Cohen, J. R., Asarnow, R. F., Sabb, F. W., Bilder, R. M., Bookheimer, S. Y., Knowlton, B. J., & Poldrack, R. A. (2010). A unique adolescent response to reward prediction errors. *Nature Neuroscience, 13,* 669–671.

Colwell, L. H., Cruise, K. R., Guy, L. S., McCoy, W. K., Fernandez, K., & Ross, H. H. (2005). The influence of psychosocial maturity on male juvenile offenders' comprehension and understanding of the Miranda warning. *Journal of the American Academy of Psychiatry and the Law Online, 33*(4), 444–454.

Cooper, M. L., Wood, P. K., Orcutt, H. K., & Albino, A. (2003). Personality and the predisposition to engage in risky or problem behaviors during adolescence. *Journal of Personality and Social Psychology, 84*(2), 390–410.

Crofts, T. (1998). Rebutting the presumption of doli incapax. *Journal of Criminal Law, 62,* 185.

Crofts, T. (2008) The Criminal Responsibility of Children. In: Monahan, G. and Young, L., (eds.) Children and the law in Australia. LexisNexis Butterworths, Chatswood, N.S.W., pp. 167–185.

Crone, E. A., & Dahl, R. E. (2012). Understanding adolescence as a period of social–affective engagement and goal flexibility. *Nature Reviews Neuroscience, 13*(9), 636–650.

Dmitrieva, J., Monahan, K. C., Cauffman, E., & Steinberg, L. (2012). Arrested development: The effects of incarceration on the development of psychosocial maturity. *Development and Psychopathology, 24,* 1073–1090.

Dreyfuss, M., Caudle, K., Drysdale, A. T., Johnston, N. E., Cohen, A. O., Somerville, L. H., & Casey, B. J. (2014). Teens impulsively react rather than retreat from threat. *Developmental Neuroscience, 36*(3–4), 220–227.

DuBois, D. L., Holloway, B. E., Valentine, J. C., & Cooper, H. (2002). Effectiveness of mentoring programs for youth: A meta-analytic review. *American Journal of Community Psychology, 30,* 157–197.

Durston, S., & Casey, B. J. (2006). What have we learned about cognitive development from neuroimaging? *Neuropsychologia ,44,* 2149–2157.

Eisenberg, N., Spinrad, T. L., & Eggum, N. D. (2010). Emotion-related self-regulation and its relation to children's maladjustment. *Annual Review of Clinical Psychology, 6,* 495.

Evans, G. W., & Kim, P. (2012). Childhood poverty and young adults' allostatic load. The mediating role of childhood cumulative risk exposure. *Psychological science, 23,* 979–983.

Ewing, S. W. F., Ryman, S. G., Gillman, A. S., Weiland, B. J., Thayer, R. E., & Bryan, A. D. (2016). Developmental cognitive neuroscience of adolescent sexual risk and alcohol use. *AIDS and Behavior, 20*(1), 97–108.

Fanniff, A. M., Schubert, C. A., Mulvey, E. P., Iselin, A. M. R., & Piquero, A. R. (2016). Risk and outcomes: Are adolescents charged with sex offenses different from other adolescent offenders? *Journal of Youth and Adolescence*. doi:10.1007/s10964-016-0536-9

Flavell, J. H. (1979). Metacognition and cognitive monitoring: A new area of cognitive–developmental inquiry. *American Psychologist, 34*, 906–911.

Fried, C. S., & Reppucci, N. D. (2001). Criminal decision making: The development of adolescent judgment, criminal responsibility, and culpability. *Law and Human Behavior, 25*, 45–61.

Galván, A., & McGlennen, K. M. (2012). Daily stress increases risky decision-making in adolescents: A preliminary study. *Developmental Psychobiology, 54*(4), 433–440.

Gardner, M., & Steinberg, L. (2005). Peer influence on risk taking, risk preference, and risky decision making in adolescence and adulthood: An experimental study. *Developmental Psychology, 41*, 625–635.

Gardner, M.R. (1989). The right of juvenile offenders to be punished: Some implications for treating kids as persons. *Nebraska Law Review, 68*, p.183–215.

Gardner, T. W., Dishion, T. J., & Connell, A. M. (2008). Adolescent self-regulation as resilience: Resistance to antisocial behavior within the deviant peer context. *Journal of Abnormal Child Psychology, 36*, 273–284.

Geier, C. F., Terwilliger, R., Teslovich, T., Velanova, K., & Luna, B. (2009). Immaturities in reward processing and its influence on inhibitory control in adolescence. *Cerebral Cortex, 20*(7), 1613–1629.

Goldenberg, D., Telzer, E. H., Lieberman, M. D., Fuligni, A., & Galván, A. (2013). Neural mechanisms of impulse control in sexually risky adolescents. *Developmental Cognitive Neuroscience, 6*, 23–29.

Graham v. Florida, 130, S. Ct. (2011).

Griffin, P., Addie, S., Adams, B., & Firestine, K. (2011). Trying juveniles as adults: An analysis of state transfer laws and reporting. Washington, DC: *US Department of Justice Office of Juvenile Justice and Delinquency Prevention*, 20–21.

Grisso, T. (1997). The competence of adolescents as trial defendants. *Psychology, Public Policy, and Law, 3*, 3–32.

Grisso, T. (1996). Society's retributive response to juvenile violence: A developmental perspective. *Law and Human Behavior, 20*(3), 229–247.

Grisso, T., Steinberg, L., Woolard, J., Cauffman, E., Scott, E., Graham, S., et al. (2003). Juveniles' competence to stand trial: A comparison of adolescents' and adults' capacities as trial defendants. *Law and Human Behavior, 27*, 333–363.

Guerra, N., Modecki, K., & Cunningham, W. (2014). Developing social-emotional skills for the labor market: the PRACTICE model. *World Bank Policy Research Working Paper*, 7123.

Guerra, N. G., Nucci, L., & Huesmann, L. R. (1994). *Moral cognition and childhood aggression*. New York, NY: Plenum Press.

Guerra, N., Williams, K, Tolan, P., & Modecki, K.L. (2008). Theoretical and research advances in understanding youth crime. In R.D. Hoge, N. Guerra, & P. Boxer (Eds.), *The Juvenile Offender: Treatment Approaches*. New York: Guilford Press.

Hains, A. A., & Ryan, E. B. (1983). The development of social cognitive processes among juvenile delinquents and nondelinquent peers. *Child Development, 54*, 1536–1544.

Hwang, K., Velanova, K., & Luna, B. (2010). Strengthening of top-down frontal cognitive control networks underlying the development of inhibitory control: a functional magnetic resonance imaging effective connectivity study. *The Journal of Neuroscience, 30*(46), 15535–15545.

Inhelder, B., & Piaget, J. (1958). The growth of logical thinking from childhood to adolescence. New York: Basic Books.

In Re Gault, 387 U.S. 1 (1967).

Izzo, R. L., & Ross, R. R. (1990). Meta-analysis of rehabilitation programs for juvenile delinquents A brief report. *Criminal Justice and Behavior, 17*, 134–142

Jacobs-Quadrel, M, Fischhoff, B, & Davis, W. (1993). Adolescent (in)vulnerability. *American Psychologist, 48*, 102–116.

Jacobs, J.E., & Klaczynski, P.A. (2002). The development of judgment and decision making during childhood and adolescence. *Current Directions in Psychological Science, 11*, 145–149.

Kann, L., Kinchen, S., Shanklin, S. L., Flint, K. H., Kawkins, J., Harris, W. A., & Zaza, S. (2014). Youth risk behavior surveillance–United States, 2013. *MMWR Surveillance Summary, 63*(Suppl 4), 1–168.

Koehler, J. A., Lösel, F., Akoensi, T. D., & Humphreys, D. K. (2013). A systematic review and meta-analysis on the effects of young offender treatment programs in Europe. *Journal of Experimental Criminology, 9*, 19–43.

Kuhn, D. (2006). Do cognitive changes accompany developments in the adolescent brain? *Perspectives on Psychological Science, 1*(1), 59–67.

Kurlychek, M. C., & Johnson, B. D. (2010). Juvenility and punishment: Sentencing juveniles in adult criminal court. *Criminology, 48*, 725–758.

Kurlychek, M.C., & Johnson, B.D. (2004). The juvenile penalty: A comparison of juvenile and young adult sentencing outcomes in criminal court. *Criminology, 42*, 485–517.

Landenberger, N. A., & Lipsey, M. W. (2005). The positive effects of cognitive–behavioral programs for offenders: A meta-analysis of factors associated with effective treatment. *Journal of Experimental Criminology, 1*, 451–476.

Lipsey, M. W. (2009). The primary factors that characterize effective interventions with juvenile offenders: A meta-analytic overview. *Victims and Offenders, 4*, 124–147.

Lowenkamp, C. T., Latessa, E. J., & Holsinger, A. M. (2006). The risk principle in action: What have we learned from 13,676 offenders and 97 correctional programs? *Crime & Delinquency, 52*, 77–93.

Luciana, M. (2013). Adolescent brain development in normality and psychopathology. *Development and Psychopathology*, 25, 1325–1345. doi: 10.1017/S0954579413000643

Luciana, M., & Collins, P. F. (2012). Incentive motivation, cognitive control, and the adolescent brain: is it time for a paradigm shift? *Child Development Perspectives, 6*(4), 392–399. doi: 10.1111/j.1750-8606.2012.00252.x

Modecki, K.L. (2016). Do risks matter? Variable and person-centered approaches to adolescents' problem behavior. *Journal of Applied Developmental Psychology, 42*, 8–20. doi:10.1016/j.appdev.2015.11.001

Modecki, K.L. (2009). "It's a rush": Psychosocial content of antisocial decision making. *Law and Human Behavior, 33*(3), 183–193.doi: 10.1007/s10979-008-9150-z

Modecki, K.L. (2008). Addressing gaps in the maturity of judgment literature: Age differences and delinquency. *Law and Human Behavior, 32*(1), 78–91. doi: 10.1007/s10979-007-9087-7

Modecki, K. L., Barber, B. L., & Eccles, J. E . (2014). Binge drinking trajectories across adolescence: Extra-curricular activities are protective for youth with early pubertal development. *Journal of Adolescent Health, 54*, 61–66. doi:10.1016/j.jadohealth.2013.07.032

Modecki, K.L. & Uink, B. (2017). How can developmental psychopathology influence social and legal policy? Adolescence, mental health, and decision making. In D. Williams & L. Certifanti (Eds.), *The Wiley-Blackwell Handbook of Developmental Psychopathology.*

Modecki, K.L., Zimmer-Gembeck, M., & Guerra, N. (2017). Emotion regulation, coping and decision-making: Three linked skills for preventing externalizing problems in adolescence. *Child Development, 88*(2). doi:10.1111/cdev.12734

Monahan, K. C., Steinberg, L., Cauffman, E., & Mulvey, E. P. (2013). Psychosocial (im) maturity from adolescence to early adulthood: Distinguishing between adolescence-limited and persisting antisocial behavior. *Development and Psychopathology, 25,* 1093–1105.

Monahan, K. C., Steinberg, L., Cauffman, E., & Mulvey, E. P. (2009). Trajectories of antisocial behavior and psychosocial maturity from adolescence to young adulthood. *Developmental Psychology, 45*(6), 1654–1668.

Mulvey, E. P. (2011). *Highlights from pathways to desistance: A longitudinal study of serious adolescent offenders.* Washington, DC: Office of Juvenile Justice and Delinquency Prevention, US Department of Justice.

Piquero, A. R., Jennings, W. G., & Farrington, D. (2013). The monetary costs of crime to middle adulthood: findings from the Cambridge study in delinquent development. *Journal of Research in Crime and Delinquency, 50,* 53–74. doi: 10.1177/0022427811424505

Preston, S. D., Buchanan, T. W., Stansfield, R. B., & Bechara, A. (2007). Effects of anticipatory stress on decision making in a gambling task. *Behavioral Neuroscience, 121*(2), 257–263.

Puzzanchera, C., & Addie, S. (2014). Delinquency cases waived to criminal court, 2010. Washington, DC.: *Office of Juvenile Justice and Delinquency Prevention.*

R v M (1977) 16 SASR 589.

Redding, R. E. (2008). Juvenile transfer laws: An effective deterrent to delinquency? *Juvenile Justice Bulletin,* August.

Riggs, N. R., Greenberg, M. T., Kusché, C. A., & Pentz, M. A. (2006). The mediational role of neuro-cognition in the behavioral outcomes of a social-emotional prevention program in elementary school students: Effects of the PATHS curriculum. *Prevention Science, 7,* 91–102.

Romer, D. (2010). Adolescent risk taking, impulsivity, and brain development: Implications for prevention. *Developmental Psychobiology, 52*(3), 263–276.

Roper v . Simmons 125 S.Ct. 1183 (2005).

Salekin, R.T. (2002). Juvenile transfer to adult court: How can developmental and child psychology inform policy decision making? In B. L. Bottoms, M. Bull Kovera, & B. D. McAuliff (Eds.), *Children, social science, and the law* (pp. 203–232). Cambridge, UK: Cambridge University Press.

Salekin, R. T., Yff, R. M. A., Neumann, C. S., Leistico, A. R., & Zalot, A. A. (2002). Juvenile transfer to adult courts. A look at the prototypes for dangerousness, sophistication-maturity, and amenability to treatment through a legal lens. *Psychology, Public Policy, and Law, 8,* 373–410. doi:10.1037/1076-8971.8.4.373.

Sandler, I., Schoenfelder, E., Wolchik, S., & MacKinnon, D. (2011). Long-term impact of prevention programs to promote effective parenting: Lasting effects but uncertain processes. *Annual Review of Psychology, 62,* 299–329.

Scott, E.S., & Grisso, T. (1997). The evolution of adolescence: A developmental perspective on juvenile justice reform. *The Journal of Criminal Law & Criminology, 88,* 137–189

Scott E.S., Reppucci, D., & Woolard, J.L. (1995). Evaluating adolescent decision making in legal contexts. *Law and Human Behavior, 19,* 221–244.

Seto, M. C., & Lalumière, M. L. (2010). What is so special about male adolescent sexual offending? A review and test of explanations through meta-analysis. *Psychological Bulletin, 136,* 526–575.

Shapiro, D. A. (2012). What's beneath the Graham Cracker: The potential impact of comparative law on the future of juvenile justice reform-after Graham v. Florida. *Pace International Law Review, 24,* 119–157.

Shulman, E. P., & Cauffman, E. (2014). Deciding in the dark: Age differences in intuitive risk judgment. *Developmental Psychology, 50*(1), 167–177.

Shulman, E. P., & Cauffman, E. (2013). Reward-biased risk appraisal and its relation to juvenile versus adult crime. *Law and Human Behavior, 37*(6), 412–423.

Silva, K., Chein, J., & Steinberg, L. (2016). Adolescents in peer groups make more prudent decisions when a slightly older adult is present. *Psychological Science,* 322–330. DOI: 10.1177/0956797615620379

Slobogin, C., Fondacaro, M.R., & Woolard, J. (1999). A prevention model of juvenile justice: The promise of Kansas V. Hendricks for children. *Wisconsin Law Review,* 186–226.

Somerville, L. H. (2013). The teenage brain sensitivity to social evaluation. *Current Directions in Psychological Science, 22,* 121–127.

Spear, L.P. (2000). Neurobehavioral changes in adolescence. Current Directions in *Psychological Science, 9,* 111–114.

Steinberg, L., Albert, D., Cauffman, E., Banich, M., Graham, S., & Woolard, J. (2008). Age differences in sensation seeking and impulsivity as indexed by behavior and self-report: evidence for a dual systems model. *Developmental Psychology, 44*(6), 1764–1778.

Steinberg, L., Cauffman, E., Woolard, J., Graham, S., & Banich, M. (2009). Are adolescents less mature than adults?: Minors' access to abortion, the juvenile death penalty, and the alleged APA" flip-flop". *American Psychologist, 64*(7), 583–594.

Steinberg, L., & Cauffman, E. (1999). The elephant in the courtroom: A developmental perspective on the adjudication of youthful offenders. *Virginal Journal of Social Policy & the Law, 6,* 389–417.

Steinberg, L., & Cauffman, E. (1996). Maturity of judgment in adolescence: Psychosocial factors in adolescent decision making. *Law and Human Behavior, 20*(3), 249–272.

Steinberg, L., & Lerner, R.M. (2004). The scientific study of adolescence: A brief history. *Journal of Early Adolescence, 24,* 45–54.

Steinberg, L., & Monahan, K. C. (2007). Age differences in resistance to peer influence. *Developmental Psychology, 43,* 1531–1543.

Steinberg, L., & Scott, E. S. (2003). Less guilty by reason of adolescence: developmental immaturity, diminished responsibility, and the juvenile death penalty. *American Psychologist, 58*(12), 1009–1018.

Tapp, J. L. (1976). Psychology and the law: an overture. *Annual Review of Psychology, 27,* 359–404.

Teslovich, T., Mulder, M., Franklin, N. T., Ruberry, E. J., Millner, A., Somerville, L. H., Simen, P., Durston, S. and Casey, B. J. (2014), Adolescents let sufficient evidence accumulate before making a decision when large incentives are at stake. *Developmental Science, 17*: 59–70. doi: 10.1111/ desc.12092

Telzer, E. H., Ichien, N. T., & Qu, Y. (2015). Mothers know best: redirecting adolescent reward sensitivity toward safe behavior during risk taking. *Social Cognitive and Affective Neuroscience,* 1383–1391.

The Annie E. Casey Foundation (2013). Youth incarceration in the United States. Retrieved from: http://www.aecf.org/m/resourcedoc/aecf-YouthIncarcerationInfographic-2013.pdf

Uink, B.N., Modecki, K.L., & Barber, B.L. (under review). Are youth high in externalizing more emotionally reactive to minor stressors? An experience sampling study with disadvantaged youth.

Uink, B.N., Modecki, K.L., & Barber, B.L. (2017). Disadvantaged youth report less negative emotion to minor stressors when with peers: An experience sampling study. *International Journal of Behavioral Development, 41(1),* 41–51. doi:10.1177/0165025416626516

Weigard, A., Chein, J., Albert, D., Smith, A., & Steinberg, L. (2014). Effects of anonymous peer observation on adolescents' preference for immediate rewards. *Developmental Science, 17,* 71–78.

Weithorn, L.A. (1984). Children's capacities in legal contexts. In N.D. Reppucci, L.A. Weithorn, E.P. Mulvet, & J. Monahan (Eds.). *Children, mental health, and the law.* (pp. 25–55). Beverly Hills: Sage Publications.

Williamson, A.A., Modecki, K.L., & Guerra, N.G. (2015). Evidence-based programming in diverse settings: high school. In J. Durlak, T. Gullotta, C. Domitrovich, P. Goren, & R. Weissberg (Eds.), *The Handbook of Social and Emotional Learning,* pp.181–196.

Woolard, J. L., Fondacaro, M. R., & Slobogin, C. (2001). Informing juvenile justice policy: Directions for behavioral science research. *Law and Human Behavior, 25*(1), 13–24.

Woolard, J., Reppucci, N., & Redding, R. (1996). Theoretical and methodological issues in studying children's capacities in legal contexts. *Law and Human Behavior, 20,* 219–228.

Zimmer-Gembeck, M. J., & Skinner, E. A. (2011). The development of coping across childhood and adolescence: An integrative review and critique of research. *International Journal of Behavioral Development, 35,* 1–17. doi: 10.1177/0165025410384923.

CHAPTER 2

Adolescent Sexual Development and Normative Behavior

Michael H. Miner

Rosemary A. Munns

This chapter describes adolescent sexual development and normative sexual behavior. It is our belief the development of sexually abusive behavior in adolescent populations is the result of developmental challenges and is often a manifestation of developmental processes (Burton & Miner, 2016). In order to understand sexually abusive behavior, one must first know what is normative and how development proceeds through adolescence when there are no major traumas or disruptions.

It is also important in understanding adolescent sexual development to distinguish between the physiological changes that characterize puberty and the interactions among physiological changes, social influences, and individual characteristics that characterize adolescent sexual development. Adolescence is a broad concept that encompasses both puberty and the social, emotional, and wider psychological changes that characterize the chronological transition from childhood to adulthood (Susman & Dorn, 2009). In this chapter, we focus on the significant physical, emotional, and cognitive changes involved in the task of becoming a healthy sexual adult.

Puberty

Pubertal development in humans involves two distinct processes: adrenarche, the maturation of adrenal gland secretion and involving the hypothalamic-pituitary-adrenal (HPA) axis; and gonadarche, reactivation of the hypothalamic-pituitary-gonadal (HPG) axis and maturation of the gonadal sex steroid secretion. Adrenarche usually occurs at ages six to eight. Adrenal androgen secretion increases gradually, continues to rise through puberty, and reaches asymptote in late adolescence. No physiological role has been ascribed to adrenal androgens, other than stimulation of growth of small amounts of pubic hair. Gonadarche usually occurs at ages 9 to 11. Gonadotropin levels rise first, followed by gonadal sex steroids, the levels of which rise more steeply than adrenal androgens and reach asymptote around mid-adolescence. The gonadal sex steroids are responsible for the development of secondary sex characteristics. Testosterone and its active metabolite 5-dihydrotestosterone masculinize boys, and estradiol is primarily responsible for feminizing girls (Nottleman, Inoff-Germain, Susman, & Chrousus, 1990).

Pubertal development results in reproductive maturation in most individuals, with the exception of cases with disorders of puberty. The process is biological, involving a complex series of neuroendocrine changes that result in changes in hormonal activity. This hormone activity begins the development of reproductive organs and physical changes in weight, height, muscle mass, and distribution of fat. These physical changes occur in a social context affecting the individual's sexual status and impacted by social reactions from others that in turn results in the individual appraising and reappraising his or her developing body, feelings about the self, sexuality, and peer and family relations (Brooks-Gunn, Graber, & Paikoff, 1994; Graber & Sontag, 2006).

Menarche is often viewed as the onset of puberty for girls, but in fact it is one of the latest events in girls' pubertal development (Tanner, 1962; 1998). Growth spurt, breast bud and genital development, growth of pubic and axillary hair, voice change, and changes in curvation and fat distribution often precede menarche (Tanner, 1962; 1998). The male equivalent of menarche is semenarche, which refers to boys' first ejaculation. Semenarche also connotes sexual maturation. The physical surge of hormones that characterizes puberty does not mark the onset of sexual interest; nor does it mark the onset of sexual activity. Studies have found that sexual arousal can begin around age 9 for boys and 10 for girls (de Graaf & Rademakers, 2006). Infants engage in touching their genitals as young as age eight months, and toward the end of their first year of life this genital touching becomes more directed (de Graaf & Rademakers, 2006). Studies also indicate that it is not uncommon for prepubertal children of both genders to engage in mutual sexual touching (de Graaf & Rademakers, 2006; Friedrich, Gamback, Broughton, Kuiper, & Beilke, 1991). However, the external manifestations of pubertal development, such as facial and axillary hair and muscle growth in boys and breast and hip development in girls, are public signals of sexual readiness that may prompt unanticipated and undesired sexual approaches from others (O'Sullivan & Thompson, 2014).

ADOLESCENT SEXUAL DEVELOPMENT

Although sexual development is typically treated as a form of individual development, sexuality and sexual behavior have strong links to interpersonal experiences. Sexual development is one of the complex aspects of adolescence and involves a multitude of difficult-to-define intrapersonal processes and a broad set of interpersonal behaviors.

Drury and Bukowski (2013) outlined four basic premises in defining adolescent sexual development.

1. Sexuality is not a single thing; it is linked to and implicated in multiple forms of functioning. These domains include urges, motivation, forms of attention, emotions, aspects of the self, biological processes, moral precepts, modes of self-presentation, relationships and interactions, and one's perceptions of others.

2. Sexuality is an integrative form of development. That is, a central process of sexuality concerns the intersection and coordination of many intrapersonal and interpersonal components. Examples of these integrations include issues related to sexual desire, sexual motivation, and one's sexual self-concept that are influenced by feelings, moral orientation, interpersonal expectations, and relationship experiences and goals.

3. Sexuality is a form of development that varies across age, and sexuality at one age is in part determined by experiences at a younger age. Thus, sexuality needs to be understood from the developmental context in which it is embedded. Sexuality must be studied from a "life span" and a "life history" perspective (Bukowski, Li, Dirks, & Bouffard, 2012). The life span approach is focused on developmental processes from within a particular moment of the life course (e.g., adolescence); the life history approach is concerned with understanding stability and change from one time of the life course to another (e.g., early adolescence to adulthood).

4. Defining normal sexuality is as difficult as defining sex. Any definition of normal sexuality would be highly abstract and would emphasize the synthesis between multiple aspects of functioning. In nearly every aspect of sexuality, variability among people and across the life span is too large for the creation of a meaningful "norm."

Complex Bio-Psycho-Social Aspects of Sexual Development

Testosterone is more closely related to sexual activity for boys and less related or unrelated to sexual activity for girls, even though there are strong associations between sexual ideation, motivation, and testosterone levels (Halpern, Udry, & Suchindran, 1998). Hormone changes contribute to sexual development at some level, but sexual development best reflects a wide and complex range of biological and psychosocial systems working in tandem (Halpern, 2006). Culture clearly moderates the expression of biological differences primarily through the socialization of gender roles and expectations regarding appropriate sexual behavior (Lam, Shi, Ho, & Fan, 2002). For example, semenarche appears to have fewer emotional associations for boys than menarche among girls (O'Sullivan & Thompson, 2014).

During the period of pubertal development, significant changes in cognitive, emotional, and social functioning also occur. These changes include more abstract, hypothetical thinking, with new abilities to incorporate long-term perspectives, less egocentric thinking, and greater empathic identification with others (Larson, Clore, & Wood, 1999). Changes in social interactions with peers come with strong emotions such as anger, self-consciousness, anxiety, and shame, which are experienced at levels not previously experienced (Larson et al., 1999). Adolescents are better able to differentiate emotions (Nannis & Cowan, 1987), gain skills in emotion regulation (McRae et al., 2012), and become more capable of characterizing blended emotions and states and attributing emotions to their behavior (Fischer, Shaver, & Carnochan, 1990) than at younger ages. Negative affective states, such as irritability and depression, increase during adolescence (e.g., Arnett, 1999), and mid-adolescent girls report more negative daily mood and negative interpersonal events than younger adolescent girls (Flook, 2011). Boys and girls become increasingly dissatisfied with their body around puberty (Graber, Peterson, & Brooks-Gunn, 1996) but also become more aware of the extent to which they are attracting sexual attention and are sexually attracted to others. Young people become more sensitive to others' appearance appraisals (Carlson Jones, 2004). Mixed-gender-group interactions appear related to higher rates of sexual harassment, sexual comments, and teasing (McMaster, Connolly, Pepler, & Craig, 1992). These cognitive abilities, personal appraisals, and interpersonal experiences all have implications for the development of sexuality and the expression of sexual behavior.

Although biology plays a central role in human sexual development, sexuality is derived from the functions of the physical body but gains meaning through interplay with the individual's surroundings. Sexual learning is embedded with the individual's social context and includes elements of motivation theory, social learning theory, and gender schema theory (Drury & Bukowski, 2013). Motivation is defined as the psychological feature that arouses an organism to action toward a desired goal. It plays a fundamental role in learning. Human beings are naturally motivated to satisfy our drives and needs, and in the process we learn optimal ways of doing so (Maslow, 1943). We are motivated to increase our experiences of pleasure (incentive theory) and decrease those of pain (drive theory). Logically, sexual behavior would satisfy different drives or needs depending on the individual's development. Physical touch plays a critical role in early development. Many studies have shown physical touch to be a necessary component of healthy development (Stack, 2007; Field, 2002). Physical contact forms the foundation of self-concept through the process of internalization.

Sullivan (1953) proposed that children use experiential information derived directly from their interactions with others to create a self-concept. He proposed that self-concept is composed of two basic components: the "good me" and the "bad me." Each develops from an integrative process that brings together physical feelings derived from interpersonal interactions with caregivers. The "good me" is the result of tenderness and satisfaction from parents and the "bad me" is the result of anxiety and rejection in these interactions.

Empirical research on childhood sexual behavior supports the notion that early sexual behavior is normal, developmentally distinct, and motivated by pleasure and curiosity (Larsson, 2002). That is, children are naturally curious about their own bodies and those of others and may take part in sexual investigation on their own body and in games with other children; however, behaviors that imitate adult sexuality are very uncommon in observations of normal groups of children (Larsson, 2002). Still, as with every other aspect of sexuality and sexual development, children vary in their interest in sexuality (Larsson, 2002). Moore and Rosenthal (2006) found that the most common motive for both boys and girls, preceding first intercourse, was curiosity. Curiosity is an important aspect through which children are motivated to learn. Learning about sexuality, like all learning, transpires within a cultural and social space. Culture, in this context, is defined as the way of life of a group of people—the values, beliefs, behaviors, and attitudes they accept, from one generation to the next. There are many cultural influences, including religion, family, government, peer groups, country, and community, that come together to determine acceptable behavior in general and—for our purposes—sexual behavior. Cultural norms are expressed through a variety of mediums, and cultural beliefs and expectations about sexuality provide the parameters within which an individual learns what is acceptable and what is unacceptable behavior (Drury & Bukowski, 2013). A complete discussion of these influences is beyond the scope of this chapter.

Children grow up in a particular social context, and over time internalize its norms and values concerning sexual behaviors (Larrson, 2002). Basic social cognitive learning theory suggests that humans learn by observing others. Behaviors that are rewarded are more likely to be repeated; those that are punished are less likely to be repeated (Bandura, 1977). According to this theory, gender differences in behaviors are created because boys and girls observe different behaviors in same-gender models, and are reinforced or punished for different behaviors. Boys and girls learn gender-appropriate behaviors when they are reinforced for gender-role-consistent behaviors and punished for gender-role-inconsistent behaviors. However, social cognitive learning suggests that boys and girls do not need to be directly rewarded or punished in order to learn which behaviors are appropriate to imitate; they may learn appropriate gender role behaviors simply by observing rewards and punishment directed toward same-gender models. Gender schema theory suggests that from a young age, children identify their own gender and gender group, and develop a belief system regarding the behaviors that are consistent with being a boy or a girl or woman or man (Ruble & Martin, 1998). Children's recognition of the social significance of gender motivates them to learn about and comply with gender norms. "What we term healthy and natural sexuality is formed from the society we live in and depends on our gender" (Larsson, 2002, p. 11). Gender differences in interactional styles are of critical importance for the sexual interaction between adolescent boys and girls and subsequently men and women (Maccoby, 1998).

Adolescent sexual development introduces new personal and interpersonal dynamics into interactions and relationships. Friendships take on new characteristics, putting extra stress on the ability to negotiate the balance between the self and others. Intimacy and security are added to the presence of friendship features. The task for adolescents is to transform their friendship relationships from activity- and interaction-based experiences to relationship experiences that include high levels of interpersonal closeness involving one's internal states (Bukowski, Simard, DuBois, & Lopez, 2011).

Sexual Self-Concept

We need to have some understanding of how adolescents construct a sense of themselves as sexual people. Self-concept is a cognitive construct that is a framework for interpreting experiences. It is multifaceted and is an integration of dynamic core and peripheral concepts as well as the idealized "possible selves" (Markus & Nurius, 1986). Sexual self-concept is one of the peripheral concepts and is important in understanding adolescent sexual behavior and motivations. Rotosky, Dekhtyar, Cupp, and Anderman (2008) define sexual self-concept as "an individual's positive and negative perceptions and feelings about himself or herself as a sexual being." The consolidation of one's sexual self-concept is considered an important development task during adolescence (Longmore, 1998). Sexual self-concepts are believed to reflect gender role socialization, including the norms of appropriate behavior, responsibilities, and obligations that come with being a man or woman (Gagnon & Parker, 1995). Girls and boys are taught different lessons about sexuality and sexual lives, almost entirely from a heterocentric perspective. Girls' socialization emphasizes participation in and maintenance of relationships (Breakwell & Millward, 1997) and romantic partnerships as the contexts for sexual expression (Fine, 1998; Thompson, 1994). Boys' socialization emphasizes sexual agency and the ability to pursue sexual opportunities with female partners wherever they arise (O'Sullivan & Thompson, 2014). The above socialization and gender role expectations, while predominantly present, have wide variations within individuals, as well as across individuals within various socioeconomic, racial, ethnic, and cultural groups. As described by Money (1997), sexual self-concept includes processes to develop and internalize gendermaps, a basic schema of masculinity and feminity, and lovemaps, which describe attractions, including sexual orientation.

Sexual Desire

Sexual desire is defined as "an interest in sexual objects or activities or a wish, need, or drive to seek out sexual objects or to engage in sexual activity" (Regan & Bershceid, 1995, p. 346). This definition combines two phenomena that are not equivalent: an interest in sexual objects and a drive to seek sexual objects. These two types of sexual desire are denoted proceptivity, the basic urge to seek and initiate sexual activity, and receptivity, the capacity to become interested in sex when encountering certain erotic stimuli (Bancroft, 1976). Variability in proceptive sexual desire is tightly linked to gonadal hormones (e.g., testosterone in men and both testosterone and estrogen in women). However, variability in arousal is not linked directly to gonadal hormones (Tolman & Diamond, 2001). This difference might explain why sharp increases in pubertal gonadal hormones correspond to sharp increases in the frequency and intensity of self-reported sexual desires (Halpern, Udry, Campbell, & Suchindran, 1993), but do not correspond to onset of sexual desire. Children first report desires and attractions as early as nine years, and some experiment with purposeful self-stimulation as early as six (Diamond & Savin-Williams, 2009).

Perhaps these early childhood experiences of sexual desire, and occasionally sexual behaviors, stem from hormonal independent arousability, whereas the classic pubertal surges in self-reported sexual desire reflect the hormonally mediated development of proceptivity (Diamond & Savin-Williams, 2009). This supports the argument that sexuality does not suddenly "switch on" at puberty, but develops gradually over the course of childhood and adolescence through a subtle and gradual intertwining of erotic and social experiences. The existing literature on distinctions between arousability and proceptivity suggests that although young children might become aroused in response to erotic stimuli, many do not experience strong urges to act on those feelings until adolescence (Diamond & Savin-Williams, 2009).

Sex Differences in Desire

Regardless of sexual orientation, boys become aware of their sexual interests and impulses several years earlier than girls, and boys report more frequent sexual arousal (several times per day versus once a week) (Knoth, Boyd, & Singer, 1998). Boys also report their sexual arousal to be more intense and distracting than do girls (Knoth et al., 1998). Variability in androgen levels in both genders has been found to be reliably associated with variability in self-reported sexual motivation (Bancroft, 1978; Udry, 1988). Correspondingly, differences between male and female experiences of sexual desire—specifically the fact that women report fewer sexual urges than do men, have fewer purely sexual fantasies, lower rates and frequencies of masturbation, and less motivation to seek or initiate sexual activity—have been attributed to well-known sex differences in testosterone levels (Diamond & Savin-Williams, 2009).

Research has also supported cultural and social factors as equally or more impor-tant in differences in sexual desire, highlighting the powerful social forces that restrict female experiences of sexual desire. Even as the role of women in society has changed and the nature of masculine and feminine behavioral expectations converge, girls still are put in the role of sexual gatekeeping, with a primary task of fending off boys' sexual overtures in order to guard themselves against pregnancy and STIs (Fine & McClelland, 2006). Girls receive powerful and consistent messages from social and religious institutions, schools, media, and family that women do not want or need sexual activity as much as men and sexuality is appropriate only within committed, monogamous relationships. This may lead to girls learning to discount their own bodily experiences of sexual desire and to dismiss their own motives for sexual con-tact (Tolman, 2002). The number one form of sexual dysfunction among adult women is low or nonexistent sexual desire (Laumenn, Paik, & Rosen, 1999). Girls are supposed to consistently suppress and deny their sexual desires from childhood through ado-lescence and then suddenly blossom into healthy sexually confident adults. Evidence suggests that the negative messages girls receive about female sexuality impedes their developing awareness of their own physical experiences of sexual arousal (Diamond & Savin-Williams, 2009). Less than half of female teenagers report they can always detect their sexual arousal, compared with nearly all of male teenagers (Knoth et al., 1988). Studies using physiological measures of genital blood flow have found that women often show distinct discrepancies between their degree of physical arousal and their subjective feelings of arousal (Chivers & Bailey, 2005; Chivers, Rieger, Latty, & Bailey, 2005).

Sexual Motivation

Sexual desire is presumed to be a fairly uniform experience propelling adolescents toward a diverse array of sexual behaviors. While there are some data available on first sexual desire, there is not sufficient detailed information on the subjective quality of this experience, and thus it is difficult to develop models of sexual motivation from childhood to young adulthood or understand its links to sexual behavior (Diamond & Savin-Williams, 2009). These blind spots reflect the tendency for developmental researchers to focus on the physical characteristics of sexual maturation rather than the experiential aspects of this behavior (Brooks-Gunn & Paikoff, 1997). These blind spots also expose the deep-seated ambivalence regarding early manifestations of sexuality and the need to control and monitor sexual behavior, rather than promote positive sexual self-concepts (Fine & McClelland, 2006).

Sexual motive can be conceptualized as providing the link between sexual desire and behavior. Many factors may explain why a particular adolescent does or does not act on his or her sexual desires; understanding these motives is critical to a systematic analysis of adolescent sexual development. Sexual intentions are among the strongest predictors of an adolescent's future sexual behavior (Buhi & Goodson, 2007). Intraindividual and interindividual differences in adolescents' motives for pursuing sex are systematically related to types of sexual contact pursued: committed versus casual, planned versus unplanned, protected versus unprotected, and with a single partner versus multiple partners (Cooper, Shapiro, & Powers, 1998).

One motivation for sexual activity is simple sexual release. Another motivation for sexual activity is curiosity and experimentation. This particular motivation may be fueled in part by increasing visibility of sexually explicit depictions and discussions available through a variety of media outlets. Achievement of social status is another important motive for adolescent sexual contact, signaling to oneself and others the realization of the desired adult sexual status (O'Sullivan & Thompson, 2014). Romantic relationships also provide numerous motives and opportunities for sexual activity. Love for the person was a primary motive for having sexual intercourse among 9th-through 11th-grade students in Canada (Boyce et al., 2006). Love proved to be more important for females than males and for older than younger adolescents. Adolescents pursue a broader range of sexual behaviors with romantic partners when they feel more emotional commitment (Halpern, Udry, & Suchindran, 1997). Another motive for adolescent sexual activity is emotion regulation. The pleasure and release associated with sexual activity can attenuate or distract from negative emotions, helping youth cope with negative events. Although emotion regulation is not as common as intimacy- and pleasure-based motives for sexual activity, it deserves attention, given that adolescents with emotional-regulation motives are less likely to pursue sexual activity within committed relationships and tend to have a greater number of sexual partners and riskier sexual practices (Cooper et al., 1998). Emotion-regulating motives for sex are particularly important when considering the well-established correlations between compromised family and community environments and problematic sexual behavior, including sexual violence (Miller et al., 1997).

Sexual Behavior

Adolescent sexual development is a complex interaction among biological, cognitive, emotional, and social changes that effect the manifestation of sexual and relationship behavior. As noted above, there are large variations in behavior, attitudes, and beliefs that make it difficult to define normative adolescent behavior. However, there are data that indicate the range of behavior in which young people are engaging, and these data provide benchmarks for determining developmentally appropriate sexual behaviors and for distinguishing those behaviors that are less likely to have detrimental effects from those that are likely to be harmful.

A limitation in our understanding of adolescent sexual behavior is that much of the research has been guided by concerns about harmful outcomes. That is, much of what we know about adolescent sexual behavior has been learned from surveys of youth at risk for negative outcomes, such as teenage pregnancy and sexually transmitted diseases. The data presented in this section come from three studies: the National Survey of Family Growth (NCHS, 2015), the Youth Risk Behavior Survey (YRBS: CDC, 2014), and the National Survey of Sexual Health and Behavior (NSSHB: Reece et al., 2010a). The National Survey of Family Growth is a household survey of men and women in the 50 states of the United States and the District of Columbia. Data collection was conducted by in-person, face-to-face interviewing with adults. Teenagers, Hispanic men and women, and non-Hispanic black men and women were oversampled (NCHS, 2010). The YRBS is conducted every two years and provides data representative of 9th- through 12th-grade students in public and private schools in the United States. The survey uses a three-stage sample design and targets populations consisting of all public, Catholic, and other private school students. The survey over-samples black and Hispanic students and applies a weighting factor to account for this oversampling (CDC, 2014). The NSSHB was a cross-sectional survey that included 820 adolescents, 14 through 17 years old. Participants were recruited via research panels of Knowledge Networks, and all recruitment and data collection was conducted online. The 820 participants represented 37 percent of the adolescents initially contacted via email (Fortenberry et al., 2010).

Initiating Sexual Behavior

Data from the National Survey of Family Growth (NCHS, 2015) indicate that both for men and women, first sexual intercourse occurs at about 17 years of age. Boys appear to be slightly younger than girls, and age has decreased slightly from 2002 to 2013 (table 2.1).

TABLE 2.1 AGE AT FIRST VAGINAL INTERCOURSE

	2002	2006–2010	2011–2013
Mean age for men	17.0 years	17.1 years	16.8 years
Mean age for women	17.4 years	17.1 years	17.2 years

The data reported in figures 2.1 and 2.2 are from the most recent High School Youth Risk Behavior Survey (YRBS: CDC, 2015). This survey is conducted every two years, so we can see trends in behavior since 1991.

The data that follow indicate that the percentage of high school boys who have had sexual intercourse is somewhat higher, ranging from almost 60 percent in 1991 to a little less than 50 percent by 2013, than for girls. However, over the years, the proportion of boys and girls who have had sexual intercourse during their high school years is converging, mainly due to what appears to be a steeper decline in the proportion of boys reporting sexual intercourse experience. In 2013, less than half of adolescent boys and girls reported ever having engaged in sexual intercourse.

Figure 2.1 Percentage of High School Boys and Girls Reporting Ever Having Sexual Intercourse

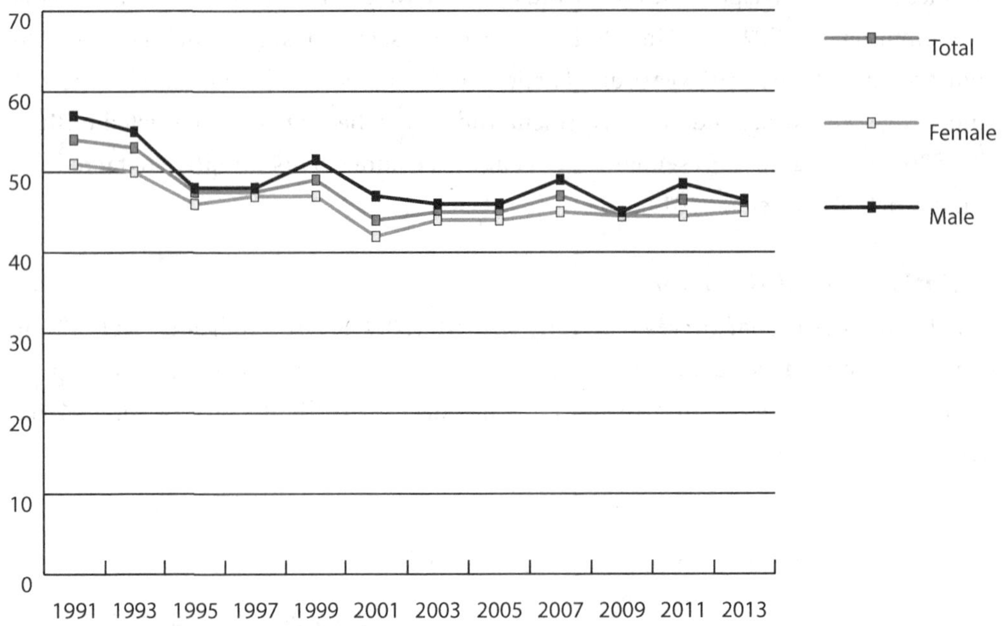

Figure 2.2 shows the percentage of teenagers reporting ever engaging in sexual intercourse by grade level. The trend lines for 9th and 10th graders indicate that the prevalence of sexual intercourse has been decreasing in these age groups since 1991. The trend for 12th graders appears pretty stable from 1991 to 2013. Additionally, sexual behavior becomes more prevalent as adolescents age, with 30 percent of 9th graders reporting having had sexual intercourse in 2013, while 64 percent of 12th graders report they have had sexual intercourse. The progression appears to be fairly linear over time until, by about age 17 years, at least 60 percent of teenagers have initiated sexual intercourse.

Data from the YRBS indicate that it is very infrequent for either boys or girls to initiate sexual intercourse before the age of 13 years. While there has been a slight decrease in the number reporting initiating sexual intercourse prior to age 13, it never exceeded 10 percent and in 2013, the last time data were collected, only 5.6 percent of adolescents reported they had engaged in sexual intercourse prior to age 13. African American youth were more likely to have engaged in sexual intercourse prior to age 13 years than any other race/ethnic group, but while the reported prevalence stayed about the same for the other groups, African American youth were less likely to have initiated sexual intercourse in 2013, 14 percent, than in 1991, 28 percent.

Figure 2.2 Percentage Reporting Engaging in Sexual Intercourse by Grade Level

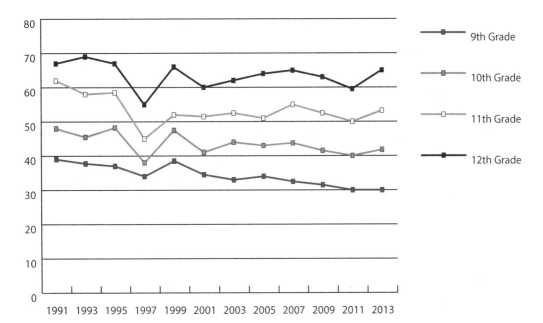

Reported Adolescent Sexual Behavior

The probability sample of 15- to 17-year-olds participating in the NSSHB report a much lower prevalence of sexual intercourse than found in the YRBS data. Lifetime vaginal intercourse is reported by a little over 30 percent of 16- to 17-year-old males and about the same number of females (Herbenick et al., 2010). This is about half the prevalence reported by 12th graders, who would be about 17 and 18 years old, and also less than 11th graders, who would be about 16 and 17 years old, in the Youth Risk Survey. The YRBS and the NSSHB use very different sampling and survey procedures, with the YRBS sampling from schools, while the NSSHB uses an available Internet-based sampling frame. These sampling and data collection differences may impact the results, however; since the YRBS includes all 12th-grade students, there are substantial numbers of participants who are 18 years old. Thus, the difference may be attributed to the different age range, since by 18 years of age, larger proportions of youth are likely to have initiated sexual activity. It is also possible that the NSSHB underestimates due to either sampling bias or social desirability. Either way, these differences highlight the difficulty defining "normal" sexual behavior and getting good estimates of the sexual behavior of adolescents.

However, despite the above, sexual behavior, including sexual intercourse, is not an uncommon behavior in teenagers. Results of the NSSHB indicate that masturbation is common in boys, with 67.5 percent of 14- and 15-year-old boys reporting having masturbated and 78.9 percent of 16- and 17-year-old boys reporting the same. Sixty-two percent of

14- to 15-year-old boys and 75 percent of 16- to 17-year-old boys reported having masturbated during the past year. The rates are somewhat less in girls, with 43.3 percent of 14- to 15-year-old girls reporting masturbating during their lifetime and 52.4 percent of 16- to 17-year-old girls. About 40 percent of 14- to 15-year-old and 45 percent of 16- to 17-year-old girls reported masturbating at least once in the past year (Herbenick et al., 2010).

Further, data from the NSSHB indicate that gay or lesbian orientation is reported by 1.8 percent of boys and 0.2 percent of girls. An additional 1.5 percent of boys indicate that they are bisexual, while 8.4 percent of girls report a bisexual orientation. Experiencing same-sex behavior is also rather rare in both adolescent boys and girls. About 2 percent of boys 14 to 15 years old and about 3 percent of boys 16 to 17 years old reported receiving oral sex from another male, with about the same proportions reporting that they have given oral sex to another male. Even smaller numbers reported receptive anal sex (1% of all males). A slightly higher proportion of girls reported having engaged in same-sex behavior. About 4 percent of 14- to 15-year-old girls and 7 percent of 16- to 17-year-old girls reported receiving oral sex from another female; 5 percent of 14- to 15-years-olds and 9 percent of 16- to 17-year-olds reported giving oral sex to another female (Herbenick et al., 2010).

While same-sex behavior is relatively rare, adolescent males receive oral sex from their female partners at a similar rate as they engage in sexual intercourse. The NSSHB data indicate that 13 percent of 14- to 15-year-old boys and 34 percent of 16- to 17-year-old boys report that they have received oral sex from a girl and about the same percentage of girls report giving oral sex to a boy. Boys, however, are less likely to engage in cunnilingus with their female partners; only 8 percent of 14- to 15-year-olds and 20 percent of 16- to 17-years-old reported that they had ever given oral sex to a female partner, with 10 percent of 14- to 15-year-old girls and 26 percent of 16- to 17-year-old girls reporting that they received oral sex from male partners. It is very rare for an adolescent girl to engage in anal intercourse, with only 7 percent of older teenage girls reporting they ever engaged in anal intercourse and 4 percent of 14- to 15-year-old girls (Herbenick et al., 2010).

Use of Condoms and Other Forms of Birth Control

The data presented in figures 2.3 and 2.4 were obtained from the YRBS online data analysis system. The data reflect the results of surveys conducted every two years between 1991 and 2013. Data are only presented for black, Hispanic, and white race/ethnicity groups because other groups either had sample sizes too small to calculate confidence intervals or were not reported for multiple time periods (see CDC, 2015). Figure 2.3 indicates that since 1991, the use of condoms has increased in all race/ethnic groups. In all cases, less than 50 percent of youth used a condom the last time they had intercourse in 1991, but in 2013, condom use has increased such that condom-less sexual intercourse occurs about 40 percent of the time. Condom use has increased substantially among Hispanic youth, who were initially the least likely to use condoms and are now at the same level as the other race/ethnicity groups. Black youth showed the highest level of condom use until about 2003, when their use declined somewhat. White youth showed a decline that leveled off about 2001 and has remained constant at about 40 percent reporting they did not use a condom the last time they had sexual intercourse. These rates are still substantial and may account for sexually transmitted illness rates for youth found in the United States.

Figure 2.3 Percentage Not Using a Condom at Last Sexual Intercourse

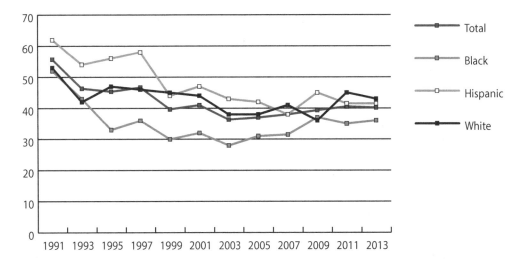

The data in figure 2.4 indicate that although there are substantial rates of unprotected sexual intercourse, most youth used some form of birth control the last time they engaged in sexual intercourse. Hispanic youth were much less likely to use birth control than any of the other race/ethnicity groups. White youth were least likely to engage in sexual intercourse without using some form of birth control. In African American youth, the year-to-year rates were unstable, but in general it appears that rates stayed fairly stable at about 12 to 15 percent of youth reporting not using some form of birth control the last time they had sexual intercourse. White youth showed an overall increase in the use of birth control when having sexual intercourse, and Hispanic youth appeared to stay fairly stable at around 20 percent reporting that they did not use any birth control the last time they engaged in sexual intercourse. For some reason, in 2013 all groups showed a decrease in birth control use. For whites, this trend started in 2011.

Figure 2.4 *Percentage Not Using Any Form of Birth Control at Last Sexual Intercourse*

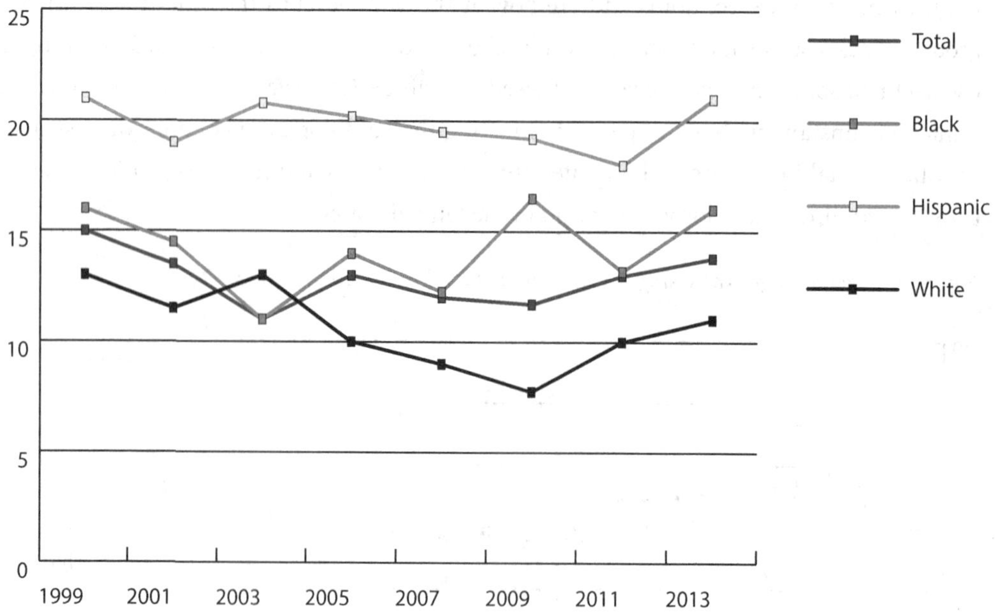

Context in Which Sexual Behavior Occurs

Adolescent sexual behavior takes place within the context of sexual and interpersonal development. Thus, the relationship context of sexual behavior provides insight into the interplay between sexuality development and the development of interpersonal intimacy. In a study of 7,470 adolescents with a mean age of 16.2, of which 54 percent were female, 38 percent were found to be sexually active and 62 percent of the sexually active youth only had sex within the context of a romantic relationship. Thus, while sexual activity usually takes place within the context of a romantic relationship, these data indicate that a substantial proportion of adolescents (38%) have engaged in sexual behavior outside such relationships (Manning, Longmore, & Giordano, 2005).

In a more recent study, Fielder, Walsh, Carey, and Carey (2013) surveyed 483 incoming female college freshmen. Twenty-six percent reported that they had engaged in a "hookup" during high school where they performed oral sex on a male partner, and 21 percent reported engaging in hookups during high school where they received oral sex or engaged in vaginal intercourse. About 25 percent of these women engaged in hookups their first year of college involving oral sex or vaginal intercourse. Again, these data indicate that substantial numbers—but not the majority—of adolescents and young adults engage in casual sexual behavior; still, most sexual behavior takes place within the context of a romantic relationship.

Digital Technology and Sexual Behavior

The way youth communicate has changed substantially over the last two decades. In 2012, over 95 percent of all adolescents had access to the Internet, although those living in families with an income less than $30,000 per year and with parents who had not attended college were less likely to have Internet access. Even in these groups, 90 percent had some type of Internet access. In 2009, 80 percent of teens had mobile phones (CTIA, 2009), and that rate is much higher today. The median number of texts sent on a typical day by those 12 to 17 years old rose from 50 in 2009 to 60 in 2011. Sixty-three percent of all teens reported that they exchange text messages every day with people in their lives, and this far surpasses the frequency with which they use any other form of daily communication. In 2011, the median number of texts sent or received by older adolescent girls was 100 per day (Lenhart, 2012). It is clear that most communication between and among adolescents today uses some form of text messaging. The specific platform may change—for example, Snapchat, Instagram—but communication is less likely to take place face-to-face or verbally, and much more likely to use digital technology and some form of written or symbolic medium.

Ehrlich (2010) reported that 10 percent of 16- to 20-year-olds ended relationships via a message on Facebook. Further, another 10 percent simply changed their relationship status on Facebook to "single." Schmitz and Siry (2011) reported that 20 percent of teens and 33 percent of young adults had sent nude or semi-nude pictures of themselves electronically and that 39 percent of teens and 59 percent of young adults had sent sexually explicit text messages. By 2013, these numbers were even higher, with 26 percent of male high school seniors and 24 percent of female high school seniors reporting that they had sent a sexually explicit picture on their cell phone, while 65 percent of senior males and 46 percent of senior females reported they had received such pictures on their cell phone (Strassberg, McKinnon, Sustaita, & Rullo, 2013).

There is little research specifically about adolescent sexting behavior (Klettke, Hallford, & Mellor, 2014), but a study by Drouin, Vogel, Surbey, and Stills (2013) on the sexting behavior of young adults reported that the majority of such behavior was text, with no pictures or video, and that such exchanges were more likely with partners in a committed relationship: 78 percent had sent text messages to committed partners, while 63 percent had sent such messages to casual partners. Higher percentages of individuals sent pictures or videos (49% and 37%), engaged in phone sex (46% and 34%), or engaged in live video (12% to 8%) with committed partners than casual sex partners.

Research is just emerging regarding the use of social networking and dating sites. There are a number of web-based and mobile sites designed for social networking, dating, or finding sexual partners. While most of the commonly known sites are for those 18 years old or older, there are social networking sites targeting adolescents. Despite the high rate of Internet and mobile phone usage in teenage samples, it appears that school is still the predominant place where they meet their potential romantic partners: 32 percent of the sample reported meeting their last romantic partner at school (Korchmaros, Ybarra, & Mitchell, 2015). Sexual minority youth (LGBTQ) tend to meet potential romantic partners online at a higher rate than heterosexual youth, but even for LGBTQ youth, about 80 percent met their last romantic partner at school. What is different from earlier generations is that while they meet their potential partners at school or through their offline social networks, most youth initiate romantic relationships online (Baker & Carreno, 2016; Korchmaros et al., 2015). So intimate, and likely sexual, exchanges are not uncommon using digital, usually mobile, technology.

SUMMARY AND IMPLICATIONS

This chapter has focused on adolescent sexual development and what we know about normative sexual behavior. Adolescence is a time of dramatic change, in terms of physiological, cognitive, emotional, and interpersonal factors. Puberty, which encompasses numerous changes in hormonal levels and the resultant development of secondary sexual characteristics and changes in body shape and composition, is accompanied by structural development in the central nervous system and interpersonal challenges that influence self-perception, interpersonal intimacy, cognitive processes, and resultant behavior. Adolescents must negotiate these changes and accommodate them within the context of their social, emotional, and spiritual environment. While there are physiological challenges, much of sexual development is driven by the way in which sexual desire is framed within the context of the adolescent's environment of school, religion, family structure, and outside influences such as media. Sexual self-concept is more a function of environmental influences and individual learning than it is a function of physiology and biological predisposition.

Perhaps the most influential process, at least in terms of understanding harmful sexual behavior, is sexual motivation. That is, what influences an individual to engage in, or seek out opportunities to engage in, sexual behavior? Motivation is driven not necessarily by sexual desire, but by environmental factors that either facilitate or inhibit motivation to engage sexually. There are gender differences, at least from the predominant heterocentric perspective, which teach girls to ignore sexual desire and pair their sexual motivation with intimacy and relationship stability. Boys are encouraged to be more motivated by sexual desire and to seek gratification for such desires.

The physiological changes that take place with puberty signal to the environment the emerging sexuality of the youth. These changes require youth to adapt to new social situations, accommodate their new bodies into their concept of self and body image, and integrate sexual desire and feelings of arousal. Gender roles for sexual behavior can be very rigid, but diverse influences may also make it difficult to integrate the differing expectations for sexual behavior presented by various cultural media. In general, girls are expected to be the sexual "gatekeepers," ensuring that boys' sexual desire is kept under control.

We didn't address the development of sexual orientation in this chapter, because it is a complex topic that requires more space than we could allocate here and because, at least from the data available to us, same-sex behavior and sexual orientation are low prevalence. Our goal was not to provide a comprehensive investigation of sexual development, but to provide a baseline from which to understand sexually harmful behavior.

As noted by Drury and Bukowski (2013), the variability among people and across the life span is large, and therefore it is difficult to create a meaningful norm of sexual behavior. Across adolescence, there are major physiological, interpersonal, and social changes that influence the expression of sexuality both within and across individuals. However, there are some trends in sexual behavior that can allow for determining normal variations between individuals from those experiences that are potentially harmful and can lead to harmful sexual behaviors.

Masturbation is very common in both boys and girls, with almost all boys having engaged in masturbation during their adolescence. Behaviors such as oral sex and vaginal intercourse are present in a substantial minority of 14- and 15-year-old males and females and in between 30 and 60 percent of 16-plus-year-old males and females. There are interesting gender differences in oral sex, in that girls are more likely to engage in fellatio than boys are to engage in cunnilingus.

Over the last 24 years there have been subtle changes in adolescent sexual behavior. Across all race/ethnic groups, there has been a decline in initiation of sexual intercourse during high school. At the same time, sexually active adolescents are more likely to use condoms or some other type of birth control during intercourse in 2013 than did adolescents in 1991. This appears to indicate more concern for unwanted pregnancy and some increased concern about sexually transmitted diseases, although most sexual intercourse events did not include the use of a condom. Early onset of sexual intercourse, before age 13 years, is very uncommon, although more common in African American youth than other race/ethnic groups.

Finally, there has been a dramatic change in the availability and use of digital technology. Although we did not present data on the use of pornography, the trends reported in sexual intercourse, condom use, and birth control use would seem to indicate that the ubiquitous availability of pornography is not having a detrimental effect on sexual decision making or leading to precocious sexual behavior. What is happening, however, is that the modes by which relationships are initiated and developed are changing dramatically. While today's youth continue to meet romantic partners in similar settings as previous generations—in school or through offline social networks—the initiation of a romantic involvement is likely to begin through online communication, especially cell phone texting. Again, sending and receiving erotic images via digital media is not an uncommon practice among adolescents and young adults engaged in romantic relationships. In general, youth are more likely to engage in sexually explicit written texts than they are to send images or to engage in live video interaction. They are also most likely to exchange sexual images and engage in sexual text exchanges with romantic partners. Thus, sexting is likely a very common occurrence, although it appears that when such behavior happens, it is done in contexts where the participants have an expectation of privacy. In general, a minority of boys and girls admit to sending nude or semi-nude images, but even when that is done, it appears to take place between romantically involved partners, using platforms in which the sender and receiver have a reasonable expectation of privacy.

The information provided in this chapter sets the stage for the explorations of sexually harmful behavior that will be the topic of the rest of this book. Our data indicate that adaptation to the challenges of adolescence leads to a wide range of behaviors and may involve a substantial level of risk taking. Adolescents engage in various sexual behaviors for a variety of reasons, not the least of which is the conception that everyone else is doing so. The hormonal changes of adolescence not only lead to bodily changes, but also precipitate strong emotional reactions, both because of the chemical action and the environmental factors that must be negotiated. Cognitive changes provide abilities that previously were absent, making the world more complex and ambiguous. The ability to form abstract concepts and differentiate complex emotions, as well as the need to negotiate the complex world of sexual interactions, leads to many opportunities for mistakes and miscalculations. In some cases, these mistakes and miscalculations may result in harmful sexual interactions.

REFERENCES

Arnett, J. J. (1999). Adolescent storm and stress reconsidered. *American Psychologist, 54*(5), 317–326.

Baker, C. K., & Carreno, P. K. (2016). Understanding the role of technology in adolescent dating and dating violence. *Journal of Child and Family Studies, 25,* 308–320.

Bancroft, J. (2006). Normal sexual development. In H. E. Barabee & W. L. Marshall (Eds.), *The juvenile sex offender* (2nd ed., pp. 19–57). New York: Guilford Press.

Bandura, J. (1997). *Social learning theory.* Englewood Cliffs, NJ: Prentice Hall.

Boyce, W., Doherty-Poirier, M., MacKinnon, D., Fortin, C., Saab, H., King, M., & Gallupe, O. (2006). Sexual health of Canadian youth: Findings from the Canadian Youth, Sexual Health, and HIV/AIDS Study. *Canadian Journal of Human Sexuality, 15*(2), 59–68.

Breakwell, G. M., & Millward, L. J. (1997). Sexual self-concept and sexual risk-taking. *Journal of Adolescence, 20,* 29–41.

Brooks-Gunn, J., Graber, J. A., & Paikoff, R. L. (1994). Studying links between hormones and negative affect: Models and measures. *Journal of Research and on Adolescence, 4,* 469–486.

Brooks-Gunn, J., & Paikoff, R. (1997). Sexuality and developmental transitions during adolescence. In J. Schulenburg, J. Maggs, K. Hurrelman (Eds.), *Health risks and developmental transitions during adolescence* (pp.190–219). New York: Cambridge University Press.

Buhi, E. R. & Goodson, P. (2007). Predictors of adolescent sexual behavior and intention: A theory-guided systematic review. *Journal of Adolescent Health, 40,* 4–21.

Bukowski, W. M., Li, K. Z., Dirks, M., & Bouffard, T. (2012). Developmental sciences and the study of successful development. *International Journal of Developmental Science 6*(1-2), 57–60.

Bukowski, W. M., Simard, M., Dubois, M., & Lopez, L. (2011). Representations, process and development: A new look at friendship in early adolescence. In E. Amsel & J. G. Smetana (Eds.), *Adolescent vulnerabilities and opportunities: Developmental and constructivist perspectives* (pp. 159–181). New York: Cambridge University Press.

Burton, D., & Miner, M. Exploring the theories explaining male adolescent perpetration of sexual crimes. In A. Beech & T. Ward (Eds.), *Wiley handbook on the theories, assessment and treatment of sexual offending: Vol. 1. Theories* (pp. 497–519). Chichester, West Sussex, UK: Wiley & Sons.

Carlson Jones, D. (2004). Body image among adolescent girls and boys: A longitudinal study. *Developmental Psychology, 40,* 823–835.

Centers for Disease Control and Prevention (2014, June). *2013 YRBS Data User's Guide.* Atlanta, GA: Author.

Chivers, M. L., & Bailey, J. M. (2000). A sex difference in features that elicit genital response. *Biological Psychology, 70,* 115–120.

Chivers, M. L., Rieger, G., Latty, E., & Bailey, J. M. (2004). A sex difference in the specificity of sexual arousal. *Psychological Science, 15,* 736–744.

Cooper, M. L., Shapiro, C. M., & Powers, A. M. (1998). Motivations for sex and risky sexual behavior among adolescents and young adults: A functional perspective. *Journal of Personality and Social Psychology, 75,* 1528–1558.

De Graaf, H., & Rademakers, J. (2006). Sexual development of prepubertal children. *Journal of Psychology and Human Sexuality, 18,* 1–21.

Diamond, L. M., & Savin-Williams, R. C. (2009). Adolescent sexuality. In R. M.Lerner & L. Steinberg (Eds.), *Handbook of adolescent psychology: Vol. 1. Individual Bases of Adolescent Development* (pp. 116–151). Hoboken, NJ: John Wiley & Sons.

Drouin, M., Vogel, K. N., Surbey, A., & Stills, J. R. (2013). Let's talk about sexting, baby: Computer-mediated sexual behavior among young adults. *Computers in Human Behavior, 29,* A25–A30.

Drury, K. M., & Bukowski, W. M. (2013). Sexual development. In D. S. Bromberg & W. T. O'Donohue (Eds.), *Handbook of child and adolescent sexuality: Developmental and forensic psychology.* Oxford, UK: Elsevier.

Ehrlich, B. (2010, November). Boy meets girl: How Facebook functions in modern romance—*Seventeen Magazine* study looks at role of Facebook in courtship. *ABC News.* Retrieved from http://media.abcnews.com/Technology/boy-meets-girl-facebook-modern-romance/stroy?id=12194479)rli

Field, T. (2002). Infants' need for touch. *Human development, 45,* 100–103.

Fielder, R. L., Walsh, J. L., Carey, K. B., & Carey, M. P. (2013). Predictors of sexual hookups: A theory-based, prospective study of first-year college women. *Archives of Sexual Behavior, 42,* 1425–1441.

Fine, M. (1998). Sexuality, schooling and adolescent females: The missing discourse of desire. *Harvard Educational Review, 58,* 29–53.

Fine, M., & McClelland, S. I. (2006). Sexual education and desire: Still missing after all these years. *Harvard Educational Review, 76,* 297–338.

Fischer, K. W., Shaver, P. R., & Carnochan, P. (1990). How emotions develop and how they organize development. *Cognition and Emotion, 4,* 81–127.

Flook, L. (2011). Gender differences in adolescents' daily interpersonal events and well-being. *Child Development, 82,* 454–461.

Fortenberry, J. D., Schick, V., Herbenick, D., Sanders, S. A., Dodge, B., & Reece, M. (2010). Sexual behaviors and condom use at last vaginal intercourse: A national sample of adolescents ages 14 to 17 years. *Journal of Sexual Medicine 7*(Suppl 5), 305–314.

Friedrich, W. N., Gramback, P., Broughton, D., Kuiper, J., & Beilke, R. L. (1991). Normative sexual behavior in children. *Pediatrics, 88,* 456–464.

Gagon, J. H., & Parker, R. G. (1995). Conceiving sexuality. In R. G. Parker & J. H. Gagnon (Eds.), *Conceiving sexuality: Approaches to sex research in a postmodern world* (pp. 3–16). New York: Routledge.

Graber, J. A., Peterson, A. C., & Brooks-Gunn, J. (1996). Pubertal processes: Methods, measures, and models. In J. A. Graber, J. Brooks-Gunn, & A. C. Peterson (Eds), *Transitions through adolescence: Interpersonal domains and context* (pp. 223–253). Mahwah, NJ: Erlbaum.

Graber, J. A., & Sontag, L. M. (2006). Puberty and girls' sexuality: Why hormones are not the complete answer. *New Directions for Child and Adolescent Development, 112,* 23–38.

Halpern, C. T. (2006). Integrating hormones and other biological factors into a developmental systems model of adolescent female sexuality. *New Directions for Child and Adolescent Development, 112,* 9–22.

Halpern, C. T., Udry, J. R., Campbell, B., & Suchindran, C. (1993). Testosterone and pubertal development as predictors of sexual activity: A panel analysis of adolescent males. *Psychosomatic Medicine, 55,* 436–447.

Halpern, C. T., Udry, J. R., & Suchindran, C. (1997). Testosterone predicts initiation of coitus in adolescent females. *Psychosomatic Medicine, 59,* 161–171.

Halpern, C. T., Udry, J. R., & Suchindran, C. (1998). Monthly measures of salivary testosterone predict sexual activity in adolescent males. *Archives of Sexual Behavior, 27,* 445–465.

Harris Interactive (2009). Teenagers: A generation unplugged. Retrieved from http://files.ctia.org/pdf/HI_TeenMobileStudy_ResearchReport.pdf

Herbenick, D., Reece, M., Schick, V., Sanders, S., Dodge, B., & Forenberry, J. D. (2010). Sexual behavior in the United States: Results from a national probability sample of men and women ages 14–94. *Journal of Sexual Medicine, 7*(Suppl 5), 255–265.

Klettke, B., Hallford, D. J., & Mellor, D. J. (2014). Sexting prevalence and correlates: A systematic literature review. *Clinical Psychology Review, 34,* 44–53.

Knoth, R., Boyd, K., & Singer, B. (1988). Empirical tests of sexual selection theory: Predictions of sex differences in onset, intensity, and time course of sexual arousal. *Journal of Sex Research, 24,* 73–89.

Korchmaros, J. D., Ybarra, M. L., & Mitchell, K. J. (2015). Adolescent online romantic relationship initiation: Differences by sexual and gender identification. *Journal of Adolescence, 40,* 54–65.

Lam, T. H., Shi, H. J., Ho, L. M., & Fan, S. (2002). Timing of pubertal maturation and heterosexual behavior among Hong Kong Chinese adolescents. *Archives of Sexual Behavior, 31*, 359–366.

Larson, R. W., Clore, G. L., & Wood, G. A. (1999). The emotions of romantic relationships: Do they wreak havoc on adolescents? In W. Furman, B. B. Brown, & C. Feiring (Eds.), *The development of romantic relationships in adolescence* (pp. 19–49). New York: Cambridge University Press.

Larsson, I. (2002). *Sexual abuse of children: Child sexuality and sexual behavior.* Report written for the Swedish National Board of Health and Welfare.

Laumann, E. O., Paik, A., & Rosen, R. C. (1999). Sexual dysfunction in the United States: Prevalence and predictors. *JAMA, 281,* 537–544.

Lenhart, A. (March 2012) *Teens, smartphones, and texting.* Pew Research Center's Internet & American Life Project. Retrieved from http://perinternet.org/Reports/2012/Teens-and-smartphones.aspx

Longmore, M. A. (1998). Symbolic interactionism and the study of sexuality. *Journal of Sex Research, 35,* 44–57.

Macoby, E. E. (1998). *The two sexes: Growing up apart, coming together.* Cambridge, MA: Belknap Press/Harvard University Press.

Manning, W. D., Longmore, M. A., & Biordano, P. C. (2005). Adolescnts' involvement in non-romantic sexual activity. *Social Science Research, 34,* 384–407.

Markus, H. & Nurius, P. (1986). Possible selves. *American Psychologist, 41,* 954–969.

Maslow, A. H. (1943) A theory of motivation. *Psychological Review, 50*(4), 370–396.

McMaster, L. E., Connolly, J., Pepler, D., & Craig, W. M. (2002). Peer to peer sexual harassment in early adolescence: A developmental perspective. *Development and Psychopathology, 14,* 91–105.

McRae, K., Gross, J J., Weber, J., Robertson, E. R., Sokol-Hessner, P., Ray, R. D., . . . Ochsner, K. N. (2012). The development of emotional regulation: An fMRI study of cognitive reappraisal in children, adolescents, and young adults. *Social Cognitive and Affective Neuroscience, 7,* 11–22.

Miller, B. C., & Benson, B. (1999). Romantic and sexual relationship development during adolescence. In W. Furman, B. B. Brown, & C. Feiring (Eds.), *The development of romantic relationships in adolescence* (pp. 99–121). New York: Cambridge University Press.

Miller, B. C., Norton, M. C., Curtis, T., Hill, E. J., Schvaneveldt, P., & Young, M. (1995). The timing of sexual intercourse among adolescents. *Youth & Society, 29,* 54–82.

Money, J. (1997). *Principles of developmental psychology.* New York: Continuum.

Moore, S., & Rosenthal, D. (2006) Sexuality in adolescence: Current trends. *Adolescent society.* London, New York: Routledge.

Nannis, E. D., & Cowan, P. A. (1987). Emotional understanding; A matter of age, dimension, and point of view. *Journal of Applied Developmental Psychology, 8,* 289–304.

National Center for Health Statistics (2010, June). *The 2006–2010 National Survey of Family Growth: Sample design and analysis of a continuous survey.* Washington, DC: Author.

National Center for Health Statistics (2015). *National Survey of Family Growth.* Washington, DC: Author.

Nottleman, E. D., Inoff-Germain, G., Susman, E. J., & Chrousos, G. P. (1990). Hormones and behavior at puberty. In J. Bancroft & J. Machover Reinisch (Eds.), *The Kinsey Institute series: Adolescence and puberty* (Vol 3., pp. 88–123). New York: Oxford University Press.

O'Sullivan, L. F., & Thompson, A. E. (2014). Sexuality in adolescence. In Tolman, L., & Diamond, L. M. (Eds.). *APA handbook of sexuality and psychology: Vol 1. Person based approaches* (pp. 433–485). Washington, DC: American Psychological Association.

Reece, M., Herbenick, D., Schick, V., Sanders, S. A., Dodge, B., & Fortenberry, J. D. (2010a). Background and considerations on the National Survey of Sexual Health and Behavior (NSSHB) from the investigators. *Journal of Sexual Medicine, 7*(Suppl 5), 243–245.

Reece, M., Herbenick, D., Schick, V., Sanders, S. A., Dodge, B., & Fortenberry, J. D. (2010b). Condom use rates in a national probability sample of males and females ages 14 to 94 in the United States. *Journal of Sexual Medicine, 7*(Suppl 5), 266–276.

Regan, P. C. & Berscheid, E. (1995). Gender differences in beliefs about the causes of male and female sexual desire. *Personal Relationships, 2,* 345–358.

Rotosky, S. S., Dekhtyar, O., Cupp, P. K., & Anderman, E. M. (2008). Sexual self-concept and sexual self efficacy in adolescents: A possible clue to promoting sexual health? *Journal of Sexual Research, 45,* 277–286.

Ruble, D. N., & Martin, C. L. (1998). Gender development. In W. Damon (Ed.), *Handbook of child psychology* (pp. 993–1016). New York: John Wiley & Sons.

Schmitz, S., & Siry, L. (2011). Teenage folly or child abuse? State responses to "sexting" by minors in the US and Germany. *Policy and the Internet, 3*(2), article 3. Retrieved from http://www.psocommons.org/policyandInternet/vol3/iss2/art3

Stack, D. M. (2007). The salience of touch and physical contact during infancy: Unraveling some of the mysteries of the somesthetic sense. In G. Bremer & A. Fogel (Eds.), *Blackwell handbook of infant development.* Oxford, UK: Blackwell Publishing.

Strassberg, D. S., McKinnon, R., Sustaita, M., & Rullo, J. (2013). Sexting by high school students: An exploratory and descriptive study. *Archives of Sexual Behavior, 42,* 15–23.

Sullivan, H. (1953). *The interpersonal theory of psychiatry.* New York: W.W. Norton.

Susman, E. J., & Dorn, L. D. (2009). Puberty: Its role in development. In R. M. Lerner & L. Steinberg (Eds.), *Handbook of adolescent psychology: Vol. 1. Individual bases of adolescent development* (pp. 116–151). Hoboken, NJ: John Wiley & Sons.

Tanner, J. M. (1962). *Growth at adolescence.* Cambridge, MA: Blackwell.

Tanner, J. M. (1998). Sequence, tempo, and individual variation in growth and development of boys and girls aged twelve to sixteen. In R. E. Muuss & H. D. Porton (Eds.), *Adolescent behavior and society: A book of readings* (5th ed., pp. 34–46). New York: McGraw-Hill.

Thompson, S. (1994). Teenage girls' narratives about sex. In A. S. Rossi (Ed.), *Sexuality across the life course* (pp. 209–232). Chicago, IL. University of Chicago Press.

Tolman, D. L. (2002). Femininity as a barrier to positive sexual health for adolescent girls. In A. E. Hunter & C. Forden, (Eds.), *Readings in the psychology of gender: Exploring our differences and commonalities* (pp. 196–206). Needham Heights, MA: Allyn & Bacon.

Tolman, D. L., & Diamond, L. M. (2001) Desegregating sexuality research: Cultural and biological perspectives on gender and desire. *Annals of Sex Research 12*(1), 33–42.

Udry, J. (1988). Biological predispositions and social control in adolescent sexual behavior. *American Sociological Review, 53,* 709–722.

CHAPTER 3

Juveniles Who Sexually Abuse: The Search for Distinctive Features

Anton van Wijk

Cyril Boonmann

Since the 1980s, sexually abusive youth have been the subject of academic research in Anglo-Saxon and other countries (Davis & Leitenberg, 1987). There are many reasons for this increased attention. First, sexual abuse in general is now spoken about more openly than in the past. Initially, the focus was on the victims (Brownmiller, 1975); eventually, however, it began to include the perpetrators as well (Bullens & Van Wijk, 2004). It also became apparent that some adult perpetrators had started to develop their problematic sexual behavior in their youth (Abel, Becker, Cunningham-Rathner, Mittelman, & Rouleau, 1987; Abel, Osborn, & Twigg, 1993; Burton, 2000). In line with developmental psychopathology models regarding other problematic symptoms and behaviors, clinicians and researchers realized that early intervention might produce more positive effects and would be more cost-effective. Secondly, the sheer number of sexually abusive youth had become a cause for concern. Estimates in the United States showed that juveniles were responsible for 20 percent of all rapes and 30 to 50 percent of all child sexual abuse cases (Barbaree & Marshall, 2006; Davis & Leitenberg, 1987). Third, the number of treatment programs targeting sexually abusive youth has risen significantly over the years because of increased prosecution and greater clinical attention to this population (Becker, 1998; Burton et al., 2000).

In 1993, Barbaree, Marshall, and Hudson edited a groundbreaking book, *The Juvenile Sex Offender,* summarizing the available knowledge about sexually abusive youth. Much of the early research and reports focused on describing the backgrounds and characteristics of sexually abusive youth (e.g., Aljazireh, 1993; Righthand & Welch, 2001; Vizard, Monck, & Misch, 1995). Many publications that appeared in the 1980s and 1990s were written mainly from a psychological or psychiatric point of view and were written by clinicians working with sexually abusive youth. Toward the beginning of the new millennium, other academic disciplines such as developmental criminology, sociology, and law became more involved in the research into juveniles who sexually offend. Sexual offenses were not necessarily the only focus: In some cases, they were considered part of a broader antisocial and/or criminal repertoire (Lussier, 2005).

As the research developed, a key issue concerned the extent to which sexually abusive youth are a separate and unique group, one that is distinct from adult sexual offenders as well as juvenile non-sexual offenders and, thus, how interventions may be directed accordingly. On the one hand, there is the idea that juveniles who sexually offend differ from other offenders and thus require specialized assessment and treatment; on the other, there is the notion that sexual offending is just another manifestation of delinquency and, as such, differs only in some respects.

In the last decade, several studies have been published in which sexually abusive youth are compared with non-sexual offenders (Van Wijk et al., 2006). This qualitative study suggested that differences exist between sexual offenders and non-sexual offenders in personality characteristics, behavioral problems, history of sexual abuse, non-sexual offending, and peer functioning. Inconsistent results were found for demographic factors, family functioning and background, antisocial attitudes, and intellectual and neurological functioning. Subsequently, Seto and Lalumière (2010) conducted a meta-analysis of 59 independent studies comparing male adolescent sexual offenders (n = 3,855) with male adolescent non-sexual offenders (n = 13,393). They found that sexually abusive youth differ from non-sexually abusive youth on some of the theoretically relevant variables including a history of sexual abuse, exposure to sexual violence, other abuse or neglect, social isolation, early exposure to sex or pornography, atypical sexual interests, anxiety, and low self-esteem. However, overall, the Seto and Lalumière (2010) meta-analysis found the groups of sexually abusive youth and non-sexual offenders homogeneous, with few differences found on most of the variables studied: "The results did not support the notion that adolescent sexual offending can be parsimoniously explained as a simple manifestation of general antisocial tendencies" (p. 526).

Studies have repeatedly shown that sexually abusive youth are a heterogeneous group (e.g., Barbaree & Marshall, 2006). In order to determine what is "so special" about adolescent sexual offending behavior, it is useful to take that heterogeneity into account. In this chapter, we describe the current state of the research literature on the backgrounds and distinguishing characteristics of subtypes of sexually abusive youth, also compared with non-sexually offending youth who commit other types of crimes, in order to gain more insight into the distinctive features of juveniles who sexually offend. First, however, we will examine the differences between youth and adults who commit sexual offenses.

SEXUALLY ABUSIVE BEHAVIOR: ADULTS VERSUS JUVENILES

It is assumed that adults and juveniles who commit sexual offenses are one and the same group. When committed at an early age, such offenses are considered expressions of a perverse disposition, to be remedied only by long-term or lifelong sentences because, it is believed, they predict future perpetration. Many studies, however, show a different picture (e.g., Letourneau & Miner, 2005). Juveniles who commit sexual offenses do not necessarily become the adult sexual offenders of the future.

Additionally, most adult sexual offenders were not sexually offending youth. For example, prospective longitudinal studies of criminal career patterns distinguish juvenile and adult sexual offenders as two separate phenomena (Lussier & Blokland, 2014). Most juveniles stop their sexual offending behavior before adulthood, and most adult offenders start their registered criminal behavior after adolescence. Studies of juvenile and adult offenders show that after 59 months, the percentage of repeated sexual offenses among juveniles is between 7 and 13 percent (Caldwell, 2010; Reitzel & Carbonell, 2006; Harris & Hanson, 2004).

Moreover, juvenile sexual offending behavior differs from that of adults in a number of areas. Based on Federal Bureau of Investigation (FBI) data, Finkelhor, Ormrod, and Chaffin (2009) investigated the differences between 13,471 juveniles and 24,344 adults who committed sexual offenses against minors. They found that juveniles were more likely to commit their offenses in groups and more frequently targeted male victims, often of a younger age, than adults. Similarly, a small-scale comparative study by Miranda and Corcoran (2000) also showed differences between juveniles and adults. Adults committed more sexual offenses, whereas the incidence of intra-familial sexual abuse was actually higher among juveniles. Juveniles committed digital fondling offenses more often than adults; adults more often committed vaginal, oral, or anal sexual abuse.

Developments in neurological and developmental criminology research have revealed significant explanations for the differences between juvenile and adult (sexual) offenders. Tolan, Walker, and Reppucci (2012) assert that these differences regard the capacity for self-management and regulation, the susceptibility to social and peer pressure, and factors related to judgment and criminal intent. All these actions, reactions, and determinations involve neurological activity. As a result of the ongoing development of their brains, juveniles have less capacity to manage their behavior and emotions than adults. Adolescence is characterized by risk-taking and sensation-seeking behavior (Steinberg, 2012; Steinberg et al., 2008). Additionally, adolescents are less adept than adults in planning ahead, and have more trouble considering the potential consequences of their decisions and conduct (Steinberg et al., 2009). Moffitt (1993) has shown that a large proportion of juvenile delinquency is age-related; juvenile offenders stop offending after their adolescence. A small number of them continue committing offenses into adulthood.

The research to date shows that juveniles who commit sexual offenses differ from adult sexual offenders. This may be due to neurological and developmental psychological factors. Decades of research have found that most juveniles who sexually offend do not continue committing sexual offenses in their adult lives (Caldwell, 2010; Zimring, 2007). Their abusive conduct may be considered age-related conduct.

CLASSIFICATION OF JUVENILES WHO COMMIT SEXUAL OFFENSES

Caldwell (2002) stated that the heterogeneity of juveniles who sexually offend is one of the most resilient findings in the research in this field. During the past 30 years, several research attempts to classify these juveniles have occurred. Some classifications were based on clinical experience, others on statistical analysis. Generally, there are five approaches to classifying juveniles who sexually offend. The first concerns classification based on the nature of the sexual offense, such as hands-on and hands-off offenses. The second form of classification uses the age of the victim and/or the age difference between the perpetrator and the victim. In the third form of classification, the nature of the criminal career is considered—in other words, whether the juvenile's offending includes non-sexual offenses as well as sexual ones. Fourth, juveniles who sexually offend sometimes are distinguished based on the numbers of perpetrators per offense. Last, in contrast with research based on offense characteristics, Worling (2001) compared subgroups of juveniles committing sexual offenses based on personality traits (see also Knight & Prentky, 1993; O'Brien & Bera, 1986; Oxnam & Vess, 2006).

A simple way to distinguish between various types of juveniles who sexually offend is to consider the nature of the sexual offenses committed. On the one hand there are hands-off offenses, which take place without physical contact between the perpetrator and the victim: Voyeurism and exhibitionism are examples of these. On the other hand, there are hands-on offenses, with physical contact, such as assault and rape (Fehrenbach et al., 1986; Saunders et al., 1986).

Within the category of hands-on offenses, further differentiation is possible if one takes into account the ages of perpetrator and victim. In this chapter, the term *youth who sexually abuse peers/adults* will be used to distinguish those adolescents who sexually abuse age mates or adults from those who sexually abuse children under 13 years when the victim is not a peer because he or she is 5 or more years younger. This division is most common in the literature (Gunby & Woodhams, 2010; Hendriks & Bijleveld, 2004; Hunter, Hazelwood, & Slesinger, 2000; 2003; Kjellgren, Wassberg, Carlberg, Långström, & Svedin, 2006; Skubic, Kemper, & Kistner, 2010). Child and peer or adult sexual abusers appear to be two different types of offenders when considering their psychosexual and social development, criminal careers, and psychological functioning (e.g., Hagan et al., 2001; Hsu & Stardinsky, 1990; Hunter, Figueredo, Malamuth, & Becker, 2003; Prentky, Harris, Frizzell, & Righthand, 2000; Weinrott, 1996).

Butler and Seto (2002) have divided juveniles who sexually offend into those who only commit sexual offenses (sex-only) and those who also commit other offenses (sex-plus). These types concur with those in Becker and Kaplan (1988), who distinguish three offender types, each with their own developmental pathway. The first type concerns "dead-end" offenders who commit a sexual offense only once and do not commit any other type of offense thereafter. The sexual criminal career of these offenders begins and ends with their first sexual offense. Hence, they may be classified as first-and-only offenders. The second type regards delinquent sexual offenders who commit several sexual offenses as well as various other, non-sexual, offenses. For these offenders, sexual offenses are only part of their entire criminal career. Since they commit both sexual and non-sexual offenses, offenders of this second type are called generalists (Hissel, Bijleveld, Hendriks, Jansen, & d'Escury-Koenigs, 2006; Van Wijk & Ferwerda, 2000). In contrast with the second type, the third type are specialists, whose conduct is based on sexual deviation; they limit themselves to committing sexual offenses, which they commit repeatedly; only very rarely do they show any other kind of criminal behavior. The typology of Becker and Kaplan fits in with research into the continuity of and changes in sexual criminal careers: At one end of the scale, many youthful sexual delinquents are dead-end offenders; at the other end, only a small number of them become specialists in sexual offenses; in between these two, a larger group of offenders commit a variety of offenses, including sexual offenses.

Another classification is between solo perpetrators and group offenders (De Wree, 2004; Looije et al., 2004). Earlier research has shown a clear distinction between these two types with regard to their age, ethnic background, and personality problems (Hendriks, 2006). Within the group offenders, another distinction can be made between leaders and followers ('t Hart-Kerkhoffs, Vermeiren, Jansen, & Doreleijers, 2010).

It is important to understand that these categorizations are made to provide a framework for studies regarding the etiology of these kinds of offenses, which can provide guidance in determining suitable treatment. In reality, offenders are not easily classifiable. There are, for example, child abusers who victimize both males and females; hands-off offenders who may become hands-on offenders as their offending behavior develops over time; offenders who change the kind of sexual offenses they commit, termed crossover offenders (e.g., Heil et al., 2003). In other words, offenders may be placed in various categories. Conversely, different typological terms may relate to the same perpetrator. Child abusers in study A may be the same group identified as specialists in study B and as solo perpetrators in study C. The same applies to offenders classified as abusers of peers, group perpetrators, or generalists. It is imperative that researchers clearly define their conceptual frameworks and how categories are defined in their studies to increase comparability.

Non-Sexual Offending

Although the sexual offense aspect of offending behaviors typically is the primary focus in publications on sexually abusive youth, attention has also long been paid to the fact that many of these youth commit other offenses as well, such as non-sexual violent offenses and property offenses (e.g., Fehrenbach et al., 1986). For two decades now, authors have focused on this problem in an attempt to figure out the difference between juveniles who sexually offend, and youth committing other offenses. In a review of the research literature (Epps & Fisher, 2004), many studies are mentioned that either fail to distinguish between the various types of (sexual) offenders, or have used small samples that were too diverse in their offending to be able to warrant robust conclusions about non-sexual offending by sexual offending juveniles. For that reason, study results vary. In some studies, lower levels of non-sexual offending were found in juveniles who sexually offend (Seto & Lalumière, 2010; Sipe et al., 1998), whereas in others, no differences with non-sexually offending juveniles were found (Hagan et al., 2001; Van Wijk et al., 2007; Van Wijk, Loeber, Vermeiren, Pardini, Doreleijers & Bullens, 2005).

In various studies, attempts were made to further differentiate between the various types of (sexual) offenders according to their offending patterns. Roughly speaking, two approaches were used: Either the homogeneity or the heterogeneity of offending patterns was taken as a point of departure (sex-only and sex-plus), or the type of sexual offense (peer/adult abusers, child abusers, and exhibitionists). Butler and Seto (2002) were some of the first to regard the heterogeneity of offending patterns as an issue. They compared 32 sexually abusive youth (22 sex-only and 10 sex-plus) with 82 non-sexual offenders. They found that the sex-only group had fewer problems than the other two groups and that in many respects the sex-plus group was similar to the group of non-sexual offenders. Wanklyn et al. (2012) reached a comparable conclusion. They compared 28 pure sexual offenders (sexual assault and related charges), 172 violent non-sexual offenders, and 24 versatile violent offenders with one another. The violent non-sexual offenders committed more property offenses than pure sexual offenders. They also committed more violent offenses; they were not distinct from the versatile sexual offenders in that respect. Yet conclusions are limited because in both studies, the groups of sexually abusive youth were very small.

Van Wijk, Mali, and Bullens (2007) adopted Butler and Seto's (2002) dichotomy. Based on police registrations, a larger group of sexually abusive youth (N = 4,430) was divided into sex-only (n = 1,945) and sex-plus (n = 2,485) offenders. The sex-only offenders had limited criminal "careers" (1.7 sexual offenses on average), but the sex-plus group had much longer criminal careers; on average, they had committed 11.9 offenses. Some of the youth in the sexual-offense-only group might be similar to Kaplan and Becker's (1988) dead-end pathway; a major proportion remained first offenders. The sex-plus group mainly committed property offenses over time. Chu and Thomas (2010) also differentiate between a group of sexually abusive youth in Singapore, in terms of specialists (sex-only; N = 71) and generalists (sex-plus; N = 77). They did not find significant differences in sexual recidivism (14.3% versus 9.9%); they did find, however, that significantly more generalists had reoffended, committing violent offenses (18.2% versus 1.4%) and non-violent offenses (37.7% versus 16.9%). Dutch research replicates the findings of Chu and Thomas (2012). Hissel et al. (2006) discriminated four subgroups in a sample of 510 sexually abusive youth who had undergone a personality test: first offenders (n = 367), generalists (sex-plus; n = 59), specialists (sex-only; n = 80), and exhibitionists (n = 4). Contrary to the authors' expectation, no differences in sexual offense recidivism were found between the specialists and the generalists. The latter group repeated property offenses sooner and more often, however.

Lussier, Van den Berg, Bijleveld, and Hendriks (2012) have mapped trajectories of 498 juveniles who sexually offended with an average follow-up period of 14 years. An added value of this study over the research mentioned earlier is that the authors take a developmental perspective by exploring offending rates over developmental periods. In addition to two sexual offending trajectories, they found five non-sexual offending trajectories. More than half the sample (53%) regarding the non-sexual offending group is in the very low-rate trajectory: They commit almost no non-sexual offenses and also rarely reoffend. Members of the second group (21%), the late starters, were not very active in their younger years; their non-sexual offending gradually increased, however, and peaked in their mid-20s. Almost the entire group of late starters reoffended as adults. Non-sexual offending in the adolescent limited group (11%) peaked at age 17, then decreased. The high-rate persisters (4%) showed the highest levels of non-sexual offending. More than half of the high-rate persisters became non-sexual repeat offenders as juveniles, and three-quarters as adults. This group showed an average of 23 convictions during the research period and peaked in their 20s. Finally, the late bloomers (10%) were like the high-rate persisters, but their non-sexual criminal careers started and peaked later. The authors also checked to what extent the types of sexually abusive youth that were distinguished (child and peer abusers and group offenders) may be placed in the various trajectories. Interestingly, it turned out that the child abusers can be found mainly in the very low-rate and late starter groups: the groups that commit—relatively speaking—few non-sexual offenses. The peer abusers are represented in all trajectories, and the group offenders mainly in the trajectories of highest activity in youth (i.e., adolescent limited, late bloomers, and high-rate persisters). As noted above, two sexual offending trajectories were identified: adolescent limited (89.6%) and high-rate slow desisters (10.4%; Lussier et al., 2012). The various types of non-sexual trajectories were represented within each of the two sexual trajectories to the same degree.

Based on police data, the crime patterns of juvenile peer/adult assaulters and rapists (n = 2,125), exhibitionists (n = 237), and child abusers (n = 491) were constructed and subsequently compared with non-sexual violent (n = 4,611) and property (n = 6,226) offenders by Bullens, Van Wijk, and Mali (2006). A large proportion of these three groups of sexually abusive youth started their official criminal careers with a sexual offense; i.e., their first contact with the police was for a sexual offense: 84 percent of the child abusers, 65 percent of the assaulters/rapists, and 71 percent of the exhibitionists. After their sexual offending, their criminal careers continue with non-sexual offenses, particularly property offenses and to a lesser extent violent offenses. Incidentally, sexual offenses have a larger share in the total number of offenses of the child molester group, compared with other sexually offending groups. When compared with juveniles with only non-sexual offense histories, the juveniles who sexually offend have shorter criminal careers than those who commit violent and property offenses; the child abusers have the shortest. The peer/adult assaulters/rapists, however, commit the most offenses of any kind. For example, Van Wijk, Mali, Bullens, and Vermeiren (2007) conducted a longitudinal comparison of the criminal careers of two specific groups of juvenile delinquents: peer/adult assaulters and rapists (N = 226) and non-sexual violent offenders (N = 4,130). Expectations were that, because of the violent nature of the offenses by both groups, the offense patterns of the two groups would be similar. The assaulters/rapists mainly committed non-sexual offenses (property offenses) after the assault/rape. Twenty percent of the new offenses committed by the assaulters/rapists were violent sexual offenses, 8 percent were other sexual offenses, and 9 percent of the offenses were non-sexual violent offenses. In contrast, the non-sexual violent offenders remain violent throughout their criminal careers: One-third of the offenses committed during those careers were violent.

Overall, research findings indicate that juveniles who commit sexual offenses either stop quickly or continue to commit mainly non-sexual offenses. As such, the non-sexual offending patterns of juveniles who sexually offend are an indispensable research theme. A meta-analysis of 63 data sets of recidivism among juveniles who sexually offend (total N = 11,219, followed for about 60 months on average) shows this clearly (Caldwell, 2010). Non-sexual general recidivism was much higher than sexual recidivism: 43.4 percent versus 7.1 percent. The dark number proviso should be considered here: Persons studied may have repeated more offenses than the police and justice departments are aware of (Fortune & Lambie, 2006; Hendriks & Bijleveld, 2008). Yet based on the registered crime data, the common denominator of the various recidivism studies is that sexual reoffending by juveniles is much less frequent than general recidivism (McCann & Lussier, 2008). Further, juveniles who sexually offend do not differ significantly from juvenile non-sexual offenders when it concerns the commission of (another) sexual offense. Official records of non-sexual offending follow the sexual offense rather than preceding it and sexually abusive youth do not become, at a different rate, the adult sexual offenders of the future (Lussier et al., 2012). When predicting sexual offending by adults, the number of offenses, of any kind, that they perpetrated as juveniles seems more significant than whether they committed sexual offenses as juveniles (Hanson & Buissière, 1996; Lussier & Blokland, 2014; Zimring, Piquero, & Jennings, 2007). The group of sexually abusive youth who commit multiple sexual offenses only—the specialists—is very small (Lussier et al., 2012).

In summary, the crime patterns (number and type of offenses committed) of juveniles who sexually offend are diverse and often vary between distinct subtypes of these youth. The sexual offense is often a small part of a youth's total criminal career. Child abusers commit the smallest number of non-sexual offenses. There are few specialists among the group of juveniles who sexually offend and relatively many onetime offenders. A small group commits many, mainly non-sexual, offenses for a longer period.

COGNITIVE DISTORTION AND ANTISOCIAL ATTITUDES AND BELIEFS

It has been suggested that "by far the most important element in the profile of an adolescent sexual offender is that of cognitive distortion" (Lakey, 1994, p. 757), manifested by "an undercurrent of misinformation and strange beliefs and attitudes" that "permeates the value systems of male juveniles who sexually offend" (Lakey, 1992). Although the concept of cognitive distortion still lacks definitional clarity, it is generally explained as opinions or beliefs that justify a criminal act (Abel, Becker, & Cunningham-Rathner, 1984; Maruna & Mann, 2006). These statements, which are not necessarily predictive, are believed to help protect the self from blame or a negative self-concept, facilitating aggressive, antisocial, or delinquent behavior (Barriga & Gibbs, 1996; Barriga, Landau, Stinson, Liau, & Gibbs, 2000; Ward, Hudson, Johnston, & Marshall, 1997). Of interest for research into juveniles who sexually offend, cognitive distortion may be subdivided into generic (e.g., attribution of carelessness to theft victims) and sex-specific cognitive distortions (e.g., attribution of promiscuity to rape victims) (McCrady et al., 2008). Juveniles who sexually offend alter the general definition of appropriate behavior in order to justify their own sexual offending behavior (Lakey, 1992). Based on her collection of observations, Lakey (1992) showed that these juvenile offenders hold incorrect information, false beliefs, and cognitive distortions about, for example, sexuality (e.g., "If a seated female crosses her legs and swings one, she is inviting sexual encounter."), sexual assault (e.g., "Compliance by a female during a sexual assault implies consent."), male dominance (e.g., "A 'real' man watches a lot of television, drinks beer, and has 'his woman' hovering over him to fulfill his slightest need or command, including sexual."), rape-supportive myths (e.g., "A female cannot be raped against her will."), and molestation (e.g., "Children [under 10 years of age] are quite capable of giving meaningful consent for a sexual experience, even if obtained under duress. Parents should allow children to become sexually active whenever they express an interest in doing so."). It is suggested that juveniles who sexually offend are more likely to endorse these fallacies than other juveniles (e.g., White & Koss, 1993). For example, juveniles who commit sexual offenses have higher levels of callous sexual attitudes toward females, and adversarial attitudes toward females and sexual minorities, than non-offending juveniles (Farr, Brown, & Beckett, 2004). However, to better understand the relationship between cognitive distortions and juvenile sexual offending behavior, over and above antisocial behavior in general, juvenile offenders with and without sexual offenses need to be compared.

As mentioned before, Seto and Lalumière (2010) conducted an extensive meta-analysis to examine "What is so special about male adolescent sexual offending?" (Seto & Lalumière, 2010, p. 1). They compared sexual and non-sexual offending juveniles in terms of various theoretically derived variables, such as cognitive abilities, mental health problems, and traumatic experiences. The two groups did not differ in antisocial attitudes and beliefs in general, including attitudes and beliefs about sex with woman and sexual offending; however, juveniles who sexually offended scored significantly lower on antisocial attitudes and beliefs that support crime in general than their non-sexually offending counterparts (Seto & Lalumière, 2010). One interpretation of these findings could be that no differences in sex-specific antisocial attitudes and beliefs were found because these attitudes and beliefs are high in both groups (e.g., Benson & Vincent, 1980). However, although the juveniles who sexually offend constitute a heterogeneous group with a variety of characteristics between subgroups (e.g., child abusers, rapists) (e.g., Hunter et al., 2003; Hunter, Hazelwood, & Slesinger, 2000), Seto and Lalumière (2010) were not able to differentiate between subgroups.

Studies regarding sex-specific cognitive distortion and antisocial attitudes and beliefs in subgroups of juveniles who sexually offend are scarce. Based on victim age, juveniles with peer/adult victims have been found more likely to endorse beliefs supportive of aggressive behavior than juveniles with child victims (i.e., generic distortion) (Davis-Rosanbalm, 2002). With regard to sexual attitudes (i.e., sex-specific distortion), Worling (1995) found no differences between the two groups. In addition, in their study into moral judgment, cognitive distortion, and implicit theories facilitating child sexual abuse in juveniles who commit sexual offenses, Van Vugt et al. (2011a) found no differences between juvenile offenders with child victims and those with peer/adult victims according to the Sociomoral Reflection Measure—Short Form (SRM-SF). However, intellectually disabled juveniles who sexually offend generally showed stage 2 moral reasoning (i.e., justifications for moral judgment dominated by instrumental and pragmatic reciprocity), whereas those without an intellectual disability generally showed transition stage 2–3 (i.e., maintenance of interpersonal relationships was considered to a certain extent in their justifications for moral decisions) (Van Vugt et al., 2011b). Finally, Butler and Seto (2002) found that within the group of juveniles who sexually offended, those who only committed sexual offenses (sex-only offenders) had significantly fewer antisocial attitudes and beliefs than juveniles committing both sexual and non-sexual offenses (sex-plus offenders).

In conclusion, juveniles who sexually offend appear to show more cognitive distortion and antisocial attitudes and beliefs than juveniles in the general population (Farr et al., 2004). Furthermore, juveniles committing sexual offenses seem to have fewer generic antisocial attitudes and beliefs than juveniles who commit other types of offenses. Although several interesting differences were revealed between sex-specific antisocial attitudes and beliefs of juvenile sexual and non-sexual offenders in a few studies, it is still unclear whether these attitudes and beliefs are actually higher in juveniles who sexually offend or whether they are equally high in both groups. Finally, although research is scarce, there are some indications that juvenile offenders with peer/adult victims exhibit more generic antisocial attitudes and beliefs than juvenile offenders who target child victims.

Mental Health Problems

Studies have shown that juveniles who sexually offend often exhibit high levels of externalizing and internalizing mental health problems (e.g., Boonmann et al., 2015; Galli et al., 1999; 't Hart-Kerkhoffs et al., 2015; Kavoussi et al., 1988; Seto & Lalumière, 2010; Van Wijk et al., 2006), as well as social skills deficits ('t Hart-Kerkhoffs et al., 2009). In addition, they often experienced childhood sexual, physical, and/or emotional abuse (e.g., Hendriks & Bijleveld, 2008; Seto & Lalumière, 2010; Van Wijk et al., 2006), which correlate with an increased risk of mental health problems (e.g., Kilpatrick et al., 2000; Ruchkin, Henrich, Jones, Vermeiren, & Schwab-Stone, 2007; Wasserman & McReynolds, 2011). In this section, we will elaborate on externalizing and internalizing mental health problems. In the subsequent section we will discuss social skills deficits and childhood traumatic experiences in more detail.

Recently, Boonmann et al. (2015) published a meta-analysis on mental disorders in juveniles who sexually offend. The main aim of the study was to estimate the prevalence of mental disorders in juveniles who sexually offended. In addition, prevalence rates of juvenile offenders with and without sexual offenses were compared. In total, 69 percent of the juveniles met the criteria for at least one disorder; 44 percent had two or more disorders. Still, 31 percent of juveniles who sexually offended were not diagnosed with a mental disorder. With regard to externalizing disorders, a conduct disorder (CD) was found in 51 percent, an oppositional defiant disorder (ODD) in 21 percent, and an attention deficit/hyperactivity disorder (ADHD) in 14 percent of the respondents. In terms of internalizing disorders, anxiety disorders were most prevalent (18%), followed by affective disorders (9%) and post-traumatic stress disorder (PTSD) (8%). In addition, 30 percent of the juvenile offenders were diagnosed with a substance use disorder (SUD). Compared with juvenile offenders without sexual offenses, however, juveniles who committed sexual offenses were less often diagnosed with a mental disorder. More specifically, sexually offending juveniles were less often diagnosed with an externalizing disorder or SUD than non-sexually offending juveniles. No differences in the prevalence of internalizing disorders were found between the two groups (Boonmann et al., 2015). These results regarding externalizing disorders and SUD are in line with the results of Seto and Lalumière's (2010) meta-analysis and the review of Van Wijk et al. (2006). In contrast with the findings of Boonmann et al. (2015), Seto and Lalumière (2010) reported more anxiety problems and lower self-esteem in sexually offending juveniles than non-sexually offending juveniles. Moreover, Van Wijk et al.'s findings (2006) also suggested that juveniles committing sexual offenses display more internalization problems than their non-sexually offending counterparts. Perhaps these characteristics prevail only in specific subgroups of juveniles who sexually offend (Boonmann et al., 2015; Seto & Lalumière, 2010; Van Wijk et al., 2006).

't Hart-Kerkhoffs et al. (2015) examined mental disorders in subgroups of juveniles who sexually offend, based on the age of the victims and the numbers of offenders. This resulted in three relevant subgroups: (a) juveniles who sexually offend against young children, (b) juveniles who sexually offend, on their own, against peers/adults, and (c) juveniles who sexually offend against peers/adults as part of a group. Juvenile offenders targeting child victims showed the most mental disorders; they demonstrated higher rates of internalizing disorders in general, of affective disorders specifically, and of ADHD than group peer/adult offenders, and a higher prevalence of affective disorders than solo peer/adult offenders. Moreover, sexually offending juveniles with child victims had lower overall level of functioning scores than either solo or group offenders with same-age or older victims. Furthermore, solo offenders exhibited higher rates of affective disorders and ADHD than group offenders ('t Hart-Kerkhoffs et al., 2015).

Other research into mental health problems in subgroups of sexually offending juveniles has revealed more internalizing problems in offenders with child victims, but fewer externalizing problems, including substance use problems, than offenders with same-age or older victims. Hunter et al. (2003), for example, found greater deficits in psychosocial functioning but less aggression (during the offense) and less substance use (at the time of the offense) in offenders with child victims than in offenders with same-age or older victims. Furthermore, Hendriks and Bijleveld (2004) identified higher rates of psychopathology, higher scores on neuroticism, more social problems, more victimization by bullies, and a more negative self-image in offenders with child victims than those with peer/adult victims. Höing, Jonker, and Van Berlo (2010) compared exhibitionists, sexual offenders targeting children, and sexual offenders targeting peers/adults. Exhibitionists and sexual offenders against children more often lacked friends, were more often bullying victims, and more often demonstrated inadequate social functioning than sexual offenders with same-age or older victims. Offenders with child victims were also more often perpetrators of bullying than offenders with peer/adult victims and exhibitionists (Höing et al., 2010). Finally, sexually offending juveniles with child victims had more internalizing problems (they were more submissive, with more anxious feelings) and fewer externalizing problems (they were less unruly and forceful, and demonstrated less social insensitivity, less impulsive propensity, and less delinquent predisposition), including fewer substance use problems (less substance abuse proneness) than juveniles who sexually offended against same-age or older victims (Glowacz & Born, 2013).

When comparing juvenile offenders with sexual offenses based on the number of offenders (group versus solo), solo offenders scored significantly higher on neuroticism, impulsiveness, and sensation seeking, but lower on sociability than group offenders (Bijleveld & Hendriks, 2003). In the study by Höing et al. (2010), the prevalence of inadequate social functioning was found to be higher, and the prevalence of negative attitudes against girls lower, in solo offenders than in group offenders. Furthermore, when Höing et al. compared juvenile offenders with only sexual offenses (sex-only offenders) and juvenile offenders with sexual and non-sexual offenses (sex-plus offenders), sex-only offenders were found to have significantly fewer conduct problems than sex-plus offenders. In addition, in their study, Butler and Seto (2002) used the Young Offender Level of Service Inventory (YO-LSI) and found that sex-only offenders had significantly fewer substance abuse problems, education/employment problems, family problems, and peer relation problems than sex-plus offenders.

In conclusion, mental health problems are highly prevalent in juveniles who sexually offend. Overall, it appears that compared with juveniles who commit non-sexual offenses, juveniles who sexually offend have fewer externalizing mental health problems, including substance abuse problems and disorders. With regard to internalizing problems, research results are inconsistent. Although sexually and non-sexually offending juveniles do not seem to differ in terms of internalizing mental disorders (i.e., official diagnoses), juveniles who sexually offend seem to have more internalizing mental health problems than their counterparts with non-sexual offenses (see also Seto & Lalumière, 2010). Within subgroups, in general, juvenile offenders with child victims seem to have more internalizing problems but fewer externalizing problems, including substance abuse problems, than juvenile offenders with same-age or older victims. Furthermore, solo offenders seem to have more mental health problems, especially inadequate social functioning, than group offenders, and sex-only offenders seem to have fewer conduct problems than sex-plus offenders.

Social Skills Deficits

Another prominent feature for some juveniles who sexually offend is the presence of social skills difficulties, such as problems in establishing and maintaining close friendships (e.g., Davis & Leitenberg, 1987; Fehrenback, Smith, Monastersky, & Deisher, 1986; Knight & Prentky, 1993). Fehrenbach et al. (1986), for example, found that 65 percent of their sample of juveniles committing sexual offenses had no close friends. It has been suggested that social skills challenges might be an important causal factor in the development of sexual offending behavior (e.g., Barbaree, Hudson, & Seto, 1993; Davis

& Leitenberg, 1987). However, in order to distinguish the relationship between social skills problems and sexual offending behavior from the relationship between such social skills difficulties and offending behavior in general, research comparing juvenile sex and non-sexual offenders is warranted.

In their meta-analysis, Seto & Lalumière (2010) compared the interpersonal problems of juveniles who sexually offended with non-sexual offenders. They found that juveniles who sexually offend were significantly more often socially isolated than juveniles committing non-sexual offenses. The two groups, however, did not differ in heterosocial and general social skill deficits, or other social problems. Hence, it was suggested that social isolation might play a bigger role in the development and persistence of sexual offending behavior than social skills in general. This does not apply only to male juveniles who sexually offend but also to female juveniles who sexually offend, who were also found to show more social isolation than female violent offenders (Van der Put et al., 2014).

As mentioned before, juveniles who sexually offend constitute a heterogeneous group with differences between subgroups (e.g., Hunter et al., 2003; Hunter et al., 2000). Accordingly, several studies have also examined the differences in social skills between subtypes of juveniles committing sexual offenses. Ford and Linney (1995), for example, not only examined differences in social skills among juveniles committing sexual offenses, violent non-sexual offenses, and status offenses, but also differentiated between juveniles who sexually offend against younger children and against peers. The researchers did not find any differences in social skills between these last two subgroups (see also Kemper & Kistner, 2010; 2007; Worling, 1995). However, the juveniles who commit sexual offenses with child victims reported the greatest need for control in interpersonal relationships (Ford & Linney, 1995). Furthermore, Hunter et al. (2003) found greater deficits in psychosocial functioning in juveniles who sexually offend against children than among those who offend against peers/adults; they lacked social confidence, viewed themselves as socially inadequate, and experienced social isolation. These results are in line with other studies in which more social problems were found, such as fewer age-appropriate friendships and lower self-esteem in juvenile offenders who commit sexual offenses against children compared with juvenile offenders who sexually offend against peers or adults (e.g., Gunby & Woodhams, 2010; Hendriks & Bijleveld, 2004).

In conclusion: Social skills difficulties are prevalent in juveniles who sexually offend. Compared with juveniles who commit other types of offenses, they are significantly more socially isolated. Although research findings have been mixed, studies have suggested that juveniles who target child victims may have more social skills deficits compared with those who have peer/adult victims. However, more research regarding these symptoms is needed to determine whether these juveniles, especially those who offend against younger children, are just socially awkward or whether these symptoms are part of autism spectrum disorder (see also chapter 11).

TRAUMATIC EXPERIENCES

Previous research has shown that traumatic experiences (e.g., sexual abuse, physical abuse, emotional abuse) are highly prevalent in juveniles who commit sexual offenses (e.g., Friedrich et al., 2001; Hunter et al., 2003). Friedrich et al. (2001), for example, found that 77 percent of their sample of juveniles in residential treatment facilities who had sexually offended (N = 70) had experienced (substantiated or suspected) sexual abuse, and 63 percent experienced physical abuse. Furthermore, 68 percent reported having been neglected, 83 percent reported emotional abuse, and 51 percent reported domestic violence in the family. Based on the results in the meta-analysis of Seto and Lalumière (2010), the mean prevalence of childhood traumatic experiences in juveniles who commit sexual offenses was calculated: 37 percent experienced childhood sexual abuse, 42 percent reported physical abuse, and 48 percent reported emotional abuse/neglect (Boonmann, 2015, p. 83).

Sexually offending juveniles more often report adverse childhood experiences than juvenile non-sexual offenders (Seto & Lalumière, 2010; Van Wijk et al., 2006). In their meta-analysis, Seto and Lalumière (2010) compared childhood traumatic experiences (sexual abuse, physical abuse, family sexual violence, family non-sexual violence, non-family non-sexual violence, emotional abuse, or neglect) in juvenile offenders with and without sexual offenses. No significant differences were found between the two groups for family sexual and non-sexual violence or for non-family non-sexual violence. However, juveniles who had committed sexual offenses reported sexual, physical, and emotional abuse significantly more often than juvenile non-sexual offenders. The effect size, "a quantitative reflection of a phenomenon and size as the magnitude of something" (Kelley & Preacher, 2012, p. 140), for physical and emotional abuse was small; the effect size for sexual abuse was medium.

Because juveniles who commit sexual offenses constitute a heterogeneous group, it is important to distinguish subgroups. In their study, Ford and Linney (1995) examined intra-familial violence and abuse experienced by juvenile child abusers and juvenile rapists. The two subgroups did not differ in their experience of family verbal aggression; child abusers reported more intrafamilial violence than rapists, however.

In addition, child abusers had been sexually abused more often than rapists (52% versus 17%) (Ford & Linney, 1995). The higher prevalence of sexual abuse in juvenile child abusers compared with rapists is in line with the results of Kemper and Kistner (2010) and 't Hart-Kerkhoffs et al. (2015). Kemper and Kistner (2010) found that sexual abuse had been more prevalent in the child abuser group or mixed sexual offender group (juvenile offenders targeting younger children and peers) than in the rapist group. 't Hart-Kerkhoffs et al. (2015) found that child abusers had experienced more sexual abuse than either solo or group rapists. Both studies, however, did not find significant differences in physical abuse between the subgroups. In contrast with the results in the aforementioned studies (Ford & Linney, 1995; 't Hart-Kerkhoffs, 2015; Kemper & Kistner, 2010), Hendriks and Bijleveld (2004) found no significant differences in sexual abuse as reported in child abusers and peer abusers; however, the two groups also failed to differ where emotional cruelty by parents, neglect by parents, and violence between parents were concerned. Höing et al. (2010) also did not find significant results regarding sexual abuse victimization between child abusers and peer/adult sexual offenders. In addition, exhibitionists did not differ in terms of their own victimization compared with hands-on offenders. In another study by Bijleveld and Hendriks (2003), where they compared juvenile solo and group sexual offenders, solo sexual offenders reported victimization significantly more often than group sexual offenders. Höing et al. (2010) found similar results. Finally, Malie and colleagues (2011) found that sexually offending juveniles who were sexually abused had higher odds of sexually reoffending than those who were not abused. No relationship was found between sexual abuse and general reoffending, or physical abuse and general or sexual reoffending (Malie, Viljoen, Mordell, Spice, & Roesch, 2011). This is in line with the results of 't Hart-Kerkhoffs et al. (2015), who found that persistent sexually offending juveniles were more often sexually abused than sexually offending juveniles who did not continue their sexual offending behavior.

In conclusion, childhood traumatic experiences are highly prevalent in the group of juveniles who commit sexual offenses. Physical, emotional, and especially sexual abuse are more often found in the histories of juveniles who sexually offend than in those of juvenile non-sexual offenders. Research findings suggest that juvenile offenders who molest younger children have been sexually abused more often than juvenile offenders targeting only peer or adult victims. Finally, a relationship between a history of childhood abuse and persistent sexual offending behavior is suggested.

COGNITIVE FUNCTIONING

Studies into the cognitive functioning of juvenile sexual offenders yield varied findings. A significant cause for this is that cognitive functioning is an umbrella for many different aspects, such as IQ, academic performance, executive functioning, learning difficulties, and intellectual and cognitive impairments. In addition, other methodological issues are involved, such as the sample diversity, research settings, and varied measuring instruments.

McCurry et al. (1998) studied 200 juveniles with serious psychiatric disorders. Half of this group also evidenced inappropriate sexual behavior such as hypersexuality, exposing, and victimizing. Lower-IQ youth engaged in more inappropriate sexual behavior than those with a higher IQ. Others also have reported that the prevalence of sexually abusive behavior is high in the intellectually disabled population group (Gilby et al., 1989).

Also, other studies make clear that a substantial proportion of juvenile sexual offenders are challenged by academic difficulties; for example, Awad et al. (1984), found about 80 percent of the juvenile sexual offenders studied had learning and/or behavioral problems at school. Ryan et al. (1996) found that 60 percent of these juveniles have problems at school, including learning difficulties.

A number of studies have investigated to what extent juvenile sexual offenders are similar to juvenile non-sexual offenders regarding their cognitive functioning, in particular their IQ and academic difficulties—with various results. Sometimes juvenile sexual offenders scored lower than juveniles who commit other offenses (e.g., Ferrara & McDonald, 1996; Van Wijk et al., 2006). Recently, Mulder et al. (2012) found that juvenile sexual offenders had lower IQs than serious violent and property offenders, and evidenced lower academic achievement. Other studies have not found any differences (e.g., Butler & Seto, 2002; Tarter et al., 1993). The latter authors suggested that sample selection likely has determined the various results.

When subgroups of juvenile sexual offenders are studied, a few interesting differences are revealed. Epps (2000; in Epps & Fisher, 2004), for example, found that juvenile child abusers have more learning problems and lower IQ scores than other types of non-sexual delinquents. Awad and Saunders (1989) found similar results: More serious chronic learning problems are more often seen in the group of child abusers than among other types of offenders. In their meta-analysis, Seto and Lalumière (2010) included 28 studies on cognitive abilities. When compared with non-sexual offenders, juvenile sexual offenders scored lower for general, verbal, and performance intelligence, but the differences were not statistically significant. Interestingly, the authors included four studies in which peer and child offenders were compared for general intelligence. They did not find a significant effect of victim age. This finding is in contrast with a study done involving adult sexual offenders (Cantor et al., 2005), where it was found that child abusers had lower intelligence scores than offenders who targeted adult victims.

More comparative studies are required for a better understanding of the similarities and differences in cognitive functioning between sexually and non-sexually offending juveniles. Similarities may be related to the finding that juvenile sexual delinquency may be partly explained by general delinquency factors (Seto & Lalumière, 2010). Neuropsychological impairments may contribute to violent offenses, whether sexual or otherwise. For example, Lewis, Shanok, and Pincus (1979) investigated possible neurological deficits in a group of juveniles who had committed sexual offenses and a group of juveniles who had committed violent non-sexual offenses. The groups did not differ in their general, verbal, or performance IQ scores. 't Hart-Kerkhoffs et al. (2010) studied a group of juvenile sexual offenders (mainly peer assaults/rapes). They distinguished between leaders and followers, and found no differences in IQ between the two groups.

Because cognitive functioning involves a wide range of skills and capabilities, specific cognitive functions should be considered as well. Recently, Miyaguchi and Shirataki (2014) compared a group of juvenile sexual offenders (mostly child abusers) with low IQs (below 69) with juvenile non-sexual offenders with low IQs. They found that the juvenile sexual offenders with low IQs had significantly lower scores than the non-sexual offenders with low IQs where it concerned attention switching, processing speed, working memory, and prospective memory. No differences were found between the groups that did not have low IQs. The authors assert: "One possible explanation for why the brain or executive functions of sexual offenders had been inconsistent in other previous studies is insufficient control of IQ in participants, such as the intermixing of participants with high IQ with those with low IQ" (p. 256) when exploring cognitive functioning among juveniles who have sexually offended.

For now, research support for the premise that the cognitive functioning of juveniles who sexually offend differs from other delinquent groups is lacking. Also, differences among the various subtypes of juveniles with sexual offenses are not consistent. Perhaps increased specificity in research—for example, by controlling for IQ scores—may further our understanding of cognitive functioning among juveniles who have sexually offended.

Conclusion

In this chapter, we have expanded on research indicating that juveniles who sexually offend differ in some ways from non-sexual offending peers. We also have noted they may be divided into various subgroups. Although there are various commonly used criteria by which to make further distinctions within the group of juveniles who sexually offend, a recurring theme is that juveniles who assault or rape peers or adults are most similar to juveniles who commit non-sexual offenses. This warrants a warning, however: The subgroup of juveniles who sexually assault peers and adults should not be considered homogeneous.

The most prominent differences between child offenders and other non-sexual offending juveniles are in the areas of mental health, psychosocial functioning, and traumatic experiences. Their increased rates of internalizing emotional problems are in contrast with the antisocial and externalizing problems of the peer abusers, and require assessment and, if indicated, appropriate treatment. This is not to say, however, that juvenile child abusers become pedophiles at a later age. Most child abusers do not continue their sexual offending careers into adulthood.

Roughly 30 years of research into juveniles who sexually offend has yielded significant information regarding their characteristics. Nevertheless, there are gaps in our knowledge that require the attention of researchers. Research has demonstrated that most juveniles who sexually offend do not seem to persist in their sexual offending behavior, although many do seem to persist in non-sexual offending behavior (e.g., Caldwell, 2010; Fortune & Lambie, 2006). Given the fact that sexually abusive youth have much in common with juvenile non-sexual offenders, Letourneau and Borduin (2008) proposed that interventions effective for reducing general delinquency, such as functional family therapy (FFT) and multisystemic therapy (MST), would also be effective in the treatment of sexually abusive youth (see also Borduin, Schaeffer, & Heiblum, 2009; Henggeler et al., 2009; Letourneau et al., 2009). Interventions such as MST may work well for juvenile sexual offenders, contrary to Lösel and Schmucker's (2005) conclusion that sexual-offender-specific treatments for adolescents are required, although promising results were made by a clinical adaptation of multisystemic therapy that has been specifically designed and developed to treat youth (and their families) for problematic sexual behavior (Letourneau et al., 2013).

Furthermore, juveniles committing sexual offenses, especially those targeting child victims, often exhibit high levels of mental health problems. More specifically, research findings suggest that juveniles who sexually reoffend have more internalizing mental health problems and have more often experienced childhood sexual abuse than juveniles who do not sexually reoffend. Therefore, assessments and treatment of juveniles committing sexual offenses, especially those with child victims, should devote special attention to internalizing mental health problems and problems related to personal childhood sexual abuse victimization.

REFERENCES

Abel, G. G., Becker, J. V., & Cunningham-Rathner, J. (1984). Complications, consent, and cognitions in sex between children and adults. *International Journal of Law and Psychiatry, 7*(1), 89–103.

Abel, G. G., Becker, J. V., Mittelman, M., Cunningham-Rathner, J., Rouleau, J. L., & Murphy, W. D. (1987). Self-reported sex crimes of nonincarcerated paraphilias. *Journal of Interpersonal Violence, 2,* 3–25.

Abel, G. G., Osborn, C. A., & Twigg, D. A. (1993). Sexual assault through the life span: Adult offenders with juvenile histories. In H. E. Barbaree, W. L. Marshall, & S. M. Hudson (Eds.), *The juvenile sex offender* (pp.104–117). New York: Guilford Press.

Aebi, M., Vogt, G., Plattner, B., Steinhausen, H. C., & Bessler, C. (2012). Offender types and criminality dimensions in male juveniles convicted of sexual offenses. *Sexual Abuse: A Journal of Research and Treatment, 24*(3), 265–288.

Aljazireh, L. (1993). Historical, environmental, and behavioral correlates of sexual offending by male adolescents: A critical review. *Behavioral Sciences and the Law, 11,* 423–440.

Awad, G. A., & Saunders, E. B. (1989). Adolescent child molesters: Clinical observations. *Child Psychiatry and Human Development, 19,* 159–206.

Babchishin, K. M., Hanson, R. K., & Hermann, C. A. (2011). The characteristics of online sex offenders: A meta-analysis. *Sexual Abuse: A Journal of Research and Treatment, 23*(1) 92–123.

Barbaree, H. E., Hudson, S. M., & Seto, M. C. (1993). Sexual assault in society: The role of the juvenile offender. In H. E. Barbaree, W. L. Marshall, & S. M. Hudson (Eds.), *The juvenile sex offender* (pp. 1–24). New York: Guilford Press.

Barbaree, H. E., & Marshall, W. L. (2006). *The juvenile sex offender* (2nd ed.). New York: Guilford Press.

Barriga, A. Q., & Gibbs, J. C. (1996). Measuring cognitive distortion in antisocial youth: Development and preliminary validation of the "How I Think" questionnaire. *Aggressive Behavior, 22*(5), 333–343.

Barriga, A. Q., Landau, J. R., Stinson, B. L., Liau, A. K., & Gibbs, J. C. (2000). Cognitive distortion and problem behaviors in adolescents. *Criminal Justice and Behavior, 27*(1), 36–56.

Becker, J. V. (1998). What we know about the characteristics and treatment of adolescents who have committed sexual offenses. *Child Maltreatment, 3,* 317–329.

Becker, J. V., & Kaplan, M. S. (1988). The assessment of juvenile sex offenders. In: R. J. Prinz (Ed.), *Advances in behavioral assessment in children and families* (Vol. 4, pp. 215–222). Greenwich, CT: JAI Press.

Benson, P. L., Institute, S., & Vincent, S. (1980). Development and validation of the Sexist Attitudes Toward Women Scale (SATWS). *Psychology of Women Quarterly, 5*(2), 276–291.

Bijleveld, C., & Hendriks, J. (2003). Juvenile sex offenders: Differences between group and solo offenders. *Psychology, Crime & Law, 9*(3), 237–245.

Boonmann, C., Nelson, R. J., DiCataldo, F., Jansen, L. M. C., Doreleijers, T. A. H., Vermeiren, R. R. J. M., . . . & Grisso, T. (2015). Mental health problems in young male offenders with and without sex offences: A comparison based on the MAYSI-2. *Criminal Behaviour and Mental Health.* 26(5), 352–365.

Boonmann, C., van Vugt, E. S., Jansen, L. M. C., Colins, O. F., Doreleijers, T. A. H., Stams, G. J. J. M., & Vermeiren, R. R. J. M. (2015). Mental disorders in juveniles who sexually offended: A meta-analysis. *Aggression and Violent Behavior, 24*, 241–249.

Borduin, C. M., Schaeffer, C. M., & Heiblum, N. (2009). A randomized clinical trial of multisystemic therapy with juvenile sexual offenders: Effects of youth social ecology and criminal activity. *Journal of Consulting and Clinical Psychology, 77*(1), 26–37.

Bovenkerk, F., & Yesilgöz, Y. (2004). Crime, ethnicity and the multicultural administration of justice. In J. Ferrel, K. Hayward, W. Morrison, & M. Presdee (Eds.), *Cultural criminology unleashed* (pp. 81–96). London: Glasshouse Press.

Brownmiller, S. (1975). *Against our will: Men, women, and rape.* New York: Simon & Schuster.

Bullens, R. A. R., & Wijk, A. Ph. van. (2004). European perspectives on juveniles who sexually abuse. In G. O'Reilly, W. L. Marshall, A. Carr, & R. Beckett (Eds.). *Handbook of clinical interventions for young people who sexually abuse* (pp. 409–418). Hove, UK: Brunner-Routledge.

Bullens, R. A. R., Wijk, A. Ph. van, & Mali, S. R. F. (2006). Similarities and differences between the criminal careers of Dutch juvenile sex offenders and non-sex offenders. *Journal of Sexual Aggression, 2*, 155–164.

Burton, D., Smith-Darden, J., Levins, J., Fiske, J., & Freeman-Longo, R. E. (2000). *1996 nationwide survey: A survey of treatment programs and models serving children with sexual behavior problems, adolescent sex offenders, and adult sex offenders.* Brandon, VT: Safer Society Press.

Butler, S. M., & Seto, M. C. (2002). Distinguishing two types of adolescent sex offenders. *Journal of the American Academy of Child & Adolescent Psychiatry, 41*(1), 83–90.

Caldwell, M. F. (2002). What we do not know about juvenile sexual reoffense risk. *Child Maltreatment, 7*(4), 291–302.

Caldwell, M. F. (2010). Study characteristics and recidivism base rates in juvenile sex offender recidivism. *International Journal of Offender Therapy and Comparative Criminology, 54*(2), 197–212.

Cantor, J. M., Blanchard, R., Robichaud, L. K., & Christensen, B. K. (2005). Quantitative reanalysis of aggregate data on IQ in sexual offenders. *Psychological Bulletin, 131*(4), 555.

Carpentier, J., & Proulx, J. (2011). Correlates of recidivism among adolescents who have sexually offended. *Sexual Abuse: A Journal of Research and Treatment, 23*(4), 434–455.

Chu, C. M., & Thomas, S. D. M. (2010). Adolescent sexual offenders: The relationship between typology and recidivism. *Sexual Abuse: A Journal of Research and Treatment, 22*(2), 218–233.

Cooper, C. L., Murphy, W. D., & Haynes, M. R. (1996). Characteristics of abused and nonabused adolescent sexual offenders. *Sexual Abuse: A Journal of Research and Treatment, 8*, 105–119.

Davis, G. E., & Leitenberg, H. (1987). Adolescent sex offenders. *Psychological Bulletin, 101*(3), 417–427.

Davis-Rosanbalm, M. K. (2002). A comparison of social information processing in juvenile sexual offenders and violent nonsexual offenders (Doctoral dissertation). Ohio University, Athens, OH.

Driemeyer, W., Spehr, A., Yoon, D., Richter-Appelt, H., & Briken, P. (2013). Comparing sexuality, aggressiveness, and antisocial behavior of alleged juvenile sexual and violent offenders. *Journal of Forensic Sciences, 58*(3), 711–718.

Epps, K. J., & Fisher, D. (2004). A review of the research literature on young people who sexually abuse. In G. O'Reilly, W. L. Marshall, A. Carr, & R. C. Beckett (Eds.), *The handbook of clinical intervention with young people who sexually abuse* (pp. 62–102). Hove, UK: Brunner-Routledge.

Farr, C., Brown, J., & Beckett, R. (2004). Ability to empathise and masculinity levels: Comparing male adolescent sex offenders with a normative sample of non-offending adolescents. *Psychology, Crime & Law, 10*(2), 155–167.

Fehrenbach, P. A., Smith, W., Monastersky, C., & Deisher, R. W. (1986). Adolescent sexual offenders: Offender and offense characteristics. *American Journal of Orthopsychiatry, 56*(2), 225.

Ferrara, M. L., & McDonald, S. (1996). Treatment of the juvenile sex offender: Neurological and psychiatric impairment. In S. Righthand & C. Welch (2001). *Juveniles who have sexually offended: A review of the professional literature.* Washington, DC: US Department of Justice Office of Juvenile Justice and Delinquency Prevention.

Finkelhor, D., Ormrod, R., & Chaffin, M. (2009). *Juveniles who commit sex offenses against minors.* Washington, DC: US Department of Justice Office of Juvenile Justice and Delinquency Prevention.

Ford, M. E., & Linney, J. A. (1995). Comparative analysis of juvenile sexual offenders, violent non-sexual offenders, and status offenders. *Journal of Interpersonal Violence, 10*(1), 56–70.

Fortune, C. A., & Lambie, I. (2006). Sexually abusive youth: A review of recidivism studies and methodological issues for future research. *Clinical Psychology Review, 26,* 1078–1095.

Friedrich, W. N., Gerber, P. N., Koplin, B., Davis, M., Giese, J., Mykelbust, C., & Franckowiak, D. (2001). Multimodal assessment of dissociation in adolescents: Inpatients and juvenile sex offenders. *Sexual Abuse: A Journal of Research and Treatment, 13*(3), 167–177.

Galli, V., McElroy, S. L., Soutullo, C. A., Kizer, D., Rauta, N., Keck, P. E. Jr., & McConville, B. J. (1999). The psychiatric diagnoses of twenty-two adolescents who have sexually molested other children. *Comprehensive Psychiatry, 42,* 1078–1095.

Gilby, R., Wolf, L., & Goldberg, B. (1989). Mentally retarded adolescent sex offenders. A survey and pilot study. *Canadian journal of psychiatry. Revue canadienne de psychiatrie, 34(6),* 542–548.

Glowacz, F., & Born, M. (2013). Do adolescent child abusers, peer abusers, and non-sex offenders have different personality profiles? *European Child & Adolescent Psychiatry, 22*(2), 117–125.

Gunby, C., & Woodhams, J. (2010). Sexually deviant juveniles: Comparisons between the offender and offence characteristics of 'child abusers' and 'peer abusers.' *Psychology, Crime & Law, 16*(1-2), 47–64.

Hagan, M. P., Gust-Brey, K. L., Cho, M. E., & Dow, E. (2001). Eight-year comparative analyses of adolescent rapists, adolescent child molesters, other delinquents, and the general population. *International Journal of Offender Therapy and Comparative Criminology, 3,* 314–324.

Hanson, R. K., & Bussière, M. T. (1998). Predicting relapse: A meta-analysis of sexual offender recidivism studies. *Journal of Consulting and Clinical Psychology, 66*(2), 348–362.

Harris, A. J. R., & Hanson, R. K. (2004). *Sex offender recidivism: A simple question.* Ottawa, Canada: Public Safety and Emergency Preparedness Canada.

't Hart-Kerkhoffs, L. A., Boonmann, C., Doreleijers, T. A. H., Jansen, L. M. C., Wijk, A. P., & Vermeiren, R. R. J. M. (2015). Mental disorders and criminal re-referrals in juveniles who sexually offended. *Child and Adolescent Psychiatry and Mental Health, 9*(4), 1–7.

't Hart-Kerkhoffs, L. A., Jansen, L. M., Doreleijers, T. A., Vermeiren, R., Minderaa, R. B., & Hartman, C. A. (2009). Autism spectrum disorder symptoms in juvenile suspects of sex offenses. *Journal of Clinical Psychiatry, 70*(2), 266–272.

't Hart-Kerkhoffs, L. A., Vermeiren, R. R. J. M., Jansen, L. M. C., & Doreleijers, T. A. H. (2011). Juvenile group sex offenders: A comparison of group leaders and followers. *Journal of Interpersonal Violence, 26*(1), 3–20.

Heil, P., Ahlmeyer, S., & Simons, D. (2003). Crossover sexual offenses. *Sexual Abuse: A Journal of Research and Treatment, 15*(4), 221–236.

Hendriks, J., & Bijleveld, C. (2008). Recidivism among juvenile sex offenders after residential treatment. *Journal of Sexual Aggression, 14*(1), 19–32.

Hendriks, J., & Bijleveld, C. C. J. H. (2004). Juvenile sexual delinquents: Contrasting child abusers with peer abusers. *Criminal Behaviour and Mental Health, 14*(4), 238–250.

Hendriks, J., & Bijleveld, C. C. J. H. (2005a). Recidive van jeugdige zedendelinquenten: Poliklinisch behandelden versus niet-behandelden. *Tijdschrift voor Seksuologie, 29*, 215–225.

Hendriks, J., & Bijleveld, C. C. J. H. (2005b). Recidive van jeugdige zedendelinquenten na residentiële behandeling. *Tijdschrift voor Seksuologie, 29*, 150–160.

Henggeler, S. W., Letourneau, E. J., Chapman, J. E., Borduin, C. M., Schewe, P. A., & McCart, M. R. (2009). Mediators of change for multisystemic therapy with juvenile sexual offenders. *Journal of Consulting and Clinical Psychology, 77*(3), 451–462.

Hissel, S., Bijleveld, C., Hendriks, J., Jansen, B., & Collot d'Escury-Koenigs, A. (2006). Jeugdige zedendelinquenten: Specialisten, generalisten en "first offenders." *Tijdschrift voor Seksuologie, 30*, 215–225.

Höing, M., Jonker, M., & Berlo, W. van (2010). Juvenile sex offenders in a Dutch mandatory educational programme: Subtypes and characteristics. *Journal of Sexual Aggression, 16*(3), 332–346.

Hsu, L. K. G., & Starzynski, J. (1990). Adolescent rapists and adolescent child sexual assaulters. *International Journal of Offender Therapy and Comparative Criminology, 34*, 23–30.

Hunter, J. A., Figueredo, A. J., Malamuth, N. M., & Becker, J. V. (2003). Juvenile sex offenders: Toward the development of a typology. *Sexual Abuse: A Journal of Research and Treatment, 15*(1), 27–48.

Hunter, J. A., Hazelwood, R. R., & Slesinger, D. (2000). Juvenile-perpetrated sex crimes: Patterns of offending and predictors of violence. *Journal of Family Violence, 15*(1), 81–93.

Jacobs, W. L., Kennedy, W. A., & Meyer, J. B. (1997). Juvenile delinquents: A between-group comparison study of sexual and nonsexual offenders. *Sexual Abuse: A Journal of Research and Treatment, 9*(3), 201–217.

Kavoussi, R. J., Kaplan, M., & Becker, J. V. (1988). Psychiatric diagnoses in adolescent sex offenders. *Journal of the American Academy for Child and Adolescent Psychiatry, 27*, 131–148.

Kelley, K., & Preacher, K. J. (2012). On effect size. *Psychological Methods, 17*(2), 137–152.

Kemper, T. S., & Kistner, J. A. (2007). Offense history and recidivism in three victim-age-based groups of juvenile sex offenders. *Sexual Abuse: A Journal of Research and Treatment, 19*(4), 409–424.

Kemper, T. S., & Kistner, J. A. (2010). An evaluation of classification criteria for juvenile sex offenders. *Sexual Abuse: A Journal of Research and Treatment, 22*(2), 172–190.

Kilpatrick, D. G., Acierno, R., Saunders, B., Resnick, H. S., Best, C. L., & Schnurr, P. P. (2000). Risk factors for adolescent substance abuse and dependence: Data from a national sample. *Journal of Consulting and Clinical Psychology, 68*(1), 19–30.

Kjellgren, C., Wassberg, A., Carlberg, M., Långström, N., & Svedin, C. G. (2006). Adolescent sexual offenders: A total survey of referrals to social services in Sweden and subgroup characteristics. *Sexual Abuse: A Journal of Research and Treatment, 18*, 357–372.

Knight, R. A., & Prentky, R. A. (1993). Exploring characteristics for classifying juvenile sex offenders. In H. E. Barbaree, W. L. Marshall, & S. M. Hudson (Eds.), *The juvenile sex offender* (pp. 45–83). New York: Guilford Press.

Lakey, J. F. (1992). Myth information and bizarre beliefs of male juvenile sex offenders. *Journal of Addictions & Offender Counseling, 13*(1), 2–10.

Lakey, J. F. (1994). The profile and treatment of male adolescent sex offenders. *Adolescence, 29*(116), 755–761.

Letourneau, E. J., & Borduin, C. M. (2008). The effective treatment of juveniles who sexually offend: An ethical imperative. *Ethics & Behavior, 18*(2-3), 286–306.

Letourneau, E. J., Henggeler, S., McCart, M., Borduin, C., Schewe, P., and Armstrong, K. (2013). Two-year follow-up of a randomized effectiveness trial evaluating MST for juveniles who sexually offend. *Journal of Family Psychology, 27*(6), 978–985.

Letourneau, E. J., Henggeler, S. W., Borduin, C. M., Schewe, P. A., McCart, M. R., Chapman, J. E., & Saldana, L. (2009). Multisystemic therapy for juvenile sexual offenders: 1-year results from a randomized effectiveness trial. *Journal of Family Psychology, 23*(1), 89–102.

Letourneau, E. J., & Miner, M. H. (2005). Juvenile sex offenders: A case against the legal and clinical status quo. *Sexual Abuse: A Journal of Research and Treatment, 17*(3), 293–312.

Lewis, D. O., Shanok, S. S., & Pincus, J. H. (1979). Juvenile male sexual assaulters. *American Journal of Psychiatry, 136*(9), 1194–1196.

Looije, D., Bijleveld, C., Weerman, F., & Hendriks, J. (2004). Gedwongen seks als groepsactiviteit: Een dossierstudie naar groepszedendelicten. *Tijdschrift voor Seksuologie, 28,* 183–196.

Lösel, F., & Schmucker, M. (2005). Effects of sexual offender treatment. *Journal of Experimental Criminology, 1,* 117–146.

Lussier, P. (2005) The criminal activity of sexual offenders in adulthood: Revisiting the specialization debate. *Sexual Abuse: A Journal of Research and Treatment, 17,* 269–292.

Lussier, P., & Blokland, A. (2014). The adolescence-adulthood transition and Robins's continuity paradox: Criminal career patterns of juvenile and adult sex offenders in a prospective longitudinal birth cohort study. *Journal of Criminal Justice, 42,* 153–163.

Lussier, P., Van den Berg, C., Bijleveld, C., & Hendriks, J. (2012). A developmental taxonomy of juvenile sex offenders for theory, research and prevention: The adolescent-limited and the high-rate slow desister. *Criminal Justice and Behavior, 39,* 1559–1581.

Mallie, A. L., Viljoen, J. L., Mordell, S., Spice, A., & Roesch, R. (2011, October). Childhood abuse and adolescent sexual re-offending: A meta-analysis. In *Child & Youth Care Forum* (Vol. 40, No. 5, pp. 401–417). Springer US.

Maruna, S., & Mann, R. E. (2006). A fundamental attribution error? Rethinking cognitive distortions. *Legal and Criminological Psychology, 11*(2), 155–177.

McCann, K., & Lussier, P. (2008). Antisociality, sexual deviance, and sexual reoffending in juvenile sex offender: A meta-analytical investigation. *Youth Violence and Juvenile Justice, 6*(4), 363–385.

McCrady, F., Kaufman, K., Vasey, M. W., Barriga, A. Q., Devlin, R. S., & Gibbs, J. C. (2008). It's all about me: A brief report of incarcerated adolescent sex offenders' generic and sex-specific cognitive distortions. *Sexual Abuse: A Journal of Research and Treatment, 20*(3), 261–271.

McCurry, C., McClellan, J., Adams, J., Norrei, M., Storck, M., Eisner, A., & Breigner, D. (1998). Sexual behavior associated with low verbal IQ in youth who have severe mental illness. *Mental Retardation, 1,* 23–30.

Miranda, A. O., & Corcoran, C. L. (2000). Comparison of perpetration characteristics between male juvenile and adult sexual offenders: Preliminary results. *Sexual Abuse: A Journal of Research and Treatment, 12*(3), 179–188.

Miyaguchi, K., & Shirataki, S. (2014) Executive functioning problems of juvenile sex offenders with low levels of measured intelligence. *Journal of Intellectual and Developmental Disability, 39*(3), 253–260.

Moffitt, T. E. (1993). Adolescence-limited and life-cycle-persistent antisocial behavior: A developmental taxonomy. *Psychological Review, 100,* 674–701.

Mulder, E., Vermunt, J., Brand, E., Bullens, R., & Marle, H. van (2012). Recidivism in subgroups of serious juvenile offenders: Different profiles, different risks? *Criminal Behaviour and Mental Health, 22*(2), 122–135.

Murphy, W. D., DiLillo, D., Haynes, M. R., & Steere, E. (2001). An exploration of factors related to deviant sexual arousal among juvenile sex offenders. *Sexual Abuse: A Journal of Research and Treatment, 13,* 91–103.

O'Brien, M., & Bera, W. (1986). Adolescent sex offenders: a descriptive typology. *A News Letter of the National Family Life Education Network, 1,* 1–5.

Oxnam, P., & Vess, J. (2008). A typology of adolescent sexual offenders: Millon Adolescent Clinical Inventory profiles, developmental factors, and offence characteristics. *Journal of Forensic Psychiatry & Psychology, 19*(2), 228–242.

Prentky, R., Harris, B., Frizzell, K., & Righthand, S. (2000). An actuarial procedure for assessing risk with juvenile sex offenders. *Sexual Abuse, 12,* 71–93.

Prentky, R. A., Li, N. C., Righthand, S., Schuler, A., Cavanaugh, D., & Lee, A. F. (2010). Assessing risk of sexually abusive behavior among youth in a child welfare sample. *Behavioral Sciences and the Law, 28,* 24–45.

Reitzel, L. R., & Carbonell, J. L. (2006). The effectiveness of sexual offender treatment for juveniles as measured by recidivism: A meta-analysis. *Sexual Abuse: A Journal of Research and Treatment, 18,* 401–421.

Righthand, S., & Welch, C. (2001). *Juveniles who have sexually offended. A review of the professional literature* (NCJ 184739). Washington, DC: US Department of Justice Office of Juvenile Justice and Delinquency Prevention.

Ruchkin, V., Henrich, C. C., Jones, S. M., Vermeiren, R., & Schwab-Stone, M. (2007). Violence Exposure and Psychopathology in Urban Youth: The Mediating Role of Posttraumatic Stress. *Journal of Abnormal Child Psychology, 35,* 578–593.

Ryan, G., Miyoshi, T. J., Metzner, J. L., Krugman, R. D., Fryer, G. E. (1996). Trends in a national sample of sexually abusive youths. *Journal of the American Academy of Child and Adolescent Psychiatry, 35*(1), 17–25.

Saunders, E., Awad, G. A., & White, G. W. (1986). Male adolescent sex offenders: The offender and the offence. *Canadian Journal of Psychiatry, 28,* 105–116.

Seto, M. C., & Lalumière, M. L. (2010). What is so special about male adolescent sexual offending? A review and test of explanations through meta-analysis. *Psychological Bulletin, 136*(4), 525.

Sipe, R., Jensen, E. L., & Everett, R. S. (1998). Adolescent sexual offenders grow up: Recidivism in young adulthood. *Criminal Justice and Behavior, 25,* 109–124.

Skubic Kemper, T., & Kistner, J. A. (2010). An evaluation of classification criteria for juvenile sex offenders. *Sexual Abuse, 22*(2), 172–190.

Steffensmeier, D., & Demuth, S. (2006). Does gender modify the effects of race–ethnicity on criminal sanctioning? Sentences for male, female, white, black, and Hispanic defendants. *Journal of Quantitative Criminology, 22,* 241–261.

Steinberg, L. (2012, Spring). Should the science of adolescent brain development inform public policy? *Issues in Science and Technology.* Retrieved from www.issues.org/28.3/steinberg.html

Steinberg, L., Albert, D., Cauffman, E., Banich, M., Graham, S., & Woolard, J. (2008). Age differences in sensation seeking and impulsivity as indexed by behavior and self-report: Evidence for a dual systems model. *Developmental Psychology, 44*(6), 1764–1778.

Steinberg, L., O'Brien, L., Cauffman, E., Graham, S., Woolard, J., & Banich, M. (2009). Age differences in future orientation and delay discounting. *Child Development, 80*(1), 28–44.

Tarter, R. E., Hegedus, A. M., Alterman, A. I., & Katz-Garris, L. (1983). Cognitive capacities of juvenile violent, nonviolent, and sexual offenders. *Journal of Nervous and Mental Disease, 171,* 564–567.

Tolan, P. H., Walker, T., & Reppucci, N. D. (2012). Applying developmental criminology to law: Reconsidering juvenile sex offenses. *Justice Research and Policy, 14*(1), 117–146.

Van der Put, C., van Vugt, E. S., Stams, G. J. J., & Hendriks, J. (2014). Psychosocial and developmental characteristics of female adolescents who have committed sexual offenses. *Sexual Abuse: A Journal of Research and Treatment, 26*(4), 330–342.

Van der Put, C. E., van Vugt, E. S., Stams, G. J. J. M., Dekovic, M., & van der Laan, P. H. (2012). Short-term general recidivism risk of juvenile sex offenders: Validation of the Washington State Juvenile Court Prescreen Assessment. *International Journal of Offender Therapy and Comparative Criminology, 57*(11), 1374–1392.

Van Vugt, E., Asscher, J., Stams, G. J., Hendriks, J., Bijleveld, C., & van der Laan, P. (2011a). Moral judgment of young sex offenders with and without intellectual disabilities. *Research in Developmental Disabilities, 32*(6), 2841–2846.

Van Vugt, E., Gibbs, J., Stams, G. J., Bijleveld, C., Hendriks, J., & van der Laan, P. (2011b). Moral development and recidivism A meta-analysis. *International Journal of Offender Therapy and Comparative Criminology, 55*(8), 1234–1250.

Venable, V. M., & Guada, J. (2014) Culturally competent practice with African American juvenile sex offenders. *Journal of Child Sexual Abuse, 23*(3), 229–246.

Vizard, E., Monck, E., & Misch P. (1995). Child and adolescent sex abuse perpetrators: A review of the research literature. *Journal of Child Psychology and Psychiatry, 5,* 731–756.

Weinrott, M. R. (1996). *Juvenile sexual aggression: A critical review.* Boulder, CO: Center for the Study and Prevention of Violence, University of Colorado.

Wijk, A. Ph. van, Blokland, A. A. J., Duits, N., & Vermeiren, R. (2006b). Psychische stoornissen bij jeugdige zedendelinquenten. *Tijdschrift voor Seksuologie, 30,* 65–74.

Wijk, A. Ph. van, & Ferwerda, H. B. (2000). Criminaliteitsprofielen van zedendelinquenten: Een analyse van politiegegevens. *Maandblad Geestelijke volksgezondheid, 12,* 1131–1145.

Wijk, A. Ph. van, Horn, J. van, Bullens, R. A. R., Bijleveld, C., & Doreleijers, Th. A. H. (2005). Juvenile sex offenders: A group on its own? *International Journal of Offender Therapy and Comparative Criminology, 49*(1), 25–36.

Wijk, A. Ph. van, Loeber, R., Vermeiren, R., Pardini, D., Doreleijers, Th. A. H., & Bullens, R. A. R. (2005). Violent juvenile sex offenders compared with violent non-sex offenders: Explorative findings from the Pittsburgh Youth Study. *Sexual Abuse: A Journal of Research and Treatment, 3,* 333–352.

Wijk, A. Ph. van, Mali, S. R. F., & Bullens, R. A. R. (2007). Juvenile sex-only and sex-plus offenders: An exploratory study on criminal profiles. *International Journal of Offender Therapy and Comparative Criminology, 51*(4), 407–419.

Wijk, A. Ph. van, Mali, S. R. F., Bullens, R. A. R., Prins, L., & Klerks, P. P. H. M. (2006a). *Zedencriminaliteit in Nederland: Delicten en delinquenten nader in beeld gebracht.* Zeist, Netherlands: Kerckebosch.

Wijk, A. Ph. van, Vermeiren, R., Loeber, R., Doreleijers, T., & Bullens, R. (2006). Juvenile sex offenders compared to non-sex offenders: A review of the literature 1995–2005. *Trauma, Violence, & Abuse, 7*(4), 227–243.

Wijk, A. Ph. van, Vreugdenhil, C., Horn, J. van, Vermeiren, R., & Doreleijers, Th. A. H. (2007). Incarcerated Dutch juvenile sex offenders compared with non-sex offender. *Journal of Child Sexual Abuse, 2,* 1–21.

Wanklyn, S. G., Ward, A. K., Cormier, N. S., Day, D. M., & Newman, J. E. (2012). Can we distinguish juvenile violent sex offenders, violent non-sex offenders, and versatile violent sex offenders based on childhood risk factors? *Journal of Interpersonal Violence, 27*(11), 2128–2143.

Ward, T., Hudson, S. M., Johnston, L., & Marshall, W. L. (1997). Cognitive distortions in sex offenders: An integrative review. *Clinical Psychology Review, 17*(5), 479–507.

Wasserman, G. A., & McReynolds, L. S. (2011). Contributors to traumatic exposure and posttraumatic stress disorder in juvenile justice youths. *Journal of Traumatic Stress, 24*(4), 422–429.

White, J. W., & Koss, M. P. (1993). Adolescent sexual aggression within heterosexual relationships: Prevalence, characteristics, and causes. In H. E. Barbaree, W. L. Marshall, & S. M. Hudson (Eds.), *The juvenile sex offender* (pp. 182–202). New York: Guilford Press.

Worling, J. R. (1995). Sexual abuse histories of adolescent male sex offenders: Differences on the basis of the age and gender of their victims. *Journal of Abnormal Psychology, 104*(4), 610.

Worling, J. R. (2001). Personality-based typology of adolescent male sexual offenders: Differences in recidivism rates, victim-selection characteristics, and personal victimization histories. *Sexual Abuse: A Journal of Research and Treatment, 13*(3), 149–166.

Wree, E. de (2004). *Daders van groepsverkrachting. Een daderprofiel in maatschappelijke context.* Antwerp, Belgium: Maklu.

Zakireh, B., Ronis, S. T., & Knight, R. A. (2008). Individual beliefs, attitudes, and victimization histories of male juvenile sexual offenders. *Sexual Abuse: A Journal of Research and Treatment, 20*(3), 323–351.

Zimring, F.E., Jennings, W.G., Piquero, A.R., & Hays, S. (2009). Investigating the Continuity of Sex Offending: Evidence from the Second Philadelphia Birth Cohort. *Justice Quarterly, 26(1),* 58–76.

CHAPTER 4

A Developmental Life Course View of Juvenile Sexual Offending

Patrick Lussier

Stéphanie Chouinard Thivierge

A widespread misconception among the general public, practitioners, and policy makers is that today's adolescents who have perpetrated a sexual offense are tomorrow's adult sexual offenders (e.g., Letourneau & Miner, 2005; Zimring, 2004). The idea that youth who have perpetrated a sexual offense are on a life-course-persistent path of sexual offending, however, is not supported by empirical evidence. These empirical observations have been raised before and the implications for prevention/ intervention outlined (e.g., Blokland & Lussier, 2014; Zimring, 2004; Zimring et al., 2007), yet American policies continue to stigmatize and label young persons as rapists and pedophiles. As a result, it is often argued that without specialized treatment programs, youth who have perpetrated a sexual offense are tomorrow's adult sexual offenders (see for a discussion, e.g., Letourneau & Miner, 2005; Lussier, Corrado, & McCuish, 2015). Retrospective studies conducted with clinical samples of adult offenders have introduced important biases (e.g., Groth, 1977; Prentky & Knight, 1993) that might have played a role in the misconception that a young person involved in sexual offenses is on such a life-course-persistent path. Furthermore, the importation of theoretical models, clinical constructs, and therapeutic approaches designed for adult offenders in the field of juvenile sexual offending might have reinforced the idea that young persons involved in sexual violence and abuse behaviors are younger versions of adult offenders. Whether the same clinical constructs explain both adolescent and adult sexual offending remains to be seen; findings from emerging prospective longitudinal research suggest that juvenile and adult sexual offending are, for the most part, two distinct phenomena (e.g., Lussier & Blokland, 2014).

In this chapter, it is posited that a program of research on the origins and developmental course of sexually deviant behavior including sexual offenses is crucial to better inform policy makers regarding prevention and intervention with young persons. A developmental life course (DLC) perspective has been recently proposed as an organizing theoretical and research framework to conduct this program of research (Lussier, 2015), and this chapter reiterates its importance by presenting and examining some key issues and concepts of the DLC perspective. While this perspective has only been recently applied to describe and explain sexual violence and abuse, it has a long tradition of research in criminology, most particularly for the description, explanation, and prediction of juvenile delinquency (e.g., Thornberry, 1997; Farrington, 2005; LeBlanc & Loeber, 1998; Morizot & Kazemian, 2015). Scholars have identified the need for and importance of a DLC perspective in the field of sexual violence and abuse to avoid confounding the behavior of children, adolescents, and adults and associated issues, but also to advance research on the origins and development of sexual violence and abuse (Barbaree & Marshall, 2008; Barbaree, Marshall, & Hudson, 1993; Chaffin, Letourneau, & Silovsky, 2002; Smallbone, 2005; Lussier, 2015). This chapter, therefore, aims to add to the growing scientific literature on a DLC view of sexual violence and abuse.

THE DEVELOPMENTAL LIFE COURSE APPROACH

In criminology, the DLC perspective originates from the influential work of criminal career researchers and the pioneer work of several scholars who conducted longitudinal studies to explore the early risk factors of adult crime and juvenile delinquency (e.g., Glueck & Glueck, 1940; Le Blanc & Fréchette, 1989; Robins, 1978; Wolfgang, Figlio, & Sellin, 1972). The criminal career perspective has been concerned with the role and influence of age and aging on crime involvement. Researchers interpreted the role and influence of age and aging differently, with some arguing that crime involvement follows a relatively predictable and uniform pattern across individuals known as the age-crime curve. The age-crime curve first observed by the sociologist Quetelet (1836) suggests that offending starts during early adolescence and quickly peaks during mid-adolescence, followed by a gradual decrease into adulthood (see also Hirschi & Gottfredson, 1983). In other words, delinquency has been described as an epiphenomenon of adolescence. Other researchers argued instead that the typical age-crime curve does not characterize all offending patterns, as some individuals show relatively stable involvement in crime and delinquency over time and into adulthood (e.g., Farrington, 1986;

Moffitt, 1993). These observations led several researchers to examine the presence of different longitudinal patterns of crime and delinquency (e.g., Piquero, Farrington, & Blumstein, 2003).

Research has shown, first and foremost, the presence of much variation in the involvement of crime and delinquency across adolescence, with a subgroup presenting a rather concerning pattern of development. In the 1980s and 1990s, researchers were focused on the description and explanation of chronic juvenile offending because, as a group, such offenders were responsible for a large amount of crime (e.g., Loeber & Farrington, 1998; Wolfgang et al., 1972). Indeed, international research has shown that about 5 to 10 percent of males from a birth cohort are responsible for about 50 percent of all arrests by the entire cohort. This proportion is higher for serious and violent crimes, including rape (e.g., Tracy, Wolfgang, & Figlio, 1990). For girls, a comparable phenomenon has also been identified characterizing about 1 percent of females in a given birth cohort (e.g., Moffitt, Caspi, Rutter, & Silva, 2002). The best method available, however, for screening chronic offenders remains the number of arrests (e.g., at least five arrests)—which only helps to identify these children after the harm is done, offending is well established, and risk factors have been operating for several years (e.g., LeBlanc, 1998).

This line of research has led some scholars to look earlier in the development to best understand the developmental processes leading someone to be involved in a long-term pattern of offending. As a result, researchers and policy makers turned their attention to child delinquency, also referred to as early onset offending. It was observed that some children were already involved in a sustained pattern of delinquency prior to the age of 12 and considered at risk for chronic juvenile offending during adolescence (e.g., Loeber & Farrington, 2001). It was also soon observed that these young persons were presenting a differential clinical profile characterized by neuropsychological issues, more specifically issues in relation to executive function (e.g., attention-deficit hyperactivity disorder) (e.g., Moffitt et al., 2002). Theoretical developmental models had already been proposed to explain the differential pattern of development of these early-onset offenders compared with late-onset offenders, which reinforced the need and importance of such policy-oriented research (e.g., Moffitt, 1993; Patterson & Yoerger, 1993). Researchers contributed to the description of the developmental risk and protective factors associated with an early onset of offending, the development of instruments and clinical tools to assess their risk and needs, as well as the development of intervention/prevention programs designed specifically to target associated treatment/intervention needs (e.g., Corrado, Roesch, Hart, & Gierowski, 2002; Greenwood & Zimring, 2007; Loeber & Farrington, 2012; Morizot & Kazemian, 2015).

Now referred to as developmental criminology (LeBlanc & Loeber, 1998), this line of research focusing on human development, especially the early years, may leave the impression that all is played out in childhood. After all, developmental researchers were also finding, among the group of early-onset children, a substantial subgroup not presenting the same challenges and difficulties during adolescence with a less important involvement in juvenile delinquency (e.g., Moffitt, Caspi, Harrington, & Milne, 2002). Relatedly, life course researchers focused on the discontinuity of antisocial and delinquent behavior, arguing that factors playing a key role extend well beyond the childhood period. These life course factors include, but are not limited to, the role and importance of life events, life transitions, and turning points. This line of research—known as life course criminology—is therefore concerned with human development beyond the childhood/adolescence period. The developmental and life course perspectives are not irreconcilable, however, as both approaches stress the importance of a longitudinal view and the dynamic nature of human behavior over time. Researchers tend to refer to these two approaches as the DLC criminology (Farrington, 2005). Key concepts from the DLC perspective are outlined in the next section—in particular, developmental concepts and issues that are relevant to the description, explanation, and prediction of juvenile sexual offending.

KEY ISSUES AND ASSUMPTIONS ABOUT THE DEVELOPMENT OF ANTISOCIAL AND CRIMINAL BEHAVIOR

In this section, key issues and assumptions from the DLC perspective are introduced. These issues and assumptions, presented and defined in table 4.1, should be seen as guiding principles to describe and explain the development of criminal and antisocial behavior. Indeed, the DLC perspective emphasizes the importance of: (a) linking past and future development; (b) recognizing the specificity of developmental stages and contextualizing the person's behavior within that context, also known as the age-graded perspective; (c) taking into account both the homotypic and the heterotypic continuity of behavioral development; (d) being aware of the presence of both continuity and discontinuity of the behavior over time; and (e) understanding the distinction between a person-oriented and a variable-oriented approach, because multiple patterns of development (rather than a single pattern) might best describe a particular phenomenon. All of these issues, considerations, and assumptions are detailed in the following text.

The scientific literature on the correlates of sexual offending can be distinguished into two broad fields of research: (a) the study of the developmental antecedents of juvenile sexual offending (e.g., Seto & Lalumière, 2010), and (b) the investigation of the risk factors of sexual recidivism (e.g., McCann & Lussier, 2008). Interestingly, there is little research linking these two broad sets of literature because of the lack of longitudinal studies in the field. From a DLC perspective, it is argued that much can be gained by *incorporating past and future* development both in terms of the onset, development course, and termination of antisocial behavior, and in terms of exposure to risk and protective factors. It raises questions such as: *What is the adolescent's past history of offending and exposure to risk/ protective factors?* and *What is the possible course of antisocial behavior and the expected exposure to risk and protective factors?* DLC researchers rely, first and foremost, on prospective longitudinal data to describe and to identify longitudinal patterns of behavioral development. Longitudinal data and repeated measurements with the same cohort of individuals at different time points and across key developmental stages are pivotal considering that DLC researchers are concerned about stability and change over time. This contrasts with traditional research within the field of juvenile offending, which is often based on retrospective data taken at one time point.

TABLE 4.1 KEY DEVELOPMENTAL CONCEPTS AND PARAMETERS FOR THE STUDY OF CRIMINAL AND ANTISOCIAL BEHAVIOR

Developmental Concept	Description
Age-graded perspective	Contextualizing the behavior and associated underlying mechanisms within a developmental stage
Cumulative risk	Developmental outcomes are better explained and predicted by a combination of risk factors than a single risk factor.
Developmental behavioral pathway	Within-individual qualitative behavioral changes over time
Developmental behavioral trajectory	Within-individual quantitative behavioral changes over time
Equifinality	A diversity of pathways can lead to the same developmental outcome
Heterotypic continuity	The continuity of a set of conceptually related behavioral manifestations over time
Homotypic continuity	The continuity of specific behavioral manifestation over time
Multifinality	Different developmental outcomes can be preceded by the same developmental starting point
Person-oriented approach	Focus on individual profiles of development
Person x environment transactions	Behavioral development is the result of ongoing exchanges between the person and his or her environment
Variable-oriented approach	Focus on the identification of risk/protection factors, irrespective of the person as a whole (i.e., person-oriented approach)

Traditionally, non-developmental research has been focused on between-individual differences associated with antisocial behavior, and the field of research on juvenile sexual offending is no exception. From this perspective, researchers have raised questions such as: *What risk factors differentiate youth involved in violent offenses from those not involved in such behaviors?* (a variable-oriented approach). In contrast, DLC researchers have focused on within-individual stability and changes, and on how individuals evolve over time (e.g., cognitive ability, beliefs and values, cognitive/emotional regulation, motor/social skills) as well as the role and impact of the changing context and environment across stages (e.g., transitioning from school to the workplace, transitioning into parenthood) and how it impacts behavioral development (a person-oriented approach). In that context, the person and his or her environment is the focal point, and research questions are formulated differently to ask, for example: *What risk factors lead someone to start acting in a criminally violent way? What risk factors lead someone to escalate to more serious forms of violent behaviors? and What factors contribute to the desistance and termination of offending?* Researchers also raise questions as to whether the risk factors for crime and delinquency during early adolescence are the same as those in middle/late adolescence, and whether new risk factors emerge in early adulthood.

DLC researchers are especially concerned by both individual and environmental factors *and their interplay* to describe and explain the onset, developmental course, and termination of antisocial behavior. While researchers have stressed the importance of child sexual abuse victimization experiences to explain juvenile sexual offending through various etiological mechanisms (social learning, conditioning) (Burton, 2003), research has consistently shown that a small minority of victims of child sexual abuse go on to become abusers themselves (e.g., Hershkowitz, 2014; Leach, Stewart, & Smallbone, 2015; Salter et al., 2003; Widom & Massey, 2015). Historically, social scientists have stressed the role of environmental factors and early exposure to social adversities (e.g., maltreatment) over genetic and biological factors. While it is generally agreed that genetic factors alone are not responsible for complex social behaviors, developmentalists recognize the importance of the interplay between genetic and environmental factors. This interplay refers, among other things, to key processes by which individual and environmental factors mutually influence each other (Caspi & Roberts, 2001; Shanahan & Boardman, 2009). Certain environmental factors can impact the presence or absence of criminal and antisocial behavior by triggering, constraining, or enhancing individual factors. For example, Caspi et al. (2002) showed that children who were victims of maltreatment with deficiencies in monoamine oxidase A (MAOA), which metabolizes neurotransmitters, are more likely to be involved in occurrence of violent criminal behaviors. The same outcome is not observed as often for maltreated children without such deficiencies.

Individual factors can also influence passively and non-passively the environment in a way that impacts the developmental course of antisocial and criminal behavior. First, an evocative process refers to situations whereby individual factors evoke certain reactions from the environment that can reinforce antisocial and criminal behaviors. For example, a child's difficult temper may evoke negative and harsh parental responses, which in turn may reinforce and exacerbate the child's negative temper and aggressive behaviors toward others (e.g., Reid, Patterson, & Snyder, 2002). Second, a proactive process refers to situations whereby the person self-selects him- or herself in specific social contexts that are conducive to antisocial and criminal behaviors. For example, adolescents with antisocial attitudes and beliefs tend to associate with other adolescents sharing similar attitudes and beliefs (e.g., Moffitt, 1993). Delinquent peer association may not only reinforce antisocial attitudes and beliefs, but also create opportunities for antisocial and criminal behaviors.

Borrowed from the field of developmental psychopathology, the terms *equifinality* and *multifinality* are also key to describing and explaining developmental patterns and outcomes among youth (Cichetti & Rogosh, 1996; 2002). Multifinality refers to the idea that from any original developmental starting point, there is a diversity of developmental outcomes. Said differently, individuals sharing certain characteristics or exposed to certain environmental factors will not exhibit the same behavioral outcomes later on. For example, research has shown over and over that children who have been sexually abused present a wide variety of developmental and behavioral outcomes (e.g., Browne & Finkelhor, 1986; Paolucci, Genuis, & Violato, 2001). In fact, not all children who have been sexually abused develop child sexual behavioral problems, and an even smaller proportion eventually become perpetrators themselves (Salter et al., 2003). Other maladaptive behaviors and outcomes may occur, such as externalizing and antisocial behaviors as well as internalizing-related behaviors such as anxiety and depression; still others might show relatively normal developmental outcomes (e.g., Friedrich, Davies, Feher, & Wright, 2003). The concept of equifinality, in contrast, refers to the idea of a common developmental outcome from distinctive developmental starting points (Cichetti & Rogosh, 2002). This suggests that a diversity of developmental processes may lead to the perpetration of a sexual offense. Some children may have a genetic predisposition toward impulsive behaviors that may manifest itself in a sexual context; others may grow up in a familial environment characterized by deviant sexual role models and experience sexual victimization; others still may develop a bond with peers characterized by negative and false beliefs that impact their view of girls and sexuality. The principle of equifinality, therefore, recognizes the presence of different developmental processes leading to juvenile sexual offending as opposed to the idea that all youth who have committed a sexual offense follow the same developmental pathway.

In the field of research on sexual violence and abuse, explanatory models of juvenile sexual offending tend to focus on the childhood period and, more specifically, the nature and quality of the familial environment and experiences of abuse, neglect, and violence. DLC explanations of criminal and antisocial behavior emphasize that risk and protective factors are *developmental-stage-specific*. DLC researchers are concerned with the person's exposure to risk/protective factors at different developmental stages: in utero, birth, infancy, preschool, elementary school, secondary school, and emerging adulthood. This age-graded perspective highlights that each developmental stage is associated with developmentally specific tasks and adaptations (e.g., development of language and communication skills, regulating positive and negative emotions, respecting rules and figures of authority, developing behavioral inhibitions). As such, the DLC model of antisocial and criminal behavior typically includes individual-, familial-, peer-, school-, and neighbourhood-level risk/protective factors (e.g., Farrington, 2005; Loeber & Farrington, 2012).

Thornberry (2005) argues that there is a continuum of onset of antisocial behavior from early childhood to adulthood, with different onset points generally associated with different causal risk factors or factors that differ in number or strength. Onset prior to school entry is said to be the result of a combination of individual characteristics (e.g., difficult temperament, attention/hyperactivity issues), ineffective parenting, and structural socioeconomic adversities (see also Moffitt, 1993). Similar factors are said to operate for onset during elementary school, but the interactions among those are less powerful, explaining the delay in antisocial, delinquent behavior. For example, not all children with a difficult temperament have parents with limited parenting skills living in a disorganized neighborhood. Onset during adolescence is described as the result of peer and school influences, the importance of establishing age-appropriate autonomy, as well the desire to experiment and seek new sensations. Finally, Thornberry (2005) describes the onset in adulthood as the combination of risk and protective factors. This adult-onset group tends to be characterized by low cognitive skills; as a result, these persons might be less successful in building the human and social capital that are necessary to find a satisfying job, to have a stable income, and to have a circle of friends providing social support and assistance during difficult and stressful periods. It is posited that their positive familial environment acted as a protective factor until these persons began to leave their home environment and, in the process, became more vulnerable to negative social influences and life stressors.

The age-graded perspective also stresses the importance of contextualizing the child's behavior. There are some behaviors considered to be age-normative, or age-appropriate, that are no longer normative at a later developmental stage and vice versa. For example, physical aggression and its various manifestations such as kicking, pushing, and biting are fairly common behaviors in toddlers in reaction to frustration and anger (e.g., Tremblay, Japel, & Pérusse, 1999). Such behaviors are considered age-normative, as toddlers are still learning to recognize these situations and to react appropriately by regulating their cognitions, emotions, and behaviors. Through a socialization process, the associated developmental tasks for this trial-and-error period are pivotal if the developing child is to learn how to regulate anger and frustration, as well as learn how to act in a prosocial way (e.g., sharing, waiting their turn). In sum, while there are age-graded norms and expectations about what is appropriate and not appropriate, there are also skills children are expected to learn, acquire, and develop at each developmental stage. Difficulties with newly added tasks at a particular stage may impact the child's ability to adapt to the next stage. In that regard, Loeber, Stouthamer-Loeber, Farrington, and White (2008) proposed a cumulative approach suggesting that the worst developmental outcomes are linked to an accumulation of risk factors across developmental stage domains and contexts. This approach suggests, therefore, that the worst antisocial behavior outcomes are the result not so much of one particular risk factor as of the accumulation of risk factors across developmental stages and across risk factor domains operating for years.

The age-graded perspective has other ramifications for the description and understanding of maladaptive behavior. Developmentalists have coined the term *heterotypic continuity* to recognize that there is continuity or persistence of conceptually similar behaviors over time and across developmental stages (e.g., Moffitt, 1993). Heterotypic continuity can be contrasted with homotypic continuity or the persistence of the same behavior over time (e.g., physical aggression during childhood and adulthood).

Patterson (1993) probably best described the heterotypic continuity of antisocial and delinquent behavior by referring to it as a chimera—a Greek-mythological character that is part lion, part dragon, part goat, and part snake. In other words, heterotypic continuity suggests that the maladaptative behavior is a moving target taking different forms and shape as it persists. Of importance, this concept highlights the dynamic aspect of antisocial behavior and the presence of qualitative changes over time. As children age, they are exposed to new environments, influences, and opportunities but also go through significant individual changes, whether cognitive, emotional, moral, verbal, physical, or social. These changes can influence the course of antisocial behaviors by favoring the addition of new behaviors to the repertoire. For example, in the context of persisting aggression during early childhood, there can be a progression from physical aggression (e.g., kicking), to verbal aggression (e.g., insulting), to social/indirect aggression (e.g., excluding someone from a group). The underlying processes are similar, but the manifestations change.

Researchers have stressed the importance of examining all forms and shapes of antisocial behavior rather than isolating and focusing one specific form—i.e., the most preoccupying or the most recent form manifested by the young person. Four types of antisocial behaviors are generally recognized by developmentalists: (a) overt and aggressive behaviors (e.g., to fight, assault, threaten, destroy property); (b) covert and sneaky behaviors (e.g., to lie frequently, be deceitful, commit fraud, steal); (c) reckless behaviors showing a disregard for another person's or one's own security and wellbeing (e.g., dangerous/reckless driving, substance use, driving while impaired, unprotected sex); and (d) defiant and oppositional behaviors (e.g., to run away, be disrespectful, break rules at home or at school) (Le Blanc & Bouthilier, 2003). Developmentalists even argue that the development of antisocial behavior is hierarchical, is predictable, and unfolds in a stage-like fashion (Loeber & Le Blanc, 1990). Loeber's developmental pathways remain one of the most comprehensive and detailed representations of the development of different types of antisocial behaviors. The concept of heterotypic continuity, however, seems to suggest that children showing one antisocial behavior will indubitably and ultimately show the most serious forms of antisocial and criminal behavior, but prospective longitudinal research shows otherwise as a result of the importance of desistance from antisocial and criminal behavior.

There is *much discontinuity albeit some continuity* of antisocial behavior over time. Robins (1978) observed that while most adults with an antisocial personality disorder were involved in antisocial behavior during adolescence, most antisocial adolescents did not develop an antisocial personality disorder in adulthood. This continuity–discontinuity paradox highlights another dynamic aspect of the developmental course of antisocial behavior over time. This paradox reminds us of the retrospective biases and the importance of not drawing conclusions about all juvenile offenders by only strictly looking at the developmental antecedents of adult offenders. It also highlights that youth presenting the same behavior or same set of behaviors at one particular time point might show very different developmental and behavioral outcomes in the future. Of importance, DLC research has shown that, irrespective of childhood exposure to adversities, desistance from crime and delinquency is the norm across individuals. The process of desistance is rapid and near immediate for some, long and gradual for others. In a follow-up longitudinal study of a sample of juvenile offenders well into their 70s, researchers have shown that most of them had desisted from a life of crime by age 30, while persisters were characterized by much intermittency, alternating sporadically between offending and non-offending states (Sampson & Laub, 2005).

The DLC perspective also stresses the importance of approaching the etiology of antisocial behavior using a *person-oriented* perspective. The person-oriented perspective can be contrasted with the variable-oriented approach, which emphasizes the identification of "risk" factors for offending and "predictors" of criminal recidivism. The variable-oriented perspective posits that these risk factors or predictors have the same value and same importance for all youth irrespective of their individual and/or familial characteristics. In other words, the variable-oriented approach suggests that a risk factor can be analyzed in isolation from other individual and environmental aspects of the person (e.g., other risk factors and protective factors). From a person-oriented approach, however, a risk factor cannot be examined in isolation; individuals need to be looked at as a whole. In that context, a single factor may be relevant and important for some individuals but not others. A single etiological model or single etiological pathway can be seen as too reductionist to account for the diversity of human development and the possible developmental course of antisocial and criminal behavior. Researchers account for the presence of such diversity through the examination and description of developmental pathways (Keenan & Shaw, 2003; Loeber & Hay, 1997) and developmental trajectories (e.g., Tremblay & Nagin, 2005). The term *developmental pathways* refers to longitudinal patterns of qualitatively different behaviors (e.g., minor aggression, physical fighting, and violence), whereas *trajectories* refers to longitudinal patterns of quantitatively different behaviors or set of behaviors (e.g., yearly number of arrests, monthly number of delinquent acts). Hence, trajectories are not informative about heterotypic continuity processes whereas pathways are not informative about the frequency (and variations in frequency) of antisocial and criminal behavior over time (Loeber et al., 2008).

Moffitt (1993) originally distinguished two developmental patterns of antisocial behavior that had a significant influence in DLC theory and research. The first trajectory, life-course-persistent (LCP) antisocial behavior, is characterized as a developmental course where the antisocial behavior is already frequent and persistent in childhood. It escalates to more serious delinquent acts, including violent offenses, during adolescence and adulthood. This LCP pattern has been said to be associated with early exposure to biological/genetic risk factors conducive to the development of neuropsychological deficits (i.e., executive functions), as well as to a criminogenic familial environment, limited in terms of parental skills, social support, and financial resources. A child with neuropsychological deficits is characterized by a more difficult temper, a shorter attention span, and behavioral inhibition issues that, in the context of a criminogenic familial environment, can exacerbate the presence, frequency, and persistence of maladaptive and antisocial behavior. In contrast, the adolescence-limited (AL) trajectory has been characterized by juvenile delinquency and antisocial behavior limited to the period of adolescence, such as status-related and property-type offenses. This AL trajectory has been associated with a maturity gap (i.e., adolescents' desire to be recognized and to behave as adults) and the role and influence of peers. In fact, adolescents' participation in delinquent acts is portrayed as being opportunistic, transitory, and involving other teens. Involvement in delinquent acts may persist into adulthood, mainly as a result of the negative consequences of their prior delinquency involvement (e.g., being kicked out of a school, developing a substance abuse problem, having a criminal record), which may limit their access to adult roles (e.g., finding a desired job). While there is limited research on the trajectories of antisocial behavior, empirical research supports the presence of multiple trajectories of offending, generally highlighting the presence of a group being labeled LCP or chronics and another being labeled AL, bell-curve pattern, or desisters (e.g., Piquero, Gonzales, & Jennings, 2015). Research examining the trajectories of offending has also helped to uncover other longitudinal patterns, such as adult-onset offending and late bloomers, that were not described by earlier etiological models of crime and delinquency.

A DEVELOPMENTAL PERSPECTIVE ON SEXUAL OFFENDING

A central aspect of the DLC perspective is the description and explanation of the development of antisocial and criminal behavior. Key to the understanding of the development of sexual offending from a DLC perspective is the description of the prevalence, onset, and developmental course of the behavior over time. These developmental parameters are important given that, from this perspective, it is argued that the factors influencing one developmental parameter may not necessarily be influencing another developmental aspect of the behavior. For example, the factors leading someone to start offending might be entirely different from those leading them to cease offending. The onset and termination of offending are only two of multiple developmental parameters that DLC researchers examine to capture the dynamic aspects of behavioral development.

Researchers distinguish a series of generic, boundary, and dynamic parameters of behavioral development (Le Blanc & Fréchette, 1989; Loeber & Le Blanc, 1990; Morizot & Kazemian, 2015). While not exhaustive, the main developmental parameters are presented and defined in table 4.2. The term *boundary parameters* refers to time-dependent aspects of behavioral development, which include the age of onset, the age of offset, and the duration of sexual offending or the time elapsed between the ages of onset and offset. *Generic parameters* relate to the frequency of offending (e.g., number of victims, number of sexual crime events) and the diversity of offenses committed (e.g., hands-on, hands-off). *Dynamic developmental parameters* refers to the relationship between boundary and generic developmental parameters. There are three main dynamic processes describing behavioral development: activation, escalation, and desistance. *Activation* refers to the link between age of onset and the process by which an early onset of sexual offending stimulates its development such that it is more likely to become persistent, frequent, and diversified. *Escalation* refers to the process by which persistent offending can stimulate offending such that it becomes chronic and characterized by a progression to more serious forms of offending. Finally, *desistance* relates to the process by which offending stops progressing, becoming more patterned and specialized (i.e., the scope of offending behavior becomes narrower and more specific) and less frequent until complete termination. In other words, for persistent offenders, over time and across offenses, the person will tend to repeat the behaviors that are providing more gratifications and/or those for which the person is less likely to get caught and apprehended.

TABLE 4.2 DEVELOPMENTAL PARAMETERS OF BEHAVIORAL DEVELOPMENT

Developmental Parameter	Description
Age of onset	Age at first offense
Age of offset	Age at last offense
Duration	Time elapsed between age of onset and age of offset
Frequency	Number of offenses
Variety	Number of different types of offenses committed
Activation	Impact of the age of onset on persistence, frequency, and versatility of delinquent acts
Escalation	Impact of persistence on progression and chronicity of offending
Desistance	Process by which offending decelerates, stops progressing, and becomes more patterned until complete termination

Together, these generic, boundary, and dynamic parameters can be organized into a dynamic developmental model of sexual offending (figure 4.1; see Le Blanc & Fréchette, 1998; Lussier, 2015). The dynamic developmental parameters of sexual offending do not suggest that all youth involved in sexual offenses become chronic persistent sexual offenders who accumulate offenses and victims over their entire life course. Quite to the contrary, these processes, first and foremost, provide a common language for researchers, practitioners, and policy makers to communicate more clearly about sexual offending. They also provide an analytical framework to examine the multidimensional aspect of the development of sexual offending among youth with the assumption that different factors could be responsible for its activation, escalation, and desistance.

Figure 4.1 A Developmental Process View of the Development of Sexual Offending

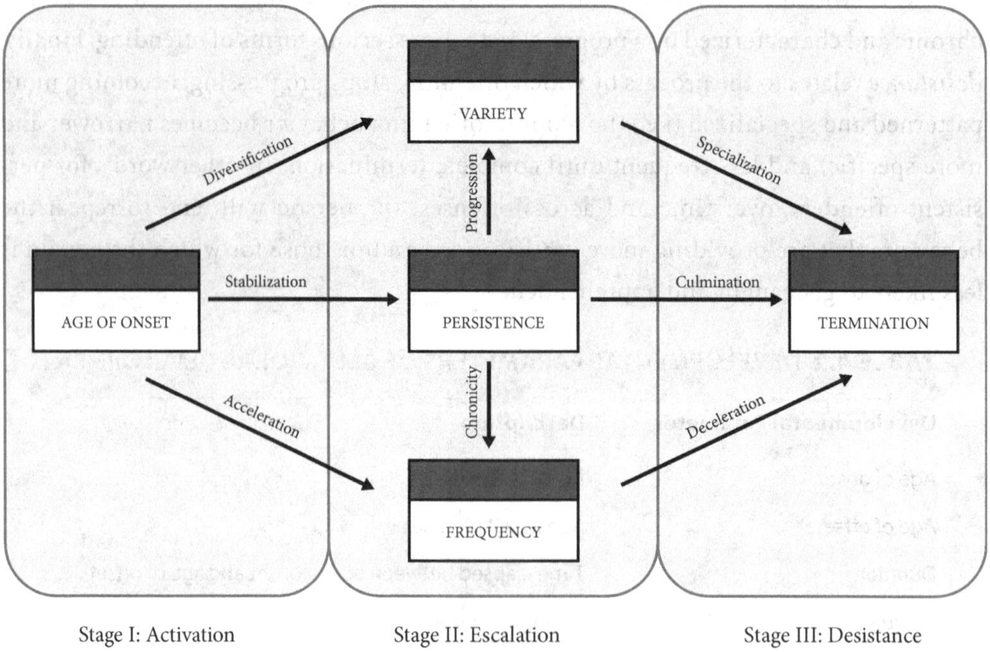

Stage I: Activation   Stage II: Escalation   Stage III: Desistance

There is limited information about the generic, boundary, and dynamic developmental parameters of sexual offending considering that longitudinal studies in the field are limited (Blokland & Lussier, 2015; Lussier & Cale, 2013). The available empirical evidence mainly stems from clinical samples, which generally include youth having committed more serious offenses and/or shown a pattern of repetitive and persistent sexual offending. Furthermore, the source of information regarding the developmental parameters is not always clearly presented in prior empirical studies. It is not always clear whether, for example, offending was measured using official data (police data, child welfare), self-reports, clinical interviews, information from collaterals, or something else. Each source of information has its methodological issues and limitations, therefore limiting the conclusions that can be drawn from the scientific literature. Also, studies reporting on the developmental parameters of juvenile sexual offending are mainly retrospective in nature and rarely include follow-up information. As a result, the reported information only represents a snapshot of a young person's possible involvement in crime and delinquency. Even when follow-up data are available, the length of the follow-up period is generally short (three to four years) and rarely covers multiple developmental stages (see McCann & Lussier, 2008). Taken together, the review below focuses on the developmental parameters pertaining mainly to juvenile sexual offending based on relatively scarce scientific literature with methodological issues and limitations; the findings need to be interpreted carefully and accordingly.

Lussier (2015) proposed a developmental model of sexual offending that recognizes the heterogeneity of the developmental course of sexual offending among young offenders. The model is presented in figure 4.2. The first dynamic aspect of sexual offending, activation, is likely to be characterized as a continuum of onset ages that can be categorized into an early-onset (childhood) and a late-onset (adolescence) group. Consistent with empirical observations (e.g., Carpentier, Leclerc, & Proulx, 2011; Vizard, Hickey, & McCrory, 2007), the model stipulates that the most common activation pattern among youth involved in sexual offenses is likely to be an adolescence-onset pattern. The second dynamic aspect of sexual offending, escalation, is likely to include a continuum of escalation involving qualitatively and quantitatively distinct sexual offending patterns. The most commonly hypothesized pattern of sexual offending is likely to involve either no or minimal progression toward serious sexual offenses and to be limited to a very small number of offenses. It is also argued that a small subgroup of young persons will follow a pattern characterized by progression toward more serious sexual offenses and a chronic, repetitive pattern of sexual offending. The third dynamic aspect of sexual offending among youth, desistance, is hypothesized by Lussier (2015) as consisting of a continuum of processes; some youth seem to stop immediately after the initial offense whereas for others, desistance is a much longer and more gradual process that unfolds over several years, into adulthood, and is more likely to include a series of lapses and relapses (i.e., sexual offense precursors or actual sexual reoffenses). It is hypothesized that the most common desistance process among youth is one where desistance from sexual offending will be rapid and near immediate.

Figure 4.2 Hypothesized Developmental Stages of Sexual Offending and Heterogeneity Across Stages

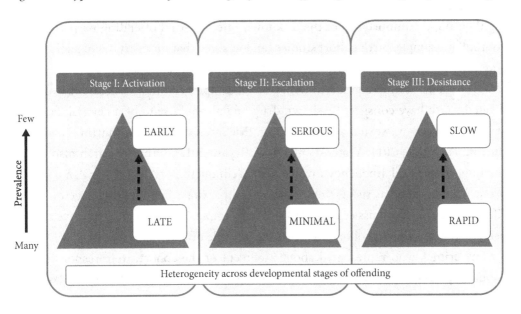

THE DEVELOPMENTAL COURSE OF
SEXUAL OFFENDING AMONG YOUTH

The term *prevalence* refers to the proportion of individuals of any given age perpetrating a sexual offense. There is limited research estimating the prevalence of sexual offending among youth. Conducting a prevalence study on deviant and illegal sexual behaviors with minors raises important ethical issues that have limited the possibilities of conducting such research. Self-report survey studies with older adolescents and young adults from the general population suggest that sexually coercive behaviors are relatively rare. Kjellgren, Priebe, Svedin, and Langström (2010) estimated that the lifetime prevalence of sexually coercive behavior in a sample of students aged between 17 and 20 years old was 5 percent. Similarly, Slotboom, Hendriks, and Verbruggen (2011) examined the self-reported prevalence of sexual aggression using a multisampling strategy by recruiting participants in low-risk (i.e., school-based sample), moderate-risk (i.e., vocational training sample), and high-risk (i.e., youth in detention) samples of adolescents. The prevalence of sexual aggression among young males varied from 1 percent (low-risk sample) to 18 percent (high-risk sample), with the moderate-risk group showing a prevalence of 7 percent. Interestingly, the rates of perpetration found for females in the low- and moderate-risk groups were similar to if not higher than those found for males. In the high-risk group, however, females showed a significantly lower prevalence of sexually coercive behavior compared with males (9.1%). For males, being a victim of sexual abuse was the most important correlate of sexual aggression, while for females, it was beliefs about sexual behaviors.

In contrast, prevalence estimates based on official data are significantly lower, highlighting the importance of the unknown rate of sexual offending perpetrated by youth. For example, birth cohort studies tend to show that for every 1,000 adolescents, about 3 to 5 are adjudicated for a sexual crime during adolescence (Lussier, 2015). Cross-sectional studies conducted with general samples and high-risk samples of adjudicated youth have consistently shown drug and alcohol use to be a key risk factor of sexual coercion and sexual aggression (e.g., Kjellgren et al., 2010; Marini, Leibowitz, Burton, & Stickle, 2014; Yeater, Lenberg, & Bryan, 2012). Other research also shows the importance of delinquency involvement, delinquent peers, and living in a crime-prone neighborhood as risk factors for adolescent sexual offending (e.g., Ageton, 1983; Kjellgren et al., 2010; Lussier et al., 2015). For example, Tracy et al. (1990) have shown, using data from a birth cohort, that chronic juvenile offenders (i.e., at least five arrests for any crime), who represented about 7 percent of the cohort, were responsible for about 75 percent of all arrests for rape among the entire cohort during adolescence.

This is not to say that all youth arrested for rape are chronic offenders, but it does suggests that, as general offending becomes chronic, there is a significant possibility that this group of adolescents becomes at risk of committing a sexual assault.

The Activation of Sexual Offending

The onset of sexual offending marks the activation of the behavior and informs us about the origin of sexual offending. Generally speaking, clinical studies have shown that the average age of onset of juvenile sexual offending is 14 years old (e.g., Carpentier et al., 2011; Christiansen & Vincent, 2013; Jacobs, Kennedy, & Meyer, 1997; Ryan, Miyoshi, Metzner, Krugman, & Fryer, 1996). The available scientific evidence suggests, therefore, that the most common age of onset of juvenile sexual offending is early to middle adolescence. Research also shows that a subgroup consisting of about 5 to 25 percent of clinical samples typically shows an early, childhood onset of sexually abusive behavior (e.g., Carpentier et al., 2011; Ryan et al., 1996; Vizard et al., 2007). There is little information concerning the presence of differential risk factors associated with childhood-onset and adolescence-onset sexual offending. Longitudinal research has shown that adolescence-onset of sexual offending is associated with criminogenic childhood risk factors such as involvement in delinquency, symptoms of an attention deficit disorder, being more sexually active early on, and living in a crime-prone neighborhood (Lussier, Blokland, Mathesius, Pardini, & Loeber, 2015).

In contrast, research has shown that the childhood onset of sexually abusive behaviors is related to both individual factors and exposure to more severe environmental risk factors. For example, Vizard et al. (2007) have shown that childhood-onset sexually abusive behaviors are related to the exposure to several indicators suggesting the presence of neuropsychological deficits (e.g., executive functioning, which may include attention deficit hyperactivity disorder, and learning disabilities) as well as several indicators typically associated with a dysfunctional familial environment, such as parental characteristics (e.g., paternal criminality and mental health problems), severe aversive familial experiences (i.e., abuse, neglect, parental conflicts), and inappropriate sexualized experiences (e.g., inappropriate sexual boundaries, sexual abuse). Similar results were also reported by Carpentier et al. (2011). These preliminary study findings show that the developmental risk factors for the childhood onset of sexually abusive behaviors are multifaceted and include a significant accumulation of individual, familial risk factors and social adversities, whereas the developmental risk factors of an adolescence onset of sexual offending are more in line with either generic criminogenic risk factors of juvenile delinquency or those associated with psychosocial development (e.g., social competence, insecure attachment issues) (e.g., Seto & Lalumière, 2010; Smallbone, 2008).

The Developmental Course of Sexual Offending

The term *individual frequency of sexual offending* refers to the number of instances in which a sexual offense was perpetrated by a person. The frequency of sexual offending is multidimensional and is best examined by looking at the number of different victims as well as the number of different times a young person sexually abused the same individual (Lussier, Bouchard, & Beauregard, 2011). It is difficult to draw conclusions regarding the individual frequency of sexual offending among youth, as researchers generally speak of frequency using official data (e.g., number of arrests), which provide very little detail about the number of victims or the number of events the person was involved in. The available evidence, however, suggests that on average, young persons offend against one or two victims (e.g., Carpentier et al., 2011; Jacobs et al., 1997). The limited research also shows that sexual offending by a minor generally involves a limited number of sexually abusive/violent incidents (e.g., Miranda & Corcoran, 2000). Therefore, sexual offending perpetrated by an adolescent is generally limited to a single victim and a single event—but there are young persons whose involvement is dramatically different. Indeed, other research highlights the presence of some heterogeneity in the frequency of sexual offending among subgroups of young persons involved in sexual offenses, but the developmental correlates of such variations are unclear (Wieckowski, Hartsoe, Mayer, & Shortz, 1998). For example, the number of victims can be somewhat higher for those having sexually abused a boy (e.g., Becker, Kaplan, Cunningham-Rathner, & Kavoussi, 1986).

Persistence or the lack thereof is perhaps one of the most documented developmental aspects of sexual offending among youth (Lussier, 2015). It is generally inferred from recidivism studies, which provide an imperfect account of persistence given the relatively short follow-up period, but also given that sexual recidivism measures only consider a portion of the sexual offending longitudinal pattern. While early empirical studies presented high sexual recidivism rates among youth (Awad, Saunders, & Levene, 1984; Awad & Saunders, 1991; Becker et al., 1986; Fehrenbach, Smith, Monastersky, & Deisher, 1986; Groth, 1977), these results were the result of sample biases and the use of retrospective as opposed to prospective longitudinal data. Meta-analyses show that sexual recidivism rates among young persons vary between 5 and 10 percent (e.g., Caldwell, 2010; McCann & Lussier, 2008). When persistence is measured using other sources of information, such as self-report data, the level of persistence does increase but not dramatically (Bremer, 1992), suggesting that persistence of sexually offending is a relatively rare phenomenon among young persons. Even when extending the follow-up into adulthood, the level of persistence does not vary much (Blokland & Lussier, 2014; Lussier, van den Berg, Bijleveld, & Hendriks, 2012; Zimring, Piquero, & Jennings, 2007). This is consistent with the observation that after five or six years, it is very uncommon for adolescents to sexually reoffend either in adolescence or in adulthood (Langström, 2002).

Of importance, the available literature does not consistently permit distinguishing two persistence-related phenomena: (a) persistence during adolescence, and (b) continuity into adulthood (some notable exceptions: Lussier & Blokland, 2014; Nisbet, Wilson, & Smallbone, 2004). Furthermore, some studies on persistence used retrospective data by examining the presence of past sexual offenses or the number of prior victims (e.g., Aebi, Plattner, Steinhausen, & Bessler, 2011; Dennison & Leclerc, 2011; Kenny, Keogh, & Seidler, 2001) whereas others used prospective longitudinal data to examine sexual recidivism (e.g., Nisbet et al., 2004; White & Smith, 2004; Zimring, Jennings, Piquero, & Hays, 2009). In all, such methodological discrepancies can therefore explain the inconsistencies observed in the scientific literature concerning the importance of certain risk factors (Worling & Langström, 2006; McCann & Lussier, 2008). This distinction is important given that different processes responsible for persistence of sexual offending might be at play during adolescence and adulthood. For example, indicators of antisociality have not been shown to be consistently related to sexual recidivism (e.g., McCann & Lussier, 2008).

An increasing number of longitudinal studies examine youth entry into adulthood. These studies have shown that there are multiple adult entry outcomes for young offenders, especially in terms of adult offending (e.g., Lussier et al., 2012; Lussier, McCuish, & Corrado, 2015; Nisbet et al., 2004). One of the key issues, of course, is to determine whether a young person having committed a sexual offense is at a greater risk of committing a sexual offense in adulthood than other youth. Longitudinal research following cohorts of adolescents into adulthood shows that adolescents having committed a sexual offense are more likely to be arrested or charged for a sexual offense in adulthood than other adolescents from the general population. This statement, however, has to be put into context. First, as stated before, while adolescents having committed a sexual offense are at a *greater* risk of adult sexual offending than other adolescents, the risk remains relatively low given the low prevalence rate of adult sexual offending observed across studies for this group (e.g., Nisbet et al., 2004; Lussier & Blokland, 2014; Lussier et al., 2015; Zimring et al., 2007). Second, prospective birth cohort longitudinal studies have shown that the vast majority of adult sexual offenders have no official record of juvenile sexual offending (e.g., Lussier & Blokland, 2014; Zimring et al., 2007). Third, prospective longitudinal studies examining the risk factors of adult sexual offending using birth cohort data have demonstrated that indicators of early-onset, chronic juvenile general offending are at least as important a risk factor in adult sexual offending as is having a record for a sexual offense during adolescence (e.g., Lussier & Blokland,

2014; Lussier et al., 2015; Zimring et al., 2007). Stated differently, adolescents who have repeated contacts with the criminal justice system for myriad offenses (e.g., breach of probation conditions, property offenses, violent offenses, drug-related offenses) are at least as likely to be involved in a sexual offense in adulthood as persons involved in sexual offenses during adolescence. In sum, the identification of youth at great risk of committing a sexual offense in adulthood is certainly not as straightforward as it might seem, and the current approach focusing on all youth having committed a sexual offense to prevent adult sexual offending appears to be misguided.

Desistance from Sexual Offending

Desistance from offending is a multifaceted phenomenon representing multiple challenges for researchers and practitioners (e.g., Harris, 2014; Laws & Ward, 2011). From a research standpoint, it is extremely challenging to conceptualize, operationalize, and measure desistance. Indeed, researchers have defined desistance in multiple ways. Traditionally, desistance has been defined simply as the termination of offending (e.g., Lussier, 2016). Researchers have relied on this conceptualization, which implies that termination of offending is rather sudden in someone's life course. This portrayal, however, leaves aside the fact that some individuals struggle for years to stop offending despite the motivation to do so. More recently, therefore, researchers have defined desistance as a process that starts with the decision to stop offending followed by gradual cognitive-behavioral changes until the complete termination of offending. From this standpoint, therefore, someone may reoffend in the process of desistance despite the motivation not to reoffend. Reoffending, in such a context, might be less serious and less repetitive, sparked by a temporary breakdown in self-efficacy as a result of difficult life circumstances and significant life stresses. At this stage and given the scarcity of research, it is probably best to approach desistance from sexual offending as involving a wide range of phenomena ranging from immediate cessation of the behavior to a long process unfolding over several years (Lussier, 2015). At one end of the continuum, therefore, desistance does not happen overnight and involves a series of lapses and relapses (e.g., Lussier et al., 2015).

The measure of desistance from offending is further complicated by a series of additional factors and issues. For example, desistance from sexual offending might be confused with crime switching. Someone may not sexually reoffend, but may take part in other types of crime (e.g., violent offenses, drug-related offenses, theft, etc.), which raises the important issue of whether that person is indeed in the process of desistance or not. Further, the measurement and assessment of desistance is challenging because of cost avoidance, or the ability to sexually offend without being caught

(Lussier et al., 2011). Indeed, a person may sexually reoffend and escape detection for long time periods while presenting a rather conventional lifestyle (e.g., Lussier & Mathesius, 2012). Moreover, the measurement and assessment of desistance is further complicated by the prevalence and importance of intermittent offending in persistent sexual offenders. Intermittency of offending implies that individuals do not offend on a regular basis, even individuals considered serial offenders (e.g., Deslauriers-Varin & Beauregard, 2014). Therefore, someone characterized by a non-offending state for a year might move to an offending state with a longer follow-up period. To date, there has been limited work examining desistance patterns among young offenders and the factors responsible for it.

The emerging scientific literature on desistance from sexual offending has been primarily focused on desistance from sexual offending in adulthood (e.g., Harris, 2014; Laws & Ward, 2011). Lussier et al. (2012) found the presence of two distinctive desistance patterns with respect to sexual offending among young persons. A first pattern, by far the most common, involves a rapid and near or immediate desistance from sexual offending during adolescence, prior to reaching adulthood. In line with Moffitt's (1993) original AL model, it is suggested that developmental, transitory, and contextual factors, rather than individual-based deficits, might be responsible for their sexual offending. With respect to this group, sexual reoffending during adolescence is a possibility if the associated risk factors are still present and operating. Worling (2013), for example, proposed a series of factors that may promote desistance from sexual offending and may be more in line with this group. More precisely, demonstrations of prosocial sexual interests, sexual attitudes, and a sexual environment; being aware of the consequences of sexual reoffending, compassion for others, positive problem-solving skills, positive affect-regulation skills, emotional intimacy with peers, a close relationship with a positive and supportive adult, adequate social controls, active involvement in prosocial structured activity with peers, hope, and successful treatment completion have been described as possible factors that may be associated with desistance from sexual offending. Furthermore, while this group desists from sexual offending during adolescence, it does not necessarily imply that the young persons who were also involved in other forms of delinquency desist from participating in non-sexual delinquent acts. For this group, desistance needs to be approached from a broader perspective by examining the role and importance of non-sexual criminogenic risk factors and factors promoting desistance more generally speaking. For example, in a follow-up study of young offenders into adulthood, van den Berg, Bijleveld, Hendriks, and Mooi-Reci (2014) found that entry into the labor market and employment were associated with lower rates of adult offending.

A second pattern found by Lussier et al. (2012), less common, involves youth who persist in sexual offending well into adulthood. For this group, the desistance process is considerably slower and more gradual compared with the previously described AL group. It is hypothesized that members of this group present a developmental trajectory characterized by exposure to earlier and accumulating risk factors in multi-domains of functioning (e.g., school, work, relationships, family). Given that slow desisters are still involved in sexual offending in adulthood, their offending is not likely to be moderated by the transition into adulthood and associated developmental issues such as maturity, increased self-control, a more long-term-oriented perspective, and a more prosocial orientation.

The findings of a qualitative study conducted by Farmer, Beech, and Ward (2012) suggest that desisters perceived treatment as a significant turning point. Desisters also showed a better sense of personal agency, and they reported the importance of belonging to a social group as opposed to being and feeling socially isolated. Farmer et al. (2012) looked at desistance in adulthood and it is unclear, from these findings, how many of them were adolescent-onset offenders. It does suggest, however, that desistance from sexual offending during adulthood might involve person x environment mechanisms such that a positive social environment can trigger and favor significant within-individual changes (e.g., beliefs about self, sexuality, women).

In the criminological literature on desistance from crime, social and familial ties are also described as hooks for change (Giordano, Cernkovitch, & Rudolph, 2002). Social ties are key factors promoting desistance from crime not only because they provide support, but also because such ties may help to stabilize risk factors that can potentially create a context conducive to a reoffense, such as unemployment and limited informal social control (e.g., prosocial friends, family members, colleagues) (e.g., Berg & Huebner, 2011; Sampson & Laub, 2005). In that regard, a longitudinal study conducted by Lussier and Gress (2014) about adult offenders returning to the community after completing their prison sentence demonstrated that one of the critical dynamic risk factors associated with short-term negative community reentry outcomes related to the social network. More specifically, the study showed that those people whose social network was composed mainly of negative social influences had more negative reentry outcomes and were more likely to breach their supervisory conditions. In other words, it is not so much that having social ties favors the desistance process; rather, the nature, stability, and quality of these ties at work, at home, and in the community may play a protective role against a reoffense. This finding may explain Kruttschnitt, Uggen, and Shelton's (2000) findings showing that recidivism rates are significantly lower among adults with a more stable job history who were court-ordered to complete a sexual offender treatment program. In other words, for treatment to impact future offending behavior, stable employment and associated features (e.g., stable income, regular interactions with prosocial influences, structured routine activities) had to characterize the person's context.

CONCLUSION

Young persons having perpetrated a sexual offense have often been portrayed as life-course-persistent sexual offenders. The scarcity of research on the origins and the developmental course of young persons who have perpetrated a sexually abusive/violent act and the reliance on retrospective developmental information about a small subgroup of adults having been convicted for a sexual offense has contributed to this misconception. The DLC perspective is presented as an organizing framework to describe, explain, and prevent sexual violence and abuse perpetrated by young persons. To date, research in the field of sexual violence and abuse has been either non-developmental or pseudo-developmental (e.g., developmentally concerned), but the field has yet to examine the issue with developmental life course lenses. Some of the key concepts from the DLC perspective suggest the importance of future research linking past and future development and examining and identifying the developmental trajectories leading to juvenile sexual offending, but also studying the developmental course of sexual offending over time and the associated developmental risk and protective factors at different developmental stages.

Lussier (2015) argued that, to date, the available evidence suggests the presence of two distinctive developmental trajectories: (a) adolescence-limited sexual offending, which refers to a late onset, minimal escalation, and near-immediate desistance from sexual offending; and (b) high-rate slow desistance, which refers to childhood-onset patterns of sexual offending characterized by a risk of progression toward more serious behaviors and a desistance process more likely to involve lapses and relapses, which may lead to termination of sexual offending in adulthood (see also Lussier et al., 2012). The portrayal of all young persons as life-course-persistent sexual offenders, therefore, is not supported by the available empirical literature. In fact, it is suggested that an age-graded perspective would be fruitful for the advancement of the field by prospectively and longitudinally examining the risk and protective factors of sexual offending from the earliest developmental stages. Such longitudinal research would not only inform us about the developmental trajectories and pathways of sexual offending among youth, but also provide key clinical and policy-relevant information for the assessment of, intervention in, and prevention of sexual violence and abuse.

REFERENCES

Aebi, M., Vogt, G., Plattner, B., Steinhausen, H. C., & Bessler, C. (2011). Offender types and criminality dimensions in male juveniles convicted of sexual offenses. *Sexual Abuse: A Journal of Research and Treatment, 24*(3), 265–288. http://dx.doi.org/10.1177/1079063210384634

Ageton, S. S. (1983). *Sexual assault among adolescents.* Lexington, MA.

Awad, A. B., & Saunders, G. A. (1991). Male adolescent sexual offenders: Exhibitionism and obscene phone calls. *Child Psychiatry & Human Development, 21,* 169–178.

Awad, G. A., Saunders, E., & Levene, J. (1984). A clinical study of male adolescent sexual offenders. *International Journal of Offender Therapy and Comparative Criminology, 28,* 105–116.

Barbaree, H. E., & Marshall, W. L. (Eds.). (2008). *The juvenile sex offender* (2nd ed.). New York: Guilford Press.

Barbaree, H. E., Marshall, W. L., & Hudson, S. M. (Eds.). (1993). *The juvenile sex offender.* New York: Guilford Press.

Becker, J. V. (1998). What we know about the characteristics and treatment of adolescents who have committed sexual offenses. *Child Maltreatment, 3,* 317–329.

Becker, J. V., & Hicks, S. J. (2003). Juvenile sexual offenders: Characteristics, interventions, and policy issues. *Annals of the New York Academy of Sciences, 398,* 397–410. http://dx.doi.org/10.1111/j.1749 6632.2003.tb07321.x

Becker, J. V., Kaplan, M. S., Cunningham-Rathner, J., & Kavoussi, R. (1986). Characteristics of adolescent incest sexual perpetrators: Preliminary findings. *Journal of Family Violence, 1,* 85–97.

Berg, M. T., & Huebner, B. M. (2011). Reentry and the ties that bind: An examination of social ties, employment, and recidivism. *Justice Quarterly, 28,* 382–410.

Bremer, J. (1992). Serious juvenile sex offenders: Treatment and long-term follow-up. *Psychiatric Annals, 22,* 326–332.

Browne, A., & Finkelhor, D. (1986). Impact of child sexual abuse: A review of the research. *Psychological Bulletin, 99,* 66–77.

Burton, D. L. (2003). Male adolescents: Sexual victimization and subsequent sexual abuse. *Child and Adolescent Social Work Journal, 20,* 277–296.

Butler, S. M., & Seto, M. C. (2002). Distinguishing two types of adolescent sex offenders. *Journal of the American Academy of Child & Adolescent Psychiatry, 41,* 83–90.

Caldwell, M. F. (2010). Study characteristics and recidivism base rates in juvenile sex offender recidivism. *International Journal of Offender Therapy and Comparative Criminology, 54*(2), 197–212. http://dx.doi.org/10.1177/0306624X08330016

Carpentier, J., Leclerc, B., & Proulx, J. (2011). Juvenile sexual offenders: Correlates of onset, variety, and desistance of criminal behavior. *Criminal Justice and Behavior, 38,* 854–873. http://dx.doi.org/10.1177/0093854811407730

Carpentier, M. Y., Silovsky, J. F., & Chaffin, M. (2006). Randomized trial of treatment for children with sexual behavior problems: Ten-year follow-up. *Journal of Consulting and Clinical Psychology, 74,* 482–488.

Caspi, A., McClay, J., Moffitt, T. E., Mill, J., Martin, J., Craig, I. W., . . . Poulton, R. (2002). Role of genotype in the cycle of violence in maltreated children. *Science, 297,* 851–854.

Caspi, A., & Roberts, B. W. (1990). Personality development across the life course: The argument for change and continuity. *Psychological Inquiry: An International Journal for the Advancement of Psychological Theory, 12*(2), 49–66. http://dx.doi.org/10.1207/S15327965PLI1202_01

Chaffin, M., Letourneau, E., & Silovsky, J. F. (2002). Adults, adolescents, and children who sexually. In J. E. B. Myers, L. Berliner, J. Briere, C. T. Hendrix, T. Reid, & C. Jenny (Eds.), *The APSAC handbook on child maltreatment* (2nd ed., pp. 205–232). Thousand Oaks, CA: Sage.

Christiansen, A. K., & Vincent, J. P. (2013). Characterization and prediction of sexual and nonsexual recidivism among adjudicated juvenile sex offenders. *Behavioral Sciences and the Law, 31*(4), 506–529. http://dx.doi.org/10.1002/bsl.2070

Chu, C. M., & Thomas, S. D. (2010). Adolescent sexual offenders: The relationship between typology and recidivism. *Sexual Abuse: A Journal of Research and Treatment, 22*(2), 218–233. http://dx.doi.org/10.1177/1079063210369011

Cicchetti, D., & Rogosch, F. A. (1996). Equifinality and multifinality in developmental psychopathology. *Development and Psychopathology, 8,* 597–600.

Corrado, R. R., Roesch, R., Hart, S. D., & Gierowski, J. K. (2002). *Multi-problem violent youth: A foundation for comparative research on needs, interventions, and outcomes.* Washington, DC: IOS Press.

Dennison, S., & Leclerc, B. (2011). Developmental factors in adolescent child sexual offenders: A comparison of nonrepeat and repeat sexual offenders. *Criminal Justice and Behavior, 38*(11), 1089–1102. http://dx.doi.org/10.1177/0093854811417076

Deslauriers-Varin, N., & Beauregard, E. (2014). Unravelling crime series patterns amongst serial sex offenders: Duration, frequency, and environmental consistency. *Journal of Investigative Psychology and Offender Profiling, 11,* 253–275.

Farmer, M., Beech, A., & Ward, T. (2012). Assessing desistance in child molesters: A qualitative analysis. *Journal of Interpersonal Violence, 27,* 1–21.

Farrington D. (1986). Age and crime. In M. Tonry & N. Morris (Eds), *Crime and justice: A review of research* (7th ed., pp. 189–249). Chicago: University of Chicago Press.

Farrington, D. P. (2005). *Integrated developmental and life-course theories of offending.* New Brunswick, NJ: Transaction Publishers.

Fehrenbach, P. A., Smith, W., Monastersky, C., & Deisher, R. W. (1986). Adolescent sexual offenders: Offender and offense characteristics. *American Journal of Orthopsychiatry, 53,* 148–151.

Friedrich, W. N., Davies, W., Feher, E., & Wright, J. (2003). Sexual behavior problems in preteen children. *Annals of the New York Academy of Sciences, 989,* 95–104.

Giordano, P., Cernkovich, S., & Rudolph, J. (2002). Gender, crime and desistance: Toward a theory of cognitive transformation. *American Journal of Sociology, 107,* 990–1064.

Glueck, S., & Glueck, E. (1940). *Juvenile delinquents grown up.* New York: Commonwealth Fund.

Greenwood, P. W., & Zimring, F. E. (2007). *Changing lives: Delinquency prevention as crime-control policy.* Chicago: University of Chicago Press.

Groth, N. (1977). The adolescent sex offender and his prey. *International Journal of Offender Therapy and Comparative Criminology, 21,* 249–254.

Harris, D. A. (2014). Desistance from sexual offending: Findings from 21 life history narratives. *Journal of Interpersonal Violence, 29*(9), 1554–1578. http://doi.org/10.1177/0886260513511532

Hershkowitz, I. (2014). Sexually intrusive behavior among alleged CSA male victims: A prospective study. *Sexual Abuse: A Journal of Research and Treatment, 26*(3), 291–305. http://dx.doi.org/10.1177/1079063213486937

Hirschi, T., & Gottfredson, M. (1983). Age and the explanation of crime. *American Journal of Sociology, 89,* 552–584.

Jacobs, W. L., Kennedy, W. A., & Meyer, J. B. (1997). Juvenile delinquents: A between-group comparison study of sexual and nonsexual offenders. *Sexual Abuse: A Journal of Research and Treatment, 9,* 201–217. http://dx.doi.org/10.1007/BF02675065

Keenan, K., & Shaw, D. S. (2003). Exploring the etiology of antisocial behavior in the first years of life. In B. B. Lahey, T. E. Moffitt, & A. Caspi (Eds.), *Causes of conduct disorder and juvenile delinquency* (pp. 153–181). New York: Guilford Press.

Kenny, D. T., Keogh, T., & Seidler, K. (2001). Predictors of recidivism in Australian juvenile sex offenders: Implications for treatment. *Sexual Abuse: A Journal of Research and Treatment, 13*(2), 131–148. http://dx.doi.org/10.1177/107906320101300206

Kjellgren, C., Priebe, G., Svedin, C. G., & Langström, N. (2010). Sexually coercive behavior in male youth: Population survey of general and specific risk factors. *Archives of Sexual Behavior, 39,* 1161–1169. http://dx.doi.org/10.1007/s10508-009-9572-9

Kruttschnitt, C., Uggen, C., & Shelton, K. (2000). Predictors of desistance among sex offenders: The interaction of formal and informal social controls. *Justice Quarterly, 17(1),* 61–87.

Langström, N. (2002). Long-term follow-up of criminal recidivism in young sex offenders: Temporal patterns and risk factors. *Psychology, Crime & Law, 8,* 1–58. http://dx.doi.org/10.1080/10683160208401808

Laws, D. R., & Ward, T. (2011). *Desistance from sex offending: Alternatives to throwing away the keys.* New York: Guilford Press.

Leach, C., Stewart, A., & Smallbone, S. (2015). Testing the sexually abused–sexual abuser hypothesis: A prospective longitudinal birth cohort study. *Child Abuse & Neglect, 51,* 144–153. http://dx.doi.org/10.1016/j.chiabu.2015.10.024

LeBlanc, M. (1998). Screening of serious and violent juvenile offenders: Identification, classification, and prediction. In R. Loeber & D. P. Farrington (Eds.), *Serious and violent juvenile offenders: Risk factors and successful interventions* (pp. 167–193). Thousand Oaks, CA: Sage.

LeBlanc, M., & Bouthillier, C. (2003). A developmental test of the general deviance syndrome with adjudicated girls and boys using hierarchical confirmatory factor analysis. *Criminal Behaviour and Mental Health, 13,* 81–105.

LeBlanc, M., & Fréchette, M. (1989). *Male criminal activity from childhood through youth: Multilevel and developmental perspectives.* New York: Springer-Verlag.

LeBlanc, M., & Loeber, R. (1998). Developmental criminology updated. *Crime and Justice: A Review of Research, 23,* 115–198.

Letourneau, E. J., & Miner, M. (2005). Juvenile sex offenders: A case against the legal and clinical status quo. *Sexual Abuse: A Journal of Research and Treatment, 17,* 293–312. http://dx.doi.org/10.1177/107906320501700304

Loeber, R., & Farrington, D. P. (1998). Never too early, never too late: Risk factors and successful interventions for serious and violent juvenile offenders. *Studies on Crime and Crime Prevention, 7,* 7–30.

Loeber, R., & Farrington, D. P. (2001). *Child delinquents: Development, intervention and service needs.* Thousand Oaks, CA: Sage.

Loeber, R., & Farrington, D. P. (2012). *From juvenile delinquency to adult crime: Criminal careers, justice policy and prevention.* Oxford, UK: Oxford University Press.

Loeber, R., & Hay, D. F. (1997). Key issues in the development of aggression and violence from childhood to early adulthood. *Annual Review of Psychology, 48,* 371–410.

Loeber, R., & LeBlanc, M. (1990). Toward a developmental criminology. *Crime and Justice, 12,* 375–473.

Loeber, R., Stouthamer-Loeber, M., Farrington, D. P., & White, H. R. (2008). *Violence and serious theft: Development and prediction from childhood and adulthood.* New York: Routledge.

Lussier, P. (2015). Juvenile sex offending through a developmental life course criminology perspective: An agenda for policy and research. *Sexual Abuse: A Journal of Research and Treatment.* http://dx.doi.org/10.1177/1079063215580966.

Lussier, P. (forthcoming). Desistance from crime: Toward an integrated conceptualization for intervention. In O'Donohue, W., & Laws, D.R. (Eds.), *Treatment of sex offenders: Strengths and weaknesses in assessment and intervention.* New York: Springer.

Lussier, P., & Blokland, A. (2014). The adolescence–adulthood transition and Robins's continuity paradox: Criminal career patterns of juvenile and adult sex offenders in a prospective longitudinal birth cohort study. *Journal of Criminal Justice, 42,* 153–163. http://dx.doi.org/10.1016/j.jcrimjus.2013.07.004

Lussier, P., & Blokland, A. (2015). Criminal careers of juvenile and adult sex offenders. In B. Francis & T. Sanders (Eds.), *Handbook of sex offenses and sex offenders.* Oxford, UK: Oxford University Press.

Lussier, P., Blokland, A., Mathesius, J., Pardini, D., & Loeber, R. (2015). The childhood risk factors of adolescent-onset and adult-onset of sex offending: Evidence from a prospective longitudinal study. In A. Blokland & P. Lussier (Eds.), *Sex offenders: A criminal career approach.* Chichester, UK: John Wiley.

Lussier, P., Bouchard, M., & Beauregard, E. (2011). Patterns of criminal achievement in sexual offending: Unravelling the "successful" sex offender. *Journal of Criminal Justice, 39,* 433–444. http://dx.doi.org/10.1016/j.jcrimjus.2011.08.001

Lussier, P., & Cale, J. (2013). Beyond sexual recidivism: A review of the sexual criminal career parameters of adult sex offenders. *Aggression and Violent Behavior, 18,* 445–457.

Lussier, P., Corrado, R., & McCuish, E. (in press). A criminal career study of the continuity and discontinuity of sex offending during the adolescence–adulthood transition: A prospective longitudinal study of incarcerated youth. *Justice Quarterly.*

Lussier, P., & Gress, C. L. Z. (2014). Community re-entry and the path toward desistance: A quasi-experimental longitudinal study of dynamic factors and community risk management of adult sex offenders. *Journal of Criminal Justice, 42,* 111–122.

Lussier, P., & Mathesius, J. (2012). Criminal achievement, criminal career initiation, and detection avoidance: The onset of successful sex offending. *Journal of Crime and Justice, 35,* 376–394.

Lussier, P., McCuish, E., & Corrado, R. R. (2015). The adolescence–adulthood transition and desistance from crime: Examining the underlying structure of desistance. *Journal of Developmental and Life-Course Criminology, 1,* 1–31.

Lussier, P., van den Berg, C., Bijleveld, C., & Hendriks, J. (2012). A developmental taxonomy of juvenile sex offenders for theory, research, and prevention. *Criminal Justice and Behavior, 39,* 1559–1581. http://dx.doi.org/10.1177/0093854812455739

Marini, V. A., Leibowitz, G. S., Burton, D. L., & Stickle, T. R. (2014). Victimization, substance use, and sexual aggression in male adolescent sexual offenders. *Criminal Justice and Behavior, 41*(5), 635–649. http://dx.doi.org/10.1177/0093854813507567

McCann, K., & Lussier, P. (2008). Antisociality, sexual deviance, and sexual reoffending in juvenile sex offenders: A meta-analytical investigation. *Youth Violence and Juvenile Justice, 6,* 363–385. http://dx.doi.org/10.1177/1541204008320260

McCuish, E., Lussier, P., & Corrado, R. (2015). Criminal careers of juvenile sex and nonsex offenders: Evidence from a prospective longitudinal study. *Youth Violence and Juvenile Justice.* http://dx.doi.org/1541204014567541

McCuish, E. C., Lussier, P., & Corrado, R. R. (2015b). Examining antisocial behavioral antecedents of juvenile sexual offenders and juvenile non-sexual offenders. *Sexual Abuse: A Journal of Research and Treatment, 27,* 414–438.

Miranda, A. O., & Corcoran, C. L. (2000). Comparison of perpetration characteristics between male juvenile and adult sexual offenders: Preliminary results. *Sexual Abuse: A Journal of Research and Treatment, 12,* 179–188. http://dx.doi.org/10.1023/A:1009582025086

Moffitt, T. E. (1993). Life-course persistent and adolescence limited antisocial behavior: A developmental taxonomy. *Psychological Review, 100,* 674–701. http://dx.doi.org/10.1037/0033-295X.100.4.674

Moffitt, T. E., Caspi, A., Harrington, H., & Milne, B. J. (2002). Males on the life-course-persistent and adolescence-limited antisocial pathways: Follow-up at age 26 years. *Development and Psychopathology, 14,* 179–207.

Moffitt, T. E., Caspi, A., Rutter, M., & Silva, P. A. (2001). *Sex differences in antisocial behaviour: Conduct disorder, delinquency, and violence in the Dunedin longitudinal study.* Cambridge, England: Cambridge University Press.

Morizot, J., & Kazemian, L. (2015). *The development of criminal and antisocial behavior: Theoretical foundations and practical applications.* New York: Springer.

Nisbet, I. A., Wilson, P. H., & Smallbone, S. W. (2004). A prospective longitudinal study of sexual recidivism among adolescent sex offenders. *Sexual Abuse: A Journal of Research and Treatment, 16,* 223–234.

Paolucci, E. O., Genuis, M. L., & Violato, C. (2001). A meta-analysis of the published research on the effects of child sexual abuse. *Journal of Psychology, 135,* 17–36.

Patterson, G. R. (1993). Orderly change in a stable world: The antisocial trait as a chimera. *Journal of Consulting and Clinical Psychology, 61,* 911.

Patterson, G. R., & Yoerger, K. (1993). Developmental models for delinquent behavior. In S. Hodgins (Ed.), *Mental disorder and crime* (pp. 140–172). Newbury Park, CA: Sage.

Piquero, A. R., Farrington, D. P., & Blumstein, A. (2003). The criminal career paradigm. *Crime and Justice, 30,* 359–506.

Piquero, A. R., Gonzales, J. M. R., & Jennings, W. G. (2015). Developmental trajectories and antisocial behavior over the life-course. In J. Morizot & L. Kazemian, The development of criminal and antisocial behavior: Theoretical foundations and practical applications (pp. 75–88). New York: Springer.

Prentky, R. A., & Knight, R. A. (1993). Age of onset of sexual assault: Criminal and life history correlates. In G. C. N. Hall, R. Hirschman, J. R. Graham, & M. S. Zaragoza (Eds.), *Sexual aggression: Issues in etiology, assessment, and treatment* (pp. 43–62). Washington, DC: Taylor & Francis.

Quetelet, A. (1836). *Sur l'homme et le développement de ses facultés, ou essai de physique sociale* (Vol. 2). Bruxelles: Louis Hauman et Comp.

Rajlic, G., & Gretton, H. M. (2010). An examination of two sexual recidivism risk measures in adolescent offenders: The moderating effect of offender type. *Criminal Justice and Behavior, 37*(10), 1066–1085. http://dx.doi.org/10.1177/0093854810376354

Reid, J. B., Patterson, G. R., & Snyder, J. E. (2002). *Antisocial behavior in children and adolescents: A developmental analysis and model for intervention.* Washington, DC: American Psychological Association.

Robins, L. N. (1978). Sturdy childhood predictors of adult anti-social behavior: Replications from longitudinal studies. *Psychological Medicine, 8,* 611–622.

Ryan, G., Miyoshi, T. J., Metzner, J. L., Krugman, R. D., & Fryer, G. E. (1996). Trends in a national sample of sexually abusive youths. *Journal of the American Academy of Child & Adolescent Psychiatry, 35,* 17–25. http://dx.doi.org/10.1097/00004583-199601000-00008

Salter, D., McMillan, D., Richards, M., Talbot, T., Hodges, J., Bentovim, A., . . . & Skuse, D. (2003). Development of sexually abusive behaviour in sexually victimised males: A longitudinal study. *The Lancet, 361,* 471–476.

Sampson, R. J., & Laub, J. H. (2005). A life-course view of the development of crime. *Annals of the American Academy of Political and Social Science, 602*(1), 12–45. http://dx.doi.org/10.1177/0002716205280075

Seto, M. C., & Lalumière, M. L. (2010). What is so special about male adolescent sexual offending? A review and test of explanations through meta-analysis. *Psychological Bulletin, 136,* 526–575.

Shanahan, M. J., & Boardman, J. D. (2009). Gene–environment interplay across the life course: Overview and problematics at a new frontier. In J. Z. Giele & G. H. Elder Jr. (Eds.), *Methods of life course research: Qualitative and quantitative approaches.* Thousand Oaks, CA: Sage.

Slotboom, A.-M., Hendriks, J., & Verbruggen, J. (2011). Contrasting adolescent female and male sexual aggression: A self-report study on prevalence and predictors of sexual aggression. *Journal of Sexual Aggression, 17,* 15–33. http://dx.doi.org/10.1080/13552600.2010.544413

Smallbone, S. (2005). Attachment insecurity as a predisposing and precipitating factor for sexually offending behaviour by young people. In M. C. Calder (Ed.), *Children and young people who sexually abuse: New theory, research and practice developments.* London, UK: Russell House.

Thornberry, T. P. (1997). *Developmental theories of crime and delinquency.* New Brunswick, NJ: Transaction Publishers.

Thornberry, T. P. (2005). Explaining multiple patterns of offending across the life course and across generations. *Annals of the American Academy of Political Science, 602,* 168–186. http://dx.doi.org/10.1177/0002716205280641

Tracy, P., Wolfgang, M. E., & Figlio, R. M. (1990). *Delinquency careers and two birth cohorts.* New York: Plenum Press.

Tremblay, R. E., Japel, C., & Pérusse, D. (1999). The search for the age of "onset" of physical aggression: Rousseau and Bandura revisited. *Criminal Behaviour and Mental Health, 9,* 8–23. http://dx.doi.org/10.1002/cbm.288

Tremblay, R. E., & Nagin, D. S. (2005). The developmental origins of physical aggression in humans. In R. E. Tremblay, W. W. Hartup, & J. Archer (Eds.), *Developmental origins of aggression* (pp. 83–106). New York: Guilford Press.

van den Berg, C., Bijleveld, C., Hendriks, J., & Mooi-Reci, I. (2014). The juvenile sex offender: The effect of employment on offending. *Journal of Criminal Justice, 42,* 145–152.

Vizard, E., Hickey, N., & McCrory, E. (2007). Developmental trajectories associated with juvenile sexually abusive behaviour and emerging severe personality disorder in childhood: 3 years study. *British Journal of Psychiatry, 49,* 27–32. http://dx.doi.org/10.1192/bjp.190.5.s27

White, J. W., & Smith, P. H. (2004). Sexual assault perpetration and reperpetration: From adolescence to young adulthood. *Criminal Justice and Behavior, 31*(2), 182–202. http://dx.doi.org/10.1177/0093854803261342

Widom, C. S., & Massey, C. (2015). A prospective examination of whether childhood sexual abuse predicts subsequent sexual offending. *JAMA Pediatrics, 169,* e143357-e143357.

Wieckowski, E., Hartsoe, P., Mayer, A., & Shortz, J. (1998). Deviant sexual behavior in children and young adolescents: Frequency and patterns. *Sexual Abuse: A Journal of Research and Treatment, 10,* 293–303. http://dx.doi.org/10.1023/A:1022194021593

Wolfgang, M. E., Figlio, R. M., & Sellin, T. (1972). *Delinquency in a birth cohort.* Chicago: University of Chicago Press.

Worling, J. R. (2013). *Desistence for adolescents who sexually harm.* Unpublished document. Retrieved from www.erasor.org.

Worling, J. R., & Långström, N. (2006). Risk of sexual recidivism in adolescents who offend sexually: Correlates and assessment. In H. E. Barbaree & W. L. Marshall (Eds.), *The juvenile sex offender* (pp. 219–247). New York: Guilford Press.

Yeater, E. A., Lenberg, K. L., & Bryan, A. D. (2012). Predictors of sexual aggression among male juvenile offenders. *Journal of Interpersonal Violence, 27,* 1242–1258. http://dx.doi.org/10.1177/0886260511425243

Zimring, F. E. (2004). *An American travesty: Legal responses to adolescent sexual offending.* Chicago: University of Chicago Press.

Zimring, F. E., Jennings, W. G., Piquero, A. R., & Hays, S. (2009). Investigating the continuity of sex offending: Evidence from the second Philadelphia birth cohort. *Justice Quarterly, 26*(1), 58–76. http://dx.doi.org/10.1080/07418820801989734

Zimring, F. E., Piquero, A. R., & Jennings, W. G. (2007). Sexual delinquency in Racine: Does early sex offending predict later sex offending in youth and young adulthood. *Criminology & Public Policy, 6,* 507–534. http://dx.doi.org/10.1111/j.1745-9133.2007.00451.x

Part II
Assessment

CHAPTER 5

Forensic Assessment of Juveniles

Laura M. Grossi

Alexandra Brereton

Robert Prentky

Forensic assessments, by definition, are psychological evaluations that assist a fact finder in answering a legal question (Otto & Heilbrun, 2002). The results of a forensic assessment may, for example, help the courts make a determination regarding a juvenile's level of criminal responsibility, adjudicative competence, appropriateness for transfer to criminal court, level of risk, or classification as a sexually violent predator (each described in more detail later in this chapter). Forensic assessments of juveniles occur at various stages of the legal process, ranging from first contact with the legal system through to the end of a sentence. A forensic assessment therefore requires knowledge of the legal system as a whole, an understanding of the relevant legal standards in the evaluator's jurisdiction of practice, familiarity with relevant ethical guidelines and recommendations, and an understanding of the recent psychological/scientific literature, as well as impartiality, honesty, and control over one's personal biases (Heilbrun & Locklair, 2016). Juvenile forensic assessments often have far-reaching implications by influencing management dispositions and labels that can have a profound impact on juveniles' long-term development. Forensic assessment results may also have onerous implications, such as detention in a secure facility or registration as a sexual offender.

In this chapter, we will address a number of legal, ethical, and practice considerations related to the assessment of juveniles in various forensic contexts. Initially, we will provide a brief history of the juvenile court, and describe the nature of mental health evaluations in forensic contexts in greater detail. Next, we will discuss the psychosocial differences between juveniles and adults who undergo forensic assessments, as well as legal considerations unique to the juvenile population. We will also refer to ethical concerns that may arise in the course of a juvenile forensic assessment, as addressed in the Ethical Principles of Psychologists and Code of Conduct (EPPCC; American Psychological Association, 2010) and the Specialty Guidelines for Forensic Psychology (SGFP; American Psychological Association, 2013). Finally, we will describe practice issues that arise in specific forensic contexts.

A BRIEF HISTORY OF THE JUVENILE COURT

Although we typically set the date of the beginning of the US juvenile justice system at 1899, due consideration of the criminal culpability of children has extended back to the turn of the 19th century. As articulated by Chief Justice Kilpatrick in *State v. Aaron* (1818), British Common Law doctrine "restated the settled common law doctrine, adapted from earlier Roman law, that since a child under seven 'cannot have discretion to discern between good and evil' he is incapable of committing crime" (cited in *State v. Monahan* [1954] and reported in Donnelly, Goldstein, & Schwartz, 1962, p. 855). Compared with contemporary standards, the age of seven as a benchmark for determining criminal responsibility is quite young, and no questions were raised at the time about mitigation of punishment or whether the state had any obligation to intervene. In *State v. Aaron*, Kilpatrick further noted that the presumption of incapacity was considered rebuttable for juveniles between the ages of 7 and 14, and juveniles 14 years of age or older were presumptively capable of committing crimes. In other words, juveniles between 7 and 14 who were charged, tried, and convicted were subjected to the full sanction of the law if they appeared to understand the difference between right and wrong. Further, children as young as seven could be sentenced to death for committing a crime. The doctrine articulated by Chief Justice Kilpatrick dated back to William Blackstone's *Commentaries on the Laws of England*, first published in the late 1760s (cf. Morrison, 2001); the *Commentaries* espoused the foundational doctrine for the founding fathers in America.

Ever so slowly, the 19th century brought about changes in the ways that juveniles were treated in the United States. In 1825, the Society for the Prevention of Juvenile Delinquency opened the House of Refuge in New York City, whose mission was to address the underpinnings of juvenile delinquency, primarily through what was called moral education. By mid-century, houses of refuge could be found all over the country. With the onset of the second industrial revolution toward the latter part of the

19th century, social reformers and academics decried the exploitation of children. Age-related legal structures began to appear, the most notable of which was the first juvenile court in 1899. Within 25 years, most states had adopted juvenile courts with a mission to carry forth the *parens patriae* doctrine that provides the authority for states to intervene to protect children and adolescents, acting on their behalf, providing them with care and treatment so that they may become prosocial, contributing members of society. Judge Julian Mack quoted Judge Lindsey as saying, "[The judiciary's] purpose is to help all it can, and to hurt as little as it can; it seeks to build character—to make good citizens rather than useless criminals. The state is thus helping itself as well as the child, for the good of the child is the good of the state" (Mack, 1909, pp. 121-122). Because these courts were not punitive, there was no need for the procedural protections afforded adults in criminal court. There was nothing adversarial about the process in the juvenile court, as the state's obligation was to protect the youthful offender. Since the focus was on rehabilitation, and not punishment, the disposition was designed for the juvenile, and not for the offense.

Over the ensuing 60 years, the attitude toward juvenile offenders and the juvenile court shifted gradually toward skepticism and eventually deep cynicism. The competence and training of clinicians assigned to treat troubled youth, and the adequacy of science informing treatment of these youth, were deemed woefully lacking, and the question of whether juveniles truly lacked criminal responsibility was revisited. A series of cases brought before the Supreme Court of the United States (SCOTUS) during the 1960s and 1970s changed profoundly the complexion and mission of the juvenile court.

Relevant Case Law

Focus on Rehabilitation

In *Kent v. United States* (1966), 16-year-old Morris Kent was transferred from juvenile court into the adult criminal court system. SCOTUS held that the *parens patriae* power of the juvenile courts was not unlimited, and that the courts were not entitled to act with procedural arbitrariness. The *Kent* decision made clear that waiving a juvenile to adult court required that the juvenile be provided with basic due process rights afforded adults: a hearing, effective assistance of counsel, and a statement of reasons for the decision: "While there can be no doubt of the original laudable purpose of juvenile courts, studies and critiques in recent years raise serious questions as to whether actual performance measures well enough against theoretical purpose to make tolerable the immunity of the process from the reach of constitutional guaranties applicable to adults" (p. 556). As Justice Abe Fortas famously remarked, "There may be grounds for concern that the child [brought before the juvenile court] gets the worst of both worlds; that he gets neither the protections accorded to adults nor the solicitous care and regenerative treatment postulated for children" (p. 556).

Kent was followed one year later by the landmark case *In re Gault* (1967). In *Gault*, SCOTUS upheld an appeal for a writ of habeas corpus, issued by the mother of a 15-year-old boy. The juvenile court had adjudicated the boy delinquent for making lewd telephone calls, and placed him in an industrial school until he reached the age of 21, although the maximum penalty for an adult committing the same offense would have been a fine or a few months in jail. *Gault* had two major effects: (a) It triggered a floodgate of questions about the limits of constitutional rights for minors and the competence of minors to exercise those rights, and (b) it effectively legalized the juvenile court by requiring that juveniles be provided the same due process rights as adults, including the right to counsel, the right of written notice of charges, the privilege against self-incrimination, the right to confrontation and cross-examination, the right to a transcript of the proceedings, and the right to appellate review. As Justice Fortas remarked, "Neither the Fourteenth Amendment nor the Bill of Rights is for adults alone" (p. 13). In effect, *Gault* converted rehabilitation-focused juvenile hearings into juvenile criminal proceedings. In the case of *In re Winship* (1970), SCOTUS further held that for adjudications of delinquency, the standard of proof required should be the same as for criminal cases (beyond a reasonable doubt). In a powerful dissent, Chief Justice Burger, joined by Justice Stewart, asserted, "Much of the judicial attitude manifested by the Court's opinion today and earlier holdings in this field is really a protest against inadequate juvenile court staffs and facilities; we 'burn down the stable to get rid of the mice.' My hope is that today's decision will not spell the end of a generously conceived program of compassionate treatment intended to mitigate the rigors and trauma of exposing youthful offenders to a traditional criminal court; each step we take turns the clock back to the pre-juvenile-court era. I cannot regard it as a manifestation of progress to transform juvenile courts into criminal courts, which is what we are well on the way to accomplishing. We can only hope the legislative response will not reflect our own by having these courts abolished" [397 US 358, 377]. In yet a further shift of the juvenile court system toward adult court, *Breed v. Jones* (1975) applied the Fifth Amendment ban on double jeopardy to convictions in juvenile court. In a noteworthy exception to this pattern, *McKeiver v. Pennsylvania* (1971) found that juveniles did not have a constitutional right to jury trial, thereby blocking full procedural parity with adult criminal trials.

A Shift Toward Punitiveness

A dramatic rise in juvenile violence in the 1990s ushered in major changes in the juvenile justice system, including easier transfer from juvenile to adult court and longer, harsher sentences. In many jurisdictions, proceedings were no longer "protected" (confidential), and court records were not always expunged when the juvenile defendant turned 18. As a result, the need for protections of juvenile defendants became apparent. In *Thompson v. Oklahoma* (1988), SCOTUS held that the 8th and 14th Amendments forbade the imposition of capital punishment on offenders who were under the age of 16 at the time of their offense. In *Stanford v. Kentucky* (1989), however, the Court upheld the imposition of capital punishment on individuals for crimes committed at 16 or 17 years of age, finding that this did *not* constitute cruel and unusual punishment under the Eighth Amendment. In *Roper v. Simmons* (2005), the Court abolished the death penalty for juveniles, holding that executing offenders who committed capital crimes before age 18 was unconstitutional, as cruel and unusual punishment under the Eighth Amendment. The majority argued that "the differences between juvenile and adult offenders are too marked and well understood to risk allowing a youthful person to receive the death penalty despite insufficient culpability" (p. 7). Citing recent research (e.g., Scott & Grisso, 1997; Steinberg & Scott, 2003), Justice Kennedy noted three broad areas in which juveniles could be distinguished from adults: (a) Juveniles lack maturity and have an underdeveloped sense of responsibility, resulting in impetuous and ill-considered actions and decisions; (b) juveniles are more susceptible to negative influences and outside pressures, including peer pressure; and (c) the character of a juvenile is not as well formed as that of an adult, and as a result, juveniles possess greater potential for rehabilitation.

In *Graham v. Florida* (2010), the Court further held that it was unconstitutional to impose the penalty of life imprisonment without the possibility of parole (LWOP) on juveniles who had not committed homicide. More recently, *Miller v. Alabama* (2012) found that juveniles also cannot be sentenced to LWOP for homicide where such a sentence is the only option; mitigating factors must be considered before a juvenile can receive an LWOP sentence. Writing for the majority, Justice Kagan stated that mandatory LWOP excludes consideration of characteristics associated with the chronological age of the defendant. As Justice Kagan elaborated, it fails to take into account the family and home environment of the juvenile—an environment, Justice Kagan noted, that can be brutal and dysfunctional. The judicial reasoning in this series of cases relies on a recognition of fundamental differences between juveniles and adults that can be subsumed under the umbrella of immaturity (cf. Heilbrun & Locklair, 2016; Steinberg & Scott, 2003).

PSYCHOLEGAL ASSESSMENTS IN FORENSIC CONTEXTS

Forensic contexts include correctional settings, juvenile justice programs, and other settings in which services are provided to forensic populations (i.e., both offenders and survivors of crime; Otto & Heilbrun, 2002). It should be noted, however, that not all tasks performed by mental health professionals within forensic contexts are forensic assessments. For example, mental health professionals may be asked to perform clinical assessments in forensic settings for the purpose of gathering information for treatment planning and implementation (e.g., to answer clinical referral questions regarding diagnostic clarification, as opposed to answering a psycholegal question; Heilbrun & Locklair, 2016). The term *psycholegal* is used throughout this chapter to refer specifically to situations in which mental health and legal constructs (e.g., concepts and methods) interact (i.e., where the focus of the psychological assessment is on a legal issue).

There are as many important differences between clinical assessments and forensic assessments as there are distinctions between therapeutic and forensic dyadic relationships (Greenberg & Shuman, 1997). In clinical settings and therapeutic contexts, the clinician is expected to be supportive and empathic. Although we appreciate that this is often not the case, the forensic evaluator must remain neutral, objective (Greenberg & Shuman, 1997), and nonpartisan. Additionally, forensic evaluators often use collateral data as additional sources of information when forming a psycholegal opinion, while this is less common in therapeutic contexts. Finally, in clinical settings, patients often seek an assessment voluntarily. In forensic contexts, however, examinees are often court-ordered and/or acutely aware that their participation (or lack thereof) may become known to the court; thus, examinees often cannot or will not refuse to participate (Zapf & Roesch, 2009).

In clinical settings, the client is the examinee, and clinician–patient privilege protects the information gathered during the assessment. In forensic settings, the client typically is either the examinee's attorney or the court, and so there is no clinician–patient privilege. For evaluations performed in some forensic settings (e.g., juvenile detention centers, forensic hospitals), assessment results are commonly expected to be available to the courts. Despite the potential risks to juveniles when they participate in forensic assessments (described in more detail below), examinees who are court-ordered to undergo an evaluation are not required to be provided informed consent. However, best practice requires that informed *assent* from juveniles is obtained. Formal informed consent is also required from the juvenile's parent, foster parent, or other designated legal guardian. Identifying the appropriate person to provide informed consent may be complicated, given factors such as nontraditional family structure, emancipation, adolescent marriage, and youth in residential and detention facilities.

Thus, the juvenile examinee should still have the evaluation process and limits of confidentiality explained to him or her in appropriate detail (Zapf & Roesch, 2009). The distinctions between clinical assessments and forensic assessments should be made explicit during the informed consent process. The evaluator should also clarify how information obtained during the assessment will be used, and should alert the examinee to the limits of confidentiality (Hoge & Andrews, 2010). For example, the mandated reporting of child or elder abuse (Zapf & Roesch, 2009) should be made explicit; as in clinical practice, an evaluator is required to report any threats of imminent harm to appropriate authorities (Hoge & Andrews, 2010). Further, the examinee should be informed about who will have access to the report that results from the assessment (Zapf & Roesch, 2009), including both those individuals who will receive the report, and those who may in turn have access to the report.

RESEARCH ON BIOPHYSICAL AND COGNITIVE DEVELOPMENT IN ADOLESCENCE

Adolescence marks an extraordinary period of change across most, if not all, domains of human development, including physical, neurocognitive, social, sexual, and emotional development (e.g., Albert & Steinberg, 2011; Bonnie & Scott, 2013; Borum & Verhaagen, 2006; Casey, Getz, & Galván, 2008; Cohen et al., 2016; Cohen & Casey, 2014; Luna & Wright, 2016; Modecki, 2008; Owen-Kostelnik, Reppucci, & Meyer, 2006; Reyna & Farley, 2006; Steinberg, 2007; 2009; van den Bos, van Dijk, Westenberg, Rombouts, & Crone, 2011). It is clear that even the adolescent central nervous system is developing (e.g., Giedd, 2004; Luna & Sweeney, 2004), and that structural development corresponds with psychological growth. For example, Cohen and her colleagues (2016) found "a developmental shift in cognitive control in negative emotional situations during young adulthood that is paralleled by dynamic developmental changes in prefrontal circuitry" (p. 11). Bostic, Thurau, Potter, and Drury (2014) similarly noted that adolescents tend to process information less through the prefrontal cortex than adults, and more through the amygdala, particularly during highly emotional situations, and that this can lead to more erratic behaviors.

In addition to structurally based neurological developments, neurobehavioral changes in adolescence have been linked to puberty (Dahl, 2004). For example, marked changes have been observed in both the reproductive and stress hormones associated with maturational changes in several domains, including: sexual arousal, emotional intensity and lability, sleep, appetite, and risk-taking behaviors. As Steinberg (2004) noted, "Increased risk taking in adolescence is normative, biologically driven, and inevitable" (p. 57). Steinberg (2007) subsequently remarked that adolescence is a period of increased vulnerability for high-risk behaviors and impulsivity, due in part to the difference in timing of puberty onset (i.e., which leads to sensation seeking) and the development of the cognitive control system (which aids in impulse control). In the brief submitted by the American Psychological Association and the Missouri Psychological Association (Brief, 2004) in *Roper v. Simmons* (2005), the authors remarked that juveniles are "moving targets" with regard to dangerousness risk and character assessment, as "the transitory nature of adolescence also means that an adolescent defendant is much more likely to change in relevant respects between the time of the offense and the time of assessment by courts and experts" (p. 3). These problems are only magnified by the hormonal paroxysm brought on by puberty (Beaver & Wright, 2005).

Overall, adolescence is characterized, even under the best of conditions, by markedly impaired decision making, as rational decisions give way to intense emotions and a notable incidence of risk taking. In addition, however, there is a complex social chemistry in which peers become powerful influences on behavior, again hormonally augmented with the onset of puberty. In other words, adolescence is a developmental twilight zone between childhood and adulthood that is often characterized by radical emotional changes in response to hormonal shifts, high-intensity feelings, emotionally charged, impulsive, risky behaviors, and poor decision making (Kelley, Schochet, & Landry, 2004).

Impact of Childhood Maltreatment

Based on the relationship between childhood abuse and developmental maturation, a comprehensive forensic assessment must include an assessment of child maltreatment. This was recently suggested by Salekin and colleagues (2016), who indicated that developmental maturity may be impaired by family dysfunction, as well as factors such as poverty, mental illness, and learning deficits (i.e., factors that are prevalent in juvenile offender populations). Of note, Conrad and colleagues (2014) found that juvenile females who reoffended over a 12-month period were more likely to have experienced childhood sexual abuse than females who did not reoffend. However, childhood sexual abuse does not appear to affect rates of male recidivism over a 12-month period. Baglivio and colleagues (2016) found that adverse childhood experiences, such as abuse, affect the likelihood of a child becoming involved in the child welfare system. However, Hispanic female and Caucasian male juveniles who had cases concurrently open in both the juvenile justice and child welfare systems were more likely to recidivate than their counterparts who were only involved in the juvenile justice system. In addition to the obvious emotional and psychological impact of maltreatment, there is a growing literature documenting neurological impairment associated with early and protracted maltreatment (e.g., Arnsten & Shansky, 2004; DeBellis, 2004; Perry, 2001; Teicher, 2002; Teicher, Andersen, Polcari, Anderson, & Navalta, 2002). Protracted abuse produces a cascade of stress-related hormones (e.g., cortisol and adrenaline) in the young, developing brain, permanently altering the development of certain structures (e.g., hippocampus, corpus callosum, and prefrontal cortex). Arnsten and Shansky (2004) stated that "exposure to even mild uncontrollable stress impairs the cognitive functioning of the prefrontal cortex," thereby undermining control capacity (p. 143). Hence, an evaluation of sophistication-maturity must take into consideration the inherently inconstant life course of those children subjected to maltreatment. In sum, a developmentally focused understanding of trauma can facilitate forensic assessments.

DEVELOPMENTAL SOPHISTICATION-MATURITY

The task of answering specific psycholegal questions in the juvenile offender population is highly complex and not to be equated with comparable evaluations of adults, and developmental sophistication-maturity is a prime consideration in assessments of children involved in the legal system. Thus, it has been argued that sophistication-maturity may in fact be the most helpful (Salekin, 2015), and most reliable, information that forensic examiners can provide as a product of their evaluations. The contribution of sophistication-maturity to answering specific psycholegal questions is described in greater detail later in this chapter.

Given the central importance of sophistication-maturity in the adjudication of adolescents, and most notably in decisions to transfer juveniles to criminal court, there has been much attention paid to the operationalization and measurement of sophistication-maturity (cf. Salekin et al., 2016). Cauffman and Steinberg (2000), for example, examined three hypothesized psychosocial factors associated with sophistication-maturity (i.e., responsibility, perspective, and temperance) in a sample of over 1,000 participants ranging in age from 12 to 48. Cauffman and Steinberg (2000) defined these three non-mutually-exclusive psychosocial factors accordingly: "(1) responsibility, which encompasses such characteristics as self-reliance, clarity of identity, and independence; (2) perspective, which refers to one's likelihood of considering situations from different viewpoints and placing them in broader social and temporal contexts; and (3) temperance, which refers to tendencies to limit impulsivity and to evaluate situations before acting" (p. 745). Adolescents were generally less responsible, more myopic, and less temperate than adults. The most dramatic changes in behavior were observed between the ages of 16 and 19, with respect to perspective and temperance. It was not until age 19 that responsible decision making and maturity of judgment began to plateau and stabilize.

Salekin and colleagues (2016) illustrated that responsibility, perspective taking, and temperance mapped onto three similar factors proposed by Salekin, Rogers, and Ustad (2001), with responsibility bearing similarity to autonomy (e.g., internal locus of control, high self-esteem, clarity of self-concept, and ability to resist peer pressure); perspective resembling cognitive capacities (e.g., ability to think abstractly, goal setting, ability to identify alternative behaviors and consequences, and ability to engage in cost–benefit analyses); and temperance having congruence with emotion regulation skills (e.g., insight, clarity about values and priorities, capacity to regulate emotions, openness to change, and ability to delay gratification). Deficits in these core characteristics exacerbate responses to adverse life experiences that undermine normal development, and thus sophistication-maturity, in youth.

Level of maturity and intellectual sophistication speaks to the rationale behind the existence of a juvenile justice system: It has long been presumed that juveniles are not sufficiently cognitively and emotionally developed to fully appreciate the nature of their offenses, and should therefore not be held fully accountable for their crimes. Assessments of sophistication-maturity must take into consideration any developmental delays, long-term cognitive deficits, and failures to achieve developmental milestones, including delays or deficits that stem from maltreatment experiences. Ewing (1990) recommended that tests of personality, intelligence, and achievement be incorporated in the assessment of factors such as emotional functioning, reality testing, cognitive processing, perception, attention, and judgment, among other factors relevant to sophistication-maturity independent of the specific legal context. Within the forensic context, the assessment of psycholegal constructs, such as culpability, criminal sophistication, the understanding of normative behaviors, and the ability to consider alternative behaviors, are considered integral (Salekin, 2002). Broadly, consideration of moral development, planning/premeditation, consideration of long-term consequences, decision-making skills, and intelligence (i.e., cognitive and emotional) are considered central to evaluation of maturity and sophistication (Salekin, 2002).

PSYCHOLEGAL CONTEXTS

Transfer of Juveniles to Adult Court

The assessment of juvenile offenders for transfer or waiver to adult court is inherently unique to the juvenile population, unlike other categories of forensic assessment described in this chapter. Juveniles may be referred for transfer to adult court when the juvenile justice system is deemed ill equipped to provide a penalty that fits the offense at hand, and in cases where the juvenile offender has demonstrated that he or she is unlikely to be responsive to juvenile justice interventions (e.g., demonstrated through repeated recidivism; Loughran et al., 2010). The requisite criteria for juvenile transfer to adult court varies by state, such as the minimum age of eligibility for transfer, and offenses that may warrant a transfer. The minimum age for transfer is as low as 10 in some jurisdictions, whereas other jurisdictions do not have an explicit minimum age, and in some jurisdictions defendants facing particular charges can be transferred regardless of age (McKee, 1998; Wynkoop, 2003).

Although Nunez and her colleagues (2007) noted that the public may believe that juveniles today are more violent and less amenable to treatment than in previous years, contributing to changes in transfer policies (e.g., decreases in the minimum age for transfer) and increases in the number of transfers, a trend toward increased use of waivers can be traced back to the 1990s (Larson & Grisso, 2016; Tate, Reppucci, & Mulvey, 1995). Although only a small percentage of delinquency cases are transferred to adult court, the absolute number of cases climbed sharply during the 1990s (Feiler & Shelley, 1999). Thus, the need for competent transfer evaluations, correspondingly, began to rise. This dramatic rise in transfers during the 1980s and 1990s began to reverse around 1998, with states increasingly reexamining transfer procedures as juvenile justice reform was seen as advantageous and less "bipartisan." The pendulum shifted again around 2010, with transfer rates returning to 1989–1990 levels. Griffin, Addie, Adams, and Firestine (2011) estimated that in 2007, juvenile courts waived approximately 8,500 cases to criminal court. This was less than 1 percent of the total juvenile court caseload. The issue of transferring any juvenile to adult court remains controversial; as recently as February 2016, an op-ed piece appeared in the *New York Times* titled "Stop Trying Children in Adult Court" (Schiraldi, 2016).

All states retain some mechanism for transferring youth from juvenile court to adult court for criminal prosecution. Discretion typically resides with the juvenile court judge, the prosecutor, or, in some cases, state law making waiver for certain types of offenses mandatory. Forensic evaluators may be retained to evaluate youth for appropriateness of transfer, and in fact, the findings of psycholegal evaluations of the juvenile are often requested regardless of the transfer mechanism (Salekin, 2002). Evaluators who assess the appropriateness of transfer to adult court must therefore be attuned to the specific transfer mechanism, among other circumstances relevant to the offender, as context may impact the outcome of the evaluation. Judicial transfer, or judicial waiver, has traditionally been the favored mechanism for transfer in the United States (Brannen et al., 2006; Grisso, 1998; Kruh & Brodsky, 1997; Snyder & Sickmund, 2006). However, as youth crime increased in the 1980s and 1990s and became a matter of public concern, states began to shift discretion away from judges and place it in the hands of prosecutors and state legislatures. With judicial transfer, the ultimate decision regarding each potential transfer case is in the hands of the juvenile court judge, often with consideration of the opinion of forensic evaluators.

Other transfer mechanisms exist that remove the authority to transfer cases from the judiciary. For example, some states provide a statutory exclusion, in which charges for serious offenses are automatically filed with the adult criminal court, without a formal evaluation or opinion from a juvenile court judge, and without the case ever entering the jurisdiction of the juvenile court. This may occur in cases where certain crimes are committed (e.g., rape), or when juveniles are repeat offenders (Kruh & Brodsky, 1997), although the exact requirements vary by jurisdiction. In states with prosecutorial direct file (Snyder & Sickmund, 2006), the prosecutors maintain the right to file charges in either the juvenile or adult court, for particular offenses. Larson and Grisso (2016) concluded that in today's court system, judicial transfers "most closely approximate the transfer procedure as it existed at the inception of the juvenile courts, but the stated rationale has changed" (p. 449). The authors went on to note that the focus of transfer has moved away from protection of juveniles in the juvenile justice system, and toward public safety concerns. Additionally, some states have once adult/always adult laws. These laws require that any juvenile who has been previously criminally prosecuted (i.e., in adult court) be criminally prosecuted in adult court for any future charges. In these cases, the seriousness of the crime usually does not matter (Griffin et al., 2011). Lastly, blended sentencing laws allow juvenile courts to impose criminal sentences, or allow criminal courts to use juvenile dispositions (Griffin et al., 2011).

Variation in mechanisms introduced during the past two decades has contributed to notable heterogeneity in juvenile offenders transferred to adult court. Most opinion-based research appears to have found support for judicial transfer, as opposed to the other transfer mechanisms. For example, in a survey of juvenile court judges, Brannen and colleagues (2006) found that 72 percent of judges reported a preference for identifying transfer cases on an individual basis; other studies have similarly found that the public does not support blanket transfers to adult courts (e.g., due to charges for a particular severe offense; Nunez, Dahl, Tang, & Jensen, 2007). Across the board, states' responses to a tough-on-crime political climate have made transfer somewhat easier (Brannen et al., 2006). As a protection against errors in decision making and inappropriate transfer, in certain jurisdictions the potential also exists for a reverse transfer or decertification from adult court back to juvenile court (Brannen et al., 2006; Griffin et al., 2011; Grisso, 1998; Marczyk, Heilbrun, Lander, & DeMatteo, 2005). In such cases, psycholegal evaluations may be required to assist in a reverse transfer determination.

Transfer from juvenile court to adult court has notable implications for the juvenile offender, and is therefore considered one of the most serious acts performed by the juvenile court (Brannen et al., 2006; Woolard, Odgers, Lanza-Kaduce, & Daglis, 2005). The magnitude of a transfer decision is not limited to the offender's adjudication and possible detention experience, but also includes stark differences in long-term consequences. For example, youth tried in adult court may face a lengthier maximum sentence, and the realities of life in adult prison (e.g., sexual abuse; Brannen et al., 2006). Additionally, juveniles tried in adult court face increased stigmatization and systematic identification as deviant, and may be deprived of normative developmental experiences with prosocial peers and family members (Tonry, 2007). In other words, the youthful offender risks possibly losing all protections and opportunities ostensibly afforded by the rehabilitation available within the juvenile justice system, while simultaneously being subjected to the adverse interpersonal consequences of detention in an adult facility (Brannen et al., 2006; Woolard et al., 2005).

Interestingly, some evidence suggests that juvenile offenders tried in adult court often are treated as first-time offenders, regardless of prior history of delinquency; in such cases, similar juvenile offenders tried in the juvenile court system may actually receive more severe sanctions than those tried in the criminal court system (Kruh & Brodsky, 1997). The outcomes within either court system, in turn, may impact an offender's risk for recidivism. Although the majority of the research notes that adolescent offenders tried in adult court have higher rates of recidivism than juvenile offenders tried within the juvenile court system (Tonry, 2007), some researchers have not identified significant distinctions with regard to recidivism (Loughran et al., 2010). For example, Loughran and colleagues (2010) used propensity score matching, a statistical procedure for reducing selection bias and controlling for factors that could be confounding the effects of treatment. The researchers found that juveniles who committed person-related crimes were less likely to reoffend after being transferred to adult court. There was no such finding for juveniles who engaged in property crimes. The extent to which findings are due to the multitude of inherent differences between transferred and non-transferred offenders remains unclear. However, the possibility exists that juveniles transferred to adult court, and therefore subject to adult sanctions, may experience iatrogenic effects of transfer (Tonry, 2007). For example, a juvenile incarcerated in a prison with adult felons will be exposed to more antisocial role models than in a juvenile justice facility.

Although transfers have been on the decline over the past decade and the present wave of public opinion appears to have shifted away from transferring youth to adult court, mental health professionals are still relied upon to provide evidence regarding the appropriateness of transfer when transfers are sought (Brannen et al., 2006). The criteria for transfer to adult court were established in *Kent,* wherein three broad domains were identified as principal foci of an evaluation for transfer: (a) potential risk to the community, (b) level of sophistication-maturity, and (c) amenability to treatment interventions. Ewing (1990) recommended that evaluators also attend to additional legal and extralegal factors. Evaluators should consider, for example, whether the possible juvenile court dispositions are likely to rehabilitate the offending juvenile before the jurisdiction of the court ends, and whether the services available in the adult criminal justice system are appropriate for meeting the juvenile's treatment and risk management needs. Heilbrun, Leheny, Thomas, and Huneycutt (1997) reported five criteria governing transfer: (a) dangerousness, (b) treatment amenability, (c) sophistication-maturity, (d) mental illness or intellectual disabilities, and (e) specific characteristics of the offense.

In a survey of juvenile court judges, Brannen and colleagues (2006) found that the overwhelming majority (97–98%) indicated that it would be useful for forensic evaluations to specifically address the criteria set forth in *Kent.* Thus, evaluators are encouraged to explicitly evaluate risk, sophistication-maturity, and amenability to treatment interventions in a comprehensive transfer assessment. In a survey of the National Council of Juvenile and Family Court Judges, Brannen and colleagues (2006) found that judges weighed dangerousness and sophistication-maturity more heavily when forming a decision regarding transfer, whereas treatment amenability did not have as significant an impact on their decisions. Of note, the weight of various aspects of the assessment findings in court varies by jurisdiction (Brannen et al., 2006; Kruh & Brodsky, 1997).

Potential for Risk

Dangerousness risk is commonly evaluated through use of formal risk assessment measures, and may consider factors such as the likelihood of persistence of offending as suggested by developmental offending histories, including age of onset, severity, and frequency, as well as personality traits (e.g., traits associated with psychopathy). Considerations regarding dangerousness risk are described in more detail below, in the section titled Assessment of Risk of Harm and in chapter 7 of this volume: Assessing Risks and Needs.

Level of Sophistication-Maturity

As described above, sophistication-maturity is a functional-legal capacity that is routinely addressed in hearings both on waiver up to criminal court and on reverse waiver back to juvenile court (Heilbrun & Locklair, 2016). Considerations in the assessment of sophistication-maturity are described above, in the section of this chapter titled Developmental Sophistication-Maturity.

Amenability to Treatment Interventions

There are essentially two separate issues raised with regard to treatment amenability: (a) clinical mental health issues presented by youth in the juvenile justice system, and (b) prognosis. With regard to clinical mental health issues, children and adolescents within the juvenile system at times present with noteworthy mental health symptoms. Approximately two-thirds of such youth within the juvenile justice system have at least one diagnosable mental illness, and many have two or more comorbid disorders (Cocozza & Skowyra, 2000; Teplin, Abram, McClelland, Dulcan, & Mericle, 2002). Details regarding the assessment of psychopathology are presented in chapter 6 of this volume: Clinical Approaches to High-Quality Assessments.

Despite the prevalence of mental illness in juvenile forensic samples, children and adolescents are considered more likely than adults to be rehabilitated, and so the juvenile justice system is significantly more focused on rehabilitation. This perception is due in part to medical and psychological research suggesting that juveniles are in fact more amenable to treatment than adults (Salekin, 2002). Thus, evaluation of amenability for treatment begins with knowledge of factors associated with treatment success, as well as treatment failure. Consistent with clinical treatment research, Salekin and colleagues (2002) identified motivation to engage in treatment, awareness of difficulties, positive expectations for treatment, remorse and guilt, empathy, moral decision making, anxiety related to their legal situation, and a stable and supportive family environment as factors related to the transfer decision, according to clinical psychologists (Salekin et al., 2001) and juvenile court judges (Salekin, Yff, Neumann, Leistico, & Zalot, 2002).

Despite the magnitude of transfer evaluations, given potential consequences of transfer to adult court, there is a paucity of systematic guidelines to assist evaluators in answering the referral question (Brannen et al., 2006). Evaluators may therefore approach transfer evaluations very differently, in a non-standardized manner, and those evaluators who wish to add more structure may opt to use adult measures of transfer-related constructs that are not normed for use with a youth sample (Salekin, 2002). There is a call for further research to develop and further validate assessment tools to aid forensic evaluators in transfer assessment decision making (Brannen, 2006). Evaluators are encouraged to be forthright regarding prognosis when expressing an opinion in which the data strongly support transfer, and to also note the limitations of the assessment process, given the high stakes involved in a juvenile transfer evaluation (Salekin, 2002).

COMPETENCE TO WAIVE MIRANDA RIGHTS

In *Miranda v. Arizona* (1966), SCOTUS determined that all suspects have a right to be informed of their legal protections (i.e., be provided with a Miranda warning), and that awareness of one's legal rights is integral for being able to provide a knowing, intelligent, and voluntary waiver of those rights. In accordance with *Miranda,* suspects must be provided information regarding: (a) their right to silence, (b) that any statement they make may be used as evidence in court, (c) their right to counsel, (d) that indigent suspects have a right to counsel, and (e) that they may assert their rights at any time. Since *Miranda,* the courts have extended the right to be informed of Fifth Amendment protections to juveniles. In *Gault,* SCOTUS noted that "the constitutional protection against self-incrimination is as applicable in the case of juveniles as it is with respect to adults" (p. 44). In *Fare v. Michael C.* (1979), the Court furthered this reasoning, finding that juveniles had an increased likelihood of incompetence to waive constitutional rights, due to their increased risk for intellectual and emotional deficits. *Fare* set the legal precedent for judges weighing the legitimacy of a juvenile's waiver of Miranda rights (Grisso, 1998).

A totality-of-the-circumstances approach was hence established with regard to Miranda waiver evaluations, in which factors such as age, experience, education, background, and the circumstances of questioning are considered. Moreover, the Court required that juveniles' capacity to comprehend the Miranda protections, understand their Fifth Amendment rights, and appreciate the consequences of waiving their legal rights should be considered in Miranda evaluations (Rogers et al., 2014). In *J.D.B. v. North Carolina* (2011), SCOTUS specified that the age of juvenile suspects should be explicitly considered in evaluations of Miranda waivers (i.e., as an indicator of developmental maturity), since chronological age has implications for perception and decision-making abilities (Rogers et al., 2014). Thus, forensic evaluators are at times asked to attest to a juvenile's ability to waive his or her legal rights under the Fifth Amendment.

Although the aforementioned legal cases set the minimum threshold for Miranda rights on a national level, individual jurisdictions may institute additional safeguards. Each jurisdiction determines the way in which Miranda warnings are provided to suspects, and each jurisdiction establishes the process by which a waiver may be obtained. For example, a few states require that an attorney be provided to a juvenile suspect before a waiver can be accepted as valid, regardless of whether the juvenile can demonstrate knowledge of his or her legal rights. Other jurisdictions require that the juvenile suspect consult with a parent, custodian, or guardian in order to jointly waive the juvenile's legal rights (Rogers et al., 2008). Regardless of the specific require-ment, these protections are in place to ensure that juvenile suspects have a factual understanding of their rights, appreciate the potential consequences associated with waiving those rights, and only provide a waiver (and any statements following that waiver) in the absence of police coercion. More specifically, Miranda rights help to minimize the likelihood of a false confession, and coerced or otherwise involuntary confession, among other legal injustices. Miranda warnings are therefore "procedural safeguards against self-incrimination and police intimidation for suspects during custodial interrogations" (Zelle, Romaine, & Goldstein, 2015, p. 281). Waiving legal rights leaves a juvenile vulnerable to the power differential that exists between an interrogator and a suspect, compounded by the differential that exists between an adult and a juvenile.

At times, juvenile suspects are provided with general Miranda warnings that are intended for suspects of all ages. In some jurisdictions, Miranda warnings specifi-cally developed to inform youth of their rights (i.e., juvenile Miranda warnings) are required. According to Rogers and colleagues (2008), more than 1.5 million juveniles are arrested and Mirandized annually, and those individuals who provide Miranda warnings to suspects often have little regard for how understandable the warnings are. Warnings vary greatly across jurisdiction with regard to length and difficulty of con-tent (Rogers et al., 2008; Rogers, Sewell, Drogin, & Fiduccia, 2012), as well as by the method of administration (i.e., oral, written, or a combined method), all of which affect comprehension (Zelle et al., 2015). Miranda warnings are sometimes lengthened in an attempt to make the warning more comprehensible to juvenile suspects, such as by providing more context (Rogers et al., 2014). Alternatively, as the legal context dif-fers between juveniles and adults, the warnings for juveniles may be lengthened due to natural expansion upon the rights that are afforded to adults. For example, Rogers and colleagues (2012) found that many juvenile Miranda warnings include the right to the presence of a parent, guardian, or another interested adult, in addition to the right to an attorney. Juveniles are occasionally also warned that any statements may be used in consideration of transfer to adult court (Rogers et al., 2014). Rogers, Sewell, Drogin, and Fiduccia (2012) found that 37.5 percent of juvenile Miranda warnings exceeded 175 words, as opposed to 9.9 percent of general Miranda warnings. Yet juveniles are less likely to recall and understand lengthy Miranda warnings, as opposed to shorter warnings, due to the sheer amount of information and/or an inability to identify what information is most important.

Aside from length, how well a juvenile understands the content of a Miranda warning often depends on the difficulty level of the information provided. Historically, the typical Miranda warning requires a reading comprehension level between seventh and eighth grade (Grisso, 1981). This is clearly problematic, as a number of juvenile suspects may have not reached the eighth grade, and many demonstrate reading abilities below grade level. In a Texas study, for example, most juvenile detainees completed at least an eighth-grade education (83% in 2013), yet their median reading level was below the sixth grade (5 years 7 months of education; Texas Juvenile Justice Department, 2013).

In a totality-of-circumstances approach, Zelle and colleagues (2015) found that age, verbal intelligence, and academic achievement were associated with Miranda understanding and comprehension, whereas gender and number of previous arrests were not. In his study of youth's abilities to understand and appreciate Miranda warnings, Grisso (1981) found that understanding of Miranda-related rights was noticeably poorer among juveniles below the age of 15, whereas 15- and 16-year-old juveniles demonstrated a level of understanding similar to that of adults. Grisso (1981) additionally found that deficits were most pronounced among youth with low intelligence, regardless of age. Memory-related abilities in particular may also contribute to a lack of understanding regarding Miranda rights. Rogers and colleagues (2014) found that all juveniles, regardless of maturity level, failed to recall at least 50 percent of the Miranda warning used in their study. Sophistication-maturity level (i.e., as opposed to age) has been shown to impact juveniles' immediate recall of a Miranda warning, with the most mature juveniles outperforming juveniles in less mature groups (Rogers et al., 2014). As alluded to above, sophistication-maturity level, corresponding with neurocognitive development, may impact decisional competence due to development of a greater future orientation, improved risk perception, and less susceptibility to the influences of others (all of which develop with age; Bonnie, 1992; Grisso, 2003).

Although the courts often assume that Miranda warnings will lead juvenile detainees toward knowledge of their legal rights, and therefore the ability to waive those rights, psycholegal research suggests that juveniles may not be as knowledgeable as may be assumed, even after psycholegal education. For example, Grisso (1981) found that a large proportion of juveniles misunderstood the extent of their legal rights; 82.8 percent of their overall sample exhibited at least 10 erroneous beliefs, highlighting the potential for ill-informed Miranda-related decisions. Almost two-thirds (61.8%) of the juveniles in their sample believed that they would be penalized for remaining silent, over half (55.3%) believed that the judge could revoke their right to remain silent, over half (57.1%) believed that Miranda rights extended to non-custodial police interviews, and 18 percent believed that a defense attorney is obligated to report incriminatory evidence to the court. Rogers and colleagues (2014) similarly found that all of the forensically involved juveniles in their sample endorsed a large number of Miranda-related misconceptions, and that this high rate of endorsement overshadowed any differences between the low-, middle-, and high-maturity groups. It goes without saying that such misunderstandings may lead juveniles to disclose information that they would not have otherwise reported (i.e., if they were more fully aware of their rights, as well as the implications of their disclosures). Thus, evaluators of competency to waive Miranda rights must perform a thorough assessment to ensure that juvenile suspects' understandings, regardless of claimed knowledge, sufficiently meets waiver standards.

ADJUDICATIVE COMPETENCY (COMPETENCY TO STAND TRIAL)

Adjudicative competency—often referred to as competency to stand trial, capacity to stand trial, or fitness to stand trial—describes the defendant's mental and behavioral ability to successfully proceed with and contribute to his or her legal case. The right of adults to adjudicative competency was established in 1960, in *Dusky v. United States,* wherein an adult male with a history of schizophrenia was charged with kidnapping and attempted rape of an underage female. In *Dusky,* SCOTUS ruled that a defendant must possess "sufficient present ability to consult with [his or her] lawyer with a reasonable degree of rational understanding" and "a rational as well as factual understanding of the charges against [him or her]," in order to proceed with his or her legal case (p. 403). Although this ruling clearly set precedent for adult defendants, the generalizability of the decision to juvenile defendants has been the subject of some debate. Specifically, it is unclear whether juveniles tried in the juvenile court system have a right to adjudicative competence, and whether juveniles transferred to adult court in particular possess that right (Soulier, 2012).

Although *Kent* (1966) and *Gault* (1967) introduced due process rights into juvenile proceedings, no mention was made of juvenile competency. By the mid-1980s, a third of the states in the United States recognized the legal necessity of being competent to stand trial in the increasingly adversarial environment of the juvenile court (Grisso, Miller, & Sales, 1987). At present, all states acknowledge the right of juveniles to be competent for adjudication (LaFortune, 2016). In Oklahoma, the state to most recently adopt a juvenile competency statute, the courts had previously determined that the juvenile adjudicative competence standard was neither appropriate nor necessary, given the rehabilitative focus of the juvenile justice system (LaFortune, 2016; Soulier, 2012). However, as noted above, the climate of the juvenile justice system has been changing. Although SCOTUS has not yet proffered a standard for juvenile adjudicative competence that is distinguished from the adult criminal standard (i.e., the *Dusky* standard), the majority of states have established some minimum standards (Scott & Grisso, 2005) and a few states have incorporated the construct of sophistication-maturity into the standard (Heilbrun et al., 2016). In nearly half of the states, there is still no specific statutory competency standard for juveniles. In such areas, decisions regarding adjudicative competence are often guided by case law, juvenile court statutes, and the standards that apply to adults (Soulier, 2012).

In practice, adjudicative competence is presumed for defendants of all ages until the presumption of competence is challenged. In fact, some have speculated that competency status is too infrequently questioned with juveniles, contributing to lack of attention to issues of juvenile adjudicative competence assessment, and a lessened demand for evaluations in practice (e.g., McKee, 1998). Regardless, the frequency of juvenile adjudicative competence assessments is on the rise (Ryba, Cooper, & Zapf, 2003). When the adjudicative competence of a defendant is questioned, a formal competence evaluation is frequently elicited. Researchers have indicated that young age (i.e., less than 12 years old), a prior diagnosis or treatment for a mental illness or intellectual disability, borderline intellectual functioning, a significant history of a learning disorder, and pretrial observations suggestive of deficits in memory, attention, or reality testing should also elicit an evaluation of adjudicative competence (Grisso, 1987). As with other psycholegal issues described in this chapter, the assessment of juvenile adjudicative competence is a relatively recent adaptation of adult adjudicative competence assessment.

In performing a competency evaluation, evaluators must be aware of the specific referral question and the legal standard in use in the applicable jurisdiction. Generally, in order to be identified as incompetent, an adult defendant must evidence a mental illness or intellectual disability, as well as a functional deficit. Further, there must be a causal connection between the mental illness/intellectual disability and functional deficit, and the deficit must impair the defendant's ability to proceed with his or her case in court (Zapf & Roesch, 2009). Thus, evaluators of adjudicative competence must perform comprehensive assessments in order to examine the aforementioned criteria.

As noted above, *Dusky* established three prongs, describing functional capacities relevant to adjudicative competence: (a) factual understanding, (b) rational under-standing, and (c) the ability to consult with counsel; these capacities are at the core of an adjudicative competence assessment. Factual understanding refers to the defen-dant's basic knowledge of the legal process, as well as details regarding the charges against him or her. Rational understanding refers to the defendant's ability to apply his or her understanding of the legal process to his or her own circumstances. The ability to consult with counsel and aid in one's own defense refers to the defendant's ability to speak and act in a facilitative manner; this includes the defendant's ability to cooperate with his or her attorney and behave appropriately in the courtroom. Jurisdictions in which *Dusky* applies to juveniles vary considerably. In some jurisdictions, the *Dusky* standard is typically applied to juveniles whose trial is in adult court, whereas in other jurisdictions it is not. With regard to the juvenile courts, the standards for competence appear to be somewhat less stringent. For example, factual and rational understanding are typically not required of juvenile defendants by current legal standards (Soulier, 2012). In certain jurisdictions, courts consider the totality of circumstances with regard to adjudicative competence in juveniles. In such an approach, the nature, severity, and ramifications of the charges, as well as availability of attorneys and caregivers for legal guidance, are considered in the context of the defendant's age, background, experience, education, and intelligence (Wynkoop, 2003). Jones (2004) found that judges, attorneys, and forensic examiners who responded to competency vignettes did so in a way sug-gesting that the perceived threshold for juvenile adjudicative competence varied based on the implications of such a determination; the threshold was higher when stakes were higher (e.g., transfer to adult court, or when the case involved a felony).

In a neuropsychological-developmental discussion of competence, Wynkoop (2003) noted that factors directly related to rational understanding, such as bidirec-tional and abstract thinking, as well as moral and complex reasoning, are developed gradually over the course of childhood and adolescence. Perceived autonomy, percep-tion of time, and perception of risks also differ between adolescents and adults, and their development has great implications for legal decision making (Grisso et al., 2003; Fogel, Schiffman, Mumley, Tillbrook, & Grisso, 2013). Thus, due to immaturity, as well as a paucity of normative life experiences, children and preadolescents may be expected to have less of an understanding of legal concepts than older adolescents. This perception is supported by the literature. In their examination of age and adjudi-cative competence, Grisso and colleagues (2003) found that juveniles under the age of 16 demonstrated poorer competency-related abilities than young adults (aged 18 to 24), with 35 percent of the youngest of the youth examined (aged 11 through 13), and one fifth of 14- to 15-year-olds, demonstrating significant impairment. Moreover, children between 11 and 13 were significantly more inclined than young adults to form legal decisions indicative of compliance with authority. Older adolescents (aged 16 and 17) demonstrated competence and decision-making abilities similar to young adults. These findings were consistent with those of other researchers, including McKee (1998), who found that 15- and 16-year-olds had competency-related abilities equivalent to adults, with the exception of knowledge of plea bargaining. Further, McKee identified that preteens were 16 times more likely than adults to be incompetent, and 15- to 16-year-olds were 3.5 times more likely.

With regard to the assessment of sophistication-maturity itself, Ryba and colleagues (2003) found that, of 52 practitioners who reported using a formal assessment tool or procedure to evaluate sophistication-maturity, 34 different tests or assessment methods were used. Of those, the vast majority (e.g., tests of intelligence or personality) were not designed explicitly for the assessment of psychosocial/neurodevelopmental sophistication-maturity. Social skills, cognitive abilities, literacy, decision making, emotional control, behavioral control, and reasoning abilities were additional factors commonly assessed by evaluators of competency when considering sophistication-maturity (Ryba et al., 2003).

In at least one case, *In re Causey* (1978), SCOTUS recognized developmental immaturity as a potential cause of adjudicative incompetence. More recently, state legislators have begun to acknowledge developmental maturity as a potential prerequisite for competency, along with mental illness and intellectual disability, specific to the adjudicative competence of juveniles (LaFortune, 2016; Fogel et al., 2013; Grisso et al., 2003; Ryba et al., 2003; Wynkoop, 2003). In other words, a young defendant may still be considered incompetent even if he or she lacks a mental illness, and also lacks an intellectual disability, but lacks the requisite level of neurocognitive maturity for due process to be achieved (e.g., due to developmental immaturity).

As with adults, juveniles who are identified as incompetent are subject to treatment efforts intended to improve their adjudicative competence. Grisso and colleagues (2003; 2005b) indicated that the attainment of competence, in cases where the barrier is immaturity or lack of experience, might be better conceptualized as competence achievement rather than competence restoration (i.e., the term used to describe the treatment of adults for competence), and that the process of increasing a juvenile defendant's capacity be referred to as the competence remediation process instead of the competence restoration process. The location of competence remediation varies by jurisdiction, with the potential to occur both in hospitals and in the community for juveniles and adults (Fogel et al., 2013). The competence remediation process typically involves psychiatric medication, group therapy focused on psychoeducation, and at times individual therapy (Zapf & Roesch, 2011). Recent studies suggest that the rate of successful competence remediation is approximately 60 to 75 percent for juveniles, although this rate is lower in cases where the defendant has an intellectual disability. In most cases, when competence was not attained after six months of competence remediation, competence is not attained despite additional treatment efforts (Fogel et al., 2013).

Continued lack of competence may be attributable to a number of factors, including neurodevelopmental immaturity. The psychosocial constructs described above, such as moral reasoning, cannot be taught to children prior to their attainment of sufficient neurodevelopmental maturity. Thus, beyond opining as to whether a defendant is incompetent or competent, forensic evaluators are at times tasked with answering the question of whether juveniles are likely to achieve competence in the foreseeable future. This question derives from *Jackson v. Indiana* (1972), in which SCOTUS found that incompetent defendants could not be hospitalized indefinitely for the purpose of competency remediation/restoration. Instead, defendants should be held no longer than "a reasonable period of time to determine whether there is a substantial probability that [they] will attain the capacity [to stand trial] in the foreseeable future" (p. 738). After a determination of non-restorability, the defendant may be hospitalized through civil commitment proceedings, or may be released. If adjudicative competence appears attainable, remediation/restoration efforts may continue. The *Jackson* decision directly applied to adult defendants, and applicability to juveniles is unclear (Soulier, 2012).

Decisions made by forensic evaluators with regard to adjudicative competence and restorability are based on assessments that vary greatly from evaluator to evaluator, but typically involve comprehensive record review, consultation with collateral sources, and a formal assessment of psychopathology and competency-related abilities inclusive of behavioral observations (Ryba et al., 2003). In their survey of juvenile and adult criminal court judges, Viljoen, Wingrove, and Ryba (2008) found that 70 percent of the judges identified forensic and psychological testing as either recommended or essential. A number of assessment measures exist that aid evaluators in the assessment of real and fabricated symptoms and impairment, and the potential for feigning or malingering in the aforementioned functional domains (for a review of measures, see Grisso, 2003; Zapf & Viljoen, 2003). Although there are many commonly used tests for assessing competency, almost all were developed for adults, none were normed on juveniles, and most were designed without consideration for developmental maturity (cf. Warren, Jackson, & Coburn, 2016). One tool, the Juvenile Adjudicative Competence Interview (JACI; Grisso, 2005b), was developed to assess juvenile defendants' understanding and appreciation of legal issues relevant to proceeding with their legal case. The JACI is not normed, however, and many have called for additional measures of juvenile competency (Warren et al., 2016). Although the MacArthur Competence Assessment Tool—Criminal Adjudication (MacCAT-CA; Hoge, Bonnie, Poythress, Monahan, & Eisenberg, 1997) has demonstrated potential for use with adolescents (Fogel et al., 2013), it too was developed to assess criminal adjudication in adults following *Dusky*. As it stands, there is a paucity of tools that can be used to assess issues of competency with juveniles. Thus, more often than not, evaluators who require use of formal assessment instruments in the evaluation of juvenile adjudicative competence are compelled to use existing measures designed for adults. Estimates suggest that adult-normed competency instruments are utilized in approximately one-third of juvenile adjudicative competence assessments (Fogel et al., 2013). The reader is encouraged to consult Grisso (2005a; 2005b), Kruh and Grisso (2009), Soulier (2012), and Wynkoop (2003) for detailed discussions regarding best practice in adjudicative competence assessment.

Sex Offender Registration, Notification, and Sexually Violent Predatory Commitment

Despite low rates of reoffense, juvenile sexual offenders are subject to registration, and community notification may be required for the remainder of a juvenile's life (Wynkoop, 2003). The Adam Walsh Act (2006) mandates the registration of adolescent sexual offenders, as well as community notification regarding their residence. According to this act, adjudicated adolescent sexual offenders are automatically registered on Tier 3, and therefore subject to indefinite sex offender registration. Under the Sex Offender Registration and Notification Act (SORNA), juveniles could also be required to register as sexual offenders. However, registration of juvenile offenders is not required under this act in response to all offenses that would lead to registration if committed by an adult. Specifically, the juvenile must be at least 14 years old and the offense must be "comparable to or more severe than aggravated sexual abuse" in order to mandate registration (Adam Walsh Act, 2006, 18 USC §2241). These federal and state statutes frequently require evaluations targeting the risk posed by juvenile sexual offenders in the community. Evaluators who conduct these risk assessments should be cognizant of the white paper issued by the Association for Treatment of Sexual Abusers (ATSA, 2012), which concluded: "Increasingly, research findings show that registration and public notification policies, especially when applied to youth, are not effective; and may do more harm than good. Such laws may have deleterious effects on pro-social development by disrupting positive peer relationships and activities and interfering with school and work opportunities, resulting in housing instability or homelessness, harassment and ostracism, social alienation and lifelong stigmatization and instability. Such practices are inconsistent with community safety and promotion of pro-social development, and in fact may actually elevate a youth's risk by increasing known risk factors for sexual and nonsexual offending such as social isolation" (pp. 5–6).

Beyond registration and community notification, in some states juveniles can be civilly committed under a Sexually Violent Predator (SVP) statute (Heilbrun & Locklair, 2016). SVP commitments occur after an individual has been incarcerated for a sexual offense, and thus SVP commitments do not require a recent crime to have occurred (i.e., the juvenile may have committed the governing offense at age 14 or 15, but is petitioned for civil commitment at age 18 or 19). For example, since 2003, Pennsylvania may petition under Act 21 to civilly commit a juvenile within 90 days of his or her 21st birthday. Civil commitments are indefinite, and may keep the individual locked up for many years past the date that he or she was due to be released from a correctional facility. To be civilly committed, an individual must evidence some type of mental abnormality that would make him or her likely to commit sexual crimes in the future (Witt & Conroy, 2009). Although committed to a facility with security features similar to a prison, civilly committed youngsters are afforded specialized treatment until they are identified as no longer posing a danger to society. When offenders are evaluated for release, the evaluators must determine if changes in dynamic risk factors outweigh the unchangeable static risk factors (Witt & Conroy, 2009).

ASSESSMENT OF RISK OF HARM

Risk assessment, in which evaluators are tasked to determine the likelihood that an examinee will offend or reoffend, is an important role of forensic evaluators. Generally, the identification, synthesis, and overview of risk and protective factors, in consideration of a particular outcome of interest, determines a person's risk (Heilbrun & Locklair, 2016). In the juvenile justice system, risk assessment is used in many different contexts; results of a risk assessment may impact decisions regarding psycholegal opinions regarding sentencing, disposition planning, transfer to adult court, parole/probation, eligibility for diversion programs, and sex offender registration and commitment (Viljoen, McLachlan, & Vincent, 2010).

Forensic evaluations provide the juvenile justice system with information regarding risk for recidivism, treatment needs, and, to some extent, sophistication-maturity (Heilbrun & Locklair, 2016). Thus, risk assessment reports tend to differ between adults and juveniles primarily due to the juvenile justice system's focus on treatment and rehabilitation (Viljoen et al., 2010). Juvenile risk assessment reports often speak to treatment needs, include discussion of protective factors, and should include a caveat that risk must be reevaluated periodically (at minimum, every six months). Such recommendations, however, are frequently unheeded. The close-to-universal appreciation of change during adolescence should be accompanied by an equally universal appreciation that a risk identified in adolescence is not fixed, but is instead variable over time. The inconstancy of emotions, behavior, and decision making during adolescence affects not just assessments of risk but diagnostic and prognostic assessments as well.

Additionally, it should be emphasized that the use of risk assessment procedures for pre-adjudication purposes raises further ethical concerns. Diversion programs, in particular, were introduced in the 1970s with the beneficent goal of avoiding the more harmful effects of the juvenile justice system, and the less heralded goal of alleviating the overburdened juvenile courts and juvenile institutions. These pre-adjudication diversion programs came with a hidden flaw—a reliance on risk *screening,* often embedded in a psychosexual evaluation. Unlike our common understanding of the utility of risk assessment post-adjudication, risk screening is introduced before there has been any judicial review and ruling and is often used, as noted, for detention—and more recently registration—decisions. Juveniles are effectively subject to the potentially harmful, enduring effects of risk assessment, including stigmatizing labels, absent any of the procedural due process rights afforded by judicial review.

Although risk assessment methodology with adults and juveniles is similar, there are critical distinctions. For one, forensic evaluators are less likely to use risk assessment tools during juvenile risk assessments, as opposed to adult risk assessments, perhaps because juvenile risk assessment measures are less well established (Viljoen et al., 2010). It may also be the case that mechanical assessment (i.e., without clinical judgment) of risk in juveniles is perceived to be contrary to the underlying principle of developmental change. There are, nevertheless, numerous juvenile risk assessment measures that are available, consistent with both mechanical and structured professional judgment (SPJ) approaches; such measures differ from adult risk assessment measures in that they incorporate risk factors thought to be uniquely relevant to juveniles. As a result of the development of such measures, risk predictions in recent years have been more accurate than prior to their development (Ewing, 1990; Borum, 1996). The more commonly used tools that aid in the prediction of general offending behaviors include: Early Assessment Risk Lists for Boys (EARL-20B; Augimeri, Koegl, Webster, & Levene, 2001) and Girls (EARL-21G; Levene et al., 2001), the Structured

Assessment of Violence Risk in Youth (SAVRY; Borum, Bartel, & Forth, 2006), and Youth Level of Service/Case Management Inventory (YLS/CMI; Hoge & Andrews, 2002). For an in-depth discussion of risk assessment of juveniles who sexually offend in particular, the reader is encouraged to refer to chapter 7 of this volume: Assessing Risks and Needs.

Factors Associated with Risk

There are many different factors positively associated with a juvenile's risk of offending, including static and dynamic risk factors. Static or historical risk factors, which cannot reflect change, can provide some assistance in identifying individuals or groups at increased risk for criminal behavior. Static risk factors include a history of prior offenses, childhood conduct problems, a history of delinquency, and low intelligence. Static "environmental" factors include peer rejection, parental antisocial behavior, and maltreatment. Maltreatment is a highly complex factor in terms of its proximal influence on behavior, often varying in its impact according to the type of abuse (e.g., physical, sexual, emotional) and, most importantly, according to morbidity factors (e.g., age of onset of the abuse, duration of the abuse, severity of the abuse, and relationship between the child and the abuser). Other risk factors may include poor performance and behavioral problems at school or at work, family history of psychiatric disorders and criminality, and family financial difficulties (Hoge & Andrews, 2010).

Children who experience adverse life experiences, most particularly severe neglect, chronic caregiver instability, and caregiver drug abuse and criminality, are more likely to end up in the child welfare system. At least one recent study found that children who are dually involved in the child welfare and juvenile justice systems were more likely to reoffend within the next year than juveniles who were only involved in the juvenile justice system (Baglivio et al., 2016). This is not a surprising finding in that wards of the child welfare system who persist in their acting out and engage in more chronic and antisocial behavior are much more likely to be adjudicated and wind up in the juvenile justice system. In regard to childhood sexual abuse, female juvenile offenders, but not male offenders, were more likely to reoffend if they had a history of childhood sexual abuse and psychiatric issues (Conrad et al., 2014). Childhood physical abuse is more likely associated with anger problems and delinquency in boys than in girls.

In contrast with static risk factors, dynamic risk factors are subject to change throughout the life span, and are often the focus of treatment; dynamic risk factors are therefore extremely important in assessment of risk posed by juveniles. Given that juveniles are in a marked state of biodevelopmental, cognitive, and emotional flux, dynamic risk factors become critically important. As discussed above, this mutability is the hallmark of adolescence. Dynamic risk factors may include anger, impulse control, antisocial peers, substance abuse, and neglectful or abusive caregivers. Juvenile risk assessments, compared with adult risk assessments, should be characterized by an explicit and thorough focus on these dynamic and protective factors, as well as increased consideration of the fluctuating quality of risk-relevant personality traits during a period of change (Childs et al., 2013). Optimizing prediction with juveniles must take into account this normative, pervasive developmental flux. Protective factors are presumed to insulate the youngster from risky events (or risky emotional responses to those events), thereby reducing the likelihood of a reoffense. These factors may include responsible caregivers, family stability, prosocial attitudes, prosocial peers, schools and neighborhoods with lower crime rates, and treatment; it is important that these factors be considered during any assessment (Hoge & Andrews, 2010). Precisely what constitutes a protective factor remains unsettled (Prentky, Righthand, & Lamade, 2015). The apparent absence of a risk factor, for example, might be considered a strength or protective factor. As Prentky and colleagues (2015) suggested, the apparent absence of a high sexual drive or preoccupation could be considered a strength. By contrast, lack of social isolation may not necessarily be a strength or protective (e.g., if the adolescent's social life involves delinquency-minded peers), although social isolation may be a risk factor for repeated sexual offending.

Base Rates and Risk Estimates

If we are to make progress in developing useful mechanisms for assessing risk of harm among juveniles, our focus must be on the life course of youth. The younger the child, the briefer the window of life experience from which to sample behavior (i.e., assess static risk) and the less stable (and hence less reliable) the behavior that is sampled. Thus, accuracy of all assessments of risk of harm/reoffense in juveniles are frequently compromised by both short time frame of follow-up and base-rate neglect (ignoring the base rates). When the estimated base rate of a new offense is low (i.e., is not likely to occur), it is extraordinarily difficult to predict accurately the probability of occurrence of that behavior, resulting, inevitably, in many false positive predictions (i.e., Type I errors; Evans, McGovern-Kondik, & Peric, 2005). Reported rates of *sexual* reoffending by juveniles are generally around 10 percent over five years (Viljoen, Mordell, & Beneteau, 2012). As Prentky et al. (2015) commented, when the base rate is as low as 10 percent or less, the true positive target is extraordinarily small, and a very high false positive rate is virtually inevitable. By contrast, base rates for general (non-sexual) delinquency reoffense among both non-sexual and sexual delinquents are moderately high. This is partially explained because the reoffense target is much larger (a single category of reoffense—sexual—compared with all categories reflecting any non-sexual offenses).

As for time frame, accuracy of prediction drops as time increases (e.g., Zara & Farrington, 2013), with short-term predictions yielding greater accuracy. With juveniles, long-term predictions are likely to be highly unreliable. That said, all estimates of risk must include the intended or implied time frame for the estimation (DeMatteo, Wolbransky, & LaDuke, 2016), and should underscore the complexity and (in)stability of accurately forecasting future behavior among juveniles. To some extent, theory can help to guide predictions in cases when base rates are low, as well as when they are not. Developmental psychopathology and developmental criminology have become the dominant paradigms (e.g., Guerra, Williams, Tolan, & Modecki, 2008; Thornberry, 2005) for examining the antecedents of proximal outcomes of delinquent behavior, including the onset, persistence, and desistence of antisocial behavior (Hoge and Andrews, 2010).

Trajectories of Offending Behaviors

An understanding of the trajectories of offending behaviors, including those based on developmental taxonomies, is important for accurate base-rate estimates, and therefore accurate estimates of risk. For example, short-term situational antisocial behavior is common among adolescents, but persistent antisocial behavior is rare (Moffitt, 1993). In other words, it may be viewed as normative for juveniles to engage in some degree of delinquent behavior. The rate of antisocial behavior typically peaks in adolescence (i.e., around age 17) then sharply decreases as juveniles age into adulthood (e.g., Moffitt, 1993). It is a small subgroup of juvenile offenders responsible for the crimes committed by juveniles (Halikias, 2000); specifically, it is estimated that about 5 to 6 percent of offenders commit 50 percent of known crimes (Moffitt, 1993). Moffitt's longitudinal study of 1,037 New Zealand children compared the base rates of persistent and temporary antisocial behavior problems (Moffitt, Caspi, Rutter, & Silva, 2001). Approximately 5 percent of boys were rated as Very Antisocial by any of three sources (parents, teachers, youth). Moffitt found clear evidence that the temporal stability of delinquency was attributable to these 5 percent of the youth whose behavior was most extreme and most persistent. When it comes to predicting risk of sexual reoffense, overcoming the low base rate among juvenile sexual offenders represents an intimidating challenge (Prentky et al., 2015).

Neurocognitive development may play a role in the persistence of juvenile offending, and thus may inform risk assessment. Some research to date has provided support for this notion, identifying neurocognitive differences in those offenders who are persistent in their offending from those who are not. However, these differences may be accounted for by environmental factors to a larger extent than organic factors. For example, Moffitt and

Caspi (2001) identified two groups: (a) juveniles who were persistent in their offending over the course of the life span (life-course-persistent offenders), and (b) those whose offending was generally limited to adolescence (adolescence-limited offenders). The researchers found that life-course-persistent offenders commonly experienced poor parenting and had neurocognitive risk factors, a difficult temperament, and inattention/hyperactivity to a greater degree than adolescence-limited offenders. Considering the initial similarity, Moffitt and her colleagues (2001) concluded that differences might be a consequence of childhood adversity (Moffitt & Capsi, 2001). Thus, it may be important to include neuropsychological testing in a comprehensive assessment of risk, in order to evaluate potential deficits associated with increased risk (Soulier, 2012).

Risk of Sexual Aggression

Risk assessment specific to juvenile sexual offenders is addressed elsewhere in this volume, so it will not be discussed here. It should be emphasized, however, that the commonly used risk scales developed for juvenile sexual offenders are methodologically different, and these differences should be understood and noted by users. None of the commonly used scales are *true* empirical actuarial scales (i.e., those that include life tables with probabilistic estimates of reoffense associated with the numeric values for the scale). Actuarial scales of the type used with adult sexual offenders (e.g., Static-99-R or SORAG) are likely to perform poorly if adapted for use with juvenile sexual offenders, given the low base-rate estimates from the samples used to derive the life table, and the reasonable assumption (based on developmental change) that the risk estimates will not be stable over time for juveniles. Unlike the adult actuarial scales, with life table estimates going out 10 to 15 years, assessments of risk with juveniles should be revisited every six months or less depending on the life circumstances of the youngster.

PSYCHOPATHY

Psychopathy is identified by the American Psychological Association as a classification that merits additional research (American Psychiatric Association, 2013). More often than not, it is considered distinct from diagnoses largely based on behaviors (e.g., CD, ODD), since psychopathy encompasses more cognitive and emotional traits such as pathological lying, lack of remorse, and irresponsibility (Hoge & Andrews, 2010). Given normative developmental changes, classifying juveniles as psychopaths is controversial. Further, the label itself is highly stigmatizing (Viljoen et al., 2010; Weaver,

2008) and can adversely affect management decisions (e.g., whether or not to provide treatment). Forensic assessments, however, do occasionally include an assessment of psychopathy, requested by an attorney, an agency, or the court, or simply deemed necessary by the examiner in order to answer a broader psycholegal question (e.g., risk of recidivism). Viljoen and colleagues (2010) found that 79 percent of clinicians have used a formal psychopathy assessment instrument at least once when conducting a juvenile risk assessment, typically using the Psychopathy Checklist: Youth Version (PCL:YV; Forth, Kosson, & Hare, 2003). In addition to the PCL:YV, which usually relies on a clinical interview, there are several other approaches to assessing psychopathy in juveniles, including a self-report measure (Youth Psychopathic Traits Inventory, or YPTI; Andershed, Kerr, Stattin, & Levander, 2002) and a personality-based measure (NEO Psychopathy Resemblance Index; Lynam & Widiger, 2007), and screeners such as the Antisocial Process Screening Device (Frick & Hare, 2001).

The PCL:YV is composed of essentially the same set of items as its adult counterpart, the Psychopathy Checklist–Revised (Hare, 1991), although it includes some modifications to scoring criteria in order to achieve a more sensitive focus on adjustment (i.e., social/peer, family, and school). Otherwise, psychopathy is assumed to manifest in the same way in juveniles as adults (MacArthur Foundation Research Network on Adolescent Development and Juvenile Justice, 2006). When juvenile psychopathy measures are used, it is imperative to note that they were developed originally for adults, not juveniles, and that any measures used must be normed for children and adolescents due to the aforementioned differences in presentation and obvious implications of false positive classifications (Seagrave & Grisso, 2002).

A study, the findings of which are significantly disquieting, was conducted by Cauffman, Kimonis, Dmitrieva, and Monahan (2009). These researchers compared 1,170 serious male juvenile offenders on the PCL:YV, YPTI, and the NEO, finding little more than a modest overlap. Often, one measure of psychopathy, and not others, identified a juvenile offender as psychopathic; Cauffman and colleagues found that the measures had low correlations with reoffense at 6 and 12 months post-assessment. The authors warned that "the lack of long-term predictive power for the PCL:YV and the inconsistent psychopathy designations obtained with different measures raise serious questions about the use of such measures as the basis for legal or clinical treatment decisions" (p. 528). These findings suggest clear practice implications, not the least of which is that great caution must be exercised when evaluating a juvenile for psychopathy, with a mandatory "black box" warning that while a youngster may evidence traits associated with psychopathy he or she should *not* be classified as "a psychopath," and that all facets of personality are in flux during adolescence.

Psychopathic traits may be considered more malleable and, perhaps even more importantly, appear to be subclinical (i.e., not rising to the level of a formal classification). In either case, juveniles identified as evidencing psychopathic traits, as opposed to a defined psychopathic personality style, may be perceived by themselves and others as more amenable to treatment. Perhaps due to sophistication-maturity, and perhaps due to treatment, juveniles appear capable of maturing out of psychopathic traits (Weaver, 2008; Lynam, Caspi, Moffitt, Loeber, & Stouthamer-Loeber, 2007).

Given that juveniles are often viewed as more receptive to treatment than adults, and that rehabilitation is a central tenet of the juvenile justice system, it follows that treatment providers routinely treat juveniles with psychopathic traits. Caldwell, Skeem, Salekin, and Van Rybroek (2006) found that juvenile offenders with high PCL:YV scores in a traditional correctional setting were twice as likely to violently reoffend during the two-year follow-up than juveniles who participated in an intensive treatment program. In regard to adults, Skeem, Monahan, and Mulvey (2002) found that psychopathic patients who received more treatment were less likely to be violent during follow-up periods than were those patients who received little (one to six sessions) or no treatment (zero sessions). Thus, it appears that both juveniles and adults labeled as "psychopathic" can benefit from intensive treatment.

Lastly, it should be pointed out that there are several risk assessment scales with substantial empirical support that are commonly used when evaluating juveniles for delinquency and violence, including the Structured Assessment of Violence Risk in Youth (SAVRY) and the Youth Level of Service/Case Management Inventory (YLS/CMI). Risk judgments using the SAVRY correlate 0.64 with the YLS/CMI and 0.68 with the PCL:YV (Borum & Verhaagen, 2006). These alternatives to the PCL:YV avoid the potential deleterious stigma of the label of psychopathy.

BIASED RESPONDING

As adults, juveniles undergoing forensic evaluations may present with a biased response style in which they understate their pathology, overstate their adjustment, or present in an otherwise non-genuine manner for one or more reasons (Rogers, 2008); such biased responding may inhibit the evaluator's ability to develop an accurate understanding of the case at hand. In particular, the evaluation of juveniles in forensic contexts should include some consideration of whether there is dissimulation in the form of malingered deficits, typically on cognitive and neuropsychological tests and feigned reports of historical information. The assessment of veracity is particularly relevant in forensic contexts, wherein examinees may be motivated to feign symptoms or impairment for external gain. In particular, the motivation to malinger cognitive impairment may be great given the obvious incentives (e.g., to increase the chances that legal charges will be dropped, to be transferred to a treatment facility from a juvenile detention center, to avoid transfer to adult court). As Grisso (1998) noted, malingering may be the cause of observed deficits on cognitive measures in particular, commenting that "the importance of assessing the potential for dissimulation in evaluations for capacities to waive Miranda rights cannot be overstated" (p. 52). Differentiating between feigning and suboptimal understanding, as in the case of Miranda comprehension, can thus pose a problem (Grisso, 1998).

Evaluators of juvenile adjudicative competence also must be especially mindful of defendants fabricating, feigning, or exaggerating symptoms for the purpose of being found incompetent (i.e., malingering; American Psychiatric Association, 2013). Within the context of adjudicative competence, malingering may take the form of feigned or exaggerated impairment with regard to any or all aspects of the *Dusky* standard: mental illness (i.e., psychiatric or somatic symptoms), intellectual disability (i.e., cognitive impairment), functional impairment (i.e., factual or rational understanding, or the ability to consult with counsel), and, in the case of juveniles, immaturity.

As Salekin (2015) pointed out, lack of veracity in general can, to some extent, be normative in childhood and adolescence; at times, however, it may be a sign of pathology (e.g., conduct disorder). For all of the aforementioned reasons, discerning intentional disclosures of inaccurate/incorrect information from true cognitive deficits or misunderstanding is critical with juveniles, just as it is with adults. The motivation for dissimulation in juveniles and adults is much the same, and the approach to feigning and dissimulating (e.g., denying and minimizing wrongdoing) in juveniles may be very similar to adults (Grisso, 1998). Veracity can be tested in a number of ways, such as by checking information provided by the juvenile against collateral sources of information, by consultation (e.g., with the youth's caregivers and teacher), and through the administration of psychological measures designed to identify biased responding. There is, however, a paucity of formal assessment tools designed specifically to aid in the detection of malingering among juveniles.

Summary

Over the past 100 years, the juvenile court system in the United States has traditionally taken a caretaking role with juveniles, guiding its errant, impulsive charges through the turbulent waters of adolescence into calmer, more civilized waters. When rates of crime and violence escalated during the 1980s and 1990s, the instant response was punitive, to treat juveniles harshly by sending them to adult court and sanctioning them in much the same way as adults. In a series of challenges to these waivers to adult court, SCOTUS confronted the problem of how juveniles were expected to navigate adult court without all of the same constitutional protections afforded to adults. The resulting conundrum was apparent—if juveniles were to be treated as adults, they needed the protections that rightly came to adults, but if juveniles were granted those protections, they were now being adjudicated as adults and the entire historical mission of the juvenile court would be subverted. Over the span of several decades, a major thrust of sound empirical literature underscored the principal finding that juveniles were not simply junior adults. Adolescence is a true stage of human development in which most systems are immature. Many of these developmental changes, most obviously neurocognitive, hormonal, and social, left teenagers with a legitimate defense against full responsibility for their criminal behavior.

Recognition of youth's developmental immaturity led to a series of landmark cases by SCOTUS. Immaturity, a functional condition that is now routinely addressed by the court, has led to significant changes in the ways that juveniles are evaluated for competency, for waiver to adult court, for Miranda warnings, and for risk of dangerousness. Juvenile courts, for the most part, have become hybrids, retaining some of the *parens patriae* features (and philosophy) of the pre-Gault era as well as features (and philosophy) of the post-Gault era. Although youth violence continues to be of concern in some large cities, trend lines have been sloping downward nationwide, and there is increased appreciation of developmental flux and that delinquency in childhood and adolescence most often does not persist into adulthood.

REFERENCES

Achenbach, T. (1991). *Manual for the child behavior checklist.* Burlington: Department of Psychiatry, University of Vermont.

Ackerman, M. J. (2010). *Essentials of forensic psychological assessment* (2nd ed.). Hoboken, NJ: John Wiley & Sons.

Adam Walsh Child Protection and Safety Act of 2006, 42 USC §§ 16901-16991 (2006). Retrieved from GPO's Federal Digital System: http://www.gpo.gov/fdsys/pkg/PLAW-109publ248/pdf/PLAW-109publ248.pdf

Albert, D., & Steinberg, L. (2011). Judgment and decision making in adolescence. *Journal of Research on Adolescence, 21,* 211–224. http://dx.doi.org/10.1111/j.1532-7795.2010.00724.x

American Psychiatric Association (2013). *Diagnostic and statistical manual of mental disorders* (5th ed.). Washington, DC: Author.

American Psychological Association (2013). Specialty guidelines for forensic psychologists. *American Psychologist, 68,* 7–19. http://dx.doi.org/10.1037/a0029889

American Psychological Association and Missouri Psychological Association. (2005). Amici curiae briefs supporting respondents in *Donald P. Roper v. Christopher Simmons,* 543 US 551 (2005) (no. 03-633) (2004).

Andershed, H., Kerr, M., Stattin, H., & Levander, S. (2002). Psychopathic traits in non-referred youths: A new assessment tool. In E. Blaauw & L. Sheridan (Eds.). *Psychopaths: Current international perspectives* (pp. 131–158). The Hague, Netherlands: Elsevier.

Archer, R. P., Handel, R. W., Ben-Porath, Y. S., & Tellegen, A. (2016). Minnesota Multiphasic Personality Inventory–Adolescent Restructured Form. Minneapolis: University of Minnesota Press.

Arnsten, A. T., & Shansky, R. M. (2004). Adolescence: Vulnerable period for stress-induced prefrontal cortical function? Introduction to part IV. In R. E. Dahl & L. P. Spear (Eds.), *Adolescent brain development: Vulnerabilities and opportunities* (pp. 143–147). New York: New York Academy of Sciences.

ATSA. (2012, October 30). Adolescents who have engaged in sexually abusive behavior: Effective policies and practices. Beaverton, OR: Association for the Treatment of Sexual Abusers. Retrieved from http://www.atsa.com/adolescents-engaged-in-sexually-abusive-behavior

Augimeri, L. K., Koegl, C. J., Webster, C. D., & Levene, K. S. (2001) *Early Assessment Risk List for Boys: EARL-20B. Version 2.* Toronto, Canada: Earlscourt Child and Family Centre.

Baglivio, M. T., Wolff, K. T., Piquero, A. R., Bilchik, S., Jackowski, K., Greenwald, M. A., & Epps, N. (2016). Maltreatment, child welfare, and recidivism in a sample of deep-end crossover youth. *Journal of Youth and Adolescence, 45*(4), 625–654. http://dx.doi.org/10.1007/s10964-015-0407-9

Beaver, K. M., & Wright, J. P. (2005). Biosocial development and delinquent involvement. *Youth Violence and Juvenile Justice, 3*(2), 168–192. http://dx.doi.org/10.1177/1541204004273318

Becker, J. V., & Kaplan, M. S. (1988). Assessment of adolescent sexual offenders. In R. J. Prinz (Ed.), *Advances in behavioral assessment of children and families* (pp. 97–118). Greenwich, CT: Elsevier Science/JAI Press.

Bonnie, R. J. (1992). The competence of criminal defendants: A theoretical reformulation. *Behavioral Science & the Law, 10*(3), 291–316. http://dx.doi.org/10.1002/bsl.2370100303

Bonnie, R. J., & Scott, E. S. (2013). The teenage brain: Adolescent brain research and the law. *Current Directions in Psychological Science, 22*(2), 158–161. http://dx.doi.org/10.1177/0963721412471678

Borum, R., Bartel, P. A., & Forth, A. E. (2006). *Manual for the Structured Assessment of Violence Risk in Youth (SAVRY).* Lutz, FL: Psychological Assessment Resources.

Borum, R., & Verhaagen, D. (2006). *Assessing and managing violence risk in juveniles.* New York: Guilford Press.

Bostic, J. Q., Thurau, L., Potter, M., & Drury, S. S. (2014). Policing the teen brain. *Journal of the American Academy of Child & Adolescent Psychiatry, 53*(2), 127–129. http://dx.doi.org/10.1016/j.jaac.2013.09.021

Brannen, D. N., Salekin, R. T., Zapf, P. A., Salekin, K. L., Kubak, F. A., & DeCoster, J. (2006). Transfer to adult court: A national study of how juvenile court judges weigh pertinent Kent criteria. *Psychology, Public Policy, and Law, 12*(3), 332–355. http://dx.doi.org/10.1037/1076-8971.12.3.332

Breed v. Jones, 421 US 519 (1975).

Brennan, T., Breitenbach, M., & Dieterich, W. (2008). Towards an explanatory taxonomy of adolescent delinquents: Identifying several social-psychological profiles. *Journal of Quantitative Criminology, 24,* 179–203. http://dx.doi.org/10.1007/s10940-008-9045-7

Butcher, J. N., Williams, C. L., Graham, J. R., Archer, R. P., Tellegen, A., Ben-Porath, Y. S., & Kaemmer, B. (1992). *MMPI-A (Minnesota Multiphasic Personality Inventory–Adolescent): Manual for administration, scoring, and interpretation.* Minneapolis: University of Minnesota Press.

Caldwell, M., Skeem, J., Salekin, R., Van Rybroek, G. (2006). Treatment response of adolescent offenders with psychopathy features: A 2-year follow-up study. *Criminal Justice and Behavior, 33*(5), 571–596. http://dx.doi.org/10.1177/0093854806288176

Caldwell, M. F., & Dickinson, C. (2009). Sex offender registration and recidivism risk in juvenile sexual offenders. *Behavioral Sciences and the Law, 27*(6), 941–956. http://dx.doi.org/10.1002/bsl.907

Casey, B. J., Getz, S., & Galván, A. (2008). The adolescent brain. *Developmental Review, 28,* 62–77. http://dx.doi.org/10.1016/j.dr.2007.08.003

Cauffman, E., Kimonis, E. R., Dmitrieva, J., & Monahan, K. C. (2009). A multimethod assessment of juvenile psychopathy: Comparing the predictive utility of the PCL:YV, YPI, and NEO PRI. *Psychological Assessment, 21*(4), 528–542. http://dx.doi.org/10.1037/a0017367

Cauffman, E., & Steinberg, L. (2000). (Im)maturity of judgment in adolescence: Why adolescents may be less culpable than adults. *Behavioral Sciences and the Law, 18*(6), 741–760. http://dx.doi.org/10.1002/bsl.416

Childs, K. K., Ryals, J. Jr., Frick, P. J., Lawing, K., Phillippi, S. W., & Deprato, D. K. (2013). Examining the validity of the Structured Assessment of Violence Risk in Youth (SAVRY) for predicting probation outcomes among adjudicated juvenile offenders. *Behavioral Sciences and the Law, 31*(2), 256–270. http://dx.doi.org/10.1002/bsl.2060

Christodoulides, T. E., Richardson, G., Graham, F., Kennedy, P. J., & Kelly, T. P. (2005). Risk assessment with adolescent sex offenders. *Journal of Sexual Aggression, 11,* 37–48. http://dx.doi.org/10.1080/13552600410001697848

Cocozza, J. J., & Skowyra, K. R. (2000). Youth with mental health disorders: Issues and emerging responses. *Juvenile Justice, 7,* 3–13. Retrieved from http://www.journalofjuvjustice.org

Cohen, A. O., Breiner, K., Steinberg, L., Bonnie, R. J., Scott, E. S., Taylor-Thompson, K. A., . . . & Casey, B. J. (2016). When is an adolescent an adult? Assessing cognitive control in emotional and nonemotional contexts. *Psychological Science.* Advance online publication. http://dx.doi.org/10.1177/0956797615627625

Cohen, A. O., & Casey, B. J. (2014). Rewiring juvenile justice: The intersection of developmental neuroscience and legal policy. *Trends in Cognitive Science, 18*(2), 63–65. http://dx.doi.org/10.1016/j.tics.2013.11.002

Conrad, S. M., Tolou-Shams, M., Rizzo, C. J., Placella, N., & Brown, L. K. (2014). Gender differences in recidivism rates for juvenile justice youth: The impact of sexual abuse. *Law and Human Behavior, 38*(4), 305–314. http://dx.doi.org/10.1037/lhb0000062

Dahl, R. E. (2001). Affect regulation, brain development, and behavioral/emotional health in adolescence. *CNS Spectrum, 6,* 1–12. http://dx.doi.org/10.1017/S1092852900022884

Dahl, R. E. (2003). Beyond raging hormones: The tinderbox in the teenage brain. *Cerebrum: The Dana Forum on Brain Science, 5*(3), 7–22. Retrieved from http://www.dana.org/Cerebrum/2003/Beyond_Raging_Hormones__The_Tinderbox_in_the_Teenage_Brain

Dahl, R. E. (2004). Adolescent brain development: A period of vulnerabilities and opportunities. In R. E. Dahl & L. P. Spear (Eds.), *Adolescent brain development: Vulnerabilities and opportunities* (pp. 1–22). New York: New York Academy of Sciences.

DeBellis, M. D. (2004). Neurotoxic effects of childhood trauma: Magnetic resonance imaging studies of pediatric maltreatment-related posttraumatic stress disorder versus nontraumatized children with generalized anxiety disorder. In J. M. Gorman (Ed.), *Fear and anxiety: The benefits of transitional research* (pp. 151–170). Arlington, VA: American Psychiatric Publishing.

DeMatteo, D., Wolbransky, M., & LaDuke, C. (2016). Risk assessment with juveniles. In K. Heilbrun, D. DeMatteo, & N. E. S. Goldstein (Eds.), *APA Handbook of Psychology and Juvenile Justice* (pp. 365–384). Washington, DC: American Psychological Association.

Department of Justice Office of the Attorney General. (2008). The national guidelines for sex offender registration and notification; Notice. *Federal Register, 73*(128), 38029-38070. Retrieved from http://ojp.gov/smart/pdfs/fr_2008_07_02.pdf

Donnelly, R. C., Goldstein, J., & Schwartz, R. D. (1962). *Criminal law: Problems for decision in the promulgation, invocation, and administration of a law of crimes.* New York: Free Press of Glencoe.

Dusky v. United States, 362 US 402 (1960).

Epperson, D. L., Ralston, C. A., Fowers, D., DeWitt, J., & Gore, K. (2006). Actuarial risk assessment with juveniles who offend sexually: Development of the Juvenile Sexual Offense Recidivism Risk Assessment Tool–II. In D. S. Prescott (Ed.), *Risk assessment of youth who have sexually abused: Theory, controversy, and emerging strategies* (pp. 118–169). Oklahoma City: Wood & Barnes.

Evans, T. M., McGovern-Kondik, M., & Peric, F. (2005). Juvenile parricide: A predictable offense?. *Journal of Forensic Psychology Practice, 5*(2), 31–50. http://dx.doi.org/10.1300/J158v05n02_02

Ewing, C. P. (1990). Juveniles or adults? Forensic assessment of juveniles considered for trial in criminal court. *Forensic Reports, 3,* 3–13. Retrieved from http://psycnet.apa.org/psycinfo/1990-22367-001

Fare v. Michael, C., 442 US 707 (1979).

Feiler, S. M., & Shelley, J. F. (1999). Legal and racial elements of public willingness to transfer juvenile offenders to adult court. *Journal of Criminal Justice, 27,* 55–64. http://dx.doi.org/10.1016/S0047-2352(98)00036-1

Fogel, M. H., Schiffman, W., Mumley, D., Tillbrook, C., & Grisso, T. (2013). Ten year research update (2001–2010): Evaluations for competence to stand trial (adjudicative competence). *Behavioral Sciences and the Law, 31,* 165–191. http://dx.doi.org/10.1002/bsl.2051

Forth, A. E., Kosson, D., & Hare, R. D. (2003). *The Hare PCL: Youth Version.* Toronto, Canada: Multi-Health Systems.

Frick, P., & Hare, R. D. (2001). *The Antisocial Processes Screening Device.* Toronto, Canada: Multi-Health Systems.

Giedd, J. N. (2004). Structural magnetic resonance imaging of the adolescent brain. In R. E. Dahl & L. P. Spear (Eds.), *Adolescent brain development: Vulnerabilities and opportunities* (pp. 77–85). New York: New York Academy of Sciences.

Graham v. Florida, 560 US 48, no. 08-7412 (2010).

Greenberg, S. A., & Shuman, D. W. (1997). Irreconcilable conflict between therapeutic and forensic roles. *Professional Psychology: Research and Practice, 28,* 50–57. http://dx.doi.org/10.1037/0735-7028.28.1.50

Griffin, P., Addie, S., Adams, B., & Firestine, K. (2011). Trying juveniles as adults: An analysis of state transfer laws and reporting. *Juvenile Offenders and Victims: National Report Series,* 1–28.

Grisso, T. (1981). *Juveniles' waiver of rights: Legal and psychological competence.* New York: Plenum.

Grisso, T. (1987). Psychological assessments for legal decisions. In D. Weisstub (Ed.), *Law and mental health: International perspectives* (Vol. 3, pp. 125–157). New York: Pergamon.

Grisso, T. (1998). *Forensic evaluation of juveniles.* Sarasota, FL: Professional Resource Press.

Grisso, T. (2003). *Evaluating competencies: Forensic assessments and instruments* (2nd ed.). New York: Plenum.

Grisso, T. (2005a). *Clinical evaluations for juveniles' competence to stand trial: A guide for legal professionals.* Sarasota, FL: Professional Resource Press.

Grisso, T. (2005b). *Evaluating juveniles' adjudicative competence: A guide for clinical practice.* Sarasota, FL: Professional Resource Press.

Grisso, T., & Barnum, R. (2006). *Massachusetts Youth Screening Instrument Version 2.* Sarasota, FL: Professional Resource Press.

Grisso, T., Miller, M. O., & Sales, B. (1987). Competency to stand trial in juvenile court. *International Journal of Law and Psychiatry, 10,* 1–20. http://dx.doi.org/10.1016/0160-2527(87)90009-4

Grisso, T., Steinberg, L., Woolard, J., Cauffman, E., Scott, E., Graham, S., . . . & Schwartz, R. (2003). Juveniles' competence to stand trial: A comparison of adolescents' and adults' capacities as trial defendants. *Law and Human Behavior, 27*(4). http://dx.doi.org/10.1023/A:1024065015717

Guerra, N. G., Williams, K. R., Tolan, P. H., & Modecki, K. L. (2008). Theoretical and research advances in understanding the causes of juvenile offending. In R. D. Hoge, N. G. Guerra, & P. Boxer (Eds.), *Treating the juvenile offender* (pp. 33–53). New York: Guilford.

Haley v. Ohio, 332 US 596 (1947).

Halikias, W. (2000). Forensic evaluations of adolescents: Psychosocial and clinical considerations. *Adolescence, 35*(139), 467–484. Retrieved from http://www.journals.elsevier.com/journal-of-adolescence

Hare, R. D. (1991). *The Hare Psychopathy Checklist—Revised.* Toronto, ON: Multi-Health Systems.

Heilbrun, K., DeMatteo, D., Goldstein, N. E. S., Locklair, B., Murphy, M., & Giallella, C. (2016). Psychology and juvenile justice: Human development, law, science, and practice. In K. Heilbrun, D. DeMatteo, & N. E. S. Goldstein (Eds.), *APA handbook of psychology and juvenile justice* (pp. 3–20). Washington, DC: American Psychological Association. http://dx.doi.org/10.1037/14643-001

Heilbrun, K., Leheny, C., Thomas, L., & Huneycutt, D. (1997). A national survey of U.S. statues on juvenile transfer: Implications for policy and practice. *Behavioral Sciences and the Law, 15*(2), 125–149. http://dx.doi.org/10.1002/(SICI)1099-0798(199721)15:2<125::AID-BSL265>3.0.CO;2-R

Heilbrun, K., & Locklair, B. (2016). Forensic assessment of juveniles. In K. Heilbrun, D. DeMatteo, & N. E. S. Goldstein (Eds.), *APA handbook of psychology and juvenile justice* (pp. 345–363). Washington, DC: American Psychological Association. http://dx.doi.org/10.1037/14643-016

Hendrix, K. S., Carney Doebbling, C., & Aalsma, M. C. (2012). Psychological and neuropsychological assessment in the juvenile justice system: Recommendations for protocols. *Criminal Justice Studies, A Critical Journal of Crime, Law & Society, 25*(3), 239–249. http://dx.doi.org/10.1080/1478601X.2012.705530

Hodges, K. (2000). *Child and Adolescent Functional Assessment Scale.* Ypsilanti: Eastern Michigan University.

Hoge, R. D., & Andrews, D. A. (2002). *Youth Level of Service/Case Management Inventory: User's manual.* Toronto, ON: Multi-Health Systems.

Hoge, R. D., & Andrews, D. A. (2010). *Evaluation for risk of violence in juveniles.* New York: Oxford University Press.

Hoge, S. K., Bonnie, R. J., Poythress, N. G., Monahan, J., & Eisenberg, M. (1997). The MacArthur Adjudicative Competence Study: Development and validation of a research instrument. *Law and Human Behavior, 21,* 141–179.

In re Causey, 363 So. 2d 472 (La. 1978).

In re Gault, 387 US 1 (1967).

In re Winship, 397 US 358 (1970).

Jackson v. Indiana, 406 US 715 (1972).

J.D.B. v. North Carolina, 131 S. Ct. 2394 (2011).

Jesness, C. F. (2003). *Jesness Inventory–Revised (JI-R) technical manual.* Odessa, FL: Psychological Assessment Resources.

Johnson, M. B., & Hunt, R. C. (2000). The psycholegal interface in juvenile Miranda assessment. *American Journal of Forensic Psychology, 18*(3), 17–36. Retrieved from http://www.forensicpsychology.org/journal.htm

Jones, M. R. (2004). The varying threshold of competence to proceed in juvenile court: Opinions of judges, attorneys, and forensic examiners. *Dissertation Abstracts International, 64,* 1498.

Kelley, A. E., Schochet, T., & Landry, C. F. (2004). Risk taking and novelty seeking in adolescence: Introduction to part I. In R. E. Dahl & L. P. Spear (Eds.), *Adolescent brain development: Vulnerabilities and opportunities* (pp. 27–32). New York: New York Academy of Sciences.

Kent v. United States, 383 US 541 (1966).

Kruh, I., & Grisso, T. (2009). *Juveniles' competence to stand trial.* New York: Oxford University Press.

Kruh, I. P., & Brodsky, S. L. (1997). Clinical evaluations for transfer of juveniles to criminal court: Current practices and future research. *Behavioral Sciences and the Law, 15,* 151–165. http://dx.doi.org/10.1002/(SICI)1099-0798(199721)15:2%3C151::AID-BSL267%3E3.0.CO;2-U

LaFortune, K. A. (2016). Oklahoma leads the way on juvenile competency. *Monitor on Psychology, 47,* 32. Retrieved from http://www.apa.org/monitor/2016/01/jn.aspx

Larson, K., & Grisso, T. (2016). Transfer and commitment of youth in the United States: Law, policy, and forensic practice. In K. Heilbrun, D. DeMatteo, & N. E. S. Goldstein (Eds.), *APA handbook of psychology and juvenile justice* (pp. 445–466). Washington, DC: American Psychological Association. http://dx.doi.org/10.1037/14643–021

Levene, K. S., Augimeri, L. K., Pepler, D., Walsh, M., Webster, C. D., & Koegl, C. J. (2001). *Early Risk Assessment Risk List for Girls: EARL-21G, Version 1, Consultation Edition.* Toronto: Earlscourt Child and Family Centre.

Liptak, A., & Bronner, E. (2012, June 25). Justices bar mandatory life terms for juveniles. *New York Times.* Retrieved from http://www.nytimes.com/2012/06/26/us/justices-bar-mandatory-life-sentences-for-juveniles.html?_r=0

Loeber, R., & Stouthamer-Loeber, M. (1986). Family factors as correlates and predictors of juvenile conduct problems and delinquency. *Crime and Justice, 7,* 29–149. http://dx.doi.org/10.1086/449112

Loughran, T. A., Mulvey, E. P., Shubert, C. A., Chassin, L. A., Steinberg, L., Piquero, A. R., . . . & Losoya, S. (2010). Differential effects of adult court transfer on juvenile offender recidivism. *Law and Human Behavior, 34,* 476–488. http://dx.doi.org/10.1007/s10979-009-9210-z

Luna, B., & Sweeney, J. A. (2004). The emergence of collaborative brain function: fMRI studies of the development of response inhibition. *Annals of the New York Academy of Sciences, 1021,* 296–309. http://dx.doi.org/10.1196/annals.1308.035

Luna, B., & Wright, C. (2016). Adolescent brain development: Implications for the juvenile criminal justice system. In K. Heilbrun, D. DeMatteo, & N. E. S. Goldstein (Eds.), *APA Handbook of psychology and juvenile justice* (pp. 91–116). Washington, DC: American Psychological Association. http://dx.doi.org/10.1037/14643-005

Lussier, P., Van Den Berg, C., Bijleveld, C., & Hendriks, J. (2012). A developmental taxonomy of juvenile sex offenders for theory, research, and prevention: The adolescent-limited and the high-rate slow desister. *Criminal Justice and Behavior, 39*(12), 1159–1581. http://dx.doi.org/10.1177/0093854812455739

Lynam, D. R., Caspi, A., Moffitt, T. E., Loeber, R., & Stouthamer-Loeber, M. (2007). Longitudinal evidence that psychopathy scores in early adolescence predict adult psychopathy. *Journal of Abnormal Psychology, 116,* 155–165. http://dx.doi.org/10.1037/0021-843X.116.1.155

Lynam, D. R., & Widiger, T. A. (2007). Using a general model of personality to identify the basic elements of psychopathy. *Journal of Personality Disorders, 21,* 160–178.

MacArthur Foundation Research Network on Adolescent Development and Juvenile Justice (2006, September 9). Assessing juvenile psychopathy: Developmental and legal implications. Retrieved from https://www.macfound.org/media/files/ADJJPSYCHOPATHY.PDF

Mack, J. W. (1909, December). The juvenile court. *Harvard Law Review, 23*(2), 104–122.

Marczyk, G. R., Heilbrun, K., Lander, T., & DeMatteo, D. (2005). Juvenile decertification: Developing a model for classification and prediction. *Criminal Justice and Behavior, 32*(2), 278–301. http://dx.doi.org/10.1177/0093854804274371

McCrory, E., Hickey, N., Farmer, E., & Vizard, E. (2008). Early-onset sexually harmful behavior in childhood: A marker for life-course-persistent antisocial behavior? *Journal of Forensic Psychiatry & Psychology, 19*(3), 382–395. http://dx.doi.org/10.1080/14789940802159371

McKee, G. R. (1998). Competency to stand trial in preadjudicatory juveniles and adults. *Journal of the American Academy of Psychiatry and the Law, 26,* 89–99. Retrieved from http://www.jaapl.org

McKeiver v. Pennsylvania, 403 US 528 (1971).

Medoff, D. (2004). Developmental considerations in the forensic assessment of adolescent sexual offenders: Victim selection, intervention, and offender recidivism rates. *Forensic Examiner, 13*(2), 26–30. Retrieved from http://www.theforensicexaminer.com

Miller v. Alabama, 567 US (2012).

Millon, T., & Davis, R. D. (1993). The Millon Adolescent Personality Inventory and the Millon Adolescent Clinical Inventory. *Journal of Counseling and Development, 71,* 570–574.

Miranda v. Arizona, 384 US 436 (1966).

Modecki, K. L. (2008). Addressing gaps in the maturity of judgment literature: Age differences and delinquency. *Law and Human Behavior, 32,* 78–91. http://dx.doi.org/10.1007/s10979-007-9087-7

Moffitt, T. E. (1993). Adolescence-limited and life-course-persistent antisocial behavior: A developmental taxonomy. *Psychological Review, 100*(4), 674–701. http://dx.doi.org/10.1037/0033-295X.100.4.674

Moffitt, T. E., & Caspi, A. (2001). Childhood predictors differentiate life-course-persistent and adolescence-limited antisocial pathways among males and females. *Development and Psychopathology, 13*(2), 355–375. http://dx.doi.org/10.1017/S0954579401002097

Moffitt, T. E., Caspi, A., Rutter, M., & Silva, P. A. (2001). *Sex differences in antisocial behaviour: Conduct disorder, delinquency, and violence in the Dunedin Longitudinal Study.* New York: Cambridge University Press. http://dx.doi.org/10.1017/CBO9780511490057

Morrison, W. (Ed.). (2001). *Blackstone's commentaries on the laws of England.* London: Routledge-Cavendish.

Naglieri, J. A., LeBuffe, P. A., & Pfeiffer, S. I. (1994). *Devereux Scales of Mental Disorders.* San Antonio: Psychological Corporation.

National Center for Juvenile Justice (2016). Juvenile Justice Geography, Policy, Practice & Statistics: Jurisdictional boundaries. Retrieved from http://www.jjgps.org/jurisdictional-boundaries

National Institutes of Health (2005, October 25). Research involving vulnerable populations. Retrieved from http://grants.nih.gov/grants/policy/hs/populations.htm

Nunez, N., Dahl, M. J., Tang, C. M., & Jensen, B. L. (2007). Trial venue decisions in juvenile cases: Mitigating and extralegal factors matter. *Legal and Criminological Psychology, 12,* 21–39. http://dx.doi.org/10.1348/135532505X73768

Odgers, C. L., Moffitt, T. E., Broadbent, J. M., Dickson, N., Hancox, R. J., Harrington, H., . . . & Caspi, A. (2008). Female and male antisocial trajectories: From childhood origins to adult outcomes. *Development and Psychopathology, 20*(2), 673–716. http://dx.doi.org/10.1017/S0954579408000333

Otto, R. K., & Heilbrun, K. (2002). The practice of forensic psychology: A look toward the future in light of the past. *American Psychologist, 57,* 5–18. http://dx.doi.org/10.1037//0003-066X.57.1.5

Owen-Kostelnik, J., Reppucci, N. D., & Meyer, J. R. (2006). Testimony and interrogation of minors: Assumptions and maturity and morality. *American Psychologist 61*(4), 286-304. http://dx.doi.org/10.1037/0003-066X.61.4.286

Patterson, G. R., & Yoerger, K. (1993). Developmental models for delinquent behavior. In S. Hodgins (Ed.), *Mental disorder and crime* (pp. 140–172). Thousand Oaks, CA: Sage Publications.

Perry, B. D. (2001). The neurodevelopmental impact of violence in childhood. In D. Schetky & E. P. Benedek (Eds.), *Textbook of child and adolescent forensic psychiatry* (pp. 221–238). Washington, DC: American Psychiatric Press.

Prentky, R. A., Harris, B., Frizzell, K., & Righthand, S. (2000). Development and validation of an actuarial instrument for assessing risk among juvenile sex offenders. *Sexual Abuse: A Journal of Research and Treatment, 12*(2), 71–93. Retrieved from sax.sagepub.com

Prentky, R. A., & Righthand, S. (2003). Juvenile Sex Offender Assessment Protocol–II: J-SOAP-II manual. Bridgewater, MA: Author.

Prentky, R. A., Righthand, S., & Lamade, R. (2015). Juvenile sexual offending: Assessment and intervention. In K. Heilbrun, D. DeMatteo, & N. E. S. Goldstein (Eds.), *Handbook of Psychology and Juvenile Justice* (pp. 641–672). Washington, DC: American Psychological Association.

Prescott, D. S. (2006). *Risk assessment of youth who have sexually abused: Theory, controversy, and emerging strategies.* Brandon, VT: Safer Society Press.

Raine, A., Brennan, P., Mednick, B., & Mednick, S. A. (1996). High rates of violence, crime, academic problems, and behavioral problems in males with both early neuromotor deficits and unstable family environments. *Archives of General Psychiatry, 53*(6), 544–549. http://dx.doi.org/10.1001/archpsyc.1996.01830060090012

Reich, W. (2000). Diagnostic interview for children and adolescents (DICA). *Journal of the American Academy of Child and Adolescent Psychiatry, 39,* 59–66. http://dx.doi.org/10.1097/00004583-200001000-00017

Reppucci, N. D. (1999). Adolescent development and juvenile justice. *American Journal of Community Psychology, 27*(3), 307–326.

Reyna, V. F., & Farley, F. (2006). Risk and rationality in adolescent decision-making: Implications for theory, practice, and public policy. *Psychological Science in the Public Interest, 7,* 1–44. http://dx.doi.org/10.1111/j.1529-1006.2006.00026.x

Reynolds, W. M. (1998). *Adolescent Psychopathy Scale: Psychometric and technical manual.* Odessa, FL: Psychological Assessment Resources.

Rogers, R. (2008). An introduction to response styles. In R. Rodgers (Ed.), *Clinical assessment of malingering and deception* (3rd ed., pp. 3–13). New York: Guilford Press

Rogers, R., Hazelwood, L. L., Sewell, K. W., Shuman, D. W., & Blackwood, H. L. (2008). The comprehensibility and content of juvenile Miranda warnings. *Psychology, Public Policy, and Law, 14,* 63–87. http://dx.doi.org/10.1037/a0013102

Rogers, R., Sewell, K. W., Drogin, E. Y., & Fiduccia, C. E. (2012). *Standardized Assessment of Miranda Abilities professional manual.* Lutz, FL: Psychological Assessment Resources.

Rogers, R., Steadham, J. A., Fiduccia, C. E., Drogin, E. Y., & Robinson, E. V. (2014). Mired in Miranda misconceptions: A study of legally involved juveniles at different levels of psychosocial maturity. *Behavioral Sciences and the Law, 32,* 104–120. http://dx.doi.org/10.1002/bsl.2099

Roper v. Simmons, 543 US 551, no. 03-633 (2005).

Ryba, N. L., Cooper, V. G., & Zapf, P. A. (2003). Assessment of maturity in juvenile competency to stand trial evaluations: A survey of practitioners. *Journal of Forensic Psychology Practice, 3*(3), 23–45. http://dx.doi.org/10.1300/J158v03n03_02

Salekin, R. T. (2002). Clinical evaluation of youth considered for transfer to adult criminal court: Refining practice and directions for science. *Journal of Forensic Psychology Practice, 2,* 55–72. http://dx.doi.org/10.1300/J158v02n01_03

Salekin, R. T. (2015). *Forensic evaluation and treatment of juveniles: Innovation and best practice.* Washington, DC: American Psychological Association. http://dx.doi.org/10.1037/14595-002

Salekin, R. T., MacDougall, E. M., & Harrison, N. A. (2016). Developmental maturity and sophistication-maturity: Learning more about its purpose and assessment. In K. Heilbrun, D. DeMatteo, & N. E. S. Goldstein (Eds.), *APA handbook of psychology and juvenile justice* (pp. 405–424). Washington, DC: American Psychological Association. http://dx.doi.org/10.1037/14643-019

Salekin, R. T., Rogers, R., & Ustad, K. L. (2001). Juvenile waiver to adult criminal courts: Prototypes for dangerousness, sophistication-maturity, and amenability to treatment. *Psychology, Public Policy, and Law, 7*(2), 381–408. http://dx.doi.org/10.1037/1076-8971.7.2.381

Salekin, R. T., Yff, R. A., Neumann, C. S., Leistico, A. R., & Zalot, A. A. (2002). Juvenile transfer to adult courts: A look at the prototypes for dangerousness, sophistication-maturity, and amenability to treatment through a legal lens. *Psychology, Public Policy, and Law, 8,* 373–410. http://dx.doi.org/10.1037/1076-8971.8.4.373

Schiraldi, V. (2016, February 26). Op-ed; Stop trying children in adult court. *New York Times,* p. A29.

Scott, E., & Grisso, T. (2005). Developmental incompetence, due process, and juvenile justice policy. *North Carolina Law Review, 83,* 101–147. Retrieved from http://www.nclawreview.org

Scott, E. S., & Grisso, T. (1997). The evolution of adolescence: A developmental perspective on juvenile justice reform. *Journal of Criminal Law and Criminology, 88,* 137–189. http://dx.doi.org/10.2307/1144076

Scott, E. S., Reppucci, N. D., & Woolard, J. L. (1995). Evaluating adolescent decision making in legal contexts. *Law and Human Behavior, 19*(3), 221–244. http://dx.doi.org/10.1007/BF01501658

Seagrave, D., & Grisso, T. (2002). Adolescent development and the measure of juvenile psychopathy. *Law and Human Behavior, 26*(2), 219–239. http://dx.doi.org/10.1023/A:1014696110850

Sharp, C., & Kine, S. (2008). The assessment of juvenile psychopathy: Strengths and weaknesses of currently used questionnaire measures. *Child and Adolescent Mental Health, 13*(2), 85–95. http://dx.doi.org/10.1111/j.1475-3588.2008.00483.x

Skeem, J. L., Monahan, J., & Mulvey, E. P. (2002). Psychopathy, treatment involvement, and subsequent violence among civil psychiatric patients. *Law and Human Behavior, 26*(6), 577–603. http://dx.doi.org/10.1023/A:1020993916404

Snyder, H. N., & Sickmund, M. (2006). *Juvenile offenders and victims: 2006 national report.* Washington, DC: US Department of Justice Office of Juvenile Justice and Delinquency Prevention.

Soulier, M. (2012). Juvenile offenders: Competence to stand trial. *Psychiatric Clinics of North America, 35,* 837–854. http://dx.doi.org/10.1016/j.psc.2012.08.005

Spear, L. P. (2000). Neurobehavioral changes in adolescence. *Current Directions in Psychological Science, 9*(4), 111–114. http://dx.doi.org/10.1111/1467-8721.00072

Stanford v. Kentucky, 492 US 361 (1989).

State v. Aaron, 4 NJL, 231, 244 [reprint 269, 277] (Sup. Ct. 1818).

State v. Monahan, 15 NJ 34, 104 A. 2d 21 (1954).

Steinberg, L. (2004). Risk taking in adolescence: What changes, and why?. In R. E. Dahl & L. P. Spear (Eds.), *Adolescent brain development: Vulnerabilities and opportunities* (pp. 51–58). New York: New York Academy of Sciences.

Steinberg, L. (2007). Risk-taking in adolescence: New perspectives from brain and behavioral science. *Current Directions in Psychological Science, 16*(2), 55–59. http://dx.doi.org/10.1111/j.1467-8721.2007.00475.x

Steinberg, L. (2009). Adolescent development and juvenile justice. *Annual review of clinical psychology, 5,* 459–485. http://dx.doi.org/10.1146/annurev.clinpsy.032408.153603

Steinberg, L., & Cauffman, E. (1996). Maturity of judgment in adolescence: Psychosocial factors in adolescent decision making. *Law and Human Behavior, 20*(3), 249–272. http://dx.doi.org/10.1007/BF01499023

Steinberg, L., & Scott, E. (2003). Less guilty by reason of adolescence: Developmental immaturity, diminished responsibility and the juvenile death penalty. *American Psychologist, 58*(12), 1009–1018. http://dx.doi.org/10.1037/0003-066X.58.12.1009

Tate, D. C., Reppucci, N. D., & Mulvey, E. P. (1995). Violent juvenile delinquents: Treatment effectiveness and implications for future action. *American Psychologist, 50*(9), 777–781. http://dx.doi.org/10.1037/0003-066X.50.9.777

Teicher, M. H. (2002). Scars that won't heal: The neurobiology of child abuse. *Scientific American, 286*(3), 68–75. http://dx.doi.org/10.1038/scientificamerican0302-68

Teicher, M. H., Andersen, S. L., Polcari, A., Anderson, C. M., & Navalta, C. P. (2002). Developmental neurobiology of childhood stress and trauma. *Psychiatric Clinics of North America, 25*(2), 397–426. http://dx.doi.org/10.1016/S0193-953X(01)00003-X

Teplin, L. A., Abram, K. M., McClelland, G. M., Dulcan, M. K., & Mericle, A. A. (2002). Psychiatric disorders in youth in juvenile detention. *Archives of General Psychiatry, 59*(12), 1133–1143. http://dx.doi.org/10.1001/archpsych.59.12.1133

Texas Juvenile Justice Department. (2013). Commitment profile for new commitments. Retrieved from http://www.tjjd.texas.gov/research/profile.aspx

Thompson v. Oklahoma, 487 US 815 (1988).

Thornberry, T. P. (2005). Explaining multiple patterns of offending across the life course and across generations. *Annals of the American Academy of Political and Social Sciences, 602,* 156–195.

Tonry, M. (2007). Treating juveniles as adult criminals: An iatrogenic violence prevention strategy if ever there was one. *American Journal of Preventative Medicine, 32*(4S), S3-S4. http://dx.doi.org/10.1016/j.amepre.2006.12.025

van den Bos, W., van Dijk, E., Westenberg, M., Rombouts, S. A. R. B., & Crone, E. A. (2011). Changing brains, changing perspectives: The neurocognitive development of reciprocity. *Psychological Science, 22,* 60–70. http://dx.doi.org/10.1177/0956797610391102

Viljoen, J. L., McLachlan, K., & Vincent, G. M. (2010). Assessing violence risk and psychopathy in juvenile and adult offenders: A survey of clinical practices. *Assessment, 17*(3), 377–395. http://dx.doi.org/10.1177/1073191109359587

Viljoen, J. L., Mordell, S., & Beneteau, J. L. (2012). Prediction of adolescent sexual reoffending: A meta-analysis of the J-SOAP-II, ERASOR, J-SORRAT-II, and Static-99. *Law and Human Behavior, 36*(5), 423–438. http://dx.doi.org/10.1037/h0093938

Viljoen, J. L., Wingrove, T., & Ryba, N. L. (2008). Adjudicative competence evaluations of juvenile and adult defendants: Judges' views regarding essential components of competence reports. *International Journal of Forensic Mental Health, 7,* 107–119. http://dx.doi.org/10.1080/14999013.2008.9914408

Vitelli, R. (1997). Comparison of early and late start models of delinquency in adult offenders. *International Journal of Offender Therapy and Comparative Criminology, 41*(4), 351–357. http://dx.doi.org/10.1177/0306624X97414005

Warren, J. I., Jackson, S. L., & Coburn, J. J. (2016). Evaluation and restoration of competency to stand trial. In K. Heilbrun, D. DeMatteo, & N. E. S. Goldstein (Eds.), *APA handbook of psychology and juvenile justice* (pp. 489–514). Washington, DC: American Psychological Association.

Wasserman, G. A., & Seracini, A. G. (2001). Family risk factors and interventions. In R. Loeber & D. P. Farrington (Eds.), *Child delinquents: Development, intervention, and service needs* (pp. 165–189). Thousand Oaks, CA: Sage Publications.

Weaver, C. M. (2008). The need for responsibly pursuing work in juvenile psychopathy. *Journal of Forensic Psychology Practice, 8*(2), 198–211. http://dx.doi.org/10.1080/15228930801964109

Witt, P. H., & Conroy, M. A. (2009). *Evaluation of Sexually Violent Predators.* New York: Oxford University Press.

Woolard, J. L., Odgers, C., Lanza-Kaduce, L., & Daglis, H. (2005). Juveniles within adult correctional settings: Legal pathways and developmental considerations. *International Journal of Forensic Mental Health, 4,* 1–18. http://dx.doi.org/10.1080/14999013.2005.10471209

Worling, J. R. (2002). Assessing risk of sexual assault recidivism with adolescent sexual offenders. In M. C. Calder (Ed.), *Young people who sexually abuse: Building the evidence base for your practice* (pp. 365–375). Lyme Regis, Dorset, UK: Russell House Publishing.

Worling, J. R., & Curwen, T. (2000). Adolescent sexual offender recidivism: Success of specialized treatment and implications for risk prediction. *Child Abuse & Neglect, 24*(7), 965–982. http://dx.doi.org/10.1016/S0145-2134(00)00147-2

Worling, J. R., & Långström, N. (2003). Assessment of criminal recidivism risk with adolescents who have offended sexually: A review. *Trauma, Violence, & Abuse: A Review Journal, 4*(4), 341–362. http://dx.doi.org/10.1177/1524838003256562

Wynkoop, T. F. (2003). Neuropsychology of juvenile adjudicative competence. *Journal of Forensic Neuropsychology, 3*(4), 45–65. http://dx.doi.org/10.1300/J151v03n04_04

Zapf, P. A., & Roesch, R. (2009). *Evaluation of competence to stand trial.* New York: Oxford University Press.

Zapf, P. A., & Roesch, R. (2011). Future directions in the restoration of competency to stand trial. *Current Directions in Psychological Science, 20,* 43–47. http://dx.doi.org/10.1177/0963721410396798

Zapf, P. A., & Viljoen, J. L. (2003) Issues and considerations regarding the use of assessment instruments in the evaluation of competency to stand trial. *Behavioral Sciences and the Law, 21*(3), 351–367. http://dx.doi.org/10.1002/bsl.535

Zara, G., & Farrington, D. P. (2013). Assessment of risk for juvenile compared with adult criminal onset implications for policy, prevention, and intervention. *Psychology, Public Policy, and Law, 19*(2), 235–249. http://dx.doi.org/10.1037/a0029050

Zelle, H., Romaine, C. R., & Goldstein, N. S. (2015). Juveniles' Miranda comprehension: Understanding, appreciation, and totality of circumstances factors. *Law and Human Behavior, 39*(3), 281–293. http://dx.doi.org/10.1037/lhb0000116

CHAPTER 6

Clinical Approaches to High-Quality Assessments

Judith V. Becker

Cassandra Valerio

There are various categories of assessment that a psychologist or other qualified mental health professional may be requested to perform when an allegation of inappropriate behavior has been made against an adolescent. One form of assessment would involve informing legal decision makers who are requesting information regarding level of risk and/or types of placements for the youth. Specifically, a forensic evaluation would determine whether the youth's treatment needs and community safety would be best served by settings such as outpatient, a group home setting, or a secure residential setting. Another form of evaluation would be to guide treatment needs of the youth, including the intensity of treatment, and the setting in which treatment may be best provided, particularly when there is no legal involvement. This clinical evaluation should address the adolescent's mental health needs, what the adolescent's strengths are, and other areas to be addressed in treatment such as social skills, empathy deficits, limited knowledge about sexuality, behavioral or emotional dysregulation, and medication needs. In either case, it is important that psychologists never address ultimate issues, such as whether the abuse occurred and the youth's guilt or innocence, as this capacity is the job of the trier of fact. Nor should the psychologist provide information about whether the youth fits the profile of a sexual offender, given that there is no one empirically supported profile of an adolescent sexual offender. Adolescents who sexually abuse others are a diverse population.

ETHICAL ISSUES AND INFORMED CONSENT

In working with adolescents, it is important to remember that they are still developing, in terms of both physical and brain development. Inappropriate sexual behaviors seen in adolescents do not necessarily indicate a lifetime pattern of inappropriate behavior. Legislatures have a number of policies that, while potentially meant to benefit the community, can have negative impacts on the adolescents and their families, including removal of the youth from the community, restrictions on involvement in normal adolescent activities, years of treatment for those who could be treated with fewer sessions, assignment to alternative schools, sex offender registration, and in some states civil commitment of the adolescent. Consequently, one must conduct an evaluation that is guided by empirical literature and that utilizes reliable and valid instruments.

Clinicians are obligated to first obtain the youth's informed assent prior to beginning the evaluation. Additionally, parent or guardian consent for the evaluation should be obtained. Clinicians should provide appropriate information regarding the nature of the interview using language that is understandable to the person being evaluated. Given current policies in some states such as community notification and registration of juvenile sexual offenders, even civil commitment, it is critical that the adolescent and family know how the results of the evaluation will be used.

EVALUATOR QUALIFICATIONS

It is important for individuals who work with adolescents who have engaged in sexually abusive behavior, as well as evaluators who are conducting assessments of these youth, to be knowledgeable about overall adolescent psychological and sexual development. Furthermore, it is important that evaluators have been trained in conducting clinical interviews with this population. Further, evaluators should be familiar with principles of psychometrics, including reliability and validity of any measures they choose to use. We strongly recommend that mental health professionals conducting such evaluations be licensed in their state and be required to have a specified number of continuing education credits, as well as receive ongoing education through conferences and presentations related to sexual offender assessment, in order to keep abreast of the empirical literature. Research shows that only about 10 percent of adolescents who sexually offend go on to recidivate sexually. The evaluator should be aware of such findings, as well as the strengths and limitations of the current literature and areas that warrant further research, such as long-term follow-up studies of the youth and the need for additional adolescent-specific sexual offender risk assessment instruments.

Relevant Research-Supported Assessment Domains

Assessment of youth with sexual offending behaviors should follow a socio-ecological model, covering not only the youth's individual functioning but also contextual factors impacting adolescents, including family relationships, peer relationships, school, and community.

The American Psychological Association's (APA) evidence-based practice guidelines (APA, 2005) suggest a number of domains relevant to assessment and case formulation that evaluators should address in their assessment of youth with sexual offending behaviors. These assessment domains include: (a) the client's presenting problem or disorder and its etiology; (b) the youth's chronological age, developmental status, and developmental history; (c) sociocultural and familial factors, including gender, ethnicity, race, social class, religion, sexual orientation, and family structure; (d) environmental context and current stressors, such as family unemployment, issues related to race or ethnicity, and major life events; and (e) the youth's personal preferences related to treatment, such as beliefs, worldviews, and treatment expectations. We recommend that evaluators follow these guidelines in conducting their assessment to be consistent with a best practice model.

Preparation for the Interview

Prior to beginning an evaluation, it is imperative that the interviewer obtain collateral material. This material should include (a) police reports, including victim statements if made available; (b) relevant educational records, given that some children may suffer from learning disabilities or intellectual disability or may have records of sexual offending behaviors at school; (c) any prior juvenile court or juvenile justice records on the youth; (d) psychological or psychiatric evaluations that have been conducted, given that it is not infrequent that such youth may suffer from ADHD, substance abuse, or other internalizing or externalizing disorders; and (e) previous institutional records if the youth has been previously detained. On occasion, youth who have engaged in sexually abusive behavior may have been involved with child welfare agencies, having been victims of neglect or sexual or physical abuse themselves. These records should also be obtained if available. Prior to interviewing the youth, it is also important to obtain a developmental history from the youth's parent(s) or guardian(s) and to assess whether there are or have been any recent losses, disruptions, or other physical, psychological, or behavioral problems occurring among family members.

The Clinical Interview

Usefulness and Limitations of the Clinical Interview

The clinical interview can provide the evaluator with a wealth of information from both the adolescent and family members. It also provides the opportunity for the evaluator to follow up on the youth's answers, to assess the youth's and family's reactions to questions, and to assess the family's interactional style. Further, the evaluator may learn whether the youth has had a typical or atypical developmental trajectory, the family's level of adversity or stress, and the impact that the youth's behavior has had on the family. The interview allows the evaluator to gain a comprehensive view of the youth and the environment in which he or she functions.

Limitations of the clinical interview should also be noted, however. For example, recall for events in the past may not always be accurate. Additionally, denial and minimization on the part of the adolescent or family members may occur. There are many reasons, however, why a youth may deny having engaged in sexually inappropriate behavior, including fear of the reaction of family members, embarrassment, shame, and fear of legal consequences. What is important to note is that research literature indicates that denial has not generally been shown to be related to recidivism (Hanson & Morton-Bourgon, 2005). In a safe and nonjudgmental setting, a youth may feel more comfortable in acknowledging the inappropriate behavior. It is also important to note that it may take more than one interview to obtain all relevant information from the adolescent and family members.

Environment

The environment in which the interview takes place is of consideration. It is important that the evaluation be conducted in a private area where the conversation will not be overheard while also taking into account the evaluator's safety. The adolescent should be seated in a comfortable chair, and when paper and pencil instruments are administered the adolescent should be seated at a table in a room without distractions.

Establishing Rapport

Establishing rapport with the adolescent being evaluated may be particularly important in order to obtain the most accurate information, particularly given the sensitive nature of taking an individual's sexual history. Additionally, judgments should never be made about the client's behavior during the interview, and the evaluator should inhibit body and facial expressions that may be interpreted negatively. Avoid euphemisms such as *hooking up* but be comfortable with vernacular the youth may use. Ask short, single, concise questions rather than complex ones. Additionally, open-ended questions, rather than more directive and closed-ended questions, allow the youth greater opportunity to respond in detail and using his or her own words. Evaluators should avoid suggesting answers to the youth. Cultural differences should be considered where appropriate. Remember that sexual histories may be falsified by exaggeration, denial, minimization, or misremembering. It is important to set the right tone when taking a sex history. As Pomeroy and colleagues (1982) described, "It is a privilege to be allowed to take anyone's sexual history and the respondent's willingness to share this material should be regarded as a sacred trust. One's sexual history is a private affair."

A controlled, even manner of speaking, a pleasant expression, and a relaxed body posture best convey an attitude of acceptance to the person being interviewed. The interviewer's objective is to obtain information about a variety of sexual behaviors, while excluding any prejudgments and prejudices (Pomeroy et al., 1982). Additionally, evaluators may find it helpful to begin the interview with less sensitive information, such the family's current functioning or information about schooling and peers. Once greater rapport has been established with the youth, the evaluator may then move on to discussing non-problematic sexual behavior, and later to the youth's problematic sexual behaviors.

When meeting with the youth for the first time, it is important to remember that he or she may feel uncomfortable discussing sexual issues. It can be helpful for the evaluator to explain to the youth that he or she has met with and interviewed many youth who have been in situations similar to the one this particular youth is currently in. It may also be helpful and useful to ask the youth what information he or she would like to gain from the evaluation, and follow through to provide this information to the extent possible. It is important to reiterate that the evaluator is not there to pass judgment, but instead to gather as much information as possible such that recommendations may be made to ensure the best interests of the youth and society. The youth should also be informed as to what records and collateral information have been reviewed by the evaluator. As noted previously, more than one interview may be necessary to obtain this information and to develop stronger rapport with the youth.

Areas to Be Covered

Family History, Parenting Practices, and Current Family Functioning

It is important to understand the ecological framework in which the adolescent functions. The interview should begin by asking demographic questions and questions about the youth's experience living within the family or circumstances in which the youth lives. It may also be helpful to begin by asking the youth who the family members are that he or she lives with at the present time and whether there have been any recent changes to this living situation. It is important to obtain information about the interaction between the caregiver(s) and the youth, including parenting style and practices and other family events that may affect the youth, such as divorce or involvement of child welfare agencies.

Youth Developmental History

Information regarding the adolescent's developmental history should also be obtained. An interview with the youth's parent or guardian may be particularly helpful in this regard, as the guardian may be able to provide more information regarding prenatal care, any complications that occurred during pregnancy, and whether the youth met typical developmental milestones. Information regarding the youth's physical health history, including any hospitalizations, surgeries, major illness or injuries (particularly head injuries), and family history of illness should be obtained from the youth as well as from a parent/guardian, and collateral information if available.

Educational History

Information should be obtained regarding educational history, including grades, special education, or repeating grades, as well as any current or history of behavior problems in school. The evaluator should also inquire whether the youth is currently attending school, and what the youth's plans are following completion of school.

Peer Relationships and Community Involvement

While we all operate within a social world, peer influence may be particularly salient in adolescence. Therefore, it is also crucial to ask the youth about peers, including whether these peers engage in antisocial or delinquent activity or use substances. The adolescent should also be asked whether he or she has a best friend or friends (and the first names of the friend or friends), and what types of activities he or she engages in with friends. Further, information about any community activities the youth may participate in should be obtained, such as clubs, sports, hobbies, or church involvement.

Mental Health History

Information about prior counseling and psychological or pharmacological treatments should be obtained directly from the youth and the parent or guardian in addition to collateral records. Importantly, ask how the youth has felt about any mental health services received to date. Additionally, if the adolescent has taken medication for mental health problems, he or she should be asked if the medication worked well or poorly, his or her attitudes about taking medication, and whether he or she was compliant in taking the medication.

Substance Abuse History

Substance use history is also crucial. It is not unusual for youth to experiment with alcohol or with illegal substances. Very often, the way the evaluator phrases a question can determine whether the youth will be at least somewhat open to disclosing this information. Sometimes it is helpful to acknowledge that adolescence is a time of experimentation and that it is not uncommon for youth to be offered or to use different substances on an experimental basis, and that it is important as part of the assessment for the clinician to know what substances the youth has tried or has been invited to try. Information should be elicited regarding not only the types of substances, but also the frequency of use, how the youth feels when using the particular substance(s), and what impact the use of the substance has on the youth's life. Sometimes youth are averse to sharing such information face-to-face, and this can be followed up by using measures such as the Adolescent Substance Abuse Subtle Screening Inventory (SASSI-A2; Miller & Lazowski, 2001), a screening measure that identifies the probability of a substance use disorder in adolescents 12 through 18 years of age.

Criminal/Delinquent History

The evaluator should inquire about the youth's history of non-sexual offending, as well as collect this information from collateral records. Research suggests that many juveniles with problematic sexual behavior have characteristics in common with juveniles who offend non-sexually (Seto & Lalumière, 2010). Additionally, youth with sexual offending behaviors are more likely to recidivate non-sexually (Caldwell, 2007; Letourneau & Miner, 2005; McCann & Lussier, 2008). Thus, obtaining a history of general delinquency is also important in addition to the youth's sexual offending history.

History of Maltreatment

Literature has indicated that a portion of youth with sexual offending behaviors may also have been the victims of physical or sexual abuse (e.g., Jespersen, Lalumière, & Seto, 2009). On occasion it is difficult for adolescents, particularly if they believe they may be taken from their parents, to acknowledge any form of maltreatment. The wording of the questions in this area is particularly important. The first author has found that if an evaluator asks children directly if they have been physically abused by their parents, sometimes children will deny this even if such behavior has occurred. Children are more likely to respond to a question such as "What form(s) of discipline do your parents (or guardians) use when they feel that you have misbehaved?" Youth may also respond more honestly to inquiries including whether a parent has ever disciplined them when they have not misbehaved, and whether a parent has ever disciplined them while the parent was drinking and/or appeared to be under a great deal of stress. Children may also be asked what rules are set for them in the home and what consequences occur if they do not follow the rules. If a child indicates abuse, the evaluator should follow up on whether the child required medical care or was not able to attend school due to the abuse. Regarding neglect, children may be asked if they have always had housing, medical care, and food to eat.

When interviewing about a history of sexual abuse, we have found that rather than responding to a direct question, youth appear to be more comfortable with a question such as, "Has anyone ever touched your body in a way that has made you feel uncomfortable?" or "Has anyone done anything to you sexually that might be considered against the law?" Then information is obtained regarding the perpetrator of the abuse and his or her relationship to the youth, the nature of the abuse, the type of behavior that occurred, the frequency of the behavior, whether the behavior was disclosed and to whom, and what happened if the behavior was disclosed. The evaluator should note that if the abuse has not been previously disclosed, a report may be required. Given that abuse is prevalent and it is not uncommon for youth to develop trauma symptoms (Chen et al., 2010), an evaluator may also wish to administer a screening measure for PTSD and trauma-related symptoms. The National Child Traumatic Stress Network (http://www.nctsn.org) provides a database of measures where clinicians may access information on a variety of trauma questionnaires.

Non-Problematic Sexual Behavior History

Following the collection of demographic information and a general social history, the evaluator may progress to taking the adolescent's sexual history. As noted previously, inquiring about non-problematic sexual behavior prior to discussion of sexual offending behavior may better facilitate rapport with the youth. Initial information to obtain from the adolescent may include family values and rules regarding sexuality, the age at which the youth learned about sex, whether the youth has been exposed to sexual behavior by parents or siblings, and the age at which the youth entered puberty. When the youth has established a greater level of comfort with discussion of sexual topics, the evaluator should inquire about more sensitive information, such as when the youth began masturbating and the current frequency of masturbation, onset of sexual interest and behavior with another person, as well as previous and current sexual relationships.

Being interested in sex and having sexual fantasies are hallmarks of adolescence. Thus, the extent and nature of the youth's fantasies are crucial for the evaluator to investigate. Areas to explore include the age and gender of individuals in the youth's fantasies, and whether any of these fantasies involve force or coercion. Further, the evaluator should inquire as to when the youth was first exposed to sexually explicit material, including books, magazines, and videos. A description of the frequency of use and the type of the material should be obtained, as well as whether any of the material involves force. Given the proliferation of sexually explicit material available online and through other technological means, the adolescent should be asked about whether he or she has used various electronic forums to obtain this material or to distribute material of his or own.

History of Sexual Offending Behaviors

Once the interviewer has obtained a history of the youth's normative sexual development and behavior, the interview may progress to sexual offending behaviors. The evaluator may go through a list of some behaviors and ask whether the youth has fantasized about or engaged in these behaviors and, if so, at what age. Given each particular case, the clinician should decide whether or not it is appropriate to ask about some behaviors. If there is no indication based on the victim's statement or collateral information that violence or weapons have been used, an evaluator may not find it necessary to delve into those areas. Behaviors that the evaluator may inquire of the youth may include (but are not limited to) exposing him- or herself, voyeurism, becoming sexually aroused by hurting another person or fantasizing about doing so, having sexual contact with children, and using alcohol or drugs to make someone engage in sexual activity with him or her.

The evaluator should conclude this line of questioning by asking if there is any sexual behavior the youth has fantasized about or engaged in that the evaluator failed to ask about. At this point in the interview, given that the adolescent has been exposed to and has discussed areas related to sexuality, the clinician can then begin to explore the alleged sexual offense(s), reminding the youth that the evaluator has reviewed collateral material and statements that were made by the victim(s) if this has occurred. The evaluator may ask the nature of the current offense, as well as information about previous referrals to the court for illegal sexual behavior. The evaluator may also use this line of questioning to probe for feelings of guilt and empathy.

Psychometric Measures

Choosing Assessment Instruments

When selecting measures to use in evaluating a youth, it is important for an evaluator to ensure that any assessment instruments used are appropriate for that youth. First, assessment measures should be developmentally appropriate, as well as normed on and intended for use with adolescent populations. Additionally, the evaluator should consider any particular characteristics of the youth being evaluated that may impact whether an assessment measure is appropriate for him or her. For example, special attention should be paid to ensure that a measure is appropriate for use with females, ethnic minorities, or youth with intellectual disabilities. Standardized instruments may provide guidelines regarding the appropriate age and sample for use of the instrument. If the evaluator is administering an assessment that is not intended for use with the particular youth being evaluated, this should be noted in any report produced based on the assessment results.

Evaluators should also ensure that any measures used in the assessment have adequate psychometric properties. Major psychometric properties an evaluator should consider regarding any particular assessment include its validity and reliability. Validity refers to the extent to which a test measures the quality or construct it is intended to measure. Reliability refers to the overall consistency of a measure, in particular its ability to obtain similar results over time (Kaplan & Saccuzzo, 2009). Several forms of reliability and validity may be of importance in determining whether a measure is psychometrically sound. Relevant forms of reliability may include: (a) internal consistency, or the correlations between items within the same measure, which should be high if the test is designed to measure a single construct; (b) test–retest reliability, or a test's stability over time, measured by administering the same test twice over a period of time; and (c) inter-rater reliability, or the degree of agreement between different raters evaluating the same behavior or trait. Forms of validity that may be of interest include: (a) predictive validity, or the extent to which a score on a measure predicts scores on a designated outcome measure; (b) concurrent validity, or the degree to which the results of a measure correspond to another measure of the same trait or construct; and (c) discriminant validity, or whether a measure is unrelated to theoretically different measures (Kaplan & Saccuzzo, 2009). An assessment instrument's specificity and sensitivity should also be considered. Sensitivity refers to the measure's ability to correctly identify those who possess a particular characteristic or trait (i.e., true positive rate), while specificity refers to the measure's ability to correctly identify those who do *not* possess the characteristic or trait (i.e., true negative rate; Lalkhen & McCluskey, 2008).

Instruments for General Psychopathology

In addition to a review of collateral information and a clinical interview with the youth, a high-quality assessment may also include the administration of measures assessing general psychopathology. Of note, previous research has indicated that adolescents who have engaged in sexually abusive behavior may present with attention, executive functioning, or other cognitive deficits (e.g., Kelly, Richardson, Hunter, & Knapp, 2010). It is important, therefore, prior to administering any standardized assessments or screening measures, that the evaluator be aware of the youth's level of intellectual functioning, including whether the youth suffers from any learning disabilities, has difficulty with attention, or has any disabilities that may interfere with test-taking ability. School records may be particularly important in this regard. Additionally, future cognitive-behavioral interventions may need to be modified depending on the cognitive ability of a particular youth (Veneziano & Veneziano, 2002). It is especially critical that the evaluator know the reading level of the youth and the reading level that is required for any particular instrument used as part of testing.

Previous research indicates that general mental health problems do not seem to be related to general recidivism with the exception of substance abuse (Schubert, Mulvey, & Glasheen, 2011). However, it may be useful to also assess for co-occurring mental health disorders. Previous research indicates that adolescents who engage in sexually abusive behavior may have comorbid depression (Becker, Kaplan, Tenke, & Tartaglini, 1991) or ADHD (Blocher et al., 2001); exposure to trauma may also be particularly prevalent in this population (McMackin, Leisen, Cusak, LaFratta, & Litwin, 2002) and may need to be addressed before sexual-offense-specific treatment can be effective. Therefore, identifying the particular mental health concerns of the youth being evaluated may be an important part of the assessment. Trauma and mental health needs, if not addressed in treatment, may impact the youth's engagement or ability to respond to sexual-offense-specific treatment. Although the goal of such treatment is to prevent recidivism, it is important that all of the youth's needs are addressed. The following are among the many measures that may be used to assess general personality or psychological functioning in adolescents:

- *Minnesota Multiphasic Personality Inventory–Adolescent* (MMPI-A; Butcher et al., 1992). The MMPI-A is an objective personality measure that describes personality functioning on 10 clinical scales, as well as three validity scales.

- *Millon Adolescent Clinical Inventory* (MACI; Millon, 2006). The MACI is also a self-report personality inventory for use in adolescents 13 through 19 years old. It consists of 12 personality pattern scales, eight expressed concerns scales, seven clinical syndrome scales, 36 personality facet scales, and one validity scale.

- *Personality Assessment Inventory–Adolescent* (PAI-A; Morey, 2007). The PAI-A is a personality measure for adolescents 12 through 18 years old. It consists of 18 clinical scales, an additional 31 subscales, and four validity scales.

- *Adolescent Psychopathology Scale* (APS; Reynolds, 1998). The APS assesses for the presence and severity of symptoms of psychological disorders and consists of 20 scales assessing clinical disorders, five scales assessing personality disorders, 11 scales assessing psychosocial problems, and four validity scales. It is intended for use with adolescents 12 through 19 years old.

- *Youth Self Report* (YSR; Achenbach, 1991). The YSR is a self-report measure assessing emotional behavioral problems in adolescents aged 11 through 18. It consists of eight symptom scales, including anxiety, depression, social problems, and oppositional behavior. The YSR may be used in conjunction with the Child Behavior Checklist (CBCL; Achenbach, 1991), which has corresponding items and scales to be completed by the youth's parent or guardian. The Teacher Report Form may be useful as well in providing a well-rounded picture of the youth's functioning.

- *Behavior Assessment System for Children, Second Edition* (BASC-2; Reynolds & Kamphaus, 2004). The BASC-2 is a comprehensive set of rating scales to assess changes in behaviors and emotions in children and adolescents. The self-report scale may be supplemented by the available parent and teacher rating scales.

SEXUAL-OFFENDER-SPECIFIC INSTRUMENTS

Fanniff and Becker (2013) reviewed sexual-offender-specific assessment instruments for adolescents who have been adjudicated for sexual offenses. The authors note that the two major goals of these assessments are to assist in treatment planning for these youth, and to identify those youth at high risk to reoffend in order to inform disposition. Three major methods of assessment have been used to achieve those goals: (a) self-report instruments, which are designed to assess sexual distortions and deviant sexual interests; (b) objective/physiological assessment measures of sexual interest and arousal; and (c) risk assessment instruments. The current chapter will review self-report and objective measures and briefly discuss risk assessment measures.

Research-based risk and needs assessments and measures are discussed in more detail in chapter 7.

Adolescent Cognitions Scale

The Adolescent Cognitions Scale (ACS) assesses cognitive distortions juveniles with sexual offending behaviors may employ to justify sexual offending. Recent research investigating the utility of the ACS is limited; however, the research that exists indicates that the internal consistency and test–retest reliability of this measure appear to be less than adequate (Fanniff & Becker, 2006). Further, the measure does not appear to distinguish juvenile sexual offenders and non-offending juveniles. Hunter, Becker, Kaplan, and Goodwin (1991) found no differences on ACS-summed scores in a comparison of juvenile sexual offenders with a group of community adolescents who were not in mental health treatment and had no history of sexual victimization or perpetration. While some clinicians may find this instrument useful with clients who are very disclosing, Fanniff and Becker (2006) note that the lack of reliability and validity data limits the usefulness of the measure.

Adolescent Sexual Interest Cardsort

The Adolescent Sexual Interest Cardsort (ASIC) is a 64-vignette self-report measure of sexual interest. The adolescent rates the sexual vignettes on a five-point Likert scale reflecting arousal. Fanniff and Becker (2006) reported that this instrument demonstrates adequate reliability. Specifically, 60 of the vignettes show significant test–retest correlations. Further, all 17 categories contained in the measure demonstrate adequate internal consistency (Hunter, Becker, & Kaplan, 1995). However, an issue with the ASIC is its limited correlation between self-reported sexual interest on the instrument and arousal as assessed by plethysmography. Plethysmography involves assessing penile tumescence to either audio or visual stimuli depicting males and females of different ages, or audiotaped descriptions of sexual contact with individuals of different ages; the erectile response is measured with a strain-gauge, a small device placed on the penis in the privacy of a laboratory setting. The only correlations found between self-reported interest and plethysmography results were for arousal to aggressive sex with a young female, consensual sex with a same-age male, aggressive sex with a same-age female, and aggressive sex with an adult female, although Hunter and colleagues (1995) note that this might be influenced by respondents' willingness to report arousal to particular inappropriate situations. Research results suggest that the ASIC might, as with the ACS, be useful with adolescents who are highly disclosing. However, further research is needed to determine its utility. For example, there is a lack of data on how non-offending juveniles would perform on this instrument. As Fanniff and Becker (2006) note, if no differences are found between adolescents who have committed sexual offenses and juveniles in the community, the utility of the ASIC would be further limited. The first author, who was one of the developers of this instrument, no longer uses this instrument for these reasons.

Multiphasic Sex Inventory–II

Another commonly utilized self-report measure is the Multiphasic Sex Inventory, Second Edition (MSI-II; Nichols & Mollinder, 1996). This is a self-report instrument that has both an adult and an adolescent version. It assesses a variety of psychosexual characteristics in adults and adolescents who have been charged or convicted of sexual offenses. Becker and Fanniff (2013) note that concerns have been raised regarding the representatives of the normal sample and the validity of the measure with adults. However, it has been shown to be related to recidivism among adult male sexual offenders and is also sometimes used as a measure of treatment progress in adult offenders. To the authors' knowledge, there is no peer-reviewed research available regarding its reliability and validity in assessment of adolescents.

Objective Assessment Instruments

Viewing-Time Measures

A number of measures have been designed to subtly record the amount of time that individuals spend looking at images of males and females of different ages. These methods are advantageous in that they are less intrusive than techniques such as plethysmography. Viewing-time measures are associated with sexual interest and/or arousal in both non-offending adults and adult sexual offenders (Faniff & Becker, 2013). Viewing-time measures have also been employed with adolescent sexual offenders. Such measures include the Abel Assessment for Sexual Interest (AASI) and the Affinity Measure of Sexual Interest (AMSI). The AASI consists of (a) the client's subjective ratings of sexual interest, (b) viewing time for slides representing 22 categories of sexual interest, and (c) a questionnaire about the adolescent's sexual history and interests (Abel et al., 2004). There is a limited amount of recent research available on the use of the AASI with adolescents who have committed sexual offenses. Smith & Fisher (1999) reported inadequate test–retest correlations on the measure. Further, these authors reported that one scoring method demonstrated high specificity (98% of non-offenders were classified as uninterested in children) but low sensitivity (15%

of offenders were classified as interested in children). An alternative scoring method improved the sensitivity but decreased the specificity. Abel (2000) noted several flaws in that study, however, including failure to ensure that members of the control group were not interested in children, and the conflation of offending against a child with sexual interest in children. Abel and colleagues (2004) conducted a large study of adolescent males who had engaged in inappropriate sexual behavior. This study found that those adolescents who had child victims viewed the slides of children longer than did the adolescents with non-child victims. However, the authors cautioned against using viewing time alone to identify male adolescents who have offended against or are specifically interested in children.

Another viewing-time measure is the Affinity Measure of Sexual Interest. This assessment instrument includes visual stimuli of males and females in four age categories. Adolescents rate these slides on sexual attractiveness while their viewing time is recorded. Though research on this measure is limited, a study by Worling (2006) found that sexual attractiveness ratings, self-report sexual arousal graphs, and the Affinity viewing-time measure all demonstrated internal consistency. Further, significant correlations were found between sexual attractiveness ratings and viewing times for the majority of the stimulus categories. In this study the author found that all three measures identified adolescents with male victims significantly better than chance. However, no measure correctly identified adolescents with female child victims. Given the accuracy of self-report found in this particular study, Becker and Fanniff (2013) question whether viewing time is necessarily a needed component for accurate assessment. Perhaps the nature of the relationship that the assessor develops with the adolescent is a more important factor. That is, if the assessor takes a non-confrontational, non-judgmental approach to working with the youth, the youth may feel comfortable enough to disclose information relevant to the offense(s) for which they were charged.

Crooks, Rostill-Brookes, Beech, and Bickley (2009) reported on a visual-reaction-based assessment of sexual interest termed the attentional blink response. Their sample included both adolescent offenders against children and adolescent non-sexual offenders. The theory underlying this assessment hypothesizes that an individual's accuracy is reduced when responding to images that quickly follow after a particularly attractive image. In this particular study, however, both groups of adolescents demonstrated reduced accuracy after they had viewed pictures of animals but not after viewing pictures of children.

Fanniff and Becker (2013) note that viewing-time measures are in need of continued investigation in the following areas: data on a large normative (i.e., non-offending) sample of youth, and data on adolescent sexual offenders who deny their offenses. Further, the authors note that the research to date has used victim choice as an indicator of sexual preference when in fact an adolescent may choose a victim for reasons other than sexual preference, and may not necessarily have a pedophilic interest or arousal pattern. Further research should consider use of samples of adolescents with a persistent pattern of offending against children. Research to date indicates that viewing time may show the most promise in assessing sexual interest in those adolescents who have targeted male children. As noted above, further research is needed given that this particular method of assessment is less invasive than others, such as plethysmography (described below).

Plethysmography

There is a large body of literature on use of the penile plethysmograph (PPG) with adult offenders (e.g., Chivers, Seto, Lalumière, Laan, & Grimbos, 2010; Howes, 1995) and a much smaller body of literature regarding its use with adolescents. This technique involves presenting video or audiotape stimuli to the client while erectile responses are measured with either penile circumference measure or penile volume measure. With adult offenders, PPG demonstrates concurrent validity in assessing pedophilic interest (Stinson & Becker, 2008). Further, Hanson and Morton-Bourgon (2005) found that deviant sexual interest is significantly associated with recidivism among adult offenders. Use of this assessment instrument with adolescents has been more controversial; it is not used by the majority of treatment programs. McGrath and colleagues (2010) reported that less than 10 percent of programs for males in the United States and less than 25 percent of programs in Canada employ this method. Of importance in deciding whether use of this controversial method for adolescents is warranted is whether the measure demonstrates adequate reliability and validity. In one of the few studies available, Becker and colleagues (1992) found adequate test–retest reliability for most of the 19 categories of stimuli investigated. A number of researchers (e.g., Clift, Rajlic, & Gretton, 2009; Rice, Harris, Lang, & Chaplin, 2012) have found that adolescents with male child victims evidenced greater sexual arousal to the stimuli. Research has also shown a positive correlation between a PPG index of sexual arousal to children and number of victims (Seto, Murphy, Page, & Ennis, 2003). Fanniff and Becker (2013) note that while findings from the studies mentioned above are promising in terms of reliability, additional research (e.g., Clift et al., 2009) has found inadequate specificity and sensitivity in distinguishing between youth with different types of victims. Further, other factors that need to be taken into account include that adolescents may suppress their sexual response (Clift et al., 2009) or deny their offense (Becker et al., 1992). Findings regarding predictive validity of PPG-assessed arousal are mixed. Some studies have found that those who demonstrate arousal to children are significantly more likely to sexually recidivate (Clift et al., 2009; Rice et al., 2012), but this finding is not consistent (Gretton, McBride, Hare, O'Shaghnessy, & Kumka, 2001). Prior to a clinician using this form of assessment, the clinician must take into consideration that it is more invasive than other forms of assessment and, given research to date, it may not provide sufficient information to inform treatment that is not otherwise available through self-report or other means of assessment (Fanniff & Becker, 2013).

Polygraphy

There appears to be an increase in the use of polygraphy with both adults and adolescents with sexual offending behaviors. McGrath and colleagues (2010) reported that about 50 percent of community and residential treatment programs in the United States utilize polygraphy. This technique may be used for a variety of reasons, such as for validating a sex history and as part of monitoring during treatment (Fanniff & Becker, 2013). The National Research Council (NRC, 2003) published a review of the evidence regarding the validity of polygraphy. To summarize this report, specific-incident polygraphs were shown to discriminate deception from truth slightly better than chance. There is currently a dearth of research on the use of polygraphy with adolescents; however, treatment programs continue to use it despite the limited evidence for validity. The rationale often put forward for use of this measure is that adolescents may disclose more victims or offenses during polygraphy, although the accuracy of these disclosures is unclear (Fanniff & Becker, 2013). Some clinicians believe treatment would be incomplete unless they know the exact number of victims or offenses. However, it is important to note that there is little evidence that denial is associated with recidivism (Hanson & Morton-Bourgon, 2005). Given the false positive and false negative rates associated with polygraphy and the lack of research on its use with adolescents, a number of ethical concerns exist regarding its use (Chaffin, 2011). As Becker and Harris (2004) note, in order for a youth to disclose truthful information, it may be most useful to provide a safe environment for him or her to do so.

Risk Assessment Measures

There are a number of risk assessment measures—including the Juvenile Sex Offender Assessment Protocol–II (JSOAP-II; Prentky & Righthand, 2003), the Estimate of Risk of Adolescent Sex Offense Recidivism (ERASOR; Worling & Curwen, 2001), and the Juvenile Sexual Offense Recidivism Risk Assessment Tool (JSORRAT-II; Epperson, Ralston, Fowers, Dewitt, & Gore, 2006)—that can be used with male adolescent sexual offenders to assess sexual reoffending. The Youth Level of Service/Case Management Inventory (YLS/CMI; Hoge & Andrews, 2006) and the Structured

Assessment of Violence Risk in Youth (SAVRY; Borum, Bartel, & Forth, 2003) can be used for predicting general reoffending and violent reoffending. As part of a comprehensive evaluation, and in an attempt to determine appropriate placement, it is important to assess risk for reoffense. Empirically supported risk assessment measures should investigate areas that the literature has found are associated with risk, including both static (non-changing or historical) and dynamic factors, which may be the targets of interventions.

The authors believe that the available risk assessment measures can be useful in identifying treatment needs, specifically those that identify dynamic risk factors. However, given that youth continue to develop during adolescence, their level of risk may change as they mature and thus the risk predicted by a given measure may be limited in its usefulness over time.

Further discussion of risk and needs assessment is provided (see chapter 7 of this volume).

Conclusion and Future Directions

In conclusion, we have attempted to provide an overview of clinical approaches to interviewing adolescents who have sexually offended, as well as to offer information regarding available self-report and other measures that have been utilized in the assessment of adolescents. The majority of literature cited has been on male adolescents because most adolescents who have sexually abused are male (Finkelhor, Ormrod, & Chaffin, 2009), and the majority of studies in peer-reviewed literature have investigated males who engage in sexual offending. Clearly more research is needed in the development of more instruments with sufficient reliability and validity. Additionally, further research is needed on existing measures to more clearly elucidate their psychometric properties. It is of course important that assessors of juveniles use instruments that have been developed for adolescents and not those that have been validated on only an adult population to ensure the best results. While ATSA has practice guidelines for the assessment of adult male sexual abusers, the field awaits practice guidelines for adolescent males and females who have engaged in inappropriate sexual behavior. It is imperative that clinicians realize that adolescence is a stage of development and that interest in sexuality is a hallmark of this stage. Out of curiosity, experimentation, or other psychological problems, some adolescents may engage in norm-violating sexual behavior. This does not necessarily mean that they will develop a paraphilic interest pattern or will be at high risk to recidivate. What is important in doing a comprehensive assessment is determining what the adolescent's needs are, what protective factors are in existence, and what level of intervention and support is needed. Given the low detected recidivism rate for this population, it is important to remember that many adolescents will not engage in such behavior again in the future, and in terms of assessment and treatment, we should "do no harm." In conducting an ethically sound, scientifically valid assessment, we will serve both the youth and the community at large.

REFERENCES

Abel, G. G. (2000). The importance of meeting research standards: A reply to Fischer and Smith's articles on the Abel Assessment for Sexual Interest. *Sexual Abuse: A Journal of Research and Treatment, 12*(2), 155–161.

Abel, G. G., Jordan, A., Rouleau, J. L., Emerick, R., Barboza-Whitehead, S., & Osborn, C. (2004). Use of visual reaction time to assess male adolescents who molest children. *Sexual Abuse: A Journal of Research and Treatment, 16*(3), 255–265. http://dx.doi.org/10.1177/107906320401600306

Achenbach, T. (1991). *Manual for the Youth Self-Report and 1991 Profile.* Burlington: University of Vermont, Department of Psychiatry.

Achenbach, T. M., (1991). *Manual for the child behavior checklist.*Child Burlington: Department of Psychiatry, University of Vermont.

Becker, J. V., & Harris, C. (2004). The psychophysiological assessment of juvenile offenders. In G. O'Reilley, W. L. Marshall, A. Carr, & R. C. Beckett (Eds.), *The handbook of clinical intervention with young people who sexually abuse* (pp. 191–202). New York: Psychology Press, Taylor and Francis Group.

Becker, J. V., Hunter, J. A., Goodwin, D., Kaplan, M. S., & Martinez, D. (1992). Test–retest reliability of audio-taped phallometric stimuli with adolescent sexual offenders. *Annals of Sex Research, 5*(1), 45–51.

Becker, J. V., Kaplan, M. S., Tenke, C. E., & Tartaglini, A. (1991). The incidence of depressive symptomatology in juvenile sex offenders with a history of abuse. *Child Abuse & Neglect, 15*(4), 531–536. http://dx.doi.org/10.1016/0145-2134(91)90037-E

Bernstein, D. P., & Fink, L. (1998). *Childhood trauma questionnaire: A retrospective self-report: Manual.* San Antonio: Psychological Corporation.

Blocher, D., Henkel, K., Retz, W., Retz-Junginger, P., Thome, J., & Rösler, M. (2001). Symptoms from the spectrum of attention-deficit/hyperactivity disorder (ADHD) in sexual delinquents. *Fortschritte Der Neurologie, Psychiatrie, 69*(10), 453–459. http://dx.doi.org/10.1055/s-2001-17562

Borum, R., Bartel, P., & Forth, A. (2003). *Manual for the Structured Assessment for Violence Risk in Youth (SAVRY).* Odessa, FL: Psychological Assessment Resources.

Briere, J. (1996). *Trauma Symptom Checklist for Children (TSCC) professional manual.* Odessa, FL: Psychological Assessment Resources.

Butcher, J. N., Williams, C. L., Graham, J. R., Archer, R. P., Tellegen, A., Ben-Porath, Y., & and Kaemmer, B. (1992). *Minnesota Multiphasic Personality Inventory–Adolescent (MMPI-A): Manual for administration, scoring, and interpretation.* Minneapolis: University of Minnesota Press.

Caldwell, M. F. (2007). Sexual offense adjudication and sexual recidivism among juvenile offenders. *Sexual Abuse: Journal of Research and Treatment, 19*(2), 107–113. doi:10.1177/107906320701900203

Chaffin, M. (2010). The case of juvenile polygraphy as a clinical ethics dilemma. *Sexual Abuse: A Journal of Research and Treatment, 23,* 314–328.

Chen, L. P., Murad, M. H., Paras, M. L., Colbenson, K. M., Sattler, A. L., Goranson, E. N., . . . & Zirakzadeh, A. (2010, July). Sexual abuse and lifetime diagnosis of psychiatric disorders: Systematic review and meta-analysis. In *Mayo Clinic Proceedings, 85*(7), 618–629.

Chivers, M. L., Seto, M. C., Lalumière, M. L., Laan, E., & Grimbos, T. (2010). Agreement of self-reported and genital measures of sexual arousal in men and women: A meta-analysis. *Archives of sexual behavior, 39*(1), 5–56.

Clift, R. J., Rajlic, G., & Gretton, H. M. (2009). Discriminative and predictive validity of the penile plethysmograph in adolescent sex offenders. *Sexual Abuse: A Journal of Research and Treatment, 21*(3), 335–362.

Cottle, C. C., Lee, R. J., & Heilbrun, K. (2001). The prediction of criminal recidivism in juveniles: A meta-analysis. *Criminal Justice and Behavior, 28*(3), 367–394. http://dx.doi.org/10.1177/0093854801028003005

Crooks, V. L., Rostill-Brookes, H., Beech, A. R., & Bickley, J. A. (2009). Applying rapid serial visual presentation to adolescent sexual offenders: Attentional bias as a measure of deviant sexual interest? *Sexual Abuse: A Journal of Research and Treatment, 21*(2), 135–148.

Epperson, D., Ralston, C., Fowers, D., DeWitt, J., & Gore, K. (2006). Juvenile Sexual Offense Recidivism Rate Assessment Tool-II (JSORRAT-II). In D. Prescott (Ed.), *Risk assessment of youth who have sexually abused* (222–236). Brandon, VT: Safer Society Press.

Fanniff, A. M., & Becker, J. V. (2006). Specialized assessment and treatment of adolescent sex offenders. *Aggression and Violent Behavior, 11*(3), 265–282. http://dx.doi.org/10.1016/j.avb.2005.08.003

Fanniff, A. M., & Becker, J. V. (2013). Adolescents adjudicated for sexual offenses. In D. S. Bromberg & W. T. O'Donohue (Eds.), *Handbook of child and adolescent sexuality: Developmental and forensic psychology* (pp. 519–546). San Diego: Elsevier Academic Press. http://dx.doi.org/10.1016/B978-0-12-387759-8.00021-0

Finkelhor, D., Ormrod, R., & Chaffin, M. (2009, December). Juveniles who commit sex offenses against minors. Retrieved from www.ojp.usdoj.gov/ojjdp

Gretton, H. M., McBride, M., Hare, R. D., O'Shaughnessy, R., & Kumka, G. (2001). Psychopathy and recidivism in adolescent sex offenders. *Criminal Justice and Behavior, 28*(4), 427–449.

Hanson, R. K., & Morton-Bourgon, K. E. (2005). The characteristics of persistent sexual offenders: A meta-analysis of recidivism studies. *Journal of Consulting and Clinical Psychology, 73*(6), 1154–1163.

Hoge, R. D., & Andrews, D. A. (2006). *Youth Level of Service/Case Management Inventory YLS/CMI: User's manual.* Toronto: Multi-Health Systems.

Howes, R. J. (1995). A survey of plethysmographic assessment in North America. *Sexual Abuse: A Journal of Research and Treatment, 7*(1), 9–24.

Hunter, J. A., Becker, J. V., & Kaplan, M. S. (1995). The Adolescent Sexual Interest Card Sort: Test-retest reliability and concurrent validity in relation to phallometric assessment. *Archives of Sexual Behavior, 24*(5), 555–561. doi:10.1007/BF01541834

Hunter, J. A., Becker, J. V., Kaplan, M., & Goodwin, D. W. (1991). Reliability and discriminitive validity of the Adolescent Cognitions Scale for juvenile offenders. *Annals of Sex Research, 4,* 281–286.

Jespersen, A. F., Lalumière, M. L., & Seto, M. C. (2009). Sexual abuse history among adult sex offenders and non-sex offenders: A meta-analysis. *Child Abuse & Neglect, 33*(3), 179–192. http://dx.doi.org/10.1016/j.chiabu.2008.07.004

Kaplan, R., & Saccuzzo, D. (2012). *Psychological testing: Principles, applications, and issues* (8th ed.). Boston: Cengage Learning.

Kelly, T., Richardson, G., Hunter, R., & Knapp, M. (2002). Attention and executive function deficits in adolescent sex offenders. *Child Neuropsychology, 8*(2), 138–143. http://dx.doi.org/10.1076/chin.8.2.138.8722

Lalkhen, A. G., & McCluskey, A. (2008). Clinical tests: Sensitivity and specificity. *Continuing Education in Anesthesia, Critical Care, and Pain, 8*(6): 221–223. http://dx.doi.org/10.1093/bjaceaccp/mkn041

Letourneau, E. J., & Miner, M. H. (2005). Juvenile sex offenders: A case against the legal and clinical status quo. *Sexual Abuse: A Journal of Research and Treatment, 17*(3), 293–312. http://dx.doi.org/10.1177/107906320501700304

McCann, K., & Lussier, P. (2008). Antisociality, sexual deviance, and sexual reoffending in juvenile sex offenders: A meta-analytical investigation. *Youth Violence and Juvenile Justice, 6*(4), 363–385. doi:10.1177/1541204008320260

McGrath, R. J., Cumming, G. F., Burchard, B. L., Zeoli, S., & Ellerby, L. (2010). *Current practices and emerging trends in sexual abuser management: The Safer Society 2009 North American survey.* Brandon, VT: Safer Society Press.

McMackin, R. A., Leisen, M. B., Cusack, J. F., LaFratta, J., & Litwin, P. (2002). The relationship of trauma exposure to sex offending behavior among male juvenile offenders. *Journal of Child Sexual Abuse: Research, Treatment, & Program Innovations For Victims, Survivors, & Offenders, 11*(2), 25–40. doi:10.1300/J070v11n02_02

Miller, F. G., & Lazowski, L. E. (2001). *The Adolescent Substance Abuse Subtle Screening Inventory-A2 (SASSI-A2) manual.* Springville, IN: SASSI Institute.

Millon, T. (with Millon, C., Davis, R. D., & Grossman, S. D.). (2006). *Millon Adolescent Clinical Inventory manual* (2nd ed.). Minneapolis: Pearson Assessments.

Morey, L. C. (2007). *Personality Assessment Inventory–Adolescent (PAI-A).* Lutz, FL: Psychological Assessment Resources.

Nichols, H. R., & Molinder, I. (1996). *Multiphasic Sex Inventory–II handbook.* Tacoma, WA: Nichols and Molinder Assessments.

Pomeroy, W. B., Wheeler, C. C., & Flax, C. C. (1982). *Taking a sex history: Interviewing and recording.* New York: Free Press Publishing.

Prentky, R. A., & Righthand, S. (2003). *Juvenile Sex Offender Assessment Protocol: Manual.* Washington, DC: US Department of Justice Office of Juvenile Justice and Delinquency Prevention.

Reynolds, C. R., & Kamphaus, R. W. (2004). *BASC-2: Behavior Assessment System for Children.* Bloomington, MN: Pearson.

Reynolds, W. M. (1998). *Adolescent Psychopathology Scale (APS).* Odessa, FL: Psychological Assessment Resources.

Rice, M. E., Harris, G. T., Lang, C., & Chaplin, T. C. (2012). Adolescents who have sexually offended: Is phallometry valid? *Sexual Abuse: A Journal of Research and Treatment, 24*(2), 133–152.

Schubert, C. A., Mulvey, E. P., & Glasheen, C. (2011). Influence of mental health and substance use problems and criminogenic risk on outcomes in serious juvenile offenders. *Journal of the American Academy of Child & Adolescent Psychiatry, 50*(9), 925–937.

Seto, M. C., Murphy, W. D., Page, J., & Ennis, L. (2003). Detecting anomalous sexual interests in juvenile sex offenders. *Annals of the New York Academy of Sciences, 989*(1), 118–130.

Smith, G., & Fischer, L. (1999). Assessment of juvenile sexual offenders: Reliability and validity of the Abel Assessment for Interest in Paraphilias. *Sexual Abuse: Journal of Research And Treatment, 11*(3), 207–216. doi:10.1177/107906329901100304

Stinson, J. D., & Becker, J. V. (2008). Assessing sexual deviance: A comparison of physiological, historical, and self-report measures. *Journal of Psychiatric Practice, 14*(6), 379–388.

Veneziano, C., & Veneziano, L. (2002). Adolescent sex offenders: A review of the literature. *Trauma, Violence, & Abuse, 3*(4), 247–260. http://dx.doi.org/10.1177/1524838002237329

Worling, J. R. (2006). Assessing sexual arousal with adolescent males who have offended sexually: Self-report and unobtrusively measured viewing time. *Sexual Abuse: A Journal of Research and Treatment, 18*(4), 383–400.

Worling, J. R., & Curwen, T. (2001). Estimate of risk of adolescent sexual offense recidivism (ERA-SOR; Version 2.0). In M. C. Calder (Ed.), *Juveniles and children who sexually abuse: Frameworks for assessment* (pp. 372–397). Lyme Regis, UK: Russell House.

CHAPTER 7

Assessing Risks and Needs

Sue Righthand

Gina Vincent

Rachael M. Huff

Public attitudes and policies regarding adolescents who have sexually abused continue to reflect a "nothing works" perspective, despite nearly half a century of debate and growing empirical research suggesting otherwise. Such attitudes may be supported by research findings indicating that some adults began their sexual offending careers as juveniles (Abel, Mittelman, & Becker, 1985; Knight & Prentky, 1993). Recently, Harris and Socia (2014) found that just the term *juvenile sex offender*, compared with more neutral terms such as *a minor youth* and *a crime of a sexual nature*, may conjure up images of a stereotypical, predatory adult sexual offender and, consequently, serious worries about the propensity of these youth to commit future sex crimes. Such fears can contribute to a perceived need for significant and severe interventions, such as public registration and Internet notifications of these youth's "sex offender" status (Harris and Socia, 2014). However, as will be discussed below and throughout this volume, a very small minority of youth who have sexually offended are identified as having perpetrated a new sexual offense (Caldwell, 2016; Finkelhor, Ormrod, & Chaffin, 2009). Thus, one-size-fits-all public policies, rather than individually tailored interventions, may cause more harm than good (Chaffin, 2008; Letourneau & Miner, 2005; Pittman & Nguyen, 2011; Zimring, 2004; Zimring, this volume, for a discussion of public policies).

Negative and pessimistic attitudes and unsupported beliefs about adolescents who sexually abuse are reminiscent of the decades-old nothing-works rehabilitation debate.

In 1974, Martinson reported the results of a review of published studies of criminal rehabilitation programs in operation between 1945 and 1967 conducted by him and his colleagues. They found that with few exceptions, rehabilitation did not significantly reduce recidivism and, hence, did not work (Martinson, 1974). The findings often were reported in the press and elsewhere under the headline "Nothing Works" (Miller, 1989).

Various researchers questioned the nothing-works findings, citing growing research evidence that some interventions did reduce criminal behavior and further, suggested that the wide acceptance of the nothing-works doctrine had more to do with social ideology than empirical research (Cullen & Gendreau, 1989). In fact, even Martinson (1979) reversed his position, remarking that "contrary to my previous position, some treatment programs do have an appreciable effect on recidivism" (p. 244). Later, Andrews, Bonta, and Hoge (1990) outlined three important guidelines (later referred to as principles; e.g., Andrews & Bonta, 2010) that can promote effective interventions and reduce criminal behavior. These principles make up the risk-need-responsivity (RNR) model (e.g., Andrews & Bonta, 2010; Hoge, 2016). While other principles (e.g., treatment integrity) are important for facilitating effective intervention as well (see, for example, Cullen & Gendreau, 1989; Lipsey, 2009), the RNR model provides a useful framework for this risk and needs assessment chapter.

According to the risk principle, recidivism rates are reduced when interventions are commensurate with one's risk of reoffending. In other words, someone presenting with many risk factors and insufficient protective factors would require the most rigorous interventions (e.g., frequent therapy sessions, multi-modal interventions, and, when necessary, placement in secure settings). In contrast, intensive and restrictive interventions with someone who has few risk factors and also has important protective ones may do more harm than good, especially when the person is mixed with individuals who present with significantly greater risk (Andrews, Bonta, & Wormith, 2011).

The need principle of the RNR model indicates that interventions are most effective when they target dynamic risk factors associated with criminal offending. A dynamic risk factor that appears to be particularly relevant to a particular individual's delinquent behavior and may increase the likelihood of future criminal behavior is referred to as a criminogenic need. Effective interventions target these criminogenic needs, for example by reducing or eliminating risk factors and by facilitating and building upon prosocial strengths (Andrews et al., 2011)—e.g., reducing negative peer association by increasing enjoyable activities with positive peers.

Finally, the responsivity principle maintains that interventions are likely to be most effective when the mode and method of treatment are matched to unique characteristics that may affect one's responsiveness to treatment (Andrews & Bonta, 2010; Hoge,

2016). General responsivity involves using interventions or treatment approaches that have been demonstrated to be effective with people involved in the juvenile and criminal justice system, such as cognitive-behavioral, social learning, and skill-building strategies. Specific responsivity includes factors that impede or facilitate treatment engagement, participation, and outcomes such as motivation to change, learning or mental health challenges, cultural factors, and so forth.

When assessing a youth's risk factors for conduct problems and intervention needs, identifying his or her assets, strengths, and protective factors is essential (Andrews et al., 2011). Thus, information about characteristics or circumstances that may buffer or moderate risk and enhance positive outcomes is relevant to the assessment and subsequent interventions.

Over the years, research studies have found the RNR model, or aspects of it, associated with lower rates of general criminal recidivism among adults (c.f. Andrews & Bonta, 2010; Wormith, Gendreau, & Bonta, 2012, for reviews of research studies) and youth (e.g., Koehler, Lösel, Akoensi, & Humphreys, 2013; Lipsey, 2009; Lowenkamp, Makarios, Latessa, Lemke, & Smith, 2010; Pealer & Latessa, 2004). In addition, Hanson, Bourgon, Helmus, and Hodgson (2009) conducted a meta-analysis of 23 individual studies of people with sexual offenses (3 studies involved adolescents) and found that the RNR principles were associated with lower sexual and non-sexual recidivism. Furthermore, programs adhering to all three RNR principles had the most reductions in both sexual and general recidivism.

In regard to risk assessment, the RNR model suggests clear, evidence-based, and relevant assessment domains. Individuals who engage in decision making and triaging youth to appropriate services, as well as other professionals who work with these youth, may find evaluations that utilize the RNR principles especially useful. These evaluations will be better able to guide the selection of interventions that may reduce the likelihood of offending and facilitate healthy, prosocial development.

THE RISK ASSESSMENT PROCESS

Risk assessment is a process of identifying factors that may increase or decrease the likelihood that a problem or harmful event, such as sexual abuse, will reoccur, and then recommending interventions that may reduce the likelihood of reoccurrence. Too often, however, when it comes to adolescents with illegal sexual behavior, the primary objectives of risk assessment overemphasize predicting the possibility of sexual reoffending and providing estimates or classifications intended to reflect the likelihood of a new sexual offense—i.e., trying to establish who is most likely to reoffend sexually

(Vitacco, Caldwell, Ryba, Malesky, & Kurus, 2009). An overemphasis on risk prediction or estimation misses the opportunity to use risk assessments in a manner that guides "prevention" of reoffending and facilitating prosocial development. If used properly, risk assessments identify criminogenic needs that, when effectively addressed, may increase desistance and reduce the aforementioned costly, severe, and potentially harmful public policy interventions. Because of the importance of the risk and the need principles for facilitating effective interventions, this chapter emphasizes both by focusing on risk assessment approaches and instruments that incorporate dynamic risk factors (criminogenic needs) that may be the best targets for intervention.

A Forensic Context

Adolescents referred for sexual offending behaviors typically have engaged in behaviors that are illegal. Consequently, clients, parents, or caregivers would rarely request an assessment of these behaviors. Generally, the youth is referred by a third party such as a child welfare worker, juvenile justice staff, school personnel, or the courts. As such, the nature of the assessment is non-voluntary and the findings are not confidential. As already discussed, assessment results also may have significant and sometimes severe, life-altering consequences for the youth and his or her family. Thus, it is imperative that the youth and family be well informed of the risks and benefits of participating in the assessment, that parents or guardians consent to the evaluation, and that the youth be provided with this information as well as the opportunity to assent to the evaluation. (See Grossi, Brereton, & Prentky, this volume, for a full discussion of forensic assessments.)

Risk assessments are requested for a variety of reasons and in diverse settings (e.g., child welfare system, schools, and the juvenile justice system) (DeMatteo, Wolbransky, & LaDuke, 2016; Prentky, Righthand, & Lamade, 2016). For examples, child protective workers may wonder about whether a youth who has sexually offended can live at home with siblings safely. School personnel may question whether a youth with illegal sexual behaviors should continue at school or be placed in an alternative school, or even taught at home with limited age-appropriate peer interaction. Juvenile justice personnel, attorneys, and judges may question the appropriateness of a diversion program or, post-adjudication, the most appropriate placement to facilitate community safety and the youth's healthy development. Although most youth who have sexually offended may be able to receive treatment in the community (Chaffin, 2008), assessment findings may indicate that a youth requires more intensive interventions than are safely available while living at home or with another caregiver and receiving outpatient treatment. Placement in a residential treatment program or a correctional facility may be needed.

Risk assessments also may be used to aid other risk-relevant determinations, such as whether a youth should be transferred from the juvenile court to the adult criminal justice system (Grossi et al., this volume), whether a juvenile should be placed on a public sexual offender registry (Vitacco et al., 2009), or, as noted by the Association for the Treatment of Sexual Abusers (2015), in Pennsylvania, whether a youth "aging out" of the juvenile system should be committed indeterminately as a sexually violent predator. The results of these assessments can have profound outcomes for adolescents and their families, outcomes that may be long-term and significantly life-altering.

Referral sources in these cases typically want to know whether the youth will engage in illegal sexual behavior again. Although the answer to such a question is elusive, risk assessments can provide referral sources with information that may facilitate safety, guide effective interventions, and promote prosocial lifestyles.

Further, it is important to emphasize that extensive research (e.g., Caldwell, 2010; 2016; McCann & Lussier, 2008; Viljoen, Mordell, & Beneteau, 2012; Zimring, 2004) has shown that most adolescents with illegal sexual behavior do not reoffend sexually. Studies suggest that generally between 85 and 95 percent do not reoffend with a sexual offense (Finkelhor et al., 2009); if they reoffend at all, it is likely to be with a non-sexual offense. Moreover, research suggests that effective treatment may further reduce recidivism rates (e.g., Heilbrun, Lee, & Cottle, 2005; Worling, Litteljohn, & Bookalam, 2010). Additionally, findings from a recent large meta-analysis suggest that the rates of sexual reoffending have declined, perhaps due to improved treatment interventions and community supervision. Caldwell (2016) conducted a large meta-analysis of 106 follow-up studies of 33,783 adjudicated youth who had offended sexually. He found that for the overall sample, the base rate for sexual recidivism was nearly 5 percent; the base rate for non-sexual recidivism was approximately 41 percent. Studies conducted between 2000 and 2015 identified an average base rate of sexual recidivism at 2.75 percent, whereas studies conducted between 1980 and 1995 showed a base rate of 10.30 percent. This is a 73 percent reduction in sexual recidivism over time.

Findings regarding the low base rate of sexual offending should inform risk assessments and related recommendations. Yet some youth do reoffend. Therefore, high-quality risk assessments are required.

The Process of Risk Assessment

As discussed in the John D. and Catherine T. MacArthur Foundation guide for implementing risk assessment in juvenile justice settings (Vincent, Guy, & Grisso, 2012), risk assessment is not simply the administration of a risk assessment instrument. It is a process. The process involves conducting high-quality assessments that systematically gather information from multiple sources, e.g., the youth, family, school, police, and others; analyzing the consistency or divergence of information across domains; and identifying dynamic or variable risk and protective factors that could increase risk or, conversely, protect against future abusive and illegal behavior. The process also involves using the assessment information, along with valid risk assessment instruments, to formulate a plan for an effective course of action that is in line with the RNR approach and also promotes and enhances protective factors.

Holistic Assessments

In order to adequately assess the RNR-related factors and provide a useful assessment of the youth and his or her circumstances, a number of risk-relevant areas should be considered. Sexual behavior in adolescents, like other aspects of human development (e.g., Bronfenbrenner, 1977; Lussier, 2015), is multi-determined. It involves the interplay of bio-psycho-social, individual, and socio-ecological factors (Cicchetti, 2010; Cicchetti & Toth, 2009). As such, characteristics and functioning of the individual, family, and other caregivers, as well as other social (e.g., peers) and community (e.g., schools, neighborhoods) factors, must be considered.

Further, high-quality assessments do not limit their focus to problematic and abusive sexual behaviors. As noted earlier, research findings have consistently indicated that if these youth reoffend at all, it is likely to be with a non-sexual offense (e.g., Caldwell, 2016; Heilbrun et al., 2005; Viljoen et al., 2012). Continued reoffending of any kind is in nobody's best interest; thus, it is important that risk assessment address non-sexual delinquent offending and related criminogenic needs, as well as sexual offending.

Consistent with the responsivity principle discussed earlier, in addition to risk and protective factors associated with offending, other characteristics and circumstances can affect treatment responsiveness and outcomes, and these must be assessed as well. For example, relevant records or clinical assessments related to possible learning challenges, personal maltreatment and traumas, and co-occurring disorders, as well as possible strengths including motivation for change, can help elucidate this domain.

In sum, evaluators can be most helpful to referral sources, as well as the youth and his or her family, by providing structured, focused, and holistic risk and needs assessments that identify individual, family, social, and situational factors associated with abusive sexual behavior and general delinquency. Such risk-relevant information is required to provide clear, practical, and case-specific recommendations for effective interventions that match the individual's and the family's unique treatment needs.

Risk and Protective Factors

A risk factor is anything that increases the possibility that an individual is going to reoffend. Risk factors can be static (e.g., prior sexual offenses, age at first sexual offense) or dynamic and capable of change (e.g., attitudes and beliefs that condone sexual abuse). For example, sexual preoccupation is a dynamic risk factor because it may increase the likelihood one will reoffend sexually; yet, it is possible that the preoccupation can subside as a result of maturation. These dynamic risk factors are often referred to as criminogenic needs, a term that technically refers to factors that, if changed, will be associated with a reduction in risk (Andrews & Bonta, 2010).

Protective factors are assets of the youth or his or her environment that may moderate or "buffer" risk factors and decrease the likelihood that the risk factors will influence offending (e.g., Cicchetti, 2010; Griffin, Beech, Print, Bradshaw, & Quayle, 2008). Like risk factors, protective factors may be static (e.g., intelligence) or can be dynamic and changeable (e.g., social competence or emotion regulation). In general, the more protective factors, the greater the likelihood of positive functioning, yet resilient functioning may be uneven across time and domains (Cicchetti, 2010; Luthar, Cicchetti, & Becker, 2000; Griffin et al., 2008).

There has been limited research on risk and, especially, protective factors specific to youth who have sexually abused others (Lussier & Chouinard Thivierge, this volume; McCann & Lussier, 2008; Prentky et al., 2016). Existing studies have been plagued with an array of conceptual, operational, and methodological problems, including small sample sizes, different definitions of reoffending, varying follow-up times, and the low base rate of sexual reoffending, to name a few (Heilbrun et al., 2005; McCann & Lussier, 2008). Findings from one study often have not been replicated in others (Worling & Långström, 2006). Meta-analyses of risk factors for sexual offending have been limited due to a lack of studies and inconsistencies in measurement across studies (Heilbrun et al., 2005; McCann & Lussier, 2008).

Because of the inconsistencies and methodological problems, research findings regarding risk factors for sexual reoffending must be considered cautiously. In their meta-analysis of nine studies of adolescents with one or more arrests for sexual offenses, ranging in age from 7 through 20, Heilbrun and colleagues (2005) found several criminal history variables related to sexual reoffenses. These static factors included younger age at first sexual offense, non-contact initial offenses, and offending against acquaintances. They also found that having participated in treatment designed to reduce sexual offending was related to lower rates of reoffending.

In 2008, McCann and Lussier conducted a meta-analysis of 18 studies of varying sizes (N = 3,189). They explored 15 risk factors related to sexual deviancy and antisociality, the two strongest risk factors associated with sexual recidivism in adult studies (Hanson & Bussière, 1998; Hanson & Morton-Bourgon, 2005). Individual risk factors that were significantly associated with sexual reoffending, and that were replicated in three or more studies, included stranger victim (not found predictive in the Heilbrun et al., 2005, study), child victim (in contrast with peers or adults), using threats/weapons, prior sexual offenses, and male victims. McCann and Lussier also found the domains of sexual deviancy and antisociality related to sexual recidivism. The authors concluded, however, that although some risk factors and domains showed promise, their relationships to reoffending (effect sizes) were small. They further emphasized that adolescents are still maturing, and that the importance of such dynamic processes had not been incorporated into the available research studies.

McCann and Lussier (2008) also replicated the common finding that most adolescents with sexual offenses who reoffend do so in non-sexual ways. Consequently, they suggested that risk factors associated with non-sexual delinquent offending may be very relevant for youth who commit sexual offenses.

Decades of research have identified eight major risk factors for delinquency and adult criminal behavior, factors that are associated with the RNR model: (a) history of conduct disorder or criminal activity, (b) family or parent dysfunction, (c) education or employment deficits, (d) antisocial peer associations, (e) substance abuse, (f) poor use of leisure time, (g) personality or behavior dysfunction, and (h) antisocial attitudes, values, and beliefs (Hoge, 2016). Given the substantial non-sexual reoffense rates among adolescents with illegal sexual behavior, these factors warrant assessment. Certainly some of these factors may be related to sexual as well as non-sexual reoffending. Yet, as Spice and colleagues recently noted, "The literature regarding risk factors for sexual recidivism among JSOs remains conflicted" (Spice, Viljoen, Latzman, Scalora, & Ullman, 2013, p. 350). Clearly, more studies regarding the most relevant risk factors for adolescents with illegal sexual behaviors are required.

Recently, Righthand and colleagues (Righthand, Baird, Way, & Seto, 2014) turned their attention to dynamic risk factors that may be relevant treatment targets when working with adolescents who have been sexually abusive. They surveyed the empirical literature on risk and protective factors associated with adolescent sexual reoffending, the research on adult sexual recidivism, and studies related to non-sexual recidivism to identify potentially relevant domains for intervention. They found research evidence supporting five primary dynamic risk factor domains that require assessment and may warrant intervention. The domains are as follows:

1. *Sexuality.* Factors within this domain include healthy attitudes and beliefs about sexual behavior in contrast with those that support sexually abusive behavior. Also included is socially appropriate, legal, and non-problematic sexual self-regulation contrasted with inappropriate and poor sexual regulation. Age-appropriate sexual interests contrasted with attraction and arousal to prepubescent children or sexual violence, and hypersexual drive and excessive sexual preoccupation are other areas to assess, although persistent patterns of non-normative sexual interests or sexual drive appear infrequent among adolescents.

2. *Social Bonds and Orientation.* This domain involves the extent to which the adolescent is prosocially engaged, particularly as contrasted with an antisocial orientation. Prosocial bonds may be exemplified by attitudes and beliefs that support lawful behavior, associating with like-minded peers, and positively contributing to benefit the good of society. In contrast, someone with an asocial orientation may disregard others and social conventions and avoid social engagement, while an antisocial orientation may be indicated by a lack of adherence to social norms and values, antisocial attitudes and beliefs, delinquent peers or gang associations, and criminal behavior.

3. *General Self-Regulation.* This domain includes problems and challenges with self-regulation, which may be exemplified by impulsivity, school behavior problems, or substance abuse, as well as emotional self-regulation difficulties, including problems identifying, expressing, and coping with negative and stressful emotions.

4. *Social Competence.* This domain includes having mutually satisfying prosocial relationships and friendships and age-appropriate intimate relationships. It involves prosocial engagement as contrasted with social isolation or emotional congruence with much younger children rather than peers and adults.

5. *Socio-Ecological Factors.* These include family and caregiver characteristics as well as community and societal factors. Family factors involve child–caregiver relationships—for example, conflicts and insufficient monitoring contrasted with positive caregiver discipline, supervision, and support—as well as help from extended family

members or other positive adults. Other socio-ecological factors may include positive community supports, such as school outreach and prosocial, supervised community activities or, in contrast, school or community rejection.

While researchers and practitioners concerned with sexually abusive behavior searched for sexual-offense-specific risk factors for reoffending, the field virtually ignored the literature on juvenile delinquency. Further, little attention was paid to the study of child and adolescent development, the field of developmental psychopathology (e.g., Cicchetti & Toth, 2009; Cicchetti & Sroufe, 2000), or life course criminology and rehabilitation, including the concepts of desistance (e.g., Lussier, 2015; Lussier & Chouinard Thivierge, this volume) and resilience (e.g., Cicchitti & Toth, 2009). These areas of study have much to offer for understanding, assessing, and intervening effectively with these youth. For example, as the developmental psychopathology field has found, static and historical risk factors are correlated with reoffending but are not necessarily causal (Cicchetti & Lynch, 1993; Cicchetti & Rogosch, 1996). Moreover, multiple risk factors may increase the likelihood of problems and negative outcomes and hence, greater risk, but they are not necessarily determinative (e.g., Cicchetti, 2010).

Many structured adult and general delinquency risk assessment tools provide algorithms for determining reoffense risk, sometimes by simply summing risk factors and sometimes by applying weights to them. Often, it is unclear how protective factors should be weighted, and these are not included in the algorithms. What is the best method for weighing these factors is an empirical question. Some risk factors may be more relevant to reoffending in a particular case—and therefore carry more weight—than other risk factors. Further, factors interact within and across the socio-ecological system. Consequently, their dynamic nature and interplay require thoughtful consideration so that appropriate, individualized treatment targets are identified and effectively addressed.

As we conduct risk and needs assessment, we would do well to remember that not only are adolescents in a rapid phase of development (e.g., see Modecki, this volume, for a discussion), but that development is multi-determined. It involves the interplay of bio-psycho-social, individual, and socio-ecological factors that contribute to adaptive and maladaptive functioning during adolescence and also across the life span (e.g., Bronfenbrenner, 1977; Cicchetti & Toth, 2009; Cicchetti, 2010; Lussier, 2015). By identifying factors that may increase risk, those that may protect against or buffer risk, and their interactions, we may be better able to help adolescents and their families increase prosocial functioning despite risk and adversity, and thereby enhance and support resilient functioning (Cicchetti, 2010) while increasing community safety.

APPROACHES TO RISK ASSESSMENT

There are three primary approaches that evaluators typically use or rely upon to organize and analyze their assessment data and evaluate risks and needs (DeMatteo et al.,
2016). These methods include unstructured professional judgments, actuarial assessment instruments, structured professional judgment, and sometimes variants of the
three (e.g., for further discussion see Melton, Petrila, Poythress, & Slobogin, 2007;
Skeem & Monahan, 2011).

Unstructured Professional Judgments

Unstructured professional judgments involve clinicians or other professionals relying
on their training and experience when conducting risk and needs assessments, including assessment of the likelihood of reoffending, without using research-based checklists or actuarial tables of risk. The accuracy of unstructured clinical judgments has
long been criticized (e.g., Dawes, Faust, & Meehl, 1989; Hanson & Morton-Bourgon,
2009) and can involve a range of problems, such as information-processing challenges and cognitive shortcuts that can hinder human judgments (Norcross, Hogan, &
Koocher, 2008). Research supporting more structured approaches and the use of risk
assessment instruments has accumulated (Hanson & Morton-Bourgon, 2009; Viljoen
et al., 2012). Despite being the least reliable risk assessment method, unstructured professional judgments are commonly used (Storey, Watt, & Hart, 2015).

Actuarial Assessment Instruments

Actuarial decision making is mechanical and "involves a formal, algorithmic, objective
procedure (e.g., equation) to reach the decision" (Grove & Meehl, 1996, p. 293). Actuarial
assessment instruments are generally (but not always) constructed using items selected
based on a statistical association with a given outcome (reoccurrence of violence) and
are scored according to some algorithm to produce a judgment about the likelihood of
reoffending. Often, these tools contain only static risk factors; however, some actuarial
tools contain both static and dynamic risk factors. These static/dynamic actuarial tools
are often constructed based on the empirical evidence of significant risk factors that
are both theoretical and relevant for case planning. When used appropriately, such as
by ensuring the individual's general characteristics (e.g., age and gender) are consistent
with the group whose outcomes are known, actuarial tools enable evaluators to report
that the subject of their evaluation scores similarly to people who typically have, or do
not have, the outcome of interest.

Despite the statistical superiority of actuarial tools relative to unstructured clinical
judgment, several critics have pointed out some limitations of actuarial assessments and

the dangers of over-reliance on actuarial decision making (Berlin, Galbreath, Geary, & McGlone, 2003; Borum, 1996; Dvoskin & Heilbrun, 2001; Grisso, 2000; Hart, 2003). This is most notably an issue with actuarial tools comprising mostly static factors, which may have limited ideographic, case-specific clinical utility. A consequence of the empirical test construction methods is that many risk factors make little sense theoretically or clinically. Consequently, assessment procedures are not tied to intervention strategies in a prescriptive manner, and they are not capable of measuring changes in risk. Researchers have cautioned that static actuarial instruments are for the most part atheoretical, cover only a limited range of predictor variables, and are not useful for intervention planning or reassessments to measure individual progress (Borum, 1996; Dvoskin & Heilbrun, 2001; Hart, 2003; Hoge & Andrews, 2010).

Structured Professional Judgment Instruments

Structured professional judgment (SPJ) assessment instruments provide professionals with checklists of risk-relevant factors that guide assessment of an individual's risk and intervention needs. In this approach to assessing risk, structure is imposed on which risk factors should be considered and how they should be measured, but the way in which factors are combined is left to the discretion of the evaluator. The evaluator's discretion similarly is valued in terms of generating the final estimate of risk. Like the static/dynamic actuarial tools, the items on SPJ tools are generally selected based on empirical research on static and dynamic factors, and include factors that guide decisions about risk and treatment planning. The intent of SPJ instruments was to improve human judgment by adding structure, and to improve actuarial decision making by adding more professional discretion (Borum & Douglas, 2003). They typically contain static and dynamic risk factors (and may contain protective factors), assuming that risk can change as a result of treatment quality and quantity, developmental factors, protective factors, context, and maturation.

The difference between SPJ tools and the static/dynamic actuarial tools is that SPJ tools can result in a final judgment by the rater regarding the overall level of risk (frequently communicated as Low, Moderate, or High) based on a combination of individual and socio-ecological risk factors, protective factors, and idiosyncratic factors present. No algorithm is used to produce a quantitative index of risk level. Despite this seeming subjectivity, meta-analyses of many SPJ instruments have determined that the predictive accuracy is equivalent to actuarial tools (Guy, 2008; Olver, Stockdale, & Wormith, 2009; Singh, Grann, & Fazel, 2011).

SEXUAL-OFFENSE-SPECIFIC RISK ASSESSMENT INSTRUMENTS: IS THE TOOL ANY GOOD?

When using risk assessment tools, whether an actuarial or SPJ instrument, or a variant thereof, an evaluator must ask him- or herself: Is the tool any good? As with any assessment measure, issues of reliability and validity need to be considered carefully. It is necessary to determine if the measure was found reliable and valid in multiple investigations, including studies by researchers not involved in the development of the risk assessment tool (Vincent et al., 2012).

There are various types of reliability, but inter-rater reliability is most important for risk assessment evaluations (Hecker, 2014; Vincent et al., 2012). Inter-rater reliability evaluates whether the assessment tool yields consistent findings when employed by different evaluators.

Another critical question is whether a risk assessment tool is valid for its intended purpose—whether it is sufficiently associated with the outcome of interest. When considering using a risk assessment tool, it is necessary to evaluate whether it assesses what it claims to measure. Thus, when responding to concerns about whether a youth may engage in future sexual offending (or non-sexual offending), it is necessary to ensure that selected risk assessment tools are associated with the possibility of repeat offending and with the type of reoffending. It is also important to determine that the risk assessment tool has been validated for use with the population characteristic of individuals being evaluated (e.g., girls, minorities, the setting) and to carefully consider its appropriateness in the absence of such research.

As discussed above, when requesting risk assessments, referral sources typically want to know: Will this youth sexually offend again? However, risk assessments and risk assessment instruments cannot identify individuals who will recidivate without mistaking many people as likely recidivists when they are not (false positives), and erroneously identifying others as unlikely to reoffend when in fact they do (false negatives). There are many reasons for erroneous predictions including insufficient research and knowledge about relevant risk and protective factors associated with sexual reoffending, how such factors may interact, and the malleability of risk. Risk, in adolescents, is especially variable due to individual characteristics, changing life circumstances, and rapid physical, cognitive, emotional, social, and behavioral developmental changes. Thus, risk ratings that describe the youth and his or her *current* circumstances in relation to other youth (i.e., few, moderate, or high number of current risks and needs), along with case plans to reduce risk while promoting protective factors, will be most helpful.

Evaluating Offense-Specific Risk Assessment Tools

Assessment tools for evaluating the risk of non-sexual and sexual reoffending by adults and juveniles have proliferated in recent years (Singh, 2013). Criticism of these measures and debates concerning their utility have evolved as well (e.g., Vitacco et al., 2009). In addition, there are questions about the research methodology used to investigate the validity of risk assessment tools (Singh, 2013; Singh, Desmarais, & Van Dorn, 2013). A full discussion of these concerns is beyond the scope of this chapter.

When reviewing studies that evaluate the predictive validity of risk assessment tools, it is important to focus on the full report, including the limitations sections. No study is without limitations. As previously noted, studies of risk and protective factors associated with sexual recidivism among youth who have prior sexual offenses often conflict. Studies of adolescent sexual-offense-specific risk assessment tools have had inconsistent results as well (e.g., Prentky et al., 2016; Viljoen et al., 2012). Given that these risk assessment instruments include risk factors reported in the professional literature, which vary in empirical support, these diverse outcomes are not surprising.

Methodological challenges likely contribute to the mixed results. For example, the low frequency of detected sexual reoffending (the base-rate problem) adds to difficulties identifying empirical risk factors associated with sexual reoffending, factors that may be included in risk assessment tools. The base-rate problem contributes to challenges validating sexual-offense-specific risk assessment tools as well; it is very difficult to predict infrequent events (Szmukler, 2001).

Other research challenges relevant to validating adolescent sexual offense risk assessment tools include the heterogeneity of adolescents who sexually abuse (Seto & Lalumière, 2010; van Wijk & Boonmann, this volume) and the necessity to rely on available samples of youth that may not be representative of other adolescents with sexual offenses. Sample sizes generally are small and vary in a number of ways, such as the youth's settings (e.g., outpatient, residential, or correctional placement) and environment (e.g., from rural, suburban, or urban environments; varying home countries). In addition, some studies only include youth with contact offenses, while others include those with both contact and non-contact offenses. Further, adolescents also vary in their histories of non-sexual offending, with some committing only sexual offenses (e.g., Lussier & Chouinard Thivierge, this volume; van Wijk & Boonmann, this volume). Age ranges vary and different racial groups may be over- or underrepresented. Further, studies often include adolescents in treatment programs, while others may include those who are not. For those in treatment, the quality of the treatment they receive generally is unknown. Understandably, such differences may contribute to varied outcomes (e.g., Rajlic & Gretton, 2010; Viljoen et al., 2008; Viljoen et al., 2015).

Additionally, most studies are archival and are limited to the data included in a case file. The quality of the information in the files may not adequately or sufficiently represent the youth and relevant risk and protective factors. This retrospective research approach, although often a necessary step for validating a measure, is inconsistent with assessment recommendations for instruments that stress the importance of gathering multiple sources of accurate information and using multiple methods of assessment (Prentky & Righthand, 2003; Worling & Curwen, 2001). Lastly, outcome measures and the procedures used to assess recidivism may also vary. Some studies may use credible reports of additional sexually abusive behavior, new charges, or other factors. The lengths of the follow-up also may differ, as may time at risk in the community.

In addition to the above procedural limitations, recent criticisms of commonly used predictive validity indicators suggest that many studies misinterpret the commonly used statistics, particularly the area under the curve (AUC) for receiver operating characteristic curves (ROCs) (Singh et al., 2013). For example, Singh (2013) observed that the AUC is commonly mistaken as a reflection of how accurate the tool is in predicting actual outcomes, while it was designed to determine how effectively the tool is able to discriminate between those who went on to have the outcome of interest and those who did not (e.g., that a randomly selected individual who sexually reoffended would have a higher score on the risk assessment measure than a randomly selected person who did not sexually recidivate). This misinterpretation is important because it can lead to confusing higher AUC coefficients with better predictive ability, and commonly used benchmarks of the effect size magnitudes (i.e., small, moderate, and large) may be misinterpreted as indicative of the strength of the tool's ability to predict outcomes. Even though AUC statistics are not as affected by fluctuations in base rates as some other statistical approaches, they are not immune and may be impacted by other factors, such as small sample sizes (n < 200; Hanczar et al., 2010, as cited in Singh, 2013). Consequently, when evaluating the predictive validity of a tool, reviewers must consider an array of research methodology factors.

ADOLESCENT SEXUAL-OFFENSE-SPECIFIC RISK ASSESSMENT TOOLS

There are an increasing number of risk assessment tools designed to facilitate risk and needs assessments of male adolescents who have sexually abused. Varied and unsupportive findings are sometimes reported, which have led some in the field to argue against the use of such measures, unless they are refined or until new tools with increased validity are developed (e.g., Vitacco et al., 2009). Yet without adequately validated measures used with fidelity to their manuals, and used appropriately as a component of the risk and needs assessment process, evaluators would be required to rely solely on unstructured professional/clinical judgment. Fortunately and more positively, some risk assessment measures, in fact, have been validated and cross-validated in multiple studies, including replications by independent researchers and/or in an independent meta-analytic review.

It is beyond the scope of this chapter to review all risk assessment instruments designed for youth with sexual offenses. Thus, this chapter focuses on sexual-offense-specific risk assessment measures that have been used frequently (McGrath, Cumming, Burchard, Zeoli, & Ellerby, 2010), have demonstrated predictive validity in multiple studies, have been available for independent investigation, and have meta-analytic evidence. These instruments are the Estimate of Risk of Adolescent Sexual Offense Recidivism (ERASOR; Version 2.0; Worling & Curwen, 2001), the Juvenile Sexual Offender Assessment Inventory II (J-SOAP-II; Prentky & Righthand, 2003), and the Juvenile Sexual Offense Recidivism Risk Assessment Tool–II (JSORRAT-II; Epperson, Ralston, Fowers, DeWitt, & Gore, 2006; Epperson, Ralston, Fowers, & DeWitt, 2016). Other sexual offense risk assessment tools available for adolescents, which are not reviewed here because they do not currently meet the above criteria, include Juvenile Risk Appraisal Scale (JRAS; New Jersey Attorney General Office, 2006) and the Multiplex Empirically Guided Inventory of Ecological Aggregates for Assessing Sexually Abusive Adolescents and Children (MEGA; Miccio-Fonseca, 2006; 2010).

Juvenile Sexual Offense Risk Assessment Instruments
Briefly, the ERASOR is a 25-item SPJ instrument with 12 static and 13 dynamic risk factors identified in the research and professional literature as related to juvenile and adult sexual recidivism (Worling & Curwen, 2001). The ERASOR was designed as a single-scale instrument, although the 25 risk items are categorized under five headings: Sexual Interests, Attitudes and Behaviors; Historical Sexual Assaults; Psychosocial Functioning; Family/Environmental Functioning; and Treatment. Items are rated as either: Present, Possibly or Partially Present; Not Present; or Unknown. The ERASOR is designed to facilitate short-term, empirically guided estimates of the risk of a sexual reoffense for youth aged 12 through 18.

The J-SOAP-II is a 28-item instrument containing 16 static and 12 dynamic items identified in the professional and research literature as associated with sexual and criminal offending. The J-SOAP-II was designed for boys in the age range of 12 through 18 who have been adjudicated for sexual offenses as well as non-adjudicated youth with a history of sexually coercive behavior. J-SOAP-II items are rated with a 0–2 format to reflect the degree of their presence or absence. The J-SOAP-II has four subscales:

(a) Sexual Drive/Sexual Preoccupation; (b) Impulsive, Antisocial Behavior; (c) Clinical Intervention; and (d) Community Stability. The J-SOAP-II is not an actuarial measure but also differs from a typical SPJ tool in that the authors recommend that evaluators calculate risk ratios for the total score and subscales and then consider these findings as information sources in comprehensive, short-term risk assessments that guide interventions and treatment planning (Prentky & Righthand, 2003).

The JSORRAT-II is a 12-item actuarial measure comprising only static risk factors designed for use with adolescents aged 12 through 18. In contrast with the ERASOR and J-SOAP-II, the JSORRAT-II's items were selected based on statistical associations between factors and reoffending using archival records of juveniles adjudicated for a sexual offense. Items are scored solely on the basis of file information. Some items are scored on a present/absent basis (i.e., 0 or 1), while others are scored on a 3-point (0–1–2) or 4-point (0–1–2–3) scale to indicate the degree to which the item is present or severe. The authors (Epperson et al., 2016) have noted that the JSORRAT-II may be used as a measure of relative risk to inform treatment decisions and similar clinical determinations. The authors also indicate that the JSORRAT-II "may be used to argue against the application of adult statutes, policies, and procedures to juveniles" (p. 1) in any state, but should be used to provide probability estimates of the risk for sexual reoffending only in states where it has been validated (currently Iowa and Utah).

Reliability and Validity Evidence

The inter-rater reliability of the ERASOR, the J-SOAP-II, and the JSORRAT-II are described in multiple studies and generally have ranged from adequate to excellent (e.g., ERASOR: Chu, Ng, Fong, & Teoh, 2012; Rajcik & Gretton, 2010; Viljoen, Elkovitch, Scalora, & Ullman, 2009; Worling, Bookalam, & Litteljohn, 2012; J-SOAP-II: Caldwell & Dickenson, 2009; Martinez, Rosenfeld, Cruise, & Martin, 2015; Viljoen et al., 2008; JSORRAT-II: Epperson & Ralston, 2015; Ralston, Epperson, & Edwards, 2016). It is important to keep in mind that once an instrument has been found reliable in multiple studies, particularly by independent evaluators, any later findings of low inter-rater reliability may be due to factors other than the instrument, such as insufficient training, rater drift, the need for booster training, or a lack of adequate information for reliable scoring.

As noted earlier, findings from individual predictive validity studies of juvenile sexual offense risk assessment tools sometimes have yielded inconsistent results. In view of these divergent findings, Viljoen and colleagues (2012) conducted a comprehensive meta-analysis of 33 published and unpublished predictive validity studies (31 independent samples) to examine the predictive validity of several juvenile sexual offense risk assessment instruments (i.e., the ERASOR, J-SOAP II, JSORRAT-II), as well as an adult tool (the Static-99; Hanson & Thornton, 1999). Meta-analyses enable researchers to aggregate data from multiple studies, increasing sample size and statistical power in the analyses, thereby alleviating some of the methodological challenges inherent in risk assessment validation research.

The meta-analytic findings (Viljoen et al., 2012) indicated that the total scores on each instrument significantly predicted sexual recidivism despite moderate to high heterogeneity across many studies. No significant differences between measures were found. Aggregate correlations ranged from 0.12 to 0.20. Although these correlations appear quite small, the authors noted that this statistic is sensitive to the low base rates of rare events (Rice & Harris, 2005). Aggregate AUC findings, which tend to be less sensitive to low base rates, ranged from 0.64 to 0.67, which Viljoen et al. noted are generally considered moderate effect sizes (Rice & Harris, 2005).

Viljoen et al. (2012) identified 11 investigations of the ERASOR; 10 were included in their meta-analysis of the total score and 9 were included in results related to the SPJ risk rating. Significant effect sizes for both the ERASOR total score (a summation of ratings) (AUC = 0.66, 95% CI [0.61, 0.72]) and the ERASOR SPJ risk rating (evaluator qualitative judgments of risk based on the ratings) (AUC = 0.66, 95% CI [0.60, 0.71]) were found in regard to sexual recidivism.

Viljoen et al. (2012) identified 15 studies of the J-SOAP-II, but not all were included in their analyses. The nine studies that investigated the J-SOAP-II total score yielded an average AUC of 0.67 (95% CI [0.59–0.75]). The researchers also found that the J-SOAP-II Scale 1, Sex Drive/Preoccupation (AUC = 0.61, 95% CI [0.53–0.69]); Scale 2, the Antisocial/Impulsive Scale (AUC = 0.63, 95% CI [0.58–0.69]); Scale 3, the Intervention Scale (AUC = 0.60, 95% CI [0.54–0.66]); and Scale 4, Community Adjustment (AUC = 0.70, 95% CI [0.60–0.80]) significantly predicted sexual recidivism. The number of individual studies that investigated the subscales varied from 8 to 13.

The meta-analysis included seven studies of the Juvenile Sexual Offense Recidivism Risk Assessment Tool–II (JSORRAT-II; Epperson et al., 2006), which also indicated a moderate effect for the total score (AUC = 0.64, 95% CI [0.54–0.74]). In addition to sexual recidivism, Viljoen et al. (2012) found the total scores of the ERASOR and J-SOAP-II were predictive of general reoffending (defined as any type of offending including non-sexual reoffending). There were an insufficient number of studies on the JSORRAT-II in the meta-analysis to evaluate its predictive validity with general reoffending.

In summary, Viljoen et al. (2012) concluded that the sexual-offense-specific risk assessment instruments provided clear benefit over unstructured clinical judgments and that they appeared to assess some unique sexual-offense-specific factors not present in general delinquency-focused risk assessment tools. They noted, how-ever, that these instruments do not have sufficient predictive accuracy for making determinations about risk that require an exceptionally high degree of accuracy, such as lifetime registration or indeterminate civil commitment. Instead, these instru-ments, particularly those including dynamic risk factors (i.e., the ERASOR and the J-SOAP-II) may be useful for identifying treatment needs and facilitating effective interventions.

Since the Viljoen et al. (2012) study, there have been several additional research publications exploring the predictive validity of these risk assessment measures. For example, Worling and Langton (2015) recently used the ERASOR to investigate the incremental validity of including protective factors when assessing risk. The predictive validity of the ERASOR was supported again, although the protective factors did not improve predictive validity.

Two additional studies that explored the predictive validity of the J-SOAP-II have been published. Ralston and Epperson (2013) included the J-SOAP-II in a large, com-parative analysis of two juvenile and two adult sexual-offense-specific risk assessment tools that investigated 636 juveniles who had offended sexually. Because the records were archival, and from many years ago, dynamic information necessary for scoring Scales 3 and 4, the Intervention and Community Adjustment scales of the J-SOAP-II, were unavailable and the scales could not be scored. Ralston and Epperson (2013) found that Scale 1 significantly predicted juvenile sexual recidivism (AUC = 0.76, 99.9% CI [0.67–0.85]), and juvenile violent sexual recidivism (AUC = 0.78, 99.9% CI [0.69–0.87]).[1] Scale 2, the Antisocial/Impulsive scale, also was predictive of juvenile sexual recidivism (AUC = 0.75, 99.9% CI [0.66–0.84]) and juvenile violent sexual recidivism (AUC = 0.77, 99.9% CI [0.67–0.87]). Scales 1 and 2 did not predict violent recidivism once sexual violence was excluded. Scale 1 significantly predicted sexual recidivism occurring in adulthood (AUC = 0.65, 99.9% CI [0.51–0.79]) as did Scale 2 (AUC = 0.66, 99.9% CI [0.53–0.80]). The reduced accuracy of the J-SOAP-II in predicting recidivism in adulthood was consistent with findings for the other tools included in this study and reflects the importance of using such adolescent measures for short-term risk assessments only.

Additionally, Martinez et al. (2015) recently considered whether the J-SOAP-II pre-dicted sexual reoffending across settings by investigating its utility in a medium-security

---

1. Ralston and Epperson (2013) reported they selected a 99.9 percent confidence interval, a more narrowly defined level of significance, to reduce the risk of a Type I error (i.e., to reduce the risk of false positives and identifying individuals as recidivists when they are not), thereby increasing the significance of their findings.

facility (n = 70) in contrast with an unlocked residential treatment center (n = 86).[2] The predictive validity for the full total score, including Scale 4, was moderate, but not statistically significant (AUC = 0.64, 95% CI [0.49, 0.80]). They also found moderate but not significant predictive validity for the total score without Scale 4; the AUC was 0.63 (95% CI [0.47, 0.78]). Regarding the J-SOAP-II subscales, they found support for the dynamic scales only. They found Scale 3 (AUC = 0.68, 95% CI [0.51, 0.85]) and 4 (AUC = 0.65, 95% [CI 0.50, 0.79]) significantly predictive of sexual reoffending. The J-SOAP-II total score with all four scales (AUC = .60, 95% CI [0.51, 0.69]) and Scales 2, 3, and 4 specifically, also significantly predicted non-sexual offending. Scale 1, the Sex Drive and Preoccupation scale, was significantly, inversely, related to general reoffending, suggesting discriminate validity for this scale; i.e., lower scores on Scale 1 were related to greater non-sexual reoffending. Interpretation of the findings from this study should consider that sample sizes were small, like other studies; only seven youth reoffended.

There also have been recent publications on the JSORRAT-II using some of the same samples included in Viljoen et al.'s (2012) meta-analysis (e.g., Epperson & Ralston, 2015; Ralston et al., 2016). In a sample of 1,095 juveniles adjudicated for sexual offending in Utah and Iowa, Ralston and colleagues (Ralston, Sarkar, Phillip, & Epperson, in press) investigated whether adding information about documented but uncharged sexual offenses to scoring the JSORRAT-II would improve its predictive accuracy. They found that including the uncharged offenses data did not improve the predictive accuracy of the JSORRAT-II over the standard scoring.

Clearly, additional and independently validated research studies focusing on existing and more recently or newly developed juvenile sexual recidivism risk assessment measures are needed. For example, Rajlic and Gretton (2010) found that the ERASOR and J-SOAP-II predicted sexual reoffending significantly better than chance in their combined sample of juveniles (medium effect sizes). When they divided the sample by criminal histories, and examined the predictive accuracy of the measures for those with and without non-sexual offenses, they found predictive validity for the youth who had sexual offenses only (large effect sizes); risk assessment findings for both measures regarding those with non-sexual as well as sexual offenses were no better than chance. It is important to replicate this study and explore whether predictive accuracy may vary among those in the mixed-offense group—e.g., whether there was improved predictive accuracy for those with multiple sexual offenses contrasted with a single sexual offense.

---

2. They noted that in a couple of analyses they used the J-SOAP-II in a manner inconsistent with Scale 4, the Community Stability/Adjustment scale, scoring rules in order to evaluate that scale's utility in their residential and institutional samples.

Yet, as this study suggests, it may be especially difficult to predict sexual recidivism among youth who engage in a wide variety of offenses. It may be, however, that even within a group of youth with diverse offenses, there are some factors that increase or decrease the risk of repeated sexual offending. Other individual and socio-ecological factors, such as age, gender, and family characteristics, as well as protective factors may be risk-relevant and also warrant investigation in risk assessment research.

ADOLESCENT SEXUAL-OFFENSE-SPECIFIC PROTECTIVE FACTORS ASSESSMENT

The sexual reoffending risk assessment tools just reviewed do not include specific protective factors, such as prosocial sexual attitudes or effective emotion regulation skills. Typically the absence of problems in particular domains (e.g., caregiver involvement) may be considered protective. Few scales have been developed to specifically assess personal, family, and community assets that support healthy sexual development and appropriate sexual behavior.

As part of the Assessment, Intervention and Moving (AIM) project, Griffin and colleagues (2008) developed a structured research-based assessment guide for assessing individual and socio-ecological risk and protective factors for males aged 12 through 18 years who had sexually abused. The AIM-2 was designed to identify relevant risk and protective factor treatment targets and guide effective interventions. The utility of the AIM-2 assessment protocol was evaluated over an average follow-up period of six years. All youth who recidivated with a sexual offense (10%, n = 7) had higher risk ratings (high concern ratings) and fewer protective factors (i.e., lower strengths). In addition, adolescents with high concern ratings, but also high protective ratings, were less likely to reoffend than those with similar concern ratings but limited strengths, suggesting that increasing numbers of protective factors may reduce the risk of repeat offending.

Recently, Worling (2013) developed the Desistence for Adolescents who Sexually Harm (DASH), a checklist of 13 protective dynamic factors such as prosocial sexual attitudes, compassion for others, and positive problem-solving skills. A preliminary study of the DASH in Singapore found that its total score was inversely related to risk as measured by the ERASOR, but the DASH lacked adequate predictive validity or any incremental validity beyond the ERASOR for sexual reoffending (Zeng, Chu, & Lee, 2015). Worling noted that studies of the DASH's psychometric properties are still under way. In the meantime, Worling suggests, the DASH should be used to help facilitate a review of possible protective factors when working with adolescents who have offended sexually.

Protective factors associated with desistance from general or non-sexual violent offending appear to have received more attention than those that may reduce juvenile sexual offending specifically. For example, the Centers for Disease Control and Prevention's Youth Violence website lists risk and protective factors associated with youth violence. The protective factors include individual characteristics, such as positive social orientation; family factors, such as parental involvement in social activities; and peer and social factors, such as close relationships with non-deviant peers and school commitment. Yet protective factor research is in its infancy compared with the risk factors research. Similar to sexual offense recidivism studies, findings pertaining to protective factors for youth violence have been described as inconsistent and based on research studies that are fraught with methodological problems (Spice et al., 2013). Clearly, more research regarding protective factors that may reduce youth violence and sexual offending is needed, as well as investigations as to if and how protective factors differ in terms of offense outcomes.

Adolescent General Violence and Delinquency Risk Assessment Tools

Because adolescents who have sexually abused are most likely to reoffend with a non-sexual offense, if they reoffend at all, assessment of risk and needs associated with non-sexual offending is an important component of risk and needs assessments. Vincent et al. (2012) noted that although there are other risk assessment instruments, the two measures that currently have the most research support are the Youth Level of Service/Case Management Inventory (YLS/CMI; Hoge & Andrews, 2010) and the Structured Assessment of Violence Risk in Youth (SAVRY; Borum, Bartel, & Forth, 2006).

The YLS/CMI is a static/dynamic actuarial risk/needs assessment tool for males and females 12 through 18 years old who have committed juvenile offenses (Hoge & Andrews, 2010). It is designed to assist assessors in evaluating historical and dynamic risk factors associated with future criminal activity as well as identifying relevant intervention needs. As noted in the YLS/CMI 2.0 manual (Hoge & Andrews, 2010), it has been evaluated in numerous studies including a new large, geographically representative US sample of 12,798 youth and the original sample of Canadians. The new US sample includes nearly 40 percent non-Caucasian youth and provides actuarial cutoff scores for risk levels by gender and setting (e.g., community or custodial samples). An updated research review is provided in the manual. The YLS/CMI was not designed to assess the risk of sexual recidivism and it does not predict sexual reoffending.

The SAVRY is an SPJ risk assessment tool. Designed for youth 12 through 18 years old, the SAVRY includes historical and dynamic risk and protective factors associated with violent behavior in adolescents. Good to excellent inter-rater reliability has been demonstrated for the SAVRY in multiple studies (Vincent, Guy, Fusco, & Gershenson, 2011). In addition, meta-analyses support the predictive validity of the SAVRY for general and violent reoffending (Olver et al., 2009; Singh et al., 2011).

Like the YLS/CMI, the SAVRY was not designed to predict sexual reoffending; however, Viljoen et al. (2008) found the SAVRY was predictive of serious non-sexual violent recidivism among adolescents who sexually abused. Its accuracy was better with older adolescents, but it was not predictive of sexual reoffending. In addition, one study found that the SAVRY's protective factors were not significantly associated with desisting from sexually reoffending, although methodological challenges such as the low base rate of sexual recidivism may have contributed to these null findings (Klein, Rettenberger, Yoon, Köhler, & Briken, 2015; Spice et al., 2013).

Progress Assessments

Risk and needs assessment is a process, not an event. Measures such as the ERASOR and J-SOAP-II that include dynamic risk factors can be used to assess change and progress over time. For example, Bourgon, Morton-Bourgon, and Madrigrano (2005) used the ERASOR to evaluate treatment progress among 53 adolescents involved in various treatment programs. They assessed whether the youth demonstrated improvement, no change, or deterioration over time. They found improvement among 50 percent or more of the youth on four of the identified treatment targets.

In addition, research (Viljoen et al., 2015) has found decreases in risk on the J-SOAP-II Scale 3, Intervention, significantly associated with decreased rates of sexual recidivism. Using the same sample as Viljoen et al. (2008), although with seven fewer subjects and a longer follow-up period, Viljoen et al. (2015) investigated reliable change indices for J-SOAP-II Scales 3 and 4 with a sample of youth in a residential treatment center. Reliable change indices (RCIs) are statistical procedures that estimate reliable or true change after taking into account measurement error. The researchers explored the relationship of risk-relevant changes, as indicated by the dynamic J-SOAP-II scales, among admission to the residential treatment program, discharge, and sexual recidivism. Findings indicated that the youth who had reliable decreases on Scale 3, the Intervention Scale, were significantly less likely to reoffend sexually. In contrast, they found that reliable decreases on Scale 4 were significantly more likely to reoffend sexually.

Certainly, the finding regarding Scale 4's inverse relationship with sexual recidivism is surprising, but Viljoen et al. (2015) provided some plausible explanations. For instance, they noted that youth who were considered improved and at lower risk at discharge may be provided with less supervision in the community; placement in the residential center may have provided needed structure and supervision. Further, as Viljoen et al. noted, the archival file records used in the study may not have had sufficient information that satisfactorily "mapped onto" J-SOAP-II Scale 4 items.

In contrast with the Viljoen et al. (2015) findings regarding Scale 4 of the J-SOAP-II, Martinez et al. (2015) found Scale 4 scores assessed at discharge were predictive of sexual reoffending, but they did not evaluate reliable change indices. Reasons for the discrepant findings are not clear. Certainly, further research evaluating how dynamic, community-based risk factors are evaluated while youth are in residential or correctional placements and how to assess factors that may facilitate safe transitions to and adjustments in the community are needed.

Another measure of treatment progress is the Juvenile Sex Offense Specific Treatment Needs and Progress Report (TNPR; Righthand, 2005). The TNPR facilitates initial and progress assessments of dynamic risk factors associated with sexual and criminal offending by adolescent males and females. The TNPR was based on a literature review conducted by Righthand and Way (unpublished), which was subsequently updated (Righthand et al., 2014). It consists of 14 items, only 2 of which pertain specifically to inappropriate sexual interests or sexual drive. Items are scored on a 0–2 basis, with higher scores reflecting significant treatment needs while 0 indicates no or minimal need for intervention and, as such, a potential protective factor. The TNPR enables clinicians to identify individual treatment needs and develop individualized treatment plans. Repeated administration of the TNPR—e.g., quarterly—allows clinicians to monitor progress, or the lack thereof, over time, as well as readiness for discharge (Righthand, Boulard, Cabral, & Serwik, 2011).

A preliminary psychometric study with 187 adolescent males adjudicated for a sexual offense indicated that the inter-rater reliability was excellent (0.82) and internal consistency (a = 0.72) was good (Righthand, Hecker, & Dore, 2012). Predictive validity for sexual recidivism was moderate (AUC = 0.71, 95% CI [0.50, 0.91]), but not statistically significant (only six youth, less than 4% of the sample, reoffended with a sexual offense). Predictive validity was significant for violent recidivism (AUC = 0.62, 95% CI [0.52, 0.70]), which had a much higher base rate. These findings are encouraging, but more research on this and additional measures for assessing treatment progress are needed.

GUIDELINES FOR RISK ASSESSMENTS

In sum, the primary goals of risk assessments are to (a) identify the level or extent of risk of reoffending; (b) identify factors that, if targeted by interventions, may reduce the likelihood of repeat sexual abuse or other types of offending (criminogenic needs); and (c) identify factors that may promote healthy, prosocial development. These goals are applicable whether the adolescent is managed within juvenile justice systems or not. This assessment process should incorporate risk assessment instruments in addition to other information gathered, and requires sound professional judgment tying it all together. Suggested guidelines for conducting high-quality risk assessments for youth who have sexually abused are presented in the following section.

Consider Developmental Issues

Adolescence is a period of rapid development (see Modecki, this volume, for a more in-depth review). The ability to think through others' perspectives, sufficiently control impulses, regulate emotions, and think of future consequences is still developing. Inappropriate or even illegal sexual behaviors by adolescents may occur with peers who do not differ substantially in age. Further, compared with adults, these youth may not have the cognitive capacity required for detailed offense planning, a significant risk factor in adults. With adolescents, sometimes abusive sexual behavior is experimental, situational, or opportunistic; typically it does not persist, especially following appropriate interventions. Evaluators help consumers of their assessments appreciate developmental factors and recognize that adolescents are not simply small or young versions of adults who commit sexual offenses.

Provide Holistic Assessments

Risk assessments are holistic. They identify individual, family, and other socio-ecological risk and protective factors that may increase or decrease the risk of sexual or non-sexual recidivism. The extent to which each of these domains is addressed, the assessment methods used, and the overall comprehensiveness of the assessment will depend on its purpose. For example, when the purpose of the assessment is for treatment planning during treatment, it may not need to be as detailed and thorough as when an evaluation is required to inform a legal decision such as a transfer to adult court. Treatment assessments help identify relevant treatment targets and needed interventions and provide baseline information about a youth, his or her family, and their circumstances. During the course of treatment, there are opportunities to observe the youth's and family's conduct, or refer out for additional assessments if indicated—e.g., when concerns develop about the possibility that a mental health disorder is interfering with successful treatment participation and may require specialized treatment interventions.

In contrast, when evaluations are conducted to inform administrative or legal decision making, these forensic assessments (as described in chapter 5) provide a "snapshot" of the youth and his or her circumstances at one point in time. Although treatment and forensic risk assessments may have some similar components, such as the importance of useful, practical RNR treatment recommendations, forensic risk assessments require a greater degree of thoroughness because, as noted earlier, they are used by legal and other administrative decision makers whose primary interest is community safety. At times, their legal decisions may result in severe and restrictive life-altering consequences for the individual youth and family.

Beware of Information-Processing Errors

Clinicians and others engaged in risk assessment, even those who are well trained and experienced, can make human errors. For example, research indicates that mental health clinicians may view clients as more dysfunctional than they are and may overestimate risk (e.g., Miller & Brodsky, 2011; Schram, Milloy, & Rowe, 1991).

When conducting risk assessments of people who have harmed others, of course evaluators want to get it right; otherwise there are grave public safety ramifications. Thus, a tendency to err on the safe side is not surprising. There are a variety of personal, social, political, and financial pressures that may contribute to a propensity to overestimate as well as underestimate risk, pressures that may operate outside our awareness (e.g., Miller & Brodsky, 2011; Norcross et al., 2008). These pressures include our concern for potential victims, as well as an awareness that our findings may, perhaps unnecessarily, result in severe, negative consequences for the youth, such as long-term or lifelong sex offender registration. Further, if a new offense occurs, negative publicity may be associated with the erroneous assessments (e.g., discharge to the community). As a result of the new offense, we may experience significant distress for the new victims and feel like we have failed. Public confidence in our professions' abilities to facilitate public safety may be diminished, and policy changes that unfairly affect other clients who are invested in positive behavior change may result.

In addition to these pressures and concerns, there are other cognitive biases to be aware of that may cloud our judgment. These errors include a variety of information-processing mistakes that people make in everyday life (e.g., Norcross et al., 2008). For example, people generally rely on vivid, unambiguous, available information in decision making. When conducting risk assessments, we may over-rely on the vivid details of an offense, rather than adequately considering statistical information, such as the low base rates of sexual reoffending. Further, people generally form first impressions based on available information, and then over-rely on this impression even if it is erroneous. Additionally, we may not recognize or may ignore contradictory information that is less apparent.

Further, despite our increased knowledge about adolescent development, people often attribute permanent characteristics to youth and do not adequately consider family and circumstantial factors, or individual circumstances, that may be transient but relevant for understanding adolescent behavior. People also tend to make assumptions of cross-situational permanence. For example, some people automatically assume that adolescents who have sexually abused a sibling pose a risk to the larger community, regardless of other factors that may suggest otherwise. Sometimes, we erroneously hold beliefs that are unsupported by research, such as the presumption that denying an offense suggests an increased risk of sexual reoffending. Such erroneous assumptions can negatively affect the accuracy of our assessments (e.g., Monahan, 1981; Norcross et al., 2008; Miller & Brodsky, 2011).

In view of these cognitive biases, which are part of human nature, professionals who conduct risk and needs assessments must do so cautiously, taking steps to control for information-processing errors. Such steps include, but are not limited to:

- Identifying personal biases and other pressures

- Considering base-rates of reoffending

- Identifying initial hypotheses and then looking for disconfirming evidence

- Checking alternative hypotheses

- Exploring situational and contextual factors

- Using appropriate, valid, and structured risk assessment instruments with fidelity

- Guarding against overconfidence

- Consulting and collaborating with other trained evaluators

Use Appropriate Risk Assessment Instruments

Risk assessment instruments provide standardized checklists based on research evidence to help evaluators and decision makers consider relevant risk and possible protective factors and determine appropriate interventions and treatment needs. A risk assessment instrument, however, does not provide a full assessment. These instruments only include selected factors associated with reoffending among groups of similar youth. There may be other issues that evaluators need to know in order to put together an effective case or treatment plan in individual cases, such as whether there are mental health disorders or trauma-related symptoms that would affect responsiveness to treatment. Moreover, on occasion there are idiosyncratic factors that may lead to sexual offending or delinquency that would not be captured on a risk assessment tool because the factors are uncommon. Thus, risk assessment instruments should be supplemented with other forms of information gathering and assessment, and sometimes include psychological tests and measures.

The increasing research base discussed in this chapter suggests that adolescent risk assessment instruments designed to assess sexual, violent, and general delinquency recidivism can facilitate the process of risk assessment. Such measures help identify relevant treatment targets and intervention domains, and provide increased accuracy over unstructured clinical assessments (Viljoen et al., 2012; Vincent et al., 2012). Evaluators should be well versed in the research base for the instrument they choose and ensure it is appropriate for use with their case. They must also be properly trained and administer the instrument as instructed in the manual to maintain its validity and avoid contamination from the evaluator's potential biases and information-processing errors. When presenting evaluation findings in assessment reports, the strengths and limitations of assessment measures used should be discussed, including their research evidence.

Finally, it is important to remember that risk assessment instruments are most important and valid for case planning, intervention, and risk management, rather than "prediction" per se. Risk assessment tools, particularly those that include dynamic risk and protective factors, provide a method for systematically assessing and reassessing risk-relevant factors and then determining the best treatment approaches and intervention strategies for individual youth at a given point in time (Martinez et al., 2015; Viljoen et al., 2012).

Provide Risk Assessment Formulations

The onset and potential reoccurrence of sexual behavior problems in youth is multifaceted and due to a combination of individual, developmental, familial, and contextual factors. Thus, findings from the risk assessment should explicate the varied individual, social, and situational factors that may exacerbate or mitigate risk, as well as the extent to which these factors are present currently, or are likely to be so in the near future. As noted previously, if adolescents who have been sexually abusive reoffend, it is more likely to be with a non-sexual offense. Thus, individual and socio-ecological risk and protective factors related to non-sexual offending also require discussion.

Risk labels, such as high, moderate, or low risk, are consistent with the RNR model and may be required for matching resources and individual need. However, given developmental fluidity and the strong influence of families and other dynamic social contexts on youth, using risk labels in absolute, person-specific terms, such as "he is a high risk," is problematic. Instead, risk classifications can be presented in dynamic ways that recognize the malleability of adolescence, such as "currently, there are a high number of risk factors, some treatable, and few protective factors." Further, when discussing risk-relevant concerns, reminders about developmental fluidity and the importance of families and other dynamic social contexts on youth are important.

Once a discussion of risks and needs is completed, specific and developmentally appropriate strategies that may reduce risk and facilitate prosocial behavior can be formulated. Consistent with the RNR model, recommendations should offer specific, individualized ways to reduce risk factors, facilitate protective factors, and promote healthy, prosocial development. It is important that recommended interventions be matched to treatment needs (e.g., more intensive interventions when there are more dynamic risk factors and fewer possibly protective ones) and individual learning styles. In addition, it is important that recommendations for interventions be feasible and not unduly burdensome, and certainly not unnecessarily detract from normative and healthy developmental pursuits.

Conduct Ongoing Reassessment

It is important to remember that risk assessment is not simply an event, but a process. Following initial and baseline assessments, ongoing reassessments are necessary for monitoring treatment progress and adjusting case and treatment plans, as indicated, to ensure their effectiveness. Further, risk assessments at discharge from community-based or residential treatment programs are necessary to evaluate the extent to which criminogenic treatment needs have been resolved or whether additional interventions are warranted.

Regardless of when an initial assessment is conducted and which assessment tools are used, risk and needs assessment reports should emphasize that findings represent *current* functioning and circumstances. The importance of periodic reassessments, responsive to developmental and situational fluctuations and current needs, requires emphasis. The short "shelf life" of the report, generally considered six months or less depending on the youth's age and circumstances, should be underscored.

Ensure Evaluator Qualifications

Because adolescence is a time of such rapid development, professionals who conduct risk assessments must be knowledgeable about adolescent development and recognize that maturational processes vary between, as well as within, individual youth.

Developmental knowledge includes awareness of the range of normative sexual behavior in adolescence. Evaluators must be able to distinguish sexual behaviors that may signify significant problems while recognizing that actions that may reflect sexual deviance in adults, such as sex with children, may not have the same serious prognostic implications when exhibited by adolescents.

Evaluators should have training and experience in assessing adolescents with sexual and other conduct problems, and specific training in clinical or forensic risk assessment. They also must recognize the limits of their own competence, biases, training, and professional role. Finally, they should complete the specialized training requirements on any of the risk assessment instruments or psychological tests they administer.

Future Research Needs

Increased research pertaining to risk and protective factors associated with sexual reoffending is required, and efforts to overcome the significant methodological problems inherent in such research should be supported. There is substantially more research about risk and protective factors in the delinquency and life course criminology fields, as well as child psychopathology. Information from these areas of study is highly relevant. Adolescents who commit sexual offenses are first and foremost adolescents. This means that various risk and protective factors may contribute to the same outcome (equifinality) and that similar factors may influence divergent outcomes (multifinality; Cicchetti, 2010). Research that helps increase our understanding of how risk and protective factors interact to facilitate resilience is required.

Due to the heterogeneity of adolescents who sexually abuse (e.g., age, race, gender, families, culture, criminal history, placement setting, etc.) and the very low base rate of sexual reoffending, overfocusing on specific risk and protective factors that may increase or decrease the likelihood of sexual recidivism, in groups of adolescents with illegal sexual behavior, may have limited utility. Differences in individual and socioecological risk and protective factors, as well as their interplay, in sufficiently large samples of youth with sexual offenses are required to adequately identify risk and protective factors and risk-relevant treatment needs, to evaluate the utility of risk and needs assessment instruments and treatment progress scales, and to facilitate effective interventions. Research that addresses factors that facilitate desistance from any type of offending and promotes prosocial engagement and lifestyles is essential.

Explorations regarding the ongoing utility of current risk assessment instruments, as well as whether and how they can be improved, are warranted (Monahan & Skeem,

2014). The reliability and validity of progress measures and the utility of such tools for measuring change in reassessments also should be studied to improve our assessment and intervention methods. Additionally, the utility of existing tools should be evaluated in the field—i.e., the settings in which they are used (for example, Worling et al.'s 2012 prospective study of the ERASOR) and used in a manner that is consistent with their assessment manuals and the purpose of the instrument (Vincent et al., 2012). It is important that researchers investigate how practitioners can successfully use dynamic risk and needs assessment to improve interventions and whether they are, in fact, doing so (Viljoen et al., 2015).

Much work remains to be done. But it should be noted that the small to moderate effect sizes of the adolescent sexual-offense-specific instruments described in this chapter are similar to those found for adult sexual risk assessment instruments (Hanson & Morton-Bourgon, 2009), measures assessing general recidivism risk in adolescents (Olver et al., 2009; Schwalbe, 2007), and those appraising other types of infrequent human behaviors such as self-harm and suicide (as noted in Viljoen et al., 2012). It is inherently difficult to assess future human behavior. When we do, we must be cautious and humble, use evidence-based practices and guidelines, and stay current with the evolving research literature.

REFERENCES

Abel, G. G., Mittelman, M. S., & Becker, J. V. (1985). Sex offenders: Results of assessment and treatment and recommendations for treatment. In M. H. Ben-Aron, S. J. Hucker, & C. D. Webster (Eds.), *Clinical criminology: Assessment and treatment of criminal behavior* (pp. 207–220). Toronto, Canada: M & M Graphics.

Andrews, D. A., & Bonta, J. (2010). *The psychology of criminal conduct* (5th ed.). Cincinnati: Anderson.

Andrews, D. A., Bonta, J., & Hoge, R. D. (1990). Classification for effective rehabilitation: Rediscovering psychology. *Criminal Justice and Behavior, 17,* 19–52.

Andrews, D. A., Bonta, J., & Wormith, S. J. (2011). The risk-need-responsivity (RNR) model: Does adding the good lives model contribute to effective crime prevention? *Criminal Justice and Behavior, 38*(7), 735–755. http://dx.doi.org/10.1177/0093854811406356

Association for the Treatment of Sexual Abusers (2015, October). Civil commitment of sexual offenders: Introduction and overview. Retrieved August 25, 2016, from http://www.atsa.com/sites/default/files/%5BCivil%20Commitment%5D%20Overview.pdf

Babchishin, K. M., & Helmus, L. M. (2015). The influence of base rates on correlations: An evaluation of proposed alternative effect sizes with real-world dichotomous data. *Behavior Research Methods, 48*(3), 1021–1031. http://dx.doi.org/10.3758/s13428-015-0627-7

Berlin, F. S., Galbreath, N. W., Geary, B., & McGlone, G. (2003). The use of actuarials at civil commitment hearings to predict the likelihood of future sexual violence. *Sexual Abuse: A Journal of Research and Treatment, 15*(4), 377–382.

Borum, R. (1996). Improving the clinical practice of violence risk assessment: Technology, guidelines, and training. *American Psychologist, 51*(9), 945–956.

Borum, R., Bartel, P., & Forth, A. (2006). *Structured Assessment of Violence Risk in Youth (SAVRY).* Lutz, FL: Psychological Assessment Resources.

Borum, R., & Douglas, K. (2003). New directions in violence risk assessment. *Psychiatric Times, 20,* 102–103.

Bourgon, G., Morton-Bourgon, K. E., & Madrigrano, G. (2005). Multisite investigation of treatment for sexually abusive juveniles. In B. K. Schwartz (Ed.), *The sex offender: Issues in assessment, treatment, and supervision of adult and juvenile populations* (Vol. 5, pp. 15–1 to 15–17). Kingston, NJ: Civic Research Institute.

Bronfenbrenner, U. (1977). Toward an experimental ecology of human development. *American Psychologist, 32,* 513–531.

Caldwell, M. F. (2010). Study characteristics and recidivism base rates in juvenile sex offender recidivism. *International Journal of Offender Therapy and Comparative Criminology, 54*(2), 197–212.

Caldwell, M. F. (2016, July 18). Quantifying the decline in juvenile sexual recidivism rates. *Psychology, Public Policy, and Law.* Advance online publication. http://dx.doi.org/10.1037/law0000094

Caldwell, M. F., & Dickinson, C. (2009). Sex offender registration and recidivism risk in juvenile sexual offenders. *Behavioral Sciences and the Law, 27*(6), 941–956.

Centers for Disease Control and Prevention. Youth violence: Risk and protective factors. Accessed May 19, 2016, from http://www.cdc.gov/ViolencePrevention/youthviolence/riskprotectivefactors.html

Chaffin, M. (2008). Our minds are made up—don't confuse us with the facts: Commentary on policies concerning children with sexual behavior problems and juvenile sex offenders. *Child Maltreatment, 13*(2), 110–121.

Chu, C. M., Ng, K., Fong, J., & Teoh, J. (2012). Assessing youth who sexually offended: The predictive validity of the ERASOR, J-SOAP-II, and YLS/CMI in a non-Western context. *Sexual Abuse: A Journal of Research and Treatment, 24,* 153–174. http://dx.doi.org/1079063211404250.

Cicchetti, D. (2010). Resilience under conditions of extreme stress: A multilevel perspective. *World Psychiatry, 9*(3), 145–154.

Cicchetti, D., & Lynch, M. (1993). Toward an ecological/transactional model of community violence and child maltreatment: Consequences for children's development. *Psychiatry, 56,* 96–118.

Cicchetti, D., & Rogosch, F. A. (1996). Equifinality and multifinality in developmental psychopathology. *Developmental Psychopathology, 8,* 597–600.

Cicchetti, D., & Sroufe, L. A. (2000). The past as prologue to the future: The times, they've been a-changin'. *Development and Psychopathology, 12*(3), 255–264.

Cicchetti, D., & Toth, S. L. (2009). The past achievements and future promises of developmental psychopathology: The coming of age of a discipline. *Journal of Child Psychology and Psychiatry, 50,* 16–25.

Cullen, F. T., & Gendreau, P. (1989). The effectiveness of correctional rehabilitation: Reconsidering the "nothing works" debate. In L. Goodstein and D. L. MacKenzie (Eds.), *The American Prison* (pp. 23–44). New York: Plenum Press.

Dawes, R. M., Faust, D., &. Meehl, P. E. (1989). Clinical versus actuarial judgment. *Science, New Series, 243*(4899), 1668–1674.

DeMatteo, D., Wolbransky, M., & LaDuke, C. (2016). Risk assessment with juveniles. In K. Heilbrun, D. DeMatteo, & N. E. S. Goldstein (Eds.), *Handbook of psychology and juvenile justice* (pp. 365–384). Washington, DC: American Psychological Association.

DiCataldo, F. (2013, August–September). Risk assessment instruments for juvenile sex offenders. *Sex Offender Law Report, 14*(5), 65–77.

Dvoskin, J. A., & Heilbrun, K. (2001). Risk assessment and release decision-making: Toward resolving the great debate. *Journal of the American Academy of Psychiatry and the Law, 29,* 6–10.

Epperson, D. L., & Ralston, C. A. (2015). Development and validation of the Juvenile Sexual Offense Recidivism Risk Assessment Tool–II (JSORRAT-II). *Sexual Abuse: A Journal of Research and Treatment, 27,* 529–558. http://dx.doi.org/10.1177/1079063213514452

Epperson, D. L., Ralston, C. A., Fowers, D., & DeWitt, J. (2016). *Juvenile Sexual Offense Recidivism Risk Assessment Tool–II (JSORRAT-II) scoring manual.* Author: dleppers@calpoly.edu

Epperson, D. L., Ralston, C. A., Fowers, D., DeWitt, J., & Gore, K. S. (2006). Actuarial risk assessment with juveniles who offend sexually: Development of the Juvenile Sexual Offense Recidivism Risk Assessment Tool–II. In D. Prescott (Ed.), *Risk assessment of youth who have sexually abused: Theory, controversy, and emerging strategies* (pp. 118–169). Oklahoma City: Wood & Barnes.

Finkelhor, D., Ormrod, R., & Chaffin, M. (2009). Juveniles who commit sex offenses against minors. *Juvenile Justice Bulletin.* Retrieved from unh.edu/ccrc/pdf/CV171.pdf

Griffin, H. L., Beech, A., Print, B., Bradshaw, H., & Quayle, J. (2008). The development and initial testing of the AIM2 framework to assess risk and strengths in young people who sexually offend. *Journal of Sexual Aggression, .14,* 211–225.

Grisso, T. (2000). *Ethical issues in evaluations for sex offender re-offending.* Paper presented at the Sex Offender Re-Offence Risk Prediction Training, Sinclair Seminars, Madison, WI.

Grove, W. M., & Meehl, P. E. (1996). Comparative efficiency of informal (subjective, impressionistic) and formal (mechanical, algorithmic) prediction procedures: The clinical–statistical controversy. *Psychology, Public Policy, and Law, 2*(2), 293–323.

Guy, L. S. (2008). Performance indicators of the structured professional judgment approach for assessing risk for violence to others: A meta-analytic survey (Doctoral dissertation). Simon Fraser University, Burnaby, BC, Canada.

Hanson, R. K., Bourgon, G., Helmus, L., Hodgson, S. (2009). The principles of effective correctional treatment also apply to sexual offenders : A meta-analysis. *Criminal Justice and Behavior, 36*(9), 865–891. http://dx.doi.org/10.1177/0093854809338545

Hanson, R. K., & Bussière, M. T. (1998). Predicting relapse: A meta-analysis of sexual offender recidivism studies. *Journal of Consulting and Clinical Psychology, 66,* 348–362.

Hanson, R. K., & Morton-Bourgon, K. (2005). The characteristics of persistent sexual offenders: A meta-analysis of recidivism studies. *Journal of Consulting and Clinical Psychology, 73*(6), 1154–1163.

Hanson, R. K., & Morton-Bourgon, K. (2009). The accuracy of recidivism risk assessments for sexual offenders: A meta-analysis of 118 prediction studies. *Psychological Assessment, 21*(1), 1–21. http://dx.doi.org/10.1037/a0014421

Hanson, R. K., & Thornton, D. (1999). *Static 99: Improving actuarial risk assessments for sex offenders* (Vol. 2). Ottawa, Canada: Solicitor General Canada.

Harris, A. J., & Socia, K. M. (2014). What's in a name? Evaluating the effects of the "sex offender" label on public opinions and beliefs. *Sexual Abuse: A Journal of Research and Treatment, 28*(7), 660–678. http://dx.doi.org/10.1177/1079063214564391

Hart, S. D. (2003). Actuarial risk assessment: Commentary on Berlin et al. *Sexual Abuse: A Journal of Research and Treatment, 15*(4), 384–388. http://dx.doi.org/10.1177/107906320301500413

Hecker, J. E. (2014). Baby with the bath water: Response to Fanniff and Letourneau. *Sexual Abuse: a Journal of Research and Treatment, 26*(5), 395–400. http://dx.doi.org/1079063214525644

Heilbrun, K., Lee, R. J., Cottle, C. C (2005). Risk factors and intervention outcomes: Meta-analyses of juvenile offending. In K. Heilbrun, N. E. S. Goldstein, & R. E. Redding, *Juvenile delinquency: Prevention, assessment, & intervention* (pp. 111–133). New York: Oxford University Press.

Hoge, R. D. (2016). Risk, need, and responsivity in juveniles. In K. Heilbrun, D. DeMatteo, & N. E. S. Goldstein (Eds.), *Handbook of psychology and juvenile justice* (pp. 179–196). Washington, DC: American Psychological Association.

Hoge, R. D., & Andrews, D. A. (2010). *The Youth Level of Service/Case Management Inventory (YLS/CMI 2.0) user's manual.* Toronto, Canada: Multi-Health Systems.

Klein, V., Rettenberger, M., Yoon, D., Köhler, N., & Briken, P. (2015). Protective factors and recidivism in accused juveniles who sexually offended. *Sexual Abuse: A Journal of Research and Treatment, 27*(1), 71–90. http://dx.doi.org/10.1177/1079063214554958

Knight, R. A., & Prentky, R. A. (1993). Exploring characteristics for classifying juvenile sex offenders. In H. E. Barbaree, W. L. Marshall, & S. M. Hudson (Eds.), *The juvenile sex offender* (pp. 45–83). New York: Guilford Press.

Koehler, J. A., Lösel, F., Akoensi, T. D., & Humphreys, D. K. (2013). A systematic review and meta-analysis on the effects of young offender treatment programs in Europe. *Journal of Experimental Criminology, 9*(1), 19–43. http://dx.doi.org/10.1007/s11292-012-9159-7

Letourneau, E., & Miner, M. (2005). Juvenile sex offenders: A case against the legal and clinical status quo. *Sexual Abuse: A Journal of Research and Treatment, 17*(3), 293–312.

Lipsey, M. W. (2009). The primary factors that characterize effective interventions with juvenile offenders: A meta-analytic overview. *Victims and offenders, 4*(2), 124–147.

Lowenkamp, C. T., Makarios, M. D., Latessa, E. J., Lemke, R., Smith, P. (2010). Community corrections facilities for juvenile offenders in Ohio: An examination of treatment integrity and recidivism. *Criminal Justice and Behavior, 37*(6), 695–708. http://dx.doi.org/10.1177/0093854810363721

Lussier, P. (2015). Juvenile sex offending through a developmental life course criminology perspective: An agenda for policy and research. *Sexual Abuse: A Journal of Research and Treatment, 29*(1), 51–80. Advance online publication. http://dx.doi.org/10.1177/1079063215580966

Luthar, S. S., Cicchetti, D., & Becker, B. (2000). The construct of resilience: A critical evaluation and guidelines for future work. *Child Development, 71*, 543–562.

Martinez, R., Rosenfeld, B., Cruise, K., & Martin, J. (2015). Predictive validity of the J-SOAP-II: Does accuracy differ across settings? *International Journal of Forensic Mental Health, 14*(1), 56–65. http://dx.doi.org/10.1080/14999013.2015.1019683

Martinson, R. (1974, Spring). What works?: Questions and answers about prison reform. *The Public Interest, 22*–54.

Martinson, R. (1979). New findings, new views: A note of caution regarding sentencing reform. *Hofstra Law Review, 7*, 242–258.

McCann, K., & Lussier, P. (2008). Antisociality, sexual deviance, and sexual reoffending in juvenile sex offenders: A meta-analytical investigation. *Youth Violence and Juvenile Justice, 6*, 363–385.

McGrath, R. J., Cumming, G. F., Burchard, B. L., Zeoli, S., & Ellerby, L. (2010). *Current practices and emerging trends in sexual abuser management: The Safer Society 2009 North American survey.* Brandon, VT: Safer Society.

Melton, G. B., Petrila, J., Poythress, N. G., & Slobogin, C. (2007). Psychological evaluations for the courts: A handbook for mental health professionals and lawyers (3rd ed.). New York: Guilford Press.

Miccio-Fonseca, L. C. (2006). *Multiplex empirically guided inventory of ecological aggregates for assessing sexually abusive children and adolescents (ages 19 and under)—MEGA.* San Diego: Author.

Miccio-Fonseca, L. C. (2010). MEGA♪: An ecological risk assessment tool of risk and protective factors for assessing sexually abusive children and adolescents. *Journal of Aggression, Maltreatment, and Trauma, 19,* 734–756.

Miller, J. G. (1989, March). The debate on rehabilitating criminals: Is it true that nothing works? *Washington Post.* http://www.prisonpolicy.org/scans/rehab.html

Miller, S. L., & Brodsky, S. L. (2011). Risky business: Addressing the consequences of predicting violence. *Journal of the American Academy of Psychiatry and the Law, 39*(3), 396–401.

Monahan, J. (1981). *The clinical prediction of violent behavior.* Rockville, MD: US Department of Health and Human Services.

Monahan, J., & Skeem, J. L. (2014). Risk redux: The resurgence of risk assessment in criminal sanctioning. *Federal Sentencing Reporter, 26*(3), 158–166. http://dx.doi.org/10.1525/fsr.2014.26.3.158

New Jersey Attorney General's Office (2006). Juvenile Risk Assessment Scale Manual. Retrieved from http://www.state.nj.us/lps/dcj/megan/jras-manual-scale-606.pdf.

Norcross, J. C., Hogan, T. P., Koocher, G. P. (2008). *Clinician's guide to evidence-based practices: Mental health and the addictions.* New York: Oxford University Press.

Olver, M. E., Stockdale, K. C., & Wormith, J. (2009). Risk assessment with young offenders: A meta-analysis of three assessment measures. *Criminal Justice and Behavior, 36,* 329–353. http://dx.doi.org/10.1177/0093854809331457

Pealer, J. A., & Latessa, E. J. (2004). Applying the principles of effective intervention to juvenile correctional programs. *Corrections Today, 66*(7), 26–29.

Pittman, N., & Nguyen, Q. (2011). *A snapshot of juvenile sex offender registration and notification laws: A survey of the United States.* Philadelphia: Defender Association of Philadelphia.

Prentky, R. A., & Righthand, S. (2003). *Juvenile Sex Offender Assessment Protocol: Manual.* Washington, DC: US Department of Justice Office of Juvenile Justice and Delinquency Prevention.

Prentky, R. A., Righthand, S., & Lamade, R. (2016). Sexual offending: Assessment and intervention. In K. Heilbrun, D. DeMatteo, & N. E. S. Goldstein (Eds.), *Handbook of psychology and juvenile justice* (pp. 641–672). Washington, DC: American Psychological Association.

Rajlic, G., & Gretton, H. M. (2010). An examination of two sexual recidivism risk measures in adolescent offenders: The moderating effect of offender type. *Criminal Justice and Behavior, 37,* 1066–1085.

Ralston, C. A., & Epperson, D. L. (2013). Predictive validity of adult risk assessment tools with juveniles who offended sexually. *Psychological Assessment, 25,* 905–916.

Ralston, C. A., Epperson, D. L., & Edwards, S. E. (2016). Cross-validation of the JSORRAT–II in Iowa. *Sexual Abuse: A Journal of Research and Treatment, 28*(6), 534–554. http://dx.doi.org/10.1177/1079063214548074

Ralston, C. A., Sarkar, A., Phillip, G., & Epperson, D. L. (2015). Impact of using documented but uncharged offense data on JSORRAT-II predictive validity. *Sexual Abuse: A Journal of Research and Treatment.* Advance online publication. http://dx.doi.org/10.1177/1079063215582011

Rice, M. E., & Harris, G. T. (2005). Comparing effect sizes in follow-up studies: ROC area, Cohen's *d,* and *r. Law and Human Behavior, 29,* 615–620. http://dx.doi.org/10.1007/s10979-005-6832-7

Righthand, S. (2005). Juvenile Sex Offense Specific Treatment Needs and Progress Report. Retrieved from http://www.csom.org/pubs/JSOProgressScale.pdf

Righthand, S., Baird, B., Way, I., & Seto, M. C. (2014). Effective intervention with adolescents who have offended sexually: Translating research into practice. Brandon, VT: Safer Society Press.

Righthand, S., Boulard, N., Cabral, J., & Serwik, A. (2011, February–March). Reducing sexual of-fending among juveniles in Maine: A systems approach. *Corrections Today,* pp. 24–27.

Righthand, S., Hecker, J., & Dore, G. (2012, October). *Using Assessments to Guide Effective Interventions & Preliminary Findings of the Treatment Needs and Progress Report.* Paper presented at presented at the Association for the Treatment of Sexual Abusers' 31st Annual Research and Treatment Conference, Denver, CO.

Schram, D. D., Milloy, C. D., & Rowe, W. E. (1991). *Juvenile sex offenders: A follow-up study of reoffense behavior.* Washington State Institute for Public Policy.

Schwalbe, C. S. (2007). Risk assessment for juvenile justice: A meta-analysis. *Law and Human Behavior, 31,* 449–462. http://dx.doi.org/10.1177/0093854808324377

Seto, M. C., & Lalumière, M. L. (2010). What is so special about male adolescent sexual offending? A review and test of explanations through meta-analysis. *Psychological Bulletin, 136,* 526–575.

Singh, J. P. (2013). Predictive validity performance indicators in violence risk assessment: A methodological primer. *Behavioral Sciences and the Law, 3,* 8–22. http://dx.doi.org/10.1002/bsl.2052

Singh, J. P., Desmarais, S. L., & Van Horn, R. A. (2013). Measurement of predictive validity in violence risk assessment studies: A second-order systematic review. *Behavioral Sciences and the Law, 31,* 55–73. http://dx.doi.org/10.1002/bsl.2053

Singh, J. P., Grann, M., & Fazel, S. (2011). A comparative study of violence risk assessment tools: A systematic review and metaregression analysis of 68 studies involving 25,980 participants. *Clinical Psychology Review, 31*(3), 499–513.

Skeem, J. L., & Monahan, J. (2011). Current directions in violence risk assessment. *Current Directions in Psychological Science, 20,* 38–42. http://dx.doi.org/10.1177/0963721410397271

Spice, A., Viljoen, J. L., Latzman, N. E., Scalora, M. J., & Ullman, D. (2013). Risk and protective factors for recidivism among juveniles who have offended sexually. *Sexual Abuse: A Journal of Research and Treatment, 25,* 347–369. http://dx.doi.org/10.1177/1079063212459086

Storey, J. E., Watt, K. A., & Hart, S. D. (2015). An examination of violence risk communication in practice using a structured professional judgment framework. *Behavioral Sciences and the Law, 33,* 39–55.

Szmukler, G. (2001). Violence risk prediction in practice. *British Journal of Psychiatry, 178*(1), 84–85. http://dx.doi.org/10.1192/bjp.178.1.84

Viljoen, J. L., Elkovitch, N., Scalora, M. J., & Ullman, D. (2009). Assessment of reoffense risk in adolescents who have committed sexual offenses: Predictive validity of the ERASOR, PCL:YV, YLS/CMI, and Static-99. *Criminal Justice and Behavior, 36*(10), 981–1000.

Viljoen, J. L., Gray, A. L., Shaffer, C., Latzman, N. E., Scalora, M. J., & Ullman, D. (2015). Changes in J-SOAP-II and SAVRY scores over the course of residential, cognitive-behavioral treatment for adolescent sexual offending. *Sexual Abuse: A Journal of Research and Treatment.* Advance online publication. http://dx.doi.org/10.1177/1079063215595404

Viljoen, J. L., Mordell, S., & Beneteau, J. L. (2012). Prediction of adolescent sexual reoffending: A meta-analysis of the J-SOAP-II, ERASOR, J-SORRAT-II, and Static-99. *Law and Human Behavior, 36*(5), 423–438. http://dx.doi.org/10.1037/h0093938

Viljoen, J. L., Scalora, M., Cuadra, L., Bader, S., Chavez, V., Ullman, D., & Lawrence, L. (2008). Assessing risk of violence in adolescents who have sexually offended: A comparison of the J-SOAP-II, J-SORRAT-II, and SAVRY. *Criminal Justice and Behavior, 35*(1), 5–23. http://dx.doi.org/10.1177/0093854807307521

Vincent, G. M., Guy, L. S., Fusco, S. L., & Gershenson, B. G. (2011). Field reliability of the SAVRY with probation officers: Implications for training. *Law and Human Behavior, 36,* 225–236. http://dx.doi.org/10.1007/s10979-011-9284-2

Vincent, G. M., Guy, L. S., & Grisso, T. (2012, November). Risk assessment in juvenile justice: A guidebook for implementation. Retrieved from http://www.modelsforchange.net/publications/346

Vitacco, M. J., Caldwell, M., Ryba, N. L., Malesky, A., & Kurus, S. J. (2009). Assessing risk in adolescent sexual offenders: Recommendations for clinical practice. *Behavioral Sciences and the Law, 27,* 929-940. http://dx.doi.org/10.1002/bsl.909

Worling, J. R. (2004). The Estimate of Risk of Adolescent Sexual Offense Recidivism (ERASOR): Preliminary psychometric data. *Sexual Abuse: A Journal of Research and Treatment, 16,* 235–254.

Worling, J. R. (2013). Desistence for Adolescents who Sexually Harm (DASH-13). Retrieved from http://www.drjamesworling.com/dash-13.html

Worling, J. R., Bookalam, D., & Litteljohn, A. (2012). Prospective validity of the Estimate of Risk of Adolescent Sexual Offense Recidivism (ERASOR). *Sexual Abuse: A Journal of Research and Treatment, 24,* 203–223.

Worling, J. R., & Curwen, T. (2001). Estimate of Risk of Adolescent Sexual Offense Recidivism (ERASOR; Version 2.0). In M. C. Calder (Ed.), *Juveniles and children who sexually abuse: Frameworks for assessment* (pp. 372–397). Lyme Regis, UK: Russell House. [The ERASOR is also available as pdf file from the author at jworling@ican.net.]

Worling, J. R., & Långström, N. (2006). Risk of sexual recidivism in adolescents who offend sexually: Correlates and assessment. In H. E. Barbaree & W. L. Marshall (Eds.), *The juvenile sex offender* (2nd ed., pp. 219–247). New York: Guilford.

Worling, J. R., & Langton, C. M. (2015). A prospective investigation of factors that predict desistance from recidivism for adolescents who have sexually offended. *Sexual Abuse: A Journal of Research and Treatment, 27*(1), 127–142.

Worling, J. R., Litteljohn, A., & Bookalam, D. (2010). 20-year prospective follow-up study of specialized treatment for adolescents who offended sexually. *Behavioral Sciences and the Law, 28,* 46–57.

Wormith, J. S., Gendreau, P., & Bonta, J. (2012). Deferring to clarity, parsimony, and evidence in reply to Ward, Yates, and Willis. *Criminal Justice and Behavior, 39*(1), 111–120.

Zeng, G., Chu, C. M., & Lee, Y. (2015). Assessing protective factors of youth who sexually offended in Singapore: Preliminary evidence on the utility of the DASH-13 and the SAPROF. *Sexual Abuse: A Journal of Research and Treatment, 27*(1), 91–108.

Zimring, F. E. (2004). *An American travesty: Legal responses to adolescent sexual offending.* Chicago: University of Chicago Press.

Part III
Intervention

CHAPTER 8

Engaging Adolescents and Families

Kevin M. Powell

Creating an environment in which youth and families feel safe to openly participate and address sensitive topics is a critical component for effective youth services. This is particularly important within sexual-offense-specific (SOS) services, where youth are often court-mandated to participate and may initially be quite guarded and defensive. In order for SOS assessment, therapy, and supervision to be most effective, youth and families must be actively engaged in the process. Low engagement and high dropout have been identified as significant threats to evidence-based interventions (NIMH, 2001). Treatment will not be effective if youth and families "no-show" for sessions or are poorly engaged in the services provided. Research on both youth and adults who have sexually offended indicates that those who do not complete sexual-offense-specific treatment are at significantly higher risk for sexual recidivism (Hanson & Bussiere, 1998; Reitzel & Carbonell, 2006; Schmucker & Lösel, 2015; Worling, Litteljohn, & Bookalam, 2010). Engagement is an essential component of effective SOS services.

Due to the paucity of research investigating client engagement within SOS services, especially the juvenile population, this chapter will also include information and research from general youth and family psychotherapy services, as well as various constructs that closely parallel engagement. A broad view of engagement will be described as it relates to definition, history, theory, empirical research, and clinical applications.

Defining Engagement

A review of the literature on client engagement reveals a multidimensional construct comprising many interrelated variables that influence engagement, which has been defined and measured in a variety of ways (Lindsey et al., 2014). Engagement has been defined as representing all the efforts that clients (youth and families) make during the course of treatment (both within and between sessions) toward the achievement of changes (Holdsworth, Bowen, Brown, & Howat, 2014). Engagement is a multifaceted, reciprocal process influenced by provider, client, and treatment factors. It also includes external, practical factors that can impede or enhance client involvement in services. A manageable means of conceptualizing engagement is to incorporate four interrelated components: practical/access engagement (e.g., access to transportation; access to services; access to child care; financial costs); behavioral engagement (e.g., client attendance; no-shows; level of participation; completion of homework/adherence; client retention and attrition); attitudinal/cognitive engagement (e.g., degree of feeling understood; perceived relevance/usefulness of treatment; buy-in and ownership of identified treatment goals; cognitive preparation—understanding of and readiness for treatment; prior negative treatment experiences; degree of confidence in treatment; treatment satisfaction; stigma about participation in mental health services); and social process engagement (e.g., alliance with therapist and the therapy process; collaboration in treatment) (Becker et al., 2014; French, Reardon, & Smith, 2003; Lindsey et al., 2014; Pullmann et al., 2013; Schley, Yuen, Fletcher, & Radovini, 2012; Staudt, 2007). Engagement is a dynamic process that youth service providers must be attentive to throughout the course of services (Ellis, Lindsey, Barker, Boxmeyer, & Lochman, 2013).

History and Theory of Engagement

The concept and importance of engagement in psychotherapy evolved out of the humanistic psychology movement, which emerged in the 1950s and 1960s. In contrast with the psychodynamic and behaviorist perspectives that primarily focused attention on problem behaviors and influential forces outside a person's control (e.g., instinctual drives and environmental stimuli), the humanistic perspective placed an emphasis on strengths and people's capacity to make choices in their lives. Humanist Abraham Maslow's hierarchy of needs theory of motivation (1954; 1962; 1970) highlighted the importance of meeting individuals' basic human needs in order to increase their capacity to engage in higher level needs (e.g., esteem and achievement needs and living up to their fullest potential/self-actualization). Humanist Carl Rogers developed the client-centered/person-centered perspective (1951; 1957; 1961), which emphasized humans' natural tendency toward healthy psychological growth and the power of relationships to foster this growth. This capacity for clients to play an active role in their personal development highlights why engagement is so crucial in youth services.

The field of SOS services for juveniles appears to be evolving in a similar fashion to the history of contemporary psychology, progressing from an approach that primarily attends to external factors and problem-focused interventions (e.g., physical management and containment; targeting risk factors) to a more holistic, client-centered approach. In the 1980s, information about youth who had sexually offended was limited, which resulted in the juvenile field applying the adult model, with the no-cure mantra, *Once a sex offender, always a sex offender.* An emphasis was placed on a punitive, deficit-based orientation, with providers delivering services in an authoritarian, confrontational manner (D'Orazio, 2013; Marshall & Hollin, 2015). Youth's interactions with others, even prosocial actions, were frequently interpreted as "grooming" behaviors used to set up sexual offense opportunities. This harsh, overpathologizing approach focused almost no attention on engaging youth and families or creating an atmosphere conducive to the internal change process. Fortunately, recidivism research on sexual reoffense rates has debunked the no-cure model, highlighting the capacity for the large majority of youth to desist from sexual reoffending (Caldwell, 2010; Langstrom & Grann, 2000; Reitzel & Carbonell, 2006; Worling et al., 2010). In response to these findings, the juvenile field is beginning to focus more attention on healthy life course development and harnessing the youth's and family's capacity to actively participate in the treatment process.

Two prominent theoretical models within the field of offender rehabilitation and SOS services include components that highlight the importance of client engagement. The risk-need-responsivity (RNR) model and the good lives model (GLM) both evolved from the adult offender population and are beginning to be explored within the juvenile field (Brogan, Haney-Caron, NeMoyer, & DeMatteo, 2015; Chua, Chu, Yim, Chong, & Teoh, 2014; Fortune, Ward, & Print, 2014; Hoge, 2016; Singh et al., 2014). The RNR model theorizes that effective offender rehabilitation requires the targeting of three core principles: risk, need, and responsivity (Andrews & Bonta, 2010). Although the RNR camp has historically focused most of their attention and research on the identification and management of dynamic risk factors (need principle) and matching the level of risk of the offender to the appropriate level of intervention (risk principle), in recent years more attention is beginning to be placed on strengths and responsivity for engaging clients in the treatment process (Andrews, Bonta, & Wormith, 2011). The responsivity principle directly focuses on engagement with its emphasis on the *how* of intervention. This principle endeavors to deliver treatment and supervision in a style and mode that consider clients' individualized needs in order to enhance receptiveness to services. Individualized needs include client motivation and readiness, intellectual functioning, learning style or disabilities, co-occurring psychiatric disorders, developmental issues, personality, anger/hostility, cultural factors, and religious beliefs.

GLM theorizes that human beings are active, goal-seeking beings whose actions reflect attempts to meet inherent human needs (primary human goods) (Collie, Ward, Ayland, & West, 2007; Ward & Gannon, 2006). Sexual offending is believed to occur when an individual attempts to get his or her human needs (e.g., friendships, romantic relationships) met in abusive ways. GLM has helped to orient the SOS field beyond goals to be avoided (avoidance of sexually abusive behaviors and managing risk factors associated with sexual offending) to prosocial goals associated with life satisfaction and enhanced well-being, which clients want to achieve (approach goals).

The RNR and GLM camps have had a lively debate within the literature (e.g., Andrews et al., 2011; Ward, Gannon, & Yates, 2008; Ward, Melser, & Yates, 2007; Ward & Stewart, 2003; Ward, Yates, & Willis, 2012; Wormith, Gendreau, & Bonta, 2012), which is helping the SOS field to become not only more holistic, but also more focused on treatment engagement. GLM's approach goals and strengths-based orientation, along with RNR's responsivity principle, delineate the importance of client engagement in SOS services.

Empirical Research Linked to Engagement

Client engagement research has been conducted within general youth and family services, as well as SOS services. Due to the multifaceted nature of the engagement construct, research has explored myriad practices and outcome variables. There are several related constructs and areas of research associated with engagement, including strengths-based orientation, therapeutic alliance, personal attributes of the provider, motivational interviewing strategies, hope promotion, approach goals, collaborative treatment atmosphere, identification of protective factors, and responsivity principle. Potential barriers to engagement have also been empirically studied.

Research on Engagement Within Youth and Family Services

The construct of engagement has been studied within general youth and family services. When there is no buy-in from caregivers, barriers to treatment effectiveness arise including increased no-shows, premature termination, and poor follow-through on treatment assignments (Dorsey et al., 2014; Lindsey et al., 2014; Saxe, Ellis, Fogler, & Navalta, 2012; Thompson, Bender, Lantry, & Flynn, 2007).

Becker et al. (2015) investigated the common elements of engagement in children's mental health services by coding 89 engagement practices and outcomes from 40 randomized controlled trials. They utilized the distillation component of the distillation and matching framework (Chorpita, Daleiden, & Weisz, 2005), which provides a way of reorganizing the accumulated empirical data beyond the evidence-based treatment protocols to the specific practice elements that are common across various studies. The outcomes (treatment engagement indicators) investigated were treatment attendance, treatment adherence (e.g., session participation; out-of-session practice), and cognitive preparation (e.g., expectations about roles or treatment outcomes; attitudes toward therapy; motivation for change; perceptions of personal stress and resources). The results of this study identified three practices that were strong interventions for promoting engagement universally across all the outcomes: accessibility promotion, individualized assessment, and psycho-education about services. The accessibility promotion practices included providing treatment at a location convenient to the youth and family, providing transportation to the treatment session, and providing child care. These practices enhanced engagement by reducing the practical barriers to attending treatment. Individualized assessment involved the practice of learning about youth's and families' individualized strengths, needs, goals, and values. While gathering this assessment information, therapists were building rapport and making therapeutic connections, which appeared to enhance engagement. The third practice involved the provision of psycho-education about services to youth and families regarding what to expect in treatment, including the type of services (e.g., theoretical approach), the logistics (e.g., the frequency and cost of treatment), the roles and responsibilities of the clients and therapist, information about why treatment could benefit them, and information to correct any misperceptions clients may have about services. Lindsey et al. (2014) similarly found that the most frequently identified practices linked to positive engagement outcomes were individualized assessment, accessibility promotion, and psycho-education about services. They also identified homework assignments as a practice to improve treatment adherence/engagement.

From what is known about the influence of family relationships and utility of the ecological perspective, engaging caregivers is essential for positively impacting the developmental trajectory of youth. Ingoldsby (2010) investigated methods for improving family/caregiver engagement and retention in child mental health programs by identifying and evaluating 17 randomized controlled trials published since 1980. The general findings revealed that interventions addressing families' motivations, expectations, and needs throughout the course of treatment were successful in improving engagement and retention. Providers who effectively engaged families were those who assisted family members in identifying the potential benefits of treatment services, had discussions about the families' expectations for the treatment process and outcomes, and collaboratively worked with families to develop a plan addressing practical barriers (e.g., transportation; scheduling) and psychological barriers (e.g., family stressors; family members' resistance to treatment). The utilization of motivational interviewing was also identified as an effective method of improving family engagement, which is a practice described later in this chapter.

Engaged caregivers can even have a positive impact on youth who are incarcerated. Research has revealed that youth who receive more frequent visits while incarcerated have a more rapid reduction in depressed symptoms, get better grades, have fewer violent incidents, and have reduced recidivism after their release back into the community. Parent visits during incarceration even appear to have a protective effect regardless of the quality of the parent–adolescent relationship (Monahan, Goldweber, & Cauffman, 2011; Shanahan & diZerega, 2016).

Research on Engagement Within Sexual-Offense-Specific Services

Research on engagement in SOS services has unfortunately been limited and has primarily targeted adult offenders. This research has included studies investigating RNR's responsivity principle (Andrews et al., 2011), GLM's strengths-based orientation with its emphasis on approach goals (McMurran & Ward, 2004; Netto, Carter, & Bonell, 2014; Yates, 2009a), as well as independent researchers investigating the engagement process as it relates to therapist qualities and the therapeutic alliance within group settings (Marshall, 2005; Beech & Fordham, 1997; Harkins & Beech, 2007; Levenson & MacGowan, 2004).

There have only been a few engagement studies targeting the juvenile population. These studies have focused primarily on treatment non-completers, investigating factors that impede engagement, as opposed to enhancing it (Edwards et al., 2005; Hunter & Figueredo, 1999; Kraemer, Salisbury, & Spielman, 1998). An exception to these engagement barrier studies is a study by Smallbone, Crissman, and Rayment-McHugh (2009) conducted in Australia with 159 adolescents participating in sexual-offense-specific group therapy. This study explored factors associated with enhancing and/or impeding client engagement, including appointment keeping (e.g., attending scheduled outpatient appointments), client–therapist interaction (the extent to which the client relates well with the therapist, helping to create a positive atmosphere during sessions), communication/openness (the extent to which the client volunteers personal information and is open in discussing his or her feelings, problems, and current situation), perceived usefulness of treatment (the extent to which the client perceives treatment to be useful), and collaboration with treatment (the extent to which the client agrees with proposed intervention plans and is involved in carrying them out). A youth attribute found to be associated with poor treatment engagement was impulsivity/antisocial behavior problems. The impulsivity and antisocial behavior attribute has been identified as an impediment to engagement in other studies as well (Edwards et al., 2005; Kraemer et al., 1998). Another attribute linked to poor engagement in this Australian study was indigenous race. In the second phase of the Smallbone et al. study (2009), a practice that was found to enhance engagement with both the indigenous race and impulsive/antisocial youth was to shift responsibility for treatment engagement to the treatment professional. Clinicians were tasked to assess potential barriers to engagement and improve their problem-solving efforts to address the barriers. Specific strategies that helped overcome barriers to engagement were scheduling appointments at locations and times most convenient to the client, framing treatment engagement as a primary treatment goal, enhancing the cultural competence of clinical staff, and recruiting indigenous adults as collaborative partners to work directly with indigenous youth. It is important to note that although these strategies did significantly enhance treatment engagement for both indigenous and non-indigenous youth, the improvement was less pronounced for the indigenous group. Further research investigating culturally sensitive practices for enhancing engagement within SOS juvenile services is needed.

More research is also needed in the area of caregiver engagement in SOS services. Pithers, Gray, Busconi, and Houchens (1998) found that caregivers of children with sexual behavior problems frequently manifest high levels of stress in many areas of life including income, criminal arrest, family violence, sexual abuse, social support, modulation of emotion, and attachment to their child. A meta-analysis of sexual-offense-specific treatment, which included some studies with juveniles, found that the most positive treatment effects (including lower recidivism rates) came from interventions that placed an emphasis on family involvement (Schmucker & Lösel, 2015). In order to maximize the efficacy of SOS treatment with youth, caregivers must be involved and receive needed services.

Research on Strengths-Based Orientation
Historically, the SOS field has primarily focused attention on risk factors associated with sexual offending. While there is clear evidence for the influence and importance of risk factors (Andrews & Bonta, 2010), if treatment only attends to deficits, client engagement can suffer. Utilization of a positive, strengths-based approach is gaining

momentum and empirical support within SOS services (Fortune et al., 2014; Marshall & Marshall, 2014; Maruna & LeBel, 2003; Powell, 2011). A strengths-based approach focuses on the identification, creation, and reinforcement of strengths and resources within youth, families, and their communities (Powell, 2015). This approach also includes a focus on solutions that can lead to potential dissolution of problems (Berg & Steiner, 2003). Within general child psychotherapy research, there is empirical support for the efficacy of a strengths-based, solution-focused orientation (Berg & Steiner, 2003; Corcoran & Stephenson, 2000; Lethem, 2002), including the enhancement of engagement (Corcoran & Ivery, 2004; Kemp, Marcenko, Lyons, & Kruzich, 2014). The many engagement-related constructs and strategies described in this chapter can be classified as strengths-based.

Research on the Therapeutic Alliance

A construct that is closely linked to client engagement is the therapeutic alliance. Over the years, researchers have defined alliance in many ways and used a variety of different terms. The most commonly used term and definition is *therapeutic alliance,* defined by Bordin (1979) to include three related but distinct dimensions—an affective bond between the client and the therapist, the agreed-upon tasks and participation in therapy activities, and collaboratively shared goals.

When there are problems with the therapeutic alliance, poor engagement and treatment dropout are common (Garcia & Weisz, 2002; Kazdin & Wassel, 1999). On the other hand, when the therapeutic alliance is strong, not only do treatment retention and participation improve, but other positive outcomes occur that likely enhance treatment engagement (e.g., improved family functioning, global functioning, and interpersonal relations, as well as decreased symptomatology and rate of new criminal offenses) (Karver, Handelsman, Fields, & Bickman, 2006; Karver et al., 2008; Kerkorian, McKay, & Bannon, 2006; Macneil, Hasty, Evans, Redlich, & Berk, 2009; Mcleod et al., 2014; Robbins et al., 2006). Although the effect sizes—i.e., the strength of the relationships—for these positive outcomes have ranged from moderate to low (McLeod, 2011; Shirk & Karver, 2011; Karver et al., 2006), they have been consistently associated with engagement. Hawley & Weisz (2005) found that the therapeutic alliance between the therapist and the parent predicted better therapy participation (attendance and retention in treatment), while the therapeutic alliance with the youth predicted symptom change.

The therapeutic alliance has also been identified as a crucial factor for client engagement in sexual-offense-specific services (Blanchard, 1995; Marshall, 2005; Marshall & Burton, 2010; Marshall & Serran, 2004; Marshall, Serran, Moulden, et al., 2002; Powell, 2010b). Although the majority of research has focused on adults, it is an important construct to consider with all populations including juveniles. Forging a therapeutic alliance with youth and families is essential for treatment engagement and positive outcomes.

Research on Personal Attributes of the Provider

Regardless of the specific interventions being implemented, the provider's personal attributes play an important role in engaging youth and families (Marshall, 2005; Miller, Hubble, Chow, & Seidel, 2015; Wampold & Imel, 2015). Marshall and colleagues (Marshall, 2005; Marshall & Burton, 2010; Marshall & Serran, 2004; Marshall, Serran, Moulden, et al., 2002) have conducted informative research on SOS therapists' attributes linked to positive treatment targets (e.g., improved relationships, decreased denial of responsibility, decreased denial of planning, decreased victim blaming, and decreased minimization of offense features), which are assumed to positively impact engagement. Although this research was conducted on adults, it is assumed to be relevant for the juvenile population due to the many common factors found in both adult and child psychotherapy (Norcross, 2011). The therapist attributes that were linked to the above treatment targets included warmth, empathy, rewardingness, and some directiveness (Marshall, 2005). The warmth and empathy attributes involve the therapist's ability to communicate acceptance and unconditional positive regard. Rewardingness is described as the verbal encouragement given to clients for their small steps toward whatever goal is being sought. Directiveness is defined as providing some direction and guidance (e.g., "Have you thought of trying . . ."; "Have you considered . . .") while still allowing clients opportunities to develop their own solutions to problems. The antithesis of these attributes is a harsh, confrontational therapist, which has been found to be negatively correlated with achieving treatment targets (Marshall, 2005).

Research on Motivational Interviewing

Motivational interviewing (MI) defines engagement as "the process of establishing a mutually trusting and respectful helping relationship" (Miller & Rollnick, 2013, p. 40). MI evolved out of the Rogerian, person-centered approach in which the therapist helps elicit the client's own motivation for change (Miller & Rollnick, 2002; 2013). This intrinsic motivation is a construct that closely parallels the attitudinal/cognitive component of engagement and has growing empirical support. Hettema, Steele, and Miller (2005) conducted a meta-analysis of MI that included 72 clinical studies covering a range of target problems, which included both adolescent and adult clients ranging in age from 16 to 62. One of the highest effect sizes (ES = 0.72) occurred for the studies investigating MI's impact on treatment engagement as measured by retention and adherence. The specific mechanism in which MI exerts its influence is not well understood due to the variable effectiveness across providers, populations, target problems, and settings, as well as the broad collection of components that are included in MI. The MI components coded for Hettema et al.'s (2005) meta-analysis included being collaborative, being client-centered, being nonjudgmental, building trust, reducing resistance, increasing readiness to change, increasing self-efficacy, increasing perceived discrepancy, engaging in reflective listening, eliciting "change" talk, exploring ambivalence, and listening empathically.

The utilization of MI continues to grow and has increasingly been incorporated into juvenile criminal justice settings and SOS services to enhance engagement and adherence (Patel, Lambie, & Glover, 2008; Stein et al., 2006; Wood, Wood, & Taylor, 2012; Zweben & Zuckoff, 2002). MI has identified specific strategies for enhancing engagement, which include asking and listening; being welcoming; getting a sense of how important particular goals are to a client; providing the client with a sense of what to expect in treatment; and offering hope about how the treatment can help them (Miller & Rollnick, 2013, p. 46). Other key MI concepts include partnership; acceptance; compassion; and rolling with resistance, which are described in the Clinical Applications section beginning on page 229.

Research on Hope Promotion

Instilling hope in clients has been identified as an important variable in the psychotherapy process and for treating many psychological issues (Larsen & Stege, 2010a; 2010b; Snyder, 2000). When clients have hope that their participation in treatment services will lead to a better life, engagement can flourish. In contrast, when hopelessness or learned helplessness is the dominant worldview (Seligman, 1975; 2006), engagement can suffer. Research has found that animals (Seligman, 1975; 1991) and humans (Witkowski, 1997) who are exposed to repeated incidents in which they do not have control of their environment (e.g., inescapable shocks, abuse, frequent failures) often develop a sense of helplessness. They come to believe they have no control of their life circumstances and often take on an apathetic, non-caring attitude.

The construct of hope in SOS services is now being considered within the adult population (Moulden & Marshall, 2005) and should also be incorporated into juvenile services, due to the many reasons for hope identified in child and adolescent development research. Developmental research findings that promote hope include the maturation of the brain's prefrontal cortex (Casey, Giedd, & Thomas, 2000; Diamond, 2002; Luna & Sweeney, 2004; Rubia et al., 2000; Sowell, Trauner, Gamst, & Jernigan, 2002; Spear, 2000), the influence of neuroplasticity (Bryck & Fisher, 2012; Nelson, 2003; Winerman, 2012), the low lifetime prevalence rate for delinquent behavior (Farrington, 2007; Loeber et al., 2012; Moffitt, 1993; 1997; 2007; Van Domburgh, Loeber, Bezemer, Stallings, & Stouthamer-Loeber, 2009;

Walters, 2011), and the low recidivism rate for sexual reoffending (Caldwell, 2010; Reitzel & Carbonell, 2006; Worling et al., 2010). Educating youth and families about these developmental research findings is hypothesized to enhance hope and engagement in juvenile SOS services, although it has not yet been empirically studied. Clinical applications of these hope-promoting research findings are described later in the chapter.

Research on Approach Goals

A construct closely linked to hope and engagement is the identification of meaningful goals. The Good Lives Model (GLM) (Collie et al., 2007) focuses attention on approach goals, which target what clients want to achieve in life, now and in the future. Within the adult research, approach goals have been linked to greater engagement in treatment (as measured by homework compliance and willingness to disclose lapses) compared with programs that primarily focus on avoidance goals (Mann, Webster, Schofield, & Marshall, 2004). Approach goals, as well as other GLM components, engage clients in the treatment process (Yates, 2009a; McMurran & Ward, 2004). Although GLM was developed for adult offenders, and research on the juvenile population has yet to be conducted, many of the identified approach goals appear relevant for adolescents to help clarify what they have and what they want to have in life. Youth are more likely to be engaged in learning how to manage their sexual behaviors in prosocial ways if it leads to something they desire (e.g., making and keeping friendships). The identified GLM approach goals are described in the Clinical Applications section of this chapter.

Research on a Collaborative Treatment Atmosphere

The identification of treatment goals that are meaningful for clients requires a collaborative atmosphere. When youth and families are actively involved in the identification of goals and the direction of treatment, a strong therapeutic alliance and client engagement are enhanced (Creed & Kendall, 2005; Defife & Hilsenroth, 2011; Russell, Shirk, & Jungbluth, 2008; Shirk & Karver, 2011; Wampold & Imel, 2015). This is an area of research that has primarily targeted general child psychotherapy populations as opposed to the juvenile SOS population.

Research on a Holistic, Ecological Perspective— Family and School Connections

There is growing interest within the juvenile SOS field in utilizing a holistic, ecological perspective that targets not only sexual offending behaviors but also non-sexual problem behaviors; prosocial, healthy behaviors; and strengths and resources within youth, their family, and their community (Leversee & Powell, 2012; Longo, 2002; Morrison,

2006). The ecological model views youth as developing within a complex network of reciprocally interacting contexts and relationships that includes individual, family, and community factors (Bronfenbrenner, 2001; Bronfenbrenner & Ceci, 1994). According to general child and family psychotherapy research, when providers successfully engage a youth's family support system, treatment engagement is augmented (Becker et al., 2015; Ingoldsby, 2010; Lindsey et al., 2014). A connectedness to school has also been linked to treatment involvement and healthy social/emotional development within residential facilities (Dornbusch, Erickson, Laird, & Wong, 2001; McNeely, Nonnemaker, & Blum, 2002; Murray & Greenberg, 2001; Nickerson, Hopson, & Steinke, 2011).

Research on Protective Factors

Focusing exclusively on risks and deficits can be stigmatizing to clients and potentially impede treatment engagement (de Vries Robbe, Mann, Maruna, & Thornton, 2015; Mann et al., 2004; Maruna & LeBel, 2003; Ward et al., 2007). There is growing interest and research investigating protective factors associated with desistance from sexual offending (Langton & Worling, 2015). Thus far, results have been mixed, with some studies identifying a link (direct and/or buffering effects) between protective factors and reduced sexual reoffense recidivism with adults (Miller, 2015; de Vries Robbe, de Vogel, Koster, & Bogaerts, 2015) and juveniles (Worling & Langton, 2015), while other studies have not found a significant link (Klien, Rettenberger, Yoon, Kohler, & Briken, 2015; Spice, Viljoen, Latzman, Scalora, & Ullman, 2013; Zeng, Chu, & Lee, 2015). However, regardless of the direct influence of protective factors on desistance from sexual offending, the impact on youth and family engagement in SOS services is a critical factor that can impact outcomes.

While research on protective factors associated with prevention and desistance from sexual offending is just under way, research on protective factors linked to general resiliency has been in motion for many decades (Gilgun, 2006; Hawkins, Graham, Williams, & Zahn, 2009; Masten & Coatsworth, 1998; Masten, Cutuli, Herbers, & Reed, 2009; Masten & Reed, 2002; Richman & Fraser, 2001; Smith, Boutte, Zigler, & Finn-Stevenson, 2004; Trickett, Kurtz, & Pizzigati, 2004). Studies have found that resilient youth are more likely to possess beliefs in self-efficacy and have lower feelings of helplessness (Lösel & Bliesener, 1994; Lösel & Farrington, 2012; Masten et al., 2009; Wyman, Cowen, Work, & Kerley, 1993), which are critical qualities for engagement in treatment.

Research on the Responsivity Principle

The risk-need-responsivity model is a prominent model within general offender reha-bilitation and sexual-offense-specific services (Andrews & Bonta, 2010). The responsivity principle (the second *R*) directly addresses the engagement process by promoting variables that enhance responsiveness to treatment. Responsivity (specific type) highlights the importance of matching the style and mode of services to the individualized needs of the client. Individualized needs include strengths, abilities, motivations, readiness to change, mental status, learning ability, learning style, circumstances, developmental issues, personality, anger/hostility, cultural factors, religious beliefs, and other demographics of individual cases (Andrews & Bonta, 2003; Andrews et al., 2011).

Juvenile offender research has found a link between meeting individualized needs and positive outcomes, including treatment responsiveness/engagement (Haqanee, Peterson-Badali, & Skilling, 2015; Nee, Ellis, Morris, & Wilson, 2012; Veira, Skilling, & Peterson-Badali, 2009). Juvenile SOS research on the responsivity principle (specific type) has been limited thus far; however, it is becoming evident that an emphasis on more than just dynamic risk factors is required to engage youth and families and avoid poor treatment responses (Brogan et al., 2015; Hoge, 2016; Ward et al., 2008; Ward et al., 2007).

Research on Engagement Barriers

Effectively engaging youth and families in treatment requires providers to be cognizant and responsive to possible barriers to engagement (McKay & Bannon, 2004; Sax, Ellis, Fogler, & Navalta, 2012). Research has identified youth and family characteristics, as well as coercion-oriented practices, that have been linked to poor engagement.

Youth Characteristics

Research on juvenile SOS treatment programs has revealed a high rate of treatment non-completion for youth who possess specific attributes including greater impulsivity (Kraemer et al., 1998), conduct and aggression problems including non-sexual offense history (Edwards et al., 2005), and school problems—expulsion and truancy (Edwards et al., 2005). Engagement barriers have also been linked to clients struggling with past trauma. Research on the prevalence of adverse childhood experiences has identified trauma-informed care as an important component within youth services, including sexual-offense-specific services, due to the high rates of trauma experienced by these youth (Anda & Felitti, 2003; Jespersen, Lalumière, & Seto, 2009; Levenson, 2013; Levenson, Willis, & Prescott, 2014; Reavis, Looman, Franco, & Rojas, 2013). Youth with victimization histories often wish to avoid anything that places them at risk of being reminded of past experiences that were traumatic. In addition, caregivers of youth who have been impacted by trauma can also be avoidant of treatment. A caregiver's feelings of guilt and shame about not being able to protect his or her child, fear of being negatively judged, and the desire to protect the child from having to rehash past traumatic incidents in treatment can all act as barriers to treatment engagement (Gopalan et al., 2010).

Within SOS services, a potential impediment to engagement involves youth who are denying and/or minimizing their culpability for sexual offending. However, providers must be cognizant that a link between denial of responsibility and risk of sexual reoffending has not been found (Hanson & Morton-Bourgon, 2005; Levenson, 2011; Yates, 2009b), and some guardedness can be a healthy response in many circumstances. Youth may be denying and/or minimizing their offense history for a variety of reasons that are non-pathological, which is highlighted in the Clinical Applications section.

Family Characteristics

Family characteristics that have been identified as barriers to engagement and retention in general mental health services include single-parent status, socioeconomic disadvantage, parent mental health problems, marital distress, residing in rural areas, and ethnic minority status. Practical/access obstacles that have been identified include time demands, scheduling conflicts, lack of transportation, child care, and high cost (Ingoldsby, 2010; Snell-Johns, Mendez, & Smith, 2004).

Coercion-Oriented Services, Including the Polygraph

A major goal of SOS services is to promote internal change so clients have the prosocial capacity to live safely within communities; however, when the majority of services are oriented toward external, coercive controls, internal change can be difficult to achieve. When comparing mandated, coercion-oriented services to voluntary services within the justice system, the mandated services have often been found to be ineffective (Parhar, Wormith, Derzken, & Beauregard, 2008). Mandatory utilization of the polygraph raises many concerns within youth services, which include the risk of undermining a trusting, collaborative relationship; the questionable validity/accuracy of the polygraph results; the fact that empirical literature has not found a clear link between denial of offenses and higher recidivism; and concerns that forced self-disclosure can heighten defensiveness and possibly cause harm when a client is not psychologically prepared to address certain content (Chaffin, 2011; Hanson & Morton-Bourgon, 2005; Harkins, Beech, & Goodwill, 2010; Levenson, 2011; McGrath, Cumming, Hoke, & Bonn-Miller, 2007; Prescott, 2012; Yates, 2009b). Forced self-disclosure with the polygraph is a coercive process, therefore caution must be used to ensure that engagement and positive outcomes are not undermined. Decisions about the utilization of polygraphs should always be made by the multidisciplinary team who are most familiar with the individualized needs of the case.

CLINICAL APPLICATIONS FOR YOUTH AND FAMILY ENGAGEMENT

The many variables associated with client engagement require an assortment of interventions to engage youth and families. Due to the dearth of research investigating client engagement in juvenile SOS services, the clinical applications described below include information from the general psychotherapy research, as well as clinically derived interventions with components that have empirical support.

Assess and Address Practical and Perceptual Barriers to Engagement

Proactively gathering information and developing practical solutions to potential engagement barriers should be a focal point from the very first phone call with families. These discussions with families should explore practical barriers (e.g., transportation challenges; financial concerns) and perceptual barriers to engagement (e.g., attitudes about mental health treatment) (McKay & Bannon, 2004). It can also be beneficial to ask caregivers about their past experiences in youth services, both good and bad, and use this information to create a positive therapeutic environment.

Maintain a Strengths-Based Orientation

Any intervention that emphasizes strengths and the exceptions to problems can be classified as strengths-based. Attending to what is right with youth rather than what is wrong can help engage youth and families in SOS services (Powell, 2010a; 2011; 2016). Openness to intervention can be enhanced when providers place an emphasis on circumstances when youth have managed their sexual thoughts, feelings, and behaviors in prosocial ways.

Do Not Address Problems Too Quickly

Having a strengths-based orientation does not mean providers are naive or ignore problems. Risk factors, problem behaviors, and accountability are addressed; however, SOS providers must first create an atmosphere in which youth are open to addressing these sensitive topics. Youth's sexually abusive actions are what bring them into the human service system; however, if providers too quickly focus attention on problem behaviors, it can increase the risk of youth becoming defensive, growing agitated, or emotionally shutting down. Initially focusing on strengths and exceptions to problems is an important first step in SOS services.

Explore Interests, Talents, and Life Goals

Engagement can be enhanced by exploring youth's interests, talents, and life goals. While some youth will easily be able to identify their passions and life goals, others will need assistance. Questions to assist in this exploratory process include, "What do you like to do in your free time?"; "What things do you do that make you most happy?"; "What would others say are your biggest talents/things you do well?"; and "What do you hope to be doing 1 year/5 years/10 years from now?"

Share Positives

A primary component of a strengths-based orientation is to ensure that there is an adequate emphasis on positives. Regularly communicating about youth's and caregivers' successes and strengths can heighten treatment engagement.

Address Dynamic Risk Factors by Targeting Strengths-Based Alternatives

Research has identified the importance of targeting dynamic risk factors (risk factors that can be changed) that have been linked to criminal behaviors (Andrews & Bonta, 2010). Addressing these risk factors can often be accomplished by identifying and reinforcing the healthy strengths-based alternatives. For example, antisocial associates is one of the big four dynamic risk factors (Andrews & Bonta, 2010, p. 59), which can be mitigated by assisting youth in developing the skills and opportunities to establish connections with prosocial peers. When providers place an emphasis on strengths-based alternatives, as opposed to exclusively dialoguing about risks, engagement is enhanced.

Establish a Positive Therapeutic Alliance

In addition to the therapeutic alliance practices already highlighted in the Empirical Research section, other strategies that assist in alliance building and engagement include being present in the here and now during sessions so youth have providers' full and undivided attention; utilizing nonverbal behaviors that communicate attentiveness and acceptance, such as open posture with arms uncrossed (Bedi, 2006; Egan, 2006); and utilizing mimesis to join with youth and families. Mimesis (also referred to as mimicking or imitating) is a family therapy technique used to form therapeutic connections (Minuchin, 1974, p. 128). It involves mimicking/matching the interpersonal style and affective range of youth and families in order to join with them. If there is too much discrepancy between the interpersonal style or affective range of a provider and that of the client, there is less likelihood of an interpersonal connection. For example, a youth who is socially introverted and struggling with depression will typically respond better to a provider who communicates in a similar low-key manner, as opposed to an overly upbeat, jovial manner.

Ensure That Providers Possess "Engagement-Promoting" Attributes

The personal attributes of providers are common factors within the psychotherapy process that influence the therapeutic alliance and treatment outcomes. Regardless of the specific techniques being implemented, therapist attributes play a major role in whether or not a youth and family engage in the treatment process. In addition to the attributes of warmth, empathy, rewardingness, and some directiveness (Marshall, 2005), other provider characteristics that can aid in the engagement process include being understanding of a client's mistrust and defensiveness, being patient and autonomous with responses, being dependable, being humble and inquisitive, and maintaining good psychological self-care.

Be Understanding of Clients' Mistrust and Defensiveness

A certain degree of mistrust and defensiveness is normal for clients when they first come into contact with the youth service system. It is a normal reaction to be guarded when facing legal consequences and having to address misdeeds. In addition, it is not uncommon for some clients to be mistrustful of the system. The youth service and juvenile justice system is not perfect, and some clients will have had negative experiences and assume all youth service providers are the same. Acknowledging that the system is not perfect and communicating your understanding of mistrust can help facilitate a healthy client–provider connection.

If providers react to clients' defensiveness in a similar fashion, the chances of healthy engagement are low. In contrast, when providers respond to clients' hardened responses with an autonomous response, engagement can flourish. An autonomous response occurs when a provider is nurturing and supportive even when a client is not eliciting such a response (Dozier et al., 2009). This includes setting limits without malice and letting clients' disrespectful actions "bounce off" while continuing to communicate in a respectful manner. Harsh, confrontational SOS services are antithetical to engagement.

Maintain a Humble, Inquisitive Interaction Style

Human behavior is complicated, and if providers ever think they have all the answers, it is not long before a youth's disruptive behavior humbles them. Providers who interpersonally come across as if they have all the answers and disregard others' input can significantly hinder a youth's and family's receptiveness to services. A humble, inquisitive interpersonal style helps facilitate client engagement.

Maintain Good Psychological Self-Care

Providers who take good care of themselves typically have a greater capacity for patience and distress tolerance, which can reduce the risk of burnout and enhance client engagement.

Utilize Motivational Interviewing

Key MI concepts that help promote youth and family engagement include partnership, acceptance, compassion, and rolling with resistance (Miller & Rollnick, 2002; 2013). Partnership highlights the importance of providers communicating a partner-like relationship that honors a youth's or family's expertise and perspective while avoiding an authoritarian one-up stance. Acceptance highlights the importance of providers seeking to understand a client's feelings and perspectives without judging, criticizing, or blaming. They communicate acceptance of the client, which is not necessarily the same as agreement or approval. Compassion is a deliberate commitment to pursue the welfare and best interests of another, to give priority to the other's needs. Rolling with resistance is a strategy in which providers do not argue for change but instead acknowledge a client's ambivalence/resistance as natural and understandable.

Promote Hope

A significant barrier to treatment engagement is learned helplessness (Seligman, 1975; 2006). When youth or family have no hope in their capacity to overcome problems and obtain a healthy, fulfilling life, they are much less likely to actively participate in services. A method for counteracting learned helplessness is to educate youth and families about developmental research and statistics, which provide strong evidence for hope (cited in the Empirical Research section).

Educate About the Maturation of the Brain's Prefrontal Cortex

The prefrontal cortex of the brain is located directly behind the forehead and governs our executive functioning abilities, which include regulating emotions/impulse control; anticipating consequences (thinking before acting); organizing, planning, and problem solving; sustaining and shifting attention; self-motivating; and having insight into self and others. Neuro-developmental research has identified the prefrontal cortex as one of the last regions to fully mature, not reaching full maturation until the mid-20s. As the brain matures into later adolescence and early adulthood (due to myelination, synaptic pruning, and other maturational processes), it more efficiently utilizes the thinking region (prefrontal cortex) in coordination with the emotional/subcortical region. Providing psycho-education about how the brain matures during adolescence and young adulthood gives youth (and caregivers) hope that their current struggles are not a life sentence.

Educate About the Neuroplasticity of the Brain

The human brain works on a "use it or lose it" principle. The neural pathways that are used on a regular basis become strong and thrive while the pathways that are not used regularly get pruned away or become less prominent. This process is referred to as neuroplasticity, and it highlights the importance of youth repeatedly practicing healthy alternatives to their sexually abusive behaviors in order to wire the brain in positive ways. Providing youth with neurophysiological explanations for the benefits of exhibiting prosocial, healthy behaviors can motivate them to walk on these positive pathways every day.

Educate About the Decreased Prevalence of Delinquent Behavior in Late Adolescence

The prevalence rate for delinquent behaviors peaks during the adolescent years and dramatically decreases in late adolescence and young adulthood. The large majority of youth who commit delinquent acts during their teenage years do not continue on this path as adults. Sharing these statistics with youth and families promotes hope.

Educate About the Low Recidivism Rate for Sexual Reoffending

A meta-analysis of 63 data sets with a total of 11,219 juveniles who had sexually offended revealed an average sexual offense recidivism rate of 7.08 percent with a range of 0 to 18 percent and an average follow-up time of approximately five years (Caldwell, 2010). This relatively low sexual recidivism rate has even been found in a 20-year follow-up study with an average rate of 9 percent (Worling et al., 2010). The large majority of youth who receive treatment do not sexually reoffend in the future. Engagement is enhanced when youth and families understand that participation in SOS treatment can lead to a healthy developmental life path.

Identify and Promote Approach Goals

There is sometimes a bias when treating delinquent youth to primarily focus on avoidance goals—i.e., goals oriented toward what not to do, including not committing future sexual offenses. In contrast, approach goals focus attention on what youth want to achieve in life, now and in the future. Motivation to manage abusive behaviors can be enhanced when it leads to things youth want (e.g., making and keeping friendships and romantic relationships; being free in the community to pursue extracurricular activities, education, and other life goals). The good lives model (Collie et al., 2007; Ward, Mann, & Gannon, 2007) includes a list of approach goals (human needs). Although these goals were developed for the adult population, most are also relevant for the juvenile population. The approach goal categories are Family (have a connection with family of origin, be a healthy spouse, be a healthy father/mother); Friendships (have platonic and romantic relationships); Excellence in Work and Play (have mastery and competency experiences); Excellence in Agency (be independent, self-directed); Life (enjoy healthy living and optimal physical functioning); Knowledge (have wisdom and information); Inner Peace (freedom from emotional turmoil and stress); Spirituality (find meaning and purpose in life); Community (feel connected to those in the environment); Happiness (feel contentment and joy in life); and Creativity (have opportunities for creative expression). When youth make the connection between how their participation in SOS services can help them achieve what they want in life (approach goals), engagement is enhanced.

Create a Collaborative Team Approach

Engagement in youth services is much stronger when everyone has a voice. Rather than providers taking on a one-sided expert role, there is a mutual exploration of what will help youth develop into healthy, prosocial adults. A quote from the field of child welfare succinctly describes the collaborative process in youth services: "To effectively engage families as partners, child welfare workers must be prepared to share power, ask for and use feedback, and see themselves as coaches or mentors who stand beside families and not in front of them" (Cahalane & Anderson, 2013). Specific strategies for establishing a collaborative, engaged environment include placing clients in the expert role, communicating that we are all on the same team, encouraging active participation on the multidisciplinary team, and helping youth and families to be informed consumers.

Place Clients in the Expert Role

Youth and their caregivers are great sources of information and truly are the experts regarding their social history and needs. Asking questions about what interventions have been tried, what has worked, and what has not worked can result in valuable information for effective services. Placing youth and caregivers in an expert role helps facilitate a collaborative, engaged process.

Encourage Active Participation on the Multidisciplinary Team

Multidisciplinary teams play a critical role in SOS services and promote collaboration (CSOM, 2008; Lobanov-Rostovsky, 2010; McGrath, Cumming, & Holt, 2002). No one person has all the answers, which is why every voice on the team should be welcomed and encouraged to participate.

Help Youth and Families to Be Informed Consumers

If someone handed you a bucket and told you to start bailing water but did not explain why, you probably would not be motivated to bail water. However, if he informed you that your house was flooding and you needed to bail water to protect your belongings, you would be motivated to do it. The same principle holds true with SOS services: When clients are provided information about what to expect and how services can benefit them, they are typically less anxious and more engaged. The goal is to help youth and their families to be their own best therapist, caseworker, probation officer, and parole officer. Research on engagement in general youth and family services has revealed that providing psycho-education about treatment services (e.g., what to expect and the benefits of participation) is linked to client engagement (Becker et al., 2015; Lindsay et al., 2014). When clients are provided information about resiliency protective factors, brain maturation, neuroplasticity, and other treatment concepts previously highlighted, motivation to participate in treatment services can grow.

Utilize a Holistic, Individualized Approach

From a holistic perspective, SOS assessment, therapy, and supervision place an emphasis on individualized needs and address not only risk management but also health promotion (Leversee & Powell, 2012). When services are oriented toward a one-size-fits-all approach, individualized needs are often not met and engagement will decline. Every youth and family is unique, and SOS services must be individualized to best address specific needs including strengths and resources, cognitive abilities, learning style, offense history, victimization history, protective factors, risk factors, and general and specific responsivity. Specific strategies for meeting clients' individualized needs include the utilization of multisensory interventions, ensuring that the treatment modalities used are a good fit, and being sensitive and encouraging of youth and family diversity.

Use Multisensory Interventions

In order to increase the chances of matching the learning style of a particular youth, delivery of services in a multisensory manner is essential. That is, engaging youth and families often requires much more than traditional talk therapy with its emphasis on auditory stimuli (sound). Whenever possible, services should be presented in ways that reach youth's multiple senses. Visual learning occurs through our sense of sight (e.g., drawing pictures and writing down concepts while communicating with youth). Tactile learning occurs through the sense of touch and is often referred to as hands-on learning (e.g., having youth draw and write down concepts they are learning). Kinesthetic learning occurs through the sensation of position, movement, and tension in various parts of the body (e.g., having youth role-play and practice skills during sessions, such as social greetings or relaxation techniques). I have worked with youth who were guarded and defensive when having conversations in a traditional therapy session (sitting in an office facing each other); however, when we walked together side by side (which required kinesthetic processing and an opportunity to talk without directly looking at each other), they began to openly share their personal thoughts and feelings. A multisensory approach increases the chances of educational and treatment material matching the individualized learning style of youth, which can significantly enhance learning acquisition and engagement.

Use Treatment Modalities That Fit Best

Treatment modality—individual therapy, family therapy, group therapy—is another area in which to consider the individualized needs of clients. When treatment modalities are used that are incongruent with the individual needs of a youth, engagement can be poor. Historically, the SOS field has placed a great deal of emphasis on group therapy; however, there are many reasons to use caution when considering group-oriented services.

A primary goal of SOS services is to create an atmosphere in which clients feel psychologically safe to openly engage. Providing SOS services in group settings must be done with caution due to a variety of factors. It is not uncommon for youth struggling with disruptive behavior problems to struggle with psychosocial deficits, which can impair their capacity to respond to other group members in prosocial, empathetic ways. When self-disclosure in group is met with insensitive and non-supportive responses, a psychologically safe environment has not been achieved. Group work can also increase risk of trust and confidentiality violations. At-risk youth's insight and moral standards with regard to respecting others' confidentiality can be quite variable. In addition, group therapy can increase exposure to narratives from other group members' abusive acts and victimization experiences. Exposure to problematic thoughts, feelings, behaviors, and situations can increase the risk of youth becoming desensitized and/or triggering unresolved trauma. Many at-risk youth have experienced adverse childhood experiences, which can impair their tolerance for hearing about others' distressing experiences. Research on the repetitive stimulation of brain pathways (neuroplasticity) would suggest caution be exercised regarding exposure to adverse content in groups. In some circumstances, exposure to delinquent youth in group settings can increase problem behaviors, a phenomenon referred to as deviancy training (Dishion & Dodge, 2005; Dodge, Dishion, & Lansford, 2006; Gifford-Smith, Dodge, Dishion, & McCord, 2005; Leve & Chamberlain, 2005; Poulin, Dishion, & Burraston, 2001). Youth may become more interested in bonding with delinquent peers than learning prosocial skills. The prosocial proclivity of the group atmosphere is a necessity, and when there are not enough positive, motivated participants, other treatment modalities should be considered.

Other individual attributes that often do not mesh well with the group therapy format include lower cognitive functioning and/or poor auditory-processing speed, which can impair youth's ability to benefit due to the faster-paced communication coming from multiple group members. Group therapy may also be contraindicated for youth struggling with social anxiety and trust issues. Providing youth with opportunities to develop social skills and interact with prosocial peers is an important component of SOS services; however, sometimes this must be accomplished outside of group therapy. The bottom line is that providers must be cautious about when and how group therapy is implemented and always be mindful of the individual needs of youth to ensure the modalities being used are optimal for engaging youth in SOS services.

Be Sensitive to and Encouraging of Diversity

Treatment engagement is an important area of study as it relates to culturally diverse youth and families (Huey & Jones, 2013), and serious barriers can occur when clients do not feel understood and valued for the qualities that are unique to them (e.g., ethnicity, culture, religious/spiritual beliefs, gender identity, body type, personality style, sexual orientation, life experiences, physical differences, intellectual differences, learning differences, socioeconomic status). Every youth and family possesses unique attributes that should be celebrated and respected. Give them opportunities to share their self-identity and personal views of the world, and engagement is enhanced. A specific area of diversity is language. Communication (both verbal and nonverbal) is a key component for active involvement in services; therefore identified language barriers must be addressed.

Promote Resiliency Protective Factors

Resiliency involves the capacity to overcome childhood adversity and to lead successful, prosocial lives. Resiliency is a common phenomenon within human beings, if enough protective factors are available to reinforce it (Masten, 2001; http://www.apa.org/help-center/road-resilience.aspx). Protective factors are individual, family, and community conditions, which increase the likelihood of a resilient response to life adversity resulting in healthy development and outcomes. Some protective factors are internal characteristics within youth, while others are external, in that they are obtained from youth's family and/or community. Research has consistently found that even possessing a few protective factors can have a positive impact on youth development (Masten & Coatsworth, 1998; Masten et al., 2009; Masten & Reed, 2002). Educating youth and families about their capacity to be resilient and introducing them to the protective factors commonly linked to resiliency can enhance engagement.

Assess and Meet Basic Human Needs

A mistake youth service providers sometimes make is to overlook meeting basic human needs before implementing interventions directed at more advanced needs. When basic needs are *not* met, it can significantly impede individuals' capacity to focus on anything else; they could not care less about treatment goals or life goals. Maslow's (1970) hierarchy of needs theory of motivation highlights the potency of unmet human needs. The most advanced need is referred to as self-actualization, which entails living up to your fullest potential. This full potential in SOS services includes learning from past offenses, repairing harm, and leading a productive, prosocial lifestyle. To be engaged at this high level, basic needs must first be met, which include physiological needs (e.g., need for food, water, sleep, comfortable body temperature); safety needs (e.g., need for stability, predictability, protection); social needs (e.g., need to love and be loved, to be accepted, and to belong to a group or family); and competency needs/esteem and achievement needs (e.g., need to gain mastery in our environment and be respected for our personal achievements and competencies). When a youth arrives at school or a therapy session hungry (unmet physiological need); or is getting bullied on a regular basis (unmet safety need); or has no friends and feels alienated from family (unmet social need); or is struggling to learn how to read (unmet competency need), his or her capacity to focus on academic or treatment assignments will be poor. Meeting basic human needs is a foundational element for engaging youth. Each session, SOS providers should consider the question, "What needs are *not* being met for this youth and how can I help meet them?"

Consider the Context of Denial and Minimization

Rather than pathologize a youth's denial of offenses, providers should consider the intent and context. Youth may be denying and/or minimizing their offense history for a variety of reasons that are non-pathological. Reasons for denial and minimization can include fear of social rejection; feelings of shame and guilt; cognitive dissonance between their offending behaviors and personal values; fear of consequences; feeling guarded due to harsh, negative responses they have encountered in the past; feeling guarded due to their own history of victimization or unresolved trauma; or having weak ego strength/self-esteem, which reduces their tolerance to openly acknowledge personal failings. Open self-disclosure, acceptance of responsibility, and acquisition of psychological insight are all processes that evolve over time. In order to facilitate engagement in SOS services, providers must be patient and understanding when youth initially deny and/or minimize their offense(s).

FUTURE RESEARCH ON ENGAGEMENT

Research investigating client (youth and family) engagement in juvenile SOS services has been quite limited. The evidence-based practice movement and SOS field has historically focused much more attention on outcome variables (e.g., the result or comparison between pre-treatment and post-treatment variables) rather than process variables (i.e., what happens during the course of therapy to effect positive change). Many engagement practices exert their influence during the course of SOS services and would be classified as process variables. The more limited empirical attention given to process variables is due to the fact that these variables are often more difficult to operationally define and measure (Hall, 2008; Kopta, Lueger, Saunders, & Howard, 1999; Messer, 2001). However, in order for the juvenile SOS field to further reduce the risk of sexual offending and promote healthy, prosocial relationships in society, more research investigating these process variables is needed.

The concept of client engagement is complex and influenced by a multitude of psychological constructs. There are many variables within SOS services that can impact engagement, including attributes of the youth service provider, attributes of the youth and family, relationship dynamics, treatment setting, specific intervention strategies, and the interaction between the provider and client characteristics. There is a need for future research to more clearly define and empirically control for these components of engagement and their link to specific SOS outcomes.

This research will assist the SOS field in gaining a more comprehensive and holistic view of youth and family engagement. The field will benefit greatly by adhering to the American Psychological Association's holistic definition of evidence-based practice (EBP), which is "the integration of the best available research with clinical expertise in the context of patient characteristics, culture, and preferences" (APA, 2006). This three-pronged emphasis on research evidence, clinical judgment, and individualized needs of youth and families is critical for engaging the heterogeneous juvenile SOS population. Much more research is needed to further understand and harness the power of engagement within juvenile SOS services.

SUMMARY

Client engagement is an essential component for effective sexual-offense-specific services. When youth and families are actively engaged in SOS services rather than passive recipients, reduced risk and positive outcomes are much more likely. The purpose of this chapter was to provide a broad understanding of engagement, including definition, history, theory, empirical research, and clinical application.

The concept of client engagement evolved out of the humanistic movement with its emphasis on individual strengths and the capacity to take an active role in healthy psychological development. The complex, multidimensional construct of client engagement, along with the variety of constructs associated with engagement (i.e., therapeutic alliance; hope; resiliency protective factors; responsivity principle), makes it a challenging concept to define and study. This multifaceted engagement process includes the interrelated influence of client, provider, and treatment factors and includes four main areas associated with engagement, which are practical/access to services (e.g., transportation; financial cost), behavioral engagement (e.g., client attendance; level of participation), attitudinal/cognitive engagement (e.g., degree of feeling understood; perceived usefulness of treatment), and social process engagement (e.g., therapeutic alliance).

There are many provider attributes and clinical strategies with empirical support that can assist providers in engaging youth and families in SOS services. Provider attributes include warmth, empathy, and directiveness, as opposed to a harsh and confrontational style. Clinical applications include ensuring that practical barriers to accessing services are addressed including transportation and costs, utilizing a strengths-based orientation, and employing motivational interviewing strategies. Engagement has also been linked to instilling hope, promoting resiliency, and establishing a collaborative atmosphere in which clients are "informed consumers" regarding treatment and the identification of approach goals. Engagement-enhancing practices also include meeting clients' basic human needs, matching the individualized needs and diversity of clients with appropriate services (i.e., modality of services provided; multisensory delivery), and considering the context of clients' denial or minimization without pathologizing it. Regardless of the theoretical orientation or treatment models being implemented, youth and family engagement is key to effective services. Providers must be vigilant to this dynamic process throughout the course of services.

REFERENCES

American Psychological Association, Presidential Task Force on Evidence-Based Practice. (2006). Evidence-based practice in psychology. *American Psychologist, 61*(4), 271–285.

Anda, R. F., & Felitti, V. J. (2003). Origins and essense of the study. *ACE Reporter, 1*(1), 1–4.

Andrews, D. A., & Bonta, J. (2010). *The psychology of criminal conduct* (5th ed.). New Providence, NJ: Matthew Bender & Company.

Andrews, D. A., Bonta, J., & Wormith, J. S. (2011). The risk-need-responsivity (RNR) model: Does adding the good lives model contribute to effective crime prevention? *Criminal Justice and Behavior, 38*(7), 735–755.

Becker, K. D., Kiser, L. J., Herr, S. R., Stapleton, L. M., Barksdale, C. L., & Buckingham, S. (2014). Changes in treatment engagement of youths and families with complex needs. *Children and Youth Services Review, 46,* 276–284.

Becker, K. D., Lee, B. R., Daleiden, E. L., Lindsey, M., Brandt, N. E., & Chorpita, B. F. (2015). The common elements of engagement in children's mental health services: Which elements for which outcomes? *Journal of Clinical Child & Adolescent Psychology, 44*(1), 30–43.

Bedi, R. P. (2006). Concept mapping the client's perspective on counseling alliance formation. *Journal of Counseling Psychology, 53*(1), 26–35.

Beech, A., & Fordham, A. S. (1997). Therapeutic climate of sexual offender treatment programs. *Sex Abuse: A Journal of Research and Treatment, 9*(3), 219–237.

Berg, I. K., & Steiner, T. (2003). *Children's solution work.* New York: W. W. Norton.

Blanchard, G. T. (1995). *The difficult connection: The therapeutic relationship in sex offender treatment.* Brandon, VT: Safer Society Press.

Bordin, E. S. (1979). The generalizability of psychanalytic concept of the working alliance. *Psychotherapy: Theory, Research, and Practice, 16,* 252–260.

Brogan, L., Haney-Caron, E., NeMoyer, A., & DeMatteo, D. (2015). Applying the risk-needs-responsivity (RNR) model to juvenile justice. *Criminal Justice Review, 40*(3), 277–302.

Bronfenbrenner, U. (2001). The bioecological theory of human development. In N. J. Smelser & P. B. Baltes (Eds.), *International encyclopedia of social and behavioral sciences* (Vol. 10, pp. 6963–6970). New York: Elsevier.

Bronfenbrenner, U., & Ceci, S. J. (1994). Nature–nurture reconceptualized in developmental perspective: A bioecological model. *Psychological Review, 101,* 568–586.

Bryck, R. L., & Fisher, P. A. (2012). Training the brain: Practical applications of neural plasticity from the intersection of cognitive neuroscience, developmental psychology, and prevention science. *American Psychologist, 67*(2), 87–100.

Cahalane, H., & Anderson, C. M. (2013). Family engagement strategies in child welfare practice. In H. Cahalane (Ed.), *Contemporary issues in child welfare practice* (pp. 39–73). New York: Springer.

Caldwell, M. F. (2010). Study characteristics and recidivism base rates in juvenile sex offender recidivism. *International Journal of Offender Therapy and Comparative Criminology, 54*(2), 197–212.

Casey, B. J., Giedd, J. N., & Thomas, K. M. (2000). Structural and functional brain development and its relation to cognitive development. *Biological Psychology, 54,* 241–257.

Center for Sex Offender Management (2008). The comprehensive approach to sex offender management. Retrieved from http://www.atsa.com/pdfs/Policy/CSOM_SOManagement.pdf

Chaffin, M. (2011). The case of juvenile polygraphy as a clinical ethics dilemma. *Sexual Abuse: A Journal of Research and Treatment, 23,* 314–328.

Chorpita, B., Daleiden, E., & Weisz, J. (2005). Identifying and selecting the common elements of evidence based interventions: A distillation and matching model. *Mental Health Services Research, 7,* 5–20.

Chua, J. R., Chu, C. M., Yim, G., Chong, D., & Teoh, J. (2014). Implementation of the risk-need-responsivity framework across the juvenile justice agencies in Singapore. *Psychiatry, Psychology, and Law, 21*(6), 877–889.

Collie, R., Ward, T., Ayland, L., & West, B. (2007). The good lives model of rehabilitation: Reducing risks and promoting strengths with adolescent sexual offenders. In M. C. Calder (Ed.), *Working with children and young people who sexually abuse: Taking the field forward* (pp. 53–64). Dorset, UK: Russell House.

Corcoran, J., & Ivery, J. (2004). Parent and child attributions for child behavior: Distinguishing factors for engagement and outcome. *Families in Society: The Journal of Contemporary Social Services, 85*(1), 101–106.

Corcoran, J., & Stephenson, M. (2000). The effectiveness of solution-focused therapy with child behavior problems: A preliminary report. *Families in Society, 81*(5), 468–474.

Creed, T., & Kendall, P. (2005). Therapist alliance-building behavior within a cognitive-behavioral treatment for anxiety in youth. *Journal of Consulting and Clinical Psychology, 73*(3), 498–505.

Defife, J. A., & Hilsenroth M. J. (2011). Starting off on the right foot: Common factor elements in early psychotherapy process. *Journal of Psychotherapy Integration, 21,* 172–191.

de Vries Robbe, M., de Vogel, V., Koster, K., & Bogaerts, S. (2015). Assessing protective factors for sexually violent offending with the SAPROF. *Sex Abuse: A Journal of Research and Treatment, 27*(1), 51–70.

de Vries Robbe, M., Mann, R. E., Maruna, S., & Thornton, D. (2015). An exploration of protective factors supporting desistance from sexual offending. *Sex Abuse: A Journal of Research and Treatment, 27*(1), 16–33.

Diamond, A. (2002). Normal development of prefrontal cortex from birth to young adulthood: Cognitive functions, anatomy, and biochemistry. In D. T. Stuss & R. T. Knight (Eds.), *Principles of frontal lobe function* (pp. 466–503). New York: Oxford University Press.

Dishion, T. J., & Dodge, K. A. (2005). Peer contagion in interventions for children and adolescents: Moving towards an understanding of the ecology and dynamics of change. *Journal of Abnormal Child Psychology, 33*(3), 395-400.

Dodge, K. A., Dishion, T. J., & Lansford, J. E. (2006). Deviant peer influences in intervention and public policy for youth. *Social Policy Report: A Publication of the Society for Research in Child Development, 20*(1), 3–19.

D'Orazio, D. M. (2013). Lessons learned from history and experience: Five simple ways to improve the efficacy of sex offender treatment. *International Journal of Behavioral Consultation and Therapy, 8*(3–4), 2–7.

Dornbusch, S. M., Erickson, K. G., Laird, J., & Wong, C. A. (2001). The relation of family and school attachment to adolescent deviance in diverse groups and communities. *Journal of Adolescent Research, 16*(4), 396–422.

Dorsey, S., Pullman, M. D., Berliner, L., Koschmann, E., McKay, M., & Deblinger, E. (2014). Engaging foster parents in treatment: A randomized trial of supplementing trauma-focused cognitive behavioral therapy with evidence-based engagement strategies. *Child Abuse & Neglect, 38,* 1508–1520.

Dozier, M., Lindhiem, O., Lewis, E., Bick, J., Bernard, K., & Peloso, E. (2009). Effects of a foster parent training program on young children's attachment behaviors: Preliminary evidence from a randomized clinical trial. *Child and Adolescent Social Work Journal, 26,* 321–332.

Edwards, R., Beech, A., Bishopp, D., Erikson, M., Friendship, C., & Charlesworth, L. (2005). Predicting dropout from a residential programme for adolescent sexual abusers using pre-treatment variables and implications for recidivism. *Journal of Sexual Aggression, 11,* 139–155.

Egan, G. (2006). *Essentials of skilled helping: Managing problems, developing opportunities.* Belmont, CA: Thomson Wadsworth.

Ellis, M. L., Lindsey, M. A., Barker, E. D., Boxmeyer, C. L., & Lochman, J. E. (2013). Predictors of engagement in a school-based family preventive intervention for youth experiencing behavioral difficulties. *Prevention Science, 14,* 456–467.

Farrington, D. P. (2007). Origins of violent behavior over the life span. In D. J. Flannery, A. T. Vazsonyi, & I. D. Waldman (Eds.), *The Cambridge handbook of violent behavior and aggression* (pp. 19–48). New York: Cambridge University Press.

Fortune, C.-A., Ward, T., & Print, B. (2014). Integrating the good lives model with relapse prevention: Working with juvenile sex offenders. In D. S. Bromberg & W. O'Donohue (Eds.), *Toolkit for working with juvenile sex offenders* (pp. 405–426). San Diego: Elsevier.

French, R., Reardon, M., & Smith, P. (2003). Engaging with a mental health service: Perspectives of at-risk youth. *Child & Adolescent Social Work Journal, 20*(6), 529–548.

Garcia, J. A., & Weisz, J. R. (2002). When youth mental health care stops: Therapeutic relationship problems and other reasons for ending youth outpatient treatment. *Journal of Consulting and Clinical Psychology, 70*(2), 439–443.

Gifford-Smith, M., Dodge, K. A., Dishion, T. J., & McCord, J. (2005). Peer influence in children and adolescents: Crossing the bridge from developmental to intervention science. *Journal of Abnormal Child Psychology, 33*(3), 255–265.

Gilgun, J. (2006). Children and adolescents with problematic sexual behaviors: Lessons from research on resilience. In R. E. Longo & D. S. Prescott (Eds.), *Current perspectives: Working with sexually aggressive youth and youth with sexual behavior problems* (pp. 383–394). Holyoke, MA: NEARI Press.

Gopalan, G., Goldstein, L., Klingenstein, K., Sicher, C., Blake, C., & McKay, M. M. (2010). Engaging families in child mental health treatment: Updates and special considerations. *Journal of the Canadian Academy of Child and Adolescent Psychiatry, 19*(3), 182–196.

Hall, J. C. (2008). A practitioner's application and deconstruction of evidence-based practice. *Family in Society: The Journal of Contemporary Social Services, 89*(3), 385–393.

Hanson, R. K., & Bussiere, M. T. (1998). Predicting relapse: A meta-analysis of sexual offender recidivism studies. *Journal of Consulting and Clinical Psychology, 66,* 348–362.

Hanson, R. K., & Morton-Bourgon, K. E. (2005). The characteristics of persistent sexual offenders: A meta-analysis of recidivism studies. *Journal of Consulting and Clinical Psychology 73*(6), 1154–1163.

Haqanee, Z., Peterson-Badali, M., & Skilling, T. (2015). Making "what works" work: Examining probation officers' experiences addressing criminogenic needs of juvenile offenders. *Journal of Offender Rehabilitation, 54,* 37–59.

Harkins L., & Beech, A. R. (2007). A review of the factors that can influence the effectiveness of sexual offender treatment: Risk, need, responsivity, and process issues. *Aggression and Violent Behavior, 12,* 615–627.

Harkins, L., Beech, A. R., & Goodwill, A. M. (2010). Examining the influence of denial, motivation, and risk on sexual recidivism. *Sexual Abuse: A Journal of Research and Treatment, 22*(1), 78–94.

Hawkins, S. R., Graham, P. W., Williams, J., & Zahn, M. A. (2009). *Resilient girls: Factors that protect against delinquency* (NCJ 220124). Washington, DC: US Department of Justice Office of Juvenile Justice and Delinquency Prevention, Girls Study Group. Retrieved from https://www.ncjrs.gov/pdffiles1/ojjdp/220124.pdf

Hawley, K. M., & Weisz, J. R. (2005). Youth versus parent working alliance in usual clinical care: Distinctive association with retention, satisfaction, and treatment. *Journal of Clinical Child and Adolescent Psychology, 34,* 117–128.

Hettema, J., Steele, J., & Miller, W. R. (2005). Motivational interviewing. *Annual Review of Clinical Psychology, 1,* 91–111.

Hoge, R. D. (2016). Risk, need, and responsivity in juveniles. In K. Heilbrun (Ed.), *APA handbook of psychology and juvenile justice* (pp. 179–196). Washington DC: APA.

Holdsworth, E., Bowen, E., Brown, S., & Howat, D. (2014). Client engagement in psychotherapeutic treatment and associations with client characteristics, therapist characteristics, and treatment factors. *Clinical Psychology Review, 34,* 428–450.

Huey, S. J., & Jones, E. O. (2013). Improving treatment engagement and psychotherapy outcomes for culturally diverse youth and families. In F. A. Paniagua & A. Yamada (Eds.), *Handbook of multicultural mental health: Assessment and treatment of diverse populations* (2nd ed., pp. 427–444). San Diego: Elsevier/Academic Press.

Hunter, J. A., & Figueredo, A. J. (1999). Factors associated with treatment compliance in a population of juvenile sexual offenders. *Sexual Abuse: A Journal of Research and Treatment, 11*, 49–67.

Ingoldsby, E. M. (2010). Review of interventions to improve family engagement and retention in parent and child mental health programs. *Journal of Child and Family Studies, 19*, 629–645.

Jespersen, A. F., Lalumière, M. L., & Seto, M. C. (2009). Sexual abuse history among adult sex offenders and non-sex offenders: A meta-analysis. *Child Abuse & Neglect, 33*, 179–192.

Karver, M. S., Handelsman, J. B., Fields, S., & Bickman, L. (2006). Meta-analysis of therapeutic relationship variables in youth and family therapy: The evidence for different relationship variables in child and adolescent treatment outcome literature. *Clinical Psychology Review, 26*, 50–65.

Karver, M. S., Shirk, S., Handelsman, J. B., Fields, S., Crisp, H., Gudmundsen, G., & McMakin, D. (2008). Relationship process in youth psychotherapy: Measuring alliance, alliance-building behaviors, and client involvement. *Journal of Emotional and Behavioral Disorders, 16*(1), 15–28.

Kazdin, A., & Wassel, G. (1999). Barriers to treatment participation and therapeutic change among children referred for conduct disorder. *Journal of Clinical Child Psychology, 28*, 160–172.

Kemp, S. P., Marcenko, M. O., Lyons, S. J., & Kruzich, J. M. (2014). Strengths-based practices and parental engagement in child welfare services: An empirical examination. *Children and Youth Services Review, 47*, 27–35.

Kerkorian, D., McKay, M., & Bannon, W. M. (2006). Seeking help a second time: Parents'/caregivers' characterizations of previous experiences with mental health services for their children and perceptions of barriers to future use. *American Journal of Orthopsychiatry, 76*, 161–166.

Klien, V., Rettenberger, M., Yoon, D., Kohler, N., & Briken, P. (2015). Protective factors and recidivism in accused juveniles who sexually offended. *Sexual Abuse: A Journal of Research and Treatment, 27*(1), 71–90.

Kopta, S. M., Lueger, R. J., Saunders, S. M., & Howard, K. I. (1999). Individual psychotherapy outcome and process research: Challenges leading to greater turmoil or a positive transition? *Annual Review of Psychology, 50*, 441–469.

Kraemer, B. D., Salisbury, S. B., & Spielman, C. (1998). Pretreatment variables associated with treatment failure in a residential juvenile sex-offender program. *Criminal Justice and Behavior, 25*, 190–202.

Langstrom, N., & Grann, M. (2000). Risk for criminal recidivism among young sex offenders. *Journal of Interpersonal Violence, 15*, 855–871.

Langton, C. M., & Worling, J. R. (Eds.) (2015). Special issue title: Protective factors. *Sexual Abuse: A Journal of Research and Treatment, 27*(1), 3–142.

Larsen, D. J., & Stege, R. (2010a). Hope-focused practices during early psychotherapy sessions: Part I: Implicit approaches. *Journal of Psychotherapy Integration, 20*(3), 271–292.

Larsen, D. J., & Stege, R. (2010b). Hope-focused practices during early psychotherapy sessions: Part II: Explicit approaches. *Journal of Psychotherapy Integration, 20*(3), 293–311.

Lethem, J. (2002). Brief solution focused therapy. *Child and Adolescent Mental Health, 7*(4), 189–192.

Leve, L. D., & Chamberlain, P. (2005). Association with delinquent peers: Intervention effects for youth in the juvenile justice system. *Journal of Abnormal Child Psychology, 33*(3), 339–347.

Levenson, J. S. (2011). "But I didn't do it!": Ethical treatment of sex offenders in denial. *Sexual Abuse: A Journal of Research and Treatment, 23*(3), 346–364.

Levenson, J. S. (2013). Incorporating trauma-informed care into evidence-based sex offender treatment. *Journal of Sexual Aggression.* http://dx.doi.org/10.1080/13552600.2013.861523

Levenson, J. S., & MacGowan, M. J. (2004). Engagement, denial, and treatment progress among sex offenders in group therapy. *Sexual Abuse: A Journal of Research and Treatment, 16*(1), 49–63.

Levenson, J. S., Willis, G. M., & Prescott, D. S. (2014). Adverse childhood experiences in the lives of male sex offenders: Implications for trauma-informed care. *Sexual Abuse: A Journal of Research and Treatment,* 1–20. http://dx.doi.org/10.1177/1079063214535819

Leversee, T., & Powell, K. M. (2012). Beyond risk management to a more holistic model for treating sexually abusive youth. In B. Schwartz (Ed.), *The sex offender: Current trends in policy and treatment practice* (Vol. 7, pp. 1–32). Kingston, NJ: Civic Research Institute.

Lindsey, M. A., Brandt, N. E., Becker, K. D., Lee, B. R., Barth, R. P., Daleiden, E. L., & Chorpita, B. F. (2014). Identifying the common elements of treatment engagement interventions in children's mental health services. *Clinical Child and Family Psychology Review, 17,* 283–298.

Lobanov-Rostovsky, C. (2010). Juvenile justice, legislation, and policy responses to juvenile sexual offenses. In G. Ryan, T. Leversee, & S. Lane (Eds.) *Juvenile sexual offending: Causes, consequences, and corrections* (3rd ed., pp. 183–197). Hoboken, NJ: Wiley.

Loeber, R., Menting, B., Lynam, D. R., Moffit, T. E., Stouthamer-Loeber, M., Stallings, R., Farrington, D. P., & Pardini, D. (2012). Findings from the Pittsburgh Youth Study: Cognitive impulsivity and intelligence as predictors of the age-crime curve. *Journal of the American Academy of Child and Adolescent Psychiatry, 51*(11), 1136–1149.

Longo, R. E. (2002). A holistic approach to treating young people who sexually abuse. In M. C. Calder (Ed.), *Young people who sexually abuse: Building the evidence base for your practice* (pp. 218–230). Dorest, UK: Russell House Publishing.

Lösel, F., & Bliesener, T. (1994). Some high-risk adolescents do not develop conduct problems: A study of protective factors. *International Journal of Behavioral Development, 17*(40), 753–777.

Lösel, F., & Farrington, D. P. (2012). Direct protective factors and buffering protective factors in the development of youth violence. *American Journal of Preventive Medicine, 43*(2S1), S8–S23.

Luna, B., & Sweeney, J. (2004). The emergence of collaborative brain function: fMRI studies of the development of response inhibition. *Annals of the New York Academy of Science, 1021,* 296–309.

Macneil, C. A., Hasty, M. K., Evans, M., Redlich, C., & Berk, M. (2009). The therapeutic alliance: Is it necessary or sufficient to engender positive outcomes? *Acta Neuropsychiatrica, 2,* 95–98.

Mann, R. E., Webster, S. D., Schofield, C., & Marshall, W. L. (2004). Approach versus avoidance goals in relapse prevention with sexual offenders. *Sexual Abuse: A Journal of Research & Treatment, 16*(1), 65–75.

Marshall, W. L. (2005). Therapist style in sex offender treatment: Influence on indices of change. *Sexual Abuse: A Journal of Research & Treatment, 17*(2), 109–116.

Marshall, W. L., & Burton, D. (2010). The importance of therapeutic processes in offender treatment. *Aggression and Violent Behavior: A Review Journal, 15,* 141–149.

Marshall, W. L., & Hollin, C. (2015). Historical developments in sex offender treatment. *Journal of Sexual Aggression, 21*(2), 125–135.

Marshall, W. L., & Marshall, L. E. (2014). Psychological treatment of sex offenders: Recent innovations. *Psychiatric Clinics North America, 37,* 163–171.

Marshall, W. L., & Serran, G. A. (2004). The role of the therapist in offender treatment. *Psychology, Crime, & Law, 10*(3), 309–320.

Marshall, W. L., Serran, G., Moulden, H., Mulloy, R., Fernandez, Y. M., Mann, R., & Thornton, D. (2002). Therapist features in sexual offender treatment: Their reliable identification and influence on behaviour change. *Clinical Psychology and Psychotherapy, 9,* 395–405.

Maruna, S., & LeBel, T. P. (2003). Welcome home? Examining the "reentry court" concept from a strengths-based perspective. *Western Criminology Review, 4*(2), 91–107.

Maslow, A. H. (1954). *Motivation and personality.* New York: Harper and Brothers.

Maslow, A. H. (1962). *Toward a psychology of being.* New York: Van Nostrand.

Maslow, A. H. (1970). *Motivation and personality* (2nd ed.). New York: Harper and Row.

Masten, A. S. (2001). Ordinary magic: Resilience processes in development. *American Psychologist, 56*(3), 227–238.

Masten, A. S., & Coatsworth, J. D. (1998). The development of competence in favorable and unfavorable environments: Lessons from research on successful children. *American Psychologist, 53*(2), 205–220.

Masten, A. S., Cutuli, J. J., Herbers, J. E., & Reed, M. G. J. (2009). Resilience in development. In C. R. Snyder & S. J. Lopez (Eds.), *Oxford handbook of positive psychology* (2nd ed., pp. 117–131). New York: Oxford University Press.

Masten, A. S., & Reed, M. G. J. (2002). Resilience in development. In C. R. Snyder & S. J. Lopez (Eds.), *The handbook of positive psychology* (pp. 74–88). New York: Oxford University Press.

McGrath, R. J., Cumming, G., & Holt, J. (2002). Collaboration among sex offender treatment providers and probation and parole officers: The beliefs and behaviors of treatment providers. *Sexual Abuse: A Journal of Research and Treatment, 14*(1), 49–65.

McGrath, R. J., Cumming, G. F., Hoke, S. E., & Bonn-Miller, M. O. (2007). Outcomes in a community sex offender treatment program: A comparison between polygraphed and matched non-polygraphed offenders. *Sexual Abuse: A Journal of Research and Treatment, 19,* 381–393.

McKay, M. M., & Bannon, W. M. (2004). Engaging families in child mental health services. *Child and Adolescent Psychiatric Clinics of North America, 13,* 905–921.

McLeod, B. D. (2011). Relation of the alliance with outcomes in youth psychotherapy: A meta-analysis. *Clinical Psychology Review, 31,* 603–616.

Mcleod, B. D., Islam, N. Y., Chiu, A. W., Smith, M. M., Chu, B. C., & Wood, J. J. (2014). The relationship between alliance and client involvement in CBT for child anxiety disorders. *Journal of Clinical Child & Adolescent Psychology, 43,* 735–741.

McMurran, M., & Ward, T. (2004). Motivating offenders to change in therapy: An organizing framework. *Legal and Criminological Psychology, 9,* 295–311.

McNeely, C. A., Nonnemaker, J. M., & Blum, R. W. (2002). Promoting school connectedness: Evidence from the national longitudinal study of adolescent health. *Journal of School Health, 72*(4), 138–146.

Messer, S. B. (2001). Empirically supported treatments: What's a nonbehaviorist to do? In B. D. Slife, R. N. Williams, & S. H. Barlow (Eds.), *Critical issues in psychotherapy: Translating new ideas into practice* (pp. 3–19). Thousand Oaks, CA: Sage.

Miller, H. A. (2015). Protective strengths, risk, and recidivism in a sample of known sexual offenders. *Sex Abuse: A Journal of Research and Treatment, 27*(1), 34–50.

Miller, S. D., Hubble, M. A., Chow, D., & Seidel, J. (2015). Beyond measures and monitoring: Realizing the potential of feedback-informed treatment. *Psychotherapy, 52*(4), 449–457.

Miller, W. R., & Rollnick, S. (2002). *Motivational interviewing: Preparing people for change* (2nd ed.). New York: Guilford.

Miller, W. R., & Rollnick, S. (2013). *Motivational interviewing: Helping people change* (3rd ed.). New York: Guilford.

Minuchin, S. (1974). *Families and family therapy.* Cambridge, MA: Harvard University Press.

Moffitt, T. E. (1993). Adolescence-limited and life-course-persistent antisocial behavior: A developmental taxonomy. *Psychological Review, 100,* 674–701.

Moffit, T. E. (1997). Adolescence-limited and life-course-persistent offending: A complementary pair of developmental theories. In T. P. Thornberry (Ed.), *Advances in criminological theory: Vol. 7. Developmental theories of crime and delinquency.* New Brunswick, NJ: Transaction Publishers.

Moffitt, T. E. (2007). A review of research on the taxonomy of life-course persistent versus adolescence-limited antisocial behavior. In D. J. Flannery, A. T. Vazdonyi, & I. D. Walman (Eds.), *The Cambridge handbook of violent behavior and aggression* (pp. 49–74). New York: Cambridge University Press.

Monahan, K. C., Goldweber, A., & Cauffman, E. (2011). The effects of visitation on incarcerated juvenile offenders: How contact with the outside impacts adjustment on the inside. *Law and Human Behavior, 35*(2), 143–151.

Morrison, T. (2006). Building a holistic approach in the treatment of young people who sexually abuse. In R. E. Longo, D. S. Prescott (Eds.), *Current perspectives: Working with sexually aggressive youth & youth with sexual behavior problems* (pp. 349–368). Holyoke, MA: NEARI Press.

Moulden, H. M., & Marshall, W. L. (2005). Hope in the treatment of sexual offenders: The potential application of hope theory. *Psychology, Crime & Law, 11,* 329–342.

Murray, C., & Greenberg, M. T. (2001). Relationships with teachers and bonds with school: Social emotional adjustment correlates for children with and without disabilities. *Psychology in the Schools, 38*(1), 25–41.

National Institute of Mental Health (2001). *Blueprint for change: Research on child and adolescent mental health's council's workgroup on child and adolescent mental health intervention development and deployment* (DHHS Publication no. CG 031-591). Washington, DC: US Government Printing Office.

Nee, C., Ellis, T., Morris, P., & Wilson, A. (2012). Addressing criminality in childhood: Is responsivity the central issue? *International Journal of Offender Therapy and Comparative Criminology, 57*(11), 1347–1373.

Nelson, C. A. (2003). Neural development and lifelong plasticity. In R. Learner, E. Jacobs, & D. Wertlieb (Eds.), *Handbook of applied developmental science* (Vol. 1). Thousand Oaks, CA: Sage.

Netto, N. R., Carter, J. M., & Bonell, C. (2014). A systematic review of interventions that adopt the "good lives" approach to offender rehabilitation. *Journal of Offender Rehabilitation, 53,* 403–432.

Nickerson, A. B., Hopson, L. M., & Steinke, C. M. (2011). School connectedness in community and residential treatment schools: The influence of gender, grades, and engagement in treatment. *Children and Youth Services Review, 33,* 829–837.

Norcross, J. C. (Ed.). (2011). *Psychotherapy relationships that work: Evidence-based responsiveness* (2nd ed.). New York: Oxford University Press.

Parhar, K. K., Wormith, J. S., Derzken, D. M., & Beauregard, A. M. (2008). Offender coercion in treatment: A meta-analysis of effectiveness. *Criminal Justice and Behavior, 35*(9), 1109–1135.

Patel, S. H., Lambie, G. W., & Glover, M. M. (2008). Motivational counseling: Implications for counseling male juvenile sex offenders. *Journal of Addictions and Offender Counseling, 28,* 86–100.

Pithers, W. D., Gray, A., Busconi, A., & Houchens, P. (1998). Caregivers of children with sexual behavior problems: Psychological and familial functioning. *Child Abuse & Neglect, 22*(2), 129–141.

Poulin, F., Dishion, T. J., & Burraston, B. (2001). Three-year iatrogenic effects associated with aggregated high-risk adolescents in cognitive-behavioral preventive interventions. *Applied Developmental Science, 5*(4), 214–224.

Powell, K. M. (2010a). Strengths-based approach. In D. S. Prescott & R. E. Longo (Eds.), *Current applications: Strategies for working with sexually aggressive youth and youth with sexual behavior problems* (pp. 55–82). Holyoke, MA: NEARI Press.

Powell, K. M. (2010b). Therapeutic relationships and the process of change. In G. Ryan, T. Leversee, & S. Lane (Eds.), *Juvenile sexual offending: Causes, consequences, and correction* (3rd ed., pp. 253–262). Hoboken, NJ: Wiley.

Powell, K. M. (2011). Working effectively with at-risk youth: A strengths-based approach. In M. Calder (Ed.), *Contemporary practice with young people who sexually abuse: Evidence-based developments* (pp. 69–91). Holyoke, MA: NEARI Press.

Powell, K. M. (2015). *A strengths-based approach for intervention with at-risk youth.* Champaign, IL: Research Press. Retrieved from https://www.researchpress.com/books/1253/strengths-based-approach-intervention-risk-youth

Powell, K. M. (2016). Case study: Strengths-based approach. In D. S. Prescott & R. J. Wilson (Eds.), *Very different voices: Perspectives and case studies in treating sexual aggression.* Holyoke, MA: NEARI Press.

Prescott, D. (2012). What do young people learn from coercion? Polygraph examinations with youth who have sexually abused. *The ATSA Forum Newsletter, 24*(2). Retrieved from http://www.davidprescott.net/pub_36.pdf

Pullmann, M. D., Ague, S., Johnson, T., Lane, S., Beaver, K., Jetton, E., & Rund, E. (2013). Defining engagement in adolescent substance abuse treatment. *American Journal of Community Psychology, 52,* 347–358.

Reavis, J., Looman, J., Franco, K., & Rojas, B. (2013). Adverse childhood experiences and adult criminality: How long must we live before we possess our own lives? *The Permanente Journal, 17,* 44–48.

Reitzel, L. R., & Carbonell, J. L. (2006). The effectiveness of sexual offender treatment for juveniles as measured by recidivism: A meta-analysis. *Sex Abuse, 18,* 401–421.

Richman, J. M., & Fraser, M. W. (Eds.). (2001). *The context of youth violence: Resilience, risk, and protection.* Westport, CT: Praeger.

Robbins, M. S., Liddle, H. A., Turner, C. W., Dakof, G. A., Alexander, J. F., & Kagan, S. M. (2006). Adolescent and parent therapeutic alliances as predictors of dropout in multidimensional family therapy. *Journal of Family Psychology, 20,* 108–116.

Rogers, C. R. (1951). *Client-centered therapy: Its current practice, implications, and theory.* Boston: Houghton Mifflin.

Rogers, C. R. (1957). The necessary and sufficient conditions of therapeutic personality change. *Journal of Consulting Psychology, 21*(2), 95–103.

Rogers, C. R. (1961). *On becoming a person: A therapist's view of psychotherapy.* Boston: Houghton Mifflin.

Rubia, K., Overmeyer, S., Taylor, E., Brammer, M., Williams, S. C. R., Simmons, A., Andrews, C., & Bullmore, E. T. (2000). Functional frontalisation with age: Mapping neurodevelopmental trajectories with fMRI. *Neuroscience and Biobehavioral Reviews, 24*(1), 13–19.

Russell, R., Shirk, S., & Jungbluth, N. (2008). First-session pathways to the working alliance in cognitive-behavioral therapy for adolescent depression. *Psychotherapy Research, 18*(1), 15–27.

Saxe, G. N., Ellis, B. H., Fogler, J., & Navalta, C. P. (2012). Innovations in practice: Preliminary evidence for effective family engagement in treatment for child traumatic stress–trauma systems therapy approach to preventing dropout. *Child and Adolescent Mental Health, 17*(1), 58–61.

Schley, C., Yuen, K., Fletcher, K., & Radovini, A. (2012). Does engagement with an intensive outreach service predict better treatment outcomes in "high-risk" youth? *Early Intervention in Psychiatry, 6,* 176–184.

Schmucker, M., & Lösel, F. (2015). The effects of sexual offender treatment on recidivism: An international meta-analysis for sound quality evaluations. *Journal of Experimental Criminology, 11*(4), 597–630.

Seligman, M. E. P. (1975). *Helplessness: On depression, development, and death.* San Francisco: Freeman.

Seligman, M. E. P. (1991). *Learned optimism*. New York: Knopf.

Seligman, M. E. P. (2006). *Learned optimism: How to change your mind and your life*. New York: Vintage Books.

Shanahan, R., & diZerega, M. (2016). White paper. Identifying, engaging, and empowering families: A charge for juvenile justice agencies. Center for Juvenile Justice Reform.

Shirk, S. R., & Karver, M. S. (2011). Alliance in child and adolescent psychotherapy. In J. C. Norcross (Ed.), *Psychotherapy relationships that work: Evidence-based responsiveness* (2nd ed., pp. 70–91). New York: Oxford University Press.

Singh, J. P., Desmarais, S. L., Sellers, B. G., Hylton, T., Tirotti, M., & Van Dorn, R. A. (2014). From risk assessment to risk management: Matching interventions to adolescent offenders' strengths and vulnerabilities. *Children and Youth Services Review, 47, Part 1*, 1–9.

Smallbone, S., Crissman, B., & Rayment-McHugh, S. (2009). Improving therapeutic engagement with adolescent sexual offenders. *Behavioral Sciences and the Law, 27*, 862–877.

Smith, E. P., Boutte, G. S., Zigler, E., & Finn-Stevenson, M. (2004). Opportunities for school to promote resilience in children and youth. In K. I. Maton, C. J. Schellenbach, B. J. Leadbeater, & A. L. Solarz (Eds.), *Investing in children, youth, families, and communities: Strengths-based research and policy* (pp. 213–231). Washington, DC: American Psychological Association.

Snell-Johns, J., Mendez, J. L., & Smith, B. H. (2004). Evidence-based solutions for overcoming access barriers, decreasing attrition, and promoting change with underserved families. *Journal of Family Psychology, 18*(1), 19–35.

Snyder, C. R. (Ed.). (2000). *Handbook of hope: Theory, measures, and applications*. San Diego: Academic Press.

Sowell, E. R., Trauner, D. A., Gamst, A., & Jernigan, T. L. (2002). Development of cortical and subcortical brain structures in childhood and adolescence: A structural MRI study. *Developmental Medicine and Child Neurology, 44*, 4–16.

Spear, L. P. (2000). The adolescent brain and age-related behavioral manifestations. *Neuroscience and Biobehavioral Reviews, 24*, 417–463.

Spice, A., Viljoen, J. L., Latzman, N. E., Scalora, M. J., & Ullman, D. (2013). Risk and protective factors for recidivism among juveniles who have offended sexually. *Sex Abuse: A Journal of Research and Treatment, 25*(4), 347–369.

Staudt, M. (2007). Treatment engagement with caregivers of at-risk children: Gaps in research and conceptualization. *Journal of Child and Family Studies, 16*, 183–196.

Stein, L. A. R., Monti, P. M., Colby, S. M., Barnett, N. P., Goelembeske, C., Lebeau-Craven, R., & Miranda, R. (2006). Enhancing substance abuse treatment engagement in incarcerated adolescents. *Psychological Services, 3*(1), 25–34.

Thompson, S. J., Bender, K., Lantry, J., & Flynn, P. M. (2007). Treatment engagement: Building therapeutic alliance in home-based treatment with adolescents and their families. *Contemporary Family Therapy, 29*, 39–55.

Trickett, P. K., Kurtz, D. A., & Pizzigati, K. (2004). Resilient outcomes in abused and neglected children: Bases for strengths-based intervention and prevention policies. In K. I. Maton, C. J. Schellenbach, B. J. Leadbeater, & A. L. Solarz (Eds.), *Investing in children, youth, families, and communities: Strengths-based research and policy* (pp. 73–95). Washington, DC: American Psychological Association.

Van Domburgh, L., Loeber, R., Bezemer, D., Stallings, R., & Stouthamer-Loeber, M. (2009). Childhood predictors of desistance and level of persistence in offending in early onset offenders. *Journal of Abnormal Child Psychology, 37*, 967–980.

Veira, T., Skilling, T., & Peterson-Badali, M. (2009). Matching court-ordered services with treatment needs. *Criminal Justice and Behavior, 36*, 385–401.

Walters, G. D. (2011). The latent structure of life-course-persistent antisocial behavior: Is Moffit's developmental taxonomy a true taxonomy? *Journal of Consulting and Clinical Psychology, 79*(1), 96–105.

Wampold, B. E., & Imel, Z. E. (2015). *The great psychotherapy debate: The evidence for what makes psychotherapy work.* New York: Routledge.

Ward, T., & Gannon, T. A. (2006). Rehabilitation, etiology, and self-regulation: The comprehensive good lives model of treatment for sex offenders. *Aggression and Violent Behavior, 11,* 77–94.

Ward, T., Gannon, T., & Yates, P. M. (2008). The treatment of offenders: Current practice and new developments with an emphasis on sex offenders. *International Review of Victimology, 15,* 179–204.

Ward, T., Mann, R. E., & Gannon, T. A. (2007). The good lives model of offender rehabilitation: Clinical implications. *Aggression and Violent Behavior, 12,* 87–107.

Ward, T., Melser, J., & Yates, P. M. (2007). Reconstructing the risk-need-responsivity model: A theoretical elaboration and evaluation. *Aggression and Violent Behavior, 12,* 208–228.

Ward, T., & Stewart, C. A. (2003). The treatment of sex offenders: Risk management and good lives. *Professional Psychology: Research and Practice, 34*(4), 353–360.

Ward, T., Yates, P. M., & Willis, G. W. (2012). The good lives model and the risk need responsivity model: A critical response to Andrews, Bonta, and Wormith (2011). *Criminal Justice and Behavior, 39*(1), 94–110.

Winerman, L. (2012). Changing our brains, changing ourselves. *Monitor on Psychology, 43*(8), 30–33.

Witkowski, T. (1997). Performance level in situations of helplessness threat and group affiliation: Egotistic mechanisms in helplessness deficits. *Journal of Social Psychology, 137,* 229–234.

Wood, A. R., Wood, R. J., & Taylor, S. M. (2012). Becoming more therapeutic: Motivational interviewing as a communication style for paraprofessionals in juvenile justice settings. In E. L. Grigorenko (Ed.), *Handbook of juvenile forensic psychology and psychiatry* (pp. 239–251). http://dx.doi.org/10.1007/978-1-4614-0905-2.

Worling, J. R., & Langton, C. M. (2015). A prospective investigation of factors that predict desistance from recidivism for adolescents who have sexually offended. *Sexual Abuse: A Journal of Research and Treatment, 27*(1), 127–142.

Worling, J. R., Litteljohn, A., & Bookalam, D. (2010). 20-year prospective follow-up study of specialized treatment for adolescents who offended sexually. *Behavioral Sciences and the Law, 28,* 46–57.

Wormith, J. S., Gendreau, P., & Bonta, J. (2012). Deferring to clarity, parsimony, and evidence in reply to Ward, Yates, and Willis. *Criminal Justice and Behavior, 39*(1), 111–120.

Wyman, P. A., Cowen, E. L., Work, W. C., & Kerley, J. H. (1993). The role of children's future expectations in self-system functioning and adjustment to life stress: A prospective study of urban at-risk children. *Development and Psychopathology, 5,* 649–661.

Yates, P. M. (2009a) Using the good lives model to motivate sexual offenders to participate in treatment. In D. S. Prescott (Ed.), *Building motivation to change in sexual offenders.* Brandon, VT: Safer Society Press.

Yates, P. M. (2009b). Is sexual offender denial related to sex offence risk and recidivism? A review and treatment implications. *Psychology, Crime, & Law, 15*(2–3), 183–199.

Zeng, G., Chu, C. M., & Lee, Y. (2015). Assessing protective factors of youth who sexually offended in Singapore: Preliminary evidence on the utility of the Dash-13 and the SAPROF. *Sexual Abuse: A Journal of Research and Treatment, 27*(1), 91–108.

Zweben, A., & Zuckoff, A. (2002). Motivational interviewing and treatment adherence. In W. R. Miller & S. Rollnick (Eds.), *Motivational interviewing: Preparing people for change* (2nd ed., pp. 299–319). New York: Guilford Press.

CHAPTER 9

Evidence-Based Practices and Treatment

James R. Worling

Calvin M. Langton

There has been movement in recent years toward more policies regarding adolescents who have sexually offended that reflect an empirically unsupported punitive orientation (Letourneau, 2006; Lobanov-Rostovsky, 2010). This stands in contrast with arguments advanced that sexual offending be approached as a public health problem (Bellis, Hughes, Perkins, & Bennett, 2012; Laws, 2000; Letourneau, Eaton, Bass, Berlin, & Moore, 2014; National Society for the Prevention of Cruelty to Children, 2011) as well as evidence suggesting that therapeutic efforts can be effective in reducing sexual recidivism among juveniles (Washington State Institute for Public Policy & University of Washington Evidence-Based Practice Institute, 2016). Unfortunately there has been little progress toward the development and implementation of a public health approach and therefore a dearth of empirical evidence to inform such efforts (Letourneau et al., 2014). This is disconcerting because the need to address sexual offending by adolescents is certainly pressing. In 2014, 15.7 percent of those arrested for rape and 17.4 percent of those arrested for other sexual offenses in the United States were under 18 years of age (Federal Bureau of Investigation, 2015). In Canada, 17 percent of those accused of sexual offenses and 26 percent of those accused of sexual offenses involving victims under 18 years of age were youth (Allen & Superle, 2016). In this chapter, a range of treatment issues, components, and targets for adolescents who have sexually abused others is critically discussed. Throughout, a developmental perspective is emphasized, as are ecological, practical, and ethical considerations, which inform what is currently known about how to reduce recidivism among these youth.

Recent History

During the mid-20th century, several authors described the treatment needs of adolescents who had committed a sexual crime (e.g., Atcheson & Williams, 1954; Doshay, 1943; North, 1956; Waggoner & Boyd, 1941). These authors referred to the heterogeneity of this population, and they underlined the need to tailor interventions to suit the unique needs of each client. It was also pointed out in these early reports that only a minority of the adolescents posed a risk of reoffending sexually as adults. There were very few publications regarding adolescent sexual aggression in the decades that followed; however, in the mid-1980s, it was pointed out by some authors that a sizable proportion of adult males who had committed sexual offenses began to offend sexually as adolescents and/or disclosed that the onset of their abuse-supportive sexual interests occurred during adolescence (e.g., Abel, Mittelman, & Becker, 1985; Longo & Groth, 1983). Findings such as these spawned increasing scientific, social, and political interest in adolescents who offended sexually.

One Size Fits All

With this increased academic focus on adolescents who committed sexual offenses, much of the research and clinical description that followed was centered on describing how adolescents who offended sexually were different from other groups of adolescents. It was not uncommon, for example, for researchers to compare a small group of adolescents who had committed a sexual crime to a group of adolescents who had offended non-sexually (e.g, Lewis, Shankok, & Pincus, 1979; Saunders, Awad, & Levene, 1984). Given this format of scientific inquiry, there was a tendency, therefore, to describe adolescents who offended sexually as though they were homogeneous. Indeed, authors used to talk about how this group of youth had shared characteristics, such as poorly developed social skills (e.g., Groth & Loredo, 1981), deviant sexual interests (e.g., Goocher, 1994; Lakey, 1994), distorted sexual values and beliefs (e.g., Underwood, Robinson, Mosholder, & Warren, 2008), and deceitfulness (Perry & Orchard, 1992). Unfortunately, this one-size-fits-all orientation prevailed until more recently when it was stressed, again, that adolescents who commit sexual crimes are, in fact, heterogeneous (e.g., Worling, 1995b) and that there is actually no such thing as a profile of an adolescent who has offended sexually (ATSA, 1997). Therefore, it is necessary to complete a comprehensive assessment of strengths, risks, and needs to determine what, if any, treatment goals should be addressed (see Leversee, 2010; Worling & Langton, 2016; and Becker & Valerio, this volume, for a description of comprehensive assessment).

APPLICATION OF ADULT-BASED PROCEDURES

With this emerging interest during the early 1980s in adolescents who offend sexually came the call for treatment, particularly given research findings suggesting that many adults who offended sexually began to engage in sexually abusive behaviors during adolescence. Given that there were already many established assessment tools and treatment programs at that time for adults who had sexually offended (Knopp, 1984), there was a tendency for program development for adolescents to be based on tools and approaches that had already been designed for adults. This included a particular emphasis on the assessment and treatment of deviant sexual interests (i.e., sexual interest in prepubescent children and/or sexual violence), which were presumed to characterize these youth, and on the use of confrontational approaches designed to extract specific details of past sexual offenses (Knopp, 1982). Perhaps the application of adult-based tools and approaches was based on observations of similarities between adults and adolescents who commit sexual crimes. For example, some of the specific sexual offense behaviors that adolescents engage in with the individuals whom they victimize look very similar to the offense behaviors perpetrated by adults, and the harm caused by adolescents is similar to that caused by adults (e.g., Cyr, Wright, McDuff, & Perron, 2002; Rudd & Herzberger, 1999). Additionally, a number of risk factors for repeated sexual offending behaviors among adult males, such as past sexual offenses against strangers, past sexual offenses against multiple victims, and past sexual offenses against a male (Hanson & Bussière, 1998), are also correlated with sexual recidivism among adolescents (McCann & Lussier, 2008).

Despite similarities such as these, however, there are clearly many critical differences between adolescents and adults that impact the goals and delivery of treatment. For example, relative to adults, adolescents experience significant developmental changes as they incorporate the meaning and salience of sexual thoughts, feelings, and attitudes in the formation of their sexual identities (Bancroft, 2006). Sisk and Foster (2004) pointed out that highly complex interactions among brain development, hormonal changes, and external stimuli for adolescents impact this gradual transition to sexual maturity. Steinberg (2010) has also noted that the maturational changes in the brain during adolescence are quite dramatic and that adolescents are much more likely to engage in risky behaviors as a result of a combination of a slowly developing prefrontal cortex and related areas of the brain that are involved in self-regulation and an increase in the drive for dopaminergic stimulating activities (i.e., activities that result in the release of dopamine) (also see Modecki, this volume). Brain maturation regarding impulse control and executive functioning actually continues well past adolescence and into the mid-20s (Casey, Getz, & Galván, 2008; Steinberg, 2005; Yurgelen-Todd, 2007), and desistance from adolescent criminal recidivism is linked to eventual psychosocial maturity and the development of mature self-regulation (Steinberg, Cauffman, & Monahan, 2015). As such, although adolescent and adult sexual offense behaviors may sometimes look similar, the motivating factors and thought processes behind an adolescent's decision to engage in sexually abusive behavior can be very different from those of an adult who engages in the same behavior.

Given these critical maturational differences, some assessment and treatment tools designed for adults may have little use when applied to adolescents, and there may even be iatrogenic harm when they are used with adolescent clients. Take the penile plethysmograph (PPG), for example: a tool developed to measure sexual interests with adult males (Freund, 1991). Although some researchers have found that this device can yield reliable and valid information regarding sexual interests with adults who have offended sexually (e.g., Lalumière & Harris, 1998; Seto, 2001), it has been demonstrated that PPG data from adolescents are influenced by a number of extraneous factors, including a history of physical and sexual abuse (Becker, Hunter, Stein, & Kaplan, 1989; Becker, Kaplan, & Tenke, 1992), cultural background (Murphy, DiLillo, Haynes, & Steere, 2001), and the adolescent's age at assessment (Kaemingk, Koselka, Becker, & Kaplan, 1995). Given that adolescents are still developing their sexual interests and identities, there are also significant ethical concerns regarding the use of the PPG and the exposure of adolescent clients to visual and/or auditory stimuli depicting sexual deviance that occurs during the use of this technology (Becker & Harris, 2004; Hunter & Lexier, 1998; Worling, 1998).

Treatment techniques designed for adults could also be problematic when applied to adolescents. Take masturbatory satiation, for example—a punishment-based technique designed to extinguish deviant sexual arousal for adult males (Marshall, 1979). With this technique, the client is instructed first to masturbate to a non-deviant sexual fantasy and then, following climax, immediately begin to masturbate to one of their deviant sexual fantasies. The assumption behind this treatment tool is that the masturbatory behavior immediately following climax—and thus during the refractory period—will be non-rewarding, and that the client will eventually associate their deviant sexual fantasies with a decreased sexual drive state (Maltetzky, 1991). Given that the refractory period can be quite brief with an adolescent (Bancroft, 2009), the use of this treatment approach with this age group could actually result in the maintenance (or, indeed, the initial development) of deviant sexual fantasy.

It is critical, therefore, to provide treatment to adolescents that is sensitive to their cognitive, sexual, social, and emotional development (Latham & Kinscherff, 2012). The age range typically found in samples of adolescents who have sexually offended is quite narrow; for example, juveniles accounted for 14 percent of forcible rape arrests in 2010 in the United States, with 67 percent of these youth aged 15 through 17 (Sickmund & Puzzanchera, 2014). In Canada in 2014, youth aged 14 through 16 had the highest rates across the age range for distinct categories of sexual assault and sexual violations against children (Allen & Superle, 2016). However, there is certainly representation across adolescence; in recent US data, for example, the 5-year age groups from across the life span that accounted for the highest percentages of known sexual offenses in 2013 were the groups of 11- through 15-year-olds (12.2%) and 16- through 20-year-olds (15.6%) (US Department of Justice, Federal Bureau of Investigation, 2013). Attention to this age range in adolescence is important if innovations in treatment are to reflect developmental differences *within* adolescence (Holmbeck et al., 2000).

THERAPIST CHARACTERISTICS AND THE THERAPEUTIC ALLIANCE

Unfortunately, there has been a focus on the tools and techniques designed to prevent a sexual reoffense at the expense of an awareness of the salience of the most important tool for intervention: the therapeutic alliance. Indeed, there has been so much attention paid in the literature to risk assessment tools, the assessment and treatment of deviant sexual interests, and relapse prevention strategies that treatment programs have tended to focus on procedures that are applied *to* clients rather than focusing on the therapeutic process used in collaboration *with* clients that contributes to positive changes (Marshall et al., 2003). This is likely a function of the persistent view that all youth who offend sexually are sexually deviant, delinquent, disordered, deficient, and deceitful, and that treatment efforts should be focused on issues such as extracting details of past offending and quashing deviant thoughts, fantasies, and interests (Chaffin, 2008; Chaffin & Bonner, 1998; Worling, 2013). Marshall et al. (2003) have argued that a warm, encouraging, empathic, flexible, and hopeful therapeutic orientation is likely to lead to maximal therapeutic gain for clients. It is difficult to see how a focus on tools designed to punish and suppress presumed deviance could be part of such a therapeutic orientation. There is also research in the general psychotherapy literature that highlights the fact that a significant amount of variability in the outcome of treatment for youth can be accounted for by the alliance that the therapist forms with the youth and the youth's parents (Shirk, Karver, & Brown, 2011). Given its likely importance in work with adolescents who have sexually offended, it is crucial to attend to the additional considerations and challenges (perhaps most obviously around confidentiality and consent for assessment and treatment) impacting such an alliance that are inherent in work with this population (see, for example, Hunter & Lexier, 1998; Langton & Barbaree, 2004).

Along with recognizing the importance of therapist characteristics and the therapeutic alliance, it is also essential to be mindful of the potential impact of this work on the therapist. There is incredible potential to enrich one's clinical skills and practices as a result of working closely in treatment with adolescents who have sexually offended. For example, the skills learned with respect to being able to talk with youth about such potentially embarrassing issues as abuse-supportive sexual interests can be transferred to work with clients who present with other concerns. Similarly, the worries that many adolescents who have offended sexually express regarding the confidentiality of their information can enhance the care that clinicians take regarding privacy and security issues. It is not surprising, therefore, that working with adolescents who offend sexually, and their families, can be incredibly rewarding for the therapist (Slater & Lambie, 2011). There is, however, also a risk of negative outcomes, including vicarious trauma, when providing treatment to this population. In addition to the potentially negative impact of being exposed to the trauma histories of the adolescents, and the details of their past sexual crimes, the therapist will also have to cope with potentially disquieting responses, such as victim blaming, minimization and denial, or a lack of remorse (Moulden & Firestone, 2007). It may also be difficult to form a strong, therapeutic alliance when one is working with an adolescent who espouses attitudes or sexual interests supportive of sexual interactions with younger children. Moulden and Firestone (2007) offered several suggestions regarding positive self-care strategies for therapists, including obtaining adequate supervision and consultation, physical exercise, spiritual practices, and being realistic about the client's and therapist's roles in the change process.

TREATMENT MODALITY

Group therapy has long been utilized in treatment programs for adolescents who have sexually offended (Knopp, 1982), and the majority of treatment programs in Canada and the United States continue to provide group-based interventions (McGrath, Cumming, Burchard, Zeoli, & Ellerby, 2010). McGrath et al. (2010) point out that there are a number of potential advantages to group therapy, including increased comfort for group members to be open regarding sexual issues with others who have engaged in harming sexual behaviors, the ability to practice new social skills in vivo, willingness of clients to receive feedback from peers rather than from therapists, and reduced treatment costs, for example. Yalom and Leszcz (2005) have outlined a number of key benefits to group-based treatment, including the reduction in group members' sense of isolation, the instillation of hope that problems can be overcome, the reduction of shame, and a sense of acceptance and belonging, for example. Group therapy also provides the clinician with some unique opportunities to use games and other creative activities with multiple participants that would otherwise be difficult to incorporate into individual treatment.

In 1999, Dishion, McCord, and Poulin published a paper outlining the potential contagion effect of group therapy for youth involved with the criminal justice system. It was suggested by these authors that group-based interventions may well be iatrogenic as a result of exposure to antisocial peers. Shortly following this publication, fears were raised regarding the use of group therapy with adolescents who had offended sexually (e.g., ATSA, 2003). It should be stressed, however, that much of the empirical support for the supposed peer-contagion argument was based on the effect of unsupervised time with peers rather than time spent in formal treatment groups (Gifford-Smith, Dodge, Dishion, & McCord, 2005). Gifford-Smith et al. (2005) also pointed to a number of factors that moderate the potential "transmission" of peer delinquency including gender, age, and initial risk level, for example. Furthermore, it should be noted that direct tests of this potential delinquency-contagion effect have not supported this conclusion (e.g., Mager, Milich, Harris, & Howard, 2005), and Weiss et al. (2005) concluded from their meta-analysis that group-based interventions do not increase levels of delinquency. Hartup (2005) has also suggested that adolescent peer interactions are highly complex and that such a simple, causal link between peer affiliation and adolescent delinquency is questionable. Finally, in a recent meta-analysis of treatment outcome, Lipsey (2009) found that group-based interventions can significantly reduce recidivism rates among youth who have committed criminal offenses.

Group-based interventions can be beneficial for adolescents who have offended sexually; however, it is important to be mindful of (a) group composition and (b) the content of the material presented in groups. Although some level of group heterogeneity is beneficial in that this can result in a more diverse array of issues being addressed, too much variability with respect to issues such as social and emotional maturity or intellectual functioning, for example, can be disadvantageous to group cohesion and participation. Likewise, a group with a high proportion of adolescents with callous and unemotional traits could negatively impact group processes as a result of issues such as non-compliance (e.g., O'Neill, Lidz, & Heilbrun, 2003). There may also be times when the nature of the sexual offending should be considered when establishing group membership. For example, it can be challenging for an adolescent to participate fully in group conversations if that youth is the only one in the group with a sexual offense involving an animal, or if there is only one adolescent who has offended against a person of a certain gender.

It was once held that it was important for adolescents who had offended sexually to disclose the details of their presumed deviant sexual fantasies and their past sexual crimes to their group members (.e.g, Margolin, 1984; Steen & Monnette, 1989). Presumably, this public sharing of sexual deviance was believed to signal that the adolescent was being accountable and was, therefore, less likely to reoffend. It should be stressed, however, that there is no evidence that this practice has any positive impact on recidivism, and there may actually be detrimental consequences to it. For example, the sharing of details of past sexual crimes could provide other group members with novel ideas regarding sexual offending behaviors, and shared details of deviant sexual fantasies may be experienced as sexually arousing for some group members, inadvertently impacting subsequent sexual fantasy and masturbatory behavior. It may be best, therefore, for discussions focused on the details of past sexual crimes and deviant sexual interests, if present, to be reserved for individual therapy. Group-based work could then be focused on issues where peer group support and encouragement can be beneficial, such as prosocial sexual attitudes, affective-regulation strategies, parent–child relationships, impact of sexual media, sexual knowledge, and dating norms and consent, for example.

Treatment Manuals and Workbooks

With a view that adolescents who offend sexually are homogeneous, it might be tempting for some therapists to utilize a treatment manual designed for this poplation, and follow it from front to back. There may even be some practitioners who would believe that the completion of a workbook signals the completion of sexual-offense-specific treatment. There are a number of workbooks designed specifically for the treatment of adolescents who have offended sexually (e.g., Bromberg & O'Donohue, 2014; Hunter, 2011; Kahn, 2011; Page, Murphy, & Way, 2007; Rich, 2009; Robinson, 2002), and they contain an array of helpful exercises for issues such as developing and practicing offense prevention strategies, enhancing accountability for past sexual offenses, and increasing awareness of victim impact, for example. Although many of the exercises in workbooks such as these can be very useful when addressing certain treatment goals, it should be stressed that (a) not all exercises in any given workbook are going to be applicable to all adolescents; (b) there will be unique treatment goals for adolescents that are not going to be addressed in the workbooks; and (c) there will be a need to adapt exercises in the workbooks to address treatment responsivity factors such as learning disabilities, particularly given the language-based demands of many of the workbooks. It is important to note that the authors of many of these workbooks have stressed that their workbooks do not represent comprehensive, sexual-offense-specific treatment and that treatment providers should employ careful judgment regarding the use and timing of any of the exercises. Marshall (2009) has also stressed that adherence to a manualized treatment regimen would necessarily limit a clinician's ability to use creativity and innovation to address the unique responsivity factors for each client. There is evidence to suggest that the use of treatment manuals does not negatively impact the therapeutic alliance in treatment with youth (Langer, McLeod, & Weisz, 2011; McLeod et al., 2016); however, the selection of various exercises from manuals and workbooks should be directly informed by an individualized assessment of needs.

In addition to workbooks designed specifically for adolescents who have offended sexually, there are also a number of helpful manuals and workbooks that can be used to address related clinical needs. Selected exercises from these workbooks can be particularly helpful to address issues related to PTSD (Palmer, 2012), social anxiety (Shannon, 2012), and general affect regulation (Langelier, 2001), for example.

TREATMENT SETTING

In the United States, the increase in incarceration rates for adolescents who have committed sexual offenses relative to those for adolescents with non-sexual offenses reported by Snyder and Sickmund (2006) has more recently reversed (Sickmund & Puzzanchera, 2014), and there has been an accompanying decline in the numbers of adolescents in residential placements (Hockenberry, 2016). But it remains the case that some adolescents with sexual offenses will be deemed poor candidates for services in open custody or community-based settings, at least initially, meaning that therapeutic efforts will have to begin in a more restrictive environment along the continuum of care (Bengis, 2010). Still, such realities do not negate the potentially highly adverse consequences of being away from families and communities at this developmentally sensitive period of life (Grant, Thornton, & Chamarette, 2006), particularly given that theory and empirical evidence point to the importance of meeting the psychological and emotional needs of adolescence and fostering of attachment bonds (Rich, 2005), and also strongly support an ecological approach with such youth (Henggeler,

Schoenwald, Borduin, & Cunningham, 2009; Loeber & Farrington, 1998). Further, the risks of both additional sexual abuse perpetration and also sexual victimization by peers and staff in secure settings (Beck, Cantor, Hartge, & Smith, 2013) must be considered. As well, there is some evidence to suggest that community-based interventions are generally more effective in reducing reoffending among adolescents than are interventions in custodial settings (Adler et al., 2016; Koehler, Lösel, Akoensi, & Humphreys, 2013). Worling and Langton (2012) discussed a number of clinical implications of service provision in secure settings with adolescents with sexual offenses. These included the importance of early discharge planning, including effective communication and collaboration with community-based agencies and caregivers to be involved with the adolescent after release, and involvement of family members (where appropriate and feasible) in therapeutic work while the adolescent is in custody to ensure consistency and commitment throughout the continuum of care from all stakeholders. Also identified as a challenge within secure settings was the establishment and maintenance of a therapeutic alliance with the adolescent that explicitly acknowledges and collaboratively manages both the limits to confidentiality associated with security concerns of institutional care as well as the threats to confidentiality that therapeutic work involving peers and staff in institutions can pose. Within the comprehensive assessment and ongoing monitoring efforts a component was deemed necessary that addresses the specifics of the institution in order to recognize offense-paralleling behaviors and inform individualized risk management strategies for the adolescent. Additional clinical implications included consideration of carefully selected case-specific clinical objectives in individual work, should a dedicated specialized residential program be unavailable, and staff screening and training to identify and address prejudicial attitudes and behaviors that are countertherapeutic. Other key considerations focused on the healthy modeling of relational and sexual behaviors as well as boundaries, and the promotion of self-care and appropriate supervision across professional, personal, and interpersonal domains.

Common Treatment Goals

Although it would certainly be easier for treatment providers to apply the same treatment to every adolescent who has been accused of a sexual crime, there is an obvious need to tailor treatment based on an assessment of each youth's strengths, risks, and needs. Given the diversity among adolescents who have offended sexually, some will need to participate in treatment that is focused particularly on traumatic distress resulting from a childhood victimization history, whereas others may need to target sexual preoccupation connected to a lengthy history of viewing sexualized media. Some adolescents may need to learn and practice very basic social skills, such as how to start a conversation, whereas others may need to target the abuse-supportive beliefs and attitudes. Despite this diversity, however, there are some goals that are reasonably common when providing specialized treatment to adolescents who have offended sexually.

Increasing Accountability and Responsibility for Past Sexual Offending

In their survey of US and Canadian treatment programs, McGrath et al. (2010) pointed out that a common treatment goal is for adolescents to acknowledge their past involvement in sexually abusive behaviors. The rationale for this goal is that, in order for a youth to develop sexual offense prevention plans that are tailored to their unique risk factors, it is necessary to be aware of the unique situational cues, triggers, cognitions, and body responses that contributed to past decisions to commit sexual offenses. As a result of the potential for significant legal, personal, and familial consequences associated with disclosing details regarding past, sexually abusive behavior, however, it is common for adolescents to be reluctant to share new details regarding past offending.

In the past, it was stressed that adolescents who offended sexually were deceitful and that they would not be honest with others. For example, Margolin (1984) explained that "the need to control others pervades the offender's every social interaction. The most prominent symptom of this compulsion to control is his [sic] proclivity to lie" (p. 3). In a similar vein, Goocher (1994) stated that, because an adolescent who offends sexually is a "manipulative, deviant person, descriptors of the treatment of choice include confrontation, insistence on accountability for the offending behavior, a punitive rather than therapeutic orientation, and a focus on self-disclosure" (p. 244). It used to be quite common, therefore, for clinicians and youth justice professionals to be instructed to work hard in their efforts to confront the minimization and denial that they were inevitably to encounter in their work with adolescents who offended sexually (e.g., Bethea-Jackson & Brissett-Chapman, 1989; Kahn & Lafond, 1988; Lakey, 1994; Perry & Orchard, 1992; Sermabeikian & Martinez, 1994; Shaw, 1999; Way & Balthazor, 1990). Indeed, Barbaree and Coronti (1993) stated that "the first stage in treatment targets denial and minimization and successful completion of this stage is a prerequisite to successful treatment" (p. 255).

Although this push to confront adolescents to acknowledge all of the details of their sexually abusive behavior may be the result of (a) the need to identify unique risk factors, and (b) the belief that one must first acknowledge a problem before it can be addressed in treatment, it is important to underscore the fact that there is no research to suggest that a disclosure of all the details of an adolescent's sexually abusive behavior is necessary to enhance future sexual and relationship health. Furthermore, although it was once held that denial of past sexual offending was a risk factor for sexual recidivism (e.g., Prentky & Righthand, 2003; Ross & Loss, 1988), there is no research with adolescents to support this conclusion (Worling & Långström, 2006). Indeed, there are empirical data to suggest that adolescents who categorically deny past sexual crimes are actually less likely to reoffend sexually relative to those adolescents who acknowledge (Kahn & Chambers, 1991; Långström & Grann, 2000; Worling, 2002).

Many clinicians would agree that it is valuable for adolescents to acknowledge key elements of their past sexually abusive behaviors, such as the individuals whom they have abused, the duration and frequency of their offending, the level of intrusiveness, and the thoughts, feelings, and situations that typically preceded their decision to offend. However, a confrontational approach to treatment with any client is likely to further entrench any defensiveness and negatively influence motivation to participate in treatment (Miller & Rollnick, 2013). In their review of the literature, Marshall et al. (2003) highlighted the fact that, when working with individuals who have offended sexually, a confrontational approach is likely to lead to an *increase* in defensiveness, denial, and resistance. As such, Marshall et al. (2003) stressed that the best approach in treatment is to use an empathic, warm, rewarding, and supportive orientation.

In addition to a fear of negative consequences, another issue that influences an adolescent's ability to be open during treatment is shame. Unlike feelings of guilt, where the focus of cognitions is on the behavior (e.g., "I have done something horrible"), feelings of shame are the result of a negative evaluation of the self (e.g., "I am a horrible person because of what I have done") (Tangney & Dearing, 2002). Although it was once thought that shame could be be used productively in the treatment of those who offend sexually (e.g., Maletzky, 1991; Serber, 1970), there is now a general consensus in the literature that shame actually *inhibits* the treatment process (Bumby, Marshall, & Langton, 1999; Jenkins, 2005; Proeve & Howells, 2002; Ward, Day, Howells, & Birgden, 2004). Feelings of shame following sexual offending often lead to reduced victim empathy, victim blaming, and social withdrawal (Bumby et al., 1999). Feelings of guilt, on the other hand, propel individuals to take responsibility for their behavior, and they motivate individuals to take corrective steps and repair the damage that they have caused. Several authors have stressed the need to help those who have offended sexually to separate their behavior (committing the sexual offenses) from their sense of identity (Bumby et al., 1999; Jenkins, 2005; McAlinden, 2005). In this way, treatment assists the individual to move gradually from a position of shame to a position of guilt (Proeve & Howells, 2002). Worling, Josefowitz, and Maltar (2011) outlined a cognitive-behavioral approach to reducing shame for adolescents who have offended sexually through building a trusting therapeutic alliance, helping the client to separate the behavior from the person, and developing a sense of personal responsibility and guilt for past sexual offending. Jenkins (2005) has stressed the need for therapists to be supportive, patient, and affirming in order to reduce the shame experienced by adolescents who have offended sexually, and he also underscored the need to reduce the shame experienced by family members.

Enhancing Healthy Sexual Interests

It was once believed that most adolescents who commit a sexual crime have deviant sexual interests (i.e., sexual interest in prepubescent children and/or sexual violence); therefore, treatment efforts were often focused on reducing these presumed sexual interests. For example, Hunter and Santos (1990) stated that "insight-oriented approaches for the treatment of these youth are of limited value . . . key components include the reduction of deviant arousal" (p. 240). Similarly, Perry and Orchard (1992) explained that a goal for all adolescents who have offended sexually is to "learn more appropriate sexual preferences" (p. 64). In 1993, the National Task Force Report from the National Adolescent Perpetrator Network stated that all adolescents who offended sexually should reduce their deviant sexual arousal, and the American Academy of Child and Adolescent Psychiatry (Shaw, 1999) also forwarded the argument that the reduction of deviant sexual arousal is key in the treatment for all youth who have offended sexually.

Despite this once widely held assumption, however, researchers have subsequently found that most adolescents who have offended sexually demonstrate maximal sexual interest in consensual sexual activities with peer-aged partners (Seto, Murphy, Page, & Ennis, 2003; Seto, Lalumière, & Blanchard, 2000; Worling, 2004; 2006; Worling, Bookalam, & Litteljohn, 2012). As such, only a minority of adolescents who offend sexually will demonstrate abuse-supportive sexual interests, so the enhancement of healthy sexual interests will be a treatment goal for only a minority of adolescent clients.

During the late 1980s and early to mid-1990s, a number of authors discussed the application of several behavioral approaches to reducing deviant sexual interests with adolescents. As in the case of masturbatory satiation, discussed above, most of these techniques were developed for adults. Furthermore, there is little to no empirical evidence from controlled trials to support these practices. For example, Becker, Kaplan, and Kavoussi (1988) and Hunter and Goodwin (1992) described the use of verbal satiation procedures to reduce deviant sexual arousal with adolescents; however, it is impossible to comment on the effectiveness of that particular treatment approach, as participants were simultaneously involved in a number of additional treatment components designed to enhance sexual health. In their work, Weinrott, Riggan, and Frothingham (1997) used a procedure called vicarious sensitization to reduce deviant sexual arousal; in it, adolescents viewed a video depicting an aversive consequence of reoffending (e.g., an actor portraying an adolescent being caught offending sexually by a father) after listening to an audio recording that the adolescent made of the details of his or her sexual offending behavior. After approximately 300 trials, the authors reported that there was a decrease in the average level of sexual interest in prepubescent females (but not prepubescent males). It is not possible to conclude that the vicarious sensitization had any impact, however, as there may have simply been a satiation effect, given that the clients had to listen to offense details up to 300 times. Also, participants were also supplied with wallet cards describing aversive events to review, and they were also explicitly instructed not to masturbate to child-oriented fantasies during the treatment phase.

In addition to the absence of empirical support regarding the use of behavioral approaches to alter sexual interests for adolescents, there are also a number of ethical issues. For instance, how old does a client need to be in order to ensure that one can obtain informed consent to utilize a treatment procedure that is punishment-based? What safeguards need to be in place when requiring adolescents to record or repeat abuse-supportive fantasies? What about safeguards to ensure that prescribed treatment approaches do not unwittingly enhance deviant sexual interests? Can masturbatory procedures or sexual fantasy logs ever be utilized ethically with adolescents? It may be interesting to mention that, in a single-case study of the effectiveness of masturbatory satiation with a teenage male, Hunter, Ryan, and Ryback (2008) reported that the client had been inadvertently masturbating to sexual fantasies of young children at one point during the treatment.

An alternative procedure intended to reduce deviant sexual arousal is to teach adolescents thought-stopping techniques whereby they suppress abuse-supportive urges, thoughts, and fantasies when they occur (e.g., Hunter, 2011; Richardson, Bhate, & Graham, 1997; Ryan, Leversee, & Lane, 2010). For example, an adolescent can be asked to describe the worst possible consequence of being detected for a subsequent sexual offense and then be instructed to think about this scenario whenever they experience an abuse-supportive thought. Alternatively, an adolescent can be taught simply to stop the abuse-supportive thought by picturing a stop sign, snapping an elastic band on their wrist, or otherwise distracting themselves with another activity. Although thought-stopping strategies may be intuitively appealing, Johnston, Ward, and Hudson (1997) and Shingler (2009) have pointed out in their reviews of the literature that the reliance on thought-stopping procedures to change behaviors actually results in an ironic rebound effect. In other words, when trying to change behaviors, the conscious suppression of unwanted thoughts actually results in an *increase* in both the frequency and intensity of the target thoughts. Shingler (2009) suggested, therefore, that thought-stopping should only be taught as a temporary, emergency measure to assist clients to avoid a sexual reoffense. Johnston et al. (1997) advised that, if thought-stopping is to be utilized with clients who have offended sexually, they should be taught to use emotionally salient rather than innocuous distractors, and they should be informed of the inevitability of the recurrence of suppressed thoughts.

Given that there is no empirical support for efforts to alter an adolescent's abuse-supportive urges and fantasies through punishment-based techniques or via thought-suppression strategies, an alternative is the use of mindfulness-based cognitive therapy. With this approach, the client learns how to notice deviant sexual thoughts and, without any judgment, simply monitor his or her thoughts, feelings, and body responses. The abuse-supportive thought is not acted upon or suppressed; rather, it inevitably subsides as it is replaced with other thoughts as they come up. The concept of just noticing deviant sexual thoughts and not actively suppressing them was actually described in 1989 by Steen and Monnette in their book on treatment for adolescents who have offended sexually. Although there is emerging evidence regarding the effectiveness of mindfulness-based approaches to address a number of different concerns with adolescents (e.g., Biegel, Brown, Shapiro, & Schubert, 2009; Kallapiran, Koo, Kirubakaran, & Hancock, 2015; Quach, Mano, & Alexander, 2016; Semple, Lee, Rosa, & Miller, 2010), there have been no empirical investigations regarding the impact of mindfulness-based techniques to address deviant sexual interests with adolescents. There has, on the other hand, been a multiple-baseline design study with a small sample of adult males demonstrating the utility of mindfulness to reduce sexual interest in young children (Singh, Lancioni, Winton, Singh, Adkins, & Singh, 2011). Given that mindfulness-based approaches do not entail punishment, masturbatory behaviors, or thought-suppression techniques that can inadvertently increase the frequency and strength of unwanted thoughts, they may be more readily embraced by clients and therapists.

Some programs in the United States and Canada use medication in an effort to address deviant sexual interests with adolescents (McGrath et al., 2010). In their review of the literature, however, Bradford and Federoff (2006) stressed that there is very little empirical basis to support this practice. These authors also underscored the fact that there may be harmful side effects for some of the medications that have been used to control an adolescent's sexual interests.

Given the lack of empirical evidence that there are any techniques that can directly alter the sexual interests of adolescents, it may be prudent for clinicians to focus their treatment efforts instead on helping adolescents to develop and practice the skills for healthy, sexual relationships (Worling, 2012). Fortunately, treatment programs for adolescents who have offended sexually have long been targeting elements of healthy sexual relationships, including communication skills, decision making, positive sexual knowledge, positive sexual attitudes, interpersonal boundaries, and affective regulation (e.g, Kahn & Lafond, 1988; Steen & Monnette, 1989). Although many of the workbooks cited earlier contain a number of helpful exercises to address these goals, a particularly helpful resource for this work is Langford (2015).

In addition to enhancing the skills, knowledge, and attitudes that would support future, healthy relationships, it may also be necessary with some adolescents to identify and remediate barriers to interpersonal intimacy. For example, if an adolescent is struggling with the formation of close, interpersonal relationships as a result of social anxiety, then it may be helpful to address this social difficulty in their treatment. Research is supportive of a cognitive-behavioral approach to reducing social anxiety with adolescents (Scaini, Belotti, Ogliari, & Battaglia, 2016), and there are several useful workbooks that contain helpful exercises to address the thoughts, feelings, behaviors, and body responses connected with social anxiety (e.g., Shannon, 2012). For some adolescents, their future sexual health also depends on reducing their preoccupation with sexual thoughts and behaviors. Given that there is no research to support the use of any punishment-based approach to achieve this goal, and that there have been no double-blind clinical trials with medication designed to reduce sexual drive for this age group, one commonsense alternative is to work with the adolescent (together with caregivers) to find highly rewarding alternative behaviors. Regular and frequent involvement in sports and/or hobbies can create new patterns of behavior, in addition to providing the adolescent with new opportunities to build prosocial friendships and practice any new interpersonal skills.

ENHANCING HEALTHY SEXUAL ATTITUDES

Although attitudes that are supportive of sexual offending represent a risk factor for continued sexual offending behavior for adolescents (Worling & Långström, 2006), there are few descriptions in the literature of treatment approaches designed to change these attitudes. One particularly promising approach was outlined by Richardson et al. (1997). The first step is to identify the adolescent's abuse-supportive beliefs via statements that he or she makes regarding their offending behavior (e.g., "My little brother didn't say no"). The next step is to work collaboratively with the adolescent to identify the possible beliefs that could be underlying such a statement (e.g., "Young children understand what they are agreeing to when they are asked to be sexual"; "Young children always voice their dissent when they do not wish to do something"; "Young children can always freely refuse to do things when asked by an elder"; "When people do not say no, it means yes," etc.). In our work with adolescents, we have found that this step works best when the clinician has taken some time to think about the several, possible underlying beliefs prior to meeting with the adolescent. The third step in the approach outlined by Richardson et al. (1997) is to help the adolescent to understand how holding such beliefs could contribute to the decision to engage in sexually abusive behavior. An adolescent is likely to see, for example, how an individual who believes that the lack of a no really means yes could potentially engage others in sexual behavior without their consent. Finally, the last step is to work together with the adolescent and assist him or her to challenge these erroneous beliefs and to develop alternative statements (e.g., "Young children do not yet understand about sex"; "Young children are sometimes afraid to refuse to do things"; "Young children often feel pressured to do what their elders tell them"; "When people don't say no, we have no idea about consent").

Of course, it is also important to address the impact of sexual media in any work addressing sexual beliefs and attitudes. There has been a significant increase in adolescents' exposure to sexualized Internet content since the mid-1990s (Peter & Valkenburg, 2006), and this material has the potential to influence and shape their sexual knowledge, beliefs, interests, and expectations. For some adolescents, the compulsive viewing of sexualized material via the Internet can even result in the use of the Internet to meet both sexual and social needs (Boies, Knudson, & Young, 2004). Although some clinicians and parents may wish for a complete ban on sexualized media, this would be quite challenging given the current levels of exposure via the Internet, television, movies, music, books, magazines, video games, etc. Rather than an outright prohibition, therefore, one approach is to work collaboratively with adolescents to develop a filter so that they can apply critical thinking when they are exposed to sexualized media of any sort—in other words, help adolescents to think critically about whether or not the sexualized media they are seeing negatively impacts their views of gender roles, their knowledge regarding sexuality, their sexual interests, and their expectations for future sexual relationships.

Adolescents' sexual beliefs are also heavily influenced by the sexual beliefs of their peers (Tolman & McClelland, 2011). Therefore, it would be beneficial to have some ability to influence the impact of the sexual attitudes of the peer network. This can be accomplished by working directly with the sexual norms and beliefs of the peer group, such as within a school or residential treatment setting. For those adolescents in community-based treatment, the focus of this work may be on working individually with the adolescent and mitigating the influence of any abuse-supportive attitudes espoused by the peer group.

Parents and caregivers (including residential staff, if applicable) will also directly influence an adolescent's sexual attitudes and values. As such, it is ideal to work closely with the adults in the adolescent's life to ensure that prosocial sexual beliefs are espoused and modeled. Particular topics to address include gender roles and expectations, interpersonal intimacy, personal space and boundaries, and the role of touch, for example.

Reducing the Impact of Traumatic Distress

Although childhood abuse and neglect will impact children in different ways, some common reactions include depression, anxiety, anger, avoidance, and negative self-attributions, for example (Cohen, Manarino, & Deblinger, 2006). For children and youth who have experienced complex trauma (i.e., repeated exposure to abuse by a primary attachment figure), there can be additional difficulties, such as an inability to form trusting relationships, extreme self-regulation challenges, and problems forming an integrated sense of self (Ford & Courtois, 2009). Given that adolescents who commit sexual crimes are more likely to have experienced childhood physical, sexual, or emotional abuse or neglect relative to adolescents who offend non-sexually (Seto & Lalumière, 2010), it is critical to ensure that post-traumatic distress is assessed and that any resultant symptoms are addressed. If the goal of treatment is to ensure that an adolescent has healthy sexual relationships in the future and, therefore, does not commit further sexual (and non-sexual) offenses, then it follows that healing from childhood trauma would be an important step in therapy. Unfortunately, it was once held by some treatment providers that clients who have sexually offended should not be permitted to discuss traumatic events from their childhood and, in particular, a history of sexual victimization, as they may somehow use this to justify and excuse their own sexually abusive behavior (Grayson, 2014).

One of the more popular, evidence-based approaches to helping adolescents to address post-traumatic distress is trauma-focused cognitive-behavioral therapy (TF-CBT; Cohen et al., 2006). Using this approach, adolescents learn to identify and regulate distressing affect connected to their trauma; participate in gradual-exposure exercises—such as completing a trauma narrative—to reduce cognitive symptoms such as intrusive reminders; alter thinking errors resulting from traumatic experiences; and learn and practice personal safety strategies. In addition to supportive evidence for TF-CBT from the model's authors (e.g., Cohen, Mannarino, & Knudsen, 2005), there is also empirical support for this approach from meta-analytic research (e.g., Hetzel-Riggin, Brausch, & Montgomery, 2007), particularly with respect to the reduction of the cognitive symptoms of post-traumatic distress. There are also a number of helpful workbooks that contain exercises specifically developed to address post-traumatic distress for teens (e.g., Chrestman, Gilboa-Schechtman, & Foa, 2009; Palmer, 2012). It is important to note, on the other hand, that not all youth who have experienced trauma benefit from or require exposure-therapy interventions and, as is the case with all treatment goals, decisions to provide such focused treatment should be based on assessment (Cohen, Berliner, & Mannarino, 2010; Lang, Ford, & Fitzgerald, 2011).

Working with Parents/Caregivers

It is clear from meta-analytic research that youth who have been involved with the criminal justice system have a more positive outcome if their parents and/or other key caregivers are directly involved in their treatment, where possible and indicated (e.g., Latimer, Dowden, Morton-Bourgon, Edgar, & Bania, 2003; Lipsey, 2009), and this has also been demonstrated in research conducted specifically with adolescents who have sexually offended (Borduin, Schaeffer, & Heiblum, 2009; Worling, Litteljohn, & Bookalam, 2010). Powell (2010) suggested that one key element of the work with parents is the installation of hope for a healthy sexual future for their children. To achieve this goal, it can be helpful to share information with parents regarding (a) the low base rate of sexual recidivism for adolescents who have sexually offended (especially for those adolescents who have completed sexual-offense-specific counseling; e.g., Reitzel & Carbonell, 2006), (b) the plasticity of sexual arousal patterns during adolescence (e.g., Bancroft, 2006), and (c) the gradual reduction in risky and impulsive behaviors concomitant with brain maturation through adolescence and early adulthood (e.g., Steinberg, 2010). When hope can be instilled for parents, their level of motivation can be enhanced to assist with interventions that encourage future sexual and relationship health for their adolescents. In addition to supporting their child to learn and practice new skills related to interpersonal and affective functioning and healthy sexuality, work with parents may also include a focus on goals pertinent to family functioning, such as parent–child communication and child management strategies, for example.

Offense Prevention Planning

When engaged in offense prevention planning, the goal is to help adolescents move from a reliance on external controls to the regular use of internal controls. Of course, the speed with which an adolescent moves in this regard is dependent on many factors including risks, needs, strengths, and treatment progress. Although the relapse prevention model (Marlatt & Gordon, 1985) was once used by most sexual-offense-specific treatment programs in the United States and Canada, it has declined in popularity since the mid-1990s (McGrath et al., 2010). This is likely a result of the many criticisms of the application of this model to individuals who have offended sexually, including a lack of empirical support for its utility (e.g., Laws, Hudson, & Ward, 2000; Marshall & Marshall, 2015). One significant criticism of this approach is the singular pathway to a reoffense that is often assumed, whereas there are many different pathways that could influence an adolescent's decision to engage in abusive sexual behavior. Another popular approach in the past was the use of "offense cycles" (e.g., Way & Balthazor, 1990). There have been criticisms of the use of offense cycles, however, as they tend to intimate that there is somewhat of a hopeless and continuous pattern whereby one sexual crime somehow cues the next (Maletzky, 1998).

An alternative to the cycle is the "offense chain," where one works with the adolescent to understand the unique pattern of situations, environmental/internal cues, thoughts, feelings, physical responses, and behaviors that contributed to past decisions to commit sexual crimes. Following this, the clinician can work together with the adolescent to develop and practice healthy, goal-oriented alternatives for each step in the chain. Common prevention plans often include features of avoiding or escaping potentially high-risk situations, using mindfulness to cope with abuse-supportive thoughts, distracting oneself with competing activities, and thinking about the potential harm that could be caused to others, for example.

Most of the offense prevention planning discussed above is based on the goal to avoid future sexual offending. It has long been recognized, however, that behavior is motivated by both a desire to approach a positive outcome *and* a desire to avoid a negative outcome (see Elliot, 1999, for a historical review). Although much of the offense prevention planning discussed in early work with adolescents who offended sexually was focused on avoidance (e.g., escaping/avoiding high-risk situations; punishing abuse-supportive thoughts/urges), there has been a growing recognition of the importance of targeting approach goals as well, i.e., goals related to achieving future relational and sexual health. Fortunately, as mentioned above, specialized treatment programs for adolescents have actually long included an emphasis on building the capacity for sexual health; therefore, offense prevention plans now more explicitly include a focus on approach goals that are identified through the assessment process. For example, adolescents may have prevention plans that include goals to have increased self-compassion, to utilize effective problem-solving strategies, to express negative affect in a socially appropriate manner, to be respectful and supportive in relationships, and to enhance their knowledge regarding human sexuality, for example.

Adolescents with Special Needs

As the field has gradually moved away from the notion that adolescents who offend sexually are homogeneous, there has also been an increasing recognition of the fact that treatment interventions need to be modified and adapted so that they can be helpful for adolescents with special needs. For example, Ray, Marks, and Bray-Garretson (2004) and Sutton et al. (2013) provide many excellent suggestions regarding how best to modify treatment for adolescents with autism spectrum disorder who have offended sexually. Specific suggestions include how to teach youth to decode social cues, how to enhance theory-of-mind for youth, how to increase sexual knowledge, and how to cope differently with negative affective states. Similarly, Regan, Spidel, Gretton, Cathpole, and Douglas (2007) have discussed the need to adapt treatment for youth with significant cognitive challenges so that there is a more gradual progression in the complexity of learning tasks, there is increased opportunity for practice and review for new learning, and opportunities to learn are multimodal wherever possible. Baumbach (2002) has similarly identified the unique learning challenges for youth with fetal alcohol spectrum disorder (FASD) who have offended sexually, including adapting treatment to address their challenges with respect to memory, response inhibition, and executive functioning. A comprehensive discussion of the unique assessment and treatment needs of youth with FASD who are involved more generally in the criminal justice system is also provided by Brown, Connor, and Adler (2012).

Working with Female Adolescents

The vast majority of individuals charged with a sexual crime are male (e.g., Brennan & Taylor-Butts, 2008; Federal Bureau of Investigation, 2015). It should not be surprising, therefore, that most of the research regarding the etiology, assessment, and treatment of sexual offending behavior is based on predominantly male samples. There have been a handful of studies of small groups of adolescent females who have offended, however, and researchers have found that these adolescents are very likely to have a childhood sexual abuse history (Giguere & Bumby, 2007; Strickland, 2008). It has also been pointed out that adolescent females who offend sexually most often commit sexual offenses on their own (unlike a subgroup of adult females who co-commit sexual offenses in the presence of a male), they typically offend against younger children who are known to them, and they frequently have access to younger children through babysitting activities (Ryan et al., 2010). Ryan et al. (2010) noted that many of these characteristics are also present for adolescent males who offend sexually, and they suggested that many of the potential differences that clinicians see between adolescent males and females who have offended sexually are socially constructed biases. Despite often strong recommendations to tailor treatment specifically for females, few authors specify just how treatment should be altered based on gender, and treatment goals for adolescent females who have offended sexually include familiar themes, including increasing accountability for past offending; enhancing healthy sexual interests, attitudes, and knowledge; developing offense prevention plans; and reducing traumatic distress, for example (e.g., Hunter, Becker, & Lexier, 2006; Robinson, 2002; Williams & Buehler, 2002). In any case, an individualized treatment plan informed by a comprehensive assessment process would be required that takes into account factors that may enhance treatment engagement and progress and addresses needs particular to the youth; such an approach may serve to partially offset the influence of gender-based assumptions that have yet to be subject to empirical scrutiny.

POSSESSION AND DISTRIBUTION OF CHILD ABUSE IMAGERY

Most research and clinical opinion in the literature is based on the assessment and treatment of adolescent males who have committed a sexual crime that involves a contact sexual offense against an identified individual. Given the increasing exposure to online sexualized imagery for children and adolescents with the advent of the Internet (Peter & Valeknburg, 2006), there has also been an increase in the number of adolescents charged with possession (and, often, distribution) of child abuse images (Moultrie, 2006). Although some treatment and community-supervision professionals might be quick to assume the need for intensive therapy focused on the reduction of sexual deviance because of a charge such as this, there exists marked heterogeneity even within this subgroup of adolescents who offend sexually (Gillespie, 2008; Wolak & Finkelhor, 2011). For example, some adolescents end up being charged with possession of child pornography because they have searched for, and downloaded, sexualized imagery depicting age mates—not young children. Other adolescents end up being charged with producing and distributing child pornography because they have taken sexualized photographs of themselves and then sent them to consenting, romantic partners. If a comprehensive evaluation reveals that there are no additional concerns related to sexual offending, then it would be difficult to justify lengthy sexual-offense-specific treatment for situations such as those described above—despite the nature of the criminal charge.

On the other hand, there are some adolescents who have been charged with possession of child pornography because they have purposely searched for sexualized imagery of prepubescent children. For these youth, many of the treatment goals will overlap with the treatment goals described above for youth who have sexually harmed an identified victim. For example, it will be important to develop prevention plans that are tailored to their unique situational triggers, thoughts, feelings, and body responses. There will also be some adolescents charged with possession of child pornography where there is evidence of a sexual interest in prepubescent children and/or attitudes that are supportive of continued sexual offending against younger children. Moultrie (2006) has argued that the frequent viewing of sexualized imagery of prepubescent children is likely to have an impact on an adolescent's developing sexual interests, attitudes, and expectations.

Sibling Sexual Abuse

There are a number of unique challenges that may be present when working with an adolescent who has offended sexually against a sibling. For example, there are often critical questions regarding both the short- and long-term residency of the adolescent who has offended as they pertain to safety considerations, and there are often issues related to divided loyalties in the family as a result of the sexual offending. Given that many agencies work only with youth who have offended sexually or with children and youth who have been abused, there can also be competing agendas and conflicting philosophies among treatment services provided to a family. There may also be considerable pressure from families and/or systems to speed up (or slow down or halt) treatment that is aimed at repairing the sibling relationship, and complications can arise when treatment readiness is different for various members of the family.

Hodges (2002) and Thomas and Viar (2005) have outlined important steps in working with adolescents who have offended against a sibling. The first important step is to complete independent assessments for the adolescent who offended and for the sibling(s) who was abused. Although sibling sexual abuse often spans many months and can involve repeated, intrusive sexual behaviors (e.g., Adler & Schutz, 1995; O'Brien, 1991), this is not always the case, and treatment and supervision requirements should be tailored to the unique risks and needs for each family. A common treatment goal when there has been sibling sexual abuse, however, is to prepare for clarification work with the family whereby the adolescent takes responsibility for the sexual offending and begins the task of restitution. Likewise, it is important to work with adolescents and their families to develop comprehensive safety plans that address all aspects of contact that the siblings are to have, with a focus on issues such as appropriate communication and physical contact, and sibling roles and responsibilities. If the adolescent who has offended has been removed from the home, and the goal is to reintegrate the youth back into the home, then treatment focused on this goal becomes critical. It is important to stress, on the other hand, that the timing and intensity of treatment aimed at sibling reunification should be based on the physical and emotional safety of the sibling(s) who were abused (ATSA, 2003).

In addition to possible pressure from parents, child welfare, or probation regarding the timing of sibling relationship repair and family reunification work, an additional challenge to this work may be that one of the siblings may be residing far from the rest of the family, and this can make dyadic and family sessions difficult. Also, parents of adolescents who have offended against a sibling may be struggling with their own issues related to family violence and/or childhood sexual abuse (Worling, 1995a), and they may require their own support to cope with issues that are now being raised by their child's sexual offending.

STATUTORY SEXUAL CRIMES

There are jurisdictions in the world where there are no "close-in-age" rules regarding consent for sexual interactions between partners and where sexual behavior that would be considered widely as developmentally normative has the potential to be criminalized. In the United States, for example, there are some states where *any* sexual behavior under a certain age is considered illegal—regardless of the context (Zimring, 2004). In a jurisdiction where it is illegal to engage in any form of sexual behavior under the age of 18, for example, and two 17-year-olds have been involved in a consensual sexual relationship, one or both of these adolescents could potentially be convicted of a sexual crime, despite the fact that this would be considered normative and legal in other parts of the world. If the results of an assessment reveal that there are no concerns related to an increased risk of sexually abusive behavior, it would be difficult to justify the need for specialized treatment beyond ensuring that the adolescent is aware of local laws and has some practical strategies to avoid further criminal charges.

OUTCOME RESEARCH REGARDING SPECIALIZED TREATMENT

Relative to areas within children's mental health, child welfare, and even juvenile justice, the outcome research with adolescents who have sexually offended is a relatively small literature, particularly when focusing on treatment evaluation studies that utilize methodologically sound designs and include recidivism as a dependent variable (see, for example, Washington State Institute for Public Policy & University of Washington Evidence-Based Practice Institute, 2016). Certainly, this is disconcerting given the growth in specialized programs (McGrath et al., 2010) and the importance of basing what is undertaken with these youth and their families on a firm empirical foundation.

Nevertheless, both qualitative and quantitative reviews have suggested that treatment is generally associated with reductions in recidivism. Fortune and Lambie (2006) reported a narrative review of 28 treatment outcome studies and concluded that recidivism rates for adolescents receiving treatment were generally lower than those for untreated adolescents. But they pointed to various methodological flaws, including the general absence of appropriate comparison groups, which render conclusions about treatment efficacy on the basis of their review tentative at best. Reitzel and Carbonell (2006) conducted a meta-analysis of nine studies (involving appropriately 3,000 adolescents with sexual offenses) in which specialized treatment was compared directly with untreated comparison groups. They reported that just over 7 percent of treated adolescents were charged with a new sexual offense over an average follow-up period of five years compared with nearly 19 percent of those in comparison groups, a moderate treatment effect in statistical terms.

Two individual studies, noteworthy for their methodological rigor and extended follow-up periods, similarly indicated positive treatment effects. Worling et al. (2010) reported that 9 percent of adolescents undergoing specialized treatment (involving individual, group, and family components) who were then followed up between 12 and 20 years later were found to have been charged with a new sexual offense, compared with 21 percent of those in an untreated comparison group. Borduin et al. (2009) used an average follow-up period of 8.9 years in their evaluation of multisystemic therapy (MST) with adolescents with sexual offenses. Sexual recidivism rates were 8 percent and 46 percent for the treated and untreated groups, respectively.

Since 2012, the Washington State Institute for Public Policy and University of Washington Evidence-Based Practice Institute have published annual meta-analyses of a comprehensive array of prevention and intervention services for children and adolescents, including juvenile justice programs and treatment for adolescents with sexual offenses specifically. In the 2016 update of this multi-year inventory, MST for this latter group was classified as evidence-based according to the current definition in law: "A program or practice that has had multiple site random controlled trials across heterogeneous populations demonstrating that the program or practice is effective for the population" (p. 7). Of note, the legal mandate under which these reviews were commissioned contained two provisions beyond this definition: consideration of available systematic evidence and cost-effectiveness. As such, along with the definition in law, a modified definition of the term *evidence-based* has been used in these reports:

A program or practice that has been tested in heterogeneous or intended populations with multiple randomized and/or statistically-controlled evaluations, or one large multiple-site randomized and/or statistically-controlled evaluation, where the weight of the evidence from a systematic review demonstrates sustained improvements in at least one of the following outcomes: child abuse, neglect, or the need for out of home placement; crime; children's mental health; education; or employment. Further, "evidence-based" means a program or practice that can be implemented with a set of procedures to allow successful replication in Washington and, when possible, has been determined to be cost-beneficial. (Washington State Institute for Public Policy & University of Washington Evidence-Based Practice Institute, 2016, p. 7)

According to this definition, MST for adolescents who have sexually offended is now considered research-based, as distinct from evidence-based, by this organization on the basis of the available evidence, with the former defined as follows:

A program or practice that has been tested with a single randomized and/or statistically-controlled evaluation demonstrating sustained desirable outcomes; or where the weight of the evidence from a systematic review supports sustained outcomes as identified in the term "evidence-based" in RCW (the above definition) but does not meet the full criteria for "evidence-based." (Washington State Institute for Public Policy & University of Washington Evidence-Based Practice Institute, 2016, p. 7)

In the 2016 update, treatment programs other than MST, which were grouped together, were classified as a promising practice. The modified definition used is: "A program or practice that, based on statistical analyses or a well-established theory of change, shows potential for meeting the 'evidence-based' or 'research-based' criteria, which could include the use of a program that is evidence-based for outcomes other than the alternative use" (Washington State Institute for Public Policy & University of Washington Evidence-Based Practice Institute, 2016, p. 7). Taken altogether, there is certainly reason for optimism but also for renewed research efforts. The multifaceted elements along which programs are evaluated in reports such as those of the Washington State Institute for Public Policy and the University of Washington Evidence-Based Practice Institute serve to clarify both what is known about and what is still in need of empirical investigation. It remains the case that more research on the effects of specific treatment programs on sexual recidivism as well as mechanisms of change and cost-effectiveness is clearly required to more firmly ground the field's efforts.

Outcome Research Regarding General Recidivism

Research on the effectiveness of specialized treatment for adolescents with sexual offenses is certainly encouraging. But a myopic focus on sexual recidivism and treatment to address it (lowering or otherwise managing that risk and optimizing or otherwise building on strengths) misses the fact that the recidivism rate for non-sexual offenses for these adolescents is considerably higher (Alexander, 1999; Caldwell, 2010; 2016; Reitzel & Carbonell, 2006). As such, treatment intended to reduce non-sexual reoffending by these adolescents must also be a central consideration.

Fortunately, the literature on what works to reduce recidivism among adolescents involved in juvenile justice more broadly is characterized by a growing number of established, empirically tested programs and practices (Adler et al., 2016; Lipsey, 2009). As is the case with adults who offend, effective interventions with adolescents have been shown to align with central tenets from Andrews and Bonta's (2010) risk-need-responsivity model (see, for example, Andrews, Bonta, & Hoge, 1990; Koehler et al., 2013); these hold that services be matched to assessed level of risk of reoffending and that the focus is placed on those at higher risk (the risk principle); that criminogenic needs (those factors that are changeable and are associated with further involvement in crime) be targeted in treatment (the needs principle); and that interventions are tailored to individuals' characteristics, such as motivation and learning styles (the responsivity principle). A meta-analysis by Hanson, Bourgon, Helmus, and Hodgson (2009) showed larger effect sizes for treatment programs for individuals who offended sexually that adhered to these principles.

Meta-analyses have also shown that the nature of the intervention (i.e., therapeutic rather than punitive or control-oriented), and particular features of the implementation of the intervention such as quality and fidelity of implementation (with staff training and adherence to the intervention protocol important), as well as duration and intensity (with longer programs and participants receiving the full dose, as intended) are all important elements associated with successful interventions (Koehler et al., 2013; Lipsey, 1999; 2009).

Further, cost-benefit analyses indicate that a range of interventions (including, for example, programs reflecting restorative justice, mediation, and mentoring approaches; therapeutic communities for substance abusers; diversion initiatives; programs representing cognitive-behavioral, multisystemic, and family therapies; and those incorporating motivational interviewing) can all be effective in reducing recidivism and also demonstrably economically viable (Adler et al., 2016; Washington State Institute for Public Policy & University of Washington Evidence-Based Practice Institute, 2016). At the systemic level, decisions about how best to address non-sexual reoffending among adolescents with sexual offenses should be firmly grounded in this literature. At the level of the adolescent, such decisions should be informed by an individualized assessment, of course, based on the use of psychometrically sound tools for the purpose.

CONCLUSION

Treatment for adolescents who have sexually abused others has evolved from an imposition and extrapolation of models, programs, and tools developed for their adult counterparts to more developmentally informed and ecologically attuned efforts. Although this is a work in progress, the field has some promising directions in which to advance in terms of clinical practices and process—the "what" and the "how" of efforts to reduce recidivism among these youth and facilitate a healthy, meaningful, prosocial transition into young adulthood. It remains the case, however, that further attention is needed regarding theory development and empirical investigations of pathways to onset, continuation, and desistance of sexual offending behavior. Such work will do much to inform program evaluation, where more research is needed across all stages of involvement in juvenile justice to firmly establish treatment for this particularly troubling behavior as evidence-based.

REFERENCES

Abel, G. G., Mittelman, M. S., & Becker, J. V. (1985). Sex offenders: Results of assessment and treatment and recommendations for treatment. In M. H. Ben-Aron, S. J. Hucker, & C. D. Webster (Eds.), *Clinical criminology: Assessment and treatment of criminal behavior* (pp. 207–220). Toronto, Canada: M & M Graphics.

Adler, J. R., Edwards, S. K., Scally, M., Gill, D., Puniskis, M. J., Gekoski, A., & Horvath, M. A. H. (2016). *What works in managing young people who offend? A summary of the international evidence.* Technical report. London, UK: Ministry of Justice.

Adler, N. A., & Schutz, J. (1995). Sibling incest offenders. *Child Abuse & Neglect, 19,* 811–819. doi: 10.1016/0145–2134(95)00040-F

Alexander, M. A. 1999. Sexual offender treatment efficacy revisited. *Sexual Abuse: A Journal of Research and Treatment, 11*(2), 101–116. http://dx.doi.org/10.1007/BF02658841

Allen, M. K., & Superle, T. (2016). *Youth crime in Canada, 2014* (Statistics Canada, Catalogue no. 85-002-X). Canadian Centre for Justice Statistics, Ottawa, Canada.

Andrews, D. A., & Bonta, J. (2010). *The psychology of criminal conduct* (5th ed.). New Providence, NJ: Mathew Bender & Company.

Andrews, D. A., Bonta, J., & Hoge, R. D. (1990). Classification for effective rehabilitation: Rediscovering psychology. *Criminal Justice and Behavior, 17,* 19–52.

Association for the Treatment of Sexual Abusers. (1997, November). *Position on the effective legal management of juvenile sexual offenders.* Beaverton, OR: Author.

Association for the Treatment of Sexual Abusers (2003). *Practice standards and guidelines for members of the Association for the Treatment of Sexual Abusers.* Beaverton, OR: Author.

Atcheson, J. D., & Williams, D. C. (1954). A study of juvenile sex offenders. *American Journal of Psychiatry, 111,* 366–370. http://dx.doi.org/10.1176/ajp.111.5.366

Bancroft, J. (2006). Normal sexual development. In H. E. Barbaree & W. L. Marshall (Eds.), *The juvenile sex offender* (2nd ed.) (pp. 19–57). New York: Guilford.

Bancroft, J. (2009). *Human sexuality and its problems* (3rd ed.). London, UK: Elsevier.

Barbaree, H. E., & Cortoni, F. A. (1993). Treatment of the juvenile sex offender within the criminal justice and mental health systems. In H. E. Barbaree, W. L. Marshall, & S. M. Hudson (Eds.), *The juvenile sex offender* (pp. 243–263). New York: Guilford.

Baumbach, J. (2002). Some implications of prenatal alcohol exposure for the treatment of adolescents with sexual offending behaviors. *Sexual Abuse: A Journal of Research and Treatment, 14,* 313–327. http://dx.doi.org/1079-0632/02/1000-0313/0

Beck, A., Cantor, D., Hartge, J., & Smith, T. (2013). *Sexual victimization in juvenile facilities reported by youth, 2012.* Washington, DC: US Department of Justice Office of Justice Programs, Bureau of Justice Statistics.

Becker, J. V., & Harris, C. (2004). The psychophysiological assessment of juvenile offenders. In G. O'Reilly, W. L. Marshall, A. Carr, & R. C. Beckett (Eds.), *The handbook of clinical intervention with young people who sexually abuse* (pp. 191–202). Hove, East Sussex, UK: Brunner-Routledge.

Becker, J. V., Hunter, J., Stein, R., & Kaplan, M. S. (1989). Factors associated with erectile response in adolescent sex offenders. *Journal of Psychopathology and Behavioral Assessment, 11,* 353–362. http://dx.doi.org/10.1007/BF00961533

Becker, J. V., Kaplan, M. S., & Kavoussi, R. (1988). Measuring the effectiveness of treatment for the aggressive adolescent sexual offender. *Annals of the New York Academy of Sciences, 528,* 215–222. http://dx.doi.org/10.1111/j.1749-6632.1988.tb50865.x

Becker, J. V., Kaplan, M. S., & Tenke, C. E. (1992). The relationship of abuse history, denial and erectile response: Profiles of adolescent sexual perpetrators. *Behavior Therapy, 23,* 87–97. http://dx.doi.org/10.1016/S0005-7894(05)80310-7

Bellis, M. A., Hughes, K., Perkins, P., & Bennett, A. (2012). *Protecting people promoting health: A public health approach to violence prevention for England.* Liverpool, UK: North West Public Health Observatory at the Centre for Public Health, Liverpool John Moores University. Retrieved from https://www.gov.uk/government/uploads/system/uploads/attachment_data/file/216977/Violence-prevention.pdf

Bengis, S. (2010). Comprehensive service delivery with a continuum of care. In G. Ryan, T. Leversee, & S. Lane (Eds.), *Juvenile sexual offending* (3rd ed.) (pp. 224–230). Hoboken, NJ: John Wiley & Sons.

Bethea-Jackson, G., & Brissett-Chapman, S. (1989). The juvenile sexual offender: Challenges to assessment for outpatient intervention. *Child and Adolescent Social Work, 6,* 127–137. http://dx.doi.org/10.1007/BF00756112

Biegel, G. M., Brown, K. W., Shapiro, S. L., & Schubert, C. M. (2009). Mindfulness-based stress reduction for the treatment of adolescent psychiatric outpatients: A randomized clinical trial. *Journal of Consulting and Clinical Psychology, 77,* 855–866. http://dx.doi.org/10.1037/a0016241

Boies, S. C., Knudson, G., & Young, J. (2004). The Internet, sex, and youths: Implications for sexual development. *Sexual Addiction & Compulsivity, 11,* 343–363. http://dx.doi.org/10.1080/10720160490902630

Borduin, C. M., Schaeffer, C. M., & Heiblum, N. (2009). A randomized clinical trial of multisystemic therapy with juvenile sexual offenders: Effects on youth social ecology and criminal activity. *Journal of Consulting and Clinical Psychology, 77*, 26–37. http://dx.doi.org/10.1037/a0013035

Bradford, J. M. W., & Federoff, P. (2006). Pharmacological treatment of the juvenile sex offender. In H. E. Barbaree & W. L. Marshall (Eds.), *The juvenile sex offender* (2nd ed.) (pp. 358–382). New York: Guilford.

Brennan, S., & Taylor-Butts, A. (2008). Sexual assault in Canada: 2004 and 2007 (Statistics Canada, Catalogue no. 85F0033M). Canadian Centre for Justice Statistics Profile Series (No. 19), Ottawa, Canada.

Bromberg, D. S., & O'Donohue, W. T. (Eds.) (2014). *Toolkit for working with juvenile sex offenders.* London, UK: Academic Press.

Brown, N. N., Connor, P. D., & Adler, R. S. (2012). Conduct-disordered adolescents with fetal alcohol spectrum disorder intervention in secure treatment settings. *Criminal Justice and Behavior, 39*, 770–793. http://dx.doi.org/10.1177/0093854812437919

Bumby, K. M., Marshall, W. L., & Langton, C. M. (1999). A theoretical model of the influences of shame and guilt on sexual offending. In B. Schwartz & H. Cellini (Eds.), *The sex offender* (Vol. 3) (pp. 5.1–5.12). Kingston, NJ: Civic Research Institute.

Caldwell, M. F. (2010). Study characteristics and recidivism base rates in juvenile sex offender recidivism. *International Journal of Offender Therapy and Comparative Criminology, 54*, 197–212. http://dx.doi.org/10.1177/0306624X08330016

Caldwell, M. F. (2016). Quantifying the decline in juvenile sexual recidivism rates. *Psychology, Public Policy, and Law.* Advance online publication. http://dx.doi.org/10.1037/law0000094

Casey, B. J., Getz, S., & Galván, A. (2008). The adolescent brain. *Developmental Review, 28*, 62–77. http://dx.doi.org/10.1016/j.dr.2007.08.003

Chaffin, M. (2008). Our minds are made up—don't confuse us with the facts: Commentary on policies concerning children with sexual behavior problems and juvenile sex offenders. *Child Maltreatment, 13*, 110–121. http://dx.doi.org/10.1177/1077559508314510

Chaffin, M., & Bonner, B.L. (1998). "Don't shoot, we're your children": Have we gone too far in our response to adolescent sexual abusers and children with sexual behavior problems? *Child Maltreatment, 3*, 314–316. http://dx.doi.org/10.1177/1077559598003004003

Chrestman, K. R., Gilboa-Schechtman, E., & Foa, E. B. (2009). *Prolonged exposure therapy for PTSD: Teen workbook.* Oxford, UK: Oxford University Press.

Cohen, J. A., Berliner, L., & Mannarino, A. (2010). Trauma focused CBT for children with co-occurring trauma and behavior problems. *Child Abuse & Neglect, 34*, 215–224. http://dx.doi.org/10.1016/j.chiabu.2009.12.003

Cohen, J. A., Mannarino, A. P., & Deblinger, E. (2006). *Treating trauma and traumatic grief in children and adolescents.* New York: Guilford.

Cohen, J. A., Mannarino, A. P., & Knudsen, K. (2005). Treating sexually abused children: 1 year follow-up of a randomized controlled trial. *Child Abuse & Neglect, 29*, 135–145. http://dx.doi.org/10.1016/j.chiabu.2004.12.005

Cyr, M., Wright, J., McDuff, P., & Perron, A. (2002). Intrafamilial sexual abuse: Brother–sister incest does not differ from father–daughter and stepfather–stepdaughter incest. *Child Abuse & Neglect, 26*, 957–973. http://dx.doi.org/10.1016/S0145-2134(02)00365-4

Dishion, T. J., McCord, J., & Poulin, F. (1999). When interventions harm: Peer groups and problem behavior. *American Psychologist, 54*, 755–764. http://dx.doi.org/10.1037/0003-066X.54.9.755

Doshay, L. J. (1943). *The boy sex offender and his later career.* New York: Grune & Stratton.

Elliot, A. J. (1999). Approach and avoidance motivation and achievement goals. *Educational psychologist, 34*, 169–189. http://dx.doi.org/10.1207/s15326985ep3403_3

Federal Bureau of Investigation (2015). *Crime in the United States (Uniform Crime Reports)*. Retrieved from https://ucr.fbi.gov/crime-in-the-u.s/2014/crime-in-the-u.s.-2014/tables/table-36

Ford, J. D., & Courtois, C. A. (2009). Defining and understanding complex trauma and complex traumatic stress disorders. In C. A. Courtois & J. D. Ford (Eds.). *Treating complex traumatic stress disorders: An evidence-based guide* (pp. 13–30). New York: Guilford.

Fortune, C., & Lambie, I. (2006). Sexually abusive youth: A review of recidivism studies and methodological issues for future research. *Clinical Psychology Review, 26,* 1078–1095. http://dx.doi.org/10.1016/j.cpr.2005.12.007

Freund, K. (1991). Reflections on the development of the phallometric method of assessing erotic preferences. *Annals of Sex Research, 4,* 221–228. http://dx.doi.org/10.1007/BF00850054

Gifford-Smith, M., Dodge, K. A., Dishion, T. J., & McCord, J. (2005). Peer influence in children and adolescents: Crossing the bridge from developmental to intervention science. *Journal of Abnormal Child Psychology, 33,* 255–265. http://dx.doi.org/10.1007/s10802-005-3563-7

Giguere, R., & Bumby, K. (2007). Female sex offenders. Silver Spring, MD: Centre for Sex Offender Management. Retrieved from www.csom.org/pubs/female_ sex_offenders_brief.pdf

Gillespie, A. A. (2008). Adolescents accessing indecent images of children. *Journal of Sexual Aggression, 14,* 111–122. http://dx.doi.org/10.1080/13552600080224802248122

Goocher, B. E. (1994). Some comments on the residential treatment of juvenile sex offenders. *Child & Youth Care Forum, 23,* 243–250. http://dx.doi.org/10.1007/BF02209088

Grant, J., Thornton, J., & Chamarette, C. (2006). Residential placement of intra-familial adolescent sex offenders. *Trends and Issues in Crime and Criminal Justice, 315,* 1–6.

Grayson, J. (2014). Back to the root: Healing potential offenders' childhood trauma with Pesso Boyden System Psychomotor. In G. H. Allez (Ed.), *Sexual diversity and sexual offending* (pp. 251–274). London, UK: Karnac Books.

Groth, N., & Loredo, C. M. (1981). Juvenile sexual offenders: Guidelines for assessment. *International Journal of Offender Therapy and Comparative Criminology, 25,* 31–39. http://dx.doi.org/10.1177/0306624X8102500104

Hanson, R. K., Bourgon, G., Helmus, L., & Hodgson, S. (2009). A meta-analysis of the effectiveness of treatment for sexual offenders: Risk, need, and responsivity (User Report, 1). Ottawa, Canada: Public Safety Canada.

Hanson, R. K., & Bussière, M. (1998). Predicting relapse: A meta analysis of sexual offender recidivism studies. *Journal of Consulting and Clinical Psychology, 66,* 348–362. http://dx.doi.org/10.1037/0022-006X.66.2.348

Hartup, W. W. (2005). Peer interaction: What causes what? *Journal of Abnormal Child Psychology, 33*(3), 387–394. http://dx.doi.org/10.1007/s10802-005-3578-0

Henggeler, S. W., Schoenwald, S. K., Borduin, C. M., Rowland, M. D., & Cunningham, P. B. (2009). *Multisystemic therapy for antisocial behavior in children and adolescents* (2nd ed.). New York: Guilford.

Hetzel-Riggin, M. D., Brausch, A. M., & Montgomery, B. S. (2007). A meta-analytic investigation of therapy modality outcomes for sexually abused children and adolescents: An exploratory study. *Child Abuse & Neglect, 31,* 125–141. http://dx.doi.org/10.1016/j.chiabu.2006.10.007

Hockenberry, S. (2016). Juveniles in residential placement, 2013 (Juvenile Justice Statistics National Report Series Bulletin). Washington, DC: US Department of Justice Office of Juvenile Justice and Delinquency Prevention.

Hodges, C. E. (2002). A 5-step family therapy protocol to treat sibling on sibling sexual abuse. In M. C. Calder (Ed.), *Young people who sexually abuse: Building the evidence base for your practice* (pp. 376–385). Lyme Regis, Dorset, UK: Russell House Publishing.

Holmbeck, G. N., Colder, C., Shapera, W., Westhoven, V., Kenealy, L., & Updegrove, A. (2000). Working with adolescents: Guides from developmental psychology. In P. C. Kendall (Ed.), *Child and adolescent therapy: Cognitive-behavioral procedures* (pp. 334–385). New York: Guilford.

Hunter, J. A. (2011). *Help for adolescent males with sexual behavior problems: A cognitive-behavioral treatment program: Therapist guide.* New York: Oxford University Press.

Hunter, J. A., Becker, J. V., & Lexier, L. J. (2006). The female juvenile sex offender. In H. E. Barbaree & W. L. Marshall (Eds.), *The juvenile sex offender* (2nd ed.) (pp. 148–165). New York: Guilford.

Hunter, J. A., & Goodwin, D. W. (1992). The clinical utility of satiation therapy with juvenile sexual offenders: Variations and efficacy. *Annals of Sex Research, 5,* 71–80. http://dx.doi.org/10.1177/107906329200500201

Hunter, J. A., & Lexier, L. J. (1998). Ethical and legal issues in the assessment and treatment of juvenile sex offenders. *Child Maltreatment, 3,* 339–348. http://dx.doi.org/10.1177/1077559598003004006

Hunter, J. A., Ram, N., & Ryback, R. (2008). Use of satiation therapy in the treatment of adolescent-manifest sexual interest in male children. *Clinical Case Studies, 7,* 54–74. http://dx.doi.org/10.1177/1534650107304773

Hunter, J. A., & Santos, D. R. (1990). The use of specialized cognitive-behavioral therapies in the treatment of adolescent sex offenders. *International Journal of Offender Therapy and Comparative Criminology, 34,* 239–247. http://dx.doi.org/10.1177/0306624X9003400307

Jenkins, A. (2005). Knocking on shame's door: Facing shame without shaming disadvantaged young people who have abused. In M. C. Calder (Ed.), *Children and young people who sexually abuse: New theory, research and practice developments* (pp. 114–127). Lyme Regis, Dorset, UK: Russell House Publishing.

Johnston, L., Ward, T., & Hudson, S. M. (1997). Deviant sexual thoughts: Mental control and the treatment of sexual offenders. *Journal of Sex Research, 34,* 121–130. http://dx.doi.org/10.1080/00224499709551876

Kaeminghk, K. L., Koselka, M., Becker, J. V., & Kaplan, M. S. (1995). Age and adolescent sexual offender arousal. *Sexual Abuse: A Journal of Research & Treatment, 7,* 249–257. http://dx.doi.org/10.1177/107906329500700402

Kahn, T. J., & Chambers, H. J. (1991). Assessing reoffense risk with juvenile sexual offenders. *Child Welfare, 70,* 333–345. PMID 2070660

Kahn, T. J., & Lafond, M. A. (1988). Treatment of the adolescent sexual offender. *Child and Adolescent Social Work, 5,* 135–148. http://dx.doi.org/10.1007/BF00778822

Kahn, T. K. (2011). *Pathways: A guided workbook for youth beginning treatment* (4th ed.). Brandon, VT: Safer Society.

Kallapiran, K., Koo, S., Kirubakaran, R., & Hancock, K. (2015). Review: Effectiveness of mindfulness in improving mental health symptoms of children and adolescents: A meta-analysis. *Child and Adolescent Mental Health, 20*(4), 182–194. http://dx.doi.org/10.1111/camh.12113

Knopp, F. H. (1982). *Remedial intervention in adolescent sex offenses: Nine program descriptions.* Orwell, VT: Safer Society.

Knopp, F. H. (1984). *Retraining adult sex offenders: Methods and models.* Brandon, VT: Safer Society.

Koehler, J. A., Lösel, F., Akoensi, T. D., & Humphreys, D. K. (2013). A systematic review and meta-analysis on the effects of young offender treatment programs in Europe. *Journal of Experimental Criminology, 9,* 19–43. http://dx.doi.org/10.1007/s11292-012-9159-7

Lakey, J. F. (1994). The profile and treatment of male adolescent sex offenders. *Adolescence, 29,* 755–761. http://dx.doi.org/10.1080/02673843.1995.9747780

Lalumière, M. L., & Harris, G. T. (1998). Common questions regarding the use of phallometric testing with sexual offenders. *Sexual Abuse: A Journal of Research and Treatment, 10,* 227–237. http://dx.doi.org/10.1177/107906329801000306

Lang, J. M., Ford, J. D., & Fitzgerald, M. M. (2010). An algorithm for determining use of trauma-focused cognitive-behavioral therapy. *Psychotherapy: Theory, Research, Practice, Training, 47,* 554. http://dx.doi.org/10.1037/a0021184

Langelier, C. A. (2001). *Mood management: A cognitive-behavioral skills-building program for adolescents.* Thousand Oaks, CA: Sage.

Langer, D. A., McLeod, B. D., & Weisz, J. R. (2011). Do treatment manuals undermine youth–therapist alliance in community clinical practice? *Journal of Consulting and Clinical Psychology, 79,* 427–432. http://dx.doi.org/10.1037/a0023821

Langford, J. (2015). *Spare me 'the talk'! A guy's guide to sex, relationships, and growing up.* Seattle: ParentMap.

Långström, N., & Grann, M. (2000). Risk for criminal recidivism among young sex offenders. *Journal of Interpersonal Violence, 15,* 855–871. http://dx.doi.org/10.1177/088626000015008005

Langton, C. M., & Barbaree, H. E. (2004). Ethical and methodological issues in evaluation research with juvenile sexual abusers. In G. O'Reilly, W. L. Marshall, A. Carr, & R. C. Beckett (Eds.), *The handbook of clinical intervention with young people who sexually abuse* (pp. 419–441). Hove, UK: Brunner-Routledge.

Latham, C., & Kinscherff, R. (2012). *A developmental perspective on the meaning of problematic sexual behavior in children and adolescents.* Holyoke, MA: NEARI.

Latimer, J., Dowden, J., Morton-Bourgon, K. E., Edgar, J., & Bania, M. (2003). *Treating youth in conflict with the law: A new meta-analysis.* Ottawa, Canada: Youth Justice Research, Department of Justice.

Laws, D. R. (2000). Sexual offending as a public health problem: A North American perspective. *Journal of Sexual Aggression, 5*(1), 30–44. http://dx.doi.org/10.1080/13552600008413294

Laws, D. R., Hudson, S. M., & Ward, T. (2000). The original model of relapse prevention with sex offenders: Promises unfulfilled. In D. R. Laws, S. M. Hudson, & T. Ward (Eds.), *Remaking relapse prevention with sex offenders: A sourcebook* (pp. 3–24). Thousand Oaks, CA: Sage.

Letourneau, E. J. (2006). Legal consequences of juvenile sexual offending in the United States. In H. E. Barbaree & W. L. Marshall (Eds.), *The juvenile sex offender* (2nd ed.) (pp. 275–290). New York: Guilford.

Letourneau, E. J., Eaton, W. W., Bass, J., Berlin, F. S., & Moore, S. G. (2014). The need for a comprehensive public health approach to preventing child sexual abuse. *Public Health Reports, 129*(3), 222–228.

Leversee, T. (2010). Comprehensive and individualized evaluation and ongoing assessment. In G. Ryan, T. Leversee, & S. Lane (Eds.), *Juvenile sexual offending* (3rd ed.) (pp. 201–223). Hoboken, NJ: John Wiley & Sons.

Lewis, D. O., Shankok, S. S., & Pincus, J. H. (1979). Juvenile male sexual assaulters. *American Journal of Psychiatry, 136,* 1194–1196. http://dx.doi.org/10.1176/ajp.136.9.1194

Lipsey, M. W. (1999). Can intervention rehabilitate serious delinquents? *The Annals of the American Academy of Political and Social Science 564*(1), 142–166.

Lipsey, M. W. (2009). The primary factors that characterize effective interventions with juvenile offenders: A meta-analytic overview. *Victims and Offenders, 4,* 124–147. http://dx.doi.org/10.1080/15564880802612573

Lobanov-Rostovsky, C. (2010). Juvenile justice, legislation, and policy responses to juvenile sexual offenses. In G. Ryan, T. Leversee, & S. Lane (Eds.), *Juvenile sexual offending* (3rd ed.) (pp. 183–200). Hoboken, NJ: John Wiley & Sons.

Loeber, R., & Farrington, D. P. (1998) (Eds.). *Serious and violent juvenile offenders: Risk factors and successful interventions.* Thousand Oaks, CA: Sage Publications.

Longo, R. E., & Groth, N. (1983). Juvenile sexual offenses in the histories of adult rapists and child molesters. *International Journal of Offender Therapy and Comparative Criminology, 27,* 150–155. http://dx.doi.org/10.1177/0306624X8302700207

Mager, W., Milich, R., Harris, M. J., & Howard, A. (2005). Intervention groups for adolescents with conduct problems: Is aggregation harmful or helpful. *Journal of Abnormal Child Psychology, 33,* 349–362. http://dx.doi.org/10.1007/s10802-005-3572-6

Maletzky, B. M. (1991). *Treating the sexual offender.* Thousand Oaks, CA: Sage.

Maletzky, B. M. (1998). Defining our field II: Cycles, chains, and assorted misnomers. *Sexual Abuse: A Journal of Research and Treatment, 10,* 1–3. http://dx.doi.org/10.1023/A:1022115813068

Margolin, L. (1984). Group therapy as a means of learning about the sexually assaultive adolescent. *International Journal of Offender Therapy and Comparative Criminology, 28,* 65–72. http://dx.doi.org/10.1177/0306624X8402800108

Marlatt, G. A., & Gordon, J. R. (Eds.). (1985). *Relapse prevention: Maintenance strategies in addictive behavior change.* New York: Guilford.

Marshall, W. L. (1979). Satiation therapy: A procedure for reducing deviant sexual arousal. *Journal of Applied Behavior Analysis, 12*(3), 377–389. http://dx.doi.org/10.1901/jaba.1979.12-377

Marshall, W. L. (2009). Manualization: A blessing or a curse? *Journal of Sexual Aggression, 25,* 109–120. http://dx.doi.org/10.1080/13552600902997320

Marshall, W. L., Fernandez, Y. M., Serran, G. A., Mulloy, R., Thornton, D., Mann, R. E., & Anderson, D. (2003). Process variables in the treatment of sexual offenders: A review of the relevant literature. *Aggression and Violent Behavior, 8,* 205–234. http://dx.doi.org/10.1016/S1359-1789(01)00065-9

Marshall, W. L., & Marshall, L. E. (2015). Psychological treatment of the paraphilias: A review and an appraisal of effectiveness. *Current Psychiatry Reports, 17,* 1–6. http://dx.doi.org/10.1007/s11920-015-0580-2

McAlinden, A. (2005). The use of "shame" with sexual offenders. *British Journal of Criminology, 45,* 373–394. http://dx.doi.org/10.1093/bjc/azh095

McCann, K., & Lussier, P. (2008). Antisociality, sexual deviance, and sexual reoffending in juvenile sex offenders: A meta-analytical investigation. *Youth Violence and Juvenile Justice, 6,* 363–385. http://dx.doi.org/10.1177/1541204008320260

McGrath, R. J., Cumming, G. F., Burchard, B. L., Zeoli, S., & Ellerby, L. (2010). *Current practices and emerging trends in sexual abuser management: The Safer Society 2009 North American survey.* Brandon, VT: Safer Society.

McLeod, B. D., Jensen-Doss, A., Tully, C. B., Southam-Gerow, M. A., Weisz, J. R., & Kendall, P. C. (2016). The role of setting versus treatment type in alliance within youth therapy. *Journal of Consulting and Clinical Psychology, 84*(5), 453. http://dx.doi.org/10.1037/ccp0000081

Miller, W. R., & Rollnick, S. (2013). *Motivational interviewing: Helping people change* (3rd ed.). New York: Guilford.

Moulden, H. M., & Firestone, P. (2007). Vicarious traumatization: The impact on therapists who work with sexual offenders. *Trauma, Violence, & Abuse, 8,* 67–83. http://dx.doi.org/10.1177/1524838006297729

Moultrie, D. (2006). Adolescents convicted of possession of abuse images of children: A new type of adolescent sex offender? *Journal of Sexual Aggression, 12,* 165–174. http://dx.doi.org/10.1080/13552600600823670

Murphy, W. D., DiLillo, D., Haynes, M. R., & Steere, E. (2001). An exploration of factors related to deviant sexual arousal among juvenile sex offenders. *Sexual Abuse: A Journal of Research and Treatment, 13,* 91–103. http://dx.doi.org/10.1023/A:1026648220419

National Society for the Prevention of Cruelty to Children (2011). *Sexual abuse: A public health challenge.* London, UK: Author. Retrieved from https://www.nspcc.org.uk/globalassets/documents/research-reports/sexual-abuse--public-health-challenge-evidence-review.pdf

National Task Force on Juvenile Sexual Offending (1993). The revised report from the National Task Force on Juvenile Sexual Offending. *Juvenile and Family Court Journal, 44,* 1–120. http://dx.doi.org/10.1111/j.1755-6988.1993.tb00929.x

North, H. M. (1956). On the management of the juvenile sex offender. *The Medical Journal of Australia, 1,* 685–688. PMID 13321217

O'Brien, M. J. (1991). Taking sibling-incest seriously. In M. Q. Patton (Ed.), *Family sexual abuse: Frontline research and evaluation* (pp. 75–92). Newbury Park, CA: Sage.

O'Neill, M. L., Heilbrun, K., & Lidz, V. (2003). Adolescents with psychopathic characteristics in a substance abusing cohort: Treatment process and outcomes. *Law and Human Behavior, 27,* 299–313. http://dx.doi.org/10.1023/A:1023435924569

Page, J., Murphy, W. D., & Way, I. F. (2007). *Manual for structured group treatment with adolescent sexual offenders.* Brandon, VT: Safer Society.

Palmer, L. (2012). *The PTSD workbook for teens: Simple, effective skills for healing trauma.* Oakland, CA: Instant Help Books.

Perry, G. P., & Orchard, J. (1992). *Assessment and treatment of adolescent sex offenders.* Sarasota, FL: Professional Resources.

Peter, J., & Valkenburg, P. M. (2006). Adolescents' exposure to sexually explicit material on the Internet. *Communication Research, 33,* 178–204. http://dx.doi.org/10.1177/0093650205285369

Powell, K. M. (2010). Therapeutic relationships and the process of change. In G. Ryan, T. Leversee, & S. Lane (Eds.), *Juvenile sexual offending* (3rd ed.) (pp. 253–262). Hoboken, NJ: John Wiley & Sons.

Prentky, R., & Righthand, S. (2003). *Juvenile Sex Offender Assessment Protocol–II: Manual.* Unpublished manuscript. Retrieved from http://www.csom.org/pubs/jsoap.pdf

Proeve, M., & Howells, K. (2002). Shame and guilt in child sexual offenders. *International Journal of Offender Therapy and Comparative Criminology, 46,* 657–667. http://dx.doi.org/10.1177/0306624X02238160

Quach, D., Mano, K. E. J., & Alexander, K. (2016). A randomized controlled trial examining the effect of mindfulness meditation on working memory capacity in adolescents. *Journal of Adolescent Health, 58*(5), 489–496. http://dx.doi.org/10.1016/j.jadohealth.2015.09.024

Ray, F., Marks, C., & Bray-Garretson, H. (2004). Challenges to treating adolescents with Asperger's syndrome who are sexually abusive. *Sexual Addition & Compulsivity, 11,* 265–285. http://dx.doi.org/10.1080/10720160490900614

Regan, K. V., Spidel, A., Gretton, H. M., Catchpole, R. E. H., & Douglas, K. S. (2007). Special needs adolescent sex offenders: Characteristics and treatment outcomes. In M. C. Calder (Ed.), *Working with children and young people who sexually abuse: Taking the field forward* (pp. 123–133). Lyme Regis, Dorset, UK: Russell House.

Reitzel, L. R., & Carbonell, J. L. (2006). The effectiveness of sexual offender treatment for juveniles as measured by recidivism. *Sexual Abuse: A Journal of Research and Treatment, 18,* 401–421. http://dx.doi.org/10.1007/s11194-006-9031-2

Rich, P. (2005). *Attachment and sexual offending: Understanding and applying attachment theory to the treatment of juvenile sexual offenders.* Hoboken, NJ: John Wiley & Sons.

Rich, P. (2009). *Stages of accomplishment workbook: Stage 1: Introduction to treatment.* Holyoke, MA: NEARI.

Richardson, G., Bhate, S., & Graham, F. (1997). Cognitive-based practice with sexually abusive adolescents. In M. S. Hoghughi (Ed.), *Working with sexually abusive adolescents* (pp. 128–143). London, UK: Sage.

Robinson, S. L. (2002). *Growing beyond: A workbook for teenage girls.* Holyoke, MA: NEARI.

Ross, J. E., & Loss, P. (1988). *Risk assessment/interviewing protocol for adolescent sex offenders.* Unpublished manuscript.

Rudd, J. M., & Herzberger, S. D. (1999). Brother–sister incest—father–daughter incest: A comparison of characteristics and consequences. *Child Abuse & Neglect, 23,* 915–928. http://dx.doi.org/10.1016/S0145-2134(99)00058-7

Ryan, G., Leversee, T., & Lane, S. (2010). Special populations: Children, female, developmentally disabled, and violent youth. In G. Ryan, T. Leversee, & S. Lane (Eds.), *Juvenile sexual offending* (3rd ed.) (pp. 380–414). Hoboken, NJ: John Wiley & Sons.

Saunders, E., Awad, G. A, & Levene, J. (1984). A clinical study of male adolescent sex offenders. *International Journal of Offender Therapy and Comparative Criminology, 28,* 105–116. http://dx.doi.org/10.1177/0306624X8402800204

Scaini, S., Belotti, R., Ogliari, A., & Battaglia, M. (2016). A comprehensive meta-analysis of cognitive-behavioral interventions for social anxiety disorder in children and adolescents. *Journal of Anxiety Disorders,* published online ahead of print. http://dx.doi.org/10.1016/j.janxdis.2016.05.008

Semple, R. J., Lee, J., Rosa, D., & Miller, L. F. (2010). A randomized trial of mindfulness-based cognitive therapy for children: Promoting mindful attention to enhance social-emotional resiliency in children. *Journal of Child and Family Studies, 19,* 218–229. http://dx.doi.org/10.1007/s10826-009-9301-y

Serber, M. (1970). Shame aversion therapy. *Journal of Behavior Therapy and Experimental Psychiatry, 1,* 213–215. http://dx.doi.org/10.1016/0005-7916(70)90005-4

Sermabeikian, P., & Martinez, D. (1994). Treatment of adolescent sexual offenders: Theory-based practice. *Child Abuse & Neglect, 18,* 969–976. http://dx.doi.org/10.1016/S0145-2134(05)80007-9

Seto, M. C. (2001). The value of phallometry in the assessment of male sex offenders. *Journal of Forensic Psychology Practice, 1,* 65–75. http://dx.doi.org/10.1300/J158v01n02_05

Seto, M. C., & Lalumière, M. L. (2010). What is so special about male adolescent sexual offending? A review and test of explanations using meta-analysis. *Psychological Bulletin, 136,* 526–575. http://dx.doi.org/10.1037/a0019700

Seto, M. C., Lalumière, M. L., & Blanchard, R. (2000). The discriminative validity of a phallometric test for pedophilic interests among adolescent sex offenders against children. *Psychological Assessment, 12,* 319–327. http://dx.doi.org/10.1037/1040-3590.12.3.319

Seto, M. C., Murphy, W. D., Page, J., & Ennis, L. (2003). Detecting anomalous sexual interests in juvenile sex offenders. *Annals of the New York Academy of Sciences, 989,* 118–130. http://dx.doi.org/10.1111/j.1749-6632.2003.tb07298.x

Shannon, J. (2012). *The shyness and social anxiety workbook for teens: CBT and ACT skills to help you build social confidence.* Oakland, CA: Instant Help Books.

Shaw, J. A. (1999). Practice parameters for the assessment and treatment of children and adolescents who are sexually abusive of others. American Academy of Child and Adolescent Psychiatry Working Group on Quality Issues. *Journal of the American Academy of Child and Adolescent Psychiatry, 38*(supplement), 55S–76S. PMID 9334566

Shingler, J. (2009). Managing intrusive risky thoughts: What works? *Journal of Sexual Aggression, 15,* 39–53. http://dx.doi.org/10.1080/13552600802542011

Shirk, S. R., Karver, M. S., & Brown, R. (2011). The alliance in child and adolescent psychotherapy. *Psychotherapy, 48,* 17–24. http://dx.doi.org/10.1037/a0022181

Sickmund, M., & Puzzanchera, C. (Eds.). (2014). *Juvenile Offenders and Victims: 2014 National Report.* Pittsburgh, PA: National Center for Juvenile Justice.

Singh, N. N., Lancioni, G. E., Winton, S. W., Singh, A. N., Adkins, A. D., & Singh, J. (2011). Can adult offenders with intellectual disabilities use mindfulness-based procedures to control their deviant sexual arousal? *Psychology, Crime & Law, 17,* 165–179. http://dx.doi.org/10.1080/10683160903392731

Sisk, C. L., & Foster, D. L. (2004). The neural basis of puberty and adolescence. *Nature Neuroscience, 7,* 1040–1047. http://dx.doi.org/10.1038/nn1326

Slater, C., & Lambie, I. (2011). The highs and lows of working with sexual offenders: A New Zealand perspective. *Journal of Sexual Aggression, 17*(3), 320–334. http://dx.doi.org/10.1080/13552600.2010.519056

Snyder, H. N., & Sickmund, M. (2006*). Juvenile offenders and victims: 2006 national report.* Washington, DC: US Department of Justice, Office of Justice Programs, Office of Juvenile Justice and Delinquency Prevention.

Steen, C., & Monnette, B. (1989). *Treating adolescent sex offenders in the community.* Springfield, IL: Charles C. Thomas.

Steinberg, L. (2005). Cognitive and affective development in adolescence. *Trends in Cognitive Sciences, 9,* 69–74. http://dx.doi.org/10.1016/j.tics.2004.12.005

Steinberg, L. (2010). A behavioral scientist looks at the science of adolescent brain development. *Brain and Cognition, 72,* 160–164. http://dx.doi.org/10.1016/j.bandc.2009.11.003

Steinberg, L., Cauffman, E., & Monahan, K. (2015). *Psychosocial maturity and desistance from crime in a sample of serious juvenile offenders* (NCJ 248391). Washington, DC: US Department of Justice Office of Juvenile Justice and Delinquency Prevention.

Strickland, S. M. (2008). Female sexual offenders: Exploring issues of personality, trauma, and cognitive distortions. *Journal of Interpersonal Violence, 23,* 474–489. http://dx.doi.org/10.1177/0886260507312944

Sutton, L. R., Hughes, T. L., Huang, A., Lehman, C., Paserba, D., Talkington, V. . . . & Marshall, S. (2013). Identifying individuals with autism in a state facility for adolescents adjudicated as sexual offenders: A pilot study. *Focus on Autism and Other Developmental Disabilities, 28,* 175–183. http://dx.doi.org/10.1177/1088357612462060

Tangney, J. P., & Dearing, R. L. (2002). *Shame and guilt.* New York: Guilford.

Thomas, J. D., & Viar, C. W. (2005). Family reunification in cases of sibling incest. In M. C. Calder (Ed.), *Children and young people who sexually abuse: New theory, research and practice developments* (pp. 354–371). Lyme Regis, Dorset, UK: Russell House.

Tolman, D. L., & McClelland, S. I. (2011). Normative sexuality development in adolescence: A decade in review, 2000-2009. *Journal of Research on Adolescence, 21,* 242–255. http://dx.doi.org/10.1111/j.1532-7795.2010.00726.x

Underwood, L. A., Robinson, S. B., Mosholder, E., & Warren, K. M. (2008). Sex offender care for adolescents in secure care: Critical factors and counseling strategies. *Clinical Psychology Review, 28,* 917–932. http://dx.doi.org/10.1016/j.cpr.2008.01.004

US Department of Justice, Federal Bureau of Investigation (2013). *National Incident-Based Reporting System 2013.* Retrieved from https://ucr.fbi.gov/nibrs/2013/data-tables

Waggoner, R. W., & Boyd, D. A. (1941). Juvenile aberrant sexual behavior. *American Journal of Orthopsychiatry, 11,* 275–292. http://dx.doi.org/10.1111/j.1939-0025.1941.tb05804.x

Ward, T., Day, A., Howells, K., Birgden, A. (2004). The multifactor offender readiness model. *Aggression and Violent Behavior, 9,* 645–673. http://dx.doi.org/10.1016/j.avb.2003.08.001

Washington State Institute for Public Policy & University of Washington Evidence-Based Practice Institute (2016). *Updated inventory of evidence-based, research-based, and promising practices: For prevention and intervention services for children and juveniles in the child welfare, juvenile justice, and mental health systems.* Olympia: Washington State Institute for Public Policy. Retrieved from http://www.wsipp.wa.gov/ReportFile/1639/Wsipp_Updated-Inventory-of-Evidence-Based-Researched-Based-and-Promising-Practices-For-Prevention-and-Intervention-Services-for-Children-and-Juveniles-in-the-Child-Welfare-Juvenile-Justice-and-Mental-Health-Systems_Report.pdf

Way, I. F., & Balthazor, T. J. (1990). *A manual for structured group treatment with adolescent sexual offenders.* Notre Dame, IN: Jalice.

Weinrott, M. R., Riggan, M., & Frothingham, S. (1997). Reducing deviant arousal in juvenile sex offenders using vicarious sensitization. *Journal of Interpersonal Violence, 12,* 704–728. http://dx.doi.org/10.1177/088626097012005007

Weiss, B., Caron, A., Ball, S., Tapp, J., Johnson, M., & Weisz, J. R. (2005). Iatrogenic effects of group treatment for antisocial youths. *Journal of Consulting and Clinical Psychology, 73,* 1036. http://dx.doi.org/10.1037%2F0022-006X.73.6.1036

Williams, D., & Buehler, M. (2002). A proposal for comprehensive community-based treatment of female juvenile sex offenders. In M. C. Calder (Ed.), *Young people who sexually abuse: Building the evidence base for your practice* (pp. 251–264). Lyme Regis, Dorset, UK: Russell House.

Wolak, J., & Finkelhor, D. (2011). *Sexting: A typology.* Durham, NH: Crimes Against Children Research Center. Retrieved from http://www.unh.edu/ccrc/pdf/CV231_Sexting%20Typology%20Bulletin_4-6-11_revised.pdf

Worling, J. R. (1995a). Adolescent sibling-incest offenders: Differences in family and individual functioning when compared to nonsibling sex offenders. *Child Abuse & Neglect, 19,* 633–643. http://dx.doi.org/10.1016/0145-2134(95)00021-Y

Worling, J. R. (1995b). Sexual abuse histories of adolescent male sex offenders: Differences based on the age and gender of their victims. *Journal of Abnormal Psychology, 104,* 610–613. http://dx.doi.org/10.1037/0021-843X.104.4.610

Worling, J. R. (1998). Adolescent sexual offender treatment at the SAFE-T Program. In W. L. Marshall, Y. M. Fernandez, S. M. Hudson, & T. Ward (Eds.), *Sourcebook of treatment programs for sexual offenders* (pp. 353–365). New York: Plenum.

Worling, J. R. (2002). Assessing risk of sexual assault recidivism with adolescent sexual offenders. In M. C. Calder (Ed.), *Young people who sexually abuse: Building the evidence base for your practice* (pp. 365–375). Lyme Regis, UK: Russell House.

Worling, J. R. (2004). The Estimate of Risk of Adolescent Sexual Offense Recidivism (ERASOR): Preliminary psychometric data. *Sexual Abuse: A Journal of Research and Treatment, 16,* 235–254. http://dx.doi.org/10.1079-0632/04/0700-0235/0

Worling, J. R. (2006). Assessing sexual arousal with adolescent males who have offended sexually: Self-report and unobtrusively measured viewing time. *Sexual Abuse: A Journal of Research and Treatment, 18,* 383–400. http://dx.doi.org/10.1007/s11194-006-9024-1

Worling, J. R. (2012). The assessment and treatment of deviant sexual arousal with adolescents who have offended sexually. *Journal of Sexual Aggression, 18,* 36–63. http://dx.doi.org/10.1080/13552600.20 11.630152

Worling, J. R. (2103). What were we thinking?: Five erroneous assumptions that have fueled specialized interventions for adolescents who have sexually offended. *International Journal of Behavioral Consultation and Therapy, 8*(3-4), 88-96. http://dx.doi.org/10.1037/h0100988

Worling, J. R., Bookalam, D., & Litteljohn, A. (2012). Prospective validity of the Estimate of Risk of Adolescent Sexual Offense Recidivism (ERASOR). *Sexual Abuse: A Journal of Research and Treatment, 24,* 203–223. http://dx.doi.org/10.1177/1079063211407080

Worling, J. R., Josefowitz, N., & Maltar, M. (2011). Reducing shame and increasing guilt and responsibility with adolescents who have offended sexually: A CBT-based treatment approach. In M. Calder (Ed.), *Contemporary practice with young people who sexually abuse* (pp. 320–334). Lyme Regis, Dorset, UK: Russell House.

Worling, J. R., & Långström, N. (2006). Assessing risk of sexual reoffending. In H. E. Barbaree & W. L. Marshall (Eds.), *The juvenile sex offender* (2nd ed., pp. 219–247). New York: Plenum.

Worling, J. R., & Langton, C. M. (2012). Assessment and treatment of adolescents who sexually offend: Clinical issues and implications for secure settings. *Criminal Justice and Behavior, 39,* 814–841. http://dx.doi.org/10.1177/0093854812439378

Worling, J. R., & Langton, C. M. (2016). Assessment of adolescents who have sexually offended. In D. P. Boer (Series Ed.) & L. A. Craig & M. Rettenberger (Vol. Eds.), *The Wiley handbook on the theories, assessment, and treatment of sexual offending: Vol. II. Assessment* (pp. 1099–1122). Chichester, UK: John Wiley & Sons.

Worling, J. R., Litteljohn, A., & Bookalam, D. (2010). 20-year prospective follow-up study of specialized treatment for adolescents who offended sexually. *Behavioral Sciences and the Law, 28,* 46–57. http://dx.doi.org/10.1002/bsl.912

Yalom, I. D., and Leszcz, M. (2005). *The Theory and Practice of Group Psychotherapy* (5th ed.). New York: Basic Books.

Yurgelen-Todd, D. (2007). Emotional and cognitive changes during adolescence. *Current Opinion in Neurobiology, 17,* 251–257. http://dx.doi.org/10.1016/j.conb.2007.03.009

Zimring, F. E. (2004). *An American travesty: Legal responses to adolescent sexual offending.* Chicago: University of Chicago Press.

CHAPTER 10

Community Reentry and Family Reunification

Jacqueline Page

William D. Murphy

Many times adolescents who sexually abuse will be removed from the community and placed in various levels of care, including residential treatment or a secure correctional setting. When the victim is within the family, removal may be required by the juvenile justice system or child welfare system. A major challenge when adolescents are removed from the community and their family is facilitating successful reentry into the community and successful reunification with their family. In this chapter we will focus on what we see as two interrelated areas. We will initially review the general literature related to difficulties youth and families face when returning to the community, drawing from the general delinquency literature and child welfare literature, as there are limited data on this issue for youth who sexually abuse (Lambie & Price, 2015). This review will discuss the empirical literature on programs for improving success in youth reentry and family reunification and review promising practices. The final section of this chapter will focus on specific clinical approaches to family reunification when youth who sexually abuse are returned to a home with their own victim(s), many of whom will be siblings.

NATURE OF THE PROBLEM

Research with youth who sexually abuse has clearly established that they are a heterogeneous group. Overall, these youth are more likely to reoffend non-sexually than sexually (Caldwell, 2010; 2016), have many characteristics similar to youth engaging in non-sexual delinquent behavior (Seto & Lalumière, 2010), have increased rates of mental health issues compared with non-offenders (Boonmann et al., 2015; also see van Wijk & Boonman, this volume), and many have significant trauma histories (see Shilling, Grimbos, & Vinik, this volume). Families of adolescents who sexually abuse are also heterogeneous, but research suggests that many of these families have multiple problems such as substance abuse, domestic violence, histories of physical abuse, mental health issues, histories of criminal behavior, frequent moves, economic challenges, and histories of children being placed outside the home for abuse and neglect (Felizzi, 2015; Graves, Openshaw, Ascione, & Ericksen, 1996; Righthand & Welch, 2001). Although there is little research on the success of adolescents who sexually abuse reuniting with families (Lambie & Price, 2015), there is an extensive literature on reentry and reunification in the general delinquency literature and child welfare literature (Bronson, Saunders, Holt, & Beck, 2008; Carnochan, Lee, & Austin, 2013; Carnochan, Rizik-Baer, & Austin, 2013; James, Stams, Asscher, De Roo, & van der Laan, 2013). This literature can provide guidance for successful approaches to community reentry and reunification for adolescents who sexually abuse.

Research consistently shows that 50 percent or more of juvenile justice youth will return to the juvenile justice system, many within the first six months (Abrams & Snyder, 2010; Chung, Schubert, & Mulvey, 2007; Lipsey, Wilson, & Cothern, 2000). For child welfare youth, 20 to 26 percent reenter care within 10 years, and for those who enter care as an adolescent, slightly less than 50 percent reunify with their birth families (Wulczyn, 2004). Juvenile justice youth have a number of other negative outcomes in addition to rearrests, including failure to achieve a high school diploma, unstable employment, dependence on welfare, and unstable housing (Abrams & Snyder, 2010; Chung et al., 2007). It is not surprising that youth have difficulties transitioning. They can spend a significant amount of time in highly structured facilities with little opportunity for independent decision making, and the structure does not parallel with what they experience in the community. Many times in placements they are associating with other delinquent peers and are apart from support systems such as families, schools, and other community supports. All of these factors disrupt normal adolescent development (Modecki, this volume; Steinberg, Chung, & Little, 2004). Although not all youth engaging in sexually abusive behavior will be in the juvenile justice system, a number may be placed in highly structured non-juvenile-justice residential treatment centers with programs specific to adolescents who sexually abuse.

The many similarities between adolescents who sexually abuse and those who engage in non-sexual general delinquency include that they are more likely to reoffend non-sexually (Caldwell, 2010; 2016) than sexually. Given this, these youth's community reintegration is more likely to be disrupted for non-sexual offenses than for sexual offenses. In addition, research with child welfare populations has found that factors such as parental substance abuse, parental mental health issues, youth mental health issues, and youth behavioral problems have been associated with difficulties achieving reunification (Carnochan, Lee, & Austin, 2013) and are linked to disruptions of reunification (Carnochan, Rizik-Baker, & Austin, 2013). These family and youth characteristics are not uncommon in adolescents who sexually abuse. Although there are no empirical studies to our knowledge of how successful reunification is and the reason reunification fails for adolescents who sexually abuse, it seems probable that most youth's reunification with family will be disrupted by factors outlined above, which can include non-sexual offenses, significant behavioral problems in the community, and parents' difficulties supervising or following safety plans rather than sexual offending.

Child welfare research is also relevant since a number of adolescents engaging in sexually abusive behavior may be placed in the child welfare system rather than in the juvenile justice system, and research suggests that risk and need factors that predict reoffending of adjudicated adolescents also predict reoffending in child welfare samples (Prentky et al., 2010). Prentky, Lee, Lamade, Grossi, Schuler, Dube, DeMarco, and Pond (2014) have also found that placement instability, a variable linked to poor outcome in youth involved in the child welfare system (Bronson et al., 2008), was predictive of future inappropriate sexual behavior in their sample of child welfare youth with sexual behavior problems.

Although the purpose of this chapter is not to review the literature on the impact of placements, it is important to note that there is no clear evidence that residential- or correctional-type placements have an impact on reducing non-sexual reoffending in juveniles (Petrosino, Turpin-Petrosino, & Guckenburg, 2010) or adult offenders (Cullen, Jonson, & Nagin, 2011); the same has been found for adult sexual offenders (Nunes, Firestone, Wexler, Jensen, & Bradford, 2007). An extensive study (Dawkins & Sorenson, 2014), drawing on data from 50 states between 1997 and 2001, found that increased rates of detention and residential placement of juveniles were related to higher rates of violent offending, property offending, and drug offending. The Pathways to Desistance Study found no incremental reduction of reoffending for length of stays beyond six months for serious delinquent juvenile offenders (Loughran et al., 2009). In addition, there is a fairly clear finding from meta-analyses with sexual offenders (Aos, Miller, & Drake, 2006; Schmucker & Lösel, 2015) that programs are more effective when delivered in the community than in correctional or residential facilities. However, most of the studies included in these meta-analyses were of adult offenders.

In the delinquency field, there has been a recognition of the potential ineffectiveness and possible iatrogenic effects of juvenile placement in residential and correctional facilities (Loughran et al., 2009). Since the 1990s, the Office of Juvenile Justice and Delinquency Prevention (OJJDP) has recognized and facilitated programs to improve reentry outcomes (Altschuler, Armstrong, & MacKenzie, 1999), and there has been a 42 percent decrease in placements in residential facilities between 1997 and 2011 (Hockenberry, 2014) for youth in the juvenile justice system. For similar reasons, the child welfare system also has a focus on achieving permanency with youth found to be abused and/or neglected. Permanency includes both timely reunification with families or adoption and avoidance of placement disruptions. Success in these outcomes is part of the federal review of state child welfare agencies through the Child and Families Services Review (CFSR) by the Children's Bureau and Administration for Children and Families within the US Department of Health and Human Services, which was initiated in 2000 (http://www.acf.hhs.gov/programs/cb/monitoring).

Although avoiding residential placements is the preferred option, the individual youth's risk and need may support removal from the community. Also, for youth who abuse within the home or where there are vulnerable children in the home, removal may be necessary for the protection of victims or potential victims. In addition, decisions on removal and placement will many times be in the hands of the juvenile or family court and/or child protective services. The potential negative impact of removal from the family would suggest that when youth are removed from the home, there should be an attempt to place the youth in the least restrictive placement consistent with their risk and needs and as close to the family home as possible. State systems that have a range of placement options, such as kinship care, foster care, or smaller community group homes—where youth have the opportunity to engage in "normal adolescent activities"—will probably be more beneficial in fostering positive adolescent development and ultimately facilitating reunification with families than highly secure facilities.

RESEARCH ON REENTRY AND REUNIFICATION

In this section, we will attempt to highlight the empirical literature on approaches to improving successful reentry and reunification, again drawing on the child welfare and juvenile justice literature, given the paucity of literature specific to adolescents who sexually abuse (Lambie & Price, 2015). There have been a number of reviews of this literature (Abrams & Snyder, 2010; Bronson et al., 2008; Carnochan, Lee, & Austin, 2013; Child Welfare Information Gateway, 2011; Chung, Gee, Schubert, & Mulvey,

2007; James et al., 2013). The goal of this chapter as well as space concerns do not allow a thorough review of this literature, so we will highlight findings from it that shed light on strategies for reuniting adolescents who sexually offend with their families.

Before actually summarizing this literature, it is important to conceptualize what we mean by family reunification. Reunification tends to be framed as a binary decision, to either reunite the family or not. However, as we will review later, there are reasons to expand our conceptualization of what reunification means. We will suggest that reunification should be seen more as a continuum ranging from no family contact to returning to living with the family. For some youth, the goal may be determining how a connection with the family can be maintained, regardless of where the youth physically live. This same issue has been raised in the child welfare literature (Carnochan, Lee, & Austin, 2013; Mapp & Steinberg, 2007). Mapp and Steinberg (2007) suggest viewing family reunification as a planned process of reconnecting children with their families so that reconnection at some level can happen based on the needs of the family and the youth.

Since the 1990s, OJJDP has supported reentry initiatives including the Intensive Aftercare Program (IAP) (Altschuler & Armstrong, 1994a; 1994b; Altschuler, Armstrong, & McKenzie, 1999). IAP is a comprehensive case management model based on the following core principles (Geis, 2003): (a) risk assessment and classification, (b) individual case planning that incorporates family and community perspective, (c) a mix of intensive surveillance and services, (d) a balance of graduated incentives and consequences, and (e) links with community resources and social networks. This model is comprehensive and appears consistent with the overall literature on effective practice with juvenile justice youth. Unfortunately, initial evaluation of the model using randomized controlled trials, in three separate locations (Wiebush, Wagner, McNulty, Wang, & Le, 2005), found no impact of these programs on reduction of recidivism. These overall were well-designed studies, with monitoring and attention to implementation. Even with this, there were some issues noted by the investigators that could have impacted results. In one site while the IAP program was being implemented the state introduced an expansion of treatment services and aftercare services within probation, which led to enhanced services to the control group—making it similar to services received by the IAP group. A second issue was that two of the program sites had difficulties engaging parents, and in all sites parents had a number of problems of their own, including substance abuse. Integrity measures did indicate that overall the IAP group received a higher intensity of services than the control group, but there was not a systematic assessment of the quality of services actually delivered. Two of the sites also experienced problems in staff turnover and/or vacancies in the institutional components of the program that interfered with service delivery for an extended period of time. These types of issues highlight the difficulties that can arise in implementing even the best-designed programs in the "real world."

Since that time, there have been multiple studies of specific reentry programs. A meta-analysis of such programs (James et al., 2013) found that such programs had a significant impact on reducing reoffending. However, the effect size was small ($d = 0.12$); an effect size provides information beyond whether findings are significant, including a measure of the strength of the findings. There was also significant heterogeneity among studies, meaning there are factors besides the program that moderate treatment effectiveness. The child welfare literature also shows a pattern of mixed findings in programs designed to improve rates of family reunification (Bronson et al., 2008; Carnochan, Lee, & Austin, 2013; Carnochan, Rizik-Baer, & Austin, 2013; Schweitzer, Pecora, Nelson, Walters, & Blythe, 2015; Al et al., 2012).

One exception to this is Treatment Foster Care Oregon—Adolescents (Chamberlain, 2003), which was formerly known as Multidimensional Treatment Foster Care. This is an evidenced-based intervention (see the OJJDP Model Program Guide, www.ojjdp. gov/mpg) that places youth with trained foster parents while simultaneously working with the youth's parents on effective parenting. However, this program does not accept youth when the primary problem is sexual offending.

Although there are not consistent findings for specific reentry programs, the remainder of this section will focus on practices that may improve rates of successful reentry. In addition, for reentry services to be effective, it is important for youth and families to engage in these services. Juvenile justice literature (Chung et al., 2007) and child welfare literature (Bronson et al., 2008) stress the key role of youth and family engagement in successful outcomes. Because research on engagement and strategies for involving youth and families in treatment are reviewed by Powell in this volume, engagement strategies will not be reviewed here.

Assessment and Case Planning
Both the child welfare and juvenile justice literature suggest that appropriate risk and needs instruments should inform the planning of aftercare services (Altschuler et al., 1999; Child Welfare Information Gateway, 2011). There are specific risk/needs instruments developed for youth in the child welfare system designed to guide reunification planning (see Child Welfare Information Gateway, 2011, for examples). There are also specific risk assessment instruments for general delinquency and risk assessments for adolescents who sexually abuse, some of which include dynamic risk factors that may help identify relevant treatment needs (Righthand, Vincent, & Huff, this volume). As

would be expected, a meta-analysis (James et al., 2013) suggests that high-risk youth have poorer reentry outcomes than low-risk youth.

It is also important that the results of risk/need instruments are applied in actual aftercare programming. Chung et al. (2007) found that 15 percent of youth reported no participation in post-release supervision and 65 percent reported no participation in community-based services (various mental health services and/or job training and job placement) following discharge. In a probation sample, Vieira, Skilling, and Peterson-Badali (2009) found that when there was a good match between needs identified on the Youth Level of Services/Case Management Inventory (YLS/CMI) (Hoge, Andrews, & Leschied, 2002) and case plans and actual services delivered, there was a significant reduction in recidivism compared with cases where there was a low match. However, many youth never receive services matched to their criminogenic needs (Peterson-Badali, Skilling, & Haqanee, 2015). Our clinical experience is that this may not be unique, and many times there is no follow-through with the reentry plans.

In terms of case planning, Geis (2003) suggests that aftercare may be a misnomer, and aftercare might be better framed as reintegrative services. Many times aftercare is what occurs following the out-of-home placement, but reintegrative services should begin at the time of removal and be a planned process throughout the youth's removal through their return to the community. There needs to be a continuum of community services available, which will require collaboration and partnership with probation and a variety of public and private service delivery agencies. As Geis points out, in many jurisdictions the juvenile justice system is compartmentalized, with the custodial services and probation services being different systems and agencies providing community intervention services not administratively connected to either the state custodial agency or state probation agency. In many jurisdictions, probation may be a distinct entity that takes over after incarceration when, from a reintegrative service perspective, there should be collaboration between probation and custodial programs from the time of removal—which may require system changes and planned efforts for establishing interagency collaboration. Early reentry planning allows one to try to link a youth's institutional programming to what his or her community experiences will be and the resources that are available in the community the youth is returning to (Schubert & Mulvey, 2014).

Treatment Considerations

A primary tenet of the risk/need/responsivity (RNR) model (Hoge, 2002) is that intensive services are reserved for youth classified as high risk. Based on the James et al. (2013) meta-analysis, this applies to not only the youth's initial treatment, but also services when they return to the community. In addition, Chung et al. (2007) found that the best outcomes in their sample of youth in the juvenile justice system appeared to be achieved with a combination of follow-up intervention services and supervision by probation. Consistent with the RNR model, the juvenile justice literature suggests that dosage matched to risk and need is related to successful reentry (Abrams, Terry, & Franke, 2011; Chung et al., 2007; Kurlycheck, Wheeler, Tinit, & Kempinen, 2011). Dosage includes both the intensity of intervention services and the frequency and intensity of supervision. Chung et al. (2007) found that each additional month of supervision reduced system involvement by 44 percent and each additional service contact (i.e., intervention) reduced system involvement by 12 percent. Frequency of caseworker contact for child welfare cases has also been related to increased rates of family reunification (Child Welfare Information Gateway, 2011).

In addition to dosage, the types of services are important. In both the juvenile justice area and the child welfare system, cognitive-behavioral and systemic interventions appear to be the most effective (Child Welfare Information Gateway, 2011; Curtis, Ronan, & Borduin, 2004; Koehler, Lösel, Adoensi, & Humphreys, 2013; Lipsey, Chapman, & Landenberger, 2001). These are also some of the treatment strategies thought to be most effective with adolescents who sexually abuse (see Worling & Langton, this volume). Meta-analyses of effective reentry practices in the juvenile justice system (James et al., 2014) found that the most effective treatments were those that were a combination of systemic and individual treatment. They also found that involvement in group therapy, especially in the absence of individual treatment, proved less effective in successful reentry. There are a number of evidence-based treatments for treating juvenile justice youth (see the OJJDP Model Program Guide, www.ojjdp.gov/mpg). One of these is multisystemic therapy (MST), which has also been found effective with youth who have engaged in sexually abusive behavior (Borduin, Schaeffer, & Heiblum, 2009). The use of evidence-based approaches during reentry holds promise for reducing reoffending and improving the likelihood of successful family reunification.

Mental Health and Substance Abuse

Both parental substance abuse (Bronson et al., 2008) and youth substance abuse (Chung et al., 2007) have been found to negatively relate to successful reentry and reunification. Effort needs to be made to involve parents with substance abuse problems in appropriate substance abuse interventions while the youth is out of the home, and it is important that the youth who are placed have services for comorbid substance abuse disorders. It is not uncommon for youth who engage in sexually abusive behavior to have comorbid substance abuse problems (Righthand & Welch, 2001), and many programs specific for adolescents with sexually abusive behavior may not always provide adequate intervention for substance abuse issues.

It is unclear if specific mental health diagnoses, except for substance abuse, are related to recidivism, at least in males (Schubert, Mulvey, & Glasheen, 2011). However, in the child welfare literature, mental health issues for youth and parents are related to length of time in care and disruption of placements (Carnochan, Lee, & Austin, 2013; Carnochan, Rizik-Baer, & Austin, 2013). The presence of mental health issues may impact the youth's ability to engage in services, disrupt performance in school, and interfere with developing appropriate peer groups.

The youth's mental health issues can increase stress for a family that is also attempting to follow guidelines and rules to maintain safety related to the sexually abusive behavior safety plan as well as providing adequate supervision of the youth. It is important in planning for reunification and reentry that the youth have adequate follow-up care for mental health issues and that this care is arranged before their release. Our clinical experience suggests that many times youth released from higher levels of care to the community face significant delays before mental health services are initiated.

Significant mental health issues experienced by the parents can complicate reunification, and depending on degree of impairment may make it difficult for a parent to implement the guidelines and rules to maintain safety and provide adequate supervision. In such instances it is important, during the youth's removal, to assist and support parents to engage in mental health services. Depending on the system the youth is involved in, this might be the youth's social service worker, probation officer, or therapist involved in family therapy with the youth and family.

It should be noted that many families may have multiple problems impacting the success of reunification. Marsh, Ryan, Choi, and Testa (2006), in a sample of 724 substance abusing families, looked at the impact of co-occurring problems in the families (substance abuse, domestic violence, housing difficulties, and mental health) on rates of reunification. Although reunification rates were low in all subjects, fewer families reunited when there were additional family problems besides substance use. In one study (Choi & Ryan, 2007), providing matched services—i.e., services that were matched to the needs of the families— led to increased rates of reunification.

Community Involvement

Another factor important to successful reunification is that the youth attends school (Shubert & Mulvey, 2014). In the Pathway to Desistance Study, it was found that youth who went to school and worked part-time (less than 20 hours) had the lowest rates of antisocial behavior. Another important factor related to successful reentry is the youth being able to appropriately use leisure time after leaving a highly structured facility (Altschuler & Brash, 2004). Misuse of leisure time is a known risk factor for general delinquent behavior and is included in validated risk assessment instruments such as the YLS/CMI (Hoge, Andrews, & Lescheid, 2002).

In one of the few studies that looked at factors in adolescents who sexually abuse transitioning back into the community (Lambie & Price, 2015), youth themselves identified being able to find appropriate activities to fill leisure time as one of their major challenges. For adolescents who sexually abuse, this is becoming increasingly complicated by juvenile registration. Discharge planning clearly needs to specifically plan for youth's leisure time rather than assuming that the youth and family will be able to fill such time.

CLINICAL APPROACHES TO REUNIFICATION IN SIBLING SEXUAL ABUSE

Opinions and practices regarding separation of the sibling who sexually abused and his or her victim vary across treatment providers and agencies involved in sibling sexual abuse cases. Some feel that the removal of the sibling who sexually abused provides an opportunity for the situation to be more thoroughly assessed, plans developed, and interventions initiated, thereby supporting sexual and physical safety as well as the emotional safety and well-being of the victim and other children in the home. Others would state that if there is an adequate plan for safety—one that may be specific to physical safety from abuse or also address the victim's emotional well-being—and a reasonable expectation that parents will follow the plan, then the sibling who sexually abused can remain in the home. Given different policies across jurisdictions and agencies, not all cases of sibling sexual abuse result in the sibling who sexually abused being removed from the home; however this does occur in a number of cases. Separation of the sibling who sexually abused and his or her victim may be temporary and short-term during the investigation process or while assessment of safety risk occurs, or it may be more long-term.

The clinical literature on family reunification for adolescents who have sexually abused in the family focuses on issues such as therapy for the victim, the sibling who has sexually abused, and caregivers; preparing for sessions involving both the victim and the sibling who sexually abused, including the structure and content of the session(s); and developing guidelines and rules, referred to as safety plans, for maintaining safety and supervising the youth (Rich, 2011; Thomas & Viar, 2003; Tabachnik & Pollard, 2016). While the initiation of the reunification process is based on the best interest of the victim, the goals of the process also encompass the sibling who sexually abused. The goals of the reunification process are to contribute to the victim's recovery and healing, for the sibling who engaged in the sexually abusive behavior to take responsibility, and to provide the sibling who sexually abused an opportunity to make amends, with the overarching goal being ensuring the safety and well-being of the victim (Rich, 2011; Thomas & Viar, 2003). A number of states such as California (https://ccoso.org/sites/default/files/familyresolution.pdf), Colorado (https://www.cobar.org/repository/Inside_Bar/JuvLawSection/2012%20JUVENILE%20STANDARDS%20FINAL.pdf), and Tennessee (www.sworps.tennessee.edu/children/pdf/reunification) have developed statewide guidelines for family reunification in cases of sibling sexual abuse.

Preconceived, absolute beliefs that reunification is always appropriate or never appropriate are to be avoided; instead, it should be recognized that reunification is often achievable, appropriate, and healthy, with the "when" and "if" being determined by the individual case situation. This section serves as an introduction to reunification and highlights important aspects and components of the reunification process.

However, there is little empirical research on many of the common practices related to family reunification and to our knowledge no studies of how often reoffenses occur when youth are returned to a home with someone they have abused. Kahn and Chambers (1991) found no significant relationship between victim–offender relationship and reoffending; Smith and Monastersky (1986) found no difference in recidivism between those with a relative victim versus an acquaintance victim. It is unclear how many subjects in these studies actually were returned to a home with their victim. Given the limited data, what will be presented in this section is based on clinical experience and the limited clinical literature on family reunification. As a final note, we will use the term *sibling sexual abuse* in this section when discussing family reunification. However, it should be noted that the definition of sibling varies from study to study and may include biological siblings, step-siblings, extended family members living in the home, or any child living in the home who has been abused by the adolescent returning to the home (Tidefors, Arvidsson, Ingevaldson, & Larsson, 2010).

Collaboration

In many instances, working toward family reunification will involve a team. The number of people involved may vary. In addition to the parents, the sibling who sexually abused's therapist, and the victim's therapist, the team may include child welfare workers, probation officers, attorneys, guardian ad litems, etc. Given the different backgrounds of the team members, it is important to recognize that there may be different perspectives about the reunification process. Therapists may view their role and responsibility as being significantly different from that of a probation officer or a child welfare worker. At times team members may feel they are at odds, thereby increasing the possibility of dismissing one another's input. It is important to recognize and understand the different roles and responsibilities of the team members working with the sibling sexual abuse case as well as the reasons for the different roles, and to discuss these differences. While the parents and the treatment providers involved have a major role in the discussion and decisions about reunification, theirs is not the only input. The different perspectives challenge the team to look at others' views and take into account all aspects of the case when making decisions. Members of the team do not have to always agree to respect and value their different roles and responsibilities. The differing roles, responsibilities, and perspectives can be beneficial in ensuring that we are moving forward in a well-thought-out manner that is in the best interest of the child who was abused, the sibling who sexually abused, and the family as a whole, as well as the larger community.

Effective collaboration means working together by keeping lines of communication open and not viewing differences of opinion with an us-against-them mentality. Collaboration requires ongoing, active effort and is not without challenges; open communication and dialogue can help minimize those challenges. Knowing who is taking responsibility for what helps tasks get completed and can also decrease stress for the family. This may be something as simple as identifying who takes the lead in obtaining the appropriate releases of information for treatment providers to be able to communicate about their respective client.

Collaboration involves sharing of knowledge and helping educate others while also learning from one another. Not every professional involved on the team may be experienced in working with sibling sexual abuse cases or have been a part of a team addressing this complex an issue. There may be unintentional inconsistencies in responses from agencies and professionals due to lack of knowledge or members being unclear about how to move forward in the best interest of the child involved given the situation.

The team members' view of reunification in general, or more specifically how to ensure the best interest of the victim, may be impacted by a lack of knowledge about treatment or the reunification process. Educating and sharing about the rationale and goals of treatment while discussing treatment progress rather than just reporting a youth is doing well or not in treatment helps provide other members with knowledge they can use in the current and future cases. Members may also struggle with incorporating their specific role and work with an individual into the bigger picture of the well-being of the victim, the sibling who sexually abused, and the family as a whole. The team approach helps individual members understand the needs of the family, victim, and sibling who sexually abused and ensures that decisions are not made in a silo.

Why Reunite

It is not uncommon for someone to voice the question about why reunification should even be considered when an adolescent has already sexually abused a sibling. Even if the question isn't voiced, it may well be in the mind of someone involved in the case. We should expect the question and be prepared to discuss it in a straightforward and thoughtful manner. Parents may vary in their view of reunification, with some not understanding why the sibling who sexually abused was removed from the home and feeling that he or she should return home immediately while other parents want the family to be reunited but are concerned and confused about safety and if and how the sibling who sexually abused can live with the victim again. Still other parents may not have any interest in reunification occurring, although some of this latter group may alter their position as treatment progresses.

Sibling relationships are important across the life span. Some consider that sibling relationships are one of the most important and enduring relational environments in the family. Groza, Mashmeier, Jamison, and Piccola (2003) noted that most children grow up with siblings and further that the time they spend together in their early years is often greater than the time they spend with their parents. The sibling relationship often lasts for a lifetime, longer than most marriages and parent–child relationships (Dunn, 1985). The abuse and the hurt from the abuse does not negate or erase aspects of the relationship between the siblings that are viewed as positive and healthy; in other words, the abuse in and of itself does not define the entire relationship. Often victims want to have a relationship with their sibling; they want the parts of the relationship that were positive. They don't want to be hurt again but they want to regain the sibling relationship.

The family system is disrupted when family members, the sibling who sexually abused, and the victim are not able to have contact or communicate with one another. In some cases, the sibling who sexually abused's contact and communication with other family members may also be limited. While restrictions may be in place for clinical and safety reasons, there is still an impact to individual family members and the family as a whole. Treatment provides an opportunity to help reestablish and rebuild families.

While reunification is not appropriate in all cases, there are many cases in which families can safely be reunited, including the abusive sibling returning to the home with his or her victim. However, as Thomas (2010) stated, "Although it is important to preserve and restore families, it is most important to keep children safe."

Continuum Perspective for Reunification

Approaching reunification from a continuum perspective allows the reunification process to be adapted to the needs of the individual family's situation and circumstances (figure 10.1). Rather than an all-or-nothing approach, the continuum approach ranges from no contact to full reunification, with the sibling who sexually abused returning home and living with his or her victim. In some cases, contact between the sibling who sexually abused and the victim is clinically supported, but full reunification may not be possible or may be premature. While the reunification process begins in joint therapy sessions, it is hoped that the process will progress past therapy sessions to encompass the family being together—although this doesn't necessarily mean the victim and sibling who sexually abused living in the same home. Family together may include spending supervised social time together, both the victim and sibling who sexually abused being involved in activities with the family, or spending holidays and special occasions together as a family. The continuum approach allows for the youth to be an active member of the family despite not living with the family. The approach supports healing through decisions that are based on what is healthy and in the best interest of the victim, the sibling who sexually abused, and the family as a whole.

Figure 10.1 Continuum Perspective for Reunification

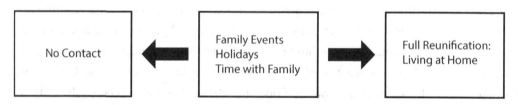

Reunification Process

Different terms and labels are used for the reunification process (e.g., family resolution, family restoration, or family reunification) and components of the process (e.g., clarification, reconciliation) (Saunders & Meinig, 2001; Tabachnik & Pollard, 2016; Thomas, 2010). At times this can be confusing or lead to misunderstandings and miscommunication. It is important that everyone involved with a specific case understand the terms being used in that case and how they are defined. Rather than exploring the reasoning behind preferences for a specific term or label or discussing which label may be more applicable, what is most important is recognizing that reunification is a process that involves several interrelated phases or steps building on one another, with each dependent on the victim, the sibling who sexually abused, and the caregiver(s). The reunification process evolves through assessment, treatment planning, family engagement, and clarification (Warsh, Pine, & Maluccio, 1994). We will use the broader descriptive term *reunification process* for purposes of our discussion.

While the literature has grown regarding sibling sexual abuse, it continues to be limited in direction and guidance related to the reunification process. One of the challenges in sibling sexual abuse cases and reunification, as identified by professionals working with this population, is the lack of research, training, and clinical direction (Harper, 2012). While there may be limitations in regard to specific information and best practices on reconciliation and reunification specific to sibling sexual abuse, we can utilize what we know about best practices in working with victims of sexual abuse, youth who sexually abuse, and families.

Previously we cited the importance of a collaborative approach and communication within the multidisciplinary team. There aren't always formal multidisciplinary teams, but the collaboration and communication between the professionals and family members involved remain important no matter how small the team or the lack of formal, regularly scheduled meetings. It is important that the treatment provider working with the victim and the treatment provider working with the sibling who sexually abused establish communication at the beginning and maintain it throughout the course of treatment, including the reunification process. In addition to the sharing of information being beneficial to the individual work with each youth, the already established relationship supports easier communication and discussion when considering the possible initiation of the reunification process. Both therapists, as well as others, such as child welfare workers, probation officers, and families, are involved in the decision about whether it is appropriate timing to initiate reunification. The clinical discussion about possible initiation of the process recognizes the valuable input of each therapist. Throughout the process, the best interest of the victim is the priority.

The process itself utilizes the strength and protective factors present within the individuals and within the family system, and builds on these to help promote the healing process. The reunification process provides an opportunity for the expression of feelings—including feelings about the abuse—and for healthy communication. The process can be viewed as reconstructing or reshaping the family, making the family stronger, and altering the family dynamics in a healthy way. The process is progressive, starting with limited contact and building toward the siblings spending more time with each other, and—in cases of full reunification—the sibling who sexually abused returning home to live where the victim resides. It is important that we are continuously assessing safety and making needed responses and adjustments. Reunification requires dedication and patience.

We will be examining main considerations and components of the reunification process through the lens of best practices. It is recognized that real-world situations at times necessitate adjustments in the process; the best practice lens is also helpful in informing the adjustments in those situations.

Treatment Highlights

While this chapter is not intended to provide details about the treatment process, we are providing broad highlights of treatment for the victim, the sibling who sexually abused, and the parents.

Victim

There are a number of resources that provide practice guidelines and information about evidence-based treatment for victims of sexual abuse, including trauma-focused cognitive-behavioral therapy and Structured Psychotherapy for Adolescents Responding to Chronic Stress (www.nctsn.org, www.samhsa.gov/nctic). The treatment of victims of sibling sexual abuse is complicated by the reality that the abuse occurred in the home and therefore has directly impacted trust, disrupted the sibling relationship, affected the family dynamics, and possibly altered how the parents respond to the victim, the sibling who sexually abused, and any other children in the home. In sibling sexual abuse cases, there are treatment issues in addition to resolving trauma-related symptoms that may be present. Given the victim was abused by a sibling, he or she is more likely to have conflicted feelings about the sibling who was abusive. The abuse may impact the victim's relationship with other siblings in the home due to possible trust issues or the other siblings' response to the situation. The victim may feel responsible for the disruption and stress in the family system, or may feel pressured to quickly have the sibling return home.

Treatment for the victim ensures that the individual needs of the child are met and provides a safe and supportive environment for the victim to be able to discuss his or her feelings and process what has happened. Treatment promotes healthy development and addresses any trauma-related symptoms that may present. While trauma symptoms may be present for some children, we need to keep in mind that children are often resilient and not immediately assume that there are trauma symptoms to be directly addressed. Trauma-focused cognitive-behavioral therapy includes reducing any negative or problematic emotional and behavioral responses as well as correcting and altering unhelpful or maladaptive beliefs related to the abuse (Child Welfare Information Gateway, 2011). Treatment for the victim assists in the child understanding that the abuse was not his or her fault and helps the child explore and be able to identify and communicate feelings, including those related to the abuse and future safety. In addition to focusing on identifying and communicating feelings, interventions support the child developing healthy coping skills and strategies. Treatment's emphasis on healthy development and individual needs serves as a safeguard that relevant issues are addressed.

One component of victim treatment that sometimes does not get mentioned is victims' input related to the development of safety guidelines. Their level of involvement is impacted by their age, but their input is important in the development of a plan that not only keeps them safe but also helps them feel safe. This will be discussed more in the section about safety guidelines.

The victim's parent(s) are involved in their child's treatment as determined by the therapist. At times the therapist may work directly with the parent(s) of the victim without the victim present and at times will include the parent(s) in specific aspects of the victim's sessions. The therapist's specific focus may be on the child, but the parent(s) play an important role in treatment and the healing process. Treatment helps them learn how to support their child and become more comfortable talking about feelings and the abuse. While it may be rare, there may be times and cases in which parent involvement is clinically contraindicated for the well-being of the child, or a parent refuses to be involved. In these cases, the therapist addresses the additional issues that this raises for the child.

The Sibling Who Sexually Abused

In regard to the sibling who sexually abused, treatment needs to be evidenced informed (see Worling & Langton, this volume). Again, as with victim treatment, the reality that the abuse occurred within the home often results in a more complex situation.

For siblings who sexually abused, treatment includes them recognizing and understanding that their behavior was abusive, learning about sexual abuse and healthy sexuality, and addressing their thinking and thoughts that may be supportive of offending. Risk and prevention are core components of the sibling who sexually abused's treatment; this includes avoidance and approach goals to help reduce risk and promote healthy functioning. Avoidance goals focus on what the youth can't do—e.g., no babysitting, not being unsupervised around children, etc. Approach goals focus on positive things the youth can do that can build on his or her strengths and reduce risk. An example would be becoming involved in organized activities with same-age peers, which decreases the likelihood of associating with children or negative peers.

Parents and/or Caregivers

For the family, it is important that the caregivers responsible for the youth be involved in the youth's treatment. There has been an increased focus on family involvement when working with youth who have engaged in sexually abusive behavior, and the need for this is even more pronounced in cases of sibling sexual abuse. In such cases the parent(s) need to be involved in both the victim's treatment and the treatment of the sibling who sexually abused. Providers recognize that this can add to an already stressful situation, and they can help in alleviating some of this stress by collaboration: being aware of other appointments, discussing content that may be overlapping, and discussing how to provide mutual support to the family. Family work involves building on strengths and positives of the family while examining the family dynamics, helping the family develop skills that promote safety and well-being, supporting the family through the healing process, and moving toward healthier family functioning.

While family involvement includes educating and helping the parent(s) understand the impact of abuse on the victim and how to support the victim, it also includes helping them understand and learn about adolescents who have engaged in sexually abusive behavior. Therapists provide information to help the parent(s) respond and cope more effectively with the sexual abuse and its effects on the family and individual children. The education provided to the parent(s), combined with interventions designed to help them recognize their family's strengths, increases their ability to realistically assess situations, helps them build skills in discussing uncomfortable topics, and provides a foundation for them understanding the issues and reasoning behind safety guidelines and their implementation.

Parents may also need services in addition to their involvement in the family therapy as a part of their children's treatment. At times it is beneficial for parents to have their own therapist to process issues due to the stress of the situation or due to the abuse having tapped into their own victim issues. In these cases we may want the parents to have a therapist who is solely focused on helping and supporting them. Also, there may be cases in which additional services are warranted due to mental health issues, substance abuse, couple discord, etc. When a parent is involved in other mental health services, releases of information need to be in place so that relevant information can be shared among the therapists.

Core Considerations

There are three considerations core to the reunification process: the victim, the sibling who sexually abused, and the parental caregiver unit. Decisions should not be made for convenience because the sibling who sexually abused is leaving a residential program or because things have become complicated in maintaining the youth out of the home. Youth may leave residential placement due to reaching maximum benefit, funding issues, or clinical readiness; clinical readiness to leave residential does not automatically equate to reunification being appropriate. It is recognized that there are often challenges to maintaining a youth out of the home, but the challenges and/or complications don't dictate the reunification decision. Decisions also should not made based on a specific length of time having elapsed or because someone arbitrarily decides it's time. It is recognized that where the sibling who sexually abused lives can be a challenge and also that it can be frustrating for families and other entities involved that the sibling who sexually abused remains out of the home; however, we have a responsibility to base decisions about the reunification on clinical information and readiness of the victim, the sibling who sexually abused, and the family.

The victim is a core consideration in the reunification process. Victims may verbalize that they want to be back around their brother or sister, or they want them to return home, and while their input and words matter we also need to observe their behaviors and how they are doing in treatment. When looking at readiness for contact with the sibling who sexually abused, the following questions are considered: Is the victim interested in having contact? Is the victim able to talk with her or his therapist or parent about feelings and thoughts? Is the victim clear that the abuse was not his or her fault and that responsibility lies with the sibling who abused them? Has there been a reduction in any abuse-related symptoms? (Bonner & Chaffin, 1998).

Where the sexually abusive youth is in his or her treatment is another core consideration for reunification. Determining readiness for reunification includes assessing the youth's progress in treatment including his or her acceptance of responsibility, understanding the impact of the abuse on the victim and family, and understanding and recognizing the need for safety guidelines (Bonner & Chaffin, 1998) as well as his or her level of emotional and behavioral stability.

The parental unit is the third core consideration in reunification. Parent involvement and progress is a crucial component of the process. The parent(s) need to provide support for both the victim and the sibling who sexually abused and be able to discuss the sexual abuse and their concerns and responsibilities with the therapist (Bonner & Chaffin, 1998). They need to be aware of details of the abuse, understand its impact on the family, and be able to talk to the victim, the sibling who sexually abused, and other children in the home about their feelings and concerns. The parent(s) recognize that because sexual abuse has occurred, there is risk present. They are involved in identifying supervision needs and developing safety guidelines, demonstrate a commitment to adhering to the guidelines, and are willing and able to do what is necessary for safety. If there are other siblings in the home, the parent then also has the responsibility of talking to the other children in the home about the rules and guidelines.

Factors Impacting If/When Reunification Occurs

There are a number of factors, situations, and circumstances that can impact if/when reunification occurs or if full reunification is possible. One situation is when the sibling who engaged in sexually abusive behavior and the sibling who was abused are not ready for contact at the same time. This needs to be respected and any initiation of the reunification process placed on hold until everyone is ready for reunification. When this situation occurs, it will need to be processed in therapy, as it can be disappointing for the sibling who is ready to move forward in the process. When the sibling who sexually abused is the one who isn't ready for the process to begin, the victim may interpret that to mean that his or her sibling doesn't care enough to do the work for the session to occur. The victim's therapist can help the parent(s) in providing support during this difficult time. When the victim is the one who isn't ready for the process to begin, the sibling who sexually abused may jump to the conclusion that his or her sibling doesn't have any interest in further contact. The therapist can work with the youth to accept that the victim isn't ready and help him or her understand that it is important that decisions are made that are in the victim's best interest.

At times, pressure is placed on victims, either by themselves, parents, or others—or they may perceive that there is pressure placed on them. This can become a barrier in regard to gaining an accurate assessment of victims' readiness for initiation of the reunification process. Helping parents understand the reason for the continued separation and why it is important that reunification is approached as a process that takes time is beneficial in trying to avoid pressure. Also, being open in discussing that the victim may be feeling responsible for the split in the family and how a parent's comments may be interpreted allows parents to be more sensitive in their interactions with their child. The team can be helpful in guarding against pressure by being alert to and openly talking about how and why pressure (and what can be perceived as pressure) sometimes occurs.

There are also situations in which the parents have made a decision that they will not support reunification efforts or allow the victim to be involved in the process. In these situations, the professional needs to respect that this is the parents' right and that parents typically make this decision because they believe it is best for their child and to protect their child. If the parents are involved in treatment, the therapist can continue to gently provide education about treatment and reunification as appropriate, but should be careful that such efforts are not perceived as pressuring. Parents may be feeling conflicted about taking the step for their children to be back around each other. They may feel that they are being pulled in different directions because the best interest of one child may not be the best interest of the other. They may be concerned that there is too much risk and that they will not be able to maintain safety if the children are reunited. Thinking about full reunification can be overwhelming for parents as they consider the restrictions that will be in place and their responsibility for safety.

In some cases, there may be barriers to full reunification occurring. This may relate to factors within the parental unit that interfere with adequate supervision and child protection (parental functioning, level of stability, or lack of commitment and follow-through) or to the composition of the home (high number of young children present in the home in addition to the victim or several victims in the home). Such factors may present too much risk for the sibling who sexually abused to live at home despite progress by the victim, the sibling who sexually abused, and the family, along with the family's desire for the youth to live at home. Parental units or families may want the youth who sexually abused to be an active part of the family, yet be unwilling to have them return home due to concern over the level of stress that this would cause or the level of supervision that is needed. Depending on the situation, there can be a level of reunification thereby allowing the family to experience being together and being a family even if the youth isn't living at home.

As noted, in some cases the parents may initially be against any reunification efforts but over time and through treatment begin to recognize that this could be positive for the victim and family. However, there are also cases in which the parental unit is not interested in the sibling who sexually abused having contact with the family again or being a part of the family again.

When contact is not possible, regardless of the reason, we need to ensure that support and guidance are provided to those impacted so they can cope with the situation and continue healing. When families are not interested in having contact, helping the affected youth build on natural support systems that are present—such as relatives, church members, positive adults they are close to—and/or develop a support system such as identifying a mentor can be beneficial.

Therapeutic Letter Writing

Therapeutic letter writing is often considered the first official contact between the sibling who sexually abused and his or her victim. Some people call this a clarification letter or ownership letter; others may refer to it as an apology letter or responsibility letter. We will use the term *therapeutic letter writing* for purposes of our discussion. Regardless of what it is labeled, letter writing appears to be a common practice

(Demaio, Davis, & Smith, 2006). Still, while therapeutic letter writing can be valuable, we should not assume that it fits for every youth.

When therapeutic letter writing is utilized, it needs to have a clear purpose and be determined by the individual case. If you are using therapeutic letters, ask yourself what is the purpose of the letter and why you are using it with that youth. Therapeutic letter writing can be used as a therapeutic tool with siblings who sexually abused related to accepting responsibility and recognizing the impact of their behavior. Therapeutic letters can also be shared with victims' therapists, to increase their knowledge of the sibling who sexually abused's view of the abuse, or can be intended to be shared with victims for their benefit. Therapeutic letter writing is not appropriate or necessary with every youth; use of this intervention needs to be determined by the individual case. For youth with low intellectual functioning or a learning disability in written expression, the therapist needs to consider other interventions or approaches that can accomplish the same purpose. Some therapists have youth make an audio recording or a video or DVD rather than writing a letter (Kahn, 2011).

Another caution about therapeutic letter writing is related to how feedback is provided and revisions that the youth is expected to make based on feedback received. Therapists review the letter, provide feedback to the youth, and—depending on the purpose of the letter—have the youth revise it. While this may be necessary if the letter is potentially to be shared with the victim, we need to guard against the letter becoming more of what we would want the youth to say than what the youth is feeling and wanting to say. Sometimes the youth is ready to write a letter to be shared with the victim, but at other times the content of the youth's letter alerts us that he or she is not ready for this step in treatment.

Apology

The role of apologies within letters or sessions warrants careful review. It is not unusual for providers to promote the use of apology in a letter or session or even refer to the session as an apology session or refer to letters as apology letters. We caution against the automatic inclusion of an apology in a letter or in a session or assuming this is in the best interest of the victim or what the victim wants or needs. What the victim wants and needs should guide whether an apology occurs and, if so, how it is incorporated into the session. The ongoing communication between therapists allows for open dialogue about apologies. There are situations in which victims are clearly expecting or stating they want siblings to apologize—they want to hear "I'm sorry"—but there are also cases in which victims may be just as clear that they don't want to hear an apology but instead want siblings to show they are sorry through their actions and behavior.

Sometimes the parent wants to hear the youth apologize or the parent thinks that the youth should have to apologize to the victim. In those situations, there can be separate sessions with the parents, but the actual session with the victim needs to be based on the victim's needs.

We also need to ensure that if an apology is a part of a session or letter, it is sincere. We do not want to script what the sibling who sexually abused should be saying in a session that incorporates an apology; we do not want an apology that doesn't appear to be sincere.

Another caution with apologies is that they have different meanings to different people and can take on unintended meanings. Small children may perceive that "I'm sorry" makes everything okay and they're supposed to forget about what happened. Others may believe that if someone apologizes to you, you are supposed to forgive them. The intent of letters or sessions is not that the abuse is forgotten, but rather that the family, victim, and sibling who sexually abused are healing from the abuse and moving forward, and that safety is maintained. How the victim views apologies is important, and communication with the victim's therapist and parents helps inform whether an apology is a part of the letter or session. It is recognized that apologies are sometimes appropriate and beneficial in letters or sessions, but it is also recognized that it is appropriate for letters and sessions to not include apologies.

Early Contact/Pre–Formal Therapeutic Contact

While many providers view the therapeutic letter (clarification letter, ownership letter, apology letter) as being the initial communication between the sibling who sexually abused and the victim, there are times when there are requests for communication between the victim and sibling who sexually abused prior to that therapeutic step. Examples include: A victim wants to send his or her sibling a Christmas card or birthday card; children beg their mother to be able to say hi to the sibling when they call home to talk to the parents; victims want the parents to give the sibling who sexually abused a message or picture they drew when the parents visit. These requests may be more common around birthdays or holidays or other special events that make victims think of their siblings not being home. There are also times when the sibling who sexually abused asks about being able to send the victim or family a holiday or birthday card. While the therapist's first reaction may be to say no, our approach should be that it depends. In these types of situations, the therapists involved need to discuss the request and situation, with the parents being included in the discussion. It may be that it is healthy and appropriate for the card to be sent or received or the child to say hi; at other times it may be determined that this isn't clinically supported.

While we want to protect victims from premature contact with the sibling who sexually abused, we need to recognize that at times the early and pre–formal contact can be a part of the healing process and help restore the healthy sibling relationship. If a young victim is missing her brother at Christmas and wanting to send him a card like the family does with relatives, it may be beneficial to the victim. However, if the victim wants to send the card due to fear of her brother being mad, to say she is sorry, or feeling she, the victim, is to blame, that is different and would raise concerns. The ongoing communication between the therapists throughout the process allows for such situations to be quickly discussed and at times anticipated.

First Session

As noted several times in this section, the first session should not occur unless it is in the victim's best interest and the victim, sibling who sexually abused, and parents have all demonstrated progress congruent with such a session. Prior to any session including the victim and the sibling who sexually abused, it is important that there is communication between the treatment providers to ensure that everyone is in agreement about the expected focus and content of the session. The victim's therapist will take the lead in what the content will be and typically will be the one to take the lead within the session. The ideal situation is for both therapists to be involved in the session, although in reality that does not always occur; it may be only one therapist working with the victim, the sibling who sexually abused, and the parents.

While there is a significant degree of preparation for the session, the session itself may not be that long. If there has been a lengthy separation, the session often becomes focused on providing an opportunity for the siblings to become reacquainted and get used to being around each other again. How much clinical work is addressed in the first session depends on the situation and the needs of the victim. While steps of accepting responsibility, addressing questions, etc., may not occur in the first session, this does not negate the sibling who sexually abused acknowledging that his or her abuse of the victim is the reason there hasn't been any contact. Sessions can be therapeutic even if there is limited clinical work.

Do not try to do too much in the first session; let it be what it is, a beginning. The individuals involved are going to be experiencing an array of emotions and will only be able to attend to or process a limited amount of information. This is often an emotional time for the parents involved, and it may also be an emotional time for the victim and the sibling who sexually abused. The victim's age also impacts the length of the session and how that session is handled. What we do with a 5-year-old in the session is much different than what we may do with a 13-year-old. If the siblings have been away from each other for a significant period of time, just seeing each other and being around each other again can easily lead to distractions that can interfere with trying to deal with other topics or content. We suggest preparing everyone that the session itself may be shorter than they expect, might have a different focus, and may be emotional.

Sessions with the victim and sibling who sexually abused continue after the initial session. At some point, the sibling who sexually abused will verbally take responsibility for the abusive behavior. The needs and age of the victim will inform how this occurs and what language is used. The sibling who sexually abused will need to provide a clear message that the abuse was not the victim's fault and that he or she is taking responsibility for the abuse having occurred.

When discussing rules for safety, it needs to be emphasized that these rules apply to all children and not just the victim. This changes some when the victim is an adolescent since the sibling who sexually abused would be supervised around his or her victim, but not around all adolescents. Questions about why the sibling who sexually abused did so, whether he or she will do it again, and what is different now will also be a focus. Sessions provide the victim an opportunity to express feelings and ask questions.

Therapists and parents need to monitor the impact the sessions have on the victim and sibling who sexually abused. This includes observations of behavior during, after, and between sessions as well as any discussion of feelings with parents and in follow-up therapy sessions. This information determines the timing and content of subsequent sessions.

Safety Guidelines and Safety Plans

Safety guidelines/safety plans are a component of the youth who sexually abused's treatment and will be in place regardless of whether there is reunification or not. However, when there is reunification, we need to ensure that the safety guidelines take into account specifics regarding the contact and interaction with the victims or other siblings living in the home. The sibling who sexually abused, parents, and victim should be involved in the development of, or have input into, the safety guidelines. The age of the victims will impact how they are involved in the development of the safety plan, but they should be provided an opportunity to have a voice in it. While safety guidelines can be developed without the victim's input, providing them an opportunity to have input reinforces healthy, open communication, which is a focus of treatment. In addition, while others may know what to put in the plan to support safety, the victim is the one who knows what will help him or her feel safe.

There will be basic guidelines, such as the sibling who sexually abused not babysitting, not being in a position of authority over children, and being supervised when around children, etc. However, it is important that the safety guidelines are also individualized based on the youth and the situation. We need to also ensure that the safety guidelines, including those specific to reunification, include both approach- and avoidance-focused components. In addition to promoting healthy functioning and thereby decreasing risk, an approach focus supports the family being family. Rather than the guidelines only focusing on what the victim and sibling who sexually abused can't do together, what they can do together with supervision is identified. Including "can-dos" supports the rebuilding of the sibling relationship and helps the family system as a whole.

Everyone involved needs to be aware of the safety guidelines. If there are other children or adults in the home, they need to understand the guidelines. It is important to make it clear that the guidelines are in place for safety, and that the sibling who sexually abused is responsible for his or her behavior and adherence to the plan; however, parents accept responsibility for implementation of the guidelines when they agree for the sibling who sexually abused to be in their care or around the victim, other children, or vulnerable persons in their home. Everyone will have responsibility for their own boundaries and communication, but we want to avoid a victim or other siblings feeling like they are responsible for the abusive youth's behavior or adherence to the guidelines.

The safety guidelines need to be reasonable, understandable, and doable. We want to give the family the skills to generalize the guidelines to a variety of situations, not just the specific examples discussed in sessions; life goes on outside treatment. Talking about how to apply the guidelines and addressing possible challenges helps the family be better prepared and feel more confident with the guidelines. While basic safety guidelines such as supervision around children and victims will remain in place, other aspects of the plan will be periodically reviewed and adjustments made as needed. The guidelines also need to include what to do and whom to contact in the event that there is a serious problem or concern, including anyone feeling uncomfortable or unsafe in the home. This involves helping the parents be prepared to assess the situation and take necessary action, with a plan in place that can be immediately implemented if safety is compromised. When safety is compromised, contact between the victim and sibling who sexually abused and other children is put on hold until physical, sexual, and emotional safety are restored.

Alarms

In some agencies, motion detectors, door alarms, and cameras are popular and viewed as an answer for safety in the home. Other agencies or areas don't use them or use them only at a minimal level. While it is recognized that those using devices are doing so because they feel it supports safety, the devices can also give a false sense of safety. If you are considering using one of these devices, there are a couple of questions to ask: (a) Would you recommend and/or agree for the youth to be in the home without the device, and if not why not? (b) Is the device the core part of your safety planning? If you would not recommend and/or agree for the youth to be in the home without the device, or if the device is the core part of the safety planning, then the decision for full reunification warrants reconsideration. Using a device as a backup to the safety plan or an extra component of it is a different strategy and does not raise the same level of concerns and questions.

Summary

Reunification is a process that includes ongoing assessment and observation of the victim, the sibling who sexually abused, other siblings, and the family as a whole. Reunification involves several interrelated phases or steps building on one another, with each dependent on the victim, the sibling who sexually abused, and the parental unit. The process takes time, and it requires collaboration and patience.

CONCLUSIONS

While removal of some youth who sexually abuse from the home and/or community may be necessary because of the youth's risk and treatment needs, or because one or more victims are in the home, inherent within the removal is the challenge of when and how the youth returns to his or her community or home. In this chapter, we reviewed relevant child welfare and juvenile delinquency literature, which provided information about the challenges associated with community reentry and family reunification, noting that many youth are not successful in their transition back to the community and their families. The literature suggests that planning for community reintegration needs to begin at the time of removal and that youth need adequate services and supervision when returning to the community and home. In addition, families need to be involved and receive appropriate services and support while the youth are in a placement and when they return home. It is important to recognize that there is little to no research specific to reentry with adolescents who sexually abuse (Lambie & Price, 2015). While we have data on reoffense rates, to our knowledge we currently lack basic information about the number of youth who are unsuccessful in other ways (truancy, behavioral problems in the school or home, etc.) when they return to the community and the reasons for their failures.

Future research needs to include a focus on reentry experiences of adolescents who sexually abuse and factors related to unsuccessful reentry. Although we can assume that factors are similar to other youth in the juvenile justice system, this population of youth may also face unique challenges that impact reentry. For example, registration and community notification may lead to youth being ostracized by prosocial peers and restrict opportunities for involvement in prosocial activities. Some school systems may be reluctant to enroll youth who have sexually abused and require placement in alternative schools, thereby further exposing them to delinquent peers and educating them in settings that isolate them from positive peer groups. Opportunities for the youth who sexually abused to engage in activities and experiences supportive of successful reentry can be directly impacted by overly strict and rigid probation requirements, general fear and apprehension of these youth, and laws and public policy that are poorly thought out and fail to take into consideration best practices and research related to this population of youth.

There are additional challenges when a sibling who sexually abused is returning to the home with his or her victim. The majority of our knowledge and practice related to these cases is derived from clinical observations. Clinical observation is important, but research that provides information about the number of youth who reoffend after returning home, including whom they reoffend against and possible factors related to the reoffense, is needed and would provide a baseline for assessing the actual risk in these situations. While this type of research would be beneficial, it does not address the question of the ongoing impact on the victim and family when the sibling who sexually abused returns to the home. Research related to immediate and long-term impact on the victim of having a sibling who abused back in the home—as well as the impact on the family as a whole—is an area that warrants attention.

In summary, there are a number of challenges for adolescents who have engaged in sexually abusive behavior returning to the community and/or home, and at times there are additional barriers such as registration and community notification. While research specific to family reunification and community reintegration with adolescents who have sexually abused is lacking, related fields provide information that is beneficial in guiding us in our efforts to be proactive in helping youth and their families prepare for and experience successful reentry.

REFERENCES

Abrams, L. S., & Snyder, S. M. (2010). Youth offender reentry: Models for intervention and directions for future inquiry. *Children and Youth Services Review, 32,* 1787–1795. http://dx.doi.org/10.1016/j.childyouth.2010.07.023

Abrams, L. S., Terry, D., & Franke, T. M. (2011). Community-based juvenile reentry services: The effects of service dosage on juvenile and adult recidivism. *Journal of Offender Rehabilitation, 50,* 492–510. http://dx.doi.org/10.1080/10509674.2011.596919

Al, C. M. W., Stams, G. J. J. M., Beck, M. S., Damen, E. M., Asscher, J. J., & van der Laan, P. H. (2012). A meta-analysis of intensive family preservation programs: Placement prevention and improvement of family functioning. *Children and Youth Services Review, 34,* 1472–1479. http://dx.doi.org/10.1016/j.childyouth.2012.04.002

Altschuler, D. M., & Armstrong, T. L. (1994a). *Intensive aftercare for high-risk juveniles: An assessment* (report). Washington, DC: US Department of Justice Office of Juvenile Justice and Delinquency Prevention.

Altschuler, D. M., & Armstrong, T. L. (1994b). *Intensive aftercare for high-risk juveniles: A community care model* (summary). Washington, DC: US Department of Justice Office of Juvenile Justice and Delinquency Prevention.

Altschuler, D. M., Armstrong, T. L., & MacKenzie, D. L. (1999). *Reintegration, supervised release, and intensive aftercare.* (NCJ 175715). Washington, DC: US Department of Justice Office of Juvenile Justice and Delinquency Prevention.

Altschuler, D. M., & Brash, R. (2004). Adolescent and teenage offenders confronting the challenges and opportunities of reentry. *Youth Violence and Juvenile Justice, 2,* 72–87. http://dx.doi.org/10.1177/1541204003260048

Aos, S., Miller, M., & Drake, E. (2006). *Evidence-based adult corrections programs: What works and what does not.* Olympia: Washington State Institute for Public Policy.

Baglivio, M. T., Wolff, K. T., Jackowski, K., & Greenwald, M. A. (2015, August 21). A multilevel examination of risk/need change scores, community context, and successful reentry of committed juvenile offenders. *Youth Violence and Juvenile Justice.* http://dx.doi.org/10.1177/1541204015596052

Bonner, B. L., & Chaffin, M. (1998). Sibling sexual behavior treatment protocol. Oklahoma City: University of Oklahoma Health Sciences Center.

Boonmann, C., van Vugt, E. S., Jansen, L. M. C., Colins, O. F., Doreleijers, T. A. H., Stams, G. J. J. M., & Vermeiren, R. R. J. M. (2015). Mental disorders in juveniles who sexually offended: A meta-analysis. *Aggression and Violent Behavior, 24,* 241–249.

Borduin, C. M., Schaeffer, C. M., & Heiblum, N. (2009). A randomized clinical trial of multisystemic therapy with juvenile sexual offenders: Effects on youth social ecology and criminal activity. *Journal of Consulting and Clinical Psychology, 77,* 26–37. http://dx.doi.org/10.1037/a0013035

Bronson, D. E., Saunders, S., Holt, M. B., & Beck, E. (2008, May). *A systemic review of strategies to promote successful reunification and to reduce re-entry to care for abused, neglected, and unruly children* (final report presented to the Ohio Department of Job and Family Services, Columbus, OH). Retrieved from http://www.ocwtp.net/pdfs/reun-reentry%20final%20report.pdf

Caldwell, M. F. (2010). Study characteristics and recidivism base rates in juvenile sex offender recidivism. *International Journal of Offender Therapy and Comparative Criminology, 54,* 197–212. http://dx.doi.org/10.1177/0306624X08330016

Caldwell, M. F. (2016, July 18). Quantifying the decline in juvenile sexual recidivism rates. *Psychology, Public Policy, and Law.* Advance online publication. http://dx.doi.org/10.1037/law0000094

Carnochan, S., Lee, C., & Austin, M. J. (2013). Achieving timely reunification. *Journal of Evidence-Based Social Work, 10,* 179–195. http://dx.doi.org/10.1080/15433714.2013.788948

Carnochan, S., Rizik-Baer, D., & Austin, M. J. (2013). Preventing re-entry to foster care. *Journal of Evidence-Based Social Work, 10,* 196–209. http://dx.doi.org/10.1080/15433714.2013.788949

Carpentier, J., & Proulx, J. (2011). Correlates of recidivism among adolescents who have sexually offended. *Sexual Abuse: A Journal of Research and Treatment, 23,* 434–455. http://dx.doi.org/10.1177/1079063211409950

Chamberlain, P. (2003). *Treating chronic juvenile offenders: Advances made through the Oregon multidimensional treatment foster care model.* Washington, DC: American Psychological Association.

Child Welfare Information Gateway. (2011). *Family reunification: What the evidence shows.* Washington, DC: US Department of Health and Human Services, Children's Bureau. Retrieved from www.childwelfare.gov/pubs/issue_briefs/family_reunification

Choi, S., & Ryan, J. P. (2007). Co-occurring problems for substance abusing mothers in child welfare: Matching services to improve family reunification. *Children and Youth Services Review, 29,* 1395–1410. http://dx.doi.org/10.1016/j.childyouth.2007.05.013

Chung, H. L., Schubert, C. A., & Mulvey, E. P. (2007). An empirical portrait of community reentry among serious juvenile offenders in two metropolitan cities. *Criminal Justice and Behavior, 34,* 1402–1426. http://dx.doi.org/10.1177/0093854807307170

Cullen, F. T., Jonson, C. L., & Nagin, D. S. (2011). Prisons do not reduce recidivism: The high cost of ignoring science. *The Prison Journal Supplement, 91,* 48S–65S. http://dx.doi.org/10.1177/0032885511415224

Curtis, N. M., Ronan, K. R., & Borduin, C. M. (2004). Multisystemic treatment: A meta-analysis of outcome studies. *Journal of Family Psychology, 18,* 411–419.

Dawkins, M., & Sorensen, J. R. (2014). The impact of residential placement on aggregate delinquency: A state-level panel study, 1997–2011. *Criminal Justice Policy Review, 26,* 85–100. http://dx.doi.org/10.1177/0887403414534854

DeMaio, C. M., Davis, J. L., & Smith, D. W. (2006). The use of clarification sessions in the treatment of incest victims and their families: An exploratory study. *Sexual Abuse: A Journal of Research and Treatment, 18,* 27–39. http://dx.doi.org/10.1007/s11194-006-9002-7

Dunn, J. (1985). *Sisters and brothers.* Cambridge, MA: Harvard University Press.

Felizzi, M. V. (2015). Family or caregiver instability, parental attachment, and the relationship to juvenile sex offending. *Journal of Child Sexual Abuse, 24,* 641–658. http://dx.doi.org/10.1080/10538712.2015.1057668

Gerhold, C. K., Browne, K. D., & Beckett, R. (2007). Predicting recidivism in adolescent sexual offenders. *Aggression and Violent Behavior, 12,* 427–438. http://dx.doi.org/10.1016/j.avb.2006.10.004

Gies, S. V. (2003). *Aftercare services* (NCJ 201800). Washington, DC: US Department of Justice, Office of Justice Programs Office of Juvenile Justice and Delinquency Prevention.

Graves, R. G., Openshaw, D. K., Ascione, F. R., & Ericksen, S. L. (1996). Demographic and parental characteristics of youthful sexual offenders. *International Journal of Offender Therapy and Comparative Criminology, 40,* 300–317.

Groza, V., Maschmeier, C., Jamison, C., & Piccola, T. (2003). Siblings and out-of-home placement: Best practices. *Families in Society: The Journal of Contemporary Human Services, 82,* 480–492.

Hanson, R. K., & Bussière, M. T. (1998). Predicting relapse: A meta-analysis of sexual offender recidivism studies. *Journal of Consulting and Clinical Psychology, 66,* 348–362.

Harper, B. M. (2012). Moving families to future health: Reunification experiences after sibling incest. *Doctorate in Social Work (DSW) Dissertations,* Paper 26.

Hockenberry, S. (2014). *Juveniles in residential placement, 2011* (NCJ 246826). Washington, DC: US Department of Justice Office of Juvenile Justice and Delinquency Prevention.

Hoge, R. D. (2002). Standardized instruments for assessing risk and need in youthful offenders. *Criminal Justice and Behavior, 29,* 38–396.

Hoge, R. D., Andrews, D. A., & Leschied, A. (2002). *The Youth Level of Service/Case Management Inventory.* Toronto, Canada: Multi Health Systems.

James, C., Stams, G. J. J. M., Asscher, J. J., De Roo, A. K., & van der Laan, P. H. (2013). Aftercare programs for reducing recidivism among juvenile and young adult offenders: A meta-analytic review. *Clinical Psychology Review, 33,* 263–274. http://dx.doi.org/10.1016/j.cpr.2012.10.013

Joyal, C. C., Carpentier, J., & Martin, C. (2016). Discriminant factors for adolescent sexual offending: On the usefulness of considering both victim age and sibling incest. *Child Abuse & Neglect, 54,* 10–22.

Kahn, T. J. (2011). *Pathways: A guided workbook for youth beginning treatment* (4th ed.). Brandon, VT: Safer Society.

Kahn, T. J., & Chambers, H. J. (1991). Assessing re-offense risk with juvenile sexual offenders. *Child Welfare, 70,* 333–345.

Koehler, J. A., Lösel, F., Akoensi, T. D., & Humphreys, D. K. (2013). A systematic review and meta-analysis on the effects of young offender treatment programs in Europe. *Journal of Experimental Criminology, 9,* 19–43.

Kurlycheck, M. C., Wheeler, A. P., Tinik, L. A., & Kempinen, C. A. (2011). How long after? A natural experiment assessing the impact of the length of aftercare service delivery on recidivism. *Crime & Delinquency, 57,* 778–800. http://dx.doi.org/10.1177/0011128710382262

Lambie, I., & Price, M. (2015). Transitioning youth with sexually harmful behavior back into the community. *Journal of Sexual Aggression: An International, Interdisciplinary Forum for Research, Theory and Practice, 21,* 244–265. http://dx.doi.org/10.1080/13552600.2013.873829

Langstrom, N. (2002). Long-term follow-up of criminal recidivism in young sex offenders: Temporal patterns and risk factors. *Psychology, Crime and Law, 8,* 41–58.

Lipsey, M., Chapman, G., & Landenberger, N. (2001). Cognitive-behavioral programs for offenders. *Annals of the American Academy of Political and Social Science, 578,* 144–157.

Lipsey, M. W., Wilson, D. B., & Cothern, L. (2000). *Effective intervention for serious juvenile offenders* (NCJ 181201). Washington, DC: US Department of Justice Office of Juvenile Justice and Delinquency Prevention.

Loughran, T. A., Mulvey, E. P., Schubert, C. A., Fagan, J., Piquero, A. R., & Losoya, S. H. (2009). Estimating a dose–response relationship between length of stay and future recidivism in serious juvenile offenders. *Criminology, 47,* 699–740. http://dx.doi.org/10.1111/j.1745-9125.2009.00165.x

Mapp, S. C., & Steinberg, C. (2007). Birthfamilies as permanency resources for children in long-term foster care. *Child Welfare, 86,* 29–51.

Marsh, J. C., Ryan, J. P., Choi, S., & Testa, M. F. (2006). Integrated services for families with multiple problems: Obstacles to family reunification. *Children and Youth Services Review, 28,* 1074–1087. http://dx.doi.org/10.1016/j.childyouth.2005.10.012

Nunes, K. L., Firestone, P., Wexler, A. F., Jensen, T. L., & Bradford, J. M. (2007). Incarceration and recidivism among sexual offenders. *Law and Human Behavior, 31,* 305–318. http://dx.doi.org/10.1007/s10979-006-9065-5

Peterson-Badali, M., Skilling, T., & Haqanee, Z. (2015). Examining implementation of risk assessment in case management for youth in the justice system. *Criminal Justice and Behavior, 42,* 304–320. http://dx.doi.org/10.1177/0093854814549595

Petrosino, A., Turpin-Petrosino, C., & Guckenburg, S. (2010). Formal system processing of juveniles: Effects on delinquency. *Campbell Systematic Reviews, 1*. http://dx.doi.org/10.4073/csr.2010.1

Prentky, R., Harris, B., Frizzell, K., & Righthand, S. (2000). An actuarial procedure for assessing risk with juvenile sex offenders. *Sexual Abuse: A Journal of Research and Treatment, 12*, 71–93. http://dx.doi.org/10.1177/107906320001200201

Prentky, R. A., Lee, A. F., Lamade, R., Grossi, L., Schuler, A., Dube, G., . . . & Pond, A. (2014). Placement instability as a risk factor in proximal sexually inappropriate and aggressive behaviors in a child welfare sample. *Journal of Child Custody, 11*, 251–277. http://dx.doi.org/10.1080/15379418.2014.987335

Prentky, R. A., Li, N., Righthand, S., Schuler, A., Cavanaugh, D., & Lee, A. F. (2010). Assessing risk of sexually abusive behavior among youth in a child welfare sample. *Behavioral Sciences and the Law, 28*, 24–45. http://dx.doi.org/10.1002/bsl.920

Rich, P. (2011). Victim awareness and clarification. In P. Rich, *Understanding juvenile sexual offenders: Assessment, treatment, and rehabilitation* (2nd ed., pp. 351–368). Hoboken, NJ: John Wiley & Sons.

Righthand, S., & Welch, C. (2001). *Juveniles who have sexually offended. A review of the professional literature (NCJ 184739)*. Washington, DC: US Department of Justice Office of Juvenile Justice and Delinquency Prevention.

Schmucker, M., & Lösel, F. (2015). The effects of sexual offender treatment on recidivism: An international meta-analysis of sound quality evaluations. *Journal of Experimental Criminology, 11*, 597–630. http://dx.doi.org/10.1007/s11292-015-9241-z

Schubert, C. A., & Mulvey, E. P., (2014). *Aftercare services are key to positive community adjustment.* Chicago: MacArthur Foundation.

Schubert, C. A., Mulvey, E. P., & Glasheen, C. (2011). Influence of mental health and substance use problems and criminogenic risk on outcomes in serious juvenile offenders. *Journal of the American Academy of Child & Adolescent Psychiatry, 50*, 925–937.

Schweitzer, D. D., Pecora, P. J., Nelson, K., Walters, B., & Blythe, B. J. (2015). Building the evidence base for intensive family preservation services. *Journal of Public Child Welfare, 9*, 423–443. http://dx.doi.org/10.1080/15548732.2015.1090363

Seto, M. C., & Lalumière, M. L. (2010). What is so special about male adolescent sexual offending? A review and test of explanations through meta-analysis. *Psychological Bulletin, 136*, 526–575. http://dx.doi.org/10.1037/a0019700

Smith, W. R., & Monastersky, C. (1986). Assessing juvenile sexual offenders' risk for reoffending. *Criminal Justice and Behavior, 13*, 115–140.

Steinberg, L., Chung, H. L., & Little, M. (2004). Reentry of young offenders from the justice system: A developmental perspective. *Youth Violence and Juvenile Justice, 2*, 21–38. http://dx.doi.org/10.1177/1541204003260045

Tabachnick, J., & Pollard, P. (2016). *Considering family reconnections and reunification after child sexual abuse: A road map for advocates and service providers.* Enola, PA: National Sexual Violence Resource Center.

Thomas, J. (2010). Family therapy: A critical component in treatment of sexually abusive youth. In G. Ryan, T. Leversee, & S. Lane (Eds.), *Juvenile sexual offending: Causes, consequences, and correction* (3rd ed., pp. 357–379). Hoboken, NJ: John Wiley & Sons.

Thomas, J., & Viar, W. (2003). Family reunification in sibling incest. In M. C. Calder (Ed.), *Children and young people who sexually abuse: New theory, research and practice developments.* Dorset, UK: Russell House Publishing.

Tidefors, I., Arvidsson, H., Ingevaldson, S., & Larsson, M. (2010). Sibling incest: A literature review and a clinical study. *Journal of Sexual Aggression: An International, Interdisciplinary Forum for Research, Theory and Practice, 16,* 347–360. http://dx.doi.org/10.1080/13552600903511667

Vieira, T. A., Skilling, T. A., & Peterson-Badali, M. (2009). Matching court-ordered services with treatment needs: Predicting treatment success with young offenders. *Criminal Justice and Behavior, 36,* 385–401. http://dx.doi.org/10.1177/0093854808331249

Warsh, R., Pine, B., & Maluccio, A. (1994). *Teaching family reunification: A sourcebook.* Washington, DC: Child Welfare League of America.

Wiebush, R. G., Wagner, D., McNulty, B., Wang, Y., & Le, T. N. (2005). *Implementation and outcome evaluation of the intensive aftercare program: Final report.* Washington, DC: National Council on Crime and Delinquency.

Worling, J. R. (2004). The Estimate of Risk of Adolescent Sexual Offense Recidivism (ERASOR): Preliminary psychometric data. *Sexual Abuse: A Journal of Research and Treatment, 16,* 235–254. http://dx.doi.org/10.1177/107906320401600305

Wulczyn, F. (2004). Family reunification. *The Future of Children, 14,* 95–113. dx.doi.org/10.2307/1602756

Part IV
Special Issues

CHAPTER 11

Interventions for Adolescents with Developmental Disabilities

Daniel Rothman

Todd Smith

Adolescents who engage in abusive sexual behaviors are a diverse group of individuals, with great variability in terms of their behaviors of concern (including the nature of their offending behaviors and the age and gender of their victims), age, maturity level, learning styles, strengths and deficits, and protective and risk factors for problem behaviors (ATSA, 2012; Seto & Lalumière, 2010). The diversity of the population calls for an individualized, holistic treatment framework (Letourneau & Bourdin, 2008; Leversee & Powell, 2012). Furthermore, interventions with youthful populations should take into consideration the overall low rates of recidivism for youth who have engaged in abusive sexual behavior: Research indicates that approximately 80 to 97 percent of these youth do not go on to reoffend, particularly if they receive targeted intervention (Reitzel & Carbonell, 2006; Caldwell, 2010; Caldwell, 2016; Worling, Litteljohn, & Bookalam, 2010). It has also been noted that there is substantial overlap between youth with sexual and non-sexual conduct problems (Seto & Lalumière, 2010; van Wijk, van Horne, Bullens, Bijleveld, & Doreleijers, 2005) and that, if these youth reoffend, they are far more likely to do so with non-sexual offenses than with sexual ones (Caldwell, 2010).

For more than two decades, researchers have found that effective interventions with individuals who have exhibited externalizing, law-violating behaviors—including youth who have engaged in sexually abusive conduct—adhere to the evidence-based principles of risk, need, and responsivity (RNR; Andrews & Bonta, 2006; Hanson, Bourgon,

Helmus, & Hodgson, 2009). According to these principles, more intensive services are provided to those who present with the most risk (risk), interventions target factors that are directly related to risk for offending behavior (need), and interventions are evidence-based and delivered in ways that are sensitive and responsive to the individual's learning style, cognitive or developmental challenges, psychological characteristics, and motivation to change as well as his or her relevant cultural, gender, and other factors that affect the individual's—and family's—ability to positively engage in and respond to interventions (responsivity). In children and adolescents who have engaged in abusive sexual behaviors, developmental disabilities can certainly be considered responsivity factors, because features of these conditions—including deficits in cognitive functioning, learning problems, communication and relational difficulties, and emotional dysregulation—can and do impact significantly on the individual youth's responsiveness to intervention (Rothman & MacKenzie, 2015).

CHARACTERISTICS OF DEVELOPMENTAL DISABILITIES

Developmental disabilities are a group of disorders characterized by an impairment in physical, learning, language, or behavior areas. These conditions begin in utero or in early childhood, often impact day-to-day functioning, and usually last throughout a person's lifetime. Developmental disabilities occur among all racial, ethnic, and socio-economic groups. Recent estimates in the United States show that about 15 percent of children aged 3 through 17 years have one or more developmental disabilities (Centers for Disease Control and Prevention, 2015a). Some of the most common forms of developmental disabilities are described briefly, below.

- *Intellectual Disability (ID),* previously known as mental retardation, describes a combination of deficits affecting general mental abilities (such as reasoning, problem solving, planning, abstract thinking, judgment, academic learning, and learning by experience) as well as adaptive functioning (such as communication, social participation, and independent living abilities) across multiple environments including home, school, work, and community settings (APA, 2013; World Health Organization, 2006). Approximately 1 percent of the general population is affected by intellectual disability, although prevalence rates vary depending on age and severity, with the lowest prevalence rates (approximately 6 per 1,000) pertaining to the most severely affected individuals (APA, 2013).

- *Attention Deficit Hyperactivity Disorder (ADHD)* is a persistent pattern of inattention and/or hyperactivity and impulsivity that interferes with a broad range of functioning. In most cultures ADHD occurs in approximately 5 percent of children and 2.5 percent of adults (APA, 2013; World Health Organization, 2006).

- *Autism Spectrum Disorder (ASD)* is characterized by persistent impairment in social communication and interaction as well as restricted, repetitive patterns of behavior, interests, and activities. Affected individuals may or may not also experience intellectual impairment. Children on the autism spectrum tend to have particular difficulty reading the subtle behavioral cues of others (including reading others' facial expressions and body language) and understanding the unwritten rules of social conduct, such as how to play with or converse interactively with someone, how to make appropriate eye contact when conversing, and the appropriate levels of personal space and boundaries inherent to different kinds of relationships. They can also be especially sensitive to sensory stimulation, resulting in unusual reactions to the way things sound, look, taste, or feel. Youth with ASDs frequently have an inflexible adherence to specific routines, tend to become preoccupied with a narrow range of interests, do not tolerate unexpected changes well, and have a tendency to interpret things very literally (Rothman, 2012). The prevalence of ASDs in the general population is approximately 1 percent and is about the same for children and adults, but with great variability in clinical presentations in terms of severity, pervasiveness, and onset (APA, 2013; Lord, Cook, Leventhal, & Amarai, 2000; World Health Organization, 2006).

- *Fetal Alcohol Spectrum Disorders (FASDs)* describe a range of disabilities that can occur in individuals exposed to maternal alcohol use during pregnancy. The effects, including alcohol-related birth defects, can vary from mild to severe and may include a range of physical, brain, and central nervous system disabilities as well as cognitive, behavioral, and emotional problems. These can include deficits in overall intellectual functioning, memory, attention, learning, language, reasoning, and judgment, as well as hyperactivity and impulsivity (Centers for Disease Control and Prevention, 2015b). Specific conditions within this spectrum include fetal alcohol syndrome (FAS) and alcohol-related neurodevelopmental disorder (ARND). The prevalence of FASDs is estimated at 2 to 5 percent in school-aged children in the United States and Western Europe (Centers for Disease Control and Prevention, 2015b).

- *Learning Disorders* describe persistent, substantial (well below age-average) difficulties mastering key academic skills associated with reading, writing, and mathematics. They are specific in nature (an individual can be affected by a disorder in one area of academic functioning and unaffected in others), and are not attributable to a more global intellectual disability (that is, an individual can function overall in the average range or above but have a specific learning disorder affecting her or his functioning in a specific area). The prevalence of learning disorders in school-aged children across the academic domains of reading, writing, and mathematics is 5 to 15 percent (APA, 2013).

Although not always discussed as often as some of the other features of developmental disabilities, affected youth also frequently experience problems with emotional regulation (Asscher, van der Put, & Stams, 2012; Laurent & Rubin, 2004). Emotional regulation refers to the key developmental capacity that underlies one's ability to manage emotional arousal, enabling one to effectively adapt to the physical and social demands of the environment and accomplish one's goals (Fox, 1994). The development of emotional regulation abilities has a significant impact on a child's ability to engage in mutually satisfying relationships, engage in extended interactions, cope with new and changing situations, and participate in group social activities and is considered essential for the optimal development of social-emotional and communication skills (Laurent & Rubin, 2004). Successfully managing one's emotions requires the ability to tolerate a range of sensory and social experiences, self-monitor emotional responses to different situations, express emotional states in socially appropriate ways, and ask others for assistance in a conventional manner (Prizant, Wetherby, Rubin, & Laurent, 2003). Disabilities in these areas often cause problems in social interaction that, in themselves, impact on emotional development and behavior, leading to an increased probability of emotional outbursts, anxiety, mood problems, oppositionality, aggression, conduct problems, social rejection, and social withdrawal (Novaco & Taylor, 2004; Semrud-Clikeman, Walkowiak, Wilkinson, & Portman, 2010).

Many developmental disorders tend to cluster together, and developmentally disabled youth often have complex combinations of mental health or behavioral problems (Gralton, 2013; Sverd, 2003). Clinicians may be prone to under-recognize comorbid mental illness in developmentally disabled young people and tend to attribute symptoms of mental health problems to either cognitive impairment alone (Mason & Scior, 2004) and/or willful conduct problems. Given how quickly and dramatically adolescents can change as they progress through normative developmental processes, it has long been recognized that diagnosis of mental health problems in youth is a challenging process requiring follow-up over long periods of time (Friedlander & Donnelly, 2004), and these challenges are heightened in adolescents with developmental disabilities (Gralton, 2013).

There is evidence that youth with developmental disabilities are at significantly higher risk of being victims of sexual and physical abuse than their non-disabled peers (Koller, 2000; Mandell, Walrath, Manteuffel, Sgro, & Pinto-Martin, 2005; Sullivan & Knutson, 2000). Studies indicate that intellectually disabled individuals, in particular, have a 4 to 10 times greater risk of being sexually abused than the neurotypical population (Denno, 1997; Morano, 2001), with a lifetime prevalence rate of exposure to sexual abuse of 25 to 53 percent for individuals with intellectual disabilities (Horner-Johnson & Drum, 2006). Features that are common among youth with developmental disabilities—such as social and communication deficits, lack of exposure to appropriate peer interactions, lifelong dependence on adults for their care, and inadequate self-protection skills—may indeed leave them especially vulnerable to sexual exploitation (Murphy & O'Callaghan, 2004; Rothman, 2012; Stromsness, 1994). Although little is known about the effects of sexual abuse on youth with developmental disabilities, the fact that this population as a whole has a higher likelihood of exposure to abuse than their neurotypical peer group makes it likely that they would be at greater risk for developmental trauma.

SEXUALITY AND DEVELOPMENTAL DISABILITIES

There has been limited research attention to the sexuality of individuals with developmental disabilities. However, caregivers often report sexual behavior problems in affected youth (Nichols & Blakeley-Smith, 2009; Ruble & Dalrymple, 1993; Stokes & Kaur, 2005), and clinicians with expertise in the developmental field are often asked by institutions and parents to give advice on sexual behavior and sexual problems (Hellemans, Colson, Verbraeken, Vermeiren, & Deboutte, 2007; Sullivan & Caterino, 2008). Nonetheless, public perception of the sexuality of individuals with developmental disabilities has been found to be largely negative (viewing sexual behavior among these populations as abnormal) and, according to current facts, largely inaccurate (Sullivan & Caterino, 2008).

There has been a historical tendency to view people with developmental disabilities as somehow unaffected by sexuality or not capable of sexual intimacy, and there has therefore been a trend toward promoting abstinence among the developmentally disabled (Gill, 2010; Sullivan & Caterino, 2008). More recently, however, it has been increasingly recognized that adolescents who are developmentally disabled have similar needs and desires as their non-disabled peers, often engage in sexual behaviors, and often desire intimate relations with others (Gill, 2010; Hellemans et al., 2007; Ray et al., 2004; Sullivan & Caterino, 2008). Adolescents with developmental disabilities generally undergo normal physical development and progress through the same developmental stages as typical teens, but the emotional changes and increasing sexual urges that go along with adolescence may be delayed or prolonged (Blasingame, 2005; Bolton, 2004; Ray, Marks, & Bray-Garretson, 2004; Sullivan & Caterino, 2008). Additionally, as with typical youth, adolescents with developmental disabilities do not progress through social-emotional stages evenly. And the social deficits in many youth and young adults with developmental disabilities (particularly those on the autism spectrum) often make it difficult for them to achieve appropriate, intimate interpersonal relations, frequently leading to frustration (Hellemans et al., 2007; Henault, 2006; Stokes & Kaur, 2005).

There have been no large-scale studies examining sexual behaviors in adolescents with developmental disabilities. The current literature has largely been limited to small samples and a focus on institutionalized populations (e.g., Gralton, 2013; Haracopos & Pedersen, 1992; Hellemans et al., 2007; van Bourgondien, Reichle, & Palmer, 1997). Additionally, these studies have looked at individuals with a wide range of developmental disabilities, which makes it difficult to distinguish between the effects of different conditions and intellectual capacities. Nonetheless, existing studies on sexuality and developmental disabilities demonstrate that affected individuals display a wide range of sexual behaviors, from masturbation (consistently the most frequently reported sexual behavior) to person-oriented sexual activities including sexually intended touching, caressing, kissing, and, more rarely, intercourse. Gender identity confusion and homosexuality have also been reported in the literature among children, adolescents, and adults with disabilities (Haracopos & Pedersen, 1992; Hellemans et al., 2007; Ray et al., 2004).

DEVELOPMENTAL DISABILITIES AND SEXUAL BEHAVIOR PROBLEMS

Caregivers of children and adolescents with developmental disabilities often express concerns about the youth's sexual conduct and report high rates of inappropriate sexual behaviors (Ballan, 2012; Banks, 2014; Hellemans et al., 2007; Hubert, Flynn, Nicholls, & Hollins, 2007; Nichols & Blakeley-Smith, 2009; Stokes & Kaur, 2005). These behaviors can impact negatively on the youth's social functioning, causing them to be ostracized, and sometimes threaten to jeopardize their placements in the least restrictive environments (Hubert et al., 2007; Sullivan & Caterino, 2008). The most frequent of these behaviors include: touching one's own genitals in public, public masturbation, inappropriately candid sex talk, removing one's own clothing in public, initiation of unwanted physical contact, and sexual behaviors directed toward strangers or other inappropriate people such as caregivers or service providers. Other reported concerns revolve around paraphilic sexual interests (fetishes) and masturbation that is self-injurious, compulsive, or unusual (for example, peculiar masturbation techniques or a repeated use of objects). Furthermore, many parents express unease that others will interpret their children's normative behaviors as sexually deviant (Ballan, 2012; Hubert et al., 2007; Nichols & Blakeley-Smith, 2009; Ruble & Dalrymple, 1993).

Published case histories suggest that most problematic behaviors lie at the minor end of the offending continuum (Barry-Walsh & Mullen, 2004; Miccio-Fonseca & Rasmussen, 2013), although the literature also details more serious problematic and illegal sexual behaviors among developmentally disabled populations, including voyeurism, child pornography viewing, frottage, stalking, sexual assault, and sexual homicide (Barry-Walsh & Mullen, 2004; Miccio-Fonseca & Rasmussen, 2013; Ray et al., 2004; Realmuto & Ruble, 1999; Silva, Ferrari, & Leong, 2002; Stokes & Kaur, 2005). Research suggests that youth with developmental disabilities are at higher risk for engaging in criminal offending than their neurotypical peers (Quinn, Rutherford, Leone, Osher, & Poirer, 2005). Adolescents with developmental disabilities who are involved in the justice system have also been found to be more aggressive and violent than their neurotypical, juvenile-justice-involved peers (Asscher et al., 2012; Banks, 2014), and high rates of aggression have been reported among some developmentally disabled youth who have offended sexually (Asscher et al., 2012). There is also compelling evidence to suggest that adolescents with developmental disabilities are overrepresented among youth who have engaged in abusive sexual behavior (Banks, 2014; 't Hart-Kerkhoffs et al., 2009; Hellemans et al., 2007; van der Put, Asscher, Wissink, & Stams, 2014; Wissink, van Vugt, Moonen, Stams, & Hendriks, 2015).

Indeed, youth with developmental disabilities have a number of characteristics that may place them at greater risk for problematic behavior—including sexually harmful behavior—than their neurotypical peer group. First, it has been noted that youth with developmental disabilities may be especially vulnerable to peer pressure to engage in delinquent behaviors (Douma, Dekker, de Ruiter, Tick, & Koot, 2007). Second, this population is known to exhibit significant problems with emotion regulation and impulse control, goal setting, problem solving, perceiving situations accurately, interpreting subtle social cues, maintaining appropriate personal boundaries, and social judgment (Asscher et al., 2012; van der Put et al., 2014). Youth with autism, in particular, are vulnerable to developing sexual preoccupations, and those preoccupations can become especially intractable if the youth lack distress tolerance abilities and rely on their sexual preoccupations to meet various other needs such as tension reduction, affiliation, and belongingness (Rothman, 2012; Rothman & MacKenzie, 2015).

These characteristics can sometimes lead to problems distinguishing between public and private behaviors as well as desired and undesired sexual contact (Ballan, 2012; Ray et al., 2004; Sullivan & Caterino, 2008). And when social impairments result in a tendency to misperceive others' intentions, youth with developmental disabilities may at times engage in inappropriate or intrusive courtship behaviors in an attempt to develop interpersonal relationships (Stokes & Newton, 2004). Combined with a desire for relationships; a lack of the necessary social skills to initiate and maintain fulfilling, appropriate friendships; and a lack of alternative outlets for sexual tension, these characteristics can lead some youth with developmental disabilities to engage in abusive sexual behavior (Allen et al., 2008; Hellemans et al., 2007; Stokes & Kaur, 2005; Realmuto & Ruble, 1999; Rothman, 2012; Rothman & MacKenzie, 2015; van Wijk et al., 2005).

It is important to note that most authorities assert that only a minority of youth with developmental disabilities engage in sexual or violent offending or otherwise illegal behavior (Ghaziuddin, Tsai, & Ghazuiddin, 1991; Murrie, Warren, Kristiansson, & Dietz, 2002; Wing, 1997; Woodbury-Smith, Clare, Holland, & Kearns, 2006). It therefore seems likely that the association between developmental disabilities and sexually abusive behaviors is mitigated by other contextual variables. It has been suggested, for example, that youth with developmental disabilities may be vulnerable to developing delinquent behaviors such as sexual behavior problems only when other factors such as adverse family conditions are present (Kumagami & Matsuura, 2009; Asscher et al., 2012; Vermeiren, Jespers, & Moffitt, 2006). And given that some individuals with developmental disabilities seem to be at risk for a wide range of psychiatric disorders (Sverd, 2003), it may be that comorbid psychopathology strengthens the association between developmental disabilities and offending behavior in some individuals (Newman & Ghaziuddin, 2008; Vermeiren et al., 2006). Certainly, there is great variability in the presentation of the conditions in different people. It therefore seems probable that the interaction between developmental disabilities and sexual offending behavior is idiosyncratic, and that the path from one to the other is quite distinct from individual to individual and situation to situation. This has significant implications on interventions for affected youth.

INTERVENTIONS

Over the past 20 years, the field of intervention for youth who have engaged in abusive sexual behavior has been largely shaped by treatment models originally designed for adults who had offended sexually, extended downward to younger populations (Chaffin, 2008; Letourneau & Borduin, 2008). These sex-offense-specific models continue to predominate in North American treatment programs for sexually abusive youth, the vast majority of which use a cognitive-behavioral, relapse prevention framework, with treatment focusing on individual-level risk factors such as: detailed disclosures of sexual offending behavior; addressing presumed atypical sexual interests and arousal (that is, sexual interests involving prepubescent children or violence); addressing the youth's own sexual victimization; changing attitudes, beliefs, and cognitions about sexual behavior; enhancing victim empathy; and self-monitoring, vigilance, and avoidance of situations deemed to be high-risk. The majority continue to utilize interventions such as sexual arousal reconditioning procedures that sometimes rely upon aversive conditioning (for example, where an individual is exposed to an aversive stimulus such as a noxious smell while simultaneously being exposed to an inappropriate sexual stimulus such as a sexualized photograph of a child) (Hanson, 2014; McGrath, Cumming, Burchard, Zeoli, & Ellerby, 2010). While some of these treatment targets and methods have been subsequently supported through research with adolescent populations, there has been a historical overfocus on these elements with youth and an unfortunate reliance on a one-size-fits-all approach to intervention (Rothman & Letourneau, 2013). And it has yet to be widely recognized that only a minority of such youth actually demonstrate atypical sexual interests or patterns of arousal (Chaffin, 2008; Worling, 2013).

Despite the predominance of these cognitive-behavioral therapy models, the current research evidence to support their use with sexually abusive youth is not especially strong, particularly when the interventions focus mainly on the youth's individual-level risk factors without also involving caregivers and other responsible adults and systems from the youth's ecology (Dopp, Borduin, & Brown, 2015; Dopp, Borduin, Rothman, & Letourneau, in press; Letourneau & Borduin, 2008; Reitzel & Carbonell, 2006; St. Amand, Bard, & Silovsky, 2008). In contrast, there has been increasing recognition over the past few years that the most successful interventions for youth who exhibit criminal sexual behaviors include high levels of caregiver involvement and are individualized to match each youth's dynamic strengths and needs (ATSA, 2012; Przybylski, 2014; Rothman & Letourneau, 2013). While some empirically supported intervention models for sexually abusive youth certainly contain behavioral and/or cognitive-behavioral elements—such as multisystemic therapy (Borduin, Schaeffer, & Heiblum, 2009; Letourneau et al., 2009) and the SAFE-T program (Worling et al., 2010)—these models also have a strong, family/caregiver-inclusive focus. Similarly, although research indicates that effective interventions for youth with general (but not necessarily sexual) delinquency problems often include cognitive-behavioral components that focus on skill building to enhance self-regulation and prosocial decision making (Lipsey, 2009; Lipsey, Howell, Kelly, Chapman, & Carver, 2010), those same studies indicate that family-focused intervention models also tend to produce considerable reductions in general recidivism.

Indeed, research indicates that effective interventions for adolescents who have engaged in abusive sexual behavior involve caregivers and other responsible adults and systems in the youth's life; occur in the youth's natural environment when possible in order to allow youth and their caregivers to practice skills and make use of social supports in real-life situations; address risk and protective factors across the youth's natural environments (such as family, peers, and school); promote safety while at the same time facilitating prosocial, healthy development; customize methods to match the individual youth's characteristics and circumstances (such as age, learning style, gender, and culture); focus on relevant dynamic (changeable) risk factors; and use evidence-based interventions that match presenting risk and needs (ATSA, 2012; Dopp et al., in press; Leversee & Powell, 2012; Letourneau & Borduin, 2008; Przybylski, 2014). And given the substantial overlap between youth who have engaged in abusive sexual conduct and those who have engaged in non-sexual aggression and/or other antisocial behaviors, clinicians are advised to be prepared to address not just sexual behavior concerns but other types of offending behavior as well (ATSA, 2012). Fortunately, current research indicates that a combination of (a) family-focused interventions (including family therapy and parent training) and (b) skill-building approaches (including such things as: cognitive-behavioral techniques to enhance self-regulation and prosocial decision making; social skills training; and academic and vocational skill building) hold promise for both sexually abusive and generally delinquent youthful populations.

In keeping with this, treatment services for sexually abusive youth are best offered and provided along a continuum of care from community-based interventions to secure residential or correctional treatment programs. That is, the level of intervention provided should match the individual youth's current treatment and supervision needs, which, depending largely on the youth's ongoing development and his or her family circumstances, may change over time (ATSA, 2006; 2012; Hunter & Longo, 2004). Mindful of the overall low rates of recidivism for youth who have engaged in abusive sexual behavior, there is consensus among experts in the field that most youth can be safely treated in community-based settings and that residential and custodial settings should be reserved for the minority of youth who present with a high risk of recidivism or other treatment needs that cannot be met in community settings (ATSA, 2006; 2012; Borduin et al., 2009; Hunter & Longo, 2004).

Similar to neurotypical youth who have engaged in sexually harmful behavior, the subpopulation of youth with developmental disabilities who have offended sexually is a vastly diverse group of individuals. As such, it is critical that clinicians appreciate the uniqueness of each individual when designing and implementing interventions (Blasingame, 2011). Unfortunately, treatment programs for developmentally disabled, sexually abusive youth have largely reflected the same shortcomings as those for their neurotypical peers. These programs have, for the most part, been modified from adult mainstream programs, often by basically simplifying the concepts using visual imagery or other tools borrowed from the disability field (West & Ayland, 2010). Treatment programs for this population have been even slower to develop than mainstream programs, and few have been supported empirically (Craig & Hutchinson, 2005; Lindsay, 2002).

Interventions with developmentally disabled youth need to be thoughtful, individualized, consistent (across settings, situations, and caregivers), and guided by a thorough assessment of each adolescent and the behaviors of concern. Given the overlap between sexual and non-sexual delinquency among youth and the high rates of aggression among some youth with developmental disabilities who have offended sexually, clinicians should be prepared to address both sexual and non-sexual conduct problems, as needed. Interventions should be designed with particular attention to the strengths and liabilities of the individual client, otherwise known as responsivity factors, or variables that enhance or detract from the individual's responsiveness to intervention (Andrews & Bonta, 2006). For youth with developmental disabilities, particularly important responsivity factors include cognitive functioning, learning style, and family functioning (Blasingame, Creeden, & Rich, 2015; Rothman & MacKenzie, 2015; van der Put et al., 2014). In some instances, disruptive behavior can actually be generated by a mismatch between behavioral expectations and the cognitive ability of the individual (for example, when a diagnosis of intellectual disability has not been recognized or otherwise rejected by the child's family). In these situations, an adjustment of expectations would be the most appropriate intervention (Myers & Plauché Johnson, 2007).

Matching Interventions to Cognitive Abilities

Interventions should be geared to the client's strengths, especially with respect to cognitive functioning and styles of learning, as these responsivity factors have significant implications on how interventions should be specifically adapted for each individual. With regard to cognitive abilities, clinicians ought to thoroughly consider the results of intellectual and speech-language testing in order to determine a youth's language abilities and cognitive strengths and weaknesses. A youth's verbal comprehension abilities should be considered to help determine the degree to which verbally based interventions are implemented, the level of vocabulary used, and the adolescent's comprehension of complex concepts and metaphors. A youth's perceptual (nonverbal) reasoning abilities can help a clinician establish the extent to which she or he will benefit from the use of visual and hands-on tools such charts, diagrams, and models, and her or his preference to actively learn by doing. An adolescent's working memory capacity can help clarify how much information can be presented at a time, how long a young client can work before requiring a break, and how often information or concepts might need to be repeated, reviewed, and practiced in order to integrate new information or skills (although frequent, active practice of newly acquired skills is generally recommended, regardless). A youth's processing speed abilities can assist in determining how much time she or he should be provided in order to make sense of information.

Matching Interventions to Learning Style

Due to the diversity of learning styles among these youth, interventions should be delivered in an active, experiential, multi-modal, and multi-sensory manner. This involves the integration of not only auditory stimuli (as in traditional "talk therapy") but also visual components (for example, drawing pictures, writing down concepts, showing video clips), tactile stimuli (for example, using squeeze balls and Play-Doh), movement (for example, role playing skills or talking while walking together or shooting baskets), tactile components (such as playing with Play-Doh or squeezing a stress ball while talking about difficult material); taste stimuli (for example, feeding youth snacks while working on treatment topics), and smell stimuli (for example, having potpourri or scented markers in the learning environment) (Leversee & Powell, 2012). In order for interventions to have a maximal positive outcome, concepts and skills need to be understood, retained, and integrated into the youth's everyday life, and an active, multi-sensory, experiential approach increases the chances that treatment material or concepts will match the individual learning style of each youth and become personally meaningful to that child (Leversee & Powell, 2012).

Because some youth with developmental disabilities may have working memory impairments and/or limited attention spans, and youth with autism, in particular, tend to more readily perceive parts or pieces of things rather than the gestalt, it may be helpful to use a parts-to-whole approach in teaching skills, where smaller and simpler steps are first introduced and later linked when adequate learning is demonstrated (Rothman, 2012; Rothman & MacKenzie, 2015). In these cases, skills and concepts should be taught explicitly and in a repetitious, rote fashion, where the individual steps are taught in the correct sequence for the behavior to be effective (Klin & Volkmar,

2000). Given that some youth with developmental disabilities also tend to perceive the world very rigidly and concretely, it may be helpful to emphasize structure, order, and routines and encourage clients to classify, label, and make lists to facilitate learning and comprehension (Latham, 2009; Vermeulen, 2008). And because strong emotions can be inherently confusing and distressing to adolescents with intellectual disabilities as well as many youth on the autism spectrum, it is further recommended that "feeling talk" be restricted or else made more concrete through the use of the above-recommended procedures (Vermeulen, 2008).

Using Social Stories

Social stories are another commonly used and effective teaching tool for individuals with autism spectrum disorders and take advantage of the visual learning strengths that are often found in youth with autism. There is good reason to believe they may be helpful for some youth with other forms of developmental disabilities as well, particularly where there are general cognitive or specific verbal limitations (see Rothman & MacKenzie, 2015, for a detailed review of the use of social stories in the treatment of youth with autism who have sexual behavior problems). Social stories are short stories used to help children "read" and understand social situations (Gray & Garand, 1993). They are written from the child's perspective and usually describe, in a very concrete fashion, a particular situation or idea that the youth finds challenging and teaches a social skill relevant to that situation (Gray, 2000). In some versions of social stories, each sentence is pictorially illustrated (in the form of a drawing or photograph), much as in a comic book. It has been suggested that visually cued instruction plays to the learning strengths of youth with autism, in that their ability to sustain attention to the pictographic stimuli enhances their attention to and encoding of the message (Quill, 1997). It has also been suggested that a visually supplemented social story enhances the concreteness and meaningfulness of the desired social behavior, further improving a youth's comprehension (Graetz, Mastropieri, & Scruggs, 2009). Although social stories have been proposed as a promising intervention for teaching sociosexual skills to youth with developmental disabilities, future research is required to examine their efficacy in this regard, particularly with youth presenting with especially compromised intellectual and verbal skills. It has also been observed that social stories may not be effective when used in isolation rather than as part of a comprehensive set of interventions (Hanley-Hochdorfer, Bray, Kehle, & Elinoff, 2010).

Intervention Format

Given the special responsivity factors discussed above, traditional cognitive-behavioral therapy (CBT) is unlikely to be effective in isolation and without significant modifications—

as discussed above—to suit developmentally disabled youth (Bolton, 2006; see Haaven & Coleman, 2000, and West & Ayland, 2010, for descriptions of some of these modifications for adults and youth with intellectual and learning disabilities who have offended sexually). It remains an empirical question whether youth with developmental disabilities, as distinct populations, would be better suited for individual or group-based treatments. However, in the absence of empirical guidance, anecdotal information currently suggests that for some youth, developmental disabilities—perhaps most particularly those on the autism spectrum—social and communication deficits, relational difficulties (often with accompanying social anxiety), cognitive inflexibility, sensory sensitivities, idiosyncratic responses, and emotional and behavioral dysregulation can make it especially difficult to tolerate being in a group. This may limit the benefits of group-based treatment, at least for more highly disturbed or disruptive youth. Individually tailored interventions, customized for the youth and his or her family or care providers, are therefore recommended over group-based ones, although skills-based group treatment might be considered as an adjunct to individual/family treatment once impediments to group participation are adequately addressed.

Caregivers and Other Supports: Primary Agents of Change

The literature on children and adolescents who have engaged in abusive sexual behavior indicates that caregiver involvement in treatment is a primary factor in treatment success (Borduin et al., 2009; Dopp et al., in press; Letourneau & Borduin, 2008; Reitzel & Carbonell, 2006; St. Amand et al., 2008; Worling et al., 2010). This likely applies especially to youth with developmental disabilities who engage in these behaviors. It is clear that the vulnerability and special needs of youth with developmental disabilities lend to an even greater dependence on external structures and supports than that required by their neurotypical peers, and that they are therefore more likely to be affected by a variety of environmental influences and systems. Depending on their age and level of impairment, youth with developmental disabilities may rely on parents or other family members, community support workers, teachers, paraprofessionals, or residential care staff to assist them in different aspects of everyday functioning. When sexual behavior problems occur, the behaviors are most often noticed or experienced by family members and care providers (Hellemans et al., 2007). Certainly, parental monitoring and supervision is well established as a primary protective factor for many kinds of antisocial conduct in adolescents (Klein, Rettenberger, Yoon, Köhler, & Briken, 2015; Spice, Viljoen, Latzman, Scalora, & Ullman, 2012; Worling & Langton, 2015). Interventions with youth—especially those addressing sexuality issues—need to be sensitive to the comfort level and value systems of the youth's families or care providers. It follows, then, that effective treatment of sexual behavior problems in developmentally disabled youth requires strong collaboration with caregivers, other responsible adults, and relevant systems in the youth's ecology, such as community support workers, teachers, child welfare workers, and criminal justice personnel.

Indeed, one critical role of clinicians is to support the adults tasked with the primary care responsibilities for these youth. Caregivers, teachers, paraprofessionals, residential staff, and community support workers bear the bulk of these responsibilities and collectively spend far more time with these adolescents than any clinician; they are naturally positioned to be the youth's primary agents of change. For adolescents who have developmental disabilities, interventions might consist largely of environmental modifications and behavioral interventions implemented in the youth's natural environments by caregivers (Rothman & Mackenzie, 2015), along with education in healthy sexuality. However, many caregivers, teachers, and support staff are unaccustomed to, uncomfortable with, and untrained in how to address sexuality issues with individuals with developmental disabilities (Ballan, 2012; Meister, Norlock, Honeyman, & Pierce, 1994; Nichols & Blakeley-Smith, 2009; van Bourgondien et al., 1997). One of the roles of clinicians is to ensure that the personnel who are primarily responsible for the youth's care are sufficiently informed about their clients' behavior problems, treatment goals, and treatment needs and that they are supported in using an active, experiential, multi-modal, and multi-sensory approach in their work, rather than relying on traditional types of instruction (Blasingame et al., 2015). To this end, in order to facilitate the strategic, complementary, and consistent targeting of risk factors and needs across the youth's social ecology, clinicians need to engage caregivers in treatment, maintaining regular communication with them and other supports and systems via telephone, by electronic communication, and through their participation in treatment sessions and attendance at regular team meetings.

An important advantage held by caregivers, teachers, paraprofessionals, and community support workers is the ability to intervene quickly and in the moment when the problematic behavior occurs. Research indicates that learning that takes place in natural settings enhances social skill development in youth with developmental disabilities such as autism (Bellini, Peters, Benner, & Hopf, 2007). However, care providers and other supports often need guidance on how to accurately interpret the youth's behavior and how to respond most helpfully and in a way that is consistent with the overall goals of treatment. For example, personnel accustomed to working with neurotypical sexually abusive youth often misinterpret a developmentally disabled youth's reactions to stress—for example, becoming especially rigid or concrete—as the "power and control" issues that conventional wisdom often characterizes as underlying sexual and/or physical aggression. However, by reframing the issue as a response to distress, the clinician can assist supports in intervening much more effectively, because youth with developmental disabilities, such as those with autism, can be especially persistent in power struggles over seemingly trivial issues (Ray et al., 2004).

It is also crucial that caregivers and other support personnel be provided with guidance on how to adequately supervise and monitor the youth in their care, balancing an attention to safety with a developmentally appropriate level of independence that allows for normative developmental experiences, whenever possible, as involvement in age-appropriate, prosocial activities is a protective factor with respect to a youth's risk for engaging in sexually abusive conduct (ATSA, 2012). Responsible adults should also ensure that the expectations of these youth remain suitable to their developmental level, with particular cautions when it comes to such things as placing them in caretaker roles with younger siblings or other younger or vulnerable children (Rothman & Letourneau, 2013). Caregivers and supports should also be taught strategies for maintaining appropriate interpersonal boundaries, because many youth with developmental disabilities are especially vulnerable to misinterpreting social interactions and failing to distinguish between different levels of intimacy (Rothman, 2012). And given the primary importance of caregivers in providing intervention—and the high levels of energy and stress involved in these tasks—it is recommended that treatment providers advocate for caregivers, where appropriate, for adequate respite, remuneration, and support.

Education in Healthy Sexuality

Most teenagers learn about appropriate behavior, including sexual behavior, through informal learning that takes place within typically developing peer groups. Adolescents with developmental disabilities frequently lack these experiences because of their social and communication deficits (Sullivan & Caterino, 2008) and tend to have less knowledge about sex and sexuality than their neurotypical peers (Nichols & Blakeley-Smith, 2009; Stokes & Kaur, 2005). Social skills instruction, particularly as it relates to sexuality and sexual behavior, is therefore another essential ingredient to intervention with youth with developmental disabilities who have offended sexually. Despite this, sexuality development and education for youth with these disabilities has received little attention in the scientific literature (Doughty & Kane, 2010; Hénault, 2004; 2006; Koller, 2000). This is especially concerning given that such youth may have difficulty interpreting the thoughts, feelings, intentions, and behavior of others or recognizing potentially risky situations, thereby increasing their potential for involvement in inappropriate or abusive sexual conduct as well as their risk of exploitation (Nichols & Blakeley-Smith, 2009). As discussed above, high rates of sexual victimization have been reported for youth with developmental disabilities (Mandell et al., 2005; Sullivan & Knutson, 2000).

Sexual arousal patterns in adolescence have been observed to be quite fluid and dynamic (Bancroft, 2006), and therefore there is good reason to expect that—at least for some adolescents—healthy, non-deviant interests can be strengthened if the youth see the possibility of forming healthy emotionally and sexually intimate relationships in their future (Worling, 2012). It is already known that most youth who have engaged in abusive sexual behavior with younger children are mainly interested in consensual activities with age-appropriate partners (Worling, 2013). Strategies that seek to build on these interests by removing obstacles to sexual health would therefore have potential for modifying sexual interests in those adolescents who present with atypical sexual interests. Consistent with what is known about risk factors for sexual offending among adolescents, some teens with sexual interests in younger children present with unhealthy attitudes about sex and sexuality, dysfunctional beliefs about intimate relationships, social anxiety and interpersonal skill deficits, and/or problems with self-regulation. Each of these factors—especially relevant to developmentally disabled youth—creates real barriers to successfully navigating the complexities of forming healthy, prosocial peer relationships. By strengthening a youth's capacity for healthy relationships, treatment approaches that target these liabilities, if present, can support adolescents in adjusting their developmental trajectories in the direction of sexual, emotional, and behavioral well-being.

For some youth who have engaged in abusive sexual behaviors, comprehensive and properly delivered sexuality education (including education about rules and laws governing sexual behavior) may be sufficient, in and of itself, to address their risk for future sexual behavior problems. At a minimum, properly delivered education in healthy sexuality should be a key component of any intervention effort for developmentally disabled adolescents who have engaged in sexually harmful conduct. A comprehensive approach to the sexuality education of youth with developmental disabilities would encompass the following topics: body parts and function, physical maturation, personal hygiene and self-care, sexual arousal, concepts of privacy, distinguishing between different types of relationships/levels of intimacy, learning about appropriate expression of affection, public and private behaviors appropriate for various relationships, safe and appropriate masturbation practices, tension release activities, sexual identity, abuse prevention, assertiveness, and attraction (Hénault, 2006; Koller, 2000; Shea & Mesibov, 2005; Sullivan & Caterino, 2008; Tissot, 2009; Tullis & Zangrillo, 2013). The curriculum of this instruction should, of course, be customized to meet the particular needs, responsivity issues (especially cognitive abilities, learning style, and developmental level), and realities (such as family culture) of the individual clients. Depending on the individual's level of cognitive and psychosocial development, it may only be necessary to cover basic topics (such as body parts, self-care, and personal hygiene), and the appropriate age to begin sexual education training may be different for each youth (Sullivan & Caterino, 2008). It is especially important to address the subtle, often implicit, rules and social values that govern sexual behavior by explicitly teaching them (Nichols & Blakeley-Smith, 2009; Sullivan & Caterino, 2008). For example, concepts related to sexuality (e.g., where to be naked) should not be taught in isolation from their social context (e.g., *why* you can be naked in some places and not others) (Nichols & Blakeley-Smith, 2009).

A number of sexuality education formats have been developed for individuals with developmental disabilities including autism spectrum disorders (see Sullivan & Caterino, 2008, and Tullis & Zangrillo, 2013, for descriptions of some of these programs). Clinicians should advocate for developmentally suitable adaptations to curricula for their clients, or become involved in these adaptations, where appropriate. Although sexuality education may be provided through schools, the person who actually delivers the instruction needs to be determined on the basis of the needs of the child, his or her family, and the setting. The range of candidates includes parents, special education teachers, therapists, psychologists, paraprofessionals, or other support staff members (Sullivan & Caterino, 2008). Service providers should be informed and trained so that they can adequately address the needs of these individuals in a manner consistent with the values and beliefs of the family (Hénault, 2006; Sullivan & Caterino, 2008).

Because sexuality is embedded in one's social environment (such as friendships), it is also essential that sexuality education for youth with developmental disabilities have a strong social skills component (Nichols & Blakeley-Smith, 2009; Stokes & Kaur, 2005). Sexuality education and social skills training should not, therefore, be conceived as two distinct processes. There is some objective evidence to support traditional and newer naturalistic behavioral strategies and other approaches to teaching general social skills to individuals on the autism spectrum (Myers & Plauché Johnson, 2007). However, a meta-analytic review of social skills programs for youth on the autism spectrum found that existing programs have only been minimally successful, overall, especially with regard to assisting students in generalizing their skills (Bellini et al., 2007). The most successful programs had high levels of intensity (more than 30 hours of instruction over the course of 10 to 12 weeks), customized and matched programs to specific skill deficits, repeatedly practiced and reinforced desired skills, and taught skills in the environments in which they were to be used (Bellini et al., 2007). It has also been suggested that effective social skills programs teach specific problem-solving strategies for handling the most frequently occurring problematic situations, and that these skills are taught explicitly, without assuming that general explanations will suffice or that generalization will occur from one situation to another (Klin & Volkmar, 2000). Consistent with this, there is some evidence that sexuality education (particularly abuse prevention education) for individuals with intellectual disabilities generalizes best if there is an emphasis on behavioral skills training, where responses to a variety of specific situations are practiced repeatedly (Doughty & Kane, 2010). Sullivan and Caterino (2008) recommend that, given the absence of research on effective approaches to teaching sexuality-related topics with individuals who have developmental disabilities, educators and service providers should utilize approaches that have been shown to be effective in teaching skills in other domains.

As youth with developmental disabilities grow older, their communication and social deficits can further limit their opportunities for positive social interactions. Youth with these disabilities often experience social rejection as they mature and often experience secondary difficulties with mood, anxiety, and social withdrawal (Ozonoff & Rogers, 2003; Semrud-Clikeman, Walkowiak, Wilkinson, & Portman Minne, 2010). Despite the unfortunate likelihood that some of the characteristics of developmental disabilities will impede youth from forming conventional sexual relationships with others, it has nonetheless been argued that healthy sexuality for adolescents can be enhanced if youth are supported to *believe* in their capacity to form mutually rewarding, intimate relationships (Worling, 2012). It has also been suggested that by enhancing an individual's self-efficacy, one could assist that person to believe she or he could enjoy sexual satisfaction in a consensual relationship without fear of humiliation or rejection (Marshall, 1989, cited in Worling, 2012). This assertion was subsequently supported by a study indicating that a focused self-esteem/self-efficacy intervention was effective in reducing unhealthy sexual interests in adult males with sexual offending histories (Marshall, 1997). Therefore, in addition to building skills for future sexual health, another important goal of sexuality education for adolescents with developmental disabilities may be to identify and address any barriers to interpersonal intimacy, such as social anxiety and/or maladaptive beliefs regarding interpersonal relationships or the self (Worling, 2012).

Managing Sexualized Media

Parents should be cautious about the influence of sexualized media on the development of healthy adolescent sexuality, particularly given the fact that adolescents have been increasingly exposed to online sexualized imagery in recent years (Peter & Valkenburg, 2006). It has been observed that frequent viewing of these materials can have a harmful impact on sexual arousal (Moultrie, 2006), potentially shaping the development of adolescents' sexual knowledge, expectations, interests, and attitudes. Some adolescents—particularly youth on the autism spectrum—are especially vulnerable to developing preoccupations with sexuality by viewing sexualized materials online (Rothman & MacKenzie, 2015), and compulsive viewing of Internet pornography can result in Internet use becoming the primary way to meet both social and sexual needs (Rothman, 2012; Worling, 2012). The relative social insulation and immediate gratification that come with Internet use may be especially appealing to youth on the autism spectrum, and can lead to rapid development of sexual fixations or preoccupations (Ray et al., 2004).

This highlights two important points for intervention. First, it is crucial to work closely with caregivers to find ways to help adolescents limit their exposure to sexualized materials. And second, acknowledging the inevitability that adolescents are going to be exposed to sexualized media through multiple means (including the Internet, television, movies, music, advertisements, and video games), it is even more important to equip them with an understanding of how what they are viewing and/or listening to may not actually be representative of healthy or typical sexual relationships, behaviors, gender roles, or physical attributes (Worling, 2012).

Caregiver Roles in Supporting Healthy Sexuality

One factor that has been associated with reduced sexual risk among youth is communication between parents and their children about sexual health (Ballan, 2012). Parent–child communication about sex and sexuality has been identified as a protective mechanism for a number of sexual behaviors that often lead to negative health outcomes, including multiple sexual partners, lack of condom use, and lack of birth control use (Miller, Benson, & Galbraith, 2001). Researchers have found that, compared with a typically developing control group, adolescents with autism spectrum disorders obtained less sexual knowledge from their peers and the media; their primary sources of romantic knowledge were their parents and their own social observations (Stokes, Newton, & Kaur, 2007). At the same time, it has been observed that parents have very limited knowledge about how to teach their children about sexuality, and adolescents' social observations are frequently lacking in critical contextual information (Nichols & Blakeley-Smith, 2009).

Understandably, parents of youth with developmental disabilities may be uneasy about conversations related to sexuality or unsure how to respond to their child's emerging sexual interests, questions, and behaviors (Meister et al., 1994). This is probably especially the case if the child is engaging in sexually inappropriate behaviors (Nichols & Blakeley-Smith, 2009). Parents of youth with developmental disabilities have identified a number of concerns about sexuality education for their children, including a lack of confidence in the parents' own abilities to adequately communicate with their children about such topics, questions about their children's ability to comprehend the information, worries that their children may overgeneralize when information about sexuality is communicated (and result in sexual misunderstandings or misbehavior), unease that sexuality education could lead to perseveration or fixation on a topic, anxiety about their child's behavioral reactions to learning about sexuality (for example, that conversations about masturbation may result in masturbation becoming a substitute for other self-soothing or repetitive behaviors such as rocking or hand flapping), worries about their children's vulnerability to sexual exploitation, and concerns that their child's odd social behavior may be misconstrued as sexual (Ballan, 2012; Blasingame, 2014; Meister et al., 1994; Nichols & Blakeley-Smith, 2009).

These quite reasonable concerns often lead parents to seek guidance and obtain additional knowledge about their child's sexual development and the skills needed to accurately and appropriately communicate this information to their children (Ballan, 2012; Blasingame, 2014; Nichols & Blakeley-Smith, 2009). However, despite the multiple professionals that are often active in their children's lives—including special educators, behavior specialists, paraprofessionals, psychologists, developmental pediatricians, and psychiatrists, among others—parents report feeling isolated and unprepared to address their child's sexuality (Ballan, 2012). Parents have commonly portrayed professionals as lacking initiative or being unreceptive to discussing aspects of children's sexual maturation unless a sexual behavior problem presents itself and, as a result, many parents have turned to other parents of children with developmental disabilities as their primary source of sexuality information (Ballan, 2012; Nichols & Blakeley-Smith, 2009). The demand for resources and individuals with expertise to address the sociosexual needs of such youth exceeds the availability of such experts, and too often these discussions are restricted to problematic sexual behaviors, failing to contextualize the youth's developmental sexual needs or promote healthy sexual behaviors (Ballan, 2012).

To this end, professionals have begun to recognize the need to support the sexual development of children and adolescents by supporting caregivers' roles in their children's sexuality education. Parenting groups have sporadically emerged over the past number of years with just this purpose in mind (Ballan, 2012; Meister et al., 1994; Nichols & Blakeley-Smith, 2009). Preliminary results indicate that these groups can be effective in alleviating parental anxiety about participating in their child's sexuality education (Nichols & Blakeley-Smith, 2009), thereby removing one barrier to their involvement.

Behavioral Interventions

While it is recognized that the sexual development of adolescents with developmental disabilities may be complicated by some of the characteristics of these conditions, very limited research to date has actually investigated the types of interventions used to treat problematic sexual behaviors with these populations (Sevlever, Roth, & Gillis, 2013). Although limited, some research has examined the effectiveness of behavioral interventions for addressing inappropriate sexual behaviors in individuals with intellectual disabilities, acquired brain injuries, and autism (e.g., Alderman, 1991; Davis et al., 2015; Youngson & Adlerman, 1995; Ylvisaker et al., 2007; LeBlanc, Hagopian, & Maglieri, 2000; Wright, Herzog, & Seymour, 1992). Similar behavioral interventions have been documented as effective for managing other problem behaviors—such as aggression, self-injurious behavior, and repetitive behavior—in youth and adults diagnosed with autism spectrum disorders (e.g., Didden, Duker, & Korzilius, 1997; Kahng, Iwata, & Lewin, 2002; Matson, Benavidez, Compton, Paclawskyj, & Baglio, 1996; Weisz, Weiss, Han, Granger, & Morton, 1995). Given the empirical support for using behavioral interventions to treat a wide range of problem behaviors exhibited by individuals with developmental disabilities (especially intellectual disabilities and autism), it follows that similar interventions may also be appropriate for addressing sexually abusive behaviors in some youth with developmental disabilities (Davis et al., 2015).

Many of the behavioral problems found in youth with these developmental disabilities can be addressed through interventions based on applied behavior analysis (ABA) principles. Applied behavior analysis as a science was established in the early 1950s as an approach to evaluating and modifying human behavior based on operant conditioning principles or what is commonly referred to as behavior modification (Ringdahl, Kopelman, & Falcomata, 2009) and is currently considered the only "well-established" comprehensive treatment for early autism (Stary, Everett, Sears, Fujiki, & Hupp, 2012). The assessment of the behavior targeted for change—referred to as functional behavioral assessment or functional behavioral analysis—is a core component emphasized in ABA interventions and is used to obtain a detailed understanding of the target behavior including its frequency, intensity, antecedents, and consequences (see Rothman, 2012, for a more detailed discussion of functional behavior analysis in the context of sexual behavior problems). From here, data are used to generate a hypothesis regarding possible functions of the target behavior and determine the most appropriate behavioral interventions (El-Ghoroury & Krackow, 2011). Overall, ABA can be understood as a conceptual framework upon which behavioral interventions are used to reinforce new behaviors and systematically reduce disruptive ones. A number of specific behavioral interventions based on ABA concepts have been identified as effective treatments for problem behaviors exhibited by individuals with developmental disabilities (e.g., Boyd, McDonough, & Bodfish, 2012; El-Ghoroury & Krackow, 2011; Patterson, Smith, & Jelen, 2010; Ylvisaker et al., 2007). A brief overview of behavioral interventions for individuals with developmental disabilities and problematic sexual behaviors is presented below. For a more detailed review, the reader is referred to Rothman and MacKenzie (2015) and Davis et al. (2015).

Punishment Procedures

Punishment involves the application of undesirable consequences contingent upon displays of inappropriate or unwanted behavior, and it has been investigated as a component of interventions for youth and adults with intellectual disabilities who have exhibited inappropriate sexual behaviors (e.g., Dozier, Iwata, & Worsdell, 2011; Fisher, Tompson, Hagopian, Bowman, & Krug, 2000; Magee & Ellis, 2001). One common punishment procedure is the time-out, wherein a youth is temporarily separated from the environment where the unwanted behavior occurred. As discussed by Davis and colleagues (2015), punishment procedures have some distinct advantages in that they provide caregivers with an appropriate response for inappropriate sexual behavior and can be effective in immediately reducing its display, thereby diminishing its negative consequences. However, a number of limitations have also been identified with respect to punishment procedures, in that they may result in avoidance or retaliation behaviors; could negatively impact the relationship between the caregiver and the individual displaying the behavior; may be physically difficult to implement, particularly if the individual is resistant; often require time and effort to implement with fidelity (e.g., time-outs must be monitored); and some procedures may pose risk of injury to the individual or caregiver, particularly in the case of physical restraint (Davis et al., 2015).

Special cautions have also been emphasized with respect to the importance of conducting a thorough functional assessment prior to implementing punishment procedures. In more than one study, the application of physical restraints as a punishment for inappropriate sexual conduct inadvertently reinforced the individual's attention-seeking behavior and actually increased the frequency of the behavior (Davis et al., 2015). And if punishment procedures are used, it has been deemed essential that they be used along with reinforcement-based procedures for teaching socially appropriate behavior (Cooper, Heron, & Heward, 2007).

Reinforcement-Based Procedures

Reinforcement describes a relationship between behavior and a consequence that follows the behavior. This relationship is only considered reinforcement if the consequence increases the probability that a behavior will occur or be maintained in the future. For example, children are often taught to ask for something politely (the target behavior) if they want to receive it (the reinforcer). The ultimate goal of reinforcement is to help individuals learn new skills and maintain their use over time in a variety of settings and with a variety of individuals. As such, it is necessary for clinicians to identify the appropriate reinforcers that motivate individuals with developmental disabilities (Neitzel, 2009).

Reinforcement is a fundamental practice that is regularly integrated into evidence-based practices. Within the ABA literature, there are several reinforcement-based procedures that have been found to be effective in attaining academic, communication, and self-help goals, teaching adaptive behavior, and reducing inappropriate and/or disruptive behaviors (including inappropriate sexual behaviors). Examples of reinforcement procedures include token economies, extinction, differential reinforcement, and functional communication training. Reinforcement strategies are frequently combined with other behavioral interventions and are rarely the sole component of treatment (Ringdahl et al., 2009).

Extinction

Extinction is a strategy used to reduce or eliminate unwanted behavior and involves withdrawing or terminating the positive reinforcers that have been determined (through a functional analysis) to maintain an inappropriate or unwanted behavior. This withdrawal results in the termination or extinction of the behavior. During extinction procedures, the unwanted behavior often increases in frequency and intensity (referred to as an extinction burst) before it is extinguished, as the individual seeks to elicit the reinforcers that were previously provided (Sullivan & Bogin, 2010). Combining extinction with intervention strategies that teach socially appropriate alternative behaviors (e.g., communication, leisure skills) can decrease the likelihood of an extinction burst, as some reinforcement is made available (Sullivan & Bogin, 2010). While extinction procedures have been found to effectively reduce problem behaviors in individuals with autism (e.g., repetitive behaviors, aggression, inappropriate sexual behavior, repetitive speech), these techniques are typically coupled with some sort of reinforcement-based procedure (Dozier et al., 2011; Kurtz, Boelter, Jarmolowicz, Chin, & Hagopian, 2006; Patterson et al., 2010), and some practitioners therefore consider it a best practice to include a teaching component in which the youth is taught a functionally equivalent replacement behavior in any treatment package that relies on extinction (Davis et al., 2015). The combination of procedures (i.e., extinction for problem behavior combined with reinforcement for another desired response) is referred to as differential reinforcement.

Given the accumulation of evidence that behavioral, reinforcement-based strategies can be effective in addressing a variety of behavior problems for a range of populations—including inappropriate sexual behavior and aggression exhibited by youth with acquired brain injuries and developmental disabilities—clinicians would benefit from considering these strategies for the treatment of youth with developmental disabilities who have engaged in sexually abusive conduct. It is important to note, however, that behavioral interventions are one of several types of interventions (as detailed elsewhere in this chapter) that can be applied in conjunction with one another—carefully matched to the individual's risk and protective factors and the family's need and responsivity factors—to address the specific and unique demands of developmentally disabled youth who have engaged in sexually abusive behaviors. Furthermore, healthy sexual development includes both (a) reducing inappropriate sexual behaviors and, often, (b) replacing those with healthy and appropriate sexual behaviors. It is therefore critical not only that clinicians strive to eliminate inappropriate or harmful sexual behaviors but that they also assist youth in building or maintaining healthy ones (Davis et al., 2015).

Emotional Regulation Strategies

As discussed above, emotional dysregulation in youth with developmental disabilities can impede their functioning in multiple arenas. Because sexuality has the potential to fulfill a wide range of physical and emotional needs for some youth with developmental disabilities (perhaps, especially, youth on the autism spectrum), sexual behavior can become a primary means by which an affected adolescent regulates her or his emotions. This can, in turn, serve to embed the sexual preoccupations and inappropriate sexual behaviors (Rothman, 2012; Rothman & MacKenzie, 2015). And when interventions attempt to deprive affected adolescents of their sexual preoccupations, those youth may become especially dysregulated, feeling as if their only outlet has been thwarted. This is especially likely when clients have not been provided with any replacement behaviors as gratifying as their previous sexual behavior or preoccupation (Ray et al., 2004).

Developing an Emotional Vocabulary

Other helpful approaches include assisting young clients in developing their emotional vocabularies and enhancing their awareness of emotional and sexual arousal (e.g., Linehan, 1993; Ogden et al., 2013). This involves instructing adolescents on how to distinguish between different emotional states by becoming better at recognizing the internal sensory phenomena associated with different emotions (for example, a racing heart might equal anxiety), facial characteristics unique to different emotions, and body language and tone of voice associated with various types of emotions. It may also involve teaching young clients about the links between distressing experiences and negative feelings, as well as describing and communicating emotions as a substitute for acting on them. Tools such as heart rate monitors can be especially helpful because they provide concrete feedback about emotional states that is easily understood.

Distress Tolerance and Self-Soothing

For these reasons, emotional regulation strategies need to be a key component of treatment for youth with developmental disabilities who have engaged in abusive sexual behaviors. Developing positive replacement behaviors is one important aspect of this, and the selection of potential replacement behaviors should be guided by a determination of the types and range of needs being served by the sexual behaviors. There is a vast literature of emotional regulation techniques to draw on to assist youth with developmentally disabilities in self-soothing. An excellent resource for children and adolescents is Saxe, Ellis, and Kaplow's (2007) *Collaborative Treatment of Traumatized Children and Teens,* which includes a number of user-friendly emotional regulation exercises for younger populations. Relaxation breathing, progressive muscle relaxation, and visualization (see Lehrer, Woolfolk, & Sime, 2008) are simple but elegant techniques for stress reduction that are easily adaptable to developmentally disabled youthful populations (although caution is warranted when using progressive muscle relaxation with clients with special sensory sensitivities, as muscle tension might be experienced as quite painful). Sensory integration exercises may also be useful; Ogden, Goldstein, and Fisher (2013) provide excellent guidelines for implementing these procedures.

On an additional note, anecdotal information indicates that, left to their own devices and competing demands and interests, some adolescents are reluctant to practice and implement self-regulation procedures on their own. The effectiveness of many emotion-regulation procedures with youth is often dependent on the availability of a supportive adult to cue the adolescent and to guide her or him through these exercises. This may be especially the case with adolescents who have developmental disabilities, whose attention and focusing abilities may be particularly compromised. Therefore, where youth are concerned, self-regulation techniques are perhaps better conceptualized as co-regulation techniques, and the adolescent's caregivers and supports should be coached on how to implement these strategies with the youth in their care, when needed.

Problem-Solving Skills

Teaching problem-solving skills to developmentally disabled youth is another method for enhancing their self-regulation capacities and has been deemed an essential component of treatment for youth with developmental disabilities who have offended sexually (Asscher et al., 2012; van der Put et al., 2014). As discussed earlier with respect to social skills instruction, given the difficulties that these youth often face generalizing skills from one situation to another, effective skills programs should explicitly teach specific problem-solving strategies for handling the most frequently occurring problematic situations, and should allow for abundant behavioral rehearsal (Doughty & Kane, 2010; Klin & Volkmar, 2000).

Mindfulness

Originally borrowed from Buddhist meditation practices and integrated in Western cognitive therapy approaches, mindfulness involves the intentional, accepting, and nonjudgmental focus of one's attention on the emotions, thoughts, and sensations occurring in the present (Kabat-Zinn, 1982; Linehan, 1993). Effective at enhancing attention and focus and reducing anxiety, stress, and depressive symptoms in adults, mindfulness-based strategies have grown considerably in popularity over the past 30 years (Tan & Martin, 2015). More recently, mindfulness approaches have been extended to adolescent populations and have demonstrated utility in enhancing overall mental health and behavior control (increasing self-esteem, mental flexibility, attention, cognitive inhibition, and behavioral regulation) and successfully reducing problems including anxiety, depression, somatic complaints, and sleep difficulties with youth (Black, Milam, & Sussman, 2009; Burke, 2010; Tan & Martin, 2015). The practice has recently shown value when integrated into interventions for adults with intellectual disabilities who have offended sexually (Singh et al., 2011).

Mindfulness approaches essentially teach individuals to notice their distressing or unwanted thoughts or urges and, without judgment, monitor their thoughts, feelings, and physiological responses without acting on them. The potential of these strategies for addressing unhealthy sexual arousal is evident: When applied to the management of sexual arousal, inappropriate or atypical arousal (that is, sexual arousal to young children or violence) is neither acted upon nor suppressed; rather, it is simply noticed by the client and experienced until it inevitably subsides. Worling (2012) notes that the practice is actually not new to treatment programs for adolescents who have offended sexually; its adaptation for this particular population has been described in at least one recent publication (Jennings, Apsche, Blossom, & Bayles, 2013). While the practice of mindfulness for addressing atypical sexual arousal in adolescents with developmental disabilities certainly needs to be evaluated, there are indications that these non-intrusive methods—devoid of aversive conditioning procedures and other elements likely to make engagement in treatment difficult for anyone—hold promise for this population.

Developmental Trauma

In cases where trauma plays an additive role in emotional and behavioral dysregulation, it is important to remember that traumatic memories and trauma reminders/cues can be extremely dysregulating and that youth with developmental disabilities may have special difficulty tolerating and managing strong emotions (Blasingame et al., 2015). Thus, standard treatment approaches for post-traumatic stress, such as exposure-based therapies, may not be appropriate. Identifying and modifying environmental triggers for traumatic reactions—in close collaboration with the child's care providers—may be a primary treatment goal. Saxe and colleagues (2011) provide a helpful structure for this process, to which the reader is referred. Latham (2009) advises that in the case of youth with autism, in particular, talking about past trauma should be avoided, except to reassure the child that she or he is safe now. Thus, emotional containment (that is, putting away thoughts, feelings, or images associated with the trauma in a manner that allows one to feel safe and function without being distracted; Goodwin, 2005), rather than "processing" or "desensitization," may be an appropriate treatment goal for some youth with developmental disabilities, although the best approaches will ultimately be determined through ongoing, individualized assessment of the youth's needs and capabilities—which, for all youth, can and do change rapidly.

Therapeutic Relationships

And finally, there is general agreement in the neurodevelopmental literature that the primary manner in which all individuals learn to regulate their emotions is in the context of early attachment relationships (DeBellis, 2001; Siegel, 1999; Schore, 2001). It is also known that, even for those unlucky enough to have been deprived of positive, early relationships, caring and responsive relationships in later childhood through adulthood can lead to the development of capacities for attunement, empathy, and self-regulation (Wallin, 2007). There is evidence that effective therapeutic relationships function in this very manner (Solomon & Siegel, 2003; Wallin, 2007), and it is well established that therapist-offered qualities of empathy, genuineness, and positive regard are universally associated with positive treatment outcomes (Norcross, 2002). There is no evidence to suggest that interpersonal connections are futile, ineffectual, or undesired by adolescents with developmental disabilities, and both research and anecdotal evidence certainly argue otherwise (Blasingame et al., 2015; Mesibov, 1992; Ray et al., 2004; Sullivan & Caterino, 2008). As with other populations, therapeutic relationships—as provided by therapists who, as indicated, also provide coaching to parents and other care providers—serve as the primary context in which most interventions occur, and it is therefore suggested that these relationships—with their inherent opportunities for positive role modeling—are also fundamental tools for supporting youth with developmental disabilities in growing their capacities for relatedness, prosocial behavior, and emotional and behavioral regulation.

CONCLUSION

Although adolescents with developmental disabilities may be at special risk for engaging in abusive sexual behaviors, there has been little research to guide intervention efforts for youth with these challenges. Fortunately, the broader developmental and sexual behavior intervention literatures provide some direction for practitioners. Features of developmental disabilities in youth (especially deficits in cognitive functioning, learning problems, communication and relational difficulties, and emotional dysregulation) can interact and lead to problematic behaviors that require thoughtful, strategic modifications to standard treatments. Nonetheless, as with most youth who have engaged in harmful sexual behaviors, effective intervention involves selecting and customizing evidence-based treatment approaches that match well to the individual youth's risk, needs, and responsivity factors, enlisting and engaging caregivers in a collaborative effort, and supporting the development of healthy sexuality.

REFERENCES

Alderman N. (1991). The treatment of avoidance behaviour following severe brain injury by satiation through negative practice. *Brain Injury, 5,* 77–86.

Allen, D., Evans, C., Hider, A., Hawkins, S., Peckett, H., & Morgan, H. (2008). Offending behaviour in adults with Asperger syndrome. *Journal of Autism & Developmental Disorders, 38*(4), 748–758.

American Psychiatric Association (2013). *The diagnostic and statistical manual of mental disorders (DSM-5)* (5th ed.) Washington, DC: Author.

Andrews, D. A., & Bonta, J. (2006). *The psychology of criminal conduct* (4th ed.). Newark, NJ: Lexis Nexis.

Asscher, J. J., van der Put, C. E., & Stams, G. J. J. M. (2012). Differences between juvenile offenders with and without intellectual disability in offense type and risk factors. *Research in Developmental Disabilities, 33,* 1905–1913.

Association for the Treatment of Sexual Abusers (2012). *Adolescents who have engaged in sexually abusive behavior: Effective policies and practices.* Beaverton, OR: Author. https://www.atsa.com/pdfs/Policy/AdolescentsEngagedSexuallyAbusiveBehavior.pdf. Accessed 4 April 2016.

Association for the Treatment of Sexual Abusers Task Force on Children with Sexual Behavior Problems (2006). *Report of the task force on children with sexual behavior problems.* Beaverton, OR: Association for the Treatment of Sexual Abusers.

Ayland, L., & West B. (2006). The Good Way model: A strengths-based approach for working with young people, especially those with intellectual disabilities, who have sexually abusive behavior. *Journal of Sexual Aggression, 12,* 189–201.

Baer, D. M., Wolf, M. M., & Risley, T. R. (1968). Some current dimensions of applied behavior analysis. *Journal of Applied Behavior Analysis, 1,* 91–97.

Ballan, M. S. (2010). Parental perspectives of communication about sexuality in families of children with autism spectrum disorders. *Journal of Autism and Developmental Disorders, 42,* 676–684.

Bancroft, J. (2006). Normal sexual development. In H. E. Barbaree & W. L. Marshall (Eds.), *The juvenile sex offender* (2nd ed., pp. 19–57). New York: Guilford.

Banks, N. (2014). Sexually harmful behavior in adolescents in a context of gender and intellectual disability: Implications for child psychologists. *Educational and Child Psychology, 31*(3), 9–21.

Barry-Walsh, J. B., & Mullen, P. E. (2004). Forensic aspects of Asperger's syndrome. *Journal of Forensic Psychiatry and Psychology, 15*(1), 96–107.

Bellini, S., Peters, J. K., Benner, L., & Hopf, A. (2007). A meta-analysis of school-based social skills interventions for children with autism spectrum disorders. *Remedial and Special Education, 28,* 153–162.

Black, D. S., Milam, J., & Sussman, S. (2009). Sitting-meditation interventions among youth: A review of treatment efficacy. *Pediatrics, 124,* 532–541.

Blasingame, G. (2005). *Developmentally disabled persons with sexual behavior problems: Treatment, management, supervision* (2nd ed.). Brandon, VT: Safer Society Press.

Blasingame, G. (2011). *An introduction to autism spectrum disorders, sexual behaviors, and therapeutic intervention.* Holyoke, MA: NEARI Press.

Blasingame, G. (2014). Practical strategies for working with youth with intellectual disabilities who have sexual behavior problems. In D. Bromberg & W. T. O'Donohue (Eds.), *Toolkit for working with juvenile sexual offenders* (pp. 479–505). San Diego: Elsevier.

Blasingame, G. D., Creeden, K., & Rich, P. (2015). *Assessment and treatment of adolescents with intellectual disabilities who exhibit sexual problems or offending behaviors.* Beaverton, OR: Association for the Treatment of Sexual Abusers. Retrieved March 3, 2016, from http://www.atsa.com/pdfs/ATSA_Adolescent_IDSPOB_packet.pdf

Bolton, W. (2006). Developmental theory and developmental deficits: The treatment of sex offenders with Asperger's syndrome. In J. Hiller, H. Wood, & W. Bolton (Eds.). *Sex, mind, and emotion: Innovation in psychological theory and practice* (pp. 41–61). London, UK: Karnac.

Borduin, C. M., Schaeffer, C. M., & Heiblum, N. (2009). A randomized clinical trial of multisystemic therapy with juvenile sexual offenders: Effects on youth social ecology and criminal activity. *Journal of Consulting and Clinical Psychology, 77,* 26–37.

Boyd, B. A., McDonough, S. G., & Bodfish, J. W. (2012). Evidence-based behavioral interventions for repetitive behaviors in autism. *Journal of Autism and Developmental Disorders, 42*(6), 1236–1248.

Burke, C. A. (2010). Mindfulness-based approaches with children and adolescents: A preliminary review of current research in an emergent field. *Journal of Child and Family Studies, 19,* 133–144.

Caldwell, M. F. (2010). Study characteristics and recidivism base rates in juvenile sex offender recidivism. *International Journal of Offender Therapy and Comparative Criminology, 54,* 197–212.

Caldwell, M. F. (2016). Quantifying the decline in juvenile sexual recidivism rates. *Psychology, Public Policy, and Law.* Advance online publication.

Centers for Disease Control and Prevention (2015a). Developmental disabilities: Facts about developmental disabilities. Retrieved May 1, 2016, from https://www.cdc.gov/ncbddd/developmentaldisabilities/facts.html

Centers for Disease Control and Prevention (2015b). Fetal alcohol spectrum disorders (FASDs): Facts about FASDs. Retrieved May 1, 2016, from http://www.cdc.gov/ncbddd/fasd/facts.html

Chaffin, M. (2008). Our minds are made up—don't confuse us with the facts: Commentary on policies concerning children with sexual behavior problems and juvenile sex offenders. *Child Maltreatment, 13,* 110–121.

Cooper, J. O., Heron, T. E., & Heward, W. L. (2007). *Applied behavior analysis* (2nd ed.). Upper Saddle River, NJ: Pearson Education.

Craig, L., & Hutchinson, R. B. (2005). Sexual offenders with learning disabilities: Risk, recidivism and treatment. *Journal of Sexual Aggression, 11,* 289–304.

Davis, T. N., Machalicek, W., Scalzo, R., Kobylecky, A., Campbell, V., Pinkelman, S., . . . & Sigafoos, J. (2015). A review and treatment selection model for individuals with developmental disabilities who engage in inappropriate sexual behavior. *Behavior Analysis in Practice,* 1–14. Advance online publication. http://dx.doi.org/10.1077/s40617-015-0062-3

De Bellis, M. D. (2001). Developmental traumatology: The psychobiological development of maltreated children and its implications for research, treatment, and policy. *Development and Psychopathology, 13,* 537–561.

Denno, D. W. (1997). Sexuality, rape, and mental retardation. *University of Illionis Law Review, 720,* 315–434.

Didden, R., Duker, P. C., & Korzilius, H. (1997). Meta-analytic study on treatment effectiveness for problem behaviors with individuals who have mental retardation. *American Journal on Mental Retardation, 101*(4), 387–399.

Dopp, A. R., Borduin, C. M., Brown, C. E. (2015). Evidence-based treatments for juvenile sexual offenders: Review and recommendations. *Journal of Aggression, Conflict and Peace Research, 7,* 223–236.

Dopp, A. R., Borduin, C. M., Rothman, D. B., & Letourneau, E. J. (in press). Evidence-based treatments for youths who engage in criminal sexual behaviors. *Journal of Clinical Child and Adolescent Psychology.*

Doughty, A. H., & Kane, L. M. (2010). Teaching abuse-protection skills to people with intellectual disabilities: A review of the literature. *Research in Developmental Disabilities, 31,* 331–337.

Douma, J. C. H., Dekker, M. C., de Ruiter, K. P., Tick, N. T., & Koot, H. M. (2007). Antisocial and delinquent behaviors in youths with mild or borderline disabilities. *American Journal on Mental Retardation, 112,* 207–220.

Dozier, C. L., Iwata, B. A., & Worsdell, A. S. (2011). Assessment and treatment of foot-shoe fetish displayed by a man with autism. *Journal of Applied Behavior Analysis, 44*(1), 133–137.

El-Ghoroury, N. H., & Krackow, E. (2011). A developmental–behavioral approach to outpatient psychotherapy with children with autism spectrum disorders. *Journal of Contemporary Psychotherapy, 41*(1), 11–17.

Fisher, W. W., Tompson, R. H., Hagopian, L. P., Bowman, L. G., & Krug, A. (2000). Facilitating tolerance of delayed reinforcement during functional communication training. *Behavior Modification, 24,* 3–29.

Fox, N. (1994). The development of emotional regulation: Biological and behavioral considerations. *Monographs for the Society for Research in Child Development, 59,* 2–3.

Friedlander, R. I., & Donnelly, T. (2004). Early-onset psychosis in youth with intellectual disability. *Journal of Intellectual Disability Research, 48,* 540–547.

Ghaziuddin, M., Tsai, L. Y., & Ghaziuddin, N. (1991). Brief report: Violence in Asperger syndrome: A critique. *Journal of Autism and Developmental Disorders, 21*(3), 349–354.

Gill, M. (2010). Sex education and young adults with intellectual disabilities: Crisis response, sexual diversity, and pleasure. In C. Dudley-Marling & A. Gurn (Eds.), *The Myth of the Normal Curve* (pp. 171–186). New York: Peter Lang.

Goodwin, J. (2005). Redefining borderline syndromes as posttraumatic and rediscovering emotional containment as a first stage in treatment. *Journal of Interpersonal Violence, 20,* 20–25.

Graetz, J. E., Mastropieri, M. A., & Scruggs, T. E. (2009). Decreasing inappropriate behaviors for adolescents with autism spectrum disorders using modified social stories. *Education and Training in Developmental Disabilities, 44*(1), 91–104.

Gralton, E. (2013). Inpatient assessment of young people with developmental disabilities who offend. *Advances in Mental Health and Intellectual Disabilities, 7*(2), 108–116.

Gray, C. (2000). *The new social story book.* Arlington, TX: Future Horizons.

Gray, C. A., & Garand, J. D. (1993). Social stories: Improving responses of students with autism with accurate social information. *Focus on Autistic Behavior, 8,* 1–10.

Haaven, J. L., & Coleman, E. M. (2000). Treatment of the developmentally disabled sex offender. In D. R. Laws, S. M. Hudson, & T. Ward (Eds.), *Remaking relapse prevention with sex offenders: A sourcebook* (pp. 369–388). Thousand Oaks, CA: Sage Publications.

Hanley-Hochdorfer, K., Bray, M. A., Kehle, T. J., & Elinoff, M. J. (2010). Social stories to increase verbal initiation in children with autism and Asperger's disorder. *School Psychology Review, 39,* 484–492.

Hanson, R. K. (2014). Treating sexual offenders: How did we get here and where are we headed? *Journal of Sexual Aggression, 20,* 3–8.

Hanson, R. K., Bourgon, G., Helmus, L., & Hodgson, S. (2009). The principles of effective correctional treatment also apply to sexual offenders: A meta-analysis. *Criminal Justice and Behavior, 36,* 865–891.

Haracopos, D., & Pedersen, L. (1992). *Sexuality and autism: Danish report.* UK: Society for the Autistically Handicapped. Retrieved May 1, 2010, from www.Autismuk.com/index9sub.htm

't Hart-Kerkhoffs, L. A., Jansen, L. M., Dorelieijers, T. A., Vermeiren, R., Minderaa, R. B., & Hartman, C. A. (2009). Autism spectrum disorder symptoms in juvenile suspects of sex offenses. *Journal of Clinical Psychiatry, 70*(2), 266–272.

Hellemans, H., Colson, K., Verbraeken, C., Vermeiren, R., & Deboutte, D. (2007). Sexual behavior in high-functioning male adolescents and young adults with autism spectrum disorder. *Journal of Autism and Developmental Disorders, 37*(2), 260–269.

Henault, I. (2006). *Asperger's syndrome and sexuality: From adolescence through adulthood.* London, UK: Jessica Kingsley Publishers.

Horner-Johnson, W., & Drum, C. E. (2006). Prevalence of maltreatment of people with intellectual disabilities: A review of recently published research. *Mental Retardation and Developmental Disabilities Research Reviews, 12,* 57–69.

Hubert, J., Flynn, M., Nicholls, L., & Hollins, S. (2007). "I don't want to be the mother of a paedophile": The perspectives of mothers whose adolescent sons with learning disabilities sexually offend. *Journal of Child Psychotherapy, 33*(3), 363–376.

Hunter, J., & Longo, R. (2004). Relapse prevention with juvenile sexual abusers. In G. O'Reilly, W. L. Marshall, A. Carr, & R. C. Beckett (Eds.), *The handbook of clinical intervention with young people who sexually abuse* (pp. 297–314). Hove, East Sussex, UK: Brunner-Routledge.

Jennings, J. L., Apsche, J. A., Blossom, P., & Bayles, C. (2013). Using mindfulness in the treatment of adolescent sexual abusers: Contributing common factor or a primary modality? *International Journal of Behavioral Consultation and Therapy, 8,* 17–22.

Kabat-Zinn, J. (1982). An outpatient program in behavioral medicine for chronic pain patients based on the practice of mindfulness meditation: Theoretical considerations and preliminary results. *General Hospital Psychiatry, 4,* 33–47.

Kahng, I. S., Iwata, B. A., & Lewin, A. B. (2002). Behavioral treatment of self-injury, 1964 to 2000. *American Journal on Mental Retardation, 107*(3), 212–221.

Klein, V., Rettenberger, M., Yoon, D., Köhler, N., & Briken, P. (2015). Protective factors and recidivism in accused juveniles who sexually offended. *Sexual Abuse, 27*(1), 71–90.

Klin, A., & Volkmar, F. R. (2000). Treatment and intervention guidelines for individuals with Asperger syndrome. In A. Klin, F. R. Volkmar, & S. S. Sparrow (Eds.), *Asperger syndrome* (pp. 340–366). New York: Guilford Press.

Koller, R. (2000). Sexuality and adolescents with autism. *Sexuality and Disability, 18,* 125–135.

Kumagami, T., & Matsuura, N. (2009). Prevalence of pervasive developmental disorder in juvenile court cases in Japan. *Journal of Forensic Psychiatry & Psychology, 20,* 974–987.

Kurtz, P. F., Boelter, E. W., Jarmolowicz, D. P., Chin, M. D., & Hagopian, L. P. (2011). An analysis of functional communication training as an empirically supported treatment for problem behavior displayed by individuals with intellectual disabilities. *Research in Developmental Disabilities, 32*(6), 2935–2942.

Latham, C. (2009, October). *Chasing the dead horse around the bush: PDD children & problematic sexual behavior.* Workshop presented at the 28th Annual Conference of the Association for the Treatment of Sexual Abusers, Dallas, TX.

Laurent, A. C., & Rubin, E. (2004). Emotional regulation challenges in Asperger's syndrome and high functioning autism. *Topics in Language Disorders, 24*(4), 286–297.

Leblanc, L. A., Hagopian, L. P., & Maglieri, K. A. (2000). Use of a token economy to eliminate excessive inappropriate social behavior in an adult with developmental disabilities. *Behavioral Interventions, 15*(2), 135–143.

Lehrer, P. M., Woolfolk, R. L., & Sime, W. E. (Eds.) (2008). *Principles and practice of stress management* (3rd ed.). New York: Guilford Press.

Letourneau, E. J., & Borduin, C. M. (2008). The effective treatment of juveniles who sexually offend: An ethical imperative. *Ethics & Behavior, 18*(2), 286–306.

Leversee, T., & Powell, K. M. (2012). Beyond risk management to a more holistic model for treating sexually abusive youth. In B. K. Schwartz (Ed.), *The Sex Offender: Vol. 7* (pp. 19-2 to 19-24). New York: Civic Research Institute.

Lindsay, W. R. (2002). Research and literature on sex offenders with intellectual and developmental disabilities. *Journal of Intellectual Disability Research, 46,* 74–85.

Linehan, M. M. (1993). *Skills training manual for treatment of borderline personality disorder.* New York: Guilford Press.

Lipsey, M. W. (2009). The primary factors that characterize effective interventions with juvenile offenders: A meta-analytic overview. *Victims and Offenders, 4,* 124–147.

Lipsey, M. W., Howell, J. C., Kelly, M. R., Chapman, G., & Carver, D. (2010). Improving the effectiveness of juvenile justice programs: A new perspective on evidence-based practice. Washington, DC: Center for Juvenile Justice Reform, Georgetown Public Policy Institute, Georgetown University. Retrieved August 17, 2016, from http://cjjr.georgetown.edu/wp-content/uploads/2014/12/ebppaper.pdf

Lord, C., Cook, E. H., Leventhal, B. L., & Amaral, D. G. (2000). Autism spectrum disorders. *Neuron, 28,* 355–363.

Magee, S. K., & Ellis, J. (2001). The detrimental effects of physical restraint as a consequence for inappropriate classroom behavior. *Journal of Applied Behavior Analysis, 34,* 501–504.

Mandell, D. S., Walrath, C. M., Manteuffel, B., Sgro, G., & Pinto-Martin, J. (2005). Characteristics of children with autistic spectrum disorders served in comprehensive community-based mental health settings. *Journal of Autism & Developmental Disorders, 35*(3), 313–321.

Marshall, W. L. (1989). Intimacy, loneliness and sexual offenders. *Behavior Research and Therapy, 27,* 691–703.

Marshall, W. L. (1997). The relationship between self-esteem and deviant sexual arousal in nonfamilial child molesters. *Behavior Modification, 21,* 86–96.

Mason, J., & Scior, K. (2004). "Diagnostic overshadowing" amongst clinicians working with people with intellectual disabilities in the UK. *Journal of Applied Research in Intellectual Disabilities, 17,* 85–90.

Matson, J. L., Benavidez, D. A., Compton, L., Paclawskyj, T., & Baglio, C. (1996). Behavioral treatment of autistic persons: A review of research from 1980 to the present. *Research in Developmental Disabilities, 17*(6), 433–465.

McGrath, R. J., Cumming, G. F., Burchard, B. L., Zeoli, S., & Ellerby, L. (2010). *Current practices and emerging trends in sexual abuser management: The Safer Society 2009 North American survey.* Brandon, VT: Safer Society Press.

Meister, C., Norlock, D., Honeyman, S., & Pierce, K. (1994). Sexuality and autism: A parenting skills enhancement group. *SIECCAN Newsletter,* in *Canadian Journal of Human Sexuality, 3,* 283–289.

Mesibov, G. B. (1992). Treatment issues with high-functioning adolescents and adults with autism. In E. Schloper & G. B. Mesibov (Eds.), *High functioning individuals with autism* (pp. 143–156). New York: Plenum Press.

Miccio-Fonseca, L. C., & Rasmussen, L. A. (2013). Applicability of MEGA to sexually abusive youth with low intellectual functioning. *Journal of Mental Health Research in Intellectual Disabilities, 6,* 42–59.

Miller, B. C., Benson, B., & Galbraith, K. A. (2001). Family relationships and adolescent pregnancy risk: A research synthesis. *Developmental Review, 21,* 1–38.

Morano, J. P. (2001). Sexual abuse of the mentally retarded patient: Medical and legal analysis for the primary care physician. *Primary Care Companion Journal Clinical Psychiatry, 3,* 126–135.

Moultrie, D. (2006). Adolescents convicted of possession of abuse images of children: A new type of adolescent sex offender? *Journal of Sexual Aggression, 12,* 165–174.

Murphy, G. H., & O'Callaghan, A. L. I. (2004). Capacity of adults with intellectual disabilities to consent to sexual relationships. *Psychological Medicine, 34*(7), 1347–1357.

Murrie, D. C., Warren, J. I., Kristiansson, M., & Dietz, P. E. (2002). Asperger's syndrome in forensic settings. *International Journal of Forensic Mental Health, 1*(1), 59–70.

Myers, S. M., & Plauché Johnson, C. (2007). Management of children with autism spectrum disorders. *Pediatrics, 120*(5), 1–21.

Neitzel, J. (2009). *Overview of reinforcement.* Chapel Hill, NC: National Professional Development Center on Autism Spectrum Disorders, Frank Porter Graham Child Development Institute, University of North Carolina. Retrieved August 20, 2013, from http://autismpdc.fpg.unc.edu/content/reinforcement

Newman, S. S., & Ghaziuddin, M. (2008). Violent crime in Asperger syndrome: The role of psychiatric comorbidity. *Journal of Autism and Developmental Disorders, 38,* 1848–1852.

Nichols, S., & Blakeley-Smith, A. (2009). "I'm not sure we're ready for this . . .": Working with families toward facilitating healthy sexuality for individuals with autism spectrum disorders. *Social Work in Mental Health, 8*(1), 72–91.

Norcross, J. C. (Ed.) (2002). *Psychotherapy relationships that work.* New York: Oxford University Press.

Novaco, R. W., & Taylor, J. L. (2004) Assessment of anger and aggression in male offenders with developmental disabilities. *Psychological Assessment, 16,* 42–50.

Ogden, P., Goldstein, B., & Fisher, J. (2013). Brain-to-brain, body-to-body: A sensorimotor psychotherapy perspective on the treatment of children and adolescents. In R. E. Longo, D. S. Prescott, J. Bergman, & K. Creeden (Eds.), *Current perspectives and applications in neurobiology: Working with young persons who are victims and perpetrators of sexual abuse* (pp. 229–257). Holyoke, MA: Neari Press.

Ozonoff, S., & Rogers, S. J. (2003). Autism spectrum disorders: A research review for practitioners. In S. Ozonoff, S. J. Rogers, & R. L. Hendren (Eds.), *Review of Psychiatry* (pp. 3–33). Washington, DC: American Psychiatric Association.

Patterson, S. Y., Smith, V., & Jelen, M. (2010). Behavioural intervention practices for stereotypic and repetitive behaviour in individuals with autism spectrum disorder: A systematic review. *Developmental Medicine & Child Neurology, 52*(4), 318–327.

Peter, J., & Valkenburg, P. M. (2006). Adolescents' exposure to sexually explicit material on the Internet. *Communication Research, 33,* 178–204.

Prizant, B. M., Wetherby, A. M., Rubin, E., & Laurent, A. C. (2003). The SCERTS Model: A family-centered, transactional approach to enhancing communication and socioemotional abilities of young children with ASD. *Infants and Young Children, 16*(4), 296–316.

Przybylski, R. (2014). Effectiveness of treatment for juveniles who sexually offend. In National Criminal Justice Association (Eds.), *Sex offender management assessment and planning initiative* (NCJ 247059). Washington, DC: US Department of Justice Office of Justice Programs.

Quill, K. A. (1997). Instructional considerations for young children with autism: The rationale for visually-cued instruction. *Journal of Autism and Developmental Disabilities, 27,* 697–714.

Quinn, M. M., Rutherford, R., Osher, D., & Poirier, J. (2005). Youth with disabilities in juvenile corrections: A national survey. *Exceptional Children, 71,* 339–345.

Ray, F., Marks, C., & Bray-Garretson, H. (2004). Challenges to treating adolescents with Asperger's syndrome who are sexually abusive. *Sexual Addiction and Compulsivity, 11,* 265–285.

Realmuto, G. M., & Ruble, L. A. (1999). Sexual behaviors in autism: Problems of definition and management. *Journal of Autism & Developmental Disorders, 29*(2), 121–127.

Reitzel, L. R., & Carbonell, J. L. (2006). The effectiveness of sexual offender treatment for juveniles as measured by recidivism: A meta-analysis. *Sexual Abuse: A Journal of Research and Treatment, 18,* 401–422.

Ringdahl, J. E., Kopelman, T., & Falcomata, T. S. (2009). Applied behavior analysis and its application to autism and autism related disorders. In J. L. Matson (Ed.), *Applied behavior analysis for children with autism spectrum disorders* (pp. 15–32). New York: Springer Science.

Rothman, D. B. (2012). Autism spectrum disorders and sexual behavior problems. In B. K. Schwartz (Ed.), *The Sex Offender: Vol. 7* (pp. 26–1 to 26–23). New York: Civic Research Institute.

Rothman, D. B., & Letourneau, E. J. (2013, October). *Adolescents who have engaged in abusive sexual behaviors: Empirically & ethically supported practice guidelines.* Invited pre-conference seminar presented at the 32nd Annual Conference of the Association for the Treatment of Sexual Abusers, Chicago, IL.

Rothman, D. B., & MacKenzie, H. K. (2015). Interventions for children and adolescents with sexual behavior problems and autism spectrum disorders. In B. K. Schwartz (Ed.), *The Sex Offender, Vol. 8* (pp. 23-2 to 23-26). New York: Civic Research Institute.

Ruble, L., & Dalrymple, N. (1993). Social/sexual awareness of persons with autism: A parental perspective. *Archives of Sexual Behavior, 22,* 229–240.

Saxe, G. N., Ellis, B. H., & Kaplow, J. B. (2007). *Collaborative treatment of traumatized children and teens: The trauma systems therapy approach.* New York: Guilford Press.

Schore, A. N. (2001). Effects of a secure attachment relationship on right brain development, affect regulation, and infant mental health. *Infant Mental Health Journal, 22,* 7–66.

Semrud-Clikeman, M., Walkowiak, J., Wilkinson, A., & Portman Minne, E. (2010). Direct and indirect measures of social perception, behavior, and emotional functioning in children with Asperger's disorder, nonverbal learning disability, or ADHD. *Journal of Abnormal Child Psychology, 38,* 509–519.

Seto, M. C., & Lalumière, M. L. (2010). What is so special about male adolescent sexual offending? A review and test of explanations through meta-analysis. *Psychological Bulletin, 136,* 526–575.

Sevlever, M., Roth, M. E., & Gillis, J. M. (2013). Sexual abuse and offending in autism spectrum disorders. *Sexuality and Disability, 31,* 189–200.

Shea, V., & Mesibov, G. B. (2005). Adolescents and adults with autism. In F. Volkmar, R. Paul, A. Klin, & D. J. Cohen (Eds.), *Handbook of autism and pervasive developmental disorders: Vol. 2. Interventions and policy* (3rd ed., pp. 288–311). Hoboken, NJ: Wiley.

Siegel, D. (1999). *The developing mind.* New York: Guilford Press.

Silva, J. A., Ferrari, M. M., & Leong, G. B. (2002). The case of Jeffery Dahmer: Sexual serial homicide from a neuropsychiatric perspective. *Journal of Forensic Science, 47,* 1347–1359.

Singh, N. N., Lancioni, G. E., Winton, A. S. W., Singh, A N., Adkins, A. D., & Singh, J. (2011). Can adult offenders with intellectual disabilities use mindfulness-based procedures to control their deviant sexual arousal? *Psychology, Crime & Law, 17,* 165–179.

Solomon, M. F., & Siegel, D. J. (Eds.) (2003). *Healing trauma: Attachment, mind, body, and brain.* New York: W. W. Norton.

Spice, A., Viljoen, J. L., Latzman, N. E., Scalora, M. J., & Ullman, D. (2012). Risk and protective factors for recidivism among juveniles who have offended sexually. *Sexual Abuse, 25,* 347–369.

St. Amand, A., Bard, D., & Silovsky, J. F. (2008). Treatment of child sexual behavior problems: Practice elements and outcomes. *Child Maltreatment [Special Issue: Children with Sexual Behavior Problems], 13,* 145–166.

Stary, A. K., Everett, G. E., Sears, K. B., Fujiki, M., & Hupp, S. D. A. (2012). Social stories for children with autism spectrum disorders: Updated review of the literature from 2004 to 2010. *Journal of Evidence-Based Practices for Schools, 13,* 123–139.

Stokes, M., & Kaur, A. (2005). High functioning autism and sexuality: A parental perspective. *Autism, 9*(3), 263–286.

Stokes, M., & Newton, N. (2004). Autistic spectrum disorders and stalking. *Autism, 8*(3), 337–339.

Stokes, M. A., Newton, N., & Kaur, A. (2007). Stalking, and social and romantic functioning among adolescents and adults with autism spectrum disorder. *Journal of Autism and Developmental Disorders, 37,* 1969–1986.

Stromsness, M. M. (1994). Sexually abused women with mental retardation: Hidden victims, absent resources. *Women & Therapy, 14,* 139–152.

Sullivan, A., & Caterino, L. C. (2008). Addressing the sexuality and sex education of individuals with autism spectrum disorders. *Education and Treatment of Children, 31*(3), 381–394.

Sullivan, L., & Bogin, J. (2010). *Overview of extinction.* Sacramento: National Professional Development Center on Autism Spectrum Disorders, MIND Institute. University of California at Davis Medical School. Retrieved August 20, 2013, from http://autismpdc.fpg.unc.edu/content/extinction

Sullivan P. M., & Knutson J. F. (2000) Maltreatment and disabilities: A population-based epidemiological study. *Child Abuse and Neglect, 24,* 1257–1273.

Sverd, J. (2003). Psychiatric disorders in individuals with pervasive developmental disorder. *Journal of Psychiatric Practice, 9,* 111–127.

Tan, L., & Martin, G. (2015). Taming the adolescent mind: A randomised controlled trial examining clinical efficacy of an adolescent mindfulness-based group programme. *Child and Adolescent Mental Health, 20,* 49–55.

Tissot, C. (2009). Establishing a sexual identity: Case studies of learners with autism and learning difficulties. *Autism, 13,* 551–556.

Tullis, C. A., & Zangrillo, A. N. (2013). Sexuality education for adolescents and adults with autism spectrum disorders. *Psychology in the Schools, 50,* 866–875.

van Bourgondien, M. E., Reichle, N. C., & Palmer, A. (1997). Sexual behavior in adults with autism. *Journal of Autism and Developmental Disorders, 27,* 113–125.

van der Put, C. E., Asscher, J. J., Wissink, I. B., & Stams G. J. J.M. (2014). The relationship between maltreatment victimisation and sexual and violent offending: Differences between adolescent offenders with and without intellectual disability. *Journal of Intellectual Disability Research, 58*(2), 979–991.

van Wijk, A., van Horne, J., Bullens, R. A. R., Bijleveld, C., & Doreleijers, T. (2005). Juvenile sex offenders: A group on its own? *International Journal of Offender Therapy and Comparative Criminology, 49*(1), 25–36.

Vermeiren, R., Jespers, I., & Moffitt, T. (2006). Mental health problems in juvenile justice populations. *Child & Adolescent Psychiatric Clinics of North America, 15,* 333–351.

Vermeulen, P. (2008). *I am special: Introducing children and young people to their autistic spectrum disorder.* London, UK: Jessica Kingsley Publishers.

Wallin, D. J. (2007). *Attachment in psychotherapy.* New York: Guilford Press.

Weisz, J. R., Weiss, B., Han, S. S., Granger, D. A., & Morton, T. (1995). Effects of psychotherapy with children and adolescents revisited: A meta-analysis of treatment outcome studies. *Psychological Bulletin, 117*(3), 450.

Wing, L. (1997). Asperger's syndrome: Management requires diagnosis. *Journal of Forensic Psychiatry, 8*(2), 253–257.

Wissink I. B., Van Vugt, E. S., Moonen, X., Stams, G. J. J. M., & Hendriks J. (2015) Sexual abuse involving children with an intellectual disability (ID): A narrative review. *Research in Developmental Disabilities, 36,* 20–35.

Woodbury-Smith, M. R., Clare, I. C. H., Holland, A. J., & Kearns, A. (2006). High functioning autistic spectrum disorders, offending and other law-breaking: Findings from a community sample. *Journal of Forensic Psychiatry and Psychology, 17*(1), 108–120.

World Health Organization (2006). *International Statistical Classification of Diseases and Related Health Problems* (10th ed.) (ICD-10). Geneva, Switzerland: World Health Organization.

Worling, J. R. (2012). The assessment and treatment of deviant sexual arousal with adolescents who have offended sexually. *Journal of Sexual Aggression, 18,* 36–63.

Worling, J. R. (2013). What were we thinking? Five erroneous assumptions that have fueled specialized interventions for adolescents who have sexually offended. *International Journal of Behavioral Consultation and Therapy, 8,* 80–88.

Worling, J. R., & Langton, C. M. (2015). A prospective investigation of factors that predict desistance from recidivism for adolescents who have sexually offended. *Sexual Abuse, 27,* 127–142.

Worling, J. R., Litteljohn, A., & Bookalam, D. (2010). 20-year prospective follow-up study of specialized treatment for adolescents who offended sexually. *Behavioral Sciences and the Law, 28,* 46–57.

Wright, G., Herzog, D., & Seymour, J. (1992). Treatment of a constellation of inappropriate sexual and social behaviors in a 20 year old man with Down's syndrome. *Sexuality and Disability, 10*(1), 57–61.

Ylvisaker, M., Turkstra, L., Coehlo, C., Yorkston, K., Kennedy, M., Sohlberg, M. M., & Avery, J. (2007). Behavioural interventions for children and adults with behaviour disorders after TBI: A systematic review of the evidence. *Brain Injury, 21*(8), 769–805.

Youngson, H. A., & Alderman, N. (1995). Fear of incontinence and its effects on a community-based rehabilitation programme after severe brain injury: Successful remediation of escape behaviour using behaviour modification. *Brain Injury, 8*(1), 23–36.

CHAPTER 12

Trauma and Mental Health Concerns in Justice-Involved Youth

Tracey A. Skilling

Teresa Grimbos

Julia Vinik

Youth involved with the justice system have much higher rates of mental health concerns compared with youth in the community (e.g., Chitsabesan & Bailey, 2006). In fact, results from some studies have estimated that more than 90 percent of justice-involved youth meet diagnostic criteria for at least one mental health disorder (e.g., Drerup, Croysdale, & Hoffmann, 2008). Further, rates of serious mental illness (mental health concerns that require significant and immediate intervention) have been estimated to be as high as 27 percent in justice-involved youth (Shufelt & Cocozza, 2006). In addition, experiences of trauma—more specifically post-traumatic stress disorder (PTSD)—are also highly prevalent among this population of youth (e.g., Abram et al., 2004). Rates of PTSD among justice-involved youth (12–55%; Abram et al., 2004; Ariga et al., 2008; Dixon et al., 2005; Moore et al., 2013; Odgers et al., 2005; Vermeiren, 2003; Cauffman, Feldman, Watherman, & Steiner, 1998) are much higher than rates of PTSD in the general population (3.5% according to the National Institute of Mental Health; Kessler, Chiu, Demler, & Walter, 2005).

Studies also indicate that the overwhelming majority of young offenders (i.e., over 90%) report having experienced at least one traumatic event over their lifetime (Ford, Chapman, Connor, & Cruise, 2012; Abram et al., 2004; Wilson et al., 2013), with comparable rates of trauma exposure in the general population estimated to be around 25 percent (Costello, Erkanli, Fairbank, & Angold, 2002). Similarly, rates of maltreatment specifically are estimated to be very high (i.e., higher than 50%; Coleman &

Stewart, 2010; Abram et al., 2004; Smith et al., 2006; Smith, Ireland, & Thornberry, 2005; Moore et al., 2013) within the youth justice population when compared with the general population.

TRAUMA AND MENTAL HEALTH IN JUVENILE SEXUAL OFFENDERS

There is some research highlighting that juvenile sexual offenders[1] (JSOs) are similar to their non-sexual offending counterparts in a variety of ways. For example, similarities have been found with respect to their negative peer relationships, antisociality, and conduct problems (Caldwell, 2002). However, other research findings suggest that there are meaningful differences between these two groups of offenders. In this regard, a number of factors that are particularly salient for JSOs have been identified, including atypical sexual interests, poor attachment relationships, sexual abuse history, physical and emotional abuse experiences, witnessing of violence, poor emotion regulation, symptoms of dissociation, and reduced empathy (for reviews, see Seto & Lalumière, 2010; Seto & Pullman, 2014).

Trauma experiences and PTSD, as well as mental health problems more generally, appear to be highly salient in this group of youthful offenders (Leibowitz et al., 2011; Jonson-Reid & Way, 2001). Compared with non-sexual offenders, JSOs have more frequently experienced multiple types of trauma, including sexual abuse, physical abuse, and emotional and physical neglect, as well as witnessing sexual or non-sexual violence (Seto & Lalumière, 2010; Jonson-Reid & Way, 2001; Van Wijk et al., 2005; Burton, Miller, & Shill, 2002; Burton, 2008; Burton & Schatz, 2003; Leibowtiz, Laser, & Burton, 2011; Davis-Rosanbalm, 2003; Ford & Linney, 1995; Veneziano, Veneziano, LeGrand, & Richards, 2004; Zakireh, Ronis, & Knight, 2008). The impact of these trauma experiences on mental health functioning is also evident in studies that have identified high rates of PTSD and other trauma-related symptoms (e.g., dissociation) among JSOs (McMackin, Leisen, Cusack, LaFratta, & Litwin, 2002; Leibowitz et al., 2011), as well as high rates of other types of psychopathology, such as mood problems and maladaptive personality traits (e.g., Cooper, Murphy, & Haynes, 1996).

More specifically, Seto and Lalumière (2010) conducted a meta-analysis in which they examined 59 direct comparison studies, with a total sample of 3,855 male JSOs and 13,393 male adolescent non-sexual offenders, on theoretically derived variables to determine which variables are most relevant to JSOs as compared with other youthful

---

1. Most of the research reviewed in this chapter focuses on male juvenile sexual offenders. See chapter 13 of this book for a specific discussion of females who sexually abuse.

offenders. The authors found the largest effect sizes for atypical sexual interests (d = 0.67, k = 8)[2] and a history of sexual abuse (d = 0.62, k = 31), indicating higher scores from JSOs than non-sexual juvenile offenders. Regarding other forms of trauma, they found small-to-medium but significant effect sizes for past experience of physical abuse (d = 0.19, k = 20), emotional abuse or neglect (d = 0.28, k = 11), and exposure to (or presence of) sexual violence in the family (d = 0.24, k = 4). There were no group differences with respect to exposure to non-sexual violence in the family or outside of the family. Therefore, while trauma is certainly evident in the lives of many young offenders, trauma and maltreatment experiences (e.g., sexual abuse, physical and emotional abuse, exposure to sexual violence) may be a particularly key part of the etiological puzzle for JSOs. How trauma relates to the development and maintenance of sexual offending, however, is less clear, although much research has centered on elucidating this link.

TRAUMA AND THE DEVELOPMENT OF ADOLESCENT SEXUAL OFFENDING

Social Learning Theory and Trauma Reenactment

Many scholars have devised theories in an attempt to explain the link between trauma and sexual offending. One of the most parsimonious and prevalent explanations is rooted in social learning theory principles in which it has been proposed that sexual offending is learned through exposure to deviant sexual role models in childhood (Burton, 2003; Burton & Meezan, 2004; Felson & Lane, 2009). The main body of evidence in support of this notion is the significantly higher rates of sexual victimization in adolescents who have sexually offended compared with non-sexually offending delinquent youth (Burton & Schatz, 2003; Hunter & Figueredo, 2000). In the victim-to-victimizer, trauma reenactment model, it is hypothesized that children learn to sexually abuse through experiences with sexual abuse, and the learning event can either be their own direct victimization or the witnessing of others being sexually victimized. In this model, children enact sexual behaviors to which they were exposed, which may then persist as a result of the physiological, cognitive, and emotional reinforcements that may follow.

To further support the notion of trauma reenactment, several researchers have shown that specific details around sexual abuse experiences are correlated with attributes of the

---

2. K indicates the number of studies included in meta-analytic comparison.

sexual offense. A relationship has been found between sexual victimization and perpetration toward a male child (Kaufman, Hilliker, & Daleiden, 1996; Worling, 1995; Cooper, Murphy, & Haynes, 1996). For example, Worling (1995) found that the majority (i.e., 75%) of male adolescents who sexually assaulted a male child reported being sexually victimized, compared with a smaller proportion of those youth who assaulted a female child. Cooper, Murphy, and Haynes (1996) also reported that male youth who had been sexually victimized were more likely to abuse male children, compared with those who had not been sexually victimized (Cooper et al., 1996). In addition, Burton (2003) found that the severity and complexity of a youth's sexual victimization were positively correlated with the severity of the youth's sexual perpetration.

Severity of sexual victimization has also been linked to early age of perpetration (Burton, 2000; Wieckowski, Hartsoe, Mayer, & Shortz, 1998). Johnson (1988) found that the earlier the sexually abusive behavior in adult sexual offenders (ASOs) begins, the more likely the individuals are to have been sexually abused themselves. Other studies found that sexual acts perpetrated by JSOs mirrored their own abuse experiences (Burton, 2003; Veneziano, Veneziano, & LeGrand, 2000). Using social learning theory principles, severity of sexual abuse experiences could increase the salience and memory of the modeled event, as well as symptomatology from the trauma of the event (Burton, 2000; Burton & Meezan, 2004). Social learning theory has also been used to explain the relationship between physically abusive experiences (witnessing violence or being physically abused) and sexual offending in adolescents. These experiences may provide models for violent behavior that combine with sexual development, sexual victimization experiences, and/or other factors, such as pornography exposure, social skills deficits, and personality traits, which in turn result in sexually aggressive behavior (Burton & Meezan, 2004).

Cognitive processes can also be modeled and learned. Adolescents may learn thoughts and interpretations of motives associated with certain behaviors, thereby altering cognitions, which may lead to sexually abusive behaviors. In an attempt to make sense of their victimization, youth may develop a cognitive schema that helps to explain the abuse (Stinson et al., 2008). A youth who has been sexually or physically abused may endorse certain maladaptive cognitions, such as normalizing abuse, believing that abuse is not harmful, believing sexual abuse will feel good or reduce anxiety, having less empathy, or attributing more blame to abuse victims (Burton & Meezan, 2004; Shahinfar, Kupersmidt, & Matza, 2001; Racey, Lopez, & Schneider, 2000; McCrady et al., 2008). Cognitive distortions may especially center on relationships and interpersonal difficulties.

The presence of maladaptive social cognitions and the misinterpretation of social cues is indeed supported by a substantial literature identifying social skills deficits, peer rejection, and higher rates of social isolation in juvenile sexual offenders (Davis-Rosanbalm, 2003; Hunter, Figueredo, Malamuth, & Becker, 2003; Miner & Munns, 2005). Attitudes toward non-consenting sex and knowledge about appropriate social boundaries can be negatively shaped by an offender's own experiences in which consent and boundaries were violated. In addition, several thinking errors and distorted cognitions about sexual behavior have been associated with sexual reoffending (Kahn & Chambers, 1991; Schram et al., 1991; Worling & Curwen, 2000), and these cognitions are often the target of treatment programs aimed to reduce sexual offending.

Deviant/Atypical Sexual Interests

Reviewing a learned event (i.e., cognitive rehearsal) under pleasurable conditions, such as masturbating, may lead to the development and/or reinforcement of atypical sexual fantasies. The prevalence of atypical sexual interests or fantasies (e.g., inappropriate partner choice, attractions to illegal or highly unusual sexual acts)—another potentially unique attribute in JSOs compared with other offenders—has also been discussed in the context of trauma; atypical sexual fantasies are indeed seen in some JSO and adult offenders (Zakireh et al., 2008; Seto & Lalumière, 2010; Langevin, Lang, & Curnoe, 1998). However, before proceeding with this discussion, it is important to note that only a minority of JSOs will exhibit atypical sexual interests (for a review, see Worling, 2012) and therefore, while relevant, atypical sexual interests are likely to be a predominant treatment need in only a small proportion of JSOs.

Johnson and Knight (2000) found that sexual victimization predicted the degree of sexual coercion used in sexual offenses perpetrated by youth, in part through misogynistic sexual fantasies. In addition, atypical sexual interests have been shown to be predictive of sexual recidivism in research examining risk prediction in adult sexual offenders and JSOs (Hanson & Morton-Bourgon, 2005; Rajlic & Gretton, 2010; Kenny, Keogh, & Seidler, 2001; Långström, 2002; Långström & Grann, 2000; Schram, Milloy, & Rowe, 1991; Worling & Curwen, 2000). As such, a number of juvenile offender treatment programs incorporate the modification of atypical sexual interests as targets of treatment when indicated.

One comprehensive explanation for the links among abuse experiences, fantasies, and sexual offending behavior was provided by Maniglio (2011), who proposed that atypical sexual fantasies provide a manner of coping with negative states that arise from abuse experiences. He suggested that atypical sexual fantasies are a source of arousal and pleasure that might serve to help an individual, lacking in coping strategies, cope with anxiety, depression, or other psychological problems that result from child sexual abuse (e.g., humiliation, rejection, anger, low self-esteem). For example, sexual offenders with post-traumatic stress might hold atypical sexual fantasies to avoid or alleviate intrusive symptoms, or offenders with depressive feelings may engage in atypical fantasies to reduce negative affect and helplessness and to increase energy, confidence, and feelings of happiness.

Maniglio also posited that engaging in atypical fantasies as a means to cope with psychological symptoms may lead to self-perpetuating cycles of fantasies and psychological distress that exacerbate the offender's social and emotional functioning difficulties. Fantasies would build more power if they are rehearsed in patterns of compulsive masturbation, also strengthening the association between fantasy content and arousal (MacCulloch et al., 2000). An individual's efforts to restrain acting out fantasies may be ineffective in the face of intense emotional states, and so actualizing fantasy (i.e., offending) may be another way of coping with these internal states. This disposition to offend may be acted upon in cases where there is a victim accessible, if inhibitions are diminished, and/or if there is disengagement from social rules (Maniglio, 2011).

Psychopathology

Affective Problems and Coping

Mental health concerns are common sequelae to trauma experiences in childhood (Hunter et al., 2003), and, as noted, high rates of mental health problems have indeed been identified among JSOs (e.g., depression, anxiety, social problems, PTSD, personality disorders or features; Galli et al., 1999; Jacobs, Kennedy, & Meyer, 1997; Cooper et al., 1996). These high rates of mental health problems have prompted researchers to investigate the known correlates of abuse and mental illness, such as emotional distress, emotion dyregulation, personality traits, and their etiological role in sexual offending. It has been postulated that emotional distress (e.g., anger, depression, anxiety), stemming from abusive experiences, may manifest externally in the form of physical or sexual aggression (Briere & Elliott, 1994). For example, in Galli et al. (1999), a group of adolescent males who sexually offended against children reported that their sexual impulses and behaviors were activated when they experienced negative mood symptoms. This finding is also in line with research on adult offenders (Cortoni & Marshall, 2001; Neidigh & Tomiko, 1991) as well as research by Hall and Hirschman (1991), who discuss a subtype of offender who engages in sexually aggressive behaviors when they are experiencing emotional distress, such as sadness or anger.

Experiencing emotional distress may also engage ineffective coping strategies that can set the stage for sexual offending. Several adult sexual offender studies have identified this link (Cortoni & Marshall, 1995; 2001), although research on juveniles is more scant. Ineffective coping is consistent with Maniglio's theory (2011) in which sexual arousal is used as a coping mechanism for affective distress. Hunter and Figueredo (2000) found that JSOs who offended against children 12 years of age and younger had greater negative attributional styles and more pessimistic views than their non-sexual offender counterparts. In addition, Pagé, Tourigny, and Renaud (2010) found that JSOs tended to use more emotion-focused coping strategies (i.e., focusing on their own emotions) than non-offending adolescents, concluding that this strategy potentially further increases distress and places JSOs at higher risk to offend. Other negative coping strategies in response to stress have been identified in JSOs, including sex as coping (Hastings et al., 1997; Cortoni & Marshall, 2001), aggressive control seeking (Spaccarelli, Bowden, Coatsworth, & Kim, 1997), and poor anger management (Van Ness, 1984).

Trauma Dissociation

Trauma, PTSD, and related symptomatology are prevalent among the JSO population, and trauma-related dissociative symptoms have been proposed to link early trauma experiences with sexual offending behaviors. More specifically, JSOs may be at greater risk for experiencing dissociative symptoms (e.g., flashbacks, amnesia, depersonalization, and derealization) and may act out in sexual and/or violent ways from trauma-related conditions. Adolescents who use dissociation to cope with abuse experiences may have those same dissociative symptoms activated during perpetration or abuse, becoming highly absorbed in the event and having distorted perceptions of their role as well as the victim's role (Becker-Blease & Freyd, 2007). Therefore, trauma could serve to initiate and/or sustain sexual offending behaviors through dissociative symptoms.

While many studies have shown a trauma–dissociation link in adult sexual offenders and youth general offenders (Carrion & Steiner, 2000; Plattner et al., 2003; Walker, 2002; Moskowitz, 2004; Becker-Blease & Freyd, 2007), some limited research also points to a preliminary trauma–dissociation link in JSOs more specifically. Leibowitz, Laser, and Burton (2011) examined dissociation and abuse experiences in 243 JSOs and 109 delinquent youth (n = 352). They investigated five types of abuse experiences (sexual abuse, physical abuse, emotional abuse, emotional neglect, and physical neglect), as well as frequency of dissociative symptoms in the last two months (e.g., flashbacks, "spacing out," dizziness, memory problems, feeling detached and as if things are unreal). The authors found that JSOs had significantly higher mean dissociation scores than other delinquent youth. In addition, using hierarchical logistic regression analysis, dissociation symptoms, as well as physical and sexual abuse experiences, best predicted membership in the sexual offender group. Further, Friedrich et al. (2001) conducted a study investigating correlates of dissociation in two samples, namely JSOs and psychiatric inpatients. They found that JSOs experienced significantly more trauma (i.e., two to five times greater) than psychiatric inpatients and that 14 percent of JSOs met the criteria for a dissociative spectrum disorder. They also found that, for JSOs, a history of physical abuse was related to a diagnosis of dissociation. Finally, in one study, trauma-associated emotions were "offense triggers" for male juvenile sex abusers, 65 percent of whom met the criteria for PTSD (McMackin et al., 2002).

Personality Traits

Maladaptive personality traits (e.g., impulsivity, empathy deficits, antisocial personality), another known correlate of trauma/abuse, have also been shown to be associated with sexual offending and reoffending among youth (Miner, 2002; Nisbet et al., 2004; Schram et al., 1991; Seto & Lalumière, 2010; Worling, 2001; McCrory, Hickey, Farmer, & Vizard, 2008). Reduced empathy and callous/unemotional traits have been a particular focus of research in JSOs and ASOs alike, and there is indeed empirical support for lower levels of empathy and more callous/unemotional traits in JSOs compared with non-offending adolescents (Lindsey, Carlozzi, & Eells, 2001; Burke, 2001; Farr, Brown, & Beckett, 2004; White Cruise & Frick, 2009; Caputo, Frick, & Brodsky, 1999; see Varker, Devilly, Ward, & Beech, 2008, for review of empathy in JSOs). It has been hypothesized that lack of empathy serves to disinhibit sexual arousal, which then contributes to sexual offending (Marshall & Barbaree, 1990). Sexual offenders may also lack concern for victims if there is an inability to fully appreciate the victim's experiences as negative (Regehr & Glancy, 2001). Importantly, while reduced empathy and callous/unemotional traits are clearly an area of concern, they may not be unique to JSOs, as some non-sexual offenders have also been shown to score high on these particular traits (Seto & Lalumière, 2010).

Some models investigating the mediating roles of personality traits in JSOs have been proposed and tested. Knight and Sims-Knight (2003) suggested that early abuse leads to sexual aggression, through certain maladaptive personality traits (e.g., impulsivity and callousness/unemotionality) and high sexualization. The combination of these traits and high sexualization may then disinhibit sexually aggressive fantasies, a known antecedent to sexual coercion. Notably, these authors recognized a unique developmental characteristic of JSOs (as compared with non-sexual offenders), namely the tendency to be sexually preoccupied and/or to have a more active sexual drive. Knight and Sims-Knight (2004) expanded on this model in an empirical investigation with 219 JSOs from inpatient treatment facilities. They examined three different (indirect) pathways through which childhood abuse experiences could lead to sexually coercive behavior toward women: (a) physical/verbal abuse and sexual abuse through callousness/unemotionality to sexual coercion; (b) physical/verbal abuse and sexual abuse through antisocial/aggressive behavior to sexual coercion; and (c) physical/verbal abuse and sexual abuse through sexual fantasies to sexual coercion. This three-pathway model was tested against alternative hypotheses, namely the direct link between sexual abuse and sexual coercion, as well as Malamuth's assertion that sexual coercion is predicted by negative masculinity (i.e., hostility toward women) and sexual promiscuity (Malamuth et al., 1993). The authors found a better fit for the three-pathway model they proposed than for Malamuth's model; in addition, a direct link between sexual abuse and sexual coercion was also supported.

Summary of Trauma and Mental Health Links to Sexual Offending

Experiences of trauma and mental health issues are clearly relevant to the lives of many justice-involved youth, including JSOs. With trauma as a central etiological backdrop, the following factors and processes appear to be associated with sexual offending in JSOs: modeling processes, learned distorted cognitions (e.g., maladaptive social cognitions), atypical sexual interests and fantasies, emotion dysregulation and maladaptive coping with emotional distress, PTSD-related dissociation, and negative personality traits (e.g., callous and unemotional traits). Although these variables are presented in turn, the etiology behind offending behaviors in JSOs is most likely a multi-factorial and complex phenomenon, in which heterotypic pathways depend on a combination of individual characteristics, circumstances, and specific trauma experiences.

AMELIORATING RISK TO REOFFEND IN JSOS

While our understanding of the development of sexual offending in JSOs is progressing, the nature of the relationships between trauma variables and sexual offending remains somewhat unclear—whether variables are directly related to offending behavior, if the relationship is in fact an indirect one, or if some of these challenges are better described as coexisting vulnerabilities in this population. Further, whether and how the aforementioned factors contribute to sexual reoffending (i.e., recidivism) in this population is even less clear. Examining unique and specific variables related to sexual reoffense has been especially difficult given the generally low rates of sexual reoffense in JSOs (McCann & Lussier, 2008; Caldwell, 2010).

While specific JSO recidivism studies are increasing in number, in the existing studies there are contradictions in results and varying definitions of sexual reoffense that make it difficult to draw comparisons across studies (Worling & Långström, 2006; Spice, Viljoen, Latzman, Scalora, & Ullman, 2013). Nevertheless, some correlates of reoffending have been identified and the field is progressing in this area of research

(McCann & Lussier, 2008; Viljoen, Latzman, Scalora, & Ullman, 2012; Viljoen, Mordell, & Beneteau, 2008; Worling & Långström, 2006). Of the developmental factors related to trauma discussed thus far, only a small subset appear to have been directly linked to sexual reoffense, namely atypical sexual interests, distorted cognitions, and social isolation (which may relate to maladaptive social cognitions; Worling & Curwen, 2000; Långström & Grann, 2000; Lipsey & Derzon, 1998). Further, what is even less clear from this research is whether the trauma-related factors discussed above have a direct relationship with offending, once well-established proximal criminogenic risk factors (i.e., factors empirically determined to be strongly and directly related to reoffending), such as those outlined in the risk-need-responsivity framework (RNR; Andrews & Bonta, 2010; Andrews, Bonta, & Hoge, 1990), are taken into account (e.g., criminal history, antisocial attitudes). Although not focused on JSOs specifically, research within the RNR framework has in fact demonstrated that symptoms resulting from, or exposure to, traumatic experiences are generally *not* empirically validated risk factors for offending. The importance of understanding how (or if) trauma and mental health issues relate to reoffending cannot be overstated, given that, from a rehabilitation framework, we must ensure we are conducting intervention practices that actually have an impact on reducing offending.

As highlighted elsewhere in this book, the RNR model is a well-established, theoretically based framework for the assessment and treatment of offenders. This framework has been widely adopted in correctional and community settings within North America, Europe, and beyond (e.g., Australia, Singapore), although its application specifically to sexual offenders has been slower to take hold (Hanson, Bourgon, Helmus, & Hodgson, 2009; Lösel & Schmucker, 2005; Zeng, Chu, Koh, & Teoh, 2015), with some concerns highlighted that RNR-based risk assessment tools may not be specialized enough for use with JSOs (Prescott, 2004; Vincent, Guy, & Grisso, 2012). Despite some concerns, recent research (Hanson et al., 2009) has demonstrated the applicability of the framework to the treatment of both youth and adults with sexual offenses.

The RNR framework highlights that, in order to ameliorate an individual's risk to reoffend, rehabilitative services must be focused on risk factors that are strongly and directly related to an individual's criminal behavior (criminogenic needs). In addition, treatment modality is important (general responsivity), as are characteristics of the individual that could impact treatment effectiveness (specific responsivity). As articulated by Taxman (2014), responsivity is not just about decreasing risk to reoffend but also about increasing an offender's receptivity to treatment programming and tailoring programming to take into account individual characteristics that can impact the success of treatment. Treatments that adhere to the RNR principles have consistently been shown to reduce rates of future general offending, violent offending, and—more recently—sexual offending as well (Andrews & Bonta, 2006; Dowden & Andrews, 1999a; Hanson et al., 2009; Lösel & Schmucker, 2005). In addition, these treatment effects have been demonstrated in both youth and adult offenders.

Mental Health in the RNR Framework

Within the general RNR framework, trauma and mental health concerns are not considered criminogenic needs in assessment and treatment planning; rather, these issues are considered specific responsivity variables. As such, mental health concerns are considered important to address in treatment because they have the potential to impact the success of criminogenic needs treatment. For example, anxiety may interfere with a youth's ability to engage in treatment programming but in and of itself would not be directly related to the likelihood of that youth reoffending. Generally, there is little support for a direct relationship between mental health and offending (for a review, see McCormick, Peterson-Badali, & Skilling, 2015). Meta-analytic studies have examined the relationship between mental health and criminal behavior and specifically whether mental health issues are predictive of recidivism (Bonta, Law, & Hanson, 1998; Lipsey & Derzon, 1998; Douglas, Guy, & Hart, 2009; Cottle, Lee, & Heilbrun, 2001). The conclusion reached from the results of these studies is that mental health issues are not a criminogenic need because these types of variables generally do not strongly predict future offending, especially when considered alongside well-established criminogenic needs (e.g., antisocial attitudes, antisocial peers). There is research to suggest, however, that mental health functioning can be related to technical violations of release conditions and therefore may impact offenders in a negative way, such as failure to complete mandated treatments (Eno Louden et al., 2008).

Meta-analyses have further shown that interventions with a clinical focus on mental health/clinical outcomes do not necessarily improve criminal outcomes (e.g., Lipsey, 1999). Research by Skeem et al. (2011) highlighted that treatment programming that focused solely on mental health issues, to the exclusion of well-established criminogenic needs, did have a positive impact on mental health outcomes, but not criminal outcomes. Skeem et al. (2011) concluded that there is a direct relationship between mental health status and criminal behavior for only a small group of mentally ill offenders, but for others, the association is fully mediated by criminogenic needs. Findings such as these have led researchers and practitioners using an RNR framework to argue that interventions should address criminogenic needs regardless of mental health symptoms, although mental health may be targeted as a responsivity variable (Bonta, 1995).

While discussion concerning the role of specific responsivity has existed in the litera-ture for decades (e.g., Bonta, 1995; McCormick et al., 2015), and it has been acknowl-edged as a very important consideration (e.g., Andrews, Bonta, & Wormith, 2011), research on responsivity has actually been quite limited to date (Andrews et al., 2011; Hubbard, 2007). Certainly this is true in the context of sexual offending.

A recent study (McCormick et al., 2016) directly examined criminal outcomes for justice-involved youth (some of whom were sexual offenders) with and without serious mental health issues, and did so alongside empirically validated criminogenic risk/need variables. Findings from this research highlighted that youth with identified mental health needs were no more likely than youth without such needs to reoffend, regardless of whether those needs were treated. Of note, youth who participated in treatment for their mental health issues were more likely than youth with untreated mental health concerns to also have their criminogenic needs targeted, suggesting that mental health treatment was associated with intermediate treatment targets. However, mental health treatment did not moderate the effectiveness of criminogenic need treatment—criminogenic need treatment reduced the risk of reoffending regard-less of whether mental health issues were treated or not. These findings lend support to the RNR research perspective that mental health needs are not in and of themselves criminogenic needs, but treating mental health may facilitate (rather than moderate) engagement in criminogenic need treatment.

Trauma in the RNR Framework

While the role of mental health in relation to offending has been quite extensively stud-ied, it is only in more recent years that increasing attention has been paid to trauma and PTSD among offenders (i.e., Abram et al., 2004). Impulsivity and emotional reac-tivity are both frequent behavioral concerns in justice-involved populations, and these issues could be sequelae of trauma experiences (Ford, Chapman, Mack, & Pearson, 2006; Greenwald, 2002); therefore, trauma could plausibly be playing a relevant role in offending. However, while exposure to traumatic events and resultant symptoms of trauma are of course relevant to the well-being of individuals involved in the justice system, researchers from an RNR framework argue that these variables have not been empirically established as criminogenic needs and therefore would not be direct targets for interventions concerned with reducing future criminal behavior. As with mental health concerns, some trauma-related factors are captured under the construct of spe-cific responsivity within the RNR framework. For example, risk-need assessment tools (e.g., YLS/CMI 2.0; Hoge & Andrews, 2012) have captured past traumatic experiences in a special consideration section, where service providers can make note of potential responsivity issues, but these issues are not considered in the determination of risk and are not considered the primary targets for intervention.

Finally, the maltreatment literature has clearly demonstrated a relationship between maltreatment in childhood and offending, and this relationship seems to be particularly true for JSOs. But again, given the notable overlap between several potential sequelae of maltreatment (e.g., difficulties with emotional regulation, familial discord and dysfunction, difficulties with learning and education) and known criminogenic needs (e.g., needs in the domains of personality, family, and education/employment), it is important to test the causal relationship between maltreatment and offending while taking into account these already established proximal risk factors. These factors represent shared vulnerabilities in both the youth justice and maltreated youth populations that could potentially better explain risk for reoffending than maltreatment exposure alone.

Recent work (Vitopoulos, 2016) exploring the relationships among various trauma constructs, criminogenic needs, and recidivism demonstrated that, while rates of PTSD symptomatology, maltreatment, and childhood adversity were significantly higher in a justice-involved sample, PTSD symptomatology and childhood adversity were not significant predictors of recidivism when entered into regression models alongside criminogenic needs. However, a history of maltreatment (physical, sexual, and/or emotional abuse and neglect) was predictive of recidivism over and above well-established criminogenic risk-need factors. This finding that maltreatment, versus other trauma variables such as PTSD symptoms and more general childhood adversity, may be more directly linked to offending behavior has some other support in the literature. For example, Smith, Leve, and Chamberlain (2006) found that maltreatment in childhood was predictive of later offending in a sample of adolescent girls—but PTSD symptoms were not. Interestingly, recent studies by Onifade, Barnes, Campbell, Anderson, Petersen, and Davidson (2014) and Li, Chu, Goh, Ng, and Zenf (2015) highlight that a well-established risk assessment tool (RNR-based YLS/CMI) was a strong predictor of reoffending in youth without serious maltreatment histories, but that the tool did not accurately predict recidivism for maltreated justice-involved youth.

Much more research is needed to unpack the relationships among maltreatment, criminogenic needs, and criminal behavior, but this recent research, along with the research described earlier highlighting a link between maltreatment and sexual offending, suggests that justice-involved youth with serious maltreatment histories, like JSOs, may have additional criminogenic needs linked to their subsequent offending that are not as readily captured by the current RNR domains of criminogenic need. Therefore, assessment tools and treatment practices may need to incorporate maltreatment variables and the psychopathology associated with severe maltreatment to effectively decrease risk to reoffend.

In summary, effectively assessing and treating mental health concerns will undoubtedly lead to better outcomes for JSOs. However, it is important to be clear that these concerns are likely to be indirectly related to criminal behavior. Therefore, while services must take into account these serious concerns (i.e., specific responsivity), they must not be to the exclusion of criminogenic needs if we are to impact offending behavior and increase public safety. Having said that, it may be the case that childhood maltreatment is a salient factor directly related to offending. As highlighted, maltreatment histories may be of particular relevance to juvenile offenders with sexual offending histories and, therefore, rehabilitative services must importantly consider these factors.

CONSIDERATIONS FOR TREATMENT SERVICES

There has been much progress in understanding sexually abusive behavior in the past several decades, as already described in this chapter. However, our understanding of the behavior and whether we can translate that understanding into effective treatments for sexual offenders continues to be debated, particularly with respect to adult offenders. This debate continues, in part, because many studies showing positive treatment effects are methodologically weak, and studies with more rigorous experimental designs have not demonstrated differences in recidivism between treated and untreated offenders (Hanson, Broom, & Stephenson, 2004; Lamade, Gabriel, & Prentky, 2011; Levenson, 2014; Marques, Wiederanders, Day, Nelson, & van Ommeren, 2005; Seto et al., 2008). Randomized trials and high-quality quasi-experimental treatment studies are needed with both youth and adult populations to provide a more solid evidence base on effective treatment for sexual offending behavior (Schmucker & Lösel, 2015).

Meta-analytic studies do, however, provide evidence that there are some promising treatment approaches to treating sexual offending behavior, with significant, if modest, reductions in recidivism noted overall across studies (Hanson et al., 2002; Lösel & Schmucker, 2005; Schmucker & Lösel, 2015). Notably, these meta-analyses primarily included studies with adult populations, although some studies (17% in Schmucker & Lösel, 2015) on adolescents are represented. Most recently, Schmucker and Lösel (2015) found an overall significant mean effect size for sexual recidivism, with a relative reduction in recidivism of about 26 percent in the treated group over the untreated group. More specifically, cognitive-behavioral therapy (CBT) and multisystemic therapy (MST) approaches with adolescents resulted in better treatment effects, as did treatments that focused on medium- to high-risk offenders, and treatments that were more individualized and provided in the community. These findings are also in keeping with the RNR principles highlighted above.

Results from another meta-analysis focused on the RNR principles of service intervention specifically suggested that treatment is effective for sexual offenders, particularly if the treatment program attends to the RNR principles (Hanson et al., 2009). This meta-analytic study demonstrated that such treatment can have an impact on sexual reoffense rates in both youth and adults, similar to the impact of RNR-based treatment on general and violent reoffending. Conclusions remain somewhat tentative, though, because of the lack of studies that were deemed high quality (Hanson et al., 2009; Hanson & Yates, 2013), which is also in keeping with the conclusions from Schmucker & Lösel (2015). While various models of intervention have been applied to the treatment of individuals who sexually offend, the vast majority of sex-offender-specific treatment programs are currently based on CBT principles (Laws, 1989; Laws, Hudson, & Ward, 2000; McGrath, Cumming, Burchard, Zeoli, & Ellerby, 2010), an approach that is clearly supported in the meta-analytic studies highlighted above. CBT and MST approaches have been found to be most effective in reducing recidivism in JSOs (e.g., Borduin, Schaeffer, & Heiblum, 2009; Reitzel & Carbonell, 2006; Walker, McGovern, Poey, & Otis, 2004) and would include treatment targets such as cognitive distortions (e.g., children as sexual beings, sexual activity does not harm children), atypical sexual behavior, emotion dysregulation, and interpersonal skills deficits (Schaffer, Jeglic, Moster, & Wnuk, 2010) through skill building, practice, and rehearsal (Hanson & Yates, 2013). Notably, these factors were highlighted earlier in this chapter as being linked to the development, and some to the continuation (i.e., recidivism), of sexual offending in JSOs.

The meta-analytic results from Schmucker and Lösel (2015), as well as Hanson et al. (2009), also highlight that programs that take a more individualized approach to treatment have stronger treatment effects. This individualized approach to treatment is clearly in keeping with the responsivity principle within an RNR framework and is also well articulated within the MST framework (e.g., Henggeler & Borduin, 1990), which incorporates elements from CBT to address youth-specific factors, as well as family work and a youth's social context. The MST approach is individualized and comprehensive in order to address multiple problems related to youth and their families (Letourneau & Borduin, 2008) and can therefore incorporate treatment targets related to youth's specific treatment needs.

Dialectical behavior therapy (DBT) is another therapeutic model, based in part on CBT principles, that has been recently utilized within forensic populations (McCann, Ivanoff, Schmidt, & Beach, 2007; Berzins & Trestman, 2004; Shelton, Sampl, Kesten,

Zhang, & Trestman, 2009). This model of treatment was developed by Marsha Linehan (1993) for outpatient intervention with individuals diagnosed with borderline personality disorder (BPD). As noted, it is based in CBT principles integrated with aspects of Eastern philosophies. DBT consists of four components—group-based skill teaching, individual therapy, telephone coaching, and group consultation—designed to address difficulties in the areas of distress tolerance, emotion regulation, and interpersonal effectiveness. One of the main principles of DBT is the balance between acceptance of the client and the need for change. DBT techniques have been extended into adult and juvenile forensic settings and have been demonstrated to be compatible with best practice principles with forensic populations (McCann et al., 2007).

More recently, it has been proposed that DBT-based therapeutic techniques could also be highly applicable to sexual offender treatment (Sakdalan & Gupta, 2014), although studies have yet to be conducted to demonstrate its effectiveness with this population. Shingler (2004) outlined several important similarities that are seen in some clients with BPD and some sexual offenders; specifically, both populations may experience emotional dysregulation, interpersonal difficulties, cognitive distortions, and challenges with impulsivity. Additionally, maltreatment experiences have been found to be prevalent in both populations (e.g., Ball & Links, 2009; Seto & Lalumière, 2010). Shingler (2004) also noted that the defining features of DBT are highly relevant for sexual offender treatment—for example, the focus on treatment-interfering behaviors in order to increase commitment to therapy as well as validation of the client's difficult emotions and circumstances. Of course, the specific needs of clients would vary because of the heterogeneity in this population of offenders; it may also be the case that the DBT model and techniques may be effective for some but not all individuals.

Trauma-Informed Care

As discussed above, the significant impact of early maltreatment experiences on functioning and trauma-related symptoms are highly prevalent in youth who have sexually offended, and are potentially related to a client's ability to fully engage and benefit from treatment (i.e., responsivity considerations). For example, McMackin and his colleagues (2002) suggested that addressing trauma-associated feelings and experiences may be an important aspect of treatment, where the goal is reducing reoffending. Singer (2013) further argued (with respect to adult sexual offenders) that most sexual offending may be better explained in the context of deficits in emotional regulation and relational patterns, which result in an underlying inability to manage one's own distress and effectively connect with others. As such, focusing entirely on strategies like cognitive reframing and relapse prevention, while leaving trauma-related symptoms and patterns of behavior unaddressed in the context of treatment, does not take into account the impact these individualized experiences may have on the client's ability to benefit from treatment and develop more adaptive cognitions, self-regulation skills, and prosocial peer relationships (Andrews & Bonta, 2010).

While there are treatment protocols designed for sexual offenders that directly address issues of trauma (e.g., Schwartz, 1994), there has recently been a push toward incorporating process-oriented and *trauma-specific* treatment approaches into existing content-oriented interventions. Trauma-informed care provides a framework, which can be incorporated into existing treatment models, such as sexual-offense-specific cognitive behavioral therapy, in order to increase their effectiveness (Levenson, 2014; Levenson, Willis, & Prescott, 2014). Although this idea has been discussed mostly in the literature related to adult sexual offenders, it is likely quite applicable to the juvenile population as well and should also be considered an area for further research for JSOs.

Trauma-informed care is based on a fundamental understanding of the impact of traumatic experiences on the individual's interpersonal and coping skills as well as his or her sense of identity and basic assumptions about the world. Delivery of assessment and intervention services within a trauma-informed care approach orients the service provider to the possibility of trauma history and its impact on the client's behavior throughout the life span. This allows for a more accurate identification of trauma-related symptoms in clients. When service providers take into account the possible impact of trauma on functioning and behavior, maladaptive behaviors are seen as clients' potential adaptations to their previous traumatic experiences or negative responses to trauma-related triggers. More specifically, it is understood that clients developed patterns of behavior and coping strategies that were appropriate and effective in the context of the traumatogenic environment; however, they are maladaptive and interfere with optimal functioning in other environments. As such, clients' maladaptive patterns of behavior are not viewed as symptoms of an underlying dysfunction but rather as survival strategies. In this way, trauma-informed care focuses on clients' strengths rather than pathology and encourages skill building rather than symptom reduction (Levenson, 2014; Elliot et al., 2005; Harris & Fallot, 2001).

A clinician operating within the trauma-informed approach strives to create a safe and client-centered environment, where the client is afforded a sense of control over the therapeutic environment and the treatment process. This approach is particularly important because it ensures that the dynamics of the traumatic interactions are not replicated within the therapeutic environment, which will serve to retraumatize the client and undermine the development of trust and a working therapeutic alliance. The service provider communicates respect and acceptance of the client and avoids judgmental messages that imply an underlying defect in the client (Levenson, 2014; Elliot et al., 2005; Harris & Fallot, 2001).

Notably, previous treatment approaches with sexual offenders often employed confrontational techniques, which may be counterproductive because such interactions serve to re-create the traumatic experiences in the therapeutic setting and could lead to lack of engagement in treatment as well as perpetuation of the client's maladaptive coping strategies (Beech & Fordham, 1997; Kear-Colwell & Pollock, 1997). In contrast, when trauma-informed care is well integrated into all aspects of the intervention, it may allow the client to develop a better therapeutic relationship, in the context of which both content (e.g., maladaptive cognitions) and process (interpersonal relatedness) issues can be addressed. Most importantly, the safe and respectful context of the trauma-informed framework provides an opportunity for the client to engage in corrective experiences. Levenson and Macgowan (2004) note that, for some clients with significant histories of abuse, the therapeutic relationship within the trauma-informed framework may be their first opportunity to experience respectful interactions and appropriate boundaries in an interpersonal relationship. In the context of these corrective experiences, clients can gain a better understanding of the impact of trauma on their behavior and are guided toward constructing more adaptive coping and interpersonal skills. This, in turn, could help to cease the cycle of abuse and potentially reduce recidivism risk.

The therapeutic process with clients who have sexually offended and have a history of trauma is undoubtedly challenging for both the service provider and the client. For the client, triggering events or processing previous traumatic events in treatment can elicit strong negative emotions and lead to emotional and behavioral dysregulation. This, in turn, may lead the client to react with hostility and resistance toward the therapeutic process. For the therapist, the client's maladaptive patterns of cognitions and behaviors may elicit negative feelings and countertransference reactions and a tendency toward confrontational interactions. It is important for service providers to consider these process issues and take steps to effectively manage them. The development of expressed empathy toward the client can provide the foundation for successful management of such challenges inherent in these interactions. In addition, service providers are encouraged to introspect about their own attitudes and beliefs and how they may impact their fostering of a safe therapeutic environment for their client. As noted above, judgmental and confrontational reactions toward the client may inadvertently re-create the dynamics that are similar to those of the traumatic environment and serve to retraumatize the client (Levenson, 2014). In contrast, responding to clients with empathy, respect, and validation not only fosters the therapeutic alliance and increases the client's engagement in treatment but also provides corrective experiences for the client.

Trauma-informed care can be applied to interventions in both individual and group therapy settings. When group dynamics are positive and supportive, the group setting provides various opportunities to model and practice effective interpersonal skills, provided that the principles of trauma-informed care have been adhered to and the group environment offers a safe and respectful environment for clients (Yalom, 1995). For example, Tougas and colleagues (2014) reported on the effectiveness of a psycho-educational group intervention for youth sexual offenders, many of whom presented with a significant history of trauma. The aim of the intervention was to enhance social skills, raise self-esteem, improve sex knowledge and attitudes, improve stress and anger control, and prevent recidivism by helping offenders better understand the process that led to the sexual assault and develop strategies to avoid sexually inappropriate behaviors in the future. Although the 24- to 30-week intervention did not include direct teaching of trauma-related topics, the authors concluded that the various activities included in the group sessions, such as those aimed at identifying triggers, likely led to discussions of past maltreatment suffered by the youth. The group setting allowed for youth to learn that others had experiences similar to theirs, which in turn may have reduced the sense of isolation and stigmatization.

Future Directions for Treatment

In summary, incorporating a trauma-informed care approach into existing intervention programs with youth who have sexually offended may serve to facilitate engagement in the therapy as well as address impairing trauma-related symptoms. As such, it could increase responsivity to existing evidence-based approaches. At the present time, there is a paucity of systematic studies evaluating the effectiveness of interventions that include a specific trauma-informed approach with youth who have sexually offended. Trauma is clearly a significant factor impacting a large proportion of these youth. Considering the encouraging, albeit very preliminary, results found in the adult literature regarding the effectiveness of trauma-informed approaches to intervention with sexual offenders (Ricci & Clayton, 2008; Ricci, 2006), it is important to evaluate this approach further in studies with both adult and youthful sexual offenders.

The following are some recommendations based on the literature on how to integrate trauma-informed approaches into existing intervention programs:

- Training therapists in understanding the potential links between trauma and sexual offending behaviors

- Screening all clients for trauma histories

- Assessing clients for the presence of PTSD symptoms

- Teaching clients to manage trauma-related difficulties with affective regulation

In addition to the recommendations outlined above, it is also important to provide training to service providers in the clinical skills required to create a safe, respectful, and nonjudgmental environment for their clients. As described above, the principles of DBT also appear to be a promising fit for, and applicable to, sexual offender treatments and hold promise in addressing important needs of this clinical population, such as emotional dysregulation and interpersonal ineffectiveness resulting in part from experiences of maltreatment. Therefore, a more systematic application and evaluation of DBT practices with youthful sexual offenders is an important next step in this field.

CONCLUSIONS

Meta-analytic research clearly suggests that the design and implementation of programs for individuals with sexual offenses should follow the RNR principles (Hanson et al., 2009). Further attention is needed to the need principle in this regard to ensure that treatment programming attends to needs that are actually criminogenic in nature for sexual offenders. Promising targets would include factors such as sexual self-regulation (e.g., atypical sexual interests, sexual preoccupation), low self-control generally, and intimate age-appropriate relationships (Hanson et al., 2009; Hanson & Morton-Bourgon, 2005; Hanson & Yates, 2013). Our current review of the literature suggests that childhood maltreatment, and not just trauma-related symptomatology and/or general mental health needs, may also be a salient risk factor for adolescent sexual offending. Obviously, this risk factor is static in nature and therefore not amenable to change, but the longer-term sequelae of maltreatment may be potential targets for change (i.e., criminogenic needs), such as emotional dysregulation, cognitive distortions, and attachment difficulties. It may also be the case that maltreatment and trauma histories are factors that are relevant to the responsivity principle within the RNR framework. Providing treatments that attend to mental health concerns, particularly those that relate to trauma through trauma-informed practices, may effectively address youth offenders' mental health concerns, which will certainly improve their functioning. In doing so, this may also allow youthful offenders to much more effectively engage in criminogenic needs services, which will in turn directly decrease their risk of reoffending.

_____

REFERENCES

Abram, K. M., Teplin, L. A., Charles, D. R., Longworth, S. L., McClelland, G. M., & Dulcan, M. K. (2004). Posttraumatic stress disorder and trauma in youth in juvenile detention. *Archives of General Psychiatry, 61*(4), 403–410. http://dx.doi.org/10.1001/archpsyc.61.4.403

Andrews, D. A., & Bonta, J. (2006). *The psychology of criminal conduct* (4th ed.). Newark, NJ: Lexis Nexis.

Andrews, D. A., & Bonta, J. (2010). Rehabilitating criminal justice policy and practice. *Psychology, Public Policy, and Law, 16*(1), 39–55. http://dx.doi.org/10.1037/a0018362

Andrews, D. A., Bonta, J., & Hoge, R. D. (1990). Classification for effective rehabilitation: Rediscovering psychology. *Criminal Justice and Behavior, 17*(1), 19–52.

Andrews, D. A., Bonta, J., & Wormith, J. S. (2011). The risk-need-responsivity (RNR) model: Does adding the good lives model contribute to effective crime prevention? *Criminal Justice and Behavior, 38*(7), 735–755. http://dx.doi.org/10.1177/0093854811406356

Andrews, D. A., Bonta, J., Wormith, J. S., Guzzo, L., Brews, A., Rettinger, J., & Rowe, R. (2011). Sources of variability in estimates of predictive validity: A specification with level of service general risk and need. *Criminal Justice and Behavior, 38*(5), 413–432. http://dx.doi.org/10.1177/0093854811401990

Ariga, M., Uehara, T., Takeuchi, K., Ishige, Y., Nakano, R., & Mikuni, M. (2008). Trauma exposure and posttraumatic stress disorder in delinquent female adolescents. *Journal of Child Psychology and Psychiatry, 49*(1), 79–87. http://dx.doi.org/10.1111/j.1469-7610.2007.01817.x

Ball, J. S., & Links, P. S. (2009). Borderline personality disorder and childhood trauma: evidence for a causal relationship. *Current psychiatry reports, 11*(1), 63–68.

Becker-Blease, K., & Freyd, J. J. (2007). Dissociation and memory for perpetration among convicted sex offenders. *Journal of Trauma & Dissociation, 8*(2), 69–80. http://dx.doi.org/10.1300/J229v08n02_05

Beech, A., & Fordham, A. (1997). Therapeutic climate of sexual offender treatment programs. *Sexual Abuse: A Journal of Research and Treatment, 9*(3), 219–238. http://dx.doi.org/10.1007/BF02675066

Berzins, L. G., & Trestman, R. L. (2004). The development and implementation of dialectical behavior therapy in forensic settings. *International Journal of Forensic Mental Health, 3*(1), 93–103. http://dx.doi.org/10.1080/14999013.2004.10471199

Bonta, J. (1995). The responsivity principle and offender rehabilitation. *Forum on Corrections Research, 7*(3), 34–37.

Bonta, J., Law, M., & Hanson, K. (1998). The prediction of criminal and violent recidivism among mentally disordered offenders: A meta-analysis. *Psychological Bulletin, 123*(2), 123–142. http://dx.doi.org/10.1037/0033-2909.123.2.123

Borduin, C. M., Schaeffer, C. M., & Heiblum, N. (2009). A randomized clinical trial of multisystemic therapy with juvenile sexual offenders: Effects on youth social ecology and criminal activity. *Journal of Consulting and Clinical Psychology, 77*, 26–37.

Briere, J. N., & Elliott, D. M. (1994). Immediate and long-term impacts of child sexual abuse. *The Future of Children, 4*(2), 54–69.

Burke D. (2001). Empathy in sexually offending and nonoffending in adolescent males. *Journal of Interpersonal Violence, 16,* 222–233. http://dx.doi.org/10.1177/088626001016003003

Burton, D. L. (2000). Were adolescent sexual offenders children with sexual behavior problems? *Sexual Abuse: A Journal of Research and Treatment, 12*(1), 37–48. http://dx.doi.org/10.1177/107906320001200105

Burton, D. L. (2003). Male adolescents: Sexual victimization and subsequent sexual abuse. *Child & Adolescent Social Work Journal, 20*(4), 277–296. http://dx.doi.org/10.1023/A:1024556909087

Burton, D. L. (2008). An exploratory evaluation of the contribution of personality and childhood sexual victimization to the development of sexually abusive behavior. *Sexual Abuse: A Journal of Research and Treatment, 20*(1), 102–115. http://dx.doi.org/10.1177/1079063208315352

Burton, D. L., & Meezan, W. (2004). Revisiting recent research on social learning theory as an etiological proposition for sexually abusive male adolescents. *Journal of Evidence-Based Social Work, 1*(1), 41–80.

Burton, D. L., Miller, D. L., & Shill, C. T. (2002). A social learning theory comparison of the sexual victimization of adolescent sexual offenders and nonsexual offending male delinquents. *Child Abuse & Neglect, 26*(9), 893–907. http://dx.doi.org/10.1016/S0145-2134(02)00360-5

Burton, D. L., & Schatz, R. (2003). *Meta-analysis of the abuse rates of adolescent sexual abusers.* Paper presented at the 8th International Family Violence Conference, Portsmouth, NH.

Caldwell, M. F. (2002). What we do not know about juvenile sexual reoffense risk. *Child Maltreatment, 7*(4), 291–302. http://dx.doi.org/10.1177/107755902237260

Caldwell, M. F. (2010). Study characteristics and recidivism base rates in juvenile sex offender recidivism. *International Journal of Offender Therapy and Comparative Criminology, 54*(2), 197–212. http://dx.doi.org/10.1177/0306624X08330016

Caputo, A. A., Frick, P. J., & Brodsky, S. L. (1999). Family violence and juvenile sex offending: The potential mediating role of psychopathic traits and negative attitudes toward women. *Criminal Justice and Behavior, 26*(3), 338–356.

Carrion, V. G., & Steiner, H. (2000). Trauma and dissociation in delinquent adolescents. *Journal of the American Academy of Child & Adolescent Psychiatry, 39*(3), 353–359.

Cauffman, E., Feldman, S. S., Waterman, J., & Steiner, H. (1998). Posttraumatic stress disorder among female juvenile offenders. *Journal of the American Academy of Child & Adolescent Psychiatry, 37*(11), 1209–1216.

Chitsabesan, P., & Bailey, S. (2006). Mental health, educational and social needs of young offenders in custody and in the community. *Current Opinion in Psychiatry, 19*(4), 355–360. http://dx.doi.org/10.1097/01.yco.0000228753.87613.01

Coleman, D., & Stewart, L. M. (2010). Prevalence and impact of childhood maltreatment in incarcerated youth. *American Journal of Orthopsychiatry, 80*(3), 343–349. http://dx.doi.org/10.1111/j.1939-0025.2010.01038.x

Cooper, C. L., Murphy, W. D., & Haynes, M. R. (1996). Characteristics of abused and nonabused adolescent sexual offenders. *Sexual Abuse: A Journal of Research and Treatment, 8*(2), 105–119.

Cortoni, F., & Marshall, W. L. (1995). Coping with sex inventory. Unpublished manuscript. Available from the Psychology Department, Queens University, Kingston, Ontario, Canada, K7L 2N6.

Cortoni, F., & Marshall, W. L. (2001). Sex as a coping strategy and its relationship to juvenile sexual history and intimacy in sexual offenders. *Sexual Abuse: A Journal of Research and Treatment, 13*(1), 27–43. http://dx.doi.org/10.1177/107906320101300104

Costello, E. J., Erkanli, A., Fairbank, J. A., & Angold, A. (2002). The prevalence of potentially traumatic events in childhood and adolescence. *Journal of Traumatic Stress, 15*(2), 99–112. http://dx.doi.org/10.1023/A:1014851823163

Cottle, C. C., Lee, R. J., & Heilbrun, K. (2001). The prediction of criminal recidivism in juveniles: A meta-analysis. *Criminal Justice and Behavior, 28*(3), 367–394. http://dx.doi.org/10.1177/0093854801028003005

Davis-Rosanbalm, M. K. (2003). A comparison of social information processing in juvenile sexual offenders and violent nonsexual offenders (Doctoral dissertation). Ohio University, Athens, OH. Dissertation Abstracts International, 64(4-B), 1897 (UMI No. 3086328).

Dixon, A., Howie, P., & Starling, J. (2005). Trauma exposure, posttraumatic stress, and psychiatric comorbidity in female juvenile offenders. *Journal of the American Academy of Child & Adolescent Psychiatry, 44*(8), 798–806. http://dx.doi.org/10.1097/01.chi.0000164590.48318.9c

Douglas, K. S., Guy, L. S., & Hart, S. D. (2009). Psychosis as a risk factor for violence to others: A meta-analysis. *Psychological Bulletin, 135*(5), 679–706. http://dx.doi.org/10.1037/a0016311

Dowden, C., & Andrews, D.A. (1999a). What works in young offender treatment: A meta-analysis. *Forum on Correction Research, 11,* 21–24.

Drerup, L. C., Croysdale, A., & Hoffmann, N. G. (2008). Patterns of behavioral health conditions among adolescents in a juvenile justice system. *Professional Psychology: Research and Practice, 39*(2), 122–128. http://dx.doi.org/10.1037/0735-7028.39.2.122

Elliott, D. E., Bjelajac, P., Fallot, R. D., Markoff, L. S., & Reed, B. G. (2005). Trauma-informed or trauma-denied: Principles and implementation of trauma-informed services for women. *Journal of Community Psychology, 33,* 461–477. http://dx.doi.org/10.1002/jcop.20063

Eno Louden, J., Skeem, J. L., Camp, J., & Christensen, E. (2008). Supervising probationers with mental disorder: How do agencies respond to violations? *Criminal Justice and Behavior, 35*(7), 832–847. http://dx.doi.org/10.1177/0093854808319042

Farr, C., Brown, J., & Beckett, R. (2004). Ability to empathize and masculinity levels: Comparing male adolescent sex offenders with a normative sample of non-offending adolescents. *Psychology, Crime & Law, 10*(2), 155–167. http://dx.doi.org/10.1080/10683160310001597153

Felson, R. B., & Lane, K. J. (2009). Social learning, sexual and physical abuse, and adult crime. *Aggressive Behavior, 35*(6), 489–501. http://dx.doi.org/10.1002/ab.20322

Ford, J. D., Chapman, J., Connor, D. F., & Cruise, K. R. (2012). Complex trauma and aggression in secure juvenile justice settings. *Criminal Justice and Behavior, 39*(6), 694–724. http://dx.doi.org/10.1177/0093854812436957

Ford, J. D., Chapman, J., Mack, M., & Pearson, G. (2006). Pathway from traumatic child victimization to delinquency: Implications for juvenile and permanency court proceedings and decisions. *Juvenile and Family Court Journal, 57*(1), 13–26.

Ford, M. E., & Linney, J. A. (1995). Comparative analysis of juvenile sexual offenders, violent nonsexual offenders, and status offenders. *Journal of Interpersonal Violence, 10*(1), 56–70.

Friedrich, W. N., Gerber, P. N., Koplin, B., Davis, M., Giese, J., Mykelbust, C., & Franckowiak, D. (2001). Multimodal assessment of dissociation in adolescents: Inpatients and juvenile sex offenders. *Sexual Abuse: A Journal of Research and Treatment, 13*(3), 167–177.

Furby, L., Weirott, M. R., & Blackshaw, L. (1989). Sex offender recidivism: A review. *Psychological Bulletin, 105*(1), 3–30. http://dx.doi.org/10.1037/0033-2909.105.1.3

Galli, V., McElroy, S. L., Soutullo, C. A., Kizer, D., Raute, N., Keck, P. E. Jr., & McConville, B. J. (1999). The psychiatric diagnoses of twenty-two adolescents who have sexually molested other children. *Comprehensive Psychiatry, 40*(2), 85–88.

Greenwald, R. (2002). The role of trauma in conduct disorder. *Journal of Aggression, Maltreatment & Trauma, 6*(1), 5–23. http://dx.doi.org/10.1300/J146v06n01_02

Groth, A. N., & Birnbaum, H. J. (1979). *Men who rape: The psychology of the offender.* New York: Plenum Press.

Hall, G. C. N., & Hirschman, R. (1991). Toward a theory of sexual aggression: A quadripartite model. *Journal of Consulting and Clinical Psychology, 59*(5), 662–669. http://dx.doi.org/10.1037/0022-006X.59.5.662

Hanson, R. K., Bourgon, G., Helmus, L., & Hodgson, S. (2009). The principles of effective correctional treatment also apply to sexual offenders: A meta-analysis. *Criminal Justice and Behavior, 36,* 865–891.

Hanson, R. K., Broom, I., & Stephenson, M. (2004). Evaluating community sex offender treatment programs: A 12-year follow-up of 724 offenders. *Canadian Journal of Behavioural Science, 36*(2), 87–96. http://dx.doi.org/10.1037/h0087220

Hanson, R. K., Gordon, A., Harris, A. J. R., Marques, J. K., Murphy, W., Quinsey, V. L., & Seto, M. C. (2002). First report of the collaborative outcome data project on the effectiveness of treatment for sex offenders. *Sexual Abuse: A Journal of Research and Treatment, 14,* 169–194.

Hanson, R. K., & Morton-Bourgon, K. (2005). The characteristics of persistent sexual offenders: A meta-analysis of recidivism studies. *Journal of Consulting and Clinical Psychology, 73*(6), 1154–1163. http://dx.doi.org/10.1037/0022-006X.73.6.1154

Hanson, R. K., & Yates, P. M. (2013). Psychological treatment of sex offenders. *Current Psychiatry Reports, 15,* 348. http://dx.doi.org/10.007/s11920-012-0348-x

Harris, M. E., & Fallot, R. D. (2001). *Using trauma theory to design service systems.* San Francisco: Jossey Bass.

Hastings, T., Anderson, S. J., & Hemphill, P. (1997). Comparisons of daily stress, coping, problem behavior, and cognitive distortions in adolescent sexual offenders and conduct-disordered youth. *Sexual Abuse: A Journal of Research and Treatment, 9*(1), 29–42.

Henggeler, S. W. and Borduin, C. M. (1990). *Family Therapy and Beyond: A multisystemic approach to treating the behavior problems of children and adolescents.* Pacific Grove, CA: Brooks/Cole.

Hoge, R. D., & Andrews, D. A. (2002; 2010). Youth Level of Service/Case Management Inventory: YLS/CMI interview guide. Toronto, Canada: Multi-Health Systems.

Hubbard, D. J. (2007). Getting the most out of correctional treatment: Testing the responsivity principle on male and female offenders. *Federal Probation, 71,* 2–8.

Hunter, J. A. Jr., & Figueredo, A. J. (2000). The influence of personality and history of sexual victimization in the prediction of juvenile perpetrated child molestation. *Behavior Modification, 24*(2), 241–263.

Hunter, J. A., Figueredo, A. J., Malamuth, N. M., & Becker, J. V. (2003). Juvenile sex offenders: Toward the development of a typology. *Sexual Abuse: A Journal of Research and Treatment, 15*(1), 27–48. http://dx.doi.org/10.1023/A:1020663723593

Jacobs, W. L., Kennedy, W. A., & Meyer, J. B. (1997). Juvenile delinquents: A between-group comparison study of sexual and nonsexual offenders. *Sexual Abuse: A Journal of Research and Treatment, 9*(3), 201–217.

Johnson, G. M., & Knight, R. A. (2000). Developmental antecedents of sexual coercion in juvenile sexual offenders. *Sexual Abuse: A Journal of Research and Treatment, 12*(3), 165–178.

Johnson, T. C. (1988). Child perpetrators—children who molest other children: Preliminary findings. *Child Abuse & Neglect, 12*(2), 219–229.

Jonson-Reid, M., & Way, I. (2001). Adolescent sexual offenders: Incidence of childhood maltreatment, serious emotional disturbance, and prior offenses. *American Journal of Orthopsychiatry, 71*(1), 120–130. http://dx.doi.org/10.1037/0002-9432.71.1.120

Kahn, T. J., & Chambers, H. J. (1991). Assessing reoffense risk with juvenile sexual offenders. *Child Welfare: Journal of Policy, Practice, and Program, 70*(3), 333–345.

Kaufman, K. L., Hilliker, D. R., & Daleiden, E. L. (1996). Subgroup differences in the modus operandi of adolescent sexual offenders. *Child Maltreatment, 1*(1), 17–24.

Kear-Colwell, J., & Pollock, P. (1997). Motivation or confrontation: Which approach to the child sex offender? *Criminal Justice and Behavior, 24*(1), 20–33. http://dx.doi.org/10.1177/0093854897024001002

Kenny, D. T., Keogh, T., & Seidler, K. (2001). Predictors of recidivism in Australian juvenile sex offenders: Implications for treatment. *Sexual Abuse: A Journal of Research and Treatment, 13*(2), 131–148. http://dx.doi.org/10.1177/107906320101300206

Kessler, R. C., Chiu, W. T., Demler, O., & Walters, E. E. (2005). Corrections: Errors in byline, author affiliations, and acknowledgment in: Prevalence, severity, and comorbidity of 12-month DSM-IV disorders in the national comorbidity survey replication. *Archives of General Psychiatry, 62*(7), 709.

Knight, R. A., & Sims-Knight, J. E. (2003). Developmental antecedents of sexual coercion against women: Testing of alternative hypotheses with structural equation modeling. In R. A. Prentky, E. S. Janus, & M. C. Seto (Eds.), *Sexually coercive behavior: Understanding and management* (Vol. 989, pp. 72–85). New York: Annals of the New York Academy of Sciences.

Knight, R. A., & Sims-Knight, J. E. (2004). Testing an etiological model for male juvenile sexual offending against females. In R. Geffner & K. Franey (Eds.), *Sex offenders: Assessment and treatment* (pp. 33–55). New York: Haworth Press.

Knopp, F. H. (1984). *Retraining adult sex offenders: Methods and models.* Syracuse, NY: Safer Society Press.

Koerner, K., & Linehan, M. M. (1997). Case formulation in dialectical behavior therapy for borderline personality disorder. In T. D. Eells (Ed.), *Handbook of psychotherapy case formulation* (pp. 340–367). New York: Guilford.

Lamade, R., Gabriel, A., & Prentky, R. (2011). Optimizing risk mitigation in management of sexual offenders: A structural model. *International Journal of Law and Psychiatry, 34,* 217–225. http://dx.doi.org/10.1016/j.ijlp.2011.04.008

Langevin, R., Lang, R. A., & Curnoe, S. (1998). The prevalence of sex offenders with deviant fantasies. *Journal of Interpersonal Violence, 13*(3), 315–327.

Långström, N. (2002). Long-term follow-up of criminal recidivism in young sex offenders: Temporal patterns and risk factors. *Psychology, Crime & Law, 8*(1), 41–58. http://dx.doi.org/10.1080/10683160208401808

Långström, N., & Grann, M. (2000). Risk for criminal recidivism among young sex offenders. *Journal of Interpersonal Violence, 15*(8), 855–871. http://dx.doi.org/10.1177/088626000015008005

Laws, D. R. (Ed.) (1989). *Relapse prevention with sex offenders.* New York: Guilford.

Laws, D. R., Hudson, S. M., & Ward, M. (2000). *Remaking relapse prevention with sex offenders: A sourcebook.* Thousand Oaks, CA: Sage.

Leibowitz, G. S., Laser, J. A., & Burton, D. L. (2011). Exploring the relationships between dissociation, victimization, and juvenile sexual offending. *Journal of Trauma & Dissociation, 12*(1), 38–52. http://dx.doi.org/10.1080/15299732.2010.496143

Letourneau, E. J., & Borduin, C. M. (2008). The effective treatment of juveniles who sexually offend: An ethical imperative. *Ethics and Behavior, 18,* 286–306.http://dx.doi.org/10.1080/105-8420802066940

Levenson, J. (2014). Incorporating trauma-informed care into evidence-based sex offender treatment. *Journal of Sexual Aggression, 20*(1), 9–22. http://dx.doi.org/10.1080/13552600.2013.861523

Levenson, J. S., & Macgowan, M. J. (2004). Engagement, denial, and treatment progress among sex offenders in group therapy. *Sexual Abuse: A Journal of Research and Treatment, 16*(1), 49–63.

Levenson, J. S., Willis, G. M., & Prescott, D. S. (2014). Adverse childhood experiences in the lives of male sex offenders: Implications for trauma-informed care. *Sexual Abuse: A Journal of Research and Treatment,* 1–20. http://dx.doi.org/10.1177/1079063214535819

Li, D., Chu, C., Goh, J., Ng, I., & Zenf, G. (2015). Impact of childhood maltreatment on recidivism in youth offenders: A matched-control study. *Criminal Justice and Behavior, 42,* 990–1007.

Lindsey, R. E., Carlozzi, A. F., & Eells, G. T. (2001). Differences in the dispositional empathy of juvenile sex offenders, non-sex-offending delinquent juveniles, and nondelinquent juveniles. *Journal of Interpersonal Violence, 16*(6), 510–522. http://dx.doi.org/10.1177/088626001016006002

Linehan, M. (1993). *Cognitive behavioral treatment of borderline personality disorder.* New York: Guilford Press.

Lipsey, M. W. (1999). Can rehabilitative programs reduce the recidivism of juvenile offenders? An inquiry into the effectiveness of practical programs. *Virginia Journal of Social Policy and the Law, 6,* 611–641.

Lipsey, M. W., & Derzon, J. H. (1998). Predictors of violent or serious delinquency in adolescence and early adulthood: A synthesis of longitudinal research. In R. Loeber & D. P. Farrington (Eds.), *Serious & violent juvenile offenders: Risk factors and successful interventions* (pp. 86–105). Thousand Oaks, CA: Sage Publications.

Lösel, F., & Schmucker, M. (2005). The effectiveness of treatment for sexual offenders: A comprehensive meta-analysis. *Journal of Experimental Criminology, 1*(1), 117–146. http://dx.doi.org/10.1007/s11292-004-6466-7

MacCulloch, M., Gray, N., & Watt, A. (2000). Britain's sadistic murderer syndrome reconsidered: An associative account of the aetiology of sadistic sexual fantasy. *Journal of Forensic Psychiatry, 11,* 401–418. http://dx.doi.org/10.1080/09585180050142606.

Malamuth, N. M., Heavey, C. L., & Linz, D. (1993). Predicting men's antisocial behavior against women: The interaction model of sexual aggression. In D. Hall (Ed.), *Sexual aggression: Issues in etiology, assessment, and treatment* (pp. 63–97). Philadelphia: Taylor & Francis.

Maniglio, R. (2011). The role of childhood trauma, psychological problems, and coping in the development of deviant sexual fantasies in sexual offenders. *Clinical Psychology Review, 31*(5), 748–756. http://dx.doi.org/10.1016/j.cpr.2011.03.003

Marques, J. K., Wiederanders, M., Day, D. M., Nelson, C., & van Ommeren, A. (2005). Effects of a relapse prevention program on sexual recidivism: Final results from California's Sex Offender Treatment and Evaluation Project (SOTEP). *Sexual Abuse: A Journal of Research and Treatment, 17*(1), 79–107.

Marshall, W. L., & Barbaree, H. E. (1990). An integrated theory of the etiology of sexual offending. In W. L. Marshall, D. R. Laws, & H. E. Barbaree (Eds.), *Handbook of sexual assault: Issues, theories, and treatment of the offender* (pp. 257–275). New York: Plenum Press.

McCann, K., & Lussier, P. (2008). Antisociality, sexual deviance, and sexual reoffending in juvenile sex offenders: A meta-analytical investigation. *Youth Violence and Juvenile Justice, 6*(4), 363–385. http://dx.doi.org/10.1177/1541204008320260

McCann R. A., Ivanoff A., Schmidt H., & Beach, B. (2007). Implementing dialectical behaviour therapy in residential forensic settings with adults and juveniles. In L. A. Dimeff & K. Koerner (Eds.), *Dialectical behaviour therapy in clinical practice: Applications across disorders and settings,* pp. 112–144. New York: Guilford Press.

McCormick, S., Peterson-Badali, M., & Skilling, T. A. (2015). Mental health and justice system involvement: A conceptual analysis of the literature. *Psychology, Public Policy, and Law, 21*(2), 213–225. http://dx.doi.org/10.1037/law0000033

McCormick, S., Peterson-Badali, M., & Skilling, T. A. (2016, January). The role of mental health and specific responsivity in juvenile justice rehabilitation. Unpublished manuscript.

McCrady, F., Kaufman, K., Vasey, M. W., Barriga, A. Q., Devlin, R. S., & Gibbs, J. C. (2008). It's all about me: A brief report of incarcerated adolescent sex offenders' generic and sex-specific cognitive distortions. *Sexual Abuse: A Journal of Research and Treatment, 20*(3), 261–271. http://dx.doi.org/10.1177/1079063208320249

McCrory, E., Hickey, N., Farmer, E., & Vizard, E. (2008). Early-onset sexually harmful behaviour in childhood: A marker for life-course persistent antisocial behaviour? *Journal of Forensic Psychiatry & Psychology, 19*(3), 382–395. http://dx.doi.org/10.1080/14789940802159371

McGrath, R., Cumming, G., Burchard, B., Zeoli, S., & Ellerby, L. (2010). *Current practices and emerging trends in sexual abuser management: The Safer Society 2009 North American survey.* Brandon, VT: Safer Society Press.

McMackin, R. A., Leisen, M. B., Cusack, J. F., LaFratta, J., & Litwin, P. (2002). The relationship of trauma exposure to sex offending behavior among male juvenile offenders. *Journal of Child Sexual Abuse: Research, Treatment, & Program Innovations for Victims, Survivors, & Offenders, 11*(2), 25–40. http://dx.doi.org/10.1300/J070v11n02_02

Miner, M. H. (2002). Factors associated with recidivism in juveniles: An analysis of serious juvenile sex offenders. *Journal of Research in Crime and Delinquency, 39*(4), 421–436. http://dx.doi.org/10.1177/002242702237287

Miner, M. H., & Munns, R. (2005). Isolation and normlessness: Attitudinal comparisons of adolescent sex offenders, juvenile offenders, and nondelinquents. *International Journal of Offender Therapy and Comparative Criminology, 49*(5), 491–504. http://dx.doi.org/10.1177/0306624X04274103

Moore, E., Gaskin, C., & Indig, D. (2013). Childhood maltreatment and post-traumatic stress disorder among incarcerated young offenders. *Child Abuse & Neglect, 37*(10), 861–870. http://dx.doi.org/10.1016/j.chiabu.2013.07.012

Moskowitz, A. K. (2004). Dissociative pathways to homicide: Clinical and forensic implications. *Journal of Trauma & Dissociation, 5*(3), 5–32. http://dx.doi.org/10.1300/J229v05n03_02

Neidigh, L. W., & Tomiko, R. (1991). The coping strategies of child sexual abusers. *Journal of Sex Education & Therapy, 17*(2), 103–110.

Nisbet, I. A., Wilson, P. H., & Smallbone, S. W. (2004). A prospective longitudinal study of sexual recidivism among adolescent sex offenders. *Sexual Abuse: A Journal of Research and Treatment, 16*(3), 223–234. http://dx.doi.org/10.1177/107906320401600304

Odgers, C. L., Reppucci, N. D., & Moretti, M. M. (2005). Nipping psychopathy in the bud: An examination of the convergent, predictive, and theoretical utility of the PCL-YV among adolescent girls. *Behavioral Sciences and the Law, 23*(6), 743–763. http://dx.doi.org/10.1002/bsl.664

Onifade, E., Barnes, A., Campbell, C., Anderson, V., Petersen, J., & Davidson, W. (2014). Juvenile offenders and experiences of neglect: The validity of the YLS/CMI with dual-status youth. *Children and Youth Services Review, 46*, 112–119. http://dx.doi.org/10.1016/j.childyouth.2014.08.004

Pagé, C. A., Tourigny, M., & Renaud, P. (2010). A comparative analysis of youth sex offenders and non-offender peers: Is there a difference in their coping strategies? *Sexologies: European Journal of Sexology and Sexual Health/Revue Européenne De Sexologie Et De Santé Sexuelle, 19*(2), 78–86.

Plattner, B., Silvermann, M. A., Redlich, A. D., Carrion, V. G., Feucht, M., Friedrich, M. H., & Steiner, H. (2003). Pathways to dissociation: Intrafamilial versus extrafamilial trauma in juvenile delinquents. *Journal of Nervous and Mental Disease, 191*(12), 781–788. http://dx.doi.org/10.1097/01.nmd.0000105372.88982.54

Prescott, D. S. (2004). Emerging strategies for risk assessment of sexually abusive youth: Theory, controversy, and practice. *Journal of Child Sexual Abuse, 13*(3–4), 83–105. http://dx.doi.org/10.1300/J070v13n03_05

Racey, B. D., Lopez, N. L., & Schneider, H. G. (2000). Sexually assaultive adolescents: Cue perception, interpersonal competence and cognitive distortions. *International Journal of Adolescence and Youth, 8*(2-3), 229–239. http://dx.doi.org/10.1080/02673843.2000.9747852

Rajlic, G., & Gretton, H. M. (2010). An examination of two sexual recidivism risk measures in adolescent offenders: The moderating effect of offender type. *Criminal Justice and Behavior, 37*(10), 1066–1085. http://dx.doi.org/10.1177/0093854810376354

Regehr, C., & Glancy, G. (2001). Empathy and its influence on sexual misconduct. *Trauma, Violence, & Abuse, 2*(2), 142–154. http://dx.doi.org/10.1177/1524838001002002003

Reitzel, L. R., & Carbonell, J. L. (2006). The effectiveness of sexual offender treatment for juveniles as measured by recidivism: A meta-analysis. *Sexual Abuse: A Journal of Research and Treatment, 18*, 401–421. http://dx.doi.org/10.1177/107906320601800407

Ricci, R. J. (2006). Trauma resolution using eye movement desensitization and reprocessing with an incestuous sex offender: An instrumental case study. *Clinical Case Studies, 5*, 248–265.

Ricci, R. J., & Clayton, C. A. (2008). Trauma resolution treatment as an adjunct to standard treatment for child molesters: A qualitative study. *Journal of EMDR Practice and Research, 2*, 41–50. doi:10.1891/1933-3196.2.1.41

Sakdalan, J. A., & Gupta, R. (2014). Wise mind–risky mind: A reconceptualization of dialectical behavior therapy concepts and its application to sexual offender treatment. *Journal of Sexual Aggression, 20*(1), 110–120. http://dx.doi.org/10.1080/13552600.2012.724457

Sakdalan, J. A., Shaw, J., & Collier, V. (2010). Staying in the here-and now: A pilot study on the use of dialectical behaviour therapy group skills training for forensic clients with intellectual disability. *Journal of Intellectual Disability Research, 54*, 568–572. http://dx.doi.org/10.1111/j.1365-2788.2010.01274.x

Schaffer, M., Jeglic, E. L., Moster, A., & Wnuk, D. (2010). Cognitive-behavioral therapy in the treatment and management of sex offenders. *Journal of Cognitive Psychotherapy: An International Quarterly, 24*, 92–103. http://dx.doi.org/10.1891/0889-8391.24.2.92

Schmuker, M., & Lösel, F. (2015). The effects of sexual offender treatment on recidivism: An international meta-analysis of sound quality evaluations. *Journal of Experimental Criminology, 11*(4), 597–630. http://dx.doi.org/10.1007/s11292-015-9241-z

Schram, D. D., Milloy, C. D., & Rowe, W. E. (1991). *Juvenile sex offenders: A follow-up study of reoffense behavior.* Olympia: Washington State Institute for Public Policy.

Schwartz, B. K., & Cellini, H. R. (Eds.). (1995). *The sex offender: Corrections, treatment and legal practice.* Kingston, NJ: Civic Research Institute.

Schwartz, M. F. (1994). The Masters and Johnson treatment program for sex offenders: Intimacy, empathy and trauma resolution. *Sexual Addiction & Compulsivity, 1*(3), 261–277. http://dx.doi.org/10.1080/10720169408400047

Seto, M. C., & Lalumière, M. L. (2010). What is so special about male adolescent sexual offending? A review and test of explanations using meta-analysis. *Psychological Bulletin, 136*, 526–575. http://dx.doi.org/10.1037/a0019700

Seto, M. C., Marques, J. K., Harris, G. T., Chaffin, M., Lalumière, M. L., Miner, M., . . . & Quinsey, V. L. (2008). Good science and progress in sex offender treatment are intertwined. *Sexual Abuse: A Journal of Research and Treatment, 20*, 247–255.

Seto, M. C., & Pullman, L. E. (2014). Risk factors for adolescent sexual offending. In G. J. N. Bruinsma & D. L. Weisburd (Eds.), *Encyclopedia of criminology and criminal justice* (pp. 4466–4475). New York: Springer.

Shahinfar, A., Kupersmidt, J. B., & Matza, L. S. (2001). The relation between exposure to violence and social information processing among incarcerated adolescents. *Journal of Abnormal Psychology, 110*(1), 136–141. http://dx.doi.org/10.1037/0021-843X.110.1.136

Shelton, D., Sampl, S., Kesten, K. L., Zhang, W., & Trestman, R. L. (2009). Treatment of impulsive aggression in correctional settings. *Behavioral Sciences and the Law, 27*(5), 787–800. http://dx.doi.org/10.1002/bsl.889

Shingler, J. (2004). A process of cross-fertilization: What sex offender treatment can learn from dialectical behavior therapy. *Journal of Sexual Aggression, 10*(2), 171–180. http://dx.doi.org/10.1080/13552600412331289050

Shufelt, J. L., & Cocozza, J. J. (2006). *Youth with mental health disorders in the juvenile justice system: Results from a multi-state prevalence study.* Delmar, NY: National Center for Mental Health and Juvenile Justice.

Singer, J. (2013). What's new in the treatment of sex offenders. *New Jersey Psychologist, 63*(1), 33–36.

Skeem, J. L., Manchak, S., & Peterson, J. K. (2011). Correctional policy for offenders with mental illness: Creating a new paradigm for recidivism. *Law and Human Behavior, 35,* 110–126. http://dx.doi.org/10.1007/s10979-010-9223-7

Smith, C. A., Ireland, T. O., & Thornberry, T. P. (2005). Adolescent maltreatment and its impact on young adult antisocial behavior. *Child Abuse & Neglect, 29*(10), 1099–1119. http://dx.doi.org/10.1016/j.chiabu.2005.02.011

Smith, D. K., Leve, L. D., & Chamberlain, P. (2006). Adolescent girls' offending and health-risking sexual behavior: The predictive role of trauma. *Child Maltreatment, 11*(4), 346–353. http://dx.doi.org/10.1177/1077559506291950

Smith, D. W., Witte, T. H., & Fricker-Elhai, A. (2006). Service outcomes in physical and sexual abuse cases: A comparison of child advocacy center–based and standard services. *Child Maltreatment, 11*(4), 354–360. http://dx.doi.org/10.1177/1077559506292277

Spaccarelli, S., Bowden, B., Coatsworth, J. D., & Kim, S. (1997). Psychosocial correlates of male sexual aggression in a chronic delinquent sample. *Criminal Justice and Behavior, 24*(1), 71–95.

Spice, A., Viljoen, J. L., Latzman, N. E., Scalora, M. J., & Ullman, D. (2013). Risk and protective factors for recidivism among juveniles who have offended sexually. *Sexual Abuse: A Journal of Research and Treatment, 25*(4), 347–369.

Stinson, J. D., Sales, B. D., & Becker, J. V. (2008). Behavioral theories. *Sex offending: Causal theories to inform research, prevention, and treatment* (pp. 63–76). Washington, DC: American Psychological Association. http://dx.doi.org/10.1037/11708-005

Taxman, F. (2014). Second generation of RNR : The importance of systemic responsivity in expanding core principles of responsivity. *Federal Probation, 78,* 32–40.

Tougas, A., Tourigny, M., Lemieux, A., Lafortune, D., & Proulx, J. (2014). Psychoeducational group intervention for juvenile sex offenders: Outcomes and associated factors. *Hellenic Journal of Psychology 11,* 184–207.

Van Ness, S. R. (1984). Rape as instrumental violence: A study of youth offenders. *Journal of Offender Counseling, Services & Rehabilitation, 9*(1-2), 161–170.

Van Wijk, A., Loeber, R., Vermeiren, R., Pardini, D., Bullens, R., & Doreleijers, T. (2005). Violent juvenile sex offenders compared with violent juvenile nonsex offenders: Explorative findings from the Pittsburgh Youth Study. *Sex Abuse, 17*(3), 333–352.

Varker, T., Devilly, G. J., Ward, T., & Beech, A. R. (2008). Empathy and adolescent sexual offenders: A review of the literature. *Aggression and Violent Behavior, 13*(4), 251–260. http://dx.doi.org/10.1016/j.avb.2008.03.006

Veneziano, C., Veneziano, L., & LeGrand, S. (2000). The relationship between adolescent sex of-fender behaviors and victim characteristics with prior victimization. *Journal of Interpersonal Violence, 15*(4), 363–374.

Veneziano, C., Veneziano, L., LeGrand, S., & Richards, L. (2004). Neuropsychological executive functions of adolescent sex offenders and nonsex offenders. *Perceptual and Motor Skills, 98*(2), 661–674. http://dx.doi.org/10.2466/PMS.98.2.661-674

Vermeiren, R. (2003). Psychopathology and delinquency in adolescents: A descriptive and devel-opmental perspective. *Clinical Psychology Review, 23*(2), 277–318. http://dx.doi.org/10.1016/S0272-7358(02)00227-1

Vincent, G. M., Guy, L. S., & Grisso, T. (2012). *Risk assessment in juvenile justice: A guidebook for implementation.* New York: Models for Change. http://modelsforchange.net/publications/346

Vitopoulos, N. (2016). What's good for the goose? Examining the impact of gender-neutral and gender-specific factors in the assessment and treatment of female and male justice-involved youth. Unpublished dissertation.

Walker, A. (2002). Dissociation in incarcerated juvenile male offenders: A pilot study in Australia. *Psychiatry, Psychology & Law, 9*(1), 56–61.

Walker, D. F., McGovern, S. K., Poey, E. L., & Otis, K. E. (2004). Treatment effectiveness for male adolescent sexual offenders: A meta-analysis and review. *Journal of Child Sexual Abuse, 13*(3-4), 281–293. http://dx.doi.org/10.1300/J070v13n03z-14

White, S. F., Cruise, K. R., & Frick, P. J. (2009). Differential correlates to self-report and parent-report of callous-unemotional traits in a sample of juvenile sexual offenders. *Behavioral Sciences and the Law, 27*(6), 910–928. http://dx.doi.org/10.1002/bsl.911

Wieckowski, E., Hartsoe, P., Mayer, A., & Shortz, J. (1998). Deviant sexual behavior in children and young adolescents: Frequency and patterns. *Sexual Abuse: A Journal of Research and Treatment, 10*(4), 293–303.

Willis, G. M., Yates, P. M., Gannon, T. A., & Ward, T. (2013). How to integrate the good lives model into treatment programs for sexual offending: An introduction and overview. *Sexual Abuse: A Journal of Research and Treatment, 25*(2), 123–142. http://dx.doi.org/10.1177/1079063212452618

Wilson, H. W., Berent, E., Donenberg, G. R., Emerson, E. M., Rodriguez, E. M., & Sandesara, A. (2013). Trauma history and PTSD symptoms in juvenile offenders on probation. *Victims & Of-fenders, 8*(4), 465–477. http://dx.doi.org/10.1080/15564886.2013.835296

Worling, J. R. (1995, November). Sexual abuse histories of adolescent male sex offenders: Differences on the basis of the age and gender of their victims. *Journal of Abnormal Psychology, 104*(4), 610–613. http://dx.doi.org/10.1037/0021-843X.104.4.610

Worling, J. R. (2001). Personality-based typology of adolescent male sexual offenders: Differences in recidivism rates, victim-selection characteristics, and personal victimization histories. *Sexual Abuse: A Journal of Research and Treatment, 13*(3), 149–166.

Worling, J. R. (2012). The assessment and treatment of deviant sexual arousal with adolescents who have offended sexually. *Journal of Sexual Aggression, 18*(1), 36–63.

Worling, J. R., & Curwen, T. (2000). Adolescent sexual offender recidivism: Success of specialized treatment and implications for risk prediction. *Child Abuse & Neglect, 24*(7), 965–982. http://dx.doi.org/10.1016/S0145-2134(00)00147-2

Worling, J. R., & Långström, N. (2003). Assessment of criminal recidivism risk with adolescents who have offended sexually: A review. *Trauma, Violence, & Abuse, 4*(4), 341–362. http://dx.doi.org/10.1177/1524838003256562

Worling, J. R., & Långström, N. (2006). Risk of sexual recidivism in adolescents who offend sexually: Correlates and assessment. In H. E. Barbaree & W. L. Marshall (Eds.), *The juvenile sex offender* (2nd ed., pp. 219–247). New York: Guilford Press.

Yalom, I. D. (1995). *The theory and practice of group psychotherapy* (4th ed.). New York: Basic Books.

Zakireh, B., Ronis, S. T., & Knight, R. A. (2008). Individual beliefs, attitudes, and victimization histories of male juvenile sexual offenders. *Sexual Abuse: A Journal of Research and Treatment, 20*(3), 323–351. http://dx.doi.org/10.1177/1079063208322424

Zeng, G., Chu, C. M., Koh, L. L., & Teoh, J. (2015). Risk and criminogenic needs of youth who sexually offended in Singapore: An examination of two typologies. *Sexual Abuse: A Journal of Research and Treatment, 27*(5), 479–495.

CHAPTER 13

Adolescent Females Who Have Sexually Abused

Lisa L. Frey

Adolescent females (i.e., 12 through 18 years old) who have sexually abused others have received some attention as a population of interest over the past 10 years (Gannon & Cortoni, 2010), although little definitive information is known about the population. The preponderance of the research has focused on the sociodemographic and clinical characteristics of adolescent females, especially those who have come to the attention of the juvenile justice system. However, there is no well-researched theoretical framework describing the developmental trajectory of adolescent females who sexually abuse and little evidence-based intervention guidance. As pointed out by Chesney-Lind and Shelden (2014), in reference to adolescent females engaged in delinquent behavior, girls' behavior is often measured against the behavior of adolescent boys and judged as less of a threat to the community, thus rendering girls' needs and their risk to the community as, at best, less pressing and, at worst, invisible. Thus, the overall purpose of this chapter is to provide an overview of what we know, do not know, and need to know about adolescent females who sexually abuse.

The chapter will begin with a review of current data regarding the prevalence of sexually abusive behavior in which adolescent females engage, followed by a review of the characteristics, including risk and protective factors, identified in this population. Adolescent females who sexually abuse will be contrasted with adolescent males who sexually abuse and adolescent females who engage in delinquent but non-sexual behaviors. The focus of these sections will be on scholarly works published in the past 5 to 10 years because the earlier literature has been extensively reviewed previously (for example, see Frey 2006; 2010; Vandiver & Teske, 2006). Theoretical frameworks for adult females who sexually offend that may have relevance to adolescent females will then be considered. Finally, assessment and treatment issues will be reviewed and comments will be offered regarding policy implications.

Given the challenges related to researching adolescent females who sexually abuse (e.g., relatively low base rates, challenges with obtaining consent for participation from parents or guardians), a brief caution about the existing research is in order. With some recent exceptions, methodological and statistical problems, including small samples, questionable psychometric integrity of instruments (i.e., unreliable survey measures), overly generous significance testing (i.e., attributing results to a true difference when the results have a relatively high likelihood of being due to chance), over-interpretation of results (i.e., interpreting results in ways that are overly broad), and limited generalizability (i.e., limitations regarding application of results beyond the study population), have been relatively common. Many of the studies investigating adolescent females who sexually offend do not report racial or ethnic identity information, nor do they report sexual orientation and/or gender identity. If race or ethnic identity is reported, most often the majority of participants are identified as white or Caucasian. The omission of ethnic or racial identity information and neglect of youth of color is particularly surprising considering the overrepresentation of girls of color in detention settings and notions of these girls (especially black girls) as more delinquent in comparison with white girls (Chesney-Lind & Shelden, 2014). In addition, oversampling of adolescent females who are incarcerated, in residential treatment, or have come to the attention of the juvenile justice system continues to occur and, while this pattern is understandable because these girls are readily available, it limits the external validity of study results. Frey (2010) pointed out that these external validity factors are especially concerning when study results are indiscriminately applied across treatment settings, particularly at the level of the individual client receiving outpatient treatment in a community agency or counseling practice due to a lower level of risk. It is recommended that mental health, child welfare, and juvenile justice professionals carefully consider these research challenges (and obtain interpretive consultation if necessary) in making assessment, treatment, and case management decisions about individual clients. To assist with assessing the research applicability, the size and type of samples will be provided in this chapter whenever possible.

Prevalence of Sexual Abuse by Adolescent Females

Finkelhor, Ormrod, and Chaffin (2009), utilizing data from the National Incident-Based Reporting System (NIBRS), reported that young females arrested for sexual abuse made up 7 percent of all juveniles arrested for sexual offending, although it should be noted that the NIBRS database included females aged 6 through 17 in their offender data. The US Department of Justice and Federal Bureau of Investigation (USDOJ-FBI) Uniform Crime Report (2014) documented that in 2013 the total number of arrests of females under 18 years old was 59 for forcible rape[1] and 773 for sexual offenses other than rape or prostitution, in contrast with 1,509 and 6,116 arrests, respectively, of males under 18 years old. Thus, arrests of females under 18 years of age accounted for 4 percent of juvenile arrests for rape and 13 percent of juvenile arrests for other sexual offenses. Five-year arrest trends for 2009–2013 indicated an increase of 59.5 percent in forcible rape and a decrease of 19.1 percent in other sexual offense arrests of females under 18 years old (USDOJ-FBI, 2014). These statistics compare with decreases of 22.4 percent in forcible rape and 19.3 percent in other sexual offense arrests of males under 18 years old.

Although the 2015 Uniform Crime Report data (USDOJ-FBI, 2016) were recently released, the 5- and 10-year trends must be interpreted with caution because the data are based on differing definitions of rape (i.e., earlier data are based on the legacy definition while later data are based on an aggregate of the legacy and newly revised definitions). The most reliable comparative data are the 2013–2014 data because both sets are based on the aggregate definitions. This one-year comparison shows that arrests of females under 18 years old decreased 2.9 percent for rape and 14.3 percent for sexual offenses other than rape and prostitution. Males under 18 years old, on the other hand, showed an increase of 5.9 percent for rape and a decrease of 8.1 percent for other sexual offenses. Until further longitudinal data using the newly revised definition are gathered, however, it is difficult to clearly interpret these data in terms of trends.

Interestingly, in 2013–2014, city arrests (i.e., by city law enforcement officials) of females under 18 years old for forcible rape increased by 11.9 percent as compared with metropolitan counties, non-metropolitan counties, and suburban areas, all of which showed decreased arrests. Comparatively, males under 18 years old showed relatively

---

1. Although the FBI recently redefined the term *forcible rape,* these statistics still fall under the legacy definition of forcible rape (i.e., the carnal knowledge of a female forcibly and against her will; FBI, 2014). The definition was recently revised to (a) include male as well as female victims, and (b) incorporate an expanded scope of sexually penetrative acts. In addition, please note that the arrest statistics could, in certain cases, include multiple arrests of the same person.

small increases in arrests for rape in all geographic areas. These data must be interpreted with caution because they are based on small absolute numbers of arrests in some geographic areas, especially metropolitan and non-metropolitan counties. Nevertheless, as pointed out by the Office for Victims of Crime (2015), there may be substantial geographic differences in responses of the criminal justice system (e.g., necessary triaging of responses to serious crimes, relationship between the criminal justice system and the community, gendered beliefs regarding crimes of female and male juveniles), and those differences have implications for crime response, data collection, and allocation of resources.

Due to the limitations of data based on arrests and juvenile justice system involvement, including under-reporting and limited generalizability, it is difficult to get a reliable estimate of the true prevalence of sexually abusive behavior engaged in by female adolescents. There is consensus, based on the available data, that adolescent males who sexually abuse significantly outnumber females, but female adolescents are still responsible for a notable number of sexually abusive incidents and victims. However, because the nature, prevalence, and impact of sexually abusive behavior enacted by females is viewed through the lens of socioculturally influenced gender role expectations (Frey, 2010), it is difficult for female adolescents who sexually abuse or their victims to disclose their experiences and seek help. Chesney-Lind and Shelden (2014) pointed out:

> . . . *girls' violence is framed within a patriarchal context, meaning that gender inequalities such as male domination, especially physical domination, lack of equal opportunities for women and girls, and pervasive control over girls and women, especially over their bodies and sexuality, are central and recurrent themes in girls' violence. (p. 169)*

CHARACTERISTICS OF FEMALE ADOLESCENTS WHO SEXUALLY ABUSE

Overall, the research related to female adolescents who sexually abuse describes a heterogeneous population in many ways. Some consensus has been reached, however, regarding the general characteristics of childhood maltreatment history, family instability, and mental health and/or school difficulties. In addition, patterns of co-offending among female adolescents who sexually abuse, a long-identified pattern among adult females (e.g., Matthews, 1989), has recently received increased attention.

Childhood Maltreatment History

Historically, the most robust finding in the literature related to female adolescents who sexually abuse has been the high rate of childhood maltreatment, including child sexual abuse, physical abuse, neglect, and exposure to family violence. Histories of child sexual abuse have been reported in 50 to 100 percent of female adolescent study participants (e.g., Bumby & Bumby, 1997; Fehrenbach & Monastersky, 1988; Kubik, Hecker, & Righthand, 2002), a higher rate than that reported among male adolescents who sexually abuse. More recently, Roe-Sepowitz and Krysik (2008) reported that 51 percent of their sample of 118 females sanctioned for sexual offenses (age range = 7–17) had experienced child maltreatment, including sexual abuse (26%), physical abuse (14%), and neglect (12%). The maltreated group differed from the non-maltreated group in several ways, including an increased likelihood of having a psychiatric diagnosis and mental health problems, and to have sexually abused a relative. In addition, Wijkman, Bijleveld, and Hendriks (2014) found a high rate of sexual abuse (37%), physical or emotional abuse (33%), and/or emotional neglect (33%) among 66 adolescent females convicted of a sexual offense in the Netherlands.

While recent studies show a relatively lower percentage of child sexual abuse, in particular, as compared with earlier studies, these studies are few in number so it is difficult to know if the findings are simply a function of methodological issues, such as small sample sizes or variations in the definitions of abuse and neglect. Nonetheless, it seems clear that child maltreatment in all its forms continues to be a significant research finding among samples of adolescent females who sexually abuse.

Notably, research focused on adolescent females who engage in delinquent behavior has also found increased rates of abuse experiences. Chesney-Lind and Shelden (2014) indicated that physical and sexual abuse rates ranging from 40 to 73 percent have been reported among delinquent girls, and have been tied to behaviors such as running away, non-abusive sexual behavior, status offenses, and school problems. Conrad, Tolou-Shams, Rizzo, Placella, and Brown (2014) reported a history of child sexual abuse in 23 percent of the female adolescents (n = 162; 11–17 years old) who received a court-ordered forensic mental health assessment at a juvenile court clinic, as compared with 8 percent among male adolescents (n = 240). Even after controlling for other risk factors, child sexual abuse was a significant predictor of recidivism for female adolescents, although not for male adolescents. Also, findings of high rates of child maltreatment, particularly sexual abuse, emotional abuse, or neglect, and exposure to domestic violence, have also been consistently documented in research examining adult females who sexually abuse (Levenson, Willis, & Prescott, 2015).

Family Instability

Findings of family instability in earlier research (e.g., Matthews, Hunter, & Vuz, 1997; Vick, McRoy, & Matthews, 2002) continue to be supported in recent literature. For instance, Roe-Sepowitz and Krysik (2008) reported that the family and/or caregiver situations of their female adolescent participants (N = 118) were characterized by poor or no caregiver supervision (74%), family disorganization (27%), unstable living situations (26%), and/or little parental contact (26%). Wijkman et al. (2014; n = 54) found their female adolescent participants reported family histories of child support or child protection agency contact (approximately 25%), family violence (17–18%), and poor sexual boundaries among family members (14%). These findings are congruent with those reported in the research on adult females who sexually abuse (e.g., Decou, Cole, Rowland, Kaplan, & Lynch, 2015; Ford, 2010).

Mental Health and/or School or Learning Difficulties

Mental health and/or school difficulties have been frequently reported among female adolescents who sexually abuse. Roe-Sepowitz and Krysik (2008) reported that about half of the adolescent females in their sample (N = 118) had a psychiatric diagnosis, although diagnoses were varied, and had clinically significant scores on scales measuring traumatic experiences (43%), depression-anxiety (39%), and anger-irritability (33%). In addition, about a third of the participants had been suspended or expelled from, or had dropped out of, school. Wijkman et al. (2014) found about a quarter of the 66 participants in their study had received a psychiatric diagnosis, with conduct disorder being the most frequent. In a study comparing female (n = 22) and male (n = 254) adolescents from the United Kingdom who had sexually abused, Hickey, McCrory, Farmer, and Vizard (2008) found that the females were more likely to be diagnosed with post-traumatic stress disorder (PTSD) or reactive attachment disorder.

Research on general adolescent populations has consistently and robustly shown that girls tend to demonstrate higher rates of internalizing (versus externalizing) behaviors as compared with boys (e.g., Crijnen, Achenbach, & Verhulst, 1997; Moffitt, Caspi, Rutter, & Silva, 2001), a pattern that has also been reported in earlier research with clinically identified adolescent females who sexually abuse (e.g., Hunter, Lexier, Goodwin, Bowne, & Dennis, 1993; Kubik et al., 2002; Matthews et al., 1997). More recently, however, findings identifying externalizing symptoms and diagnoses (e.g., conduct disorder, anger-irritability; Roe-Sepowitz & Krysik, 2008; Wijkman et al., 2014) suggest it may be too early to draw firm conclusions. It is certainly plausible that internalizing–externalizing behavior differences may be related to the type and/or characteristics of the sexually abusive behavior, such as whether the adolescent sexually abused alone or with a group.

Regarding learning difficulties, Tardif, Auclair, Jacob, and Carpentier (2005) reported learning disabilities/disorders in 80 percent of the adolescent females in their sample (n = 15). Also, several studies have reported below-average intellectual functioning in 29 to 50 percent of female adolescent participants who sexually abused (Hendriks & Bijleveld, 2006; Hickey et al., 2008; Wijkman et al., 2014; Wijkman, Weerman, Bijleveld, & Hendriks, 2015), although the generalizability of the findings may be limited due to sample characteristics (e.g., sample size, over-representation of lower-functioning females due to susceptibility to influence of co-offenders or to increased likelihood of being apprehended).

Patterns of Co-Offending

As previously noted, the issue of co-offending among adolescent females who sexually abuse is increasingly receiving attention in the literature. Studies by Finkelhor et al. (2009) and Vandiver (2010) found that 36 and 49 percent, respectively, of adolescent females who sexually abused had co-offended, as compared with 23 and 19 percent, respectively, of adolescent males. Among other samples of female adolescents who sexually abused, percentages of co-offending have varied from 16 to 60 percent (McCartan, Law, Murphy, & Bailey, 2011; Roe-Sepowitz & Krysik, 2008; Wijkman et al., 2014).

In regard to characteristics of group offenses, Finkelhor et al. (2009) and Vandiver (2010) each found an increased probability of multiple victims in incidents involving female as compared with male adolescents who sexually abused. In addition, Finkelhor et al. reported increased involvement of multiple offenders and adult offenders in group offending incidents including female adolescents.

Focusing on female adolescents from the Netherlands who sexually abused in a group (N = 35), Wijkman et al. (2015) outlined several characteristics of the group offenses. The participants had sexually abused in 26 groups of two or more individuals that included adolescent males, adult males, and/or adult women; in about 92 percent of the groups, co-offenders were male and female. Other group characteristics included prior preparation and the use of physical or verbal violence during the majority of the offenses, active participation in the sexual or non-sexual violent acts by the majority of the adolescent females, and sexual penetration of the victim in more than half of the incidents. In terms of individual characteristics, 54 percent reported a history of abuse or neglect, and 29 percent had a borderline IQ or less.

While the sample size of the Wijkman et al. (2015) study is small, it is particularly interesting due to its exploration of the possible dynamics of the co-offending patterns. Three main findings were emphasized. First, the adolescent females who sexually abused presented with significant personal childhood abuse and other interpersonal and behavioral problems. Also, three central motivators for the abuse were identified: a desire to "harass" (i.e., make fun of; p. 346) the victim, to obtain sexual gratification, or to seek revenge on and humiliate the victim for prior behavior. Last, Wijkman et al. identified various reasons for participation in the abuse. Group pressure and dynamics were identified by a majority of the participants, followed by participation for instrumental or practical reasons, such as making it possible to perpetrate the abusive behavior (e.g., physically restraining the victim).

CONTRASTING ADOLESCENT FEMALES WHO SEXUALLY ABUSE WITH OTHER POPULATIONS

Adolescent Females and Males Who Sexually Abuse

Finkelhor et al. (2009) compared data from the 2004 NIBRS database on females (n = 979) and males (n = 12,450) aged 6 through 17 who sexually abused. Several differences were reported, including that the females who abused were younger and their victims were more frequently under 11 years old and male. In addition, the females were more likely to co-offend, abusing multiple victims, and to be viewed by investigators as victims of the co-offense as well as abusers. In contrast, using a subsample of the 2002 NIBRS data (i.e., limiting the age range to 12–17), Vandiver (2010) compared female and male adolescents who sexually abused (total female n of 177; randomly selected male n of 177) and found no meaningful between-group difference[2] in their age at the time of the abuse or in victim age patterns. However, like the Finkelhor et al. study, Vandiver reported that adolescent females were more likely to target male victims and to co-offend. In an earlier study, Vandiver and Teske (2006) compared adolescent females (n = 61) and males (n = 122) who were registered as sexual offenders. Congruent with the 2009 findings of Finkelhor et al., females were arrested at a younger age and had younger victims. Vandiver and Teske found that males more frequently abused female victims, whereas females abused male and female victims equally.

Last, Hickey et al. (2008) reported that female adolescents were more likely than males to experience inadequate sexual boundaries within their families and have a history of childhood sexual abuse, with a younger age of abuse onset. They were also more likely to abuse younger victims and less likely to engage in sexual penetration

---

2. Keeping in mind the number of statistical analyses performed, only results significant at the $p < 0.01$ level are reported here.

of victims. However, the validity of the results is limited by the small sample size of female adolescents (n = 22), resulting in a significant imbalance in female and male group sizes, and a much higher proportion of female adolescents with IQs less than 70 as compared with males (i.e., 41% vs. 23%).

Adolescent and Adult Females Who Sexually Abuse

In Tardif et al.'s (2005) examination of female adolescents (n = 15) and adults (n = 13) who sexually abused, a majority of participants in both groups reported a history of experiencing sexual and/or physical abuse. Differences between the groups were found, including (a) adult females were diagnosed with personality disorders at a higher rate; (b) adolescent females reported chiefly abusing males (60%), with adults reporting primarily abusing females (i.e., 77%); and (c) the frequency of abuse engaged in by adult females was more intrusive (e.g., sexual intercourse, digital vaginal penetration). It is likely, however, that at least some of these findings (i.e., formal diagnosis of personality disorder, intrusiveness of abuse) are rooted in developmental differences between the groups. In addition, due to the small size of the samples and the lack of additional studies comparing these populations, the applicability of the findings may be limited.

Other recent studies comparing adult and adolescent females who sexually abuse were not found. At first glance, this may seem logical given the tendency to assume that adolescent and adult females who sexually abuse are similar. However, developmental differences between adolescents and adults probably have a significant impact on characteristics and outcomes of their sexually abusive behavior, including recidivism, and must be factored into assessment and treatment. Certainly the salience of these differences has been consistently emphasized in studies comparing adolescent and adult males who sexually abuse (e.g., Batastini, Hunt, Present-Koller, & DeMatteo, 2011).

Adolescent Females Who Sexually Abuse and Those Who Engage in Non-Sexual Delinquent Behavior

McCarten et al. (2011) examined the records of female adolescents who received services from a forensic treatment service specializing in adolescents, comparing 31 who had sexually abused with 222 who had engaged in non-sexual delinquent behavior. Keeping in mind the limitations due to the small sample of female adolescents who sexually abused, as well as the imbalance between group sizes, findings indicated that the girls who sexually abused were significantly less likely to engage in physically violent or aggressive behavior and more likely to engage in self-harm behavior, have learning difficulties, and have a history of childhood abuse. It is noteworthy that the history of childhood maltreatment was high in both groups (i.e., 87% vs. 55%), but was comparatively higher among the adolescents who had sexually abused.

THEORETICAL CONSIDERATIONS REGARDING FEMALE ADOLESCENTS WHO SEXUALLY ABUSE

There is currently no well-developed, structured theoretical model that describes the dynamics of or pathways to sexually abusive behavior among adolescent females, although there is a pressing need for an evidence-based model to guide prevention, assessment, and treatment efforts. However, there have been theoretical frameworks proposed, primarily emerging from the literature related to adult females who sexually abuse and adolescent females who engage in delinquent behavior, that have applicability to adolescent females who sexually abuse.

Theory Regarding Adult Females Who Sexually Abuse

Recent theoretical developments pertaining to adult females who sexually abuse may have some relevance to adolescent females. Gannon, Rose, and Ward (2008; 2010) developed the Descriptive Model of the Offense Process for Female Sex Offenders (DMFSO) based on a qualitative analysis (i.e., grounded theory; e.g., Creswell, 2013) of 22 adult females in prison or on probation in the UK. DeCou et al. (2015), using the same qualitative methodology with 24 incarcerated adult women in the United States, extended the DMFSO by exploring dynamic social and environmental vulnerabilities. While there are aspects of these theories that are not pertinent to adolescent females who sexually abuse, they do provide some guidance regarding theoretical directions to explore.

The DMFSO model includes three phases: (a) background factors, which includes the dimensions of family environment, abusive experiences, lifestyle outcomes (i.e., defined as women's late-adolescent and early-adulthood behavioral, cognitive, and affective patterns in response to early abuse and/or family experiences), vulnerability factors (e.g., mental health issues, low level of social support), and major life stressors; (b) pre-offense period, which describes the process by which vulnerabilities are transformed into risk factors that influence motivations and offense planning; and (c) offense and post-offense period, which outlines the approaches leading to the sexually abusive behavior, as well as possible victim responses and offense consequences and outcomes (Gannon et al., 2008). In a later study reexamining the 2008 data, Gannon et al. (2010) identified three pathways leading to sexual offending: explicit (i.e., explicit planning and intention), directed avoidant (i.e., directed to offend by co-offenders), and implicit disorganized (i.e., minimal planning and intention and poor self-control). It was found that the background factors phase did not discriminate among offending pathways because the women presented as relatively similar in severity of developmental dysfunction. Although there are details of the model that are not directly applicable to adolescents (e.g., approaches leading directly to offense; lifestyle outcomes, due to the focus on late adolescence and early adulthood), the overall framework may provide a starting point for exploration of pathways to abusive behavior among adolescent females. For instance, it is possible that background factors (e.g., sexual victimization) may play a more prominent role in adolescent females due to the proximal nature of these factors. Interestingly, Wijkman et al. (2015) found certain goals for group co-offending among female adolescents that were reminiscent of Gannon et al.'s (2008) study—specifically, sexual gratification and seeking revenge or humiliation. Gannon et al. also identified these as two potential goals or motivations for offending that were established by adult women during the pre-offense period.

DeCou et al. (2015) developed an ecological model with offense-related factors embedded within social, psychological, and environmental contexts. This is a complex model, based on a limited sample size, yet underscores the importance of looking beyond individual risk factors. A similar approach seems especially important for female adolescents who are in the midst of intersecting developmental processes and subject to multiple levels of systemic influences and controls. That is, female adolescents are subject to the multiple demands, expectations, and laws or rules of, for example, schools, communities, and parents, and often have little power to influence those systems. These influences occur when adolescents are also negotiating multiple developmental processes such as defining social identities (e.g., racial and ethnic identity, sexual orientation, gender identity) and building intimate relationships and connections outside the family. Thus, in working toward a theoretical framework explaining adolescent female sexual abusing, it will be critical to embed processes related to abusing behavior within these multiple levels of influence, including microsystem (e.g., family, peers) belief systems.

Additional Theory with Implications for Female Adolescents Who Sexually Abuse

Gender Responsive Theory

Chesney-Lind and Shelden (2014) provided a critique of current theoretical models explaining adolescent female delinquent behavior in general, and pointed out the problematic tendency to simply apply the models developed for adolescent males to adolescent females. In particular, Chesney-Lind and Shelden emphasized the importance of keeping gender role norms and inequities in the forefront of theoretical development, while at the same time not ignoring intersecting identities (i.e., overlapping and interconnecting social identities):

> . . . there are fixed and universal gender inequalities that cut across all contexts in which girls and boys grow up. These are large-scale, broad, and central, rather than marginal, concerns that need to be addressed when looking at adolescent violence . . . understanding the context of girls' violence will result in perspectives of girls as vulnerable within a sex/gender system as well as resilient in crafting strategies to maximize their power and self-protection in particular contexts. (pp. 174–175)

This perspective has also been discussed in relation to adult females who have committed criminal offenses. Harris (2010) offered a preliminary etiological explanation for sexual offending behavior in adult females as viewed through the lens of feminist criminology, identifying two pathways to offending: powerlessness through patriarchy (i.e., originating in the broad societal context of gender-related bias, inequality, and institutional barriers) and powerlessness through victimization (i.e., originating in experiences of child sexual abuse). Bloom, Owen, and Covington (2003) applied this perspective to the criminal justice system, underscoring the social and environmental contexts that differentiate females and males within the system, including differences in gender-related socialization, roles, and inequities. Congruent with Chesney-Lind and Shelden's (2014) assertion, Bloom et al. pointed out that most theories of crime have been "developed by male criminologists to describe male crime" (p. 51).

This theoretical viewpoint, embedded in a feminist theoretical framework, is generally identified as the gender responsive perspective. In regard to adolescent females, the approach is positioned as a way to bridge the gap between developmental processes and juvenile justice practices, informing intervention strategies "rooted in the experience of girls" (Peters, 1998, p. 8). Bloom et al. (2003) explicated a number of multidisciplinary guiding principles to implement gender responsive perspectives in the adult criminal justice system, including developing a climate of safety, respect, and dignity; creating policies, practices, and programs that are relational and foster healthy connections; and providing integrative and culturally relevant services to address substance abuse, trauma, and mental health issues (p. 76). These guiding principles are congruent with the gender responsive principles specific to female juveniles who have engaged in delinquent behaviors (e.g., recognition of the impact of sexism, victimization, poverty, and racism; need to foster healthy relationships) that have been identified by Peters.

Female adolescents who engage in violent behavior are often aware of the influence of these gender role norms and inequities. For instance, in a qualitative study of adolescent females incarcerated at a juvenile corrections facility (Frey & Beesley, 2010), a comment related to the identified theme of awareness of gender bias was articulated by an adolescent female focus group participant: "They [male residents] can say all kinds of stuff and make all kinds of remarks and you have to be quiet. But when you say it, it's a whole other story because there are expectations that we should be a lady & be quiet." The message from corrections staff to "act like a young lady" is one that came up repeatedly in the participants' narratives. This illustrates, as Chesney-Lind and Shelden (2014) remind us, the ways in which the gender-based assumptions we make about the nature, thinking, and behavior of adolescent girls directly influence the punishment and controls that are put in place, as well as the types of prevention, assessment, and treatment interventions made available.

Trauma-Informed Framework

The trauma-informed framework is a strengths-based model embedded in a full understanding of the impact of trauma, including the impact on high-risk behaviors (Levinson et al., 2015). The Substance Abuse and Mental Health Services Administration (SAMHSA; 2014a) draws a distinction between the trauma-informed model and trauma-specific interventions. That is, the trauma-informed framework incorporates the entire context of care and ensures the provision of a healing experience that avoids replication of traumatic experiences; builds safety, empowerment, and coping; and can be incorporated into many types of treatment.

It has been pointed out that "public institutions and service systems that are intended to provide services and supports to individuals are often themselves trauma-inducing" (SAMHSA, 2014a, p. 2) through the use of coercive or harsh policies and practices. The criminal and juvenile justice systems have been identified as having the potential to retraumatize individuals with histories of trauma, resulting in a negative impact on outcomes (e.g., Ko et al., 2008; SAMHSA, 2014a). In addition, SAMHSA (2014a) cautions that the behavioral consequences of individuals' trauma experiences (e.g., aggression as a reaction to powerlessness) can function to increase involvement with the criminal and juvenile justice system.

Several key principles of the trauma-informed framework have been proposed, including providing a milieu that (a) is physically and psychologically safe, (b) is transparent and trustworthy, (c) is collaborative and mutual, (d) fosters peer support, (e) builds on client strengths with a goal of increasing empowerment and choice, and (f) is responsive to racial, ethnic, and cultural needs of clients (SAMHSA, 2014a, p. 11). A key assumption is that the framework must be embedded at every level of an organization or system.

The trauma-informed framework clearly has treatment relevance to adolescent females who sexually abuse based on the strong and consistent findings of child maltreatment, including sexual abuse, in their histories. A challenge, however, is to clearly define strategies incorporating a trauma-informed approach into intervention models, such as the risk-need-responsivity model, aimed primarily at reducing recidivism.

Risk-Need-Responsivity Model

The risk-need-responsivity (RNR) model was introduced as an alternative to an increasingly punitive versus rehabilitative criminal justice system, and has been extended to the juvenile justice system. RNR is conceptualized as a framework of principles from which specific correctional interventions can be derived (Looman & Abracen, 2013). Three research-based principles have been delineated: (a) risk, which is aimed at identifying characteristics associated with criminal activity and matching intensity of intervention to the degree of individual risk; (b) need, which underscores the importance of focusing on criminogenic needs (i.e., dynamic, or changeable, factors that have been shown to be associated with youth who engage in delinquent or sexually abusive behavior); and (c) responsivity, which asserts that effective interventions must be based on cognitive social learning practices and individualized to attributes, characteristics, and sociodemographics (including gender) of the client (Andrews & Bonta, 2010; Loomis & Abracen, 2013).

Dowden and Andrews (1999) completed a meta-analysis to examine the applicability of the RNR principles to adult and juvenile females who had engaged in a variety of criminal behaviors. Of note is that age ranges for the included studies were not provided and the studies sampling adults and juveniles were combined for the meta-analysis. The results reportedly supported the applicability of the RNR principles to females, with the strongest treatment effects observed when focusing on interpersonal criminogenic needs and family process variables. Dowden and Andrews recommended further research regarding the importance of determining if past trauma is a criminogenic need in females, because none of the studies included focused on trauma experiences. This point is well taken in view of the previously cited research finding (i.e., Conrad et al., 2014) that indicated child sexual abuse was a significant predictor of recidivism in a sample of female adolescents engaged in delinquent behavior, although not for male adolescents.

In regard to the treatment modalities that are most compatible with the RNR model, Hoge (2015) stated that empirically supported treatment models with behavioral, social learning, or cognitive-behavioral approaches are preferred. Further, Hubbard and Matthews (2008) reported that the literature supports cognitive-behavioral models as most effective. Cognitive skills training (i.e., focusing on skills such as decision making and critical thinking) and cognitive restructuring (i.e., focusing on reinterpreting and revising beliefs, values, and attitudes supportive of delinquent behavior) have been identified as types of cognitive-behavioral approaches that result in positive outcomes.

Applicability of the Theories to Adolescent Females Who Sexually Abuse

Hubbard and Matthews (2008) provided an overview of the gender responsive approach and the RNR model, discussing the tensions among proponents of each model and offering suggestions for integrating the frameworks. A primary difference between the two models is that the focus of the former is on gendered differences in roles, norms, and socialization experiences and the subsequent importance of centering girls' needs in program and treatment development, whereas the focus of the latter is on a central set of program and treatment characteristics that are applicable across genders (Hubbard & Matthews, 2008). This difference is reflected in the implementation of the models, with two of the central areas of conflict being (a) the conceptualization of risk and need, and (b) the therapeutic treatment approach.

Identification and Targeting of Risk and Need

While the RNR model conceptualizes risk as factors that increase the likelihood of recidivism, the gender responsive approach examines the concept of risk in relation to females through a critical lens. That is, the latter approach proposes that the terminology of *high risk* as applied to female populations is only pertinent relative to other females who sexually abuse (Cortoni, 2010). In reference to adult females who sexually abuse, Cortoni (2010) pointed out that women consistently show lower recidivism rates than adult males. Likewise, adolescent females who have engaged in delinquent behaviors demonstrate lower recidivism rates than adolescent males (e.g., Chesney-Lind & Shelden, 2014; Conrad et al., 2014). Although there is no clear estimate of recidivism rates for adolescent girls who engage in sexually abusive behavior, it is not illogical to speculate that, while some adolescent girls pose a greater risk than others, they are unlikely to be high risk as a population.

Hubbard and Matthews (2008) pointed out that a related philosophical difference regarding risk exists within the two frameworks. The RNR perspective claims that, among adult offender (Looman & Abracen, 2013) and adolescent delinquent (Hoge, 2015; Hubbard & Matthews, 2008) populations, risk factors and criminogenic needs are essentially the same across genders. Also, Hubbard and Matthews noted that current risk assessment instruments are able to predict delinquency in both female and male adolescents. On the other hand, the gender responsive framework asserts that the majority of the research related to risk factors has been conducted with boys and simply applied to girls. Interestingly, the multicultural research has long emphasized the threats to research validity, including measurement (e.g., non-equivalence in meaning of factors) and interpretation (e.g., researcher bias and value judgments) challenges, posed by the application of findings across sociocultural groups (e.g., Matsumoto, 2003). Accordingly, it is possible that there are factors that are unique to female adolescents or that function differently or have varying potency depending on gender. Conrad et al. (2014), for example, pointed out that most RNR assessments are applied to all genders and "do not include abuse history as a factor or possible intervention point for risk reduction" (p. 312). Given research findings suggesting there may be a link between child sexual abuse and recidivism in female adolescents engaging in delinquent behavior, and the increased rates of child maltreatment in female vs. male adolescents who sexually abuse, further research regarding whether abuse history functions as a criminogenic need is a significant gender responsive consideration for the RNR model. The concerns regarding the cross-gender applicability of risk factors have implications for interpretation of risk assessment measures (see the assessment section for further discussion of this issue).

Therapeutic Treatment Approach

Kerig and Ford (2014) described gender responsive programming within the juvenile justice system as holistic, safe, strengths-based, and culturally responsive. Also, due to the significance of relationships (e.g., Levinson et al., 2015; Miller, 1984; Miller & Stiver, 1997) and the histories of relational disruption in the lives of female adolescents who sexually abuse, gender responsive treatment highlights the need to focus on relational quality (Kerig & Ford, 2014). In perhaps the only study examining gender responsive treatment for female adolescents, Day, Zahn, and Tichavsky (2015) found tentative support for the effectiveness of a gender responsive approach to treatment among girls placed in a detention center. Although there were some limitations related to the design of the study, the findings indicated support for this approach with girls who experienced "gender-sensitive risk factors" (p. 94), particularly a trauma history.

Although cognitive-behavioral interventions are central to RNR treatment approaches, Andrews and Bonta (2010) also emphasized the importance of attention to the therapeutic alliance and the need to individualize treatment. Despite this assertion, the majority of the RNR literature related to the responsivity principle concentrates exclusively on cognitive-behavioral treatment modalities. Proponents of the gender responsive perspective view this focus as reductionistic and argue there is a lack of research related to the effectiveness of cognitive-behavioral interventions with females who engage in delinquent or criminal behavior (Hubbard & Matthews, 2008). RNR proponents contend, however, that RNR implementation leads to reductions in recidivism, which is the central goal of rehabilitation (e.g., Andrews & Bonta, 2010; Looman & Abracen, 2013).

Some of the literature regarding the gender responsive and RNR frameworks offer broad suggestions for tailoring interventions to integrate assumptions from both models, such as modifying the process and content of cognitive-behavioral approaches to be more relational and to target gender-specific needs (e.g., Conrad et al., 2014; Hubbard & Matthews, 2008; Matthews & Hubbard, 2009). However, little attention seems to have been paid to developing a hybrid, integrated, structured intervention program. Ford, Chapman, Hawke, and Albert (2007) described a phase program, including need- and skill-based (phase 1), individual or trauma-focused (phase 2), and recovery sustainability (phase 3) interventions, for youth who are involved in the juvenile justice system. Whether such a multidimensional intervention model for female adolescents who sexually abuse would be viewed as feasible to policy makers, however, depends on ideological and funding priorities and, thus, remains to be seen.

ASSESSMENT OF FEMALE ADOLESCENTS WHO SEXUALLY ABUSE

Risk, Need, and Protective Factors

Risk Factors for Developing Abusive Sexual Behaviors Specific to Adolescent Girls

Risk and risk-need assessment, of course, must be guided by the empirical literature related to these factors. Although the research examining this topic in adolescent females who sexually abuse is limited, some risk factors have been identified. As previously reviewed, there is empirical support regarding the relevance of childhood maltreatment history, family instability (e.g., adequacy of supervision and monitoring, stability of living situation, boundaries among family members, family violence), mental health difficulties (e.g., pre-existing diagnoses, internalizing and externalizing behaviors, post-traumatic symptoms), and school difficulties (e.g., learning disorders, lower intellectual functioning) as risk factors in adolescent females who sexually abuse; thus, these risk factors must be thoroughly assessed. In particular, given the prevalence of trauma histories in adolescent females who sexually abuse, thorough trauma screening must be done by professional staff who have been trained in this area. The administration of a trauma screening instrument (e.g., MAYSI-2, Traumatic Events Screening Inventory, Trauma Symptom Checklist for Children) should be considered (Ford et al., 2007).

Risk, Need, and Protective Factors Specific to Female Adolescents Who Sexually Abuse

There is considerable literature related to risk, need, and protective factors associated with reoffending for male adolescents who sexually abuse and for youth who engage in delinquent behavior. Due to the limited literature specific to adolescent females who sexually abuse, it is prudent for those completing assessments to consult the wider body of literature on risk, need, and protective factors for guidance. There is one caveat, however: The underlying dynamics related to risks and needs must be carefully assessed and not assumed to be identical to that of male adolescents. As has been found in adult females who sexually abuse (e.g., DeCou et al., 2015; Gannon, Hoare, Rose, & Parrett, 2012), the dynamics underlying female adolescent abusive behavior are not well understood and may differ from those of male adolescents (e.g., Frey, 2006; 2010). Zahn et al. (2010) noted in regard to adolescents who engage in delinquent behavior, "Boys and girls experience many of the same risk factors, but they appear to differ in sensitivity to and rates of exposure to these factors" (p. 3).

Risk, Need, and Protective Factors Identified in Primarily Male Adolescent Populations

Righthand, Baird, Way, and Seto (2014) synthesized the research on criminogenic needs associated with adolescents (primarily males) who engaged in illegal sexual behavior and grouped them into domains: (a) sexuality, including sexual interests, drive and preoccupation, self-regulation, and attitudes and beliefs; (b) social bonds and orientation, including antisocial orientation, antisocial beliefs and attitudes, and peer associations; (c) general self-regulation, including self-regulation problems, impulsivity, school-related behavior problems, substance abuse, and emotional self-regulation deficits; (d) social competence, including social and intimate relationships, social isolation, and emotional congruence with children; and (e) socio-ecological factors, including family and caregiver availability and support, additional adult support, and community ties. All of these needs must be assessed in female adolescents who sexually abuse, with the understanding that the salience of each factor may vary for adolescent females versus males. For instance, as has been previously discussed, interpersonal relationships may be particularly influential for girls in terms of risk and need factors and should be thoroughly assessed. In addition, the importance of thoroughly assessing general self-regulation is indicated by the literature suggesting increased mental health difficulties in female adolescents who sexually abuse.

Risk, Need, and Protective Factors Identified in Female Adolescents Who Engage in Delinquent Behavior

Zahn et al. (2008) reviewed more than 2,300 articles and book chapters to identify correlates of delinquent behavior in girls aged 11 to 18. Family dynamics (i.e., poor supervision and monitoring, family criminal behavior, child maltreatment), lack of involvement in school, neighborhood factors (e.g., poverty level, crime rate), and reduced availability of community-based programs were found to increase the risk for delinquency in both girls and boys. However, four risk factors specific to girls were also identified: (a) early puberty, especially when combined with living in a disadvantaged neighborhood and within a dysfunctional family; (b) a history of sexual victimization; (c) experiencing depression and anxiety; and (d) influence from delinquent romantic partners (i.e., for less serious crimes only; similar gender effects found for serious crimes).

Many of the specific factors that have been found to protect against engagement in delinquent behavior among adolescent girls have been found to be influenced by complex relationships among risk factors (Hawkins, Graham, Williams, & Zahn, 2009). For example, the importance of religion served as a protective factor for some delinquent behaviors in certain situations (e.g., simple assault for girls from disadvantaged neighborhoods). In general, Hawkins et al. (2009) found three protective factors: a relationship with a caring adult, being successful in school (as measured by grade point average), and feeling connected and involved with school.

Process of Assessment

The Multiplex Empirically Guided Inventory of Ecological Aggregates for Assessing Sexually Abusive Adolescents and Children (MEGA; Miccio-Fonseca, 2006; Miccio-Fonseca & Rasmussen, 2011) is currently the only measure that reportedly assesses risk for sexually abusive behavior in female adolescents (as well as children under 12 years old and youth who are lower functioning intellectually). However, the MEGA has not been independently validated, and there are limitations to the existing validity studies as they pertain to adolescent females. For example, Miccio-Fonseca (2013) conducted a predictive validity study on a sample of 969 youth aged 4 to 19 years. However, only 99 (10.2%) of the youth were female, with just 34 percent (n = 334) of the total participants available for the six-month follow-up. The number of female youth who presented for follow-up is not clearly delineated—in fact, based on the figures provided, it appears that perhaps none of the youth were female. This, of course, makes it difficult to accurately determine the MEGA's effectiveness in predicting reoffending among female participants. Also, the recidivism outcome measure was described as "a sexually related probation or parole violation" (Miccio-Fonseca, 2013, p. 628) with no identification of the specific sexual behaviors included. Overall, the validity of the MEGA for use with female adolescents who engage in sexual behavior is unclear.

Risk assessment instruments have also been developed to assess male adolescents (e.g., J-SOAP-II [Prentky & Righthand, 2003]; ERASOR [Worling & Curwen, 2001]). However, the J-SOAP-II is not recommended for use with adolescent females, and Worling and Curwen (2001) point out that conclusions based on ERASOR results in adolescent females are risky due to the lack of research establishing validity with this population (e.g., Hunter, Becker, & Lexier, 2006; Worling & Långström, 2006).

Cortoni (2010) reminded professionals that accurately assessing risk of recidivism in adult female offenders is not yet possible in view of insufficient knowledge related to static and dynamic factors; we know even less about static and dynamic risk factors in adolescent females who sexually abuse. As an alternative, it should be noted that the Girls Study Group of the Office of Juvenile Justice and Delinquency Prevention evaluated 143 risk assessment and treatment-focused instruments to determine those that had favorable gender-based performance in juvenile-justice-involved youth (Zahn, Hawkins, Chiancone, & Whitworth, 2008). Seventy-three measures were found that were favorable, with 20 of those demonstrating gender-based instrument development and favorable gender-based analysis. It is recommended that these analyses be consulted for further guidance in assessing adolescent females for whom a delinquency-based measure would be relevant.

Given our current level of knowledge specific to female adolescents who sexually abuse, therefore, it is also necessary to rely on clinical interviewing and the use of psychometric measures pertinent to presenting issues. Three ethically related issues are especially salient for professionals who are responsible for these evaluations: Evaluators must be (a) familiar with the scholarly literature related to female adolescents who sexually abuse, (b) aware of and include assessment of risk and need factors that have been found to be associated with sexually abusive behavior in female adolescents, and (c) familiar with all relevant medical, psychological, physical, child welfare, and juvenile court records related to the client.

Psychological testing can be a valuable adjunct to clinical interviewing for female adolescents needing more comprehensive assessment due to concerns about risk level, mental health difficulties, and/or concerns related to intellectual or educational functioning. Interestingly, formal psychological and mental health measures have been found to be among the assessment instruments that are most sensitive to gender difference (Zahn et al., 2008). Based on our level of current knowledge regarding adolescent females who abuse, measures that are reliable, well validated, normed on adolescent females, and assess level of intellectual and personality functioning, externalizing and internalizing problems, emotional self-regulation, and interpersonal and social competencies are recommended. Considering the reported levels of childhood maltreatment and family instability among this population, measures related to trauma history and post-traumatic symptoms, as well as rating scales of family functioning and parental supervision and monitoring, are also suggested. Last, the adolescent female client's individual characteristics must be used as a guide regarding additional testing needs. For example, measures related to attention deficit disorder symptoms, suicidal behavior, substance use, or other psychological problems can provide supplementary information crucial to decision making about placement and necessary intervention.

TREATMENT OF FEMALE ADOLESCENTS WHO SEXUALLY ABUSE

Treatment Programs

McGrath, Cumming, Burchard, Zeoli, and Ellerby (2010) summarized the data from the 2009 Safer Society Foundation's survey of 1,370 community and residential treatment programs in the United States and Canada providing services to individuals who sexually abuse. McGrath et al. reported that 102 community-based and 19 residential programs in the US indicated treating female adolescents who sexually abused. To offer some comparative context, this contrasts with 275 community-based and 98 residential programs for adolescent males who sexually abuse. The top three theoretical models guiding the community-based programs specifically serving female adolescents were cognitive-behavioral (86%), relapse prevention (36%), and family systems or psycho-socio-educational (34% each); for residential programs, the top three were cognitive-behavioral (90%), psycho-socio-educational (57%), and sexual trauma (32%).[3] Notably, although relapse prevention was among the top three theoretical models used in adolescent female community-based programs, Gannon et al. (2010) found the DMFSO implicit disorganized pathway (in males, labeled the avoidance pathway; e.g., Pithers, 1990), which seems to be the pathway best dealt with through a relapse prevention framework, accounted for the fewest adult females who sexually abused. Given the probable low base rate of sexual reoffending among female adolescents, programs using a relapse prevention treatment framework and/or interventions that focus on the likelihood of reoffending may be missing the mark.

---

3. For adolescent males, the top three theoretical models for community-based programs matched those reported for females. Regarding residential programs, sexual trauma was not in the top three for males; instead, relapse prevention fell between cognitive-behavioral and psycho-socio-educational.

Evidence-Based Practice

Evidence-based practice in psychology (EBPP) is defined as "the integration of the best available research with clinical expertise in the context of patient characteristics, culture, and preferences" (APA Presidential Task Force on Evidence-Based Practice, 2006, p. 273). EBPP acknowledges multiple types of research evidence in making decisions regarding psychological interventions. In that sense, the material presented in this chapter is evidence-based.

On the other hand, empirically supported treatments (ESTs) are "specific psychological treatments that have been shown to be efficacious in controlled clinical trials" (APA Presidential Task Force on Evidence-Based Practice, 2006. p. 273), and are generally manualized treatments. There are no ESTs that have been specifically developed for adolescent females who sexually abuse, although multisystemic therapy for problematic sexual behavior (MST-PSB) shows promise. Also, there are ESTs that may be relevant as treatment components for certain adolescent females who sexually abuse.

MST-PSB is a service delivery model that has strong empirical support for treating adolescents who have engaged in illegal sexual behavior. Dopp, Borduin, and Brown (2015) reviewed four studies examining the effectiveness of MST-PSB and reported favorable outcomes. Although the participants included females in two of the four studies, the percentages were quite small (i.e., 2.4%, n = 3 and 4.2%, n = 2), a concern regarding MST-PSB also noted on SAMHSA's National Registry of Evidence-Based Programs and Practices (http://samhsa.gov/ViewIntervention.aspx?id=46). However, MST-PSB may be an effective treatment model to consider for female adolescents who sexually abuse due to its dual focus on youth's socio-ecological context (i.e., family, school, neighborhood, community, culture), a need emphasized by the gender responsive literature as crucial to the treatment of female adolescents, and their specific sexual behavior problems.

Ford, Steinberg, Hawke, Levine, and Zhang (2012) completed a randomized clinical comparison of Trauma Affect Regulation: Guide for Education and Therapy (TARGET) to a relational supportive treatment with female adolescents engaged in delinquent behavior who had been diagnosed with PTSD. TARGET was designed to teach skills for dealing with PTSD symptoms. Notably, the study sample (n = 59) was racially and ethnically diverse, as is not often the case in clinical trials, which tend to be limited to white populations. TARGET was found to be more effective than the comparison intervention in reducing PTSD symptoms, with some evidence that it also improved affect self-regulation. On the other hand, the relational supportive treatment was related to decreased anger. Ford et al. concluded that TARGET may have a greater impact on internalizing versus externalizing behaviors and suggested that relational therapies may also be a necessary treatment component in targeting improved self-efficacy and decreased anger. Of note, the current online Model Programs Guide of the Office of Juvenile Justice and Delinquency Prevention (http://www.ojjdp.gov/mpg/Topic/Details/128) has rated TARGET as the only effective program (out of eight) for girls engaged in delinquent behavior with PTSD.

Trauma-focused cognitive-behavioral therapy has also been shown to be effective in the treatment of PTSD, but has primarily been tested with children and early adolescents. There are also a number of other trauma-specific treatments, including integrated models, that are ESTs and/or evidence-based (see, for example, Substance Abuse and Mental Health Services Administration, 2014b). None, however, have been researched in regard to effectiveness or outcome with adolescent females who have sexually abused. Considering the reported prevalence of child maltreatment within the population of female adolescents who sexually abuse, however, these adjunctive treatments might be considered with certain female adolescents at particular points in treatment.

ESTs targeting other issues or symptoms (e.g., aggression, anxiety, substance abuse) may also be useful as supplementary treatment components for adolescent females who sexually abuse, depending on the individual needs of the adolescent. For instance, Multidimensional Treatment Foster Care (MTFC; currently labeled Treatment Foster Care Oregon, or TFCO) is a multisystemic intervention for delinquency that may be useful for youth with histories of delinquent behavior as well as sexually abusive behavior (Righthand et al., 2014). MTFC/TFCO has been examined in randomized clinical trials with girls who have engaged in delinquent behaviors with improvement observed in several areas, including psychotic symptoms, violent behaviors, and risky sexual behaviors (see http://www.tfcoregon.com/publications/peer-reviewed-journal-articles for further information). Overall, however, it must be again emphasized that many of these supplementary interventions have not been validated for application with females who engage in delinquent and/or sexually abusive behavior. Zahn et al. (2008) completed a review of 29 model programs for females engaging in delinquent behavior from the Blueprints for Violence Prevention database; none were rated as effective or effective with reservation, and Zahn et al. noted, "Most programs could be rated as having insufficient evidence" (p. 6). MTFC/TFCO may be one exception to this conclusion, at least as applied to delinquent girls.

As a final caution, the American Psychological Association Task Force on Evidence-Based Practice (2006) emphasized the importance of cultural considerations in ensuring evidence-based practice. As previously noted, the lack of consistent demographic reporting of female adolescents' ethnic or racial identity, sexual orientation, and gender identities in the research literature limits our understanding of the impact of intersectional identities on sexually abusive behavior and the cultural relevance of evidence-based treatments.

Additional Treatment Considerations

Gannon et al. (2008), in regard to adult females who abuse, pointed out that identifying pathways to sexually abusive behavior provides guidance regarding treatment goals. Unfortunately, the empirical literature related to adolescent females who sexually abuse cannot yet provide a great deal of guidance. Despite this concern and the heterogeneity of the population, though, some tentative recommendations can be offered based on developmental considerations and the consensus reached in the research related to characteristics of female adolescents who sexually abuse. Of course, as noted previously, treatment goals must build from a comprehensive assessment that identifies individual needs and vulnerabilities. In addition, all interventions must be implemented within an overall approach to clients that facilitates responsible behavior, increases awareness of impact on others, and supports the development of behavior management strategies regarding abusive behavior.

Treatment Considerations Regarding Trauma-Informed Care

The need to address trauma and maltreatment experiences is noted in virtually all the literature related to treatment needs of adolescent and adult females who sexually abuse. Levinson et al.'s (2015) application of trauma-informed care (TIC) with adult females who have sexually offended and have experienced childhood trauma has implications for the treatment of adolescent females. For instance, an important treatment component of TIC involves fostering the development of mutual, empowering, and authentic relationships. Levinson et al. offer three principles of TIC services: (a) Therapeutic services must acknowledge the prevalence and impact of trauma; (b) services must be client-centered and grounded in an understanding of problematic behavior, emotions, and psychological responses as coping strategies developed to survive trauma; and (c) there must be an emphasis on understanding the meanings each client attributes to the trauma experience, as well as the impact of these meanings intrapersonally and interpersonally. A critical aspect of TIC is the implementation of all the principles in all aspects of the therapeutic environment and relationships. TIC is not the same as therapeutic treatment targeting specific trauma symptoms; it is an overarching perspective that can be integrated into any program of treatment for adolescent females who have sexually abused.

Treatment Considerations Emerging from Literature on Adult Females Who Sexually Offend and Female Adolescents Who Engage in Delinquent Behavior

Chesney-Lind and Shelden (2014) identified three treatment needs based on the outcomes of effective programs serving female adolescents engaged in delinquent behaviors: (a) counseling that addresses personal experiences of abuse and violence; (b) general skill building (e.g., emotional regulation, interpersonal skills, empowerment, assertiveness); and (c) interventions that foster stable living situations and ensure access to resources that meet medical, dental, educational, employment, and housing needs. An additional level of complexity is added for adolescent girls who have sexually abused in that restrictions related to, for example, housing or employment may be imposed as a result of their history of sexually abusive behavior.

Extrapolating from the treatment literature on adult females who sexually abuse, some additional recommendations can be offered, keeping in mind developmental differences in the populations. Denov and Cortoni (2006) enumerated the broad goals of treatment as identifying contributors to the sexually abusive behavior, understanding the needs met by the behavior, and developing healthier ways to meet the needs. Thus, treatment targets that may be applicable include cognitions related to the sexually abusive behavior, intimacy and social relationship problems, and maladaptive coping skills, including emotional dysregulation (Decou et al., 2015; Denov & Cortoni, 2006; Ford, 2010); and mental health problems and dependency on males (Ford, 2010).

A well-developed framework explaining women's relational and interpersonal patterns that has been referenced in the literature related to adolescent and adult females who engage in sexually abusive or criminal behavior (e.g., Bloom et al., 2003; Frey, 2010; Hubbard & Matthews, 2007) is relational-cultural theory (RCT; Miller, 1984; Miller & Stiver, 1997). RCT is built on the assumption that meaningful, shared connection with others leads to the development of a healthy "felt sense of self" (Jordan, 1997, p. 15). Contrary to traditional models based on the "myth of the separate self" (Jordan, 2010, p. 2)—that is, models that consider separation-individuation to be the primary path to self-development—relational-cultural theory proposes that differentiation and growth of the felt sense of self develops through meaningful and mutual connections with others (Miller & Stiver, 1997). In relational-cultural terms, connection occurs in relationships that incorporate the four relational characteristics of engagement, authenticity, empowerment, and the ability to express, receive, and process diversity, difference, or conflict in the relationship; disconnection, which can be situational or chronic, occurs when these characteristics are not present (Jordan, 2010;

Miller & Stiver, 1997). The chronic absence of these qualities in important relation-ships results in a pervasive lack of interpersonal connection and a sense of isolation (Miller, 1986).

Treatment Considerations Regarding Group Patterns of Sexually Abusive Behavior

Wijkman et al. (2015) offered treatment suggestions related to group patterns of sexually abusive behavior involving adolescent females, although the recommendations must be viewed as tentative due to the small sample size and the limited number of stud-ies examining this population. First, Wijkman et al. cautioned that the risks of treat-ment in a therapy group focused on abusive behavior be carefully weighed due to the importance of not replicating peer group dynamics involved in the abusive incident(s). Also, it was suggested that potential treatment goals be linked to the behavioral inten-tions identified in the study. For instance, skill-based treatment, with a focus on social-cognitive interventions related to building social, problem-solving, and/or aggression management skills, was suggested for females who abused to harass the victim or to get revenge. For those whose intention was sexual gratification, suggested treatment tar-gets included a focus on sexual content (presumably, for example, cognitive distortions and deviant fantasies), as well as on improving self-esteem and self-efficacy. In general, interpersonal problems and personal sexual victimization histories were also identified as treatment targets.

IMPLICATIONS FOR RESEARCH AND PUBLIC POLICY

At this point in time, two pressing needs are the development of a theoretical frame-work explaining sexually abusive behavior among adolescent females and a clearer understanding of the effectiveness of treatment interventions with adolescent females who sexually abuse. This is a formidable challenge given the difficulties in recruit-ing a broad range of adolescent females who have sexually abused—that is, those with diverse ethnic/racial, sexual, and gender identities; those in community-based settings, not just involved in the juvenile justice system or in residential treatment programs; and so on. Considering the potential recruitment problems, Frey (2010) pointed out the importance of smaller sample size studies focusing on rigorous research designs incorporating control groups, matching of participants on multiple factors, use of psy-chometrically sound instruments, and well-defined and developmentally appropriate participant groupings. In addition, it would be helpful to expand the research base from the present focus on descriptive characteristics to the development and testing of tentative theoretical frameworks explaining adolescent female sexually abusive behavior and measuring the effectiveness and outcome of existing treatment programs for female adolescents.

To aid in overcoming these recruitment and research design challenges, one consideration might be the formation of a task force related to adolescent females who sexually abuse by a national center focused on prevention and treatment of juvenile crime (e.g., Office of Juvenile Justice and Delinquency Prevention). Central goals of the task force could include exploring creative solutions for addressing research challenges and developing best practice and research guidelines. For instance, recommended research guidelines regarding sociodemographic and offense-related data to be gathered in studies and measures that have been found to be psychometrically robust for use with female adolescents could be developed. In addition, the task force might explore the development of a database repository containing deidentified data voluntarily submitted by researchers conducting studies with adolescent females who sexually abuse. These data could be made available for continued research. While similar databases currently exist (e.g., NIBRS database), they are generally restricted to youth who have been arrested and/or involved in the juvenile justice system.

On a policy level, the point is often made that increased numbers of male versus female adolescents who sexually abuse provide a clear rationale for directing the majority of resources to programs targeting male adolescents. However, the real problem is not simply resource allocation but the lack of attention to identifying the needs of, and to developing services for, adolescent females at multiple levels of system intervention (Frey, 2006). Regarding services for girls engaged in a range of delinquent behaviors, Chesney-Lind and Shelden (2014) stated, "What has emerged . . . [is] a pattern of 'throwaway services' (Wells, 1994) for girls who were an afterthought in a juvenile justice system designed for boys in trouble" (p. 298). We can do better.

REFERENCES

Andrews, D. A., & Bonta, J. (2010). Rehabilitating criminal justice policy and practice. *Psychology, Public Policy, and Law, 16,* 39–55. http://dx.doi.org/10.1037/a0018362

APA Presidential Task Force on Evidence-Based Practice. (2006). Evidence-based practice in psychology. *American Psychologist, 61,* 271–285. http://dx.doi.org/10.1037/0003-066X.61.4.271

Batastini, A. B., Hunt, E., Present-Koller, & DeMatteo, D. (2011). Federal standards for community registration of juvenile sexual offenders: An evaluation of risk prediction and future implications. *Psychology, Public Policy, and Law, 17,* 451–474. http://dx.doi.org/10.1037/a0023637

Bloom, B., Owen, B., & Covington, S. (2003). *Gender-responsive strategies: Research, practice, and guiding principles for women offenders.* Retrieved from http://nicic.gov/library/018017

Bumby, N. H., & Bumby, K. M. (1997). Adolescent female sexual offenders. In B. K. Schwartz & H. R. Cellini (Eds.), *The sex offender: Corrections, treatment, and legal practice* (pp. 10.1–10.16). Kingston, NJ: Civic Research Institute,.

Chesney-Lind, M., & Shelden, R. G. (2014). *Girls, delinquency, and juvenile justice* (4th ed.). West Sussex, UK: Wiley-Blackwell.

Conrad, S. M., Placella, N., Tolou-Shams, M., Rizzo, C. J., & Brown, L. K. (2014). Gender differences in recidivism rates for juvenile justice youth: The impact of sexual abuse. *Law and Human Behavior, 38,* 305–314. http://dx.doi.org/10.1037/lhb0000062

Cortoni, F. (2010). The assessment of female sexual offenders. In T. A. Gannon & F. Cortoni (Eds.), *Female sexual offenders: Theory, assessment, and treatment* (pp. 87–100). West Sussex, UK: Wiley-Blackwell. http://dx.doi.org/10.1002/9780470666715.ch6

Creswell, J. W. (2013). *Qualitative inquiry & research design: Choosing among five approaches* (3rd ed.). Thousand Oaks, CA: Sage.

Crijnen, A. A. M., Achenbach, T. M., & Verhulst, F. C. (1997). Comparisons of problems reported by parents of children in 12 cultures: Total problems, externalizing, and internalizing. *Journal of the American Academy of Child & Adolescent Psychiatry, 36,* 1269–1277.

Day, J. C., Zahn, M. A., & Tichavsky, L. P. (2015). What works for whom? The effects of gender responsive programming on girls and boys in secure detention. *Journal of Research in Crime and Delinquency, 52,* 93–129. http://dx.doi.org/10:1177/0022427814538033

DeCou, C. R., Cole, T. T., Rowland, S. E., Kaplan, S. P., & Lynch, S. M. (2015). An ecological process model of female sex offending: The role of victimization, psychological distress, and life stressors. *Sexual Abuse: A Journal of Research and Treatment, 27,* 302–323. http://dx.doi.org/10.1077/1079063214556359

Denov, M. S., & Cortoni, F. (2006). Women who sexually abuse children. In C. Hilarski & J. Wodarski (Eds.), *Comprehensive mental health practice with sex offenders and their families* (pp. 71–99). New York: Haworth.

Dopp, A. R., Borduin, C. M., & Brown, C. E. (2015). Evidence-based treatments for juvenile sexual offenders: Review and recommendations. *Journal of Aggression, Conflict, and Peace Research, 7,* 223–236. http://dx.doi.org/10.1108/JACPR-01-2015-0155

Dowden, C., & Andrews, D. A. (1999). What works for female offenders: A meta-analytic review. *Crime & Delinquency, 45,* 438–452. http://dx.doi.org/10.1177/0011128799045004002

Fehrenbach, P. A., & Monastersky, C. (1988). Characteristics of female adolescent sexual offenders. *American Journal of Orthopsychiatry, 58*(1), 148–151. http://dx.doi.org/10.1111/j.1939-0025.1988.tb01575.x

Finkelhor, D., Ormrod, R., & Chaffin, M. (2009). Juveniles who commit sex offenses against minors. *Office of Justice Programs Juvenile Justice Bulletin* (December 2009). Retrieved from www.ojp.usdoj.gov

Ford, H. (2010). The treatment needs of female sexual offenders. In T. A. Gannon & F. Cortoni (Eds.), *Female sexual offenders: Theory, assessment, and treatment* (pp. 101–117). West Sussex, UK: Wiley-Blackwell. http://dx.doi.org/10.1002/9780470666715.ch7

Ford, J. D., Chapman, J. F., Hawke, J., & Albert, D. (2007). *Trauma among youth in the juvenile justice system: Critical issues and new directions.* Retrieved from www.ncmhjj.com

Ford, J. D., Steinberg, K. L., Hawke, J., Levine, J., & Zhang, W. (2012). Randomized trial comparison of emotion regulation and relational psychotherapies for PTSD with girls involved in delinquency. *Journal of Clinical Child & Adolescent Psychology, 41,* 27–37. http://dx.doi.org/10.1080/15374416.2012.632343

Frey, L. L. (2006). Girls don't do that, do they? Adolescent females who sexually abuse. In R. E. Longo & D. S. Prescott (Eds.), *Current perspectives: Working with sexually aggressive youth & youth with sexual behavior problems* (pp. 255–272). Holyoke, MA: NEARI Press.

Frey, L. L. (2010). The juvenile female sexual offender: Characteristics, treatment and research. In T. A. Gannon & F. Cortoni (Eds.), *Female sexual offenders: Theory, assessment, and treatment* (pp. 53–71). West Sussex, UK: Wiley-Blackwell. http://dx.doi.org/10.1002/9780470666715.ch4

Frey, L. L., & Beesley, D. (2010, August). *Incarcerated female adolescents: A phenomenological study.* Poster presented at the 2010 Annual Conference of the American Psychological Association, San Diego, CA.

Gannon, T. A., & Cortoni, F. (2010). *Female sexual offenders: Theory, assessment, and treatment.* West Sussex, UK: Wiley-Blackwell. http://dx.doi.org/10.1002/9780470666715

Gannon. T. A., Hoare, J. A., Rose, M. R., & Parrett, N. (2012). A re-examination of female child molesters' implicit theories: Evidence of female specificity? *Psychology, Crime & Law, 18,* 209–224. http://dx.doi.org/10.1080/10683161003752303

Gannon, T. A., Rose, M. R., & Ward, T. (2008). A descriptive model of the offense process for female sexual offenders. *Sexual Abuse: A Journal of Research and Treatment, 20,* 352–374. http://dx.doi.org/10.1177/1079063208322495

Gannon, T. A., Rose, M. R., & Ward, T. (2010). Pathways to female sexual offending: Approach or avoidance? *Psychology, Crime & Law, 16,* 359–380. http://dx.doi.org/10.1080/10683160902754956

Harris, D. A. (2010). Theories of female sexual offending. In T. A. Gannon & F. Cortoni (Eds.), *Female sexual offenders: Theory, assessment, and treatment* (pp. 31–51). West Sussex, U.K.: Wiley-Blackwell. doi: 10.1002/9780470666715.ch3

Hawkins, S. R., Graham, P. W., Williams, J., & Zahn, M. A. (2009). *Resilient girls—factors that protect against delinquency* (NCJ 220124). Washington, DC: US Department of Justice Office of Juvenile Justice and Delinquency Prevention. Retrieved from https://www.ncjrs.gov/pdffiles1/ojjdp/220124.pdf

Hendriks, J., & Bijleveld, C. C. J. H. (2006). Female adolescent sex offenders—an exploratory study. *Journal of Sexual Aggression, 12,* 31–41. http://dx.doi.org/10.1080/13552600600568937

Hickey, N., McCrory, E., Farmer, E., & Vizard, E. (2008). Comparing the developmental and behavioural characteristics of female and male juveniles who present with sexually abusive behavior. *Journal of Sexual Aggression, 14,* 241–252. http://dx.doi.org/10.1080/13552600802389793

Hoge, R. D. (2015). Risk/need/responsivity in juveniles. In K. Heilbrun, D. DeMatteo, & N. Goldstein (Eds.), *APA handbook of psychology and juvenile justice* (pp. 179–196). Washington, DC: American Psychological Association.

Hubbard, D. J., & Matthews, B. (2008). Reconciling the differences between the "gender-responsive" and the "what works" literatures to improve services for girls. *Crime & Delinquency, 54,* 225–258. http://dx.doi.org/10.1177/0011128706296733

Hunter, J. A., Becker, J. V., & Lexier, L. J. (2006). The female juvenile sex offender. In H. E. Barbaree & W. L. Marshall (Eds.), *The juvenile sex offender* (2nd ed., pp. 148–165). New York: Guilford.

Hunter, J. A., Lexier, L. J., Goodwin, D. W., Browne, P. A., & Dennis, C. (1993). Psychosexual, attitudinal, and developmental characteristics of juvenile female sexual perpetrators in a residential treatment setting. *Journal of Child and Family Studies, 2,* 317–326.

Jordan, J. V. (2010). *Relational-cultural therapy.* Washington, DC: American Psychological Association.

Kerig, P. K., & Ford, J. D. (2014). Trauma among girls in the juvenile justice system. Retrieved from National Child Traumatic Stress Network website: www.NCTSNet.org

Ko, S. J., Kassam-Adams, N., Wilson, C., Ford, J. D., Berkowitz, S. J., Wong, M., . . . & Layne, C. M. (2008). Creating trauma-informed systems: Child welfare, education, first responders, health care, juvenile justice. *Professional Psychology: Research and Practice, 39,* 396–404. http://dx.doi. org/10.1037/0735-7028.39.4.396

Kubik, E. K., Hecker, J. E., & Righthand, S. (2002). Adolescent females who have sexually offended: Comparisons with delinquent adolescent female offenders and adolescent males who sexually offend. *Journal of Child Sexual Abuse, 11*(3), 63–83. http://dx.doi.org/10.1300/J070v11n03_04

Levenson, J. S., Willis, G. M., & Prescott, D. S. (2015). Adverse childhood experiences in the lives of female sex offenders. *Sexual Abuse: A Journal of Research and Treatment, 27,* 258–283. http:// dx.doi.org/10.1177/1079063214544332

Looman, J., & Abarcen, J. (2013). The risk need responsivity model of offender rehabilitation: Is there really a need for a paradigm shift? *International Journal of Behavioral Consultation and Therapy, 8*(3-4), 30–36.

Matsumoto, D. (2003). Cross-cultural research. In S. F. Davis (Ed.), *Handbook of research methods in experimental psychology* (pp. 189–208). Malden, MA: Blackwell.

Matthews, B., & Hubbard, D. J. (2009). Moving ahead: Five essential elements for working effectively with girls. *Journal of Criminal Justice, 36,* 494–502.

Matthews, R., Hunter, J. A., & Vuz, J. (1997). Juvenile female sexual offenders: Clinical characteristics and treatment issues. *Sexual Abuse: A Journal of Research and Treatment, 9*(3), 187–199.

Matthews, R., Matthews, J. K., & Speltz, K. (1989). *Female sex offenders: An exploratory study.* Orwell, VT: Safer Society Press.

McCarten, F. M., Law, H., Murphy, M., & Bailey, S. (2011). Child and adolescent females who present with sexually abusive behaviours: A 10-year UK prevalence study. *Journal of Sexual Aggression, 17,* 4–14. http://dx.doi.org/10.1080/13552600.2010.488302

McGrath, R. J., Cumming, G. F., Burchard, B. L., Zeoli, S., & Ellerby, L. (2010). *Current practices and emerging trends in sexual abuser management: The Safer Society 2009 North American survey.* Brandon, VT: Safer Society Press.

Miccio-Fonseca, L. C. (2006). *Multiplex Empirically Guided Inventory of Ecological Aggregates for Assessing Sexually Abusive Adolescents and Children (ages 10 and under)—MEGA.* San Diego: Author.

Miccio-Fonseca, L. C. (2013). MEGA: A new paradigm in risk assessment tools for sexually abusive youth. *Journal of Family Violence, 28,* 623–634. http://dx.doi.org/10.1007/s10896-013-9527-8

Miccio-Fonseca, L. C., & Rasmussen, L. A. (2011). A concise review on validated risk assessment tools for sexually abusive youth. *Sexual Offender Treatment, 6*(2). Retrieved from http://www. sexual-offender-treatment.org/99.html

Miller, J. B. (1984). *The development of women's sense of self* (Work in Progress No. 12). Wellesley, MA: Wellesley College Stone Center.

Miller, J. B. (1986). *Toward a new psychology of women* (2nd ed.). Boston: Beacon.

Miller, J. B., & Stiver, I. P. (1997). *The healing connection: How women form relationships in therapy and in life.* Boston: Beacon Press.

Moffitt, T. E., Caspi, A., Rutter, M., & Silva, P. A. (2001). Sex differences in antisocial behaviour: Conduct disorder, delinquency, and violence in the Dunedin Logitudinal Study. New York: Cambridge University Press.

Office for Victims of Crime. (2015). *2015 NCVRW resource guide.* Retrieved from www.ovc.gov/ ncvrw201

Peters, S. (1998). *Guiding principles for promising female programming: An inventory of best practices.* Washington, DC: US Department of Justice Office of Juvenile Justice and Delinquency Prevention.

Pithers, W.D. (1990). Relapse prevention with sexual aggressors: A method for maintaining therapeutic gain and enhancing external supervision. In W. L. Marshall, D. R. Laws, & H. E. Barbaree (Eds.), *Handbook of sexual assault: Issues, theories and treatment of the offender* (pp. 346–361). New York: Plenum.

Prentky, R. A., & Righthand, S. (2003). *Juvenile Sex Offender Assessment Protocol: Manual* (NCJ 202316). Washington, DC: US Department of Justice Office of Juvenile Justice and Delinquency Prevention.

Righthand, S., Baird, B., Way, I., & Seto, M. C. (2014). *Effective intervention with adolescents who have offended sexually: Translating research into practice.* Brandon, VT: Safer Society.

Roe-Sepowitz, D., & Krysik, J. (2008). Examining the sexual offenses of female juveniles: The relevance of childhood maltreatment. *American Journal of Orthopsychiatry, 78,* 405–412. http://dx.doi.org/10.1037/a0014310

Substance Abuse and Mental Health Services Administration. (2014a). *SAMHSA's concept of trauma and guidance for a trauma-informed approach* (HHS Publication No. [SMA] 14-4884). Retrieved from http://store.samhsa.gov/shin/content/SMA14-4884/SMA14-4884.pdf

Substance Abuse and Mental Health Services Administration. (2014b). *Treatment improvement protocol (TIP) series 57: Trauma-informed care in behavioral health services* (HHS Publication No. [SMA] 13-4816). Retrieved from http://store.samhsa.gov/shin/content//SMA14-4816/SMA14-4816.pdf

Tardif, M., Auclair, N., Jacob, M., & Carpentier, J. (2005). Sexual abuse perpetrated by adult and juvenile females: An ultimate attempt to resolve a conflict associated with maternal identity. *Child Abuse & Neglect, 29,* 153–167. http://dx.doi.org/10.1016/j.chiabu.2004.05.006

US Department of Justice & Federal Bureau of Investigation. (2014). *Crime in the United States 2013: Uniform crime reports.* Retrieved from https://www.fbi.gov/about-us/cjis/ucr/crime-in-the-u.s/2013/crime-in-the-u.s.-2013

US Department of Justice & Federal Bureau of Investigation. (2015). *Crime in the United States 2014: Uniform crime reports.* Retrieved from https://www.fbi.gov/about-us/cjis/ucr/crime-in-the-u.s/2013/crime-in-the-u.s.-2014

Vandiver, D. M. (2010). Assessing gender differences and co-offending patterns of a predominantly "male-oriented" crime: A comparison of a cross-national sample of juvenile boys and girls arrested for a sexual offense. *Violence and Victims, 25,* 243-264. http://dx.doi.org/0.1891/0886-6708.25.2.243

Vandiver, D. M., & Teske, R. Jr. (2006). Juvenile female and male sex offenders: A comparison of offender, victim, and judicial processing characteristics. *International Journal of Offender Therapy and Comparative Criminology, 50,* 148–165. http://dx.doi.org/10.1177/0306624X05277941

Vick, J., McRoy, R., & Matthews, B. M. (2002). Young female sex offenders: Assessment and treatment issues. *Journal of Child Sexual Abuse, 11*(2), 1–23. http://dx.doi.org/10.1300/J070v11n02_01

Wijkman, M., Bijleveld, C., & Hendriks, J. (2014). Juvenile female sex offenders: Offender and offence characteristics. *European Journal of Criminology, 11,* 23–38. http://dx.doi.org/10.1177/1477370813479077

Wijkman, M., Weerman, F., Bijleveld, C., & Hendriks, J. (2015). Group sexual offending by juvenile females. *Sexual Abuse: A Journal of Research and Treatment, 27,* 335–356. http://dx.doi.org/10.1077/1079063214561685

Worling, J. R., & Curwen, T. (2001). *The ERASOR: Estimate of Risk of Adolescent Sexual Recidivism* (Version 2.0). Toronto, Canada: Safe-T Program, Thistletown Regeional Centre.

Worling, J. R., & Långström, N. (2006). Risk of sexual recidivism in adolescents who offend sexually: Correlates and assessment. In H. E. Barbaree & W. L. Marshall (Eds.), *The juvenile sex offender* (2nd ed., pp. 219–247). New York: Guilford.

Zahn, M. A., Agnew, R., Fishbein, D., Miller, S., Winn, D., Dakoff, G., . . . & Chesney-Lind, M. (2010). *Causes and correlates of girls' delinquency* (NCJ 226358). Washington, DC: US Department of Justice Office of Juvenile Justice and Delinquency Prevention. Retrieved from https://www.ncjrs.gov/pdffiles1/ojjdp/226358.pdf

Zahn, M. A., Hawkins, S. R., Chiancone, J., & Whitworth, A. (2008). *The Girls Study Group: Charting the way to delinquency prevention for girls* (NCJ 223434). Washington, DC: US Department of Justice Office of Juvenile Justice and Delinquency Prevention. Retrieved from https://www.ncjrs.gov/pdffiles1/ojjdp/223434.pdf

CHAPTER 14

Pornography Use and Youth-Produced Sexual Images Among Adolescents

Abigail M. Judge

The effects of the Internet and mobile communications technology on adolescent sexual behavior have caused considerable concern, speculation, and alarm in the mainstream media as well as professional circles. This is particularly true in the case of "sexting," a media-derived term to describe the production and electronic exchange of sexually explicit images between adolescents. Analysis of popular and professional reports about youth-produced sexual images has likened this discourse to a moral or media panic (Angelides, 2013; Draper, 2012; Hasinoff, 2015). These reactions are continuous with previous historical responses to new technology that alternatively glorify the potential effects of novel devices and condemn the same for their disruption of social relationships and hierarchies (Marvin, 1998). These dynamics are even more complex in the case of adolescent sexual behavior, however, a topic long since associated with danger (Moran, 2000).

The assumption that the Internet is a deviance-amplifying context for teens' sexual behavior is remarkably persistent, despite research that suggests it is not more dangerous than previous offline settings (e.g., neighborhood, school) for the majority of youth (Finkelhor, 2014)—on balance, for example, research that has shown that online risk for youth is highly related to offline adversity, thus children and adolescents with psychiatric vulnerability and other forms of psychosocial difficulty and are more likely to engage with technology in problematic ways (Finkelhor, 2011; 2014; Livingstone & Smith, 2014; Mitchell, Finkelhor, & Becker-Blease, 2007; Wolak, Finkelhor, Mitchell, &

Ybarra, 2010). Because technology use may be more complicated for youth already facing developmental challenges, it is important for clinicians, educators, and policy makers to distinguish alarmist assumptions about the Internet from reliable information in order to guide decision making.

Clinical and anecdotal evidence suggests an uptick in the number of youth who present to treatment and evaluation settings for problems with some Internet nexus (Mitchell & Wells, 2007; Pridgen, 2010; Scott, 2011). This includes youth who sexually abuse (Hunter & Figueredo, 2010). Although there has been much speculation about the Internet as a new platform for sexually abusive behaviors, a recent review concluded that the role of the Internet among youth who sexually abuse remains poorly understood (Boonmann, Grudzinskas, & Aebi, 2014). It is therefore critical that professionals working with this population be aware of the limited evidence base on these topics given the ways in which this group's treatment needs overall, including recidivism, are commonly misperceived (DiCataldo, 2009; Zimring, 2009).

Accordingly, this chapter will review the empirical literature on two intersections between the Internet and adolescent sexual behavior: adolescents' use of pornography and its effects, and the less developed research base on youth-produced sexual images (i.e., "sexting"). Because there is very little research that addresses these phenomena among youth who sexually abuse, findings from the overall literature are presented with possible implications for this population discussed later. The structure of the chapter is as follows. First, data on patterns of Internet use among US adolescents are presented and integrated with current theories about adolescent sexuality development. Next, this chapter will review research on the attitudinal and behavioral effects of pornography exposure among adolescents, including equivocal findings and areas of consensus. Research on youth-produced sexual images is then discussed, literature that is much scarcer. Research-derived typologies that help differentiate among potentially normative and problematic forms of youth-produced sexual images will be emphasized. Finally, although most extant research on both topics is based on non-clinical populations, the chapter concludes with discussion of practice implications for youth with more complicated developmental trajectories, including adolescents who sexually abuse. This includes considerations for assessment, treatment, parent consultation, and educational responses.

The Normative Context of Internet Use

The Internet, along with related mobile communications technologies, has become a mainstream facet of social development among US adolescents. According to the Pew Research Center, three-quarters of surveyed US youth aged 13 through 17 have access to a smartphone, 30 percent have a basic phone, and only 12 percent have no phone access (Lenhart, 2015). Smartphones have revolutionized how adolescents access online content such that online activity may be done wirelessly, via handheld devices, and presumably with less adult monitoring. Teens who access the Internet via smartphones report higher rates of at least daily online activity than youth who access the Internet without such devices (94% and 68%, respectively) (Lenhart, 2015).

Data also indicate that teens' use of social networking sites is increasingly diverse, with 71 percent of youth using more than one social networking site (Lenhart, 2015). The Pew Center data indicated that Facebook remains the most popular site among surveyed youth, although ethnographic research suggests regional and ethnic differences in the popularity of social networking sites (Boyd, 2014). Novel applications and their popularity change frequently among youth (e.g., Facebook, Tumblr, Instagram, Twitter, Google+, Snapchat, YikYak, Vine, Kik), which is a known limitation of research in this area (Saleh, Grudzinkas, & Judge, 2014). A key developmental function of these applications is constant access to and surveillance of one's peers, either via messaging or picture- and video-sharing technology. Seen in this way, social media is continuous with normative adolescent social development, where interactions with peers are paramount (Steinberg, 2008; Subrahmanyam, Smahel, & Greenfield, 2006).

Sociologist Danah Boyd (2014) has conducted years of ethnographic research with teens on their use of networked publics—public spaces that are restructured by networked technologies. Boyd asserts that teens have always been passionate about finding their place in society and that this enduring drive for social connection and autonomy is now expressed in networked publics like social media. Her research suggests that none of the capabilities enabled by social media are new: "What is new is the way in which social media alters and amplifies social situations by offering technical features that people can use to engage in these well established practices" (Boyd, 2014, p. 13). In the case of adolescent social behavior, technical features such as "liking" an Instagram post or maintaining a Snapchat "streak" with friends are novel ways to publicly demonstrate social connection and status, perennial adolescent concerns. In the realm of sexual development, networked publics likewise offer technical features that either facilitate developmental aims (e.g., sexual curiosity and exploration) or else enhance risk or harm.

In order to understand the effects of the Internet on adolescent sexual behavior, data on teens' technology use must be considered relative to theory and research on adolescent sexuality development. Over the last 30 years, theorists have argued that research on adolescent sexuality should not assume that sexual behavior is associated solely with dangerous outcomes. As reviewed by Tolman and McClelland (2011), research over the last decade has produced a body of empirical research that highlights the limits of a risk-centric approach. This includes, for example, a singular emphasis on the negative outcomes of sexual behavior during adolescence as opposed to the opportunity for sexual activity to promote growth (Savin-Williams & Diamond, 2009). This paradigm shift in research has been described as a normative perspective on adolescent sexuality—one that emphasizes sexuality as an expected developmental phenomenon (while recognizing the contested nature of the term *normative* in sexuality studies) (Tolman & McClelland, 2011).

A normative perspective provides a conceptual framework for the study of adolescent sexuality "not only in terms of sexual risks and how to avert them but also of querying what enables and challenges the expected development of healthy sexuality in adulthood, previously posited as 'positive sexual development'" (Tolman & McClelland, 2011, p. 250). As applied to the Internet and mobile communications technology, a normative perspective on adolescent sexuality aims to identify the ways in which technology use may propel healthy sexual development (e.g., asking questions about sexual topics; healthful exploration of emerging sexual identity), in addition to consideration of possible risk (Suzuki & Calzo, 2004; Subrahmanyam, Greenfield, & Tynes, 2004). It may be assumed that teens' digital worlds are connected to the developmental processes of their lives, including sexuality development (Smahel & Subrahmanyam, 2014). In a related theoretical vein, Johnson and Puplampu (2008) extended Brofenbrenner's (1979) ecological systems theory to include a techno-subsystem, a dimension of the microsystem (i.e., the immediate environment, which comprises family, school, peer interactions, etc.). Ethnographic research with diverse US youth supports the notion of online spaces as an extension of traditional "hangouts" such as malls, playgrounds, and other youth-only spaces (Boyd, 2014). Much as there are youth who can more and easily manage the freedoms of offline youth-only contexts, individual differences and pre-existing vulnerabilities will moderate Internet risk (Livingstone & Smith, 2014).

Sexual Behavior Online: What Is Different?

As reviewed elsewhere in this volume (see chapters 1 and 2), sexual curiosity is developmentally typical during adolescence (Crockett, Raffaelli, & Moilanen, 2003; Ponton & Judice, 2004). As an expression of this curiosity, young people have consulted sexually explicit materials for hundreds of years in order to understand their own bodies, to learn how sex is performed, and to arouse themselves sexually (Brown & Bryant, 1989). One key difference between previous print-based forms of sexually explicit material and contemporary online content is the level of unrestricted access that the Internet and its ancillary technologies offer (Brown & D'Engle, 2009; Owens et al., 2012). Access to the Internet is no longer limited to a personal computer attached to a telephone line and is now most commonly accessed wirelessly via smartphones and other handheld devices (e.g., tablet, gaming console, laptop).

Almost two decades ago, Cooper (1998) coined the term *Triple A engine* to describe three characteristics of online environments that can make sexual behavior in this context more problematic or compulsive: accessibility, affordability, and anonymity. Although youth may possess greater facility navigating online applications than adults, they lack the same decision-making capacities due to key developmental differences. The heightened sexual urges and curiosity of adolescence occur during a time of neurodevelopmental immaturity, particularly with respect to how youth make decisions about rewards (e.g., money, novelty and excitement, social connection, peer group acceptance, sexual activity, and substance use) (Steinberg, 2007). As summarized by Giedd (2008; 2012), a theme of neuroimaging research with adolescents is the shifting balance during this period between frontal (executive control) and limbic (emotional) systems. Abilities encompassed by the term *executive functions* (e.g., attention, organization, long-term planning, response inhibition) are believed to rely on frontal lobe circuitry, which is relatively late to mature in a process that continues through late adolescence. Thus, behaviors such as youth-produced sexual images, consistent with neurobiological development, may be viewed as emotionally driven behavior that is often impulsive and without a clear anticipation or understanding of the potential adverse consequences (Judge, 2012).

Importantly, teens themselves do not necessarily describe their use of social media and mobile communications in the same terms as adults. As Boyd (2014) explains, "More often than not, [teens] are unaware of why the networked publics they inhabit are different than other publics or why adults find networked publics so peculiar" (p. 15). This echoes earlier writing where adolescents did not necessarily make distinctions between on- and offline activities and selves in the same manner as adults (Palfrey & Gasser, 2008). This does not mean that adolescents are naive to basic differences between on- and offline realms, but that they psychologically shift more seamlessly between contexts than older individuals who did not come of age tethered to mobile communications technologies (Turkle, 2006). This difference in perspective may have important implications for interpreting the literature on the topics of adolescents' exposure to pornography and youth-produced sexual images, where different perspectives on these topics between youth and adults may be assumed (Harris & Davidson, 2014).

For the purposes of this chapter, the term *Internet* is used broadly and refers to online activities as well as ancillary technologies and social networking applications that youth access via smartphones. This chapter employs a normative perspective on adolescent sexuality and also technology use, a framework that considers but does not limit itself to analysis of risk, and that also queries the potentially developmentally adaptive functions of sexual behaviors both on- and offline.

Pornography Exposure and Developmental Consequences

Academics expressed concern about the effects of pornography on youth even before Internet connectivity became mainstream (Wright, 2014). The proliferation of Internet-enabled technology has only increased these concerns among researchers and policy makers, even as data to inform these debates are limited. Conducting research on the effects of pornography on youth is difficult, in part because experiments with porno-graphic stimuli are illegal in many countries due to the age-based restrictions on the consumption of sexually explicit media. There are also ethical difficulties of asking youth what exactly they have seen without introducing them to unfamiliar ideas, which also limits research (Livingstone & Smith, 2014). The study of children's access to por-nography, distinguished from illegal viewing of child abuse images, is based largely in the tradition of research on children's exposure to mass media.

Prevalence of Pornography Use and Exposure

Research distinguishes between deliberate (or wanted) use of Internet pornography and accidental (or unwanted) exposure to pornography (e.g., resulting from pop-ups, unsolicited emails, or ambiguous search terms) (Boonmann et al., 2014). Representative and large-scale studies suggest that children's exposure to pornography is common: 73 percent of US college students reported viewing online pornography prior to age 18 (Sabina, Wolak, & Finkelhor, 2008).

The most widely cited and representative studies of voluntary and unwanted por-nography exposure among US adolescents are the First, Second, and Third Youth Internet Safety Surveys (YISS-1, YISS-2, and YISS-3; Jones et al., 2012; Mitchell, Wolak, & Finkelhor, 2007; Wolak, Finkelhor, & Mitchell, 2007; Ybarra & Mitchell, 2005). The YISS-1, -2, and -3 examined patterns of online sexual behavior among US adolescents in two nationally representative, independent samples of Internet users (aged 10 through 17) by telephone survey. Thirteen to 25 percent of surveyed youth intentionally viewed X-rated material, a figure that remained relatively stable over the 10 years surveyed (Jones et al., 2012). Unwanted exposure to online pornography, including distressing exposures, declined during the final two waves of data collection from 34 percent of the sample to 23 percent, which could reflect industry effort to control pop-ups and spam (Jones et al., 2012).

Older youth (i.e., 14 through 17 years old) in the YISS-1, -2, and -3 studies were more likely to report intentionally seeking out pornography, ages when it is developmentally appropriate to be sexually curious. The authors suggested that concerns about large numbers of young children accessing pornographic material online may be overstated (Ybarra & Mitchell, 2005). Exposure to pornography prior to age 13 is uncommon (Sabina et al., 2008).

As reviewed by Wright (2014), international samples of youth suggest similarly high rates of pornography exposure. A representative survey of Dutch children (aged 12 through 17) reported that a quarter had viewed pornographic pictures online in the prior six months (Peter & Valkenburg, 2011). Similar exposure rates (i.e., a quarter of the sample) were found among a representative sample of Greek high school students (Tsitsika et al., 2009). More than three-quarters of males and females reported accidental exposure to Internet pornography among a representative sample of Australian youth aged 16 and 17, with gender differences observed in rates of deliberate access (i.e., 38% of males, and 2% of females) (Flood, 2007). A representative sample of middle and high school students in Taiwan found that nearly 40 percent viewed pornography online in the last few years (Lo & Wei, 2005). In general, studies have reported greater pornography consumption among adolescent males than females (Brown & L'Engle, 2009; Carroll et al., 2008; Owens et al., 2012; Peter & Valkenburg, 2006; Svedin et al., 2011; Ybarra & Mitchell, 2005).

When unintended and intentional pornography users are compared, youth who sought pornography were more likely to cross-sectionally report delinquent behavior and substance use in the previous year (Ybarra & Mitchell, 2005; Wolak et al., 2007). Online seekers were more likely to report clinical symptoms associated with depression and lower levels of emotional bonding with their caregiver. Although study design prevents conclusions about causality, these differences merit additional research to define youth for whom pornography use corresponds with poor functioning offline. A meta-analysis of studies comparing adolescent males who committed sexual offenses and male adolescents who committed non-sexual offenses identified early exposure to sex or pornography as unique to youth who had sexually abused (Seto & Lalumière, 2010). This finding was correlational as well but suggests an area for additional research.

It is important for future research to measure not only exposure to pornography but also its effects on young viewers and the question of harm. When Jones et al. (2012) asked 10- through 17-year-olds who had viewed online pornography if they were "very or extremely upset," nearly half the 10- to 12-year-olds endorsed this response but only a fifth of the 16- to 17-year-olds described the experience in this way. Similarly, a European study reported that around one-third of the 9- through 16-year-olds who viewed online pornography reported being bothered or upset by it (Livingstone & Smith, 2014).

In addition to self-reported harm, researchers have raised concerns about the effects of pornography consumption on sexual socialization. Such concern is based on the assumption that young people may develop unrealistic and/or undesirable patterns of sexual behavior due to pornography exposure (Brown & L'Engle, 2009; Nathan, 2007). Sexual socialization theory posits that frequent exposure to consistent themes about gender and sexual behavior can affect a young person's developing sense of what is expected for males and females and may affect subsequent behavior as well (Brown & L'Engle, 2009). As Zillmann (2000, p. 41) suggested, "because consensually accepted programs of sexual education are lacking, erotica have come to serve as a primary agent of sexual socialization." The next section reviews studies that have considered associations between pornography exposure and sexual attitudes and behavior.

Effects of Pornography on Attitudes and Behavior

There is agreement in the literature that adolescents can learn sexual behaviors from observing behaviors depicted in sexually explicit media, including pornography (Alexy, Burgess, & Prentky, 2009; Häggström-Nordin et al., 2006; Owens, Behun, Manning, & Reid, 2012). Quantitative investigations have documented the ways that teenagers utilize pornography as a sexual instructional resource (Smith, 2013; Trostle, 2003). A recent qualitative study of low-income black and Hispanic youth (aged 16 through 18) found that almost every participant reported learning how to have sex by watching pornography (Rothman, Kaczmarsky, Burke, Jansen, & Baughman, 2015). This included acquiring knowledge about sexual positions, what opposite-sex partners may enjoy sexually, and how to engage in particular sex acts. A theme among female respondents was that watching pornography led them to engage in sex acts that they would not have tried otherwise, which resulted in positive and negative experiences. A minority of male respondents described producing their own sexually explicit videos with their partners using smartphones, sometimes using coercion, suggesting that pressure to produce pornography may be an element of some unhealthy dating relationships.

Since one common motivation for adolescents who view pornography is to learn about sexual activity, researchers have raised concern about adolescents' uncritical acceptance of pornography as a realistic depiction of sexual activity (Peter & Valkenburg, 2006). This includes depictions of sexual behaviors that are objectively unsafe (e.g., lack of contraception), nonrelational sexual activity, and depictions of women as sexual objects who are subordinate to men. Condom use is the exception in pornography, with condomless intercourse observed in 97 percent of surveyed scenes

(Grudzen et al., 2009), and nonrelational sexual activity (e.g., casual sex, group sex, and sex with strangers) is a common pornographic trope (Monk-Turner & Purcell, 1999; Palys, 1986).

Depictions of women as sexual objects who are subordinate to men, as well as male-on-female aggression, are common in pornographic scenes. Content analysis studies show that the majority (55%) of free adult Internet websites promote hypermasculinity, male domination, and the prioritization of male sexual pleasure as normative sexual scripts (Gorman, Monk-Turner, & Fish, 2010). An analysis of pornographic US films found that more than three-quarters of movies included scenes of dominance, with 80 percent of the dominators as men (Cowan, Lee, Levy, & Snyder, 1988). A random sample of pornographic movies defined as bestsellers or highly rented by the Adult Video Network found that 90 percent of scenes depicted aggressive acts such as choking, gagging, or spanking, with females the recipients of aggression approximately 95 percent of the time (Bridges, Wosnitzer, Scharre, Sun, & Liberman, 2010).

Research has documented a relationship between the degree and/or frequency of pornography exposure and non-progressive sexual attitudes and behaviors among adolescents. This includes positive associations between more frequent pornography exposure and increased sexual callousness (Zillman, 2000), greater alcohol consumption and greater likelihood of involvement in commercial sex among Swedish male adolescents (Svedin, Äkerman, & Priebe, 2011), non-condom-use among Swiss high school males (Luder, 2011), and reduced likelihood of contraceptive use among adolescent females aged 14 through 18 and testing positive for chlamydia (Wingood et al., 2001). Other studies have failed to report associations between online pornography exposure and risky sexual behaviors (Luder et al., 2011), with another study indicating that only 12 percent of male and 18 percent of female adolescents reported an important impact on their emotions or attitudes as a result of viewing online pornography (Sabina et al., 2008). It is important to note that the majority of these studies are cross-sectional and correlational; longitudinal designs may provide the most rigorous form of evidence for the effects of pornography on later sexual behavior, and more are needed (Livingstone & Smith, 2014).

One widely cited prospective study of ethnically diverse early adolescents (aged 13 through 15) found that early exposure to sexually explicit material, including online pornography, for males predicted less progressive gender role attitudes, more permissive sexual norms, and greater sexual harassment perpetration at two-year follow-up (Brown & L'Engle, 2009). For females, early exposure to sexually explicit media predicted less progressive gender role attitudes at follow-up. For both male and female adolescents, exposure to sexually explicit media at baseline significantly predicted the likelihood of having intercourse and oral sex by middle adolescence. This research suggests that exposure to sexually explicit material such as pornography is not inert for certain youth and can significantly impact later attitudes and sexual practices.

Associations with Sexual Aggression

Among the most important outcomes to consider relative to adolescent pornography use is the possible association with sexual aggression. Research in this area suggests that the relationship between pornography exposure and sexual aggression is strongest among youth with predisposing risk levels toward aggressive behavior. This line of research again highlights some continuity between offline psychological functioning and the effects of Internet use. It is also consistent with research on adult males where those at high risk for sexual aggression are particularly affected by frequent pornography consumption (Vega & Malamuth, 2007).

A nationally representative study of adolescents (n = 1,501) reported that frequent exposure to sexually explicit materials is not linked cross-sectionally to sexual aggression for the majority of males (Ybarra & Mitchell, 2005). The authors found, however, that males with "predisposing risk levels" toward aggressive behavior who frequently consume pornography have more than four times greater levels of sexual aggression compared with their peers who infrequently seek out pornography (p. 283). As reviewed previously, Brown & L'Engle (2009) used a prospective, longitudinal design to evaluate the effects of exposure to sexually explicit material, including online pornography, on measures of sexual aggression (e.g., perpetration of sexual harassment) and related variables (e.g., less progressive gender role attitudes, more permissive sexual norms) among males and females. Exposure to sexually explicit material in middle school predicted less progressive gender role attitudes, more permissive sexual norms, and sexual harassment perpetration at two-year follow-up among adolescent males (Brown & L'Engle, 2009).

A more recent longitudinal study evaluated linkages between exposure to sexually explicit material and sexually aggressive behavior among US youth (aged 10 through 15) (Ybarra, Mitchell, Hamburger, Diener-West, & Leaf, 2011). After adjusting for characteristics related to sexual aggression (i.e., substance use, being victims of sexual harassment/solicitation online or via text messaging), intentional exposure to violent, X-rated material during the 36-month follow-up period predicted an almost sixfold increase in the odds of self-reported sexually aggressive behavior. Associations were similar for male and female respondents. Of note, exposure to nonviolent, X-rated material was not related to self-reported sexually aggressive behavior, highlighting the unique effects of violent pornography on later sexual behavior.

A related, albeit small, body of research is based on the handful of studies that have evaluated the effects of pornography on youth who have sexually abused. Hunter and Figueredo (2010) evaluated the effects of four exogenous variables, including exposure to pornography, on non-sexual delinquency offenses and number of male victims in a sample of adolescent males with a history of sexually abusing children (n = 256). Using a cross-sectional design and structural equation modeling, exposure to pornography prior to age 13 contributed to "psychopathic and antagonistic attitudes" (p. 146). The authors postulated a relationship between such attitudes and non-sexual delinquency, a more common outcome for youth who sexually abused that are discharged from treatment programs (Caldwell, 2010; Waite et al., 2005).

Becker and Stein (1991) examined the use of sexually explicit materials among 160 male adolescents who had sexually abused. The majority (89%) of the sample reported using sexually explicit materials and that pornography increased their arousal. No significant relationships were found between pornography use and the number of victims and self-reported arousal. The majority (70%) reported that pornography played no role in the commission of their sexual offense; self-report in this context may or may not be a reliable measure of possible impact. Alexy, Burgess, and Prentky (2009) examined correlates of pornography use in a sample of youth with sexual behavior problems (mean age 13.10 for males, 12.54 for females), finding that youth who used pornography were significantly more likely than those who did not to engage in a prominent pattern of lying and manipulation, stealing, truancy, arson/fire-setting behaviors, coerced vaginal penetration and other forced sexual acts, sexually aggressive remarks, and sex with animals. Of note, surveyed youth had been removed from abusive families of origin and placed outside of the home, usually in foster homes, which may limit the generalizability of study findings. Although more research on pornography and youth who sexually abuse is needed, especially longitudinal studies, even in the absence of data this domain should be assessed when working with this population as well as delinquent and aggressive youth without problematic sexual behavior (Boonmann et al., 2014).

Summary of Pornography Exposure Research

Examined together, the research suggests that exposure to pornography is relatively common among US teens. Deliberate seeking of pornography is less frequent, is more common among males, and has been associated with antisocial behavior. Consistent with sexual socialization theory, viewing pornography can inform sexual attitudes and behaviors among certain youth. Content analysis of mainstream pornography suggests the need to counter the images of sex that are predominantly depicted with relational representations of sexuality. A recent systematic review of the research on young users (i.e., under the age of 18) of online and mobile technologies emphasized the importance of distinguishing between mere exposure to online sexual risk via pornography and the question of harm (Livingstone & Smith, 2014). Thus, research on individual differences and moderators of risk is particularly important in order to design appropriate responses. Regarding youth at greatest risk, teenagers who are already prone to sexual aggression are uniquely vulnerable to the negative effects of pornography, especially when the sexually explicit content is violent. As stated at the outset, the effect of the Internet on adolescent sexual behavior is highly related to offline vulnerability, and research in this area confirms this theme.

Mobile communications technologies allow youth to produce their own sexually explicit images, some of which may meet statutory definitions of child pornography. It is most common, however, for youth to produce sexual images as a means to express or invite sexual interest rather than to forward images or otherwise cause harm (for a review, see Klettke, Hallford, & Mellor, 2014). There remains relatively limited empirical research on the phenomenon of youth-produced sexual images ("sexting"), and despite the research that does exist, youth and adults have different opinions about the function, meaning, and perceived harms (Harris & Davidson, 2014). The next section reviews the available evidence base on youth-produced sexual images. This includes research that has begun to demarcate for whom adolescent youth-produced sexual images may be understood as developmentally appropriate sexual exploration as opposed to a higher-risk behavior.

RESEARCH ON YOUTH-PRODUCED SEXUAL IMAGES/"SEXTING"

Previous writing has described how alarmist media coverage beginning around 2008 about sexting shaped early discourse about this topic as well as social policy and legal interventions (Angelides, 2013; Draper, 2012; Hasinoff, 2015; Judge, 2012). The effect of this history is worth summarizing here given its continued influence on professional ideas about youth-produced sexual images. In late 2008, the National Campaign for the Prevention of Teen Pregnancy and cosmogirl.com released a study that reported a 25 percent prevalence rate of youth-produced sexual images among US teens (National Campaign for the Prevention of Pregnancy, 2008). The study was widely reported in the popular press and coincided with several high-profile cases involving seemingly disproportionate social and legal responses to individual teens. This included, for example, felony charges of child pornography possession, production, and dissemination as well as stories linking the unwanted distribution of sexted images to teen suicide (Hasinoff, 2015).

In addition, in October 2008, school officials in Pennsylvania confiscated a number of student cell phones and discovered images of nude and semi-nude adolescent females (*Miller, Day, Doe v. Mitchell,* 2010). The phones were handed over to the police, and the then district attorney began a criminal investigation. Although ultimately unsuccessful, with the teens' parents obtaining a temporary restraining order to block criminal charges (a motion granted and later affirmed on appeal), the possibility of criminal charges for sexting had entered the national conversation on youth-produced sexual images (Angelides, 2013). These early landmarks informed research, with most of the psychological scholarly literature on youth-produced sexual images assuming that there is something unusual or troubling about teens who engage in this behavior: "Though many people assume that teen sexting is always wrong and dangerous, the problematic effect of this assumption is that it becomes very difficult to see the distinctions between consensual sexting and the nonconsensual production or distribution of personal sexual images" (Hasinoff, 2015, p. 2).

At the forefront of popular and scholarly interest in youth-produced sexual images have been the potentially serious legal consequences for youth and the possible incongruity between these consequences and the behavior itself (Weins & Hallstead, 2009). It is illegal under federal and state child pornography laws to create, possess, or distribute explicit images of a minor. Child pornography laws were drafted to address the adult exploitation of minors but they do not exempt minors who create and distribute their own images via "sexting." Thus, youth who take and exchange sexual images of themselves or others via cell phone may be subject to the same laws designed to curb the distribution of child pornography among adults. The illogic of applying laws designed to curb adults' sexual exploitation of children to the consensual exchange of sexual images between teenagers spurred vigorous legal scholarship on possible reforms (Calvert, 2009; Ostrager, 2010; Weins & Hallstead, 2009). By the end of 2009, at least 20 states had introduced sexting legislation with many more considering legislation subsequently; a Victorian parliamentary hearing was also convened to address the issue in Australia (Angelides, 2013). Although beyond the scope of this chapter to review, many state legislatures have since considered laws that reduce the charges for minors creating or exchanging explicit images of minors by text from felonies to misdemeanors (for a review of reforms by state, see Sacco et al., 2010; for a critique of such statutes, see Hasinoff, 2015).

Fortunately, a modest empirical literature has evolved since the media originally coined the term *sexting*. Research has begun to clarify the average experience of youth-produced sexual images in order to inform the creation of more effective and tailored social responses. A recent review article critically evaluated the extant literature and identified 31 studies on the topic (Klettke et al., 2014). This review summarized main findings across a number of domains and is relied on in the following section: prevalence, motivations, and associations with sexual behavior and high-risk behaviors.

How Common Is Sexting?

The topic of prevalence remains controversial with respect to youth-produced sexual images. Some experts have asserted that "there are no consistent and reliable findings at this time to estimate the true prevalence of the problem" (Lounsbury, Mitchell, & Finkelhor, 2011, p. 4). Studies since the 2008 National Campaign study have been more methodologically sophisticated and have also tended to generate lower estimates. Estimates vary based on what behaviors count as sexting, and definitions vary widely in the literature—from the willing exchange of sexual images between romantic partners (Lenhart, 2009), to sexually explicit images that meet the legal definition of child pornography (Mitchell, Finkelhor, Jones, & Wolak, 2011), to coercion of females by males to induce sexual activity or to conform to stereotypical gender expectations (Ringrose, Gill, Livingstone, & Harvey, 2012). When sexted images include sexually explicit images that potentially violate child pornography laws, estimates may be lower (1%) than images that are sexually suggestive (9.6%) rather than sexually explicit (Mitchell, Finkelhor, Jones, & Wolak, 2012).

Varying definitions of sexting and different sampling techniques result in large differences in estimates across studies as well as large confidence intervals of means.[1] With these caveats in mind, Klettke et al. (2014) concluded that prevalence of sexting is substantially greater among adults than adolescents, with age positively predicting this behavior among adolescents as well. Studies therefore suggest that sexting is more common among older adolescents, young adults, and adults than children or young adolescents. Overall, studies suggest that more adolescents receive sexual images rather than send them. According to the review by Klettke and colleagues (2014), the estimated mean prevalence rate across studies that used random or representative samples was 11.96 percent, 95 percent CIs (range: 5.06% to 18.85%). The estimated mean prevalence across studies that used non-representative or non-random samples of adolescents yielded higher rates: 15.48 percent, 95 percent CI (range: 11.08% to 19.98%). Another review of available research concluded that one in five adolescents may be involved in self-producing sexual images (Livingstone & Smith, 2014).

---

1. In statistics, a confidence interval describes the amount of uncertainty associated with a sample estimate. It refers to a range of values such that there is a specified probability that the value of a parameter lies within it.

Motivations for Youth-Produced Sexual Images

One key dimension to assess in any given sexting encounter is the motivations of each involved party. Research suggests that the majority of youth cite romantic and/or sexual motivations for self-producing sexual images (Henderson & Morgan, 2011; e.g., "to be sexy or initiate sexual activity," Klettke et al., 2014). As discussed, however, females have reported pressure or coercion as a salient motivation for sexting (Englander, 2012; Sacco et al., 2010). Wolak and Finkelhor (2011) produced a typology of youth-produced sexual images based on a review of 550 known cases obtained from a national survey of law enforcement agencies. All cases involved sexually explicit images of minors that could qualify as child pornography under applicable criminal statutes (therefore the most rare sexted images and also those associated with the greatest legal sanctions). The typology differentiates between two contexts in which youth send and receive self-produced sexual images: experimental and aggravated. Experimental refers to images created or sent due to romantic interest, sexual attention seeking, or in the context of a relationship. Aggravated contexts include criminal or abusive elements beyond the creation, sending, or possession of sexual images. This includes a number of possibilities: adult involvement, or criminal or abusive behavior by minors such as sexual abuse, extortion, threats, and creation or sending of images without the knowledge or against the will of the minor pictured.

Another research group created a typology, or motivational continuum, of sexting behaviors based on a mixed-methods study that combined questionnaire and focus group data among youth, parents, and educators across three states. The authors presented a motivational continuum of youth-produced sexual images: situations of mutual trust (i.e., closed, trusting relationships), self-interest (i.e., attention seeking; bragging rights; subtle coercion; joking around), and intent to harm (i.e., adults involved; explicit peer-based aggression) (Harris & Davidson, 2014). The researchers acknowledge that the boundaries among these categories may be porous and the parties involved may have different perspectives on how best to define what has transpired. Both typologies (Harris & Davidson, 2014; Wolak & Finkelhor, 2011) distinguish between youth-produced sexual images that are developmentally typical (e.g., romantic in nature; sexual attention seeking) and forms that include potential harm, whether intended or not.

Typologies help ground professional understanding of behaviors such as sexting, but the complexities of real-life sexual encounters between teens, consensual or nonconsensual, inevitably muddy the waters. Distinctions among these categories could shift rapidly due to neurodevelopmental immaturity and vicissitudes of peer relationships (Judge, 2012). As exemplified in one highly publicized case, Philip Alpert had received sexually explicit pictures from his then girlfriend (experimental). When the relationship ended, Alpert emailed these same images to his ex-girlfriend's contact list (aggravated), which resulted in felony charges of child pornography distribution and registration as a sex offender, among other penalties (Richards & Calvert, 2009). Another widely publicized case illustrates the ways in which the meaning of text-based communications between teenagers, even without images, may have consequences when consent to sexual activity is contested.

In August 2015, 18-year-old Owen Labrie was found guilty of one count misdemeanor sexual assault, one count endangering a child (his 15-year-old victim), and of using a computer to lure a child (a felony). Labrie was sentenced to a year in jail, and five years probation; as a result of the count involving use of a computer, he is required to register as a sex offender for life. The defense argued that Labrie made plans via email to meet a 15-year-old freshman girl as part of a tradition known as the "Senior Salute," in which seniors attempted to have sexual intercourse with as many underclassmen as possible. Text messages between Labrie and his 15-year-old victim that followed the sexual assault were evidence at trial. As reported by the *Boston Globe*, Labrie texted the girl, "You're an angel." She responded, "You're quite an angel yourself. But would you mind keeping the sequence of events to yourself?" Defense attorneys argued that the victim's text messages to Labrie following her sexual assault suggested that no rape had in fact occurred (Manning & Toussaint, 2015). Thus, research-derived typologies provide an important foundation to professional understanding of the varying motivations for adolescent sexting. Since these typologies model sexual behavior, however, it is likely for these motivations to shift rapidly or be contested after the fact.

Associations with Sexual Activity

A consistent finding in the literature on youth-produced sexual images is the association between this behavior and a greater likelihood of sexual activity. As summarized by Klettke et al. (2014), 11 studies investigated the relationship between sexting and sexual and sexual risk behaviors, eight of which measured sexual activity. All eight studies found that youth who had reported previous "sexting" were significantly more likely to be sexually active than non-sexters (AP-MTV, 2009; Dake et al., 2012; Dir, Cyders, et al., 2013; Giroux, 2011; Gordon-Messer et al., 2012; Rice et al., 2012; Temple, 2012). Some researchers have reported associations between prior sexting behavior and a higher number of reported sexual partners (Benotsch et al., 2013; Dake et al., 2012; Dir, Cyders, et al., 2013). Other studies report this positive association for girls but not boys (Temple et al., 2012); some report a higher number of romantic partners but not casual sex encounters (Henderson & Morgan, 2011); and some found no significant association (Gordon-Messner et al., 2012). Studies that report an association between youth-produced sexual images and sexual behavior is unsurprising when conceptualized itself as a form of sexual behavior and form of adolescent sexual development (Temple & Choi, 2014) rather than activity artificially divorced from "real life," which is not how youth perceive their online activity (Boyd, 2014).

It is important to emphasize that the majority of research on youth-produced sexual images is cross-sectional; therefore, no causal relationship between sexting and sexual behavior may be inferred. One exception is a longitudinal study on the temporal sequence of sexting and sexual intercourse, as well as the role of "active sexting" (i.e., sending a nude picture) in mediating the relationship between "passive sexting" (i.e., asking or being asked for a nude picture) on sexual behavior (Temple & Choi, 2014). The authors followed an ethnically diverse sample of high school students in southeast Texas (n = 964) for six years. Using path analysis, sexting predicted sexual behavior at one-year follow-up and also mediated the relationship between sexting and sexual behavior. More specifically, active sexting at Wave 2 mediated the relationship between asking or being asked for a sext and having sex over the next year. The authors assert that results support sexting as a viable indicator of adolescent sexual activity.

Associations with High-Risk Behavior

Given the association between youth-produced sexual images and other sexual behaviors, a natural follow-up question is sexting's relationship with high-risk sexual behaviors. As reviewed more extensively in chapter 1, adolescents' neurodevelopmental immaturity results in emotion-driven decision making. Sexting may therefore be understood for some teens as an expression of impulsivity, which may be situational and/or part of a broader repertoire of risky sexual behaviors. However, research on this topic is equivocal. For example, some studies have reported associations between previous sexting and a higher likelihood of having unprotected sex (Benotsch et al., 2013; Dake et al., 2012; Ferguson, 2011). Others have reported non-significant findings in the same direction (Rice et al., 2012), or no significant association at all (Gordon-Messner, 2012). Ybarra and Mitchell (2014) reported a greater number of past-year sex partners among teens who sext.

Other studies have considered the association between youth-produced sexual images and other risky behavior such as substance use. One study reported greater odds of substance use among youth who had sexted (Ybarra & Mitchell, 2014), and another found significant associations between previous sexting and higher reported use of alcohol and other drugs in general (Benotsch et al., 2013; Dake et al., 2012; Di, Cyders, et al., 2013). Previous sexting has also been associated with a greater likelihood of consuming alcohol and/or drugs prior to sex when compared with youth who had not sexted (Benotsch et al., 2013; Temple et al., 2012).

There have also been mixed results regarding the relationships among sexting, mental health, and other wellbeing variables. One study found no significant correlations between self-esteem and sexting (Hudson, 2011); another found no significant differences in self-reported levels of depression, anxiety, or self-esteem among teens who had received sexts, had received and sent sexts, and had neither received nor sent sexts in their lifetime (Gordon-Messer et al., 2012). The role of pressure from others to send sexts may mediate these associations. For example, Englander (2012) reported that individuals who had sexted (either under pressure from others or not) were significantly less likely to report depression during high school when compared with those who had never sexted. Of note, individuals who had sexted under pressure from others were more likely to report problems during high school with anxiety and prior dating violence than non-sexters and those who sexted without pressure (Englander, 2012).

A presumed association between youth-produced sexual images and suicidality/completed suicide was popularized in 2009 by the tragic story of Ohio teen Jessica Logan. Following a breakup, Logan's former boyfriend forwarded a nude picture she had sexted only to him to others at her school, which was in turn circulated to a number of nearby schools. Logan was subsequently harassed and bullied; she reportedly informed the school but eventually committed suicide by hanging. Logan's parents alleged that the school conducted no formal investigation (*Logan and Logan v. Sycamore,* 2009) and the case was widely covered with the language of "sexting suicide" framing popular coverage. More recent research has emphasized the complex and more nuanced association between cyberharassment/bullying and suicidality, including the role of multiple, interacting factors as opposed to one primary cause (Saleh, Feldman, Grudzinkas, Ravven, & Cody, 2014). In the case of youth-produced sexual images, Dake et al. (2012) found that youth who had previously sexted were significantly more likely to have contemplated or attempted suicide, and to have reported feeling sad or hopeless for at least two continuous weeks in the last year. Thus, although not well studied, there is evidence for an association between depressive symptoms and sexting behavior among certain youth, although other studies have failed to report associations with mental health outcomes.

Another high-risk outcome associated with youth-produced sexual images is third-party distribution of private sexual images without the original sender's consent, a scenario associated with great distress for the photographed individual (Lenhart, 2009; Mitchell et al., 2012; Wolak & Finkelhor, 2011). Fortunately, research suggests that the unwanted distribution of sexual images is relatively rare. A national study of Internet users aged 10 through 17 reported that only a small proportion of youth had forwarded youth-produced sexual images. Images were distributed in 10 percent of incidents when a youth appeared in or created the image and 3 percent when the youth received it (Mitchell et al., 2012). Since forwarded images are arguably among the most concerning class of youth-produced sexual images, available data should provide some reassurance that this is relatively uncommon. More concern is therefore warranted when such situations occur given its statistical rarity.

Gender Differences

Gender difference in the youth-produced sexual images literature bears elaboration, as it remains a source of some controversy. Several studies found no gender differences in rates of sending or receiving youth-produced sexual images (Dake et al., 2012; Kopecky, 2011; Temple, 2012), with some evidence that females are more likely to send images than males, and males correspondingly more likely to receive images (Klettke et al., 2014). Regarding the experience of sexting, however, studies have reported important gender differences. Specifically, females have reported perceived pressure to send sexually explicit images (Englander, 2012; Henderson & Morhan, 2011; Sacco et al., 2010). Girls were significantly more likely to report being "bothered a great deal" by being asked to send sexts than boys (Temple et al., 2012).

Qualitative studies comport with these findings and suggest important gender differences in the meaning of sexting. One qualitative study of males and females aged 12 through 18 found no gender difference in rates of sending sexts; females reportedly felt judged harshly whether they sent sexts or not (e.g., judged as a "slut" or "prude," respectively), with males not endorsing this same experience (Lippman & Campbell, 2014). Another qualitative investigation in the UK triangulated data from youth interviews and focus groups with teens' texting records in a sample of male and female adolescents (aged 12 through 15). This research suggests that being asked for "nudes" is a new form of female desirability, but this is a practice embedded in gender-related contradictions (Ringrose, Harvey, Gill, & Livingstone, 2013). Males in this study curried respect from peers through collected and rated images of females while females were blamed for being photographed in the first place. Female respondents describe the practice as risky and potentially shaming of sexual reputation ("slut shaming"). Additional qualitative research based in the United States suggested similar gender differences. As one female respondent noted, "If you're a guy . . . you do this . . . and you was the man. You getting backed up and all this good stuff." Another female teen observed girls being called "slut" for the same behavior (Harris & Davidson, 2014, p. 276).

Past research has shown that adolescent females' sexual behavior of any kind—not just that involving technology—is judged more harshly than males' (Maccoby, 1998; Milhausen & Herold, 1999). Seen in this way, activities like sexting may extend and reproduce historical gender inequities and sexual double standards (Hasinoff, 2015; Ringrose et al., 2013). Accordingly, existing sexual education curricula should be modified to address these problematic aspects of sexting.

Of note, available research on gender differences in youth-produced sexual images has emphasized heterosexual relationships and therefore may obscure the experience of homosexual, bisexual, and transgender teens (Draper, 2012; Ringrose et al., 2013). Ybarra and Mitchell (2015) found a higher frequency of sharing sexual pictures both online and in person among lesbian, gay, and bisexual (LGB) males and females, including queer, questioning, and unsure youth. The authors speculated, consistent with previous research, that higher rates of sexual exploration via sharing photos may reflect LGBT youth efforts to solidify their psychosexual development in a heteronormative culture (Hillier, Mitchell, & Ybarra, 2012; Ybarra & Mitchell, 2015). Additional research that expands on these preliminary findings is needed to best address the role of youth-produced sexual images for sexual minority youth, especially transgendered teens for whom no data are available. Such research is particularly important given the continuing problem of gay, lesbian, and trans people experiencing disproportionate legal responses in the criminal justice system (Hasinoff, 2015; Himmelstein & Brückner, 2011). For example, one study of people's attitudes about requiring minors who sext to register as sex offenders found that respondents were significantly more likely to recommend this punishment for gay and lesbian youth than heterosexuals (Comartin, Kernsmith, & Kernsmith, 2013).

Criminalization of Sexting

Following early high-profile cases and the legacy of *Miller, Day, Doe v. Skumanick,* there is relative consensus that use of the criminal justice system, and child pornography laws in particular, is neither a tenable nor an effective primary intervention for the majority of adolescents who self-produce sexual images (Hasinoff, 2015; Zhang, 2010). There will remain cases where aggravated forms of sexting (e.g., third-party distribution of private images, extortion, etc.) reach the attention of law enforcement and prosecutors. Research has begun to identify factors associated with these cases.

The Third National Juvenile Online Victimization Study (NJOV-3) collected information from a national sample of law enforcement agencies to assess the prevalence of arrests for and characteristics of technology-facilitated sexual exploitation crimes. Wolak, Finkelhor, and Mitchell (2012) described 3,477 cases of sexting handled by law enforcement in 2006–2009 as part of the NJOV-3. Two-thirds of sexting cases handled by law enforcement involved aggravating circumstances that went beyond creation and dissemination of sexually explicit images. This included an adult's involvement (46%) or a minor engaged in nonconsensual or malicious behavior (13%).

There is limited research on which sexting cases result in charges against juveniles. A convenience sample of state prosecutors who handled cases involving juveniles and sexting identified variables associated with prosecutors bringing charges against juveniles (Walsh, Wolak, & Finkelhor, 2013). Over one-third (36%) of surveyed prosecutors had filed charges in these cases; 16 percent had cases where the youth defendant had to register on the sex offender registry. Four main themes described when prosecutors filed charges against a minor involved in sexting: malicious intent, bullying, coercion, or harassment (36%); distribution, including of one's own image or forwarding of someone else's (25%); the existence of a large age difference between the parties (22%); and graphic nature of the images (9%) (Walsh et al., 2013). Thus, the presence of aggravating factors is typically required for arrests and prosecutions. Such incidents represent a minority of sexting activity overall but may be particularly germane data for assessment with youth who sexually abuse.

Conclusions About Research on Youth-Produced Sexual Images
Examined overall, the literature on this topic is in its infancy. Possible gender differences, with females reporting pressure to send sexual images and double binds vis-à-vis traditional gender roles ("damned if I do, damned if I don't"), require additional study (Lippman & Campbell, 2014). Indeed, findings related to the socialization of gender inequalities and sexual double standards through the practice of youth-produced sexual images may be the most common and pernicious aspect of the behavior.

Associations between youth-produced sexual images and sexual activity suggest that sexting be understood as a form of sexual behavior in itself and not an activity dissociated from other forms of sexual experience decision making (Temple & Choi, 2014). Such findings comport with Boyd's (2014) ethnographic research in which youth experience continuity between on- and offline worlds. The predictive effect of active sexting on the later initiation of sex among teens is intriguing and bears replication (Temple & Choi, 2014). Equivocal findings about associations between sexting and mental health variables require additional research to identify for which sub-populations of youth sexting may be maladaptive as opposed to reflecting developmental curiosity.

Given the low rates of unwanted third-party distribution of sexts and the fact that sexual exploration is the most common motivation for sexting cited by teens, there is merit to recent scholarship that argues for bolder distinctions between consensual sexting and the nonconsensual production or distribution of personal sexual images

(Hasinoff, 2015). A normative perspective on adolescent sexuality helps emphasize that not all youth-produced sexual images are equivalent in form or function; the term *sexting* is overly broad and encompasses a range of behaviors, meanings, and reasons for concern. Evaluation of individual circumstances is therefore critical, including the possibility for sexting to represent private sexual communication between consenting adolescents (Hasinoff, 2015). The research on sexting is evolving but in the meantime this topic, like pornography exposure, has created many practice dilemmas for professionals who work closely with children and adolescents. These challenges and suggested best practices are discussed next.

IMPLICATIONS FOR EMPIRICALLY INFORMED PRACTICES

Research on the topics of pornography use among adolescents as well as youth-produced sexual images is in its infancy, especially in the latter case. It is therefore premature to recommend "best practices" at this juncture. That said, some practice recommendations based on the foregoing review and broader developmental literature may be considered empirically informed and thus judiciously applied to settings where youth present.

Clinical Challenges

As emphasized in this chapter, the majority of youth use mobile communications technology and social media in the service of typical development (i.e., social, psychosexual) (Finkelhor, 2014; Livingstone & Smith, 2014; Smahel & Subrahmanyam, 2014). Mental health professionals are most likely to see youth whose interactions online may be more problematic. There are limited data linking psychiatric diagnoses to particular forms of technology misuse; routine assessment of Internet use across diagnostic presentations is therefore recommended (Scott, 2011). It is important for clinicians to assess whether the technology concern is a primary consideration or simply a vehicle for the expression of underlying emotional difficulties (Mitchell et al., 2007). This requires knowledge of the normative context of youth-produced sexual images and pornography use, with caveats about this literature in mind, and some methodology to assess risk. The lack of longitudinal data about for whom sexting or pornography use is a harbinger of risk is a major limitation to the assessment process.

There has been limited writing to date on the assessment of problematic sexual behavior involving technology (Boonmann et al., 2014). Research shows that juvenile sex crimes with an Internet nexus are much less frequent than those where individuals meet online (Wolak et al., 2008). Online harassment has increased over time and is frequently perpetrated by youth, however, and this includes sexual harassment (Jones et al., 2013). A key goal of assessing technology-mediated sexual behavior is distinguishing between the impulsive use of social media and an emerging or established pattern of impulse dyscontrol, boundary violations, or other psychopathology. Impulsive misuse may still be associated with harm, of course, but recommended strategies for management will differ based on these scenarios.

Pornography exposure and use should be assessed among youth who sexually abuse to help clinicians determine whether a child has imitated a behavior observed in pornography as well as to help identify youth who are at risk of developing aggressive behavioral responses to such exposure (Alexy et al., 2009). Research suggests that pornography may most negatively affect older adolescent boys and young men who are already at risk for aggressive behavior. Factors associated with risk include impulsivity, hostility to women, and promiscuity. In this group, frequent pornography use is associated with a much higher rate of sexual aggression than among youth of the same risk level who use pornography somewhat, seldom, or never (Malamuth, Addison, & Koss, 2000). Thus, a history of prior sexual aggression and/or the presence of other empirically derived risk factors should increase evaluator concern when technology misuse is also present. The limits of our empirical knowledge about these topics cannot be overstated, however, especially when opining about risk in a forensic context (Scott, 2011). This, coupled with limited data about the longitudinal significance of technology misuse, and also the heterogeneity among adolescents overall, indicates caution when assessing risk.

It bears repeating that an abiding theme of the literature on Internet risk is the role of offline psychosocial and psychiatric vulnerability and adversity on the likelihood of online difficulties (Finkelhor, 2014; Livingstone & Smith, 2014). Accordingly, evaluators should not allow the role of mobile communications technology to distract from careful assessment of the offline context, areas for which more established, standardized methodologies exist.

Parent Guidance and Parental Monitoring

The research reviewed here places sexting squarely in the context of adolescent sexual behavior, and as such it is a topic that parents should include in conversations about sexuality development, sex, and sexual decision making. Research has demonstrated that the *manner* in which parents communicate with their adolescents about topics such as sex matters more than the mere fact of communication. Nonjudgmental, open, and receptive communication among parents is most likely to result in the reduction of sexual risk among adolescents (Akers, Holland, & Bost, 2011; Fasula & Miller, 2006). It may be, then, that youth with parents who engage in this kind of communication about sexuality and sexual development more broadly may be better equipped to manage the challenges of decision making about sexting. Children raised in families where sex is taboo are more susceptible to sexually explicit media influence than those raised in homes where sex is a permissible topic (Gunter, 2002; Malamuth & Billings, 1986). When sexuality education is explored as part of treatment for youth who sexually abuse, use of the Internet should be included, both the positive and potentially negative aspects.

Clinicians should therefore coach parents to adopt a non-evaluative, open stance when speaking with their teenagers about sex. When parents' own anxiety about the topic interferes, clinicians should help parents bracket this in the service of their child's need to develop the skills necessary to make healthy decisions. Clinicians should inform parents that conversations about sexuality development are protective, and that avoidance or undue alarm fails to promote teens' ability to make self-protective choices about sexual behavior.

The role of parental monitoring is an important aspect of adolescents' safe technology use. As described in the child development literature, parental monitoring refers to monitoring in the traditional, offline sense: a set of parenting practices through which parents are aware of their teens' whereabouts, peers, and activities (Borawski, Levers-Landis, Lovegreen, & Trapl, 2003; Stattin & Kerr, 2000). There is some debate in the literature as to whether this construct may reflect children's willingness to disclose information to parents, rather than a parental behavior per se (Stattin & Kerr, 2000). These controversies aside, research has shown that parental monitoring and similar constructs (e.g., parent–child cohesion; parent involvement) are associated with lower rates of teen exposure to sexual and violent online content and online interactions with strangers (Cho & Cheon, 2005). Thus, parental monitoring in the traditional sense may impact teens' behavior in online settings.

Adolescents' perception of the extent to which parents monitor them in general predicted lower rates of involvement in a range of online activities (e.g., instant message/chat, online social networking, video streaming, online gaming). Conversely, the more adolescents perceived that their parents tracked their Internet use specifically, the more they engaged in the surveyed online activities (Vaala & Bleakley, 2015). Thus, improving parental practices overall (e.g., parental monitoring, authoritative parenting, etc.) and not just monitoring technology use may have equal impacts and also promote adolescents' autonomous decision making.

Improved parental monitoring (e.g., knowledge of adolescents' peer groups), as well as effective discipline, are key targets of multisystemic therapy, an intervention with efficacy and effectiveness for youth with problematic sexual behavior (Borduin, Henggeler, Blaske,

& Stein, 1990; Borduin, Schaeffer, & Heiblum, 2009; Henggeler et al., 2009, Letourneau et al., 2009). Thus, parental monitoring is already a known treatment target for families of youth who sexually abuse. Although research has not evaluated the effects of parental monitoring on Internet safety for this population, the possibility of improved monitoring having an indirect effect comports with evidence-based interventions.

For typically developing teens, the direct monitoring of technology use is diffi-cult, if not impossible, and as a stand-alone intervention does not foster the capacities that youth need to self-regulate and behave safely. Restricting access may be neces-sary, however, for certain clinical populations where youth have engaged in frankly unsafe behavior. There are few guidelines available to inform such sanctions, but attention should be given to benchmarks youth may demonstrate to show improved self-control.

Parental modeling of Internet use also affects teens' own behavior. Fifty-eight per-cent of surveyed US adolescents named parents as most influential on their use of the Internet (Lenhart et al., 2011). Recent cross-sectional research has shown that teens emulate the Internet behaviors in which their parents engage (Vaala & Bleakley, 2015). Thus, even when adolescents minimize their parents' influence, data suggest that in the realm of technology use, parental modeling has a significant impact. Advising par-ents about the influence of their own Internet use on their teens' behavior is there-fore another area that parent guidance should address. When working with parents of youth who sexually abuse, some discussion of parents' Internet use as it pertains to sex-ual behavior (e.g., pornography use, cybersex, online prostitution) should be addressed given the potent role of modeling problematic family norms about sexuality.

Future Directions for Administrators, Research, and Policy

It is important that educational messages about youth-produced sexual images have credibility with youth (Harris & Davidson, 2014). Although scare tactics are com-monly used (e.g., most images are ultimately distributed; child pornography charges are a likely outcome), this is likely an ineffective approach. Several lines of evidence support this recommendation. First, meta-analytic evaluations of "scared straight" approaches to the prevention of health risk behaviors among teens indicate their lim-ited efficacy and, for some youth, iatrogenic effects (Petrosino, Turpin-Petrosino, & Buehler, 2003). Second, research suggests that teens know it is unacceptable for some-one to forward an intimate sexual image that was intended to be private to a third party (Allbury & Crawford, 2012; Hasinoff & Shepherd, 2014), highlighting the limits of simply providing this information. Third, most teenage sexts are shared consensu-ally among peers and not distributed without permission (Mitchell et al., 2012).

Early Internet educational programming used an information-deficit approach where the provision of corrective information was emphasized (e.g., sexting is illegal). In this author's experience, providing information alone is rarely effective, and in the case of the Internet and social media, it lacks credibility for teens who themselves are likely to know more about the local meanings of mobile communications than the presenter. Research supports this position. A review of 31 meta-analyses of youth prevention education found that the most effective programs help youth develop cognitive and behavioral skills related to the problem of interest. Active strategies such as role playing, rehearsal, and problem solving over several sessions are also key components, as is the use of research-based knowledge about sexting and pornography (Jones, Mitchell, & Walsh, 2014a; 2014b).

It is not clear that Internet education programming has by and large identified the problems that underpin problematic Internet use, and therefore many still rely on ineffective techniques similar to anti-drug messaging of the 1990s. Given that problems with pornography use or youth-produced sexual images are complex behaviors with multi-factorial causes, it is likely that providing information alone will not be sufficient. Topics related to sexting depend on the particular youth audience (e.g., non-clinical groups versus youth who have sexually abused) but should target the developmental capacities associated with technology use. Programs that discourage privacy violations are particularly relevant to sexting, as are skills related to emotion identification and regulation, boundaries, sexual decision making broadly defined, and affirmative consent (Finkelhor, 2014; Hasinoff, 2015; see Hasinoff, 2015, and Jones et al., 2014a, for empirically supported messages about sexting to use in educational programs).

SUMMARY

Online contexts and mobile communications technologies are another setting for and influence on adolescent sexuality development (Subrahmanyam et al., 2006; Smahel & Subrahmanyam, 2014). As such, they are contexts with the potential for growth-enhancing experiences as well as risk. As captured in the broader literature on risk and resiliency, risk has the potential for positive and negative outcomes relative to one's behavior: "Resilience can only develop through exposure to risk or to stress" (Coleman & Hagell, 2007, p. 15). Sexual identity is discovered through exploration, and the challenge is that adolescents are participating in the process of acquiring sexual experience *and* skills for assessing risk at the same time (Ponton & Judice, 2004). Like adolescent sexual behavior itself, technology use may be associated with growth promotion and resilience as well as negative outcomes.

Accordingly, stakeholders who work with youth must maintain a developmental perspective on Internet use and a sense of humility regarding the limits of our empirical knowledge about the effects of this context on longitudinal outcomes. This moderate stance is challenging to maintain when novel technologies are unfamiliar and rapidly changing. It is even more difficult when safety concerns are present, as is the case with treatment for youth who sexually abuse. These dilemmas speak to the great need for additional research on the role of technology for this population of youth to guide professional decision making.

In a seminal work on youth and digital technology, Palfrey and Gasser (2008) observed years ago: "Too often, the Internet is a metaphor for all that is hard to understand about youth culture" (p. 220). This remains no less true today, with related assumptions strongly informing early psychological and legal scholarship on the topics reviewed here (Calvert, 2009; Finkelhor, 2014). Left unchallenged, however, this metaphor and the discourse it produces provide a poor foundation for evidence-informed interventions and social policy. The criminalization of adolescent sexting has highlighted the ways in which historical notions about adolescent sexuality and novel technologies as inherently dangerous have produced imprecise social responses (Hasinoff, 2015). Moreover, in practice the criminalization of youth sexual behavior typically has a disproportionate effect on already marginalized youth (e.g., sexual minorities, those of low socioeconomic status) (Comartin et al., 2013; Odem, 1995), which has implications for the population of youth with problematic sexual behavior. Moving forward, a normative perspective on adolescent sexuality development and Internet use may help temper these historical biases, limit reactionary discourse, and clarify true vulnerability and risk (Livingstone & Smith, 2014; McClelland & Tolman, 2011). In turn, such work may provide an alternative foundation for more developmentally sensitive interventions and policy.

REFERENCES

Akers, A. Y., Holland C. L., & Bost, J. (2011). Interventions to improve parental communication about sex: A systematic review. *Pediatrics, 127,* 494–510.

Albury, K., & Crawford, K. (2012). Sexting, consent and young people's ethic: Beyond Megan's story. *Continuum, 26,* 3, 463–473.

Alexy, E. M., Burgess, A. W., & Prentky, R. A. (2009). Pornography use as a risk marker for an aggressive pattern of behavior among sexually reactive children and adolescents. *Journal of the American Psychiatric Nurses Association, 14*(6), 442–453.

Angelides, S. (2013). "Technology, hormones and stupidity": The affective politics of teenage sexting. *Sexualities, 16*(5-6), 665–689.

Becker, J. V., & Stein, R. M. (1991). Is sexual erotica associated with sexual deviance in adolescent males? *International Journal of Law and Psychiatry, 14,* 85–95.

Benotsch, E. G., Snipes, D. J., Martin, A.M., & Bull, S. S. (2013). Sexting, substance use, and sexual risk behaviour in young adults. *Journal of Adolescent Health, 52,* 307–313.

Boonmann, C., Grudzinskas, A., & Aebi, M. (2014). Juveniles, the Internet and sexual offending. In F. Saleh, A. Grudzinskas, & A. Judge (Eds.) *Adolescent sexual behavior in the digital age: Considerations for clinicians, legal professionals and educators* (pp. 161–180). New York: Oxford University Press.

Borawski, E. A, Levers-Landis, C. E., Lovegreen, L. D., & Trapl, E. S. (2003). Parental monitoring, negotiated unsupervised time, and parental trust: The role of perceived parenting practices in adolescent health risk behaviors. *Journal of Adolescent Health, 33,* 60–70.

Borduin, C. M., Henggeler, S. W., Blaske, D. M., & Stein, R. (1990). Multisystemic treatment of adolescent sexual offenders. *International Journal of Offender Therapy and Comparative Criminology, 35,* 105–114.

Borduin, C. M., Schaeffer, C. M., & Heiblum, N. (2009). A randomized clinical trial of multisystemic therapy with juvenile sexual offenders: Effects on youth social ecology and criminal activity. *Journal of Consulting and Clinical Psychology, 77,* 26–37.

Boyd, D. (2014). *It's complicated: The social lives of networked teens.* New Haven, CT: Yale University Press.

Breakwell, G. M. (2009). *The psychology of risk.* Cambridge, UK: Cambridge University Press.

Bridges, A. J., Wosnitzer, R., Scharrer, E., Sun, C., & Liberman, R. (2010). Aggression and sexual behavior in best-selling pornography videos. *Violence Against Women, 16,* 1065–1085.

Brofenbrenner, U. (1979). *The ecology of human development: Experiments by nature and design.* Cambridge, MA: Harvard University Press.

Brown, D., & Bryant, J. (1989). The manifest content of pornography. In D. Zillmann & J. Bryant (Eds.), *Pornography: Research advances and policy considerations* (pp. 3–24). Hillsdale, NJ: Lawrence Erlbaum.

Brown, J. D., & D'Engle, K. L. (2009). X-rated: Sexual attitudes and behaviors associated with US early adolescents' exposure to sexually explicit media. *Communication Research, 36,* 129–151.

Caldwell, M. F. (2010). Study characteristics and recidivism base rates in juvenile sex offender recidivism. *International Journal of Offender Therapy and Comparative Criminology, 54,* 197–212.

Calvert C. (2009). Sex, cell phones, privacy and the First Amendment: When children become child pornographers and the Lolita Effect undermines the law. *CommLaw Conspectus: Journal of Communications Law and Technology Policy, 18*(1), 1–71.

Carroll, J. S., Padilla-Walker, L. M., Nelson, L. J., Olson, C. D., McNamara Barry, C., Madsen, S. D. (2008). Generation XXX: Pornography Acceptance and Use Among Emerging Adults. *Journal of Adolescent Research, 23*(1), 6–30.

Cho, C. H., & Cheon, H. J. (2005). Children's exposure to negative Internet content: Effects of family context. *Journal of Broadcasting & Electronic Media, 49,* 488–509.

Coleman, J., & Hagell, A. (Eds). (2007). *Adolescence, risk and resilience: Against the odds.* New York: Wiley Press.

Comartin, E., Kernsmith, R., & Kernsmith, P. (2013). "Sexting" and sex offender registration: Do age, gender and sexual orientation matter? *Deviant Behavior, 34*(1), 38–52.

Cooper, A. (1998). Sexuality and the Internet: Surfing into the new millennium. *Cyberpsychology & Behavior, 1,* 181–187.

Cooper, A., Boies, S., Maheu, M., & Greenfield, D. (1999). Sexuality and the Internet: The next sexual revolution. In F. Muscarella & L. Szuchman (Eds.), *The psychological science of sexuality: A research based approach* (pp. 519–545). New York: Wiley.

Cowan, G., Lee, C., Levy, D. & Snyder, D. (1988). Dominance and inequality in X-rated videocassettes. *Psychology of Women Quarterly, 12*(3), 299311.

Crockett, L. J., Raffaelli, M., & Moilanen, K. (2003). Adolescent sexuality: Behavior and meaning. In G. R. Adams & M. D. Berzonsky (Eds.), *Blackwell Handbook of Adolescence* (pp. 371–392). Oxford: Blackwell Publishing.

Dake, J. A., Price, D. H., Mazriaz, L., &Ward, B. (2012). Prevalence and correlates of sexting behaviour in adolescents. *American Journal of Sexuality Education, 7*, 1–15.

DiCataldo, F. (2009). *The perversion of youth: Controversies in the assessment and treatment of juvenile sex offenders.* New York: New York University Press.

Dir, A. L., Cyders, M. A., & Coskunpinar, A. (2013). From the bar to the bed via mobile phone: A first test of the role of problematic alcohol use, sexting, and impulsivity related traits in sexual hookups. *Computers in Human Behavior, 29*, 1664–1670.

Draper, N. (2012). Is your teen at risk? Discourses of adolescent sexting in United States television news. *Journal of Children and Media, 6*, 221–236.

Drouin, M., Vogel, K. N., Surbey, A., & Stills, J. R. (2013). Let's talk about sexting, baby: Computer-mediated sexual behaviors among young adults. *Computers in Human Behavior, 29*(5), 25–30.

Englander, E. (2012). *Low risk associated with most teenage sexting: A study of 617 18-year-olds.* Retrieved on February 1, 2016, from. http://webhost.bridgew.edu/marc/SEXTING%20AND%20 COERCION%20report.pdf

Fasula, A. M., & Miller, K. S. (2006). African American and Hispanic adolescents' intentions to delay first intercourse: Parental communication as a buffer for sexually active peers. *Journal of Adolescent Health, 38*, 193–200.

Ferguson, C. J. (2011). Sexting behaviours among young Hispanic women: Incidence and association with other high-risk sexual behaviours. *Psychiatric Quarterly, 82*, 239–243.

Finkelhor, D. (2011). *The Internet, youth safety and the problem of "juvenoia."* University of New Hampshire, Crimes Against Children Research Center.

Finkelhor, D. (2014). Commentary: Cause for alarm? Youth and Internet risk research—a commentary on Livingstone and Smith. *Journal of Child Psychology and Psychiatry, 55*(6), 655–658.

Flood, M. (2007). Exposure to pornography among youth in Australia. *Journal of Sociology, 43*, 45–60.

Giedd, J. N. (2008). The teen brain: Insights from neuroimaging. *Journal of Adolescent Health, 42*(4), 335–343.

Giedd, J. N. (2012). The digital revolution and adolescent brain evolution. *Journal of Adolescent Health, 51*, 101–105.

Giroux, A. M. (2011). Sexting: Connections to sexual and social development. Masters Thesis. The University of Arizona. Unpublished manuscript.

Gordon-Messer, D., Bauermeister, J. A., Grodzinski, A., & Zimmerman, M. (2012). Sexting among young adults. *Journal of Adolescent Health, 52*, 301–306.

Gorman, S., Monk-Turner, E., & Fish, J. N. (2010). Free adult Internet web sites. *Gender Issues, 27*, 131–145.

Grudzen, C. R., Elliott, M. N., Kerndt, P. R., Schuster, M. A., Brook, R. H., & Gelberg, L. (2009). Condom use and high-risk sexual acts in adult films. *American Journal of Public Health, 99*, 1732–1733.

Gunter, B. (2002). *Media sex: What are the issues?* Mahwah, NJ: Erlbaum.

Haggstrom-Nordin, E., Sandberg, J., Hanson, U., & Tyde, T. (2006). "It's everywhere!" Young Swedish people's thoughts and reflections about pornography. *Scandanavian Journal of Caring Science, 20*, 386–393.

Hald, G. M., & Malamuth, N. M. (2008). Self-perceived effects of pornography consumption. *Archives of Sexual Behavior, 37,* 614–625.

Harris, A., & Davidson, J. (2014). Teens, sex and technology: Implications for educational systems and practice. In F. Saleh, A. Grudzinskas, & A. Judge (Eds.) *Adolescent sexual behavior in the digital age: Considerations for clinicians, legal professionals and educators* (pp. 262–292). New York: Oxford University Press.

Hasinoff, A. A. (2015). *Sexting panic: Rethinking criminalization, privacy and consent.* Chicago: University of Illinois Press.

Hasinoff, A. A., & Shepherd, T. (2014). Sexting in context: Privacy norms and expectations. *International Journal of Communication, 8,* 2932–2955.

Henderson, L., & Morgan, E. (2011). Sexting and sexual relationships among teens and young adults. *McNair Scholars Research Journal, 7*(1), 31–39.

Henggeler, S., Letourneau, E. J., Chapman, J. E., Borduin, C., Schewe, P. A., McCart, M. (2009). Mediators of change for multisystemic therapy for juvenile sex offenders. *Journal of Consulting and Clinical Psychology, 77*(3), 451–462.

Hillier, L., Mitchell, K. J., & Ybarra, M. L. (2012). The Internet as a safety net: Findings from a series of online focus groups with LBG and non-LBG young people in the US. *Journal of LGBT Youth, 9,* 225–246.

Himmelstein, K. E. W., & Brückner, H. (2011). Criminal-justice and school sanctions against non-heterosexual youth: A national longitudinal study. *Pediatrics, 127,* 49–57.

Hudson, H. K. (2011). Factors affecting sexting behaviours among selected undergraduate students. Unpublished doctoral thesis, Southern University Illinois Carbondale, Illinois. Unpublished doctoral thesis.

Hunter, J. A., & Figueredo, A. J. (2010). Developmental pathways into social and sexual deviance. *Journal of Family Violence, 25,* 141–148.

Johnson, G. M. (2010). Internet use and child development: Validation of the ecological techno-subsystem. *Educational Technology & Society, 13*(1), 176–185.

Johnson, G. M., & Puplampu, P. (2008). A conceptual framework for understanding the effect of the Internet on child development: The ecological techno-subsystem. *Canadian Journal of Learning and Technology, 34,* 19–28.

Jones, L. M., Mitchell, K. J., & Finkelhor, D. (2012). Trends in youth Internet victimization: Findings from three youth Internet safety surveys 2000-2010. *Journal of Adolescent Health, 50,* 179–186.

Jones, L. M., Mitchell, K. J., & Walsh, W. A. (2014a). *A systematic review of effective youth prevention education: Implications for Internet safety education.* Durham, NH: Crimes Against Children Research Center, University of New Hampshire.

Jones, L. M., Mitchell, K. J., & Walsh, W. A. (2014b). *A content analysis of youth Internet safety programs: Are effective prevention strategies being used?* Durham, NH: Crimes Against Children Research Center, University of New Hampshire.

Judge, A. M. (2012). "Sexting" among US adolescents: Psychological and legal implications. *Harvard Review of Psychiatry, 20,* 86–96.

Klettke, B., Halliford, D. J., & Mellow, D. J. (2014). Sexting prevalence and correlates: A systematic literature review. *Clinical Psychology Review, 34,* 44–53.

Kopecký, K. (2011). Sexting among Czech preadolescents and adolescents. *New Educational Review, 28*(2), 39–48.

Lenhart, A. (2009). *Teens and sexting: How and why minor teens are sending sexually suggestive nude or nearly nude images via text messaging.* Washington, DC: Pew Internet and American Life Project.

Lenhart, A. (2015). *Teen, social media and technology overview.* Washington, DC: Pew Internet and American Life Project.

Lenhart, A., Madden, M., Smith, A., Purcell, K., Zickuhr, K., & Rainie, L. (2011). *Teens, kindness and cruelty on social network sites: How American teens navigate the new world of "digital citizenship."* Washington, DC: Pew Internet and American Life Project.

Letourneau, E. J., Henggeler, S. W., Borduin, C. M., Schewe, P. A., McCart, M. R., Chapman, J. E., & Saldana, L. (2009). Multisystemic therapy for juvenile sexual offenders: 1-year results from a randomized effectiveness trial. *Journal of Family Psychology, 23,* 89–102.

Lippman, J. R., & Campbell, S. W. (2014). Damned if you do, damned if you don't . . . if you're a girl: Relational and normative contexts of adolescent sexting in the United States. *Journal of Children and Media,* 1–16.

Livingstone, S., & Smith, P. K. (2014). Annual research review: Harms experienced by child users of online and mobile technologies: The nature, prevalence and management of sexual and aggressive risks in the digital age. *Journal of Child Psychology and Psychiatry, 55*(6), 635–654.

Lo, V. & Wei, R. (2005). Exposure to internet pornography and Taiwanese adolescents' sexual attitudes and behavior. *Journal of Broadcasting and Electronic Media, 49*(2), 221–237.

Logan and Logan v. Sycamore Community School Board of Education, Paul Payne, and City of Montgomery (2009). Civil Complaint and Jury Demand, 12 February 2009, Case No. 1:09-cv–885, US District Court (S.d Oh.). See information available at http://law.justia.com/cases/federal/district-courts/ohio/ohsdce/1:2009cv00885/134738/70 (accessed December 12, 2015).

Lounsbury, K., Mitchell, K. M., & Finkelhor, D. (2011). *The true prevalance of sexting.* Durham, NH: Crimes Against Children Research Center, University of New Hamphore. Retrieved January 3, 2016, from http://www.unh.edu/ccrc/pdf/Sexting%20Fact%20Sheet%204_29_11.pdf

Luder, M., Pittet, I., Berchtold, A., Akre, C., Michaud, P., & Suris, J. (2011). Associations between online pornography and sexual behavior among adolescents: Myth or reality? *Archives of Sexual Behavior, 40,* 1027–1035.

Maccoby, E. E. (1998). *The two sexes growing up apart, coming together.* Cambridge: The Belknap Press.

Malamuth, N. M., Addison, T., & Koss, M. (2000). Pornography and sexual aggression: Are there reliable effects and can we understand them? *Annual Review of Sex Research, 11,* 26–91.

Malamuth, N. M., & Billings, V. (1986). The functions and effects of pornography: Sexual communication vs. the feminist models in the light of research findings. In J. Bryant & D. Zillman (Eds.), *Perspectives on Media Effects* (pp. 83–108). Hillsdale, NJ: Erlbaun.

Manning, A., & Toussaint, K. (2015). *Why was the prep school girl so nice to the man she says raped her?* Retrieved February 2, 2016, from http://www.boston.com/news/local/massachusetts/2015/08/19/why-was-the-prep-school-girl-nice-the-man-she-says-raped-her/kxjGahzod-7dTWbAbA9uZIN/story.html

Marvin, C. (1998). *When old technologies were new: Thinking about electric communication in the late nineteenth century.* New York: Oxford University Press.

Milhausen, R. R. & Herold, E. S. (1999). Does the sexual double standard still exist? Perceptions of university women. *The Journal of Sex Research, 36*(4), 361–368.

Miller, Day, Doe v. Skumanick (2010). Case No. 3:09cv540, US District Court (M.D Pa). Available at http://www.pamd.uscourts.gov/opinions/munley/09v540.pdf (accessed January 4, 2016).

Mitchell, K. J., Finkelhor, D., & Becker-Blease, K. A. (2007). Linking youth Internet and conventional problems: Findings from a clinical perspective. *Journal of Aggression, Maltreatment & Trauma, 15,* 2, 39–58.

Mitchell, K. J., Finkelhor, D., Jones, L. M., Wolak, J. (2011). Prevalence and characteristics of youth sexting: A national study. *Pediatrics, 129,* 1–8.

Mitchell, K. J., Finkelhor. D., & Wolak, J. (2007). Youth Internet users at risk for the most serious online sexual solicitations. *American Journal Preventive Medicine, 32*(6), 532–537.

Mitchell, K. J., & Wells, M. (2007). Problematic Internet experiences: Primary or secondary presenting problems in persons seeking mental health care? *Social Science & Medicine, 65,* 1136–1141.

Mitchell, K. J., Wolak, J., & Finkelhor, D. (2007). Trends in youth reports of sexual solicitations, harassment and unwanted exposure to pornography on the Internet. *Journal of Adolescent Health, 40,* 116–126.

Monk-Turner, E., & Purcell, H. C. (1999). Sexual violence in pornography. *Gender Issues, 17,* 58–67.

Moran, J. P. (2000). *Teaching Sex: The shaping of adolescence in the twentieth century.* Cambridge, MA: Harvard University Press.

Nathan, D. (2007). *Pornography.* Toronto, Canada: Groundwork Books.

National Campaign to Prevent Teen and Unplanned Pregnancy (2008). *Sex and Tech: Results from a survey of teens and young adults.* Retrieved December 15, 2015, from http://www.thenational-campaign.org/sextech/pdf/sextech_summary.pdf

Odem. M. E. (1995). *Delinquent daughters: Protecting and policing adolescent female sexuality in the United States: 1885–1920.* Chapel Hill: University of North Carolina Press.

Ostrager, B. (2010). SMS. OMG! LOL! TTYL: Translating the law to accommodate today's teens and the evolution from texting to sexting. *Family Court Review, 48,* 712–726.

Ouytsel, J. V., Ponnet, K., & Walrave, M. (2014). The associations between adolescents' consumption of pornography and music videos and their sexting behavior. *Cyberpsychology, Behavior and Social Networking, 17*(12), 772–778.

Owens, E. W., Behun, R. J., Manning, J. C., et al. (2012). The impact of pornography on adolescents: A review of the research. *Sexual Addiction & Compulsivity, 19,* 99–122.

Palfrey, J., & Gasser, U. (2008). *Born digital: Understanding the first generation of digital natives.* New York: Perseus Books.

Palys, T. S. (1986). The social content of video pornography. *Canadian Psychology, 27,* 22–35.

Peter, J., & Valkenburg, P. M. (2006). Adolescents' exposure to sexually explicit online material and recreational attitudes toward sex. *Communication Research, 56,* 639–660.

Peter, J., & Valkenburg, P. M. (2011). The use of sexually explicit Internet material and its antecedents: A longitudinal comparison of adolescents and adults. *Archives of Sexual Behavior, 40,* 1015–1025.

Petrosino, A., Turpin-Petrosino, C., & Buehler, J. (2003). Scared Straight and other juvenile awareness programs for preventing juvenile delinquency: A systematic review of the randomized experimental evidence. *Annals of the American Academy of Political and Social Science, 589,* 41–62.

Ponton, L. E., & Judice, S. (2004). Typical adolescent sexual development. *Child and Adolescent Psychiatric Clinics of North America, 13,* 497–511.

Pridgen, B. (2010). Navigating the Internet safely: Recommendations for residential programs targeting at-risk adolescents. *Harvard Review of Psychiatry, 18,* 131–138.

Priebe, G., Mitchell, K. J., & Finkelhor, D. (2013). To tell or not to tell? Youth's responses to unwanted Internet experiences. *Cyberpsychology: Journal of Psychosocial Research on Cyberspace, 7*(1).

Rice, E., Rhoades, H., Winetrobe, H., Sanchez, M., Montoya, J., Plant, A., et al. (2012). Sexually explicit cell phone messaging associated with sexual risk among adolescents. *Pediatrics, 130,* 667–673.

Richards, R. D., & Calvert, C. (2009). When sex and cell phones collide: Inside the prosecution of a teen sexting case. *Hastings Communications & Entertainment Law Journal, 32,* 1–31.

Ringrose, J., Harvey, L., Gill, R., et al. (2012). *A qualitative study of children, young people and "sexting": A report prepared for the NSPCC.* London: National Society for the Prevention of Cruelty to Children.

Ringrose, J., Harvey, L., Gill, R., & Livingstone, S. (2013). Teen girls, sexual double standards and "sexting": Gendered value in digital image exchange. *Feminist Theory, 14*(3), 305–323.

Rothman, E. F., Kaczmarsky, C., Burke, N., Jansen, E., & Baughman, A. (2015). "Without porn . . . I wouldn't know half the things I know now": A qualitative study of pornography use among a sample of urban, low-income, black and Hispanic youth. *Journal of Sex Research, 52*(7), 736–746.

Sabina, C., Wolak, J., & Finkelhor, D. (2008). The nature of dynamics of Internet pornography exposure for youth. *CyberPsychology & Behavior, 11,* 691–693.

Sacco, D. T., Argudin, R., Maguire, J., & Tallon, K. (2010). *Sexting: Youth practices and legal implications.* The Berkman Center for Internet & Society, Harvard University. Retrieved January 1, 2016, from http://cyber.law.harvard.

Saleh, F. M., Feldman, B. N., Grudzinskas, A. J., Ravven, S. E., & Cody, R. Cybersexual harassment and suicide. In F. Saleh, A. Grudzinskas, & A. Judge (Eds.) *Adolescent sexual behavior in the digital age: Considerations for clinicians, legal professionals and educators* (pp. 139–160). New York: Oxford University Press.

Saleh, F. M., Grudzinskas, A., & Judge, A. (2014). *Adolescent sexual behavior in the digital age: Considerations for clinicians, legal professionals and educators.* New York: Oxford University Press.

Savin-Williams, R. C., & Diamond, L. M. (2009). Adolescent sexuality. In R. M. Lerner & L. Steinberg (Eds.), *Handbook of adolescent psychology: Vol. 1. Individual bases of adolescent development* (3rd ed., pp. 479–523). Hoboken, NJ: Wiley.

Scott, C. L., & Temporini, H. (2011). Forensic issues and the Internet. In E. Benedek, P. Ash, & C. L. Scott (Eds.), *Principles and practice of child and adolescent forensic mental health.* Washington, DC: American Psychiatric Publishing.

Seto, M. C., & Lalumière, M. L. (2010).What is so special about male adolescent sexual offending? A review and test of explanations through meta-analysis. *Psychological Bulletin, 136*(4), 526–575.

Smahel, D., & Subrahmanyam, K. (2014). Adolescent sexuality on the Internet: A developmental perspective. In F. Saleh, A. Grudzinskas, & A. Judge (Eds.) *Adolescent sexual behavior in the digital age: Considerations for clinicians, legal professionals and educators* (pp. 62–88). New York: Oxford University Press.

Smith, M. (2013). Youth viewing sexually explicit material online: Addressing the elephant on the screen. *Sexuality Research and Social Policy, 10*(1), 62–75.

Stattin, H., & Kerr, M. (2000). Parental monitoring: A reinterpretation. *Child Development, 71,* 1072–1085.

Steinberg, L. (2007). Risk taking in adolescence: New perspectives from brain and behavioral science. *Current Directions in Psychological Science, 16*(2), 55–59.

Steinberg, L. (2008). A social neuroscience perspective on adolescent risk-taking. *Developmental Review, 28,* 78–106.

Subrahmanyam, K., Greenfield, P., & Tynes, B. (2004). Constructing sexuality and identity in an online teen chat room. *Journal of Applied Developmental Psychology, 25,* 651–666.

Subrahmanyam, K., Smahel, D., & Greenfield, P. (2006). Connecting developmental constructions to the Internet: Identity presentation and sexual development in online teen chat rooms. *Developmental Psychology, 42*(3), 395–406.

Suzuki, L. K., & Calzo, J. P. (2004). The search for peer advice in cyberspace: An examination of online teen bulletin boards about health and sexuality. *Journal of Applied Developmental Psychology, 25,* 685–698.

Svedin, C. G., Akerman, I., & Priebe, G. (2011). Frequent users of pornography. A population based epidemiological study of Swedish male adolescents. *Journal of Adolescence,* 779–788.

Temple, J. R., & Choi, H. (2014). Longitudinal association between teen sexting and sexual behavior. *Pediatrics, 134,* 1–6.

Temple, J. R., Paul, J. A., van den Berg, P., Le, V. D., McElhany, A., & Temple, B. W. (2012). Teen sexting and its associations with sexual behaviours. *Archives of Pediatrics and Adolescent Medicine, 166,* 828–833.

Tolman, D. L. & McClelland, S. I. (2011). Normative sexuality development in adolescence: A decade in review, 2000–2009. *Journal of Research on Adolescence, 21*(1), 242–255.

Trostle L. C. (2003). Overrating pornography as a source of sex information for university students: Additional consistent findings. *Psychological Reports, 921,* 143–150.

Tsitsika, A., Critselis, E., Kormas, G., Konstantoulaki, E., Constantopoulos, A., & Kafetzis, D. (2009). Adolescent pornographic Internet site use: A multivariate regression analysis of the predictive factors of use and psychosocial implications. *CyberPsychology & Behavior, 12,* 545–550.

Turkle, S. (2006). Tethering. In C. Jones (Ed.), *Embodied experience, technology and contemporary art* (pp. 220–226). Cambridge, MA: MIT Press.

Vaala, S. E., & Bleakley, A. (2015). Monitoring, mediating and modeling: Parental influence on adolescent computer and Internet use in the United States. *Journal of Children and Media, 9*(1), 40–57.

Vega, V., & Malamuth, N. M. (2007). Predicting sexual aggression: The role of pornography in the context of general and specific risk factors. *Aggressive Behavior, 22,* 104–117.

Waite, D., Keller, A., McGarvey, E., Wieckowski, E., Pinkerton, R., & Brown, G. L. (2005). Juvenile sex offender re-arrest rates for sexual, violent nonsexual and property crimes: A 10-year follow-up. *Sexual Abuse: A Journal of Research and Treatment, 17*(3), 313–331.

Walsh, W., Wolak, J., & Finkelhor, D. (2013). *Sexting: When are state prosecutors deciding to prosecute? The Third National Juvenile Online Victimization Study (NJOV-3).* Durham, NH: Crimes Against Children Research Center, University of New Hampshire.

Weber, M., Quiring, O., & Daschmann, G. (2012). Peers, parenting and pornography: Exploring adolescents' exposure to sexually explicit material and its developmental correlates. *Sexuality & Culture, 16,* 408–427.

Weins, W. J., Hiestand, T. C. (2009). Sexting, statutes and saved by the bell: Introducing a lesser juvenile charge with "aggravating factors" framework. *Tennessee Law Review 1,* 77.

Wingood, G. M., DiClemente, R. J., Harrington, K., Davies, S., Hook, E. W. III, & Oh, M. K. (2001). Exposure to X-rated movies and adolescents' sexual and contraceptive-related attitudes and behaviors. *Pediatrics, 107,* 1116–1119.

Wolak, J., & Finkelhor, D. (2011). *Sexting: A typology.* Durham, NH: Crimes Against Children Research Center, University of New Hampshire. Retrieved from http://www.unh.edu/ccrc/pdf/CV231_Sexting%20Typology%20Bulletin_4-6-11_revised.pdf

Wolak, J., Finkelhor, D., & Mitchell, K. (2008). Online "predators" and their victims: Myths, realities, and implications for prevention and treatment. *American Psychologist 63,* 111–128.

Wolak J., Finkelhor, D., Mitchell, K. J., Ybarra, M. L. (2010). Online "predators" and their victims: myths, realities, and implications for prevention and treatment. *American Psychologist, 63*(2), 111–128.

Wright, P. J. (2014) Pornography and the sexual socialization of children: Current knowledge and a theoretical future. *Journal of Children and Media, 8*(3), 305–312.

Ybarra, M., & Mitchell, K. J. (2005). Exposure to Internet pornography among children and adolescents: A national survey. *CyberPsychology & Behavior, 8,* 473–486.

Ybarra, M. L., & Mitchell, K. J. (2014). "Sexting" and its relation to sexual activity and sexual risk behavior in a national survey of adolescents. *Journal of Adolescent Health, 55,* 757–764.

Ybarra, M. L., & Mitchell, K. J. (2015). A national study of lesbian, gay, bisexual (LGB) and non-LGB youth sexual behavior online and in-person. *Archives of Sexual Behavior, 45*(6), 1357–1372.

Ybarra, M. L., Mitchell, K. J., Hamburger, M., Diener-West, M., Leaf, P. J. (2011). X-rated material and perpetration of sexually aggressive behavior among children and adolescents: is there a link? *Aggressive Behavior, 37*(1), 1–18.

Zhang, X. (2010). Charging children with child pornography—Using the legal system to handle the problem of "sexting." *Computer Law & Security Review, 26,* 251–259.

Zillman, D. (2000). Influence of unrestrained access to erotica on adolescents' and young adults' dispositions toward sexuality. *Journal of Adolescent Health, 27*(2 Suppl), 41–44.

Zimring, F. E. (2009). *An American travesty: Legal responses to adolescent sexual offending.* Chicago: University of Illinois Press.

Criminological Perspective on Juvenile Sexual Offender Policy

Franklin E. Zimring

The subject of this chapter is juvenile sexual offenses and offenders, and the method of my report is conventional statistical criminological analysis. So the analysis that follows will parallel the approach that sociologists and criminal justice scholars use in reports on specific offenses like auto theft or assault and with analysis of the behavioral prospects of juvenile and adult offenders over time in future exposure in the community.

What gives the use of this method some degree of novelty is that criminologists and sociologists have not done much work in the nature of sexual offending or in the criminal careers and prospects for recidivism of sexual offenders. Because of the presumed importance of sexual disorders to sexual offending, the treatment and diagnosis of sexual offending was considered a more appropriate specialization for clinicians in psychology with special training in sexual disorders, and this comparative advantage in offender treatment also produced what was presumed to be expertise in criminal justice policy toward sexual offenses and offenders.

One major set of questions that were never sufficiently investigated by either psychologists or criminologists in the second half of the 20th century concerned the causes, character, and persistence of juvenile sexual offending and juvenile sexual offenders. The psychiatrist who directed New York City's program for counseling juvenile sexual offenders published a book, *The Boy Sex Offender and His Later Career,* in 1943. Dr. Lewis Doshay reported on the minimal treatment and later offending of 256 males who had been referred by the family court in New York City for sexual offenses in the six years beginning in 1928. Doshay's data set studied the juvenile sexual offenders for a period of up to six years after their 16th birthdays. While these young men had a modest rate of police arrest for any charge over this period (15.1%), the six-year risk of arrest for a sexual offense was 3.1 percent. Doshay concluded that "male juvenile sex delinquency is self-curing, providing the latent forces of shame and guilt . . . are properly stimulated into action" (Doshay, 1943, p. 168). For more than half a century after the publication of this volume, there was no book published of scholarship on juvenile sexual offenders in the English language. Sociologists studied large cohorts of children, following them into youth and young adulthood to determine the nature and correlates of criminal behavior, but sexual offending was not a significant issue in the analysis (see Wolfgang, Figlio, & Sellin, 1972). There was also practically no empirical scholarship about juvenile sexual offenders in the psychological literature.

For a long time, the lack of scholarship and statistical analysis about juvenile sexual offending was accompanied by inattention to justice system resources for juvenile sexual offenders. In this sense, no news was good news for young persons arrested for criminal sexual behavior other than forcible rape. By the mid-1980s, however, public concern about sexual crime had produced sustained efforts to increase criminal penalties for sexual offenders, particularly for child molesters, and there was particular concern about repeat sexual offenders and particularly about children killed by sexual predators. And these concerns produced major criminal prosecutions such as the McMartin preschool episode in Los Angeles and proposed sex offender registration and notification systems.

While children were the paradigm victims in the moral panic about sexual offenders in the 1980s and 1990s, their slightly older siblings were being targeted at the receiving end of a punitive turn in legislative policy. This was yet another illustration of a spillover from trends in criminal justice to policies toward juvenile offenders. Longtime students of American youth justice policy have noticed that when the American criminal justice system sneezes, the juvenile justice system catches cold. The problem with the mindless application of punitive criminal justice assumptions to juvenile sexual offenders is that it flies in the face of known facts about juvenile sexual offenders. It embraces strategies that combine harm to young offenders with stupid and grossly inefficient sexual offender prevention and registration policies. And the road to these terrible current policies was paved not only with political posturing but also with factually ignorant and extreme rhetoric from an organization of professionals in the treatment of juvenile sexual offenders.

The four sections in the following analysis provide an empirical narrative of the known facts about juvenile sexual offending and offenders and the misfit between facts and current policy. The first and longest section of this chapter provides a statistical portrait of juvenile sexual offenses and offenders. A second section addresses three linked issues about juvenile sexual offenders—whether they are specialists or generalists in patterns of law violation, whether most or much juvenile sexual offending is a product of clinical sexual disorders, and whether a sexual offense by a juvenile predicts either future sexual offending or the need for specialized and intensive treatment programs. The third section of the chapter compares the assumptions in the report of a vocal and well-organized group that called itself the National Adolescent Perpetrator Network that was published in 1993 with actual facts and should serve as a cautionary tale for sex treatment clinicians. A fourth section contrasts the current policy framework in the "Amy Zyla" extension of reporting to juveniles portion of the federal Adam Walsh Act of 2006 with the facts about juvenile sexual offenders and outlines two less outrageous policies that would improve the current worst-case regulatory policy in the United States for juvenile sexual offenders.

JUVENILE SEX CRIME AND CRIMINALS

There are two ways an observer might estimate the number of children and adolescents under 18 whose sexual behavior violates the criminal law, and the contrasting methodologies lead to very different results.

Seven Million Juvenile Sexual Offenders?

One method of estimating the incidence of juvenile sex crimes is to combine current knowledge of juvenile sexual behavior with estimates of the population of children and adolescents in the United States. This methodology would confidently predict many million juvenile sexual felons each year in the US.

The essential reason for this crime wave is the comprehensive attempt of the criminal codes to prohibit almost all interpersonal sexual contact with children and younger adolescents. There are over 230 million persons over 18 in the United States, and the members of this population probably have sexual intercourse tens of millions of times each week. But the vast majority of sexual relations among adults in the United States are not the criminal law's business.

For children and younger adolescents, however, the aim of the criminal law is to prohibit interpersonal sexual contact completely. The laws of the federal government and every state make the sexually motivated touching of the genitals of any minor under 14 or 15 or 16 into "lewd conduct," a felony punishable by substantial prison terms. All states also make sexual intercourse with girls under an age of consent (typically 18 or 16) into an offense traditionally called statutory rape whether or not the minor actually consented.

The objective of these strict criminal prohibitions is protection of sexually vulnerable young people. But the gap between legal standards and adolescent conduct is rather substantial. A longitudinal study by the National Institute of Child Health and Human Development reported that about half of all US children have engaged in genital play by age 15 (Zimring, 2004, p. 53) and more than one-third at 14. Figure 15.1 reports the prevalence in the United States of sexual intercourse by high school grade level; figure 15.2 shows the prevalence of oral sex.

Figure 15.1 Prevalence in US of Sexual Intercourse by Grade, 2013

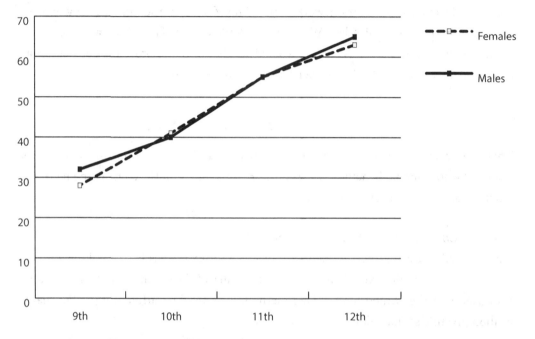

Source: Centers for Disease Control and Prevention. Ever had sexual intercourse: High School Youth Risk Behavior Survey, 2013. Youth online: High School Youth Risk Behavior Surveillance System (YRBSS). Retrieved from https://nccd.cdc.gov/youthonline.

The share of kids at each age reporting genital play is much larger (see Zimring, 2004, p. 53). Combining these surveys with population estimates produces very rough estimated prevalence rates. There were 20 million persons between 10 and 14 in the 2010 US Census, and another 22 million between 15 and 19. Reducing the older population to eliminate 18- and 19-year-olds generates an estimate of 16 million males and just under 16 million females aged 10 through 17. Assuming both that all the females should be considered victims rather than co-offenders and that most of the genital play and intercourse reported involves partners of the same age, the number of (mostly male) sexual offenders guilty of either lewd conduct or statutory rape would be in the neighborhood of seven million.

Figure 15.2 Prevalence in US of Oral Sex Experience by Age, 2011–2013

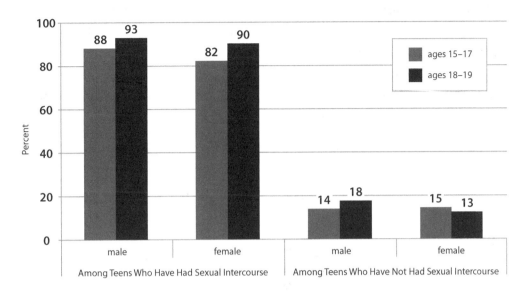

Source: Child Trends Data Bank. Oral sex behaviors among teens. Retrieved from http://www.childtrends. org/?indicators=oral-sex-behaviors-among-teens. Raw data for their graphs taken from Centers for Disease Control and Prevention, National Survey of Family Growth (NSFG), 2011-2013, retrieved from http://www.cdc.gov/nchs/NSFG.htm.

Official Statistics

A second method of estimating the number of juvenile sexual offenders in the United States is by using official arrest statistics. Figure 15.3 reports the volume of juvenile sexual offenders arrested during 2014 according to the FBI annual report. The three offense categories in the figure are the only sexual offenses reported in the Uniform Crime Reports.

The total number of sexual offense arrests reported during 2014 by the Uniform Crime Reporting program was just over 10,000. Only arrest statistics provide the age of the suspect, so these are the only age distributions available. The number of juveniles arrested for any sexual offense is a tiny fraction of both the adolescent population and of the seven million or so persons whose conduct might have been a law violation. The prevalence of sexual offenders is 700 times the volume of juveniles arrested, so the official arrests are a tiny and unrepresentative sample of kids who violate laws about sexual behavior.

The three classes of sex crimes reported in figure 15.3 are very different. The "forcible rape" arrests are for what the FBI calls Part I crime, one of the eight crime categories that make up what the agency calls "the crime index" and where, presumably, some effort will be invested in auditing the accuracy of arrests. The total number of arrests in this category is just under 2,500 in 2014, or about one-fourth of the sexual offense total. The number of juveniles arrested for prostitution and commercial vice is tiny, just over 1 percent of the 42,000 arrests of all ages in this category. Given the limited opportunities that adolescent runaways have to obtain money and their vulnerability to exploitation, the small number of prostitution arrests probably reflects the police regarding the teen in such settings as a victim rather than an offender.

Figure 15.3   US Arrests of Persons Under 18 for Three Types of Sex Crime, 2014

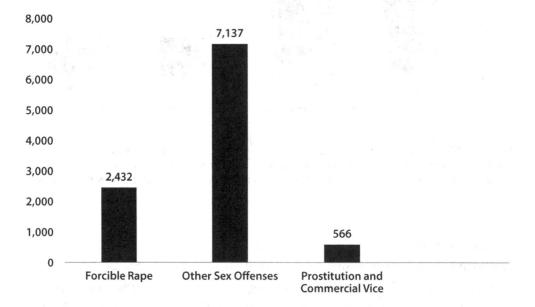

Source: US Department of Justice. Crime in the United States, table 36, Current year over previous year arrest trends. Federal Bureau of Investigation, Criminal Justice Information Services Division (2014). Retrieved from https://www.fbi.gov/about-us/cjis/ucr/crime-in-the-u.s/2014/crime-in-the-u.s.-2014/tables/table-36.

What of the more than seven thousand arrests for "other sex offenses" reported in figure 15.3? This is a "non-index" crime category, which means that the FBI puts no effort into precise definitions or auditing police department reports to discover and disclose what the departments include in this rubric. The "other sex offenses" in this category are essentially defined by what they are not: Namely, this is a residual collection of any arrests where the crime has a sexual element—child molestation including the indecent liberties offenses where consent is not a defense, indecent exposure and pornography and obscenity. This vague and never audited "other sex offense" category is the location of more than 70 percent of all juvenile offenders, so gaining insight into the nature of this category of offending is essential for policy analysis. But the only data available, to be discussed later in this section, come from statistics generated by a smaller number of states that are not national in scope.

Figure 15.4 compares the share of all arrests of several offenses that are of persons under 18 so that the rape and "other sex offense" arrests shown in figure 15.3 can be measured against juvenile involvement in other crimes.

Figure 15.4 Percentage of Total Arrests That Involve Persons Under 18, Eight Index Crimes and "Other Sex Offenses," United States, 2014

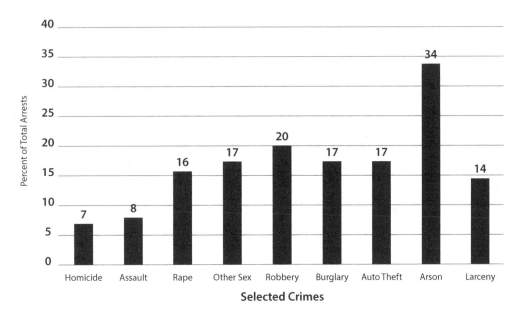

Source: US Department of Justice. Crime in the United States, table 36, Current year over previous year arrest trends. Federal Bureau of Investigation, Criminal Justice Information Services Division (2014). Retrieved from https://www.fbi.gov/about-us/cjis/ucr/crime-in-the-u.s/2014/crime-in-the-u.s.-2014/tables/tablew-36.

As figure 15.4 shows, the juvenile share of rape arrests, at 16 percent of the total, is higher than the share of arrests for homicide and aggravated assault but lower than the juvenile share of arrests for robbery, burglary, and auto theft, and just under half the share of arrests for arson committed by juveniles. More remarkable, the under-18 share of "other sex offense" arrests at 17 percent is also no higher than for property crimes despite the fact that much larger proportions of the sexual behavior of juveniles are prohibited by the criminal law. Both the low percentage of total arrests for "other sex offenses" and the very modest number of such juvenile arrests suggests that the vast majority of technically criminal sexual contact between juveniles of the same age in consensual sexual relationships does not involve either arrest or criminal charges.

Figure 15.5 profiles the relative vulnerability to arrest at each different age in the decade between age 10 and age 20 using the ages at arrest reported by the FBI in 2014. The figure shows the relative number of arests at each age compared with arrests for the same offense at age 20.

Figure 15.5 Arrest Share as Proportion of Age 20 Rate at Different Ages Between Age 10 and Age 20, FBI, 2014

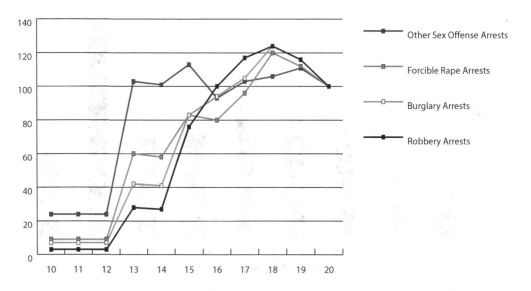

Sources: US Census Bureau. National population estimate for 12/1/2014. Retrieved from https://www.census.gov/popest/data/national/asrh/2014/2014-nat-res.html; US Department of Justice. Crime in the United States, table 38, Arrests by age, 2014. Federal Bureau of Investigation, Criminal Justice Information Services Division (2014). Retrieved from https://www.fbi.gov/about-us/cjis/ucr/crime-in-the-u.s/2014/crime-in-the-u.s.-2014/tables/table-38.

For each offense, the figure assigns the arrest rate per 100,000 at age 20 the value 100, and then shows the arrest rate for each age under 20 as its percentage. So if the rate per 100,000 of burglary arrests at age 20 is 191.8, and the rate at age 10 is 15.2, the figure shows the age 20 rate as 100 and expresses the age 10 rate as proportional to that number, in this case 7.9.

For three of the four offenses profiled in figure 15.5, the pattern with advancing age is similar. Arrest rates for robbery, burglary, and rape start very low, stay well under half the age 20 rates through age 15, and then increase to rates over that of age 20 by age 18, dropping off slightly in the last two years. The exception to this pattern is the mysterious "other sex offense" collection of unknown acts, the dotted line in figure 15.5. At ages 10, 11, and 12, when the arrest rate for robbery, burglary, and rape is below 10 percent of the age 20 rate, it is already more than 20 percent of the young adult rates at age 20 for other sex offenses. While arrests for street crime at age 10 and 11 are rare, the arrest of kids just approaching puberty for sexual offending is already quite substantial. The second major difference between "other sex crime" arrest propensity and that for street crime involves the three years from age 13 through age 15. For street crimes, the rates grow gradually during this period, only to accelerate further from 16 to 18. But the arrest risk at age 13 for "other sex offenses" is already almost as high as it will ever get, and the period from age 13 to age 18 is one where arrest risks stay at the high level established at 13. There is a bigger difference between the age pattern for rape and that for "other sex crimes" than there is between rape and either robbery or burglary. Why are the juvenile "other sex crime" arrests so concentrated at the youngest end of the spectrum?

To gain further insight into the types of activities and victims that are involved in juvenile sex crime arrests, we obtained data from a multi-state program of longitudinal arrest statistics on the age of the victims of sexual conduct and on the character of the sexual content.

Table 15.1 shows both the age of the arrested juvenile and the age of the person the juvenile was accused of victimizing. These data were originally published as part of a book published in 2004 (Zimring, 2004) and was provided by Howard Snyder of the National Center for Juvenile Justice in Pittsburgh

TABLE 15.1 AGE DISTRIBUTION OF VICTIMS BY AGE OF OFFENDER, NIBRS JURISDICTIONS, 1991–1996 (%)

	Offender Age							
Victim Age	10 and under	11	12	13	14	15	16	17
5 and under	46	39	34	27	22	17	10	7
6–8	32	33	25	24	18	16	9	6
9–11	15	19	17	17	16	13	11	9
12	1	3	9	8	8	7	8	4
13	1	3	7	12	12	12	13	12
14	1	1	3	6	12	12	14	16
15	—	1	1	3	5	11	13	15
16	—	—	—	1	2	5	10	11
17	—	—	—	—	1	2	4	7
18 and over	1	—	3	1	4	5	9	13
Sample size	1,323	612	990	1,633	1,950	1,946	1,913	1,955

Source: Zimring, 2004 p. 50

Table 15.1 shows clearly that even when the youth arrested are very young, the targets of their sexual contact are very much younger. For this reason, the age difference between offender and victim assures police that the sexual contact is predatory and inappropriate.

Figure 15.6 rounds out the portrait of the "other sex offense" category by reporting on the percentage of cases where the criminal act was classified as "forcible fondling" for the six years from 2008 through 2013. The "forcible" part of the definition does not require any assault or injury because the incapacity of the object of the fondling to give an effective consent becomes the equivalent of force. Fondling in this context is contact between the offender's hands and the target's sexual organs.

Figure 15.6 Percentage of Total Arrests of Juveniles for Sex Offenses Where the Criminal Act Was Classified as "Forcible Fondling," 2008–2013

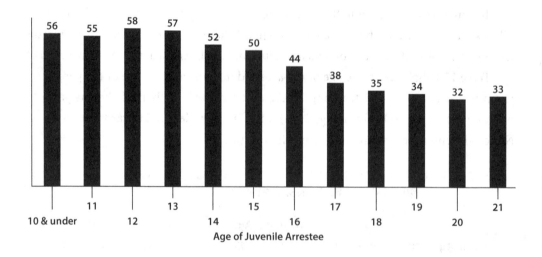

Age of Juvenile Arrestee

Source: US Department of Justice. Crime in the United States, table 36, Current year over previous year arrest trends. Federal Bureau of Investigation, Criminal Justice Information Services Division (2014). Retrieved from https://www.fbi.gov/about-us/cjis/ucr/crime-in-the-u.s/2014/crime-in-the-u.s.-2014/tables/table-36.

Figures 15.5 and 15.6 tell us both why younger boys get arrested for Part II sexual offenses (their victims are much younger) and what it is they are accused of doing (usually touching or manually caressing a younger child's sexual organs—in the majority of all arrests for offenders under age 16).

The youth of the victim of these explorations not only generates a willingness to invoke the criminal process on the part of a victim's parents and police, but also makes a record of any sexual contact with a young child a very serious event justifying both registration and community notification in current federal law—and that of many states as well (see *Raised on the Registry,* available at https://www.hrw.org/report/2013/05/01/ raised-registry/irreparable-harm-placing-children-sex-offender-registries-us).

Does the very high percentage of young children as victims mean that the juvenile offenders are pedophiles in the making? The quick answer to that is no from the *Diagnostic and Statistical Manual* of the American Psychiatric Association, which restricts evidence of pedophilia to situations where "the person is at least 16 years of age and at least 5 years older than the prepubescent child or children" (American Psychiatric Association, 2013, p. 697). But the concentration of young children as targets is highest among offenders in precisely the age groups excluded from any clinical indications of pedophilia: ages 10, 11, 12, 13, 14, and 15. And the tendency to select prepubescent targets falls away at the later ages of adolescence. I will return to this issue in the next section.

A final set of crime statistics sheds some light on whether the large volume of rape arrests of juveniles is an indication that young offenders are involved in the most serious and feared variety of sex crime, rape or child molestation leading to murder, a question that figure 15.7 answers in the negative.

Figure 15.7 Proportion Under 18 for Arrests for Forcible Rape and Other Sex Crimes, and Proportion of Identified Juvenile Offenders in Sex Crime Killings, 2012–2013

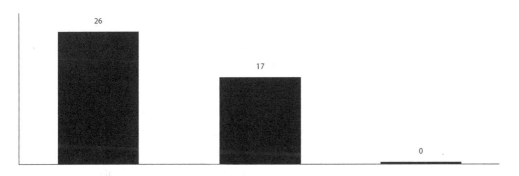

Other Sex Crime Arrests (N = 6,499/29,317)   Forcible Rape Arrests (N = 1,955/11,570)   Sex Crime Killings, Offender Age 17 and Under

Source: FBI [CRFR] Supplemental Homicide Reports 2012–2013.

Even though 17 percent of all persons arrested for rape were under 18 in 2012 and 2013, none of the persons identified as responsible for rape killings in those two years was under 18.

From Boy to Man—Long-Range Sex Recidivism and Its Implications About the Nature of Juvenile Sexual Offending

The paradigm of the sexual offender feared by the public combines three characteristics—long-term dangerousness, disordered sexual orientation, and specialization. The sexual offender image that inspired Megan's Law was a sexually disordered person with little control over sexual urges who specializes in predatory sexual offending and who becomes a repetitive sexual recidivist.

There are a wide variety of empirical inquiries following up juveniles involved in a sexual offense, which consistently indicate that none of these stereotypical patterns holds for the great majority of juvenile sexual offenders (see Caldwell, 2014). But in this section I will focus on the largest and longest assessment of involvement with the criminal justice system, the second Philadelphia birth cohort study, an attempt to follow every boy and girl born in Philadelphia during 1958 who entered school in the city and continued to live there. The 1958 birth cohort study was an attempt to replicate and improve a study of boys born in Philadelphia in 1945, which was reported in the classic criminological study *Delinquency in a Birth Cohort* by Marvin E. Wolfgang, Robert M. Figlio, and Thorsten Sellin in 1972. The 1958 study followed both boys and girls and continued to collect data all through the young adult years ending on the 26th birthday, thereby being able to report on the first eight years of adult careers. The original follow-up study for this cohort was published in the late 1980s but did not report any analysis of juvenile sexual offenders or their later careers. Sexual offending wasn't a priority for criminological research in the 1970s and early 1980s. But all of the data collected by this study were on deposit in the University of Michigan and were made available to a group of researchers interested in juvenile sexual offenses and registration. Our analysis of sexual offending in this study was published in 2009 (Zimring, Piquero, Jennings, & Hays, 2009).

What makes this cohort follow-up data set of unique and definitive value is the breadth of the sample followed and the length of the adult career captured. The cohort of 13,000-odd boys were not just a group of juveniles arrested for sexual offenses or a group of boys selected because they were arrested as juveniles, but *every* boy born in Philadelphia who stayed through to school age. And because this study followed every boy until his 26th birthday, not only can it tell us how many sexual offenses were committed in adulthood by boys who had a police contact for a juvenile sexual offense, but it can also compare the rates of sexual offending as adults for boys with a juvenile sexual offense contact with other boys who were not juvenile sexual offenders. Finally, because all boys were followed into young adulthood, we can determine the ultimate value of juvenile sex offender registration as a prediction of adult sexual danger for law enforcement and public notice—what percentage of the total adult sexual offenses committed *by this cohort of boys* were committed by those involved in a sexual offense as a juvenile?

Figure 15.8, adopted from the original research report in *Justice Quarterly* (Zimring et al., 2009), divides the total population of boys in the cohort into five groups: one group that had no police contacts prior to age 18, one group with fewer than five total police contacts prior to their 18th birthday but no sexual offenses, one group with fewer than five total contacts but at least one of them was for a sexual offense, a fourth group with more than five total police contacts but none for a sexual offense, and a final group with more than five total contacts including at least one for sexual offense of any kind. The bar for each group is the percentage of persons in that category with a sex arrest during the eight years after their 18th birthday.[1]

Figure 15.8 Distinguishing Adult Sex Offenders Based on Juvenile Record

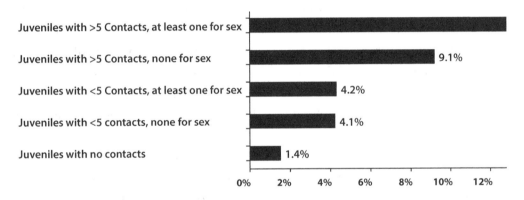

Source: Zimring, Piquero, Jennings, and Hays, 2009.

While there is variation in eight-year arrest risk among the five groups, the sexual offending levels are low for all groups, and most of the variation among groups is not related to the presence or absence of a sexual offense as a juvenile.

Boys with no police contacts of any kind prior to age 18 have tiny rates of sex-related arrest after 18: 1.4 percent over an 8-year span. The two groups of boys with only some police contacts but not many have very low rates of any sex arrest in young adulthood—4 chances in 100. And the presence or absence of a juvenile sexual offense in the under-five contact group makes *no* difference in the chances that a sex arrest

---

1. Data are also available for girls, but the sexual offense rates in adulthood are small and the sex contacts as juveniles are frequently family conflict and non-predatory.

will occur in young adulthood. The two groups with the highest number of total police contacts under age 18 also have the two highest rates of adult sex arrests, 9.1 and 15.6 percent. But it is a high juvenile arrest record for anything that best predicts adult sexual offending, not the presence or absence of a sexual offense as a juvenile. This is exactly the opposite of a pattern that would be produced if teen sexual offenders either specialized in sexual offending as youth or showed any substantial continuity in sexual offending conduct in young adulthood. For kids with low general rates of juvenile offense, the presence of a juvenile sex crime adds no weight to the likelihood of young adult sexual offending. And the kids with no juvenile sex arrests but more than five arrests for anything else as a juvenile have *twice* the chances of being arrested for a sexual offense as a young adult than do low-arrest-rate boys with a juvenile sex arrest. It is literally true in Philadelphia that an 18-year-old with five arrests for only theft and burglary will have twice the chance of being arrested for a sex crime as a young adult as an 18-year-old who was arrested for a sexual offense but had fewer than five total police contacts.

So what these aggregate statistics show is the opposite of sexual offense specialization. What generates the minimal risks that any juveniles seem to pose for adult sexual offending is high numbers of arrests for anything. There may be a very small number of youth with early-onset sexual disorders (although not pedophilia), but the overwhelming majority of juvenile sexual offenders are neither sick nor sexually dangerous.

The fact that these Philadelphia data follow every boy in the cohort into adulthood means that we have a comprehensive record for this population of who is and who is not going to be a sexual danger to the community in young adulthood. The most important statistic from this study is that fewer than 8 percent of all the adult police contacts that these boys have for sexual offending involve men who committed a sexual offense as a boy. The boys who didn't have a sexual offense arrest as boys committed 92 percent of all the adult sexual offenses attributed to this population (Zimring et al., 2009).

Some Policy Implications

Is there substantial similarity between adolescent sexual offending and habitual sexual offending in adulthood? Most probably not. And any clinical treatment of adolescent sexual offenders must begin with a sophisticated understanding of adolescence as a developmental stage with substantial impact on behavior and motivation. That is precisely what the strident and fact-free National Adolescent Perpetrator Network's 1993 report on juvenile sexual offenders was missing. This report never addressed any developmental issues or any part of the vast literature on adolescent development (see Zimring, 2015, p. 82). Instead, it provided a list of sexual abnormalities, including between "florophilia" (the sexual attraction to plants) and "pedophilia," a disorder the group called "hebephilia," which was defined by the task force as "sexual interest in adolescents." But since all of the subjects the network was considering were themselves adolescents, why was "hebephilia" for them a sexual disorder? Who should they be sexually interested in?

This kind of idiocy would be amusing except that the ignorant assumptions of a treatment group invited the catastrophic extension of compulsory sex offender registration and community notification for sexual offenders over 14.

Because so many of these cases involve young kids as targets of opportunity, the Amy Zyla amendments that treat adolescent offenders the same way as adults require long periods of stigma and tight regulation for behaviors that carry no greater likelihood of a sexual offense as an adult than would a juvenile arrest for auto theft (see figure 15.8).

The extension of sexual offender rules to juveniles is a perfect combination of punitive and destructive impact on individuals and completely ineffective impact on community protection. The idea of registration is to give enforcement authorities a method of finding those who commit sexual offenses after a first conviction—but the Philadelphia analysis shows that 92 percent of all the adult sexual offense contacts in the cohort were for boys who didn't have a juvenile offense. If the authorities did "round up the usual suspects" from the juvenile offenders, they would strike out more than nine times out of ten. Consider also the preventive logic of Megan's Law community notification. Families with children can avoid living close to the sexual offenders with addresses on the registry. The two problems with this strategy with the Amy Zyla extension are (a) the men who will be identified have a very small likelihood of future sex arrest and no evidence of any proclivity to offend against kids, and (b) 92 percent of the future sexual offenders from this age group won't be on the registry. In any competition for the world's stupidest penal law, the Amy Zyla amendment of 2006 should be a serious contender.

What Should Be Done

The simplest road to reason in treatment of juvenile sexual offending would be the repeal of the Amy Zyla amendment. If that doesn't happen, juvenile courts should favor non-adjudicative outcomes for their juvenile sexual offenders to keep them out of the legislation's mandate. A juvenile court judge either can mechanically adjudicate to generate Amy Zyla eligibility, or can observe the youth protective principles of juvenile justice, but that judge can't do both.

If the toxic politics of the matter requires some extension of registration and records to the juvenile years, the least bad approach to providing coverage would be a program of time-conditional sealing of juvenile records.

Under this approach, any records of juvenile offenders would not generate required registration or public notice unless and until the same person is convicted as an adult for a serious sexual offense. This adult conviction would then allow a full and detailed record of the juvenile portion of an active sexual offender's career—the only data of value to either the community or law enforcement. That system would also protect the more than 90 percent of all former sexual offenders who pose no hazard of sexual offending as adults.

REFERENCES

American Psychiatric Association (2013). *The diagnostic and statistical manual of mental disorders (DSM-5)* (5th ed.) Washington, DC: Author.

Caldwell, M. F. (2014). Juvenile sexual offenders. In F. E. Zimring & D. S. Tanenhaus (Eds.), *Choosing the future for American juvenile justice* (pp. 55–93). New York: New York University Press.

Centers for Disease Control and Prevention. Ever had sexual intercourse: High School Youth Risk Behavior Survey, 2013 Youth online: High School Youth Risk Behavior Surveillance System (YRBSS) Retrieved from https://nccd.cdc.gov/youthonline/App/Results.aspx?TT=A&OUT=0& SID=HS&QID=QQ&LID=XX&YID=2013&LID2=&YID2=&COL=S&ROW1=N&ROW2=N& HT=QQ&LCT=LL&FS=S1&FR=R1&FG=G1&FSL=S1&FRL=R1&FGL=G1&PV=&TST=False &C1=&C2=&QP=G&DP=1&VA=CI&CS=Y&SYID=&EYID=&SC=DEFAULT&SO=ASC

Child Trends Data Bank. Oral sex behaviors among teens. Retrieved from http://wwwchildtrends. org/?indicators=oral-sex-behaviors-among-teens. Raw data for their graphs taken from Centers for Disease Control and Prevention, National Survey of Family Growth (NSFG), 2011-2013, retrieved from http://www.cdc.gov/nchs/NSFG.htm

Doshay, L. J. (1943). *The boy sex offender and his later career.* New York: Grune & Stratton, 1943.

FBI [CRFR] Supplemental Homicide Reports, 2012–2013.

Human Rights Watch Raised on the registry: The irreparable harm of placing children on sex offender registries in the US. Retrieved from https://www.hrw.org/report/2013/05/01/raised-registry/irreparable-harm-placing-children-sex-offender-registries-us

US Census Bureau. National population estimate for 12/1/2014. Retrieved from https://www. census.gov/popest/data/national/asrh/2014/2014-nat-res.html

US Department of Justice. Crime in the United States, table 36, Current year over previous year arrest trends. Federal Bureau of Investigation, Criminal Justice Information Services Division (2013–14). Retrieved from https://www.fbi.gov/about-us/cjis/ucr/crime-in-the-u.s/2014/crime-in-the-u.s.-2014/tables/table-36 and https://www.fbi.gov/about-us/cjis/ucr/crime-in-the-u.s/2013/crime-in-the-u.s.-2013/tables/table-36

US Department of Justice. Crime in the United States, table 36, Current year over previous year arrest trends. Federal Bureau of Investigation, Criminal Justice Information Services Division (2014). Retrieved from https://www.fbi.gov/about-us/cjis/ucr/crime-in-the-u.s/2014/crime-in-the-u.s.-2014/tables/table-36

Wolfgang, M. E., Figlio, R. M., & Thorsten Sellin (1972). *Delinquency in a birth cohort.* Chicago: Chicago University Press, 1972).

Zimring, F. E. (2004). *An American travesty: Legal responses to adolescent sexual offending.* Chicago: Chicago University Press.

Zimring, F. E. (2015). The wages of ignorance. In S. M. Coupet & E. Marrus (Eds.), *Children, sexuality, and the law* (pp. 72–86). New York: New York University Press.

Zimring, F. E., Piquero, A., Jennings, W., & Hays, S. (2009, March). Investigating the continuity of sex offending: Evidence from the Second Philadelphia Birth Cohort. Justice Quarterly, 26(59), 58–76.

About the Authors

The Editors

Sue Righthand, PhD, is an associate research professor at the University of Maine. She has a BA in sociology, a MS in criminal justice and a doctorate in clinical psychology. Early in her career she worked primarily with adults who had offended sexually. Recognizing the importance of early intervention she began focusing on children and adolescents. Dr. Righthand is a consultant to the National Center for Sexual Behavior in Youth, the Maine Department of Health and Human Services and other agencies and projects. She provides presentations and training and assists with program development and evaluation. She was a member of the recently concluded ATSA Adolescent Guidelines Committee. She is the co-author of the *Juvenile Sex Offender Assessment Protocol II* and related research publications, as well as *Effective Intervention with Adolescents Who Have Offended Sexually: Translating Research into Practice* and other publications. She currently is involved in a multistate collaborative project to develop and implement an evidence-based treatment needs and progress scale.

William D. Murphy, PhD, is a professor in the Department of Psychiatry at the University of Tennessee Health Sciences Center where he was the past director of the APA accredited professional psychology internship program. Dr. Murphy has provided evaluation and treatment for adolescent and adult sex offenders. He has served on international accreditation panels for the United Kingdom and Canada and on treatment advisory boards for a number of program in the United States. He has published a number of articles and chapters related to these populations. Dr. Murphy is past president of the Association for the Treatment of Sexual Abusers, is on the editorial board of *Sexual Abuse: A Journal of Research and Treatment*, and a recipient of ATSA's Significant Achievement Award in 1999.

CHAPTER 1

Kathryn L. Modecki, PhD, is a developmental psychologist and faculty member in the School of Applied Psychology at Griffith University, Queensland, Australia. Before earning a PhD in psychology and taking up a NIMH post-doctoral fellowship at Arizona State University's Prevention Research Center, she worked with adjudicated teenagers for Outward Bound. Her work with adjudicated delinquent youth, leading month-long wilderness rehabilitation programs, helped shape her programmatic research on adolescents' risk pathways. Dr. Modecki works to chart adolescents' development of risky, delinquent, and aggressive behaviors, and better pin-point factors that serve to escalate or dampen their involvement. She aims to especially unpack how the developmental period of adolescence serves to shape antisocial decision making as well as the implications for prevention, intervention, and juvenile justice policy. In this vein, her work is cited in a number of Amicus Briefs to the US Supreme Court regarding juveniles' reduced criminal culpability for their crimes and she continues to consult for organizations such as Outward Bound at-risk programs, Florida Alliance of Boys & Girls Clubs, and the World Bank.

CHAPTER 2

Michael H. Miner, PhD, LP, is professor of Family Medicine and Community Health and Research Director for the Program in Human Sexuality (PHS) at the University of Minnesota. He began his work in sex offender research as the research psychologist for California's Sex Offender Treatment and Evaluation Project and since joining the Program in Human Sexuality his research has focused on the etiology of sexual abuse perpetration in adolescence, risk assessment, and sexual compulsivity. Dr. Miner coordinated sex offender treatment at PHS until 2008 and currently coordinates forensic assessment services. He is president of the Association for the Treatment of Sexual Abusers and past vice president of the International Association for the Treatment of Sexual Offenders. Dr. Miner is on the editorial board of *Archives of Sexual Behavior* and past associate editor of *Sexual Abuse: A Journal of Research and Treatment.*

Rosemary A. Munns, PsyD, LP, is an assistant professor in the Department of Family Medicine and Community Health at the University of Minnesota. She is a licensed psychologist specializing in sex therapy at the Program in Human Sexuality. She is the coordinator of Sexual Offender Treatment. She has 20 years of experience in assessment and treatment of sex offenders in an outpatient setting. In addition to sex offender treatment, she provides individual and group therapy to adults with sexual dysfunctions, compulsive sexual behavior, gender variant expression, and relationship and sex therapy with couples. She is a member of the Association for Treatment of Sex Abusers (ATSA). She has served on the Minnesota chapter (MnATSA) conference planning committee for 7 years and is the current co-chair of the committee. She is an American Association of Sexuality Educators, Counselors, and Therapists (AASECT) certified sex therapist and supervisor.

CHAPTER 3

Anton van Wijk, PhD, is criminologist and psychologist, and director of Bureau Beke, a private company that conducts research for the government. Before that he was a researcher at the Police Academy of the Netherlands. In 2005 he got his PhD on Juvenile Sex Offenders and Non-Sex Offenders—A Comparative Study. He has also taken part in the prestigious Violent Crime Behavior training presented by the Academy Group Inc., a forensic behavioral science firm in the United States. He publishes about juvenile sex offenders, criminal careers of sex offenders, downloaders of child pornography, and serial offenders.

Cyril Boonmann, PhD, is a research psychologist at the Child and Adolescent Psychiatric Research Department and the Department of Forensic Child and Adolescent Psychiatry of the University of Basel Psychiatric Hospital in Switzerland. He conducted his PhD on mental health problems and juvenile sexual behavior at the Department of Child and Adolescent Psychiatry of the VU University Medical Center Amsterdam.

CHAPTER 4

Patrick Lussier, PhD, is a full professor of criminology at the Université Laval, Quebec, Canada. Previously, he was an associate professor at the School of Criminology at Simon Fraser University, in British Columbia, Canada. Dr. Lussier is also a researcher at the Centre Jeunesse de Québec—Institut Universitaire and currently conducting research on the child welfare and youth justice response to inappropriate sexual behaviors in youth. He has published extensively in the area of sexual offending and developmental life course criminology. Dr. Lussier is the co-principal investigator of the Vancouver Longitudinal Study on the psychosocial development of children, which examines the development of non-normative and normative sexual behaviors during childhood. His work has been published in journals such as *Criminology, Criminal Justice and Behavior, Psychology, Public Policy and*

Law, Sexual Abuse: A Journal of Research and Treatment. He is an associate editor for the *Canadian Journal of Criminology and Criminal Justice* and an editorial board member of the *Journal of Criminal Justice.*

Stéphanie Chouinard Thivierge, is a graduate student at Université Laval, in Quebec City, Canada, and a research assistant at Centre Jeunesse de Québec—Institut Universitaire. She is currently conducting a longitudinal study on the continuity and the discontinuity of non-normative sexual behaviors in children and adolescents.

CHAPTER 5

Laura M. Grossi, MA, is a doctoral candidate in Fairleigh Dickinson University's Clinical Psychology PhD Program (Forensic Track), and holds an MA in forensic psychology. Ms. Grossi has presented and published research related to forensic assessment, predictors of feigning/malingering, and physical and sexual aggression exhibited by children, adolescents, and adults. Her dissertation research involves the assessment of malingering with pre-trial defendants hospitalized for restoration of adjudicative competence. She currently serves as clinical liaison for the American Psychology-Law Society's Student Committee, and she was recently awarded the American Psychological Foundation's 2016 Steven O. Walfish Student/ECP Grant to support her research endeavors in the field of psychology.

Alexandra Brereton, MA, completed her master's degree in forensic psychology at Fairleigh Dickinson University. She is currently a first year student in the university's Clinical Psychology PhD program forensic track. Miss Brereton's current research interests include campus sexual misconduct, suicidal, and self-injurious behaviors, and children and adolescents who engage in delinquent or sexually harmful behaviors.

Robert Prentky, PhD, is professor of psychology at Fairleigh Dickinson University. His research on sexual offenders, spanning 36 years, has been published more than 80 papers and chapters, as well as six books. His most recent book, *Sexual Predators: Society, Risk, and the Law,* was published in 2015. He has served as an *ad hoc* reviewer for 18 professional journals, and has chaired two conferences on sexual offenders for the New York Academy of Sciences (1988 & 2002). He was elected a fellow of the American Psychological Association in 2003 and the Association for Psychological Science in 2006.

Chapter 6

Judith V. Becker, PhD, is a professor in the Psychology Department at the University of Arizona. She has been conducting research and evaluations and treatment of adult sexual offenders and youth with sexual behavior problems for over 35 years. She is a past president of ATSA and past president of the International Academy of Sex Research. She has co-authored two books on sex offenders and has published over 150 articles and chapters, in which she has been the author or co-author.

Cassandra Valerio, MA, is a fourth year doctoral student in the Clinical Psychology program at the University of Arizona. Her research and clinical interests include evaluation and treatment of justice involved children and adolescents and youth with problem sexual behaviors. She has also conducted research in the area of sex-offender risk assessment and restoration of competency to stand trial

Chapter 7

Sue Righthand, PhD (See The Editors.)

Gina Vincent, PhD, is an associate professor, co-director of the Law & Psychiatry Program, and director of Translational Law & Psychiatry Research in the Department of Psychiatry at the University of Massachusetts Medical School. Dr. Vincent has funding from NIMH, the MacArthur Foundation, NIDA, and OJJDP for studies relevant to risk for reoffending and the implementation of risk assessment tools, mental health problems, and substance abuse among youth involved in the juvenile justice system. She is author of the *Risk Assessment in Juvenile Probation: A Guidebook for Implementation,* a manual designed to walk agencies through an effective implementation strategy for risk assessment. She has published, lectured, and presented research at over 100 international and national conferences and juvenile justice facilities in the areas of risk/needs assessment, adolescent substance abuse, and mental health symptoms in juvenile justice.

Rachael M. Huff, MA, is a doctoral candidate in the Clinical Psychology program at the University of Maine. She was awarded a Bachelor of Science degree in psychology from Michigan Technological University. Through her doctoral training program, she served as a consultant for the Department of Corrections, conducting forensic evaluations with adolescents, including violence and sexual risk assessments. Ms. Huff has also received training in a recently-developed treatment protocol for college students who engage in sexual misconduct, Science-based Treatment, Accountability, and Risk Reduction for Sexual Assault (STARRSA). She has reviewed extensively the established literature base for juvenile sexual offenses and recidivism, including studies investigating the psychometric properties for related assessment protocols.

CHAPTER 8

Kevin M. Powell, PhD, is the clinical director and a licensed psychologist for a 103-bed youth correctional facility in Colorado. He is also an adjunct assistant professor at Colorado State University in the Department of Psychology. He has been working with children, adolescents, and their families in a variety of settings (schools, community-based youth service agencies, hospital, and correctional/residential facilities) for the past three decades. Dr. Powell has authored several book chapters on the topic of working effectively with youth and families, and recently published a book, *A Strengths-Based Approach for Intervention with At-Risk Youth* (2015). He also has a children's book, *Our Very Special Bodies* (2014), which helps facilitate open communication between parents/loving caregivers and their young children in order to reduce the risk of childhood sexual abuse. Dr. Powell presents nationally and internationally on a variety of strengths-based topics to help youth service providers and caregivers promote healthy child and adolescent development.

CHAPTER 9

James R. Worling, PhD, is a clinical and forensic psychologist who has worked extensively since 1988 with adolescents who sexually offend and their families. During this time, he has presented many workshops internationally, and he has written a number of articles and book chapters regarding the etiology, assessment, and treatment of adolescent sexual aggression. In addition to his full-time consulting and clinical practice, he serves as an associate editor for *Sexual Abuse: A Journal of Research & Treatment.*

Calvin M. Langton, PhD, is a clinical and forensic psychologist who has been involved in assessment, treatment, and research with adolescents and adults who sexually offend, since 1997. As well as maintaining his clinical practice, Dr. Langton is on faculty at the University of Windsor. He is also an associate faculty member at the University of Toronto and a senior fellow at the University of Nottingham, United Kingdom. He serves on the editorial boards for *Sexual Abuse: A Journal of Research and Treatment* and *Criminal Justice and Behavior.*

CHAPTER 10

Jacqueline Page, PsyD, is an associate professor in the Department of Psychiatry at the University of Tennessee Health Science Center. She specializes in working with children with sexual behavior problems, adolescents who have engaged in sexually abusive behavior, and victims of sexual abuse. Currently, the majority of her time is spent as a consultant with the Tennessee Department of Children's Services and their efforts toward effective management and best practices for youth with problematic sexual behavior. Dr. Page is regularly involved in providing training on a state and national level and has also presented internationally. She has been actively involved with the Association for the Treatment of Sexual Abusers for over 25 years including serving on the board for six years and co-chairing the Adolescent Guidelines Committee.

William D. Murphy, PhD (See The Editors.)

CHAPTER 11

Daniel Rothman, PhD, is a clinical and forensic psychologist who specializes in the assessment and treatment of children, adolescents, and adults with sexual, aggressive and antisocial behavior problems. He has provided assessment, consultation, and treatment services in child protection, hospital, and correctional settings and has served as an advisor to child welfare and forensic mental health programs in Manitoba, Ontario and British Columbia. He has special interests in the roles of trauma, attachment and developmental disabilities (including autism spectrum disorders) on child development; prevention initiatives for youth at risk for engaging in sexual offending; multisystemic and holistic approaches to intervention and risk management for high-risk youth; and how to tailor therapeutic relationships to enhance clinical outcomes. Dr. Rothman has written articles and book chapters on these and other topics and provides training for child welfare, mental health, and criminal justice organizations locally, nationally, and internationally.

Todd Smith, BA, is a therapist with Forensic Psychological Services in Winnipeg, Manitoba, Canada, and a probation officer within the Manitoba Provincial Program Unit. He has provided assessment and treatment services for adolescent and adults involved in the criminal justice system in a range of institutional and community-based environments for the past 30 years. Mr. Smith has presented research at local and international conferences, provided training and consultation for the Winnipeg Police Service, Vancouver Police Department, and a variety of community-based organizations. He has stood on several Federal and Provincial Offender Management Committees and is the co-recipient of the Manitoba Attorney General Crime Prevention Award and the Canadian Criminal Justice Association National Crime Prevention Award.

CHAPTER 12

Tracey A. Skilling, PhD, CPsych, received her doctorate in Forensic Psychology at Queen's University in Kingston, Ontario, Canada. She is currently a clinical and forensic psychologist specializing in work with adolescents and emerging adults at the Centre for Addiction and Mental Health (CAMH) in Toronto, Canada. Her main area of clinical practice at the CAMH is conducting comprehensive assessments for youth involved with the justice system and over the past decade she has been involved in the assessment of close to a thousand adolescents, including many youth engaging in sexual offending behaviours. Dr. Skilling is also a clinician-scientist at the CAMH and an assistant professor with the Department of Psychiatry at the University of Toronto. She is currently conducting a longitudinal study, now involving more than 700 justice-involved youth, following them through the justice system after their mental health assessments are complete. Her specific research interests include examining the impact of mental health issues and treatment programming on mental health and legal outcomes for these youth, including a current study examining the specific outcomes for a group of youth charged with sexual offenses. She has published extensively on topics related to mental health needs and antisocial behavior in both adults and youth involved in the justice system.

Teresa Grimbos, PhD, CPsych (Supervised Practice), received her doctorate in developmental psychology and education at Ontario Institute for Studies in Education. She is a registered clinical and forensic psychologist (in supervised practice) and is currently providing court-ordered assessments for justice-involved youth at the Centre for Addiction and Mental Health (CAMH) in Toronto, Ontario, Canada. She sees a diverse range of young clients in this service, including females, young persons charged with sexual offences and those with trauma histories. Dr. Grimbos previously worked as a researcher in the Complex Mental Illness-Forensic Division at CAMH, and she has published several peer-reviewed articles and given a number of presentations in the areas of child and youth development, risk assessment, and human sexuality. Dr. Grimbos also works as a psychologist in private practice on a part-time basis, providing therapeutic services to children and adolescents with a wide-variety of referral concerns.

Julia Vinik, PhD, CPsych, received her doctorate in school and clinical child psychology at the Ontario Institute for Studies in Education, University of Toronto. She is a registered clinical and forensic psychologist and is currently conducting court-ordered mental health, psychoeducational, and risk of recidivism assessments with justice-involved youth at the Centre for Addiction and Mental Health (CAMH) in Toronto, Ontario, Canada. She works with justice-involved youth with a variety of complex clinical presentations. Dr. Vinik trained at the CAMH for several years during both her pre-doctoral internship and her supervised practice year. In addition to her work at the CAMH, Dr. Vinik also previously provided psychological intervention services in a private practice setting, with a focus on trauma-focused therapy as well as parent management. She is involved in research at the Social Development Lab in the area of parenting and value acquisition, publishing several peer-reviewed articles.

CHAPTER 13

Lisa L. Frey, PhD, is an associate professor at the University of Oklahoma (OU) and the director of the univerisity's Counseling Psychology Clinic. Dr. Frey operated a private clinical and consulting practice for many years, where she specialized in working with female and male juvenile sexual offenders and victims of violence and abuse. Her research and teaching emphases have been shaped by her extensive practice background and by her feminist orientation. Dr. Frey's research interests are in the areas of delinquent youth, particularly delinquent and aggressive behavior in girls; diversity issues; relational-cultural theory; and sociocultural influences on relational development and gender-role development.

CHAPTER 14

Abigail M. Judge, PhD, is a clinical and forensic child psychologist who works as a therapist, consultant, author, and expert witness. She maintains a private practice in Cambridge, Massachusetts where she specializes in the treatment of adolescents and young adults, as well as family intervention following high conflict divorce and other trauma. In addition, Dr. Judge is on the faculty at the Harvard Medical School and the staff at the Freedom Clinic at the Massachusetts General Hospital, a clinic for survivors of human trafficking. Dr. Judge has co-edited two books, *Adolescent Sexual Behavior in the Digital Age: Considerations for Clinicians, Legal Professionals and Educators* (Oxford University Press, 2014) and *Overcoming Parent-Child Contact Problems: Family-Based Interventions for Resistance, Rejection, and Alienation* (Oxford University Press, 2017).

CHAPTER 15

Franklin E. Zimring, JD, is the William G. Simon Professor of Law and faculty director of Criminal Justice Studies. His major fields of interest are criminal justice and family law, with special emphasis on the use of empirical research to inform legal policy. He is the author or co-author of many books and other publications on topics including deterrence, the changing legal world of adolescence, capital punishment, and juvenile sex offending. He is the author of *American Travesty: An American Travesty: Legal Responses to Adolescent Sexual Offending (2004), The City That Became Safe: New York's Lessons For Urban Crime and Its Control (2012) and When Police Kill (2017).*

Name Index

493

Subject Index